The firstwriter.com

Writers' Handbook
2024

The firstwriter.com

Writers' Handbook
2024

EDITOR
J. PAUL DYSON

Published in 2023 by JP&A Dyson
27 Old Gloucester Street, London WC1N 3AX, United Kingdom
Copyright JP&A Dyson

https://www.jpandadyson.com
https://www.firstwriter.com

ISBN 978-1-909935-47-1

Registered with the IP Rights Office
Copyright Registration Service
Ref: 3399119217

Foreword

The firstwriter.com Writers' Handbook returns for its 2024 edition with over 1,500 listings of literary agents, literary agencies, publishers, and magazines that have been updated in firstwriter.com's online databases between 2021 and 2023. This includes revised and updated listings from the previous edition and 400 new entries.

Previous editions of this handbook have been bought by writers across the United States, Canada, and Europe; and ranked in the United Kingdom as the number one bestselling writing and publishing directory on Amazon. The 2024 edition continues this international outlook, giving writers all over the English-speaking world access to the global publishing markets.

Finding the information you need is made quick and easy with multiple tables, a detailed index, and unique paragraph numbers to help you get to the listings you're looking for.

The variety of tables helps you navigate the listings in different ways, and includes a Table of Authors, which lists over 5,000 authors and tells you who represents them, or who publishes them, or both.

The number of genres in the index has expanded to over 900. So, for example, while there was only one option for "Romance" in previous editions, you can now narrow this down to Historical Romance, Fantasy Romance, Supernatural / Paranormal Romance, Contemporary Romance, Diverse Romance, Erotic Romance, Feminist Romance, Christian Romance, or even Amish Romance.

The handbook also provides free online access to the entire current firstwriter.com databases, including over 2,200 magazines, over 2,400 literary agents and agencies, over 2,700 book publishers that don't charge fees, and constantly updated listings of current writing competitions, with typically more than 50 added each month.

For details on how to claim your free access please see the end of this book.

Included in the subscription

A subscription to the full website is not only free with this book, but comes packed with all the following features:

Advanced search features

- Save searches and save time – set up to 15 search parameters specific to your work, save them, and then access the search results with a single click whenever you log in. You can even save multiple different searches if you have different types of work you are looking to place.
- Add personal notes to listings, visible only to you and fully searchable – helping you to organise your actions.
- Set reminders on listings to notify you when to submit your work, when to follow up, when to expect a reply, or any other custom action.
- Track which listings you've viewed and when, to help you organise your search – any listings which have changed since you last viewed them will be highlighted for your attention.

Daily email updates

As a subscriber you will be able to take advantage of our email alert service, meaning you can specify your particular interests and we'll send you automatic email updates when we change or add a listing that matches them. So if you're interested in agents dealing in romantic fiction in the United States you can have us send you emails with the latest updates about them – keeping you up to date without even having to log in.

User feedback

Our agent, publisher, and magazine databases all include a user feedback feature that allows our subscribers to leave feedback on each listing – giving you not only the chance to have your say about the markets you contact, but giving a unique authors' perspective on the listings.

Save on copyright protection fees

If you're sending your work away to publishers, competitions, or literary agents, it's vital that you first protect your copyright. As a subscriber to firstwriter.com you can do this through our site and save 10% on the copyright registration fees normally payable for protecting your work internationally through the Intellectual Property Rights Office (https://www.CopyrightRegistrationService.com).

Monthly newsletter

When you subscribe to firstwriter.com you also receive our monthly email newsletter – described by one publishing company as "the best in the business" – including articles, news, and interviews for writers. And the best part is that you can continue to receive the newsletter even after you stop your paid subscription – at no cost!

For details on how to claim your free access please see the back of this book.

Contents

Free Access

Glossary of Terms

This section explains common terms used in this handbook, and in the publishing industry more generally.

Academic

Listings in this book will be marked as targeting the academic market only if they publish material of an academic nature; e.g. academic theses, scientific papers, etc. The term is not used to indicate publications that publish general material aimed at people who happen to be in academia, or who are described as academic by virtue of being educated.

Adult

In publishing, "adult" simply refers to books that are aimed at adults, as opposed to books that are aimed at children, or young adults, etc. It is not a euphemism for pornographic or erotic content. Nor does it necessarily refer to content which is unsuitable for children; it is just not targeted at them. In this book, most ordinary mainstream publishers will be described as "adult", unless their books are specifically targeted at other groups (such as children, professionals, etc.).

Advance

Advances are up-front payments made by traditional publishers to authors, which are off-set against future royalties.

Agented

An *agented* submission is one which is submitted by a literary agent. If a publisher accepts only *agented* submissions then you will need a literary agent to submit the work on your behalf.

Author bio

A brief description of you and your life – normally in relation to your writing activity, but if intended for publication (particularly in magazines) may be broader in scope. May be similar to *Curriculum Vitae* (CV) or résumé, depending on context.

Bio

See *Author bio*.

Curriculum Vitae

A brief description of you, your qualifications, and accomplishments – normally in this context in relation to writing (any previous publications, or awards, etc.), but in the case of nonfiction proposals may also include relevant experience that qualifies you to write on the subject. Commonly abbreviated to "CV". May

also be referred to as a résumé. May be similar to *Author bio*, depending on context.

CV

See *Curriculum Vitae*.

International Reply Coupon

When submitting material overseas you may be required to enclose *International Reply Coupons*, which will enable the recipient to send a response and/or return your material at your cost. Not applicable/available in all countries, so check with your local Post Office for more information.

IRC

See *International Reply Coupon*.

Manuscript

Your complete piece of work – be it a novel, short story, or article, etc. – will be referred to as your manuscript. Commonly abbreviated to "ms" (singular) or "mss" (plural).

MS

See *Manuscript*.

MSS

See *Manuscript*.

Professional

Listings in this book will be marked as targeting the professional market if they publish material serving a particular profession: e.g. legal journals, medical journals, etc. The term is not used to indicate publications that publish general material aimed at a notional "professional class".

Proposal

A proposal is normally requested for nonfiction projects (where the book may not yet have been completed, or even begun). Proposals can consist of a number of components, such as an outline, table of contents, CV, marketing information, etc. but the exact requirements will vary from one publisher to another.

Query

Many agents and publishers will prefer to receive a query in the first instance, rather than your full *manuscript*. A query will typically

consist of a cover letter accompanied by a *synopsis* and/or sample chapter(s). Specific requirements will vary, however, so always check on a case by case basis.

Recommendation

If an agent is only accepting approaches by recommendation this means that they will only consider your work if it comes with a recommendation from an established professional in the industry, or an existing client.

RoW

Rest of world.

SAE

See *Stamped Addressed Envelope*. Can also be referred to as SASE.

SASE

Self-Addressed Stamped Envelope. Variation of SAE. See *Stamped Addressed Envelope*.

Simultaneous submission

A simultaneous submission is one which is sent to more than one market at the same time. Normally you will be sending your work to numerous different magazines, agents, and publishers at the same time, but some demand the right to consider it exclusively – i.e. they don't accept simultaneous submissions.

Stamped Addressed Envelope

Commonly abbreviated to "SAE". Can also be referred to as Self-Addressed Stamped Envelope, or SASE. When supplying an SAE, ensure that the envelope and postage is adequate for a reply or the return of your material, as required. If you are submitting overseas, remember that postage from your own country will not be accepted, and you may need to provide an *International Reply Coupon*.

Synopsis

A short outline of your story. This should cover all the main characters and events, including the ending. It is not the kind of "teaser" found on a book's back cover. The length of synopsis required can vary, but is generally between one and three pages.

TOC

Table of Contents. These are often requested as part of nonfiction proposals.

Unagented

An unagented submission is one which is not submitted through a literary agent. If a publisher accepts unagented submissions then you can approach them directly.

Unsolicited mss

A manuscript which has not been requested. Many agents and publishers will not accept unsolicited mss, but this does not necessarily mean they are closed to approaches – many will prefer to receive a short *query* in the first instance. If they like the idea, they will request the full work, which will then be a solicited manuscript.

The Writer's Roadmap

With most objectives in life, people recognise that there is a path to follow. Whether it is career progression, developing a relationship, or chasing your dreams, we normally understand that there are foundations to lay and baby steps to take before we'll be ready for the main event.

But for some reason, with writing (perhaps because so much of the journey of a writer happens in private, behind closed doors), people often overlook the process involved. They often have a plan of action which runs something like this:

1. Write novel.
2. Get novel published.

This is a bit like having a plan for success in tennis which runs:

1. Buy tennis racket.
2. Win Wimbledon.

It misses out all the practice that is going to be required; the competing in the minor competitions and the learning of the craft that will be needed in order to succeed in the major events; the time that will need to be spent gaining reputation and experience.

In this roadmap we'll be laying out what we think is the best path to follow to try and give yourself the best shot of success in the world of writing. You don't necessarily have to jump through all the hoops, and there will always be people who, like Pop Idol or reality TV contestants, get a lucky break that propels them to stardom without laying any of the foundations laid out below, but the aim here is to limit your reliance on luck and maximise your ability to shape your destiny yourself.

1: Write short material

Writers will very often start off by writing a novel. We would advise strongly against this. It's like leaving school one day and applying for a job as a CEO of an international corporation the next. Novels are the big league. They are expensive to produce, market, and distribute. They require significant investment and pose a significant financial risk to publishers. They are not a good place for new writers to try and cut their teeth. If you've already written your novel that's great – it's great experience and you'll have learned a lot – but we'd recommend shelving it for now (you can always come back to it later) and getting stuck into writing some short form material, such as poetry and short fiction.

This is what novelist George R. R. Martin, author of *A Game of Thrones*, has to say on the subject:

> "I would also suggest that any aspiring writer begin with short stories. These days, I meet far too many young writers who try to start off with a novel right off, or a trilogy, or even a nine-book series. That's like starting in at rock climbing by tackling Mt Everest. Short stories help you learn your craft."

You will find that writing short material will improve your writing no end. Writing short fiction allows you to play with lots of different stories and characters very quickly. Because you will probably only spend a few days on any given story you will quickly gain a lot of experience with plotting stories and will learn a lot about what works, what doesn't work, and what you personally are good at. When you write a novel, by contrast, you may spend years on a single story and one set of characters, making this learning process much slower.

Your writing will also be improved by the need to stick to a word limit. Writers who start their career by writing a novel often produce huge epics, the word counts of which they wear as a badge of honour, as if they demonstrate their commitment to and enthusiasm for writing. What they actually demonstrate is a naivety about the realities of getting published. The odds are already stacked against new writers getting a novel published, because of the cost and financial risk of publishing a novel. The bigger the novel, the more it will cost to print, warehouse, and distribute. Publishers will not look at a large word count and be impressed – they will be terrified. The longer the novel, the less chance it has of getting published.

A lengthy first novel also suggests that the writer has yet to learn one of the most critical skills a writer must possess to succeed: brevity. By writing short stories that fit the limits imposed by competitions and magazines you will learn this critical skill. You will learn to remove unnecessary words and passages, and you will find that your writing becomes leaner, more engaging, and more exciting as a result. Lengthy first novels are often rambling and sometimes boring – but once you've been forced to learn how to "trim the fat" by writing short stories, the good habits you've got into will transfer across when you start writing long form works, allowing you to write novels that are pacier and better to read. They will stand a better chance of publication not just because they are shorter and cheaper to produce, but they are also likely to be better written.

2: Get a professional critique

It's a good idea to get some professional feedback on your work at some point, and it's probably better to do this sooner, rather than later. There's no point spending a long time doing something that doesn't quite work if a little advice early on could have got you on the right track sooner. It's also a lot cheaper to get a short story critiqued than a whole novel, and if you can learn the necessary lessons now it will both minimise the cost and maximise the benefit of the advice.

Should you protect the copyright of short works before showing them to anyone?

This is a matter of personal preference. We'd suggest that it certainly isn't as important to register short works as full novels, as your short works are unlikely to be of much financial value to you. Having said that, films do sometimes get made which are based on short stories, in which case you'd want to have all your rights in order. If you do choose to register your short works this can be done for a relatively small amount online at https://www.copyrightregistrationservice.com/register.

3: Submit to competitions and magazines, and build a list of writing credits

Once you have got some short works that you are happy with you can start submitting them to competitions and small magazines. You can search for competitions at https://www.firstwriter.com/competitions and magazines at https://www.firstwriter.com/magazines. Prize money may not be huge, and you probably won't be paid for having your work appear in the kind of small literary magazines you will probably be approaching at first, but the objective here is to build up a list of writing credits to give you more credibility when approaching agents and publishers. You'll be much more likely to grab their attention if you can reel off a list of places where you have already been published, or prizes you have won.

4: Finish your novel and protect your copyright

Okay – so you've built up a list of writing credits, and you've decided it's time to either write a novel, or go back to the one you had already started (in which case you'll probably find yourself cutting out large chunks and making it a lot shorter!). Once you've got your novel to the point where you're happy to start submitting it for publication you should get it registered for copyright. Unlike the registration of short works, which we think is a matter of personal preference, we'd definitely recommend registering a novel, and doing so before you show it to anybody. That *includes* family and friends. Don't worry that you might want to change it – as long as you don't rewrite it to the point where it's not recognisable it will still be protected – the important thing is to get it registered without delay. You can protect it online at https://www.copyrightregistration service.com/register.

If you've already shown it to other people then just register it as soon as you can. Proving a claim to copyright is all about proving you had a copy of the work before anyone else, so time is of the essence.

5: Editing

These days, agents and publishers increasingly seem to expect manuscripts to have been professionally edited before being submitted to them – and no, getting your husband / wife / friend / relative to do it doesn't count. Ideally, you should have the whole manuscript professionally edited, but this can be expensive. Since most agents and publishers aren't going to want to see the whole manuscript in the first instance you can probably get away with just having the first three chapters edited. It may also be worth having your query letter and synopsis edited at the same time.

6: Submit to literary agents

There will be many publishers out there who will accept your submission directly, and on the face of it that might seem like a good idea, since you won't have to pay an agent 15% of your earnings.

However, all the biggest publishers are generally closed to direct submissions from authors, meaning that if you want the chance of getting a top publisher you're going to need a literary agent. You'll also probably find that their 15% fee is more than offset by the higher earnings you'll be likely to achieve.

To search for literary agents go to https://www.firstwriter.com/Agents. Start by being as specific in your search as possible. So if you've written a historical romance select "Fiction", "Romance", and "Historical". Once you've approached all the agents that specifically mention all three elements broaden your search to just "Fiction" and "Romance". As long as the new results don't specifically say they don't handle historical romance, these are still valid markets to approach. Finally, search for just "Fiction", as there are many agents who are willing to consider all kinds of fiction but don't specifically mention romance or historical.

Don't limit your approaches to just agents in your own country. With more and more agents accepting electronic queries it's now as easy to approach agents in other countries as in your own, and if you're ignoring either London or New York (the two main centres of English language publishing) you're cutting your chances of success in two.

7: Submit directly to publishers

Once you're certain that you've exhausted all potential agents for your work, you can start looking for publishers to submit your work directly to. You can search for publishers at https://www.firstwriter.com/publishers. Apply the same filtering as when you were searching for agents: start specific and gradually broaden, until you've exhausted all possibilities.

8: Self-publishing

In the past, once you got to the point where you'd submitted to all the publishers and agents who might be interested in your book, it would be time to pack away the manuscript in the attic, chalk it up to experience, and start writing another. However, these days writers have the option to take their book directly to market by publishing it themselves.

Before you decide to switch to self-publishing you must be sure that you've exhausted all traditional publishing possibilities – because once you've self-published your book you're unlikely to be able to submit it to agents and publishers. It will probably take a few years of exploring the world of traditional publishing to reach this point, but if you do then you've nothing to lose by giving self-publishing a shot. See our guide to self-publishing for details on how to proceed.

Why Choose Traditional Publishing

When **firstwriter.com** first started, back in 2001, there were only two games in town when it came to getting your book published: traditional publishing, and vanity publishing – and which you should pick was a no-brainer. Vanity publishing was little more than a scam that would leave you with an empty bank account and a house full of unsold books. If you were serious about being a writer, you had to follow the traditional publishing path.

Since then, there has been a self-publishing revolution, with new technologies and new printing methods giving writers a genuine opportunity to get their books into the market by themselves. So, is there still a reason for writers to choose traditional publishing?

The benefits of traditional publishing

Despite the allure and apparent ease of self-publishing, the traditional path still offers you the best chance of making a success of being a writer. There are rare cases where self-published writers make staggering fortunes and become internationally renowned on the back of their self-published books, but these cases are few and far between, and a tiny drop in the rapidly expanding ocean of self-published works. The vast majority of successful books – and the vast majority of successful writers – have their homes firmly in the established publishing houses. Even those self-published authors who find success usually end up moving to a traditional publisher in the end.

This is because the traditional publishers have the systems, the market presence, and the financial clout to *make* a book a bestseller. While successful self-published authors often owe their success in no small part to a decent dose of luck (a social media comment that goes viral; the right mention on the right media outlet at the right time), traditional publishers are in the business of engineering that success. They might not always succeed, but they have the marketing budgets and the distribution channels in place to give themselves, and the book they are promoting, the best possible chance.

And it's not just the marketing and the distribution. Getting signed with a traditional publisher brings a whole team of people with a wealth of expertise that will all work towards the success of the book. It will provide you with an editor who may have experience of working on previous bestsellers, who will not only help you get rid of mistakes in your work but may also help you refine it into a better book. They will help make sure that the quality of your content is good enough to make it in the marketplace.

The publishers will source a professional cover designer who will make your book look the part on the shelves and on the pages of the bookselling websites. They will have accountants who will handle the technicalities of tax regimes both home and abroad. They will have overseas contacts for establishing foreign publishing rights; translations; etc. They may even have contacts in the film industry, should there be a prospect of a movie adaptation. They will have experts working on every aspect of your book, right down to the printing and the warehousing and the shipping of the physical products. They will have people to manage the ebook conversion and the electronic distribution. As an author, you don't need to worry about any of this.

This means you get more time to simply be a writer. You may have to go on book tours, but even these will be organised for you by PR experts, who will also be handling all the press releases, etc.

And then there's the advances. Advances are up-front payments made by traditional publishers to authors, which are off-set against future royalties. So, an author might receive a $5,000 advance before their book is published. When the royalties start coming in, the publisher keeps the first $5,000 to off-set the advance. The good news for the author is that if the book flops and doesn't make $5,000 in royalties they still get to keep the full advance. In an uncertain profession, the security of an advance can be invaluable for an author – and of course it's not something available to self-published authors.

The drawbacks of traditional publishing

The main downside of traditional publishing is just that it's so hard to get into. If you choose to self-publish then – provided you have enough perseverance, the right help and advice, and perhaps a little bit of money – you are guaranteed to succeed and see your book in print and for sale. With traditional publishing, the cold hard fact is that most people who try will not succeed.

And for many of those people who fail it may not even be their fault. That aspect of traditional publishing which can bring so many benefits as compared to self-publishing – that of being part of a team – can also be part of its biggest drawback. It means that you have to get other people to buy into your book. It means that you have to rely on other people being competent enough to spot a bestseller. Many failed to spot the potential of the Harry Potter books. How many potential bestsellers never make it into print just because none of the professionals at the publishers' gates manage to recognise their potential?

So if you choose traditional publishing your destiny is not in your own hands – and for some writers the lack of exclusive control can also be a problem. Sometimes writers get defensive when editors try to tinker with their work, or annoyed when cover artists don't realise their vision the way they expect. But this is hardly a fair criticism of traditional publishing, as most writers (particularly when they are starting out) will benefit from advice from experienced professionals in the field, and will often only be shooting themselves in the foot if they insist on ignoring it.

The final main drawback with traditional publishing is that less of the sale price of each copy makes it to the writer. A typical royalty contract will give the writer 15%. With a self-published book, the author can expect to receive much more. So, all other things being equal, the self-published route can be more profitable – but, of course, all things are not equal. If self-publishing means lower sales (as is likely), then you will probably make less money overall. Remember, it's better to have 15% of something than 50% of nothing.

Conclusion

In conclusion, our advice to writers would be to aim for traditional publishing first. It might be a long shot, but if it works then you stand a much better chance of being successful. If you don't manage to get signed by an agent or a publisher then you still have the option of self-publishing, but make sure you don't get tempted to resort to self-publishing too soon – most agents and publishers won't consider self-published works, so this is a one-way street. Once you've self-published your work, you probably won't be able to change your mind and go back to the traditional publishers with your book unless it becomes a huge hit without them. It's therefore important that you exhaust all your traditional publishing options before making the leap to self-publishing. Be prepared for this to take perhaps a few years (lots of agents and publishers can take six months just to respond), and make sure you've submitted to everyone you can on *both* sides of the Atlantic (publishing is a global game these days, and you need to concentrate on the two main centres of English-language publishing (New York and London) equally) before you make the decision to self-publish instead.

Formatting Your Manuscript

Before submitting a manuscript to an agent, magazine, or publisher, it's important that you get the formatting right. There are industry norms covering everything from the size of your margins to the font you choose – get them wrong and you'll be marking yourself out as an amateur. Get them right, and agents and editors will be far more likely to take you seriously.

Fonts

Don't be tempted to "make your book stand out" by using fancy fonts. It *will* stand out, but not for any reason you'd want. Your entire manuscript should be in a monospaced font like Courier (not a proportional font, like Times Roman) at 12 points. (A monospaced font is one where each character takes up the same amount of space; a proportional font is where the letter "i" takes up less space than the letter "m".)

This goes for your text, your headings, your title, your name – everything. Your objective is to produce a manuscript that looks like it has been produced on a simple typewriter.

Italics / bold

Your job as the author is to indicate words that require emphasis, not to pick particular styles of font. This will be determined by the house style of the publisher in question. You indicate emphasis by underlining text; the publisher will decide whether they will use bold or italic to achieve this emphasis – you shouldn't use either in your text.

Margins

You should have a one inch (2.5 centimetre) margin around your entire page: top, bottom, left, and right.

Spacing

In terms of line spacing, your entire manuscript should be double spaced. Your word processor should provide an option for this, so you don't have to insert blank lines manually.

While line spacing should be double, spaces after punctuation should be single. If you're in the habit of putting two spaces after full stops this is the time to get out of that habit, and remove them from your manuscript. You're just creating extra work for the editor who will have to strip them all out.

Do not put blank lines between paragraphs. Start every paragraph (even those at the start of chapters) with an indent equivalent to five spaces. If you want a scene break then create a line with the "#" character centred in the middle. You don't need blank lines above or below this line.

Word count

You will need to provide an estimated word count on the front page of your manuscript. Tempting as it will be to simply use the word processor's word counting function to tell you exactly how many words there are in your manuscript, this is not what you should do. Instead, you should work out the maximum number of characters on a line, divide this number by six, and then multiply by the total number of lines in your manuscript.

Once you have got your estimated word count you need to round it to an approximate value. How you round will depend on the overall length of your manuscript:

- up to 1,500 words: round to the nearest 100;
- 1,500–10,000 words: round to the nearest 500;
- 10,000–25,000 words: round to the nearest 1,000;
- Over 25,000 words: round to the nearest 5,000.

The reason an agent or editor will need to know your word count is so that they can estimate how many pages it will make. Since actual pages include varying amounts of white space due to breaks in paragraphs, sections of speech, etc. the formula above will actually provide a better idea of how many pages will be required than an exact word count would.

And – perhaps more importantly – providing an exact word count will highlight you immediately as an amateur.

Layout of the front page

On the first page of the manuscript, place your name, address, and any other relevant contact details (such as phone number, email address, etc.) in the top left-hand corner. In the top right-hand corner write your approximate word count.

If you have registered your work for copyright protection, place the reference number two single lines (one double line) beneath your contact details. Since your manuscript will only be seen by agents or editors, not the public, this should be done as discreetly as possible, and you should refrain from using any official seal you may have been granted permissions to use. (For information on registering for copyright protection see "Protecting Your Copyright", below.)

Place your title halfway down the front page. Your title should be centred and would normally be in capital letters. You can make it bold or underlined if you want, but it should be the same size as the rest of the text.

From your title, go down two single lines (or one double line) and insert your byline. This should be centred and start with the word "By", followed by the name you are writing under. This can be your name or a pen name, but should be the name you want the work published under. However, make sure that the name in the top left-hand corner is your real, legal name.

From your byline, go down four single lines (or two double lines) and begin your manuscript.

Layout of the text

Print on only one side of the paper, even if your printer can print on both sides.

In the top right-hand corner of all pages except the first should be your running head. This should be comprised of the surname used in your byline; a keyword from your title, and the page number, e.g. "Myname / Mynovel Page 5".

Text should be left-aligned, *not* justified. This means that you should have a ragged right-hand edge to the text, with lines ending at different points. Make sure you don't have any sort of hyphenation function switched on in your word processor: if a word is too long to fit on a line it should be taken over to the next.

Start each new chapter a third of the way down the page with the centred chapter number / title, underlined. Drop down four single lines (two double lines) to the main text.

At the end of the manuscript you do not need to indicate the ending in any way: you don't need to write "The End", or "Ends", etc. The only exception to this is if your manuscript happens to end at the bottom of a page, in which case you can handwrite the word "End" at the bottom of the last page, after you have printed it out.

Protecting Your Copyright

Protecting your copyright is by no means a requirement before submitting your work, but you may feel that it is a prudent step that you would like to take before allowing strangers to see your material.

These days, you can register your work for copyright protection quickly and easily online. The Intellectual Property Rights Office operates a website called the "Copyright Registration Service" which allows you to do this:

- *https://www.CopyrightRegistrationService.com*

This website can be used for material created in any nation signed up to the Berne Convention. This includes the United States, United Kingdom, Canada, Australia, Ireland, New Zealand, and most other countries. There are around 180 countries in the world, and over 160 of them are part of the Berne Convention.

Provided you created your work in one of the Berne Convention nations, your work should be protected by copyright in all other Berne Convention nations. You can therefore protect your copyright around most of the world with a single registration, and because the process is entirely online you can have your work protected in a matter of minutes, without having to print and post a copy of your manuscript.

What is copyright?

Copyright is a form of intellectual property (often referred to as "IP"). Other forms of intellectual property include trade marks, designs, and patents. These categories refer to different kinds of ideas which may not exist in a physical form that can be owned as property in the traditional sense, but may nonetheless have value to the people who created them. These forms of intellectual property can be owned in the same way that physical property is owned, but – as with physical property – they can be subject to dispute and proper documentation is required to prove ownership.

The different types of intellectual property divide into these categories as follows:

- **Copyright:** copyright protects creative output such as books, poems, pictures, drawings, music, films, etc. Any work which can be recorded in some way can be protected by copyright, as long as it is original and of sufficient length. Copyright does not cover short phrases or names.

- **Trade marks:** trade marks cover words and/or images which distinguish the goods or services of one trader from another. Unlike copyright, trade marks can cover names and short phrases.

- **Designs:** designs cover the overall visual appearance of a product, such as its shape, etc.

- **Patents:** patents protect the technical or functional aspects of designs or inventions.

The specifics of the legal protection surrounding these various forms of intellectual property will vary from nation to nation, but there are also generally international conventions to which a lot if not most of the nations of the world subscribe. The information provided below outlines the common situation in many countries but you should be aware that this may not reflect the exact situation in every territory.

The two types of intellectual property most relevant to writers are copyright and trade marks. If a writer has written a novel, a short story, a poem, a script, or any other piece of writing then the contents themselves can be protected by copyright. The title, however, cannot be protected by copyright as it is a name. An author may therefore feel that they wish to consider protecting the title of their work by registering it as a trade mark, if they feel that it is particularly important and/or more valuable in itself than the cost of registering a trade mark.

If a writer wants to register the copyright for their work, or register the title of their work as a trade mark, there are generally registration fees to be paid. Despite the fact that copyright covers long works that could be hundreds of thousands of words long, while trade marks cover single words and short phrases, the cost for registering a trade mark is likely to be many times higher than that for registering a work for copyright protection. This is because trade marks must be unique and are checked against existing trade marks for potential conflicts. While works to be registered for copyright must also not infringe existing works, it is not practical to check the huge volume of new works to be registered for copyright against the even larger volume of all previously copyrighted works. Copyright registration therefore tends to simply archive the work in question as proof of the date at which the person registering the work was in possession of it.

In the case of both copyright and trade marks the law generally provides some protection even without any kind of registration, but registration provides the owner of the intellectual property with greater and more enforceable protection. In the case of copyright, the creator of a work usually automatically owns the copyright as soon as the work is recorded in some way (i.e. by writing it down or recording it electronically, etc.), however these rights can be difficult to prove if disputed, and therefore many countries (such as the United States) also offer an internal country-specific means of registering works. Some countries, like the United Kingdom, do not offer any such means of registration, however an international registration is available through the Intellectual Property Rights Office's Copyright Registration Service, and can be used regardless of any country-specific provisions. This can help protect copyright in all of the nations which are signatories of the Berne Convention.

In the case of trade marks, the symbol "™" can be applied to any mark which is being used as a trade mark, however greater protection is provided if this mark is registered, in which case the symbol "®" can be applied to the mark. It is often illegal to apply the "®" symbol to a trade mark which has not been registered. There are also options for international registrations of trade marks, which are administered by the World Intellectual Property Organization, however applications cannot be made to the WIPO directly – applications must be made through the relevant office of the applicant's country.

Copyright law and its history

The modern concept of copyright can be traced back to 1710 and the "Statute of Anne", which applied to England, Scotland, and Wales. Prior to this Act, governments had granted monopoly rights to publishers to produce works, but the 1710 Act was the first time that a right of ownership was acknowledged for the actual creator of a work.

From the outset, the attempt to protect the creator's rights was beset with problems due to the local nature of the laws, which applied in Britain only. This meant that lots of copyrighted works were reproduced without the permission of the author in Ireland, America, and in European countries. This not only hindered the ability of the London publishers to sell their legitimate copies of their books in these territories, but the unauthorised reproductions would also find their way into Britain, harming the home market as well.

A natural progression for copyright law was therefore its internationalisation, beginning in 1846 with a reciprocal agreement between Britain and Prussia, and culminating in a series of international treaties, the principal of which is the Berne Convention, which applies to over 160 countries.

Traditionally in the United Kingdom and the United States there has been a requirement to register a work with an official body in order to be able to claim copyright over it (Stationers Hall and the US Library of Congress respectively), however this has been changed by the Berne Convention, which requires signatory countries to grant copyright as an automatic right: i.e. the creator of a work immediately owns its copyright by virtue of creating it and recording it in some physical way (for instance by writing it down or making a recording of it, etc.). The United Kingdom and the United States have both been slow to fully adopt this approach. Though the United Kingdom signed the Berne Convention in 1887, it took 100 years for it to be fully implemented by the Copyright Designs and Patents Act 1988. The United States did not even sign the convention until 1989.

In the United States the US Library of Congress continues to provide archiving services for the purposes of copyright protection, but these are now optional. US citizens no longer need to register their work in order to be able to claim copyright over it. It is necessary, however, to be able to prove when the person who created it did so, and this is essentially the purpose of the registration today. In the United Kingdom, Stationers Hall has ceased to exist, and there is no longer any state-run means of registering the copyright to unpublished works, leaving the only available options as independent and/or international solutions such as the copyright registration service provided by the IP Rights Office.

Registering your work for copyright protection

Registering your work for copyright protection can help you protect your rights in relation to your work. Generally (particularly if you live in a Berne Convention country, as most people do) registration will not be compulsory in order to have rights over your work. Any time you create a unique original work you will in theory own the copyright over it, however you will need to be able to prove when you created it, which is the purpose of registering your work for copyright protection. There are other ways in which you might attempt to prove this, but registration provides better evidence than most other forms.

There are a range of different options for protecting your copyright that vary depending on where you live and the kind of coverage you want. Some countries, like the United States, provide internal means of registering the copyright of unpublished works, however the scope of these will tend to be restricted to the country in question. Other countries, like the United Kingdom, do not offer any specific government-sponsored system for registering the copyright of unpublished works. An international option is provided by the Intellectual Property Rights Office, which is not affiliated to any particular government or country. As long as you live in a Berne Convention country you should be able to benefit from using their Copyright Registration Service. You can register your work with the Intellectual Property Rights Office regardless of whether or not there are any specific arrangements in your home country (you may even choose to register with both to offer your work greater protection). Registration with the Intellectual Property Rights Office should provide you with protection throughout the area covered by the Berne Convention, which is most of the world.

Registering your work for copyright protection through the Intellectual Property Rights Office is an online process that can be completed in a few

minutes, provided you have your file in an accepted format and your file isn't too large (if your file is too large and cannot be reduced you may have to split it and take out two or more registrations covering it). There is a registration fee to pay ($45 / £25 / €40 at the time of writing) per file for registration, however if you are a subscriber to **firstwriter.com** you can benefit from a 10% discount when you start the registration process on our site.

When registering your work, you will need to give some consideration to what your work actually consists of. This is a straightforward question if your work is a novel, or a screenplay, but if it is a collection of poetry or short stories then the issue is more difficult. Should you register your collection as one file, or register each poem separately, which would be more expensive? Usually, you can answer this question by asking yourself what you propose to do with your collection. Do you intend to submit it to publishers as a collection only? Or do you intend to send the constituent parts separately to individual magazines? If the former is the case, then register the collection as a single work under the title of the collection. If the latter is the case then this could be unwise, as your copyright registration certificate will give the name of the collection only – which will not match the names of the individual poems or stories. If you can afford to, you should therefore register them separately. If you have so many poems and / or stories to register that you cannot afford to register them all separately, then registering them as a collection will be better than nothing.

Proper use of the copyright symbol

The first thing to note is that for copyright there is only one form of the symbol (©), unlike trade marks, where there is a symbol for registered trade marks (®) and a symbol for unregistered trade marks (™).

To qualify for use of the registered trade mark symbol (®) you must register your trade mark with the appropriate authority in your country, whereas the trade mark symbol (™) can be applied to any symbol you are using as a trade mark. Use of the copyright symbol is more similar to use of the trade mark symbol, as work does not need to be registered in order to use it.

You can place the copyright symbol on any original piece of work you have created. The normal format would be to include alongside the copyright symbol the year of first publication and the name of the copyright holder, however there are no particular legal requirements regarding this. While it has historically been a requirement in some jurisdictions to include a copyright notice on a work in order to be able to claim copyright over it, the Berne Convention does not allow such restrictions, and so any country signed up to the convention no longer has this requirement. However, in some jurisdictions failure to include such a notice can affect the damages you may be able to claim if anyone infringes your copyright.

A similar situation exists in relation to the phrase "All Rights Reserved". This phrase was a requirement in order to claim international copyright protection in countries signed up to the 1910 Buenos Aires Convention. However, since all countries signed up to the Buenos Aires Convention are now also signed up to the Berne Convention (which grants automatic copyright) this phrase has become superfluous. The phrase continues to be used frequently but is unlikely to have any legal consequences.

The Berne Convention

The Berne Convention covers 162 of the approximately 190 countries in the world, including most major nations. Countries which are signed up to the convention are compelled to offer the same protection to works created in other signatory nations as they would to works created in their own. Nations not signed up to the Berne Convention may have their own arrangements regarding copyright protection.

You can check if your country is signed up to the Berne Convention at the following website:

- *https://www.CopyrightRegistrationService.com*

The status of your country should be shown automatically on the right side of the screen. If not, you can select your country manually from the drop-down menu near the top right of the page.

Should You Self-Publish

Over recent years there has been an explosion in self-published books, as it has become easier and easier to publish your book yourself. This poses writers with a new quandary: continue to pursue publication through the traditional means, or jump into the world of self-publishing? As the rejections from traditional publishers pile up it can be tempting to reach for the control and certainty of self-publishing. Should you give into the temptation, or stick to your guns?

Isn't it just vanity publishing?

Modern self-publishing is quite different from the vanity publishing of times gone by. A vanity publisher would often pose or at least seek to appear to be a traditional publisher, inviting submissions and issuing congratulatory letters of acceptance to everyone who submitted – only slowly revealing the large fees the author would have to pay to cover the cost of printing the books.

Once the books were printed, the vanity publisher would deliver them to the author then cut and run. The author would be left with a big hole in their pocket and a mountain of boxes of books that they would be unlikely to ever sell a fraction of.

Modern self-publishing, on the other hand, is provided not by shady dealers but by some of the biggest companies involved in the publishing industry, including Penguin and Amazon. It doesn't have the large fees that vanity publishing did (depending on the path you choose and your own knowledge and technical ability it can cost almost nothing to get your book published); it *does* offer a viable means of selling your books (they can appear on the biggest bookselling websites around the world); and it *doesn't* leave you with a house full of unwanted books, because modern technology means that a copy of your book only gets printed when it's actually ordered.

That isn't to say that there aren't still shady characters out there trying to take advantage of authors' vanity by charging them enormous fees for publishing a book that stands very little chance of success, but it does mean that self-publishing – done right – can be a viable and cost effective way of an author taking their book to market.

The benefits of self-publishing

The main benefit of self-publishing, of course, is that the author gets control of whether their book is published or not. There is no need to spend years submitting to countless agents and publishers, building up countless heartbreaking rejection letters, and possibly accepting in the end that your dreams of publication will never come true – you can make them come true.

And this need not be pure vanity on the author's part. Almost every successful book – even such massive hits as *Harry Potter* – usually build up a string of rejections before someone finally accepts them. The professionals that authors rely on when going through the traditional publishing process – the literary agents and the editors – are often, it seems, just not that good at spotting what the public are going to buy. How many potential bestsellers might languish forever in the slush pile, just because agents and editors fail to spot them? What if your book is one of them? The traditional publishing process forces you to rely on the good judgment of others, but the self-publishing process enables you to sidestep that barrier and take your book directly to the public, so that readers can decide for themselves.

Self-publishing also allows you to keep control in other areas. You won't have an editor trying to change your text, and you'll have complete control over what kind of cover your book receives.

Finally, with no publisher or team of editors and accountants taking their slice, you'll probably get to keep a lot more of the retail price of every book you sell. So if you can sell the same amount of books as if you were traditionally published, you'll stand to make a lot more money.

The drawbacks of self-publishing

While self-publishing can guarantee that your book will be available for sale, it cannot guarantee that it will actually sell. Your self-published book will probably have a much lower chance of achieving significant sales than if it had been published traditionally, because it will lack the support that a mainstream publisher could bring. You will have no marketing support, no established position in the marketplace, and no PR – unless you do it yourself. You will have to arrange your own book tours; you will have to do your own sales pitches; you will have to set your own pricing structure; and you will have to manage your own accounts and tax affairs. If you're selling through Amazon or Smashwords or Apple (and if you're not, then why did you bother self-publishing in the first place?) you're going to need to fill in the relevant forms with the IRS (the US tax office) – whether you're a US citizen or not. If you're not a US citizen then you'll have to register with the IRS and complete the necessary tax forms, and potentially other forms for claiming treaty benefits so that you don't get taxed twice (in the US and your home country). And then of course you'll also have to register for tax purposes in your home nation and complete your own tax return there (though you would also have to do this as a traditionally published author).

It can all get very complicated, very confusing, and very lonely. Instead of being able to just be a writer you can find yourself writing less and less and becoming more and more embroiled in the business of publishing a book.

And while it's great to have control over your text and your cover, you'd be ill advised to ignore the value that professionals such as editors and cover designers can bring. It's tempting to think that you don't need an editor – that you've checked the book and had a friend or family member check it too, so it's probably fine – but a professional editor brings a totally different mindset to the process and will check things that won't have even occurred to you and your reader. Without a professional editor, you will almost certainly end up publishing a book which is full of embarrassing mistakes, and trust me – there is no feeling quite as deflating as opening up the first copy of your freshly printed book to see an obvious error jump out – or, even worse, to have it pointed out in an Amazon review, for all to see.

The cover is also incredibly important. Whether for sale on the shelf or on a website, the cover is normally the first point of contact your potential reader has with your book, and will cause them to form immediate opinions about it. A good cover can help a book sell well, but a bad one can kill its chances – and all too often self-published books have amateurish covers that will have readers flicking past them without a second glance.

Finally, the financial benefits of self-publishing can often be illusory. For starters, getting a higher proportion of the retail price is pretty irrelevant if you don't sell any copies. Fifty per cent of nothing is still nothing. Far better to have 15% of something. And then there's the advances. Advances are up-front payments made by traditional publishers to authors, which are off-set against future royalties. So, an author might receive a $5,000 advance before their book is published. When the royalties start coming in, the publisher keeps the first $5,000 to off-set the advance. The good news for the author is that if the book flops and doesn't make $5,000 in royalties they still get to keep the full advance. In an uncertain profession, the security of an advance can be invaluable for an author – and of course it's not something available to self-published authors.

Conclusion

Self-publishing can seem like a tempting shortcut to publication, but in reality it has its own challenges and difficulties. For the moment at least, traditional publishing still offers you the best shot of not only financial success, but also quality of life as a writer. With other people to handle all the other elements of publishing, you get to concentrate on doing what you love.

So we think that writers should always aim for traditional publishing first. It might be a long shot, but if it works then you stand a much better chance of being successful. If you don't manage to get signed by an agent or a publisher then you still have the option of self-publishing, but make sure you don't get tempted to resort to self-publishing too soon – most agents and publishers won't consider self-published works, so this is a one-way street. Once you've self-published your work, you probably won't be able to change your mind and go back to the traditional publishers with your book unless it becomes a huge hit without them. It's therefore important that you exhaust all your traditional publishing options before making the leap to self-publishing. Be prepared for this to take perhaps a few years (lots of agents and publishers can take six months just to respond), and make sure you've submitted to everyone you can on *both* sides of the Atlantic (publishing is a global game these days, and you need to concentrate on the two main centres of English-language publishing (New York and London) equally) before you make the decision to self-publish instead.

However, once you have exhausted all options for traditional publishing, modern self-publishing does offer a genuine alternative path to success, and there are a growing number of self-published authors who have managed to sell millions of copies of their books. If you don't think traditional publishing is going to be an option, we definitely think you should give self-publishing a shot.

For directions on your path through the traditional publishing process see our Writers' Roadmap, above.

If you're sure you've already exhausted all your options for traditional publishing then see below for our quick guide to the self-publishing process.

The Self Publishing Process

Thinking about self-publishing your book? Make sure you go through all these steps first – and in the right order! Do them the wrong way round and you could find yourself wasting time and/or money.

1. Be sure you want to self-publish

You need to be 100% sure that you want to self-publish, because after you've done it there is no going back. Publishers and literary agents will not normally consider books that have been self-published, so if you wanted to get your book to print the old fashioned way you should stop now and rethink. Make absolutely sure that you've exhausted every possible opportunity for traditional publishing before you head down the self-publishing path.

For more information, see "Why choose traditional publishing?" and "Should you self-publish?", above.

2. Protect your copyright

Authors often wonder about what stage in the process they should protect their copyright – often thinking that it's best to leave it till the end so that there are no more changes to make to the book after it is registered.

However, this isn't the case. The key thing is to protect your work before you let other people see it – or, if you've already let other people see it, as soon as possible thereafter.

Don't worry about making small changes to your work after registering it – as long as the work is still recognisable as the same piece of work it will still be protected. Obviously, if you completely change everything you've written then you're going to need another registration, as it will effectively be a different book, but if you've just edited it and made minor alterations this won't affect your protection.

You can register you copyright online at https://www.copyrightregistrationservice.com.

3. Get your work edited

Editing is a vital step often overlooked by authors who self-publish. The result can often be an amateurish book littered with embarrassing mistakes. Any professionally published book will go through an editing process, and it's important that the same applies to your self-published book. It's also important to complete the editing process before beginning the layout, or you could find yourself having to start the layout again from scratch.

4. Choose your self-publishing path

Before you can go any further you are going to need to choose a size for your book, and in order to do that you are going to need to choose a self-publishing path.

There are various different ways of getting self-published, but in general these range from the expensive hands off approach, where you pay a company to do the hard work for you, to the cheap DIY approach, where you do as much as you can yourself.

At the top end, the hands off approach can cost you thousands. At the bottom end, the DIY approach allows you to publish your book for almost nothing.

5. Finalise your layout / typesetting

Before you can finalise your layout (often referred to in the industry as "typesetting") you need to be sure that you've finalised your content – which means having your full work professionally edited and all the necessary changes made. If you decide to make changes after this point it will be difficult and potentially costly, and will require you to go through many of the following steps all over again.

You also need to have selected your path to publication, so that you know what page sizes are available to you, and what page margins you are going to need to apply. If you create a layout that doesn't meet printing requirements (for instance, includes text too close to the edge of the page) then you will have to start the typesetting process all over again.

6. Organise your ISBN

Your book needs to have an ISBN. If you are using a self-publishing service then they may provide you with one of their own, but it is likely to come with restrictions, and the international record for your book will show your self-publishing service as the publisher.

You can acquire your own ISBNs directly from the ISBN issuer, but they do not sell them individually, so you will end up spending quite a lot of money buying more ISBNs than you need. You will, however, have control of the ISBN, and you will be shown as the publisher.

Alternatively, you can purchase a single ISBN at a lower price from an ISBN retailer. This should give you control over the ISBN, however the record for the book will show the ISBN retailer as the publisher, which you may not consider to be ideal.

Whatever you choose, you need to arrange your ISBN no later than this point, because it needs to appear in the preliminary pages (prelims) of your book.

7. Compile your prelims

Your prelims may include a variety of pages, but should always include a title page, a half title page, and an imprint/copyright page. You might then also include other elements, such as a foreword, table of contents, etc. You can only compile your table of contents at this stage, because you need to know your ISBN (this will be included on the copyright/imprint page) and the page numbers for your table of contents. You therefore need to make sure that you are happy with the typesetting and have no further changes to make before compiling your prelims.

8. Create your final press proof

Depending on the self-publishing path you have chosen, you may be able to use a Word file as your final document. However, you need to be careful. In order to print your book it will have to be converted into a press-ready PDF at some point. If a self-publishing service is doing this for you then you will probably find that they own the PDF file that is created, meaning you don't have control over your own press files. Some services will impose hefty charges (hundreds or even more than a thousand dollars) to release these press files.

It might also be the case that you won't get to see the final PDF, and therefore won't get chance to check it for any errors introduced by the conversion process. If it's an automated system, it may also be difficult to control the output you get from it.

We'd suggest that it's best to produce your own PDF files if possible. To do this you will need a copy of Adobe Acrobat Professional, and you will need to be familiar with the correct settings for creating print ready PDFs. Be careful to embed all fonts and make sure that all images are at 300 DPI.

9. Create your cover

Only once your press proof is finalised can you complete your cover design. That's because your cover includes not only the front cover and the back cover, but also (critically) the spine – and the width of the spine will vary according to the number of pages in your final press proof. In order to complete your cover design you therefore need to know your page size, your page count (including all prelims), and your ISBN, as this will appear on the back cover. You also need to get a barcode for your ISBN.

10. Produce your book

Once your cover and press proof are ready you can go through whichever self-publishing path you have chosen to create your book. With some

pathways the production of a print proof can be an optional extra that is only available at an extra cost – but we'd recommend standing that cost and getting a print version of your book to check. You never know exactly how it's going to come out until you have a physical copy in your hand.

If you're happy with the proof you can clear your book for release. You don't need to do anything to get it on online retailers like Amazon – they will automatically pick up the ISBN and add your book to their websites themselves.

11. Create an ebook version

In the modern day, having an ebook version of your book is imperative. Ebooks account for a significant proportion of all book sales and are a particularly effective vehicle for unknown and self-published authors.

There are various different file formats used by the different platforms, but .epub is emerging as a standard, and having your book in .epub format should enable you to access all the platforms with a single file.

12. Distribute your ebook

Unlike with print books, you will need to act yourself to get your ebooks into sales channels. At a minimum, you need to ensure that you get your ebook available for sale through Amazon, Apple, and Google Play.

Table of US Literary Agencies

Table of UK Literary Agencies

Table of US Literary Agents

Table of UK Literary Agents

Table of US Magazines

Table of UK Magazines

Table of Canadian Magazines

Table of US Book Publishers

Table of UK Book Publishers

Table of Authors

Literary Agents and Agencies

For the most up-to-date listings of these and hundreds of other literary agents and agencies, visit https://www.firstwriter.com/Agents

To claim your free access to the site, please see the back of this book.

L001 3 Seas Literary Agency

Literary Agency
PO Box 444, Sun Prairie, WI 53590
United States
Tel: +1 (608) 332-3430

https://www.threeseasagency.com
https://www.facebook.com/3-Seas-Literary-Agency-75205869856/
https://twitter.com/threeseaslit?lang=en

ADULT > **Fiction** > *Novels*
Fantasy; Romance; Science Fiction; Thrillers; Women's Fiction

CHILDREN'S > **Fiction** > *Middle Grade*

YOUNG ADULT > **Fiction** > *Novels*

How to send: Query Manager
How not to send: Email

Accepts queries through online submission system only. See website for full guidelines.

Literary Agents: Cori Deyoe; Stacey Graham (**L264**); Kara Grajkowski (**L266**); Michelle Grajkowski (**L267**); Stephanie Stevens (**L585**)

L002 A.M. Heath & Company Limited, Author's Agents

Literary Agency
6 Warwick Court, Holborn, London, WC1R 5DJ
United Kingdom
Tel: +44 (0) 20 7242 2811

submissions@amheath.com

https://amheath.com
https://twitter.com/AMHeathLtd
https://www.instagram.com/a.m.heath

Professional Body: The Association of Authors' Agents (AAA)

Fiction > *Novels*

Nonfiction > *Nonfiction Books*

Send: Query; Synopsis; Writing sample
How to send: Online submission system
How not to send: Post; Email

Handles general commercial and literary fiction and nonfiction. Submit work with cover letter, synopsis, and writing sample up to 10,000 words, via online submission system only. No paper submissions or submissions by email. Aims to respond within six weeks.

Agency Assistant: Jessica Lee

Agency Assistant / Associate Agent: Florence Rees

Literary Agents: Julia Churchill; Bill Hamilton; Victoria Hobbs (**L306**); Oli Munson; Rebecca Ritchie (**L529**); Euan Thorneycroft

L003 A3 Artists Agency

Literary Agency
The Empire State Building, 350 Fifth Ave. 38th Floor, New York, NY 10118, 8305 Sunset Blvd., 5th Floor, Los Angeles, CA 90069
United States
Tel: +1 (646) 486-4600

contact@a3artistsagency.com

https://www.a3artistsagency.com/

Scripts
  Film Scripts; TV Scripts

Closed to approaches.

L004 Above the Line Agency

Literary Agency; Consultancy
468 N. Camden Drive, #200, Beverly Hills, CA 90210
United States
Tel: +1 (310) 859-6115

abovethelineagency@gmail.com

http://www.abovethelineagency.com

Professional Body: Writers Guild of America (WGA)

ADULT > **Scripts**
  Film Scripts; TV Scripts
CHILDREN'S > **Scripts**
  Film Scripts; TV Scripts

Send: Query
How to send: Online submission system

Costs: Offers services that writers have to pay for.

Send query via online web system only. Represents writers and directors; feature films, movies of the week, animation. Offers consultations at a rate of $200 per hour.

Literary Agents: Bruce Bartlett; Rima Greer

L005 Seren Adams

Associate Agent
United Kingdom

SAdams@unitedagents.co.uk

https://www.unitedagents.co.uk/sadamsunitedagentscouk
https://twitter.com/serenadams

Literary Agency: United Agents (**L619**)
Literary Agent: Anna Webber (**L639**)

Fiction > *Novels:* Literary

Nonfiction > *Nonfiction Books:* Narrative Nonfiction

Send: Query; Synopsis; Pitch; Market info
How to send: Email

Her list focuses on literary fiction and narrative non-fiction, and she has a particular passion for precise prose and unconventional storytelling.

Author Estates: The Estate of Dornford Yates; The Estate of Maurice Baring OBE

Authors: Esme Allman; Tia Bannon; Nivedita Barve; Akwasi Brenya-Mensa; Jen Calleja; Sean Patrick Cooper; Al Crow; Lauren Aimee Curtis; Sam Diamond; Olivia Douglass; Lucie Elven; Rakaya Fetuga; Ronan Fitzgerald; Amaryllis Gacioppo; Maria Giron; Lili Hamlyn; Catherine Humble; Blair James; Liza St. James; Ammar Kalia; Line Kallmayer; Ana Kinsella; Molly Lipson; Benoît Loiseau; Aileen Maguire; Megan Marz; Laura Maw; Jamal Mehmood; Sinéad Mooney; Luke Neima; Caleb Azumah Nelson; Timothy Ogene; Anna Chapman Parker; Rebecca Perry; Joanna Pocock; Karina Lickorish Quinn; Gemma Reeves; Laura Robertson; Olivia Rosenthall; Alan Rossi; Taylor-Dior Rumble; Thomas Rutter; Michael Salu; Lina Scheynius; Laura Southgate; Olivia Spring; Sean Stoker; Jordan Sullivan; Georgina Terry; Alessandra Thom; Zakia Uddin; Kenechi Uzor; Lauren Wallach; Eva Warrick; Ralf Webb; Kate West

L006 Phil Adie

Literary Agent
United Kingdom

http://nickturnermanagement.com/about-us/

Literary Agency: Nick Turner Management Ltd (**L475**)

Represents writers and directors for film and television, and is currently building his client list.

L007 Alex Adsett
Literary Agent; Consultant
Australia

https://alexadsett.com.au/literary-agency/
https://querymanager.com/query/
AlexAdsettQueries
https://twitter.com/alexadsett

Literary Agency: Alex Adsett Literary (**L016**)

ADULT
Fiction > *Novels*
 General, and in particular: Crime; Fantasy; Romance; Science Fiction

 Nonfiction > *Nonfiction Books*: Narrative Nonfiction

CHILDREN'S > **Fiction**
 Chapter Books: General
 Early Readers: General
 Middle Grade: General, and in particular: Fantasy; Science Fiction
 Picture Books: General

YOUNG ADULT > **Fiction** > *Novels*
 General, and in particular: Crime; Fantasy; Romance; Science Fiction

Send: Query; Author bio; Synopsis
How to send: Query Manager; By referral

Costs: Offers services that writers have to pay for. Provides commercial and strategic advice to authors and independent publishers, particularly regarding publishing contracts.

Always seeking amazing manuscripts, with a focus on fiction and narrative non-fiction, especially SFF, crime and romance, for all ages from picture books to adults. Accepts submissions from authors in Australia, New Zealand, SE Asia and the Pacific only.

L008 Aevitas Creative Management (ACM) UK
Literary Agency
49 Greek Street, London, W1D 4EG
United Kingdom

ukenquiries@aevitascreative.com

https://aevitascreative.com/home/acm-uk/
https://twitter.com/AevitasCreative
https://www.facebook.com/AevitasCreative/

Literary Agency: Aevitas
Professional Body: The Association of Authors' Agents (AAA)

UK branch of a US agency, founded in 2019, representing writers and brands throughout the world.

Authors: Tim Adams; James Aldred; James Ashton; Odafe Atogun; Philip Augar; Hannah Barnes; Rahul Bhatia; Chris Bickerton; Innes Bowen; Uri Bram; Ruth Brandon; Marcus Bridgewater; Tobias Buck; Stephen Bush; Joshua Chaffin; James Crabtree; Graham Daseler; Jonathan Derbyshire; Michael Dine; John Dunn; Armand D'Angour; Iyad El-Baghdadi; Graham Farmelo; Eliza Filby; Danny Finkelstein; John Gapper; Michael Gibson; Julian Glover; David Goodhart; Samuel Graydon; Rachel Halliburton; Liam Halligan; Charles Handy; Andrew Hankinson; Jonathan Hillman; Katja Hoyer; Nicholas Humphrey; Gavin Jacobson; Tiffany Jenkins; Joanna Jolly; Andrew Keen; Ivan Krastev; Graham Lawton; Charles Leadbeater; Frances Leech; Mark Leonard; Ian Leslie; Oliver Letwin; John Lloyd; Isabel Losada; Andrew Lycett; Polly Mackenzie; Gary Madden; Mark Makepeace; Kenan Malik; Owen Matthews; Tom McTague; Anand Menon; Daniel Metcalfe; Chris Miller; Munira Mirza; Paul Morland; Geoff Mulgan; Clive Myrie; David Omand; Arkady Ostrovsky; Tomiwa Owolade; Nicolas Pelham; Leigh Phillips; Mary Poffenroth; Alice Rawsthorn; Assaad Razzouk; Richard Reeves; Tim Revell; Peter Ricketts; Jonathan Rowson; Donald Sassoon; Mark Sedgwick; Nigel Shadbolt; Oliver Shah; Raymond Tallis; Sudhir Thomas Vadaketh; Georgios Varouxakis; Jeevan Vasagar; James Vogl; James Waddell; Owen Walker; Justin Webb; Frances Weetman; Geoffrey Wheatcroft; James Williams; Keely Winstone; Christian Wolmar; Jon Yates; Emma Young

Chief Executive Officer / Literary Agent: Toby Mundy

Literary Agents: Trevor Dolby (**L172**); Max Edwards (**L189**); Sara O' Keeffe (**L350**); Maria Cardona Serra (**L563**); Emily Sweet (**L601**)

L009 The Agency (London) Ltd
Literary Agency
24 Pottery Lane, Holland Park, London, W11 4LZ
United Kingdom

info@theagency.co.uk
submissions@theagency.co.uk

http://www.theagency.co.uk

Professional Body: The Association of Authors' Agents (AAA)

ADULT > **Scripts**
 Film Scripts; *TV Scripts*; *Theatre Scripts*
CHILDREN'S > **Fiction**
 Middle Grade; *Novels*; *Picture Books*
TEEN > **Fiction** > *Novels*

YOUNG ADULT > **Fiction** > *Novels*

Send: Query; Synopsis; Writing sample
How to send: Email

Represents writers and authors for film, television, radio and the theatre. Also represents directors, producers, composers, and film and television rights in books, as well as authors of children's books from picture books to teen fiction. More likely to consider material from script writers if it has been recommended by a producer, development executive or course tutor. If this is the case send CV, covering letter and details of your referee by email. Do not email more than one agent at a time. For directors, send CV, showreel and cover letter by email. For children's authors, send query by email with synopsis and first three chapters (middle grade, teen, or Young Adult) or complete ms (picture books). All submissions should be sent directly to the relevant agent. Film, TV and theatre writers and composers should also CC the submissions email address.

Literary Agents: Gina Andrews (**L025**); Ian Benson; Nicola Biltoo; Simon Blakey; Hannah Boulton; Hilary Delamere; Stephen Durbridge; Bethan Evans; Katie Haines; Jessica Hare (**L288**); Jonathan Kinnersley; Julia Kreitman; Norman North; Leah Schmidt; Emily Smith; Tanya Tillett

L010 AHA Talent Ltd
Literary Agency
22-23 James Street, Covent Garden, London, WC2E 8NS
United Kingdom
Tel: +44 (0) 20 7250 1760

mail@ahacreatives.co.uk

https://www.ahatalent.co.uk
https://twitter.com/AHAcreatives

Scripts
 Film Scripts; *Radio Scripts*; *TV Scripts*; *Theatre Scripts*

Send: Query; Author bio; Writing sample

Handles actors and creatives. Send query with CV/bio, and examples of your work.

Literary Agent: Amanda Fitzalan Howard

L011 The Ahearn Agency, Inc
Literary Agency
3436 Magazine St., #615, New Orleans, LA 70115
United States
Tel: +1 (504) 589-4200
Fax: +1 (504) 589-4200

pahearn@aol.com

http://www.ahearnagency.com

Fiction > *Novels*
 Suspense; Women's Fiction

Closed to approaches.

Send one page query with SASE, description, length, market info, and any writing credits. Accepts email queries without attachments. Response in 2-3 months.

Specialises in women's fiction and suspense. No nonfiction, poetry, juvenile material or science fiction.

Authors: Michele Albert; Rexanne Becnel; Wendy Hilton; Sabrina Jeffries; Connie Koslow; Sandra Landry; Deb Marlowe; Meagan McKinney; Kate Moore; Gerri Russell; Susan Sipal

Literary Agent: Pamela G. Ahearn

L012 Clementine Ahearne
Literary Agent; Company Director
United Kingdom

clementine.ahearne@ila-agency.co.uk

Literary Agency: ILA (Intercontinental Literary Agency) (**L316**)

Closed to approaches.

L013 Alan Brodie Representation
Literary Agency
Paddock Suite, The Courtyard, 55 Charterhouse Street, London, EC1M 6HA
United Kingdom
Tel: +44 (0) 20 7253 6226

ABR@alanbrodie.com

https://www.alanbrodie.com
https://www.facebook.com/Alan-Brodie-Representation-Ltd-407206926050145/
https://twitter.com/abragency
https://www.instagram.com/abragency/?hl=en

Scripts
 Film Scripts; *Radio Scripts*; *TV Scripts*; *Theatre Scripts*

Send: Query; Author bio
Don't send: Writing sample; Full text
How to send: By referral

Handles scripts only. No books. Approach with preliminary letter, recommendation from industry professional, and CV. Do not send a sample of work unless requested. No fiction, nonfiction, or poetry.

Literary Agents: Alan Brodie; Kara Fitzpatrick; Victoria Williams

L014 Michael Alcock
Literary Agent
United Kingdom

michael@johnsonandalcock.co.uk

http://www.johnsonandalcock.co.uk/michael-alcock

Literary Agency: Johnson & Alcock (**L330**)

Nonfiction > *Nonfiction Books*
 Arts; Biography; Current Affairs; Food; Health; History; Popular Science

Send: Query; Writing sample; Synopsis

Client list covers non-fiction mainly in the fields of history and biography, current affairs, food, health, the arts and popular science.

L015 Keir Alekseii
Associate Agent
United States

http://www.azantianlitagency.com/pages/team-ka.html
https://querymanager.com/query/keiralekseii

Literary Agency: Azantian Literary Agency (**L039**)

ADULT > **Fiction** > *Novels*
 Fantasy; Science Fiction

YOUNG ADULT > **Fiction** > *Novels*
 Contemporary; Fantasy; Science Fiction

Closed to approaches.

An educator and anti-GBV activist born and raised in Trinidad and Tobago, a twin island country in the West Indies. She is a writer, gamer, lover of folklore, and former research scientist. As a neurodivergent, queer woman of color, she is invested in discovering engaging work with similar representation, and is passionate about creating space for voices not often recognized. She is especially interested in stories from BIPOC who are born and raised in the Global South.

She is seeking YA & Adult SFF and YA contemporary. She is ONLY open to receiving queries from writers who identify as belonging to a marginalized or underrepresented group such as (but not limited to) BIPOC, LGBTQ+, immigrants, ND, folks who speak English as a second language, and DIS people.

L016 Alex Adsett Literary
Literary Agency
PO Box 694, Tugun, QLD 4224
Australia

alexadsett@alexadsett.com.au

https://alexadsett.com.au
https://twitter.com/alexadsett
http://www.facebook.com/Alexadsett.publishing
https://www.instagram.com/alexadsett

ADULT
 Fiction > *Novels*
  Commercial Women's Fiction; Commercial; Crime; Fantasy; Literary; Mystery; Romance; Romantic Comedy; Science Fiction

 Nonfiction > *Nonfiction Books*: Narrative Nonfiction

CHILDREN'S > **Fiction**
 Chapter Books; *Middle Grade*
YOUNG ADULT > **Fiction** > *Novels*

How to send: Query Manager; Email

Only represents authors in Australia, New Zealand, the Pacific or SE Asia, not USA or Europe. Only accepts submissions by invitation or referral, or from authors from an under-represented background – First Nations, authors of colour, authors from marginalised

cultures, neuroatypical authors, authors with disability, or authors from varied socio-economic circumstances.

Consultant / Literary Agent: Alex Adsett (**L007**)

Literary Agents: Rochelle Fernandez (**L215**); Abigail Nathan (**L470**)

L017 Alice Williams Literary
Literary Agency
United Kingdom
Tel: +44 (0) 20 7385 2118

submissions@alicewilliamsliterary.co.uk

https://www.alicewilliamsliterary.co.uk
https://twitter.com/aliceloveabooks
http://instagram.com/agentalicewilliams

Professional Body: The Association of Authors' Agents (AAA)

CHILDREN'S
 Fiction
  Middle Grade; *Novels*; *Picture Books*
 Nonfiction > *Nonfiction Books*

YOUNG ADULT
 Fiction > *Novels*
 Nonfiction > *Nonfiction Books*

Closed to approaches.

A specialist literary agency proudly representing writers and illustrators of picture books, young fiction, middle-grade, YA and non-fiction.

Literary Agent: Alice Williams (**L650**)

L018 Alive Literary Agency
Literary Agency
5001 Centennial Blvd #50742, Colorado Springs, CO 80908
United States

https://aliveliterary.com

Nonfiction > *Nonfiction Books*
 Lifestyle; Personal Development; Religion

How to send: By referral

Accepts queries from referred authors only. Works primarily with well-established, best-selling, and career authors.

Authors: Jamie Blaine; Michael Hyatt; Karen Kingsbury

Literary Agents: Lisa Jackson; Rachel Jacobson (**L321**); Kathleen Kerr (*L353*); Bryan Norman

L019 Beniamino Ambrosi
Literary Agent
United States

beniamino@cheneyagency.com
submissions@cheneyagency.com

https://www.cheneyagency.com/beniamino-ambrosi

Literary Agency: The Cheney Agency

Fiction in Translation > *Novels*: Literary

Fiction > *Novels*: Literary

Nonfiction in Translation > *Nonfiction Books*

Nonfiction > *Nonfiction Books*

Represents English-language nonfiction and literary fiction, and authors in translation.

L020 Eric Amling
Literary Agent; Foreign Rights Director
United States

submissions@dvagency.com

https://www.dvagency.com/aboutus

Literary Agency: Darhansoff & Verrill Literary Agents (**L156**)

Fiction > *Novels*: Literary

Nonfiction > *Nonfiction Books*
   Art Criticism; Cookery

Poetry > *Poetry Collections*

Business Manager and Foreign Rights Director, coordinating relationships with subagents across all major territories. As an agent, he is currently considering literary fiction, poetry, art criticism and cookbooks.

L021 Darley Anderson
Literary Agent
United Kingdom

https://www.darleyanderson.com/our-team

Literary Agency: The Darley Anderson Agency

ADULT > **Fiction** > *Novels*
   Romance; Thrillers

CHILDREN'S > **Fiction** > *Novels*: Animals

How to send: Email; Post

Looking specifically for thrillers with a strong central character set in America or Ireland or other internationally appealing locations and tear-jerking love stories. He is looking specifically for children's books featuring an original series character and animal stories. Email submissions should be sent to the agent's assistant.

Agency Assistant / Junior Agent: Rebeka Finch (**L219**)

Authors: Constance Briscoe; Chris Carter; Cathy Cassidy; Lee Child; Martina Cole; Margaret Dickinson; Clare Dowling; Jack Ford; Tana French; Paul Hauck; Joan Jonker; Annie Murray; Abi Oliver; Adrian Plass; Hazel Prior; David Rhodes; Jacqui Rose; Stephen Spotswood; Erik Storey; Anna-Lou Weatherley; Lee Weeks

L022 Hannah Andrade
Literary Agent
United States

https://bradfordlit.com/hannah-andrade-agent/
https://twitter.com/hhandrade93
https://querymanager.com/hannahandrade

Literary Agency: Bradford Literary Agency (**L073**)

ADULT
   Fiction > *Novels*: Mystery

   Nonfiction > *Nonfiction Books*
      Commercial; Crime; Investigative Journalism; Narrative Nonfiction

CHILDREN'S > **Fiction**
   Graphic Novels: General
   Middle Grade: General, and in particular: Dark Humour; Folklore, Myths, and Legends; Ghost Stories; Historical Fiction
YOUNG ADULT > **Fiction**
   Graphic Novels: General
   Novels: General, and in particular: Dark Fantasy; Folklore, Myths, and Legends; Historical Fiction; Mystery

Send: Query; Synopsis; Writing sample
How to send: Query Manager

Likes to think of herself as an editorial-focused agent and is particularly eager to acquire BIPOC/underrepresented voices. She is prioritizing stories of joy where identity isn't the focus and is especially excited about stories rooted in history, mythology, and legends, particularly those that are lesser-known or underrepresented in traditional publishing.

Very interested in stories that explore the intricacies of multicultural identities. She loves stories of immigration (not relegated to America) and of first/second generation Americans who struggle balancing the values of their country with the culture and heritage of their parents (as in the tv shows Ramy or Gentefied). As a Mexican-American, she would particularly love to see the stories that she grew up with showcased in new and creative ways.

L023 Nelle Andrew
Literary Agent
United Kingdom

nelle@rmliterary.co.uk

Literary Agency: Rachel Mills Literary (**L517**)

Fiction > *Novels*
   Commercial; Crime; Family; Historical Fiction; Literary; Magical Realism; Political Thrillers; Psychological Thrillers; Romantic Comedy; Speculative; Suspense; Thrillers; Women's Fiction

Nonfiction > *Nonfiction Books*
   History; Literary Memoir; Narrative Nonfiction; Politics

Send: Author bio; Synopsis; Writing sample
How to send: Email

Interested in excellent writing, compelling plots, diverse and unexpected voices and thoroughly engrossing reads. She loves books that are as escapist as they are explorative; as transportive as they are reflective. Her tastes are omnivorous. She particularly loves literary/commercial crossover fiction, psychological thrillers and suspense, intense or funny family dramas, savvy romantic comedies; gasp out loud crime and thriller, rich historical and even magical realism but that has to be done really well. She is interested in speculative and cross genre writing as well as clever female fiction. Mostly she wants stories that make her care as well as compel her to read on. In narrative nonfiction, she loves literary memoir, historical and smart politics but mainly it has to be non fiction for people who don't generally read non-fiction – aka, slightly zeitgeist, illuminative and ultimately a gripping read. She does not do straight sci-fi/Fantasy/children's and YA although that does not mean she wouldn't look at an adult novel with a child protagonist. She does not do short stories and collections or poetry. She does not do espionage thrillers either but she would be interested in a political thriller like HOUSE OF CARDS.

L024 Davinia Andrew-Lynch
Literary Agent
United Kingdom

Literary Agency: Curtis Brown (**L147**)

L025 Gina Andrews
Literary Agent
United Kingdom

gandrews@theagency.co.uk

https://theagency.co.uk/the-agents/gina-andrews/

Literary Agency: The Agency (London) Ltd (**L009**)

L026 Anne Clark Literary Agency
Literary Agency
United Kingdom

submissions@anneclarkliteraryagency.co.uk

https://www.anneclarkliteraryagency.co.uk

Professional Body: The Association of Authors' Agents (AAA)

CHILDREN'S
   Fiction
      Middle Grade; *Picture Books*
   Nonfiction > *Nonfiction Books*

YOUNG ADULT
   Fiction > *Novels*
   Nonfiction > *Nonfiction Books*

Closed to approaches.

Handles fiction and picture books for children and young adults. Send query by email only with the following pasted into the body of the email (not as an attachment): for fiction, include brief synopsis and first 3,000 words; for picture books, send complete ms; for nonfiction, send short proposal and the text of three sample pages. No submissions by post. See website for full guidelines.

Literary Agent: Anne Clark

L027 Anne Edelstein Literary Agency
Literary Agency
258 Riverside Drive #8D, New York, NY 10025
United States
Tel: +1 (212) 414-4923

information@aeliterary.com

https://aeliterary.com

Professional Body: Association of American Literary Agents (AALA)

Fiction > *Novels*
Commercial; Literary

Nonfiction > *Nonfiction Books*
Memoir; Narrative History; Psychology; Religion

Closed to approaches.

Send query letter with SASE and for fiction a summary of your novel plus the first 25 pages, or for nonfiction an outline of your book and one or two sample chapters. No queries by email.

Authors: Roderick Anscombe; Stephen Batchelor; Sophy Burnham; Mark Epstein; Kathleen Finneran; James Goodman; Patricia Hersch; His Holiness the Dalai Lama with Jeffrey Hopkins; Peter Levitt; Josip Novakovich; Natasha Rodijcic-Kane; James Shapiro; Jody Shields; Russell Shorto; Rachel Simon; Sasha Troyan; Phyllis Vane

Literary Agent: Anne Edelstein

L028 Jason Anthony
Literary Agent
United States

Literary Agency: Massie & McQuilkin

Closed to approaches.

L029 Antony Harwood Limited
Literary Agency
103 Walton Street, Oxford, OX2 6EB
United Kingdom
Tel: +44 (0) 1865 559615

mail@antonyharwood.com

http://www.antonyharwood.com

Fiction > *Novels*

Nonfiction > *Nonfiction Books*

Send: Query; Synopsis; Writing sample; Self-Addressed Stamped Envelope (SASE)
How to send: Email; Post

Handles fiction and nonfiction in every genre and category, except for screenwriting and poetry. Send brief outline and first 50 pages by email, or by post with SASE.

Authors: Christine Berry; Alastair Bonnett; Michael Bracewell; Peter Bunzl; Amanda Craig; Candida Crewe; David Dabydeen; Tracy Darnton; Roy Dennis; Louise Doughty; Robert Edric; Anna Fleming; Sarah Gibson; Bob Gilbert; Caspar Henderson; Jill Hopper; Sally Huband; Gwyneth Lewis; Amy Liptrot; Fraser MacDonald; Stephen Rutt; Guy Shrubsole; Hugh Warwick

Literary Agents: Antony Harwood; Jo Williamson (**L652**)

L030 Kurestin Armada
Literary Agent
Canada

https://www.rootliterary.com/agents
https://querymanager.com/query/kurestinarmada
https://www.publishersmarketplace.com/members/kurestinarmada/

Literary Agency: Root Literary (**L535**)

ADULT > **Fiction** > *Novels*
High / Epic Fantasy; Historical Romance; Horror; Romance; Science Fiction; Space Opera; Speculative; Supernatural / Paranormal Romance; Upmarket

CHILDREN'S > **Fiction**
Chapter Books: General
Graphic Novels: General
Middle Grade: Contemporary; Fantasy; Historical Fiction; Literary; Mystery; Science Fiction; Upmarket
Picture Books: Comedy / Humour

YOUNG ADULT > **Fiction**
Graphic Novels: Romance
Novels: Fantasy; Mystery; Science Fiction; Supernatural / Paranormal Romance; Supernatural / Paranormal

How to send: Query Manager

I love working with creators to form a roadmap for the rest of their career. Talking to people with projects that are ambitious, strange, personal, and just outrageously fun is the spark that keeps me going. I'm here to be their advocate and make sure they can keep writing for years and years to come.

L031 Victoria Wells Arms
Literary Agent
United States

victoria@hgliterary.com

https://www.hgliterary.com/victoria
https://twitter.com/VWArms

https://querymanager.com/query/VictoriaWellsArms

Literary Agency: HG Literary (**L305**)
Professional Bodies: Association of American Literary Agents (AALA); Society of Children's Book Writers and Illustrators (SCBWI)

ADULT
Fiction > *Novels*

Nonfiction > *Nonfiction Books*: Food

CHILDREN'S > **Fiction**
Middle Grade; *Picture Books*
YOUNG ADULT > **Fiction** > *Novels*

Closed to approaches.

Represents authors of children's books of all ages, select adult authors, food authors, and many talented picture book illustrators.

L032 Susan Armstrong
Literary Agent
United Kingdom
Tel: +44 (0) 20 7393 4200

susan.submissions@cwagency.co.uk
susan.armstrong@cwagency.co.uk

https://cwagency.co.uk/agent/susan-armstrong
https://twitter.com/SusanW1F

Literary Agency: C&W (Conville & Walsh) (**L092**)

Fiction > *Novels*
Book Club Fiction; Contemporary; Crime; Family Saga; Historical Fiction; Literary; Magical Realism; Speculative; Suspense; Thrillers; Upmarket Commercial Fiction; Women's Fiction

Does not want:

Fiction > *Novels*: Spy Thrilllers

How to send: Word file email attachment

I love to see literary fiction, book group/upmarket commercial women's fiction, contemporary stories, family dramas, historical, crime, thrillers and suspense. I'm also keen to see high-quality magical realism and speculative fiction. I enjoy novels that blend genres, are unusual in setting or circumstance, have unexpected twists, have a little darkness, pull at the heart-strings, and/or contain some sort of moral dilemma. Ultimately a cracking story is what I want to read.

I'm not currently taking on new YA/children's books or genre SF / Fantasy and am not the right agent to send espionage or spy thrillers to.

I am open to submissions from anyone anywhere in the world but I particularly love to hear from British-based writers, and Irish, Greek and ANZ novelists.

Authors: Jo Callaghan; Joanna Cannon; Maxine Beneba Clarke; Daniel Cole; Marianne Cronin; Joanna Glen; Anne Griffin; Miranda Cowley Heller; Crystal Jeans; Jess Kidd; Olivia Kiernan; Ali Shaw; Kim Sherwood; Natasha Solomons; M L Stedman; Jo Browning Wroe

L033 Arthur B Pulitzer Agency
Literary Agency
236 Moreland Street, Worcester, MA 01609
United States
Tel: +1 (646) 279-3118

arthur@pulitzer.biz

http://www.pulitzer.biz
http://www.pulitzer.biz/other-opportunities.html

ADULT
Nonfiction > *Nonfiction Books*: Crime

Scripts
Film Scripts: Crime
TV Scripts: Crime

CHILDREN'S > **Fiction** > *Middle Grade*

PROFESSIONAL > **Nonfiction** > *Nonfiction Books*: Education

Send: Query
How to send: Email

Costs: Offers services that writers have to pay for.

True Crime Manuscripts, Screenplays, Poems based on real people.

As their literary agent, I am in personal contact with each of these authors Since 2009 I have been corresponding with inmates by mail, email, telephone. I have corresponded via letters, email, and phone calls to inmates and some of their relatives. I have thoroughly read all manuscripts, correspondence and taken notes during direct phone calls and researched the court documents (including appeals) of each inmate. Each story, manuscript as written by the inmate, includes such injustices as: wrongful conviction, ineffective counsel, racially biased juries, police wrongdoing, evidence withheld, prosecutorial misconduct, racism in the courtroom, and constitutional rights' violations. Inmate backgrounds include horrific conditions such as: incest, parental abuse, domestic violence, poverty, drugs, and sexual abuse. All original screenplays, manuscripts were sourced by me directly from men and women inmates. Most are still in prison.

Literary Agent: Arthur B. Pulitzer (*L515*)

L034 Wayne Arthurson
Literary Agent
Canada

https://www.therightsfactory.com/Agents/Wayne-Arthurson

Literary Agency: The Rights Factory

ADULT
Fiction > *Novels*
Crime; Fantasy; Literary; Science Fiction

Nonfiction > *Nonfiction Books*
Memoir; Narrative Nonfiction

YOUNG ADULT
Fiction > *Novels*
Crime; Fantasy; Literary; Science Fiction

Nonfiction > *Nonfiction Books*
Memoir; Narrative Nonfiction

Currently building his list of talent, looking specifically for YA or adult literary, crime and SFF and narrative nonfiction and memoir. He's actively seeking works by Indigenous writers.

Authors: Greg Bechtel; Eric Beetner; Deryn Collier; Candas Jane Dorsey; Trevor Duplessis; Brittlestar aka Stewart Reynolds; Marsheila (Marcy) Rockwell; Steven Sandor; Coltrane Seesequasis

L035 ASH Literary
Literary Agency
United Kingdom

info@ashliterary.com
submissions@ashliterary.com

https://www.ashliterary.com/
https://twitter.com/ashliterary
https://instagram.com/aliceisagenting
https://querymanager.com/query/ASH_Literary

Professional Body: The Association of Authors' Agents (AAA)

CHILDREN'S > **Fiction**
Chapter Books: General
Graphic Novels: Contemporary; Fantasy; Magical Realism; Surreal
Middle Grade: Contemporary; Magical Realism
YOUNG ADULT > **Fiction**
Graphic Novels: Contemporary; Fantasy; Magical Realism; Surreal
Novels: General

Send: Synopsis; Writing sample
How to send: Query Manager

Looking for extraordinary stories for children that reflect and celebrate the diversity of our world. As of July 2021, our focus is on Middle Grade, particularly illustrated Middle Grade, and graphic novels across all ages.

Authors: Dina Al-Sabawi; HF Brownfield; Ryan Crawford; Alex Falase-Koya; Abimbola Fashola; Kereen Getten; Gina Gonzales; Sarah Guillory; Ravena Guron; Radiya Hafiza; Anika Hussain; Jennifer Iacopelli; Nansubuga Isdahl; Amy Leow; Richard Mercado; Yasmine Naghdi; Samuel Pollen; Ryan Robinson; Elizabeth Rounding; Cynthia So; Chitra Soundar; Ashley Thorpe; Claire Tomasi; Ryan Rose Vinson-Jacobs; Anna Wenner; Adelle Yeung

Literary Agents: Saffron Dodd (**L171**); Alice Sutherland-Hawes (**L599**)

L036 Charlotte Atyeo
Literary Agent
United Kingdom

charlotte@greyhoundliterary.co.uk

https://greyhoundliterary.co.uk/agent/charlotte-atyeo/
https://twitter.com/EverSoBookish

Literary Agency: Greyhound Literary (**L271**)

ADULT
Fiction > *Novels*: Literary

Nonfiction > *Nonfiction Books*
General, and in particular: Biography; Equality; Feminism; Gender Issues; Memoir; Music; Nature; Sport

CHILDREN'S
Fiction > *Picture Books*

Nonfiction
Middle Grade; *Nonfiction Books*
YOUNG ADULT > **Fiction** > *Novels*

Does not want:

> **CHILDREN'S** > **Fiction** > *Middle Grade*: Fantasy
>
> **YOUNG ADULT** > **Fiction** > *Novels*: Fantasy

Send: Query; Synopsis; Writing sample; Outline
How to send: Email
How not to send: Post

Represents non-fiction authors as well as a select number of children's and fiction authors. Primarily looking for original and brilliantly written general non-fiction, biography and memoir, sport, music, nature writing, and feminism, gender and equality issues. She is not currently taking on books about religion or memoirs that deal with abuse and/or trauma. When it comes to children's books, she is open to submissions of picture books and non-fiction (particularly from authors with expert knowledge of their subject). She is especially excited to hear from author/illustrators and from under-represented voices. For MG & YA, she is not currently considering anything on the fantasy side. On the adult fiction side, she is taking on a small number of literary novels. (She is not looking for crime and thriller, romance, or SFF.)

Authors: Carol Atherton; Saskia Gwinn; Ed Hawkins; Michael Holding; Michael Hutchinson; Jennifer Lane; Michelle Lovric; Susan Richardson; Sarah Shephard; Tatton Spiller; Jen Wight

L037 AVAnti Productions & Management
Literary Agency
22 Timms Close, Parsonage Road, Horsham,
West Sussex, RH12 4TN
United Kingdom
Tel: +44 (0) 7999 193311

avantiproductions@live.co.uk

https://www.avantiproductions.co.uk

Scripts > *Film Scripts*

Send: Full text
How to send: Email
How not to send: Post

Costs: Author covers sundry admin costs.

Talent and literary representation. Open to screenplay submissions for short films and feature films, but no theatre scripts.

Literary Agent: Veronica Lazar

L038 Ayesha Pande Literary
Literary Agency
United States
Tel: +1 (212) 283-5825

queries@pandeliterary.com

https://www.pandeliterary.com

A New York based boutique literary agency with a small and eclectic roster of clients. Submit queries via form on website. No poetry, business books, cookbooks, screenplays or illustrated children's books.

Literary Agents: Madison Smartt Bell; Stephany Evans (**L204**); Serene Hakim (**L280**); Annie Hwang (**L315**); Kayla Lightner (**L389**); Luba Ostashevsky; Ayesha Pande (**L487**); Anjali Singh

L039 Azantian Literary Agency
Literary Agency
United States

http://www.azantianlitagency.com
https://www.facebook.com/azantianlitagency/
https://twitter.com/jenazantian
https://www.instagram.com/azantianbooknerd/

Fiction > *Novels*

Nonfiction > *Nonfiction Books*

Committed to guiding the careers of both new and established voices in fiction and nonfiction, particularly those who have been historically underrepresented.

Associate Agents: Keir Alekseii (**L015**); Masha Gunic (**L277**); Shannon Lechon (**L382**); Alexandra Weiss (**L640**)

Literary Agents: Jennifer Azantian (**L040**); T.S. Ferguson (**L213**)

L040 Jennifer Azantian
Literary Agent
United States

http://www.azantianlitagency.com/pages/team-ja.html

Literary Agency: Azantian Literary Agency (**L039**)

ADULT > **Fiction** > *Novels*
General, and in particular: Fantasy; Psychological Horror; Science Fiction

CHILDREN'S > **Fiction**
Graphic Novels: Contemporary; Fantasy; Magical Realism
Middle Grade: General

YOUNG ADULT > **Fiction**
Graphic Novels: Contemporary; Fantasy; Magical Realism
Novels: General, and in particular: Mystery; Psychological Thrillers; Speculative

How to send: Query Manager

Focuses primarily on fiction across genres for mg, YA, and adult readers. Currently accepting submissions of graphic novels only.

L041 Lauren Bajek
Junior Agent
United States

https://www.lizadawsonassociates.com/lauren-bajek

Literary Agency: Liza Dawson Associates (**L397**)

Fiction > *Novels*
Fantasy; Horror; Literary; Science Fiction; Speculative; Upmarket

Nonfiction > *Nonfiction Books*
Nature; Science

Closed to approaches.

Currently building a select list of fiction and nonfiction, with an emphasis in SFFH and upmarket speculative fiction. Across the board, she is drawn to literary prose, queer and anticolonial perspectives, unusual or hybrid forms, and an ambitious sense of imagination. She is always interested in animal cognition, translation, and sentient houses.

L042 Emma Bal
Literary Agent
United Kingdom

https://madeleinemilburn.co.uk/looking-for/emma-bal-what-im-looking-for/

Literary Agency: Madeleine Milburn Literary, TV & Film Agency (**L417**)

Nonfiction > *Nonfiction Books*
Anthropology; Arts; Cookery; Culture; Economics; Food; Geography; History; Literature; Memoir; Narrative Nonfiction; Nature; Philosophy; Politics; Psychology; Science; Travel

Actively looking for: new perspectives in history, arts & culture, politics, economics, philosophy, psychology, and science; original

approaches to travel and nature writing; unusual illustrated projects; thoughtful and dynamic cookery and food writing; and atypical narrative non-fiction and memoir. See agency listing for submission guidelines.

L043 Sarah Ballard
Literary Agent
United Kingdom

sballard@unitedagents.co.uk

https://www.unitedagents.co.uk/
sballardunitedagentscouk

Literary Agency: United Agents (**L619**)

Fiction > *Novels*

Nonfiction > *Nonfiction Books*
Feminism; History; Memoir

Does not want:

> **Fiction** > *Novels*
> Saga; Science Fiction

Send: Full text; Synopsis; Author bio
How to send: Email

I have extremely broad taste in fiction and non-fiction, but the underlying quality of the work that I'm interested in is a sense of urgency, and an attempt to make a change in the world, whether that is fiction with a compelling plot or structure overlaying a set of big ideas; memoir-ish non fiction flavoured with obsession and unfolding a hidden agenda; or meticulously researched history which changes our world view. I have a particular interest in feminism and feminist approaches – but exploring ideas or angles which are completely new to me is one of the great joys of my job. I prefer to work with writers who are more-or-less based in the UK, and are aiming to deliver a book every one or two years, and for whom I can add something to every area of their creative lives.

Associate Agent: Eli Keren (**L352**)

L044 Dan Balow
Literary Agent
United States

vseem@stevelaube.com

https://stevelaube.com/what-i-am-looking-for/

Literary Agency: The Steve Laube Agency

Nonfiction > *Nonfiction Books:* Christianity

Send: Query; Proposal; Writing sample
How to send: Email attachment
How not to send: Post; In the body of an email

Represents nonfiction works mainly to Christian-themed publishers. No fiction.

L045 Gaia Banks
Literary Agent

Literary Agency: Sheil Land Associates Ltd (**L567**)

L046 Anjanette Barr
Literary Agent
United States

query@dunhamlit.com

https://www.dunhamlit.com/anjanette-barr.html
https://aalitagents.org/author/anjanettebarr/
https://www.facebook.com/BookBarrista
https://twitter.com/bookbarrista
https://www.instagram.com/bookbarrista/
https://www.linkedin.com/in/anjanette-barr-34193765/
https://youtube.com/AnjanetteBarrtheBookBarr

Literary Agency: Dunham Literary, Inc. (**L180**)
Professional Bodies: Association of American Literary Agents (AALA); Society of Children's Book Writers and Illustrators (SCBWI)

ADULT
  Fiction > *Novels*
    General, and in particular: Gothic; Magical Realism

  Nonfiction > *Nonfiction Books*
    Arts; Biography; Culture; Folklore, Myths, and Legends; History; Memoir; Nature; Popular Science; Poverty; Religion

CHILDREN'S > **Fiction** > *Picture Books*

Send: Query; Writing sample
How to send: In the body of an email
How not to send: Google Docs shared document; Email attachment

She loves genre and popular fiction with substance, and literary and non-fiction titles infused with living ideas that leave readers with a new desire to immerse themselves in the subject matter. In non-fiction she is looking for well-researched biography written in beautiful literary prose, popular science and other disciplines titles that make lay-people enchanted and invested in topics previously over their heads, and memoir with the ability to connect diverse readers. She's also interested in books that shed light on poverty and justice in a new way. She prefers picture books that are winsome and pleasant to read aloud. Particular interests are the exploration of culture, history, faith, myth, fine arts, and nature. She has a soft spot for gothic novels and magical realism. As a mother of four, she's is especially fond of books that can be read aloud and shared with the whole family.

L047 Jason Bartholomew
Literary Agent
United Kingdom

https://www.thebksagency.com/submissions

Literary Agency: The BKS Agency (**L063**)

Fiction > *Novels*
  Crime; Thrillers

Nonfiction > *Nonfiction Books*
  Biography; Current Affairs; History; Memoir; Narrative Nonfiction; Politics

Send: Query; Outline; Author bio
How to send: Online submission system

Originally from America. Spent ten years working in New York publishing, primarily for Hachette Book Group USA. He moved to Hachette UK in 2008 where he was the Rights Director across Hodder & Stoughton, Headline Publishing Group, Quercus Books, and John Murray Press.

L048 Tim Bates
Senior Agent
United Kingdom

tbates@pfd.co.uk

https://petersfraserdunlop.com/agent/tim-bates/

Literary Agency: Peters Fraser + Dunlop (**L501**)

Fiction > *Novels*

Nonfiction > *Nonfiction Books*
  Commercial; Food; Narrative Nonfiction; Nature; Popular Culture; Sport

Send: Query; Synopsis; Writing sample; Proposal; Author bio
How to send: Email
How not to send: Post

Represents a wide range of authors and is particularly interested in pop culture, narrative and serious non-fiction, food-writing, nature and the outdoors, sport and commercial non-fiction and fiction of all forms.

Authors: Iain Ballantyne; Tom Blass; Brian Blessed; Kevin Brennan; Whitney Brown; Leland Carlson; Kimberley Chambers; Richard Coles; Brendan Cooper; Sara Dallin; Len Deighton; Pepsi Demacque-Crockett; Naomi Devlin; Martin Dorey; Jon Dunn; Caroline Fleming; Will Francis; Irina Georgescu; Caro Giles; Romy Gill; Jean G Goodhind; Jonathan Gornall; Delayed Gratification; Annie Gray; Simon Halfon; Eddie Hall; Tony Hannan; Angela Hartnett; James Hogg; Becky Holmes; Amari Koryang; Lizzie Lane; Jack Lowe; Gary Numan; Chris Paling; David Papineau; Jo Pavey; Lesley Pearse; Nigel Reed; Andrew Ridgeley; Debora Robertson; Noble Rot; Neil 'Razor' Ruddock; Romla Ryan; Rupert Shortt; Susannah Stapleton; Colin Taylor; Caroline Tremlett; Valentine Warner; Emma J. Wells; Keren Woodward; Jacqueline Yallop

L049 Bath Literary Agency
Literary Agency
5 Gloucester Road, Bath, BA1 7BH
United Kingdom

submissions@bathliteraryagency.com

https://www.bathliteraryagency.com
https://twitter.com/BathLitAgency
http://instagram.com/bathlitagency

Professional Body: The Association of Authors' Agents (AAA)

CHILDREN'S
  Fiction
    Middle Grade; *Picture Books*
  Poetry > *Picture Books*
YOUNG ADULT
  Fiction > *Novels*
  Nonfiction > *Nonfiction Books*

Send: Query; Synopsis; Writing sample; Full text; Self-Addressed Stamped Envelope (SASE)
How to send: Email; Post

Handles fiction and nonfiction for children, from picture books to Young Adult. Send query by email or by post with SAE for reply and return of materials if required, along with the first three chapters (fiction) or the full manuscript (picture books). See website for full details.

Literary Agent: Gill McLay

L050 Erica Bauman
Literary Agent
United States

https://aevitascreative.com/agents/
https://querymanager.com/query/EricaBauman

Literary Agency: Aevitas

ADULT > > **Fiction**
  Graphic Novels: General
  Novels: Commercial; Folklore, Myths, and Legends; Magic; Romantic Comedy; Speculative
CHILDREN'S > **Fiction** > *Graphic Novels*
YOUNG ADULT > **Fiction** > *Graphic Novels*

Closed to approaches.

Most interested in commercial novels that feature an exciting premise and lyrical, atmospheric writing; imaginative, genre-blending tales; speculative worlds filled with haunting, quietly wondrous magic; fresh retellings of mythology, ballet, opera, and classic literature; sharply funny rom-coms; graphic novels for all ages; fearless storytellers that tackle big ideas and contemporary issues; and working with and supporting marginalized authors and stories that represent the wide range of humanity.

Authors: Telênia Albuquerque; Jessica Benoist; Melissa Benoist; Abigail Rayner

L051 Jan Baumer
Literary Agent
United States

jan@foliolitmanagement.com

https://www.foliolit.com/agents-1/jan-baumer

Literary Agency: Folio Literary Management, LLC

Fiction > *Novels*
Allegory; Literary

Nonfiction > *Nonfiction Books*
Business; Comedy / Humour; Cookery; Health; Memoir; Narrative Nonfiction; Parenting; Prescriptive Nonfiction; Religion; Self Help; Spirituality; Wellbeing

Closed to approaches.

Interests as an agent are largely nonfiction, specifically spirituality, religion, self-help, health and wellness, parenting, memoir, and business with a spirituality or self-help angle. Also open to allegorical fiction, but it must have a literary voice and an author with the writing credentials to pull it off.

L052 **Veronique Baxter**
Literary Agent; Company Director
United Kingdom

veroniquemanuscripts@davidhigham.co.uk
childrenssubmissions@davidhigham.co.uk

https://www.davidhigham.co.uk/agents-dh/veronique-baxter/

Literary Agency: David Higham Associates Ltd (**L159**)

ADULT
Fiction > *Novels*
Historical Fiction; Literary; Speculative; Upmarket Crime; Upmarket Thrillers

Nonfiction > *Nonfiction Books*
Current Affairs; Feminism; History; Memoir; Narrative Nonfiction

CHILDREN'S > **Fiction** > *Middle Grade*: Adventure

YOUNG ADULT > **Fiction** > *Novels*: Adventure

Send: Query; Synopsis; Writing sample
How to send: Email

Drawn to writing that is both distinctive and fluid in both fiction and non-fiction. In fiction she is currently looking for: literary fiction, fiction with a speculative edge, historical fiction that surprises and upmarket crime and thrillers. In non-fiction, she is particularly drawn to feminism, history, current affairs, memoir and narrative non-fiction. In children's books, she is looking for standout middle-grade and YA with heart or adventure, or preferably both! Children's submissions should be sent to the children's submissions email address.

Agency Assistant: Sara Langham

Authors: Richard Adams; Naomi Alderman; Tina Baker; Belinda Bauer; Hannah Begbie; Carys Bray; Kevin Brockmeier; Glen Brown; Nick Butterworth; Camilla Chester; Jamie Costello; Cressida Cowell; Nick Crumpton; Nicola Davies; Jonathan Dimbleby; Berlie

Doherty; Ellie Eaton; David Edmonds; Maz Evans; Jamila Gavin; Guinevere Glasfurd; Holly Gramazio; Candy Guard; Oliver Harris; Mo Hayder; Lisa Heathfield; Emma Henderson; Sarah Hilary; Edward Hogan; Phil Hogan; Ian Holding; Lucy Hounsom; Tristan Hughes; William Hussey; Will Iredale; Diana Wynne Jones; Claire King; Saci Lloyd; Kesia Lupo; Patrick Marnham; Geraldine McCaughrean; Jean McNeil; Sarah Mitchell

L053 **Diana Beaumont**
Literary Agent
United Kingdom

diana@marjacq.com

https://www.marjacq.com/diana-beaumont.html

Literary Agency: Marjacq Scripts Ltd (**L421**)

Fiction > *Novels*

Nonfiction > *Nonfiction Books*

Closed to approaches.

Represents adult fiction and nonfiction.

Authors: Tanya Atapattu; Holly Baxter; Alexandra K Benedict; Daisy Buchanan; Cecil Cameron; James Campbell; Angela Clarke; Mathew Clayton; Fiona Collins; Caroline Corcoran; Isabel Costello; Hannah Dolby; Francesca Dorricott; Lilly Ebert; Dov Forman; Eve Harris; Louise Hulland; Catriona Innes; Harriet Johnson; Amy Jones; Eve Makis; Andrea Mara; Francesca May; Claire McGowan; Emma Orchard; Adam Pearson; Fiona Perrin; Alice Peterson; Das Petrou; Rachel Phipps; Carmen Reid; Samantha Renke; Lee Ridley; Diana Rosie; Frances Ryan; Jennifer Savin; Hema Sukumar; Lucy Vine; James Wallman; Roz Watkins; Eva Woods

L054 **Maria Bell**
Associate Agent
United States

Literary Agency: Sterling Lord Literistic, Inc. (**L583**)
Literary Agent / Vice President: Douglas Stewart (**L586**)
Senior Agent: Neeti Madan (**L416**)

Fiction > *Novels*
Baseball; LGBTQIA; Literary; Nature

Nonfiction > *Nonfiction Books*
Baseball; LGBTQIA; Nature

Send: Query; Synopsis; Proposal; Writing sample
How to send: Online submission system

Drawn to literary fiction that breaks conventions in form, voice and character. In both fiction and nonfiction, she's partial to stories involving the natural world, queer identities, baseball, and all those that grapple

with conflicts and truths from which most of us instinctively distance ourselves.

L055 **Maddy Belton**
Associate Agent
United Kingdom

https://www.madeleinemilburn.co.uk/agents/maddy-belton/
https://twitter.com/MadsPhyllis

Literary Agency: Madeleine Milburn Literary, TV & Film Agency (**L417**)

ADULT > **Fiction** > *Novels*
Contemporary Fantasy; Cozy Fantasy; Dark; Fairy Tales; Fantasy; Folklore, Myths, and Legends; High / Epic Fantasy; Historical Fiction; LGBTQIA; Romance; Science Fiction; Thrillers

CHILDREN'S
Fiction > *Middle Grade*
Comedy / Humour; Fantasy; Magic

Nonfiction > *Nonfiction Books*

YOUNG ADULT > **Fiction** > *Novels*
Contemporary Fantasy; Cozy Fantasy; Fantasy; High / Epic Fantasy; LGBTQIA; Romance

Send: Outline; Author bio; Market info; Marketing Plan; Writing sample
How to send: Email

SFF across all genres for all ages, including: grim dark, thriller, historical, romance, cosy fantasy, sci-fi, epic, YA fantasy, dark academia, contemporary fantasy, fantasy middle-grade, mythology, fairy tale and queer fantasy. Inspiring children's non-fiction.

L056 **Laura Bennett**
Associate Agent; Editor
United Kingdom

https://www.liverpool-literary.agency/about

Literary Agency: The Liverpool Literary Agency (**L396**)

ADULT > **Fiction** > *Novels*
Dystopian Fiction; Fantasy; Post-Apocalyptic; Science Fiction; Steampunk; Urban Fantasy

YOUNG ADULT > **Fiction** > *Novels*
Dystopian Fiction; Fantasy; Post-Apocalyptic; Science Fiction; Steampunk; Urban Fantasy

Closed to approaches.

L057 **The Bent Agency (UK)**
Literary Agency
Greyhound House, 23/24 George Street, Richmond, TW9 1HY
United Kingdom

info@thebentagency.com

https://www.thebentagency.com
https://www.instagram.com/thebentagency/

Professional Body: The Association of Authors' Agents (AAA)

Literary Agency: The Bent Agency (**L058**)

ADULT
Fiction
Graphic Novels; *Novels*
Nonfiction > *Nonfiction Books*

CHILDREN'S > **Fiction**
Chapter Books; *Graphic Novels*; *Middle Grade*
YOUNG ADULT
Fiction
Graphic Novels; *Novels*
Nonfiction > *Nonfiction Books*

Send: Query
How to send: Email; Query Manager

UK office of established US agency. See website for individual agent interests and contact details and approach appropriate agent. Do not send submissions to general agency email address. See website for full submission guidelines.

Associate Agent: Martha Perotto-Wills (**L497**)

Literary Agent / Managing Director: Molly Ker Hawn (**L299**)

L058 The Bent Agency

Literary Agency
45 Lyme Road, Suite 206, Hanover, NH 03755
United States

info@thebentagency.com

https://www.thebentagency.com
https://www.instagram.com/thebentagency/

ADULT
Fiction
Graphic Novels; *Novels*
Nonfiction > *Nonfiction Books*

CHILDREN'S > **Fiction**
Chapter Books; *Graphic Novels*; *Middle Grade*
YOUNG ADULT
Fiction
Graphic Novels; *Novels*
Nonfiction > *Nonfiction Books*

Send: Query
How to send: Email; Query Manager

Accepts email or Query Manager queries only. See website for agent bios and specific interests and email addresses, then query one agent only. See website for full submission guidelines.

Authors: Arvin Ahmadi; Samantha M. Bailey; Gary John Bishop; Tera Lynn Childs; Yangsze Choo; Dhonielle Clayton; Liv Constantine; Spencer Coursen; Susan Crispell; Lisa Doyle; Kerry Douglas Dye; Deborah Falaye; Michael Farquhar; Mina Fears; Delores Fossen; Stephanie Garber; J. T. Geissinger; Seressia Glass; Shannon Greenland; Alexis Henderson; Rita Herron; A. G. Howard; Robert Isaacs;

Tiffany D. Jackson; Meredith Jaeger; Elise Kova; Roselle Lim; Julia London; Iman Mahoui; Jo Manning; Barry Martin; Marta McDowell; Luann McLane; Goldy Moldavsky; Laura Morelli; Joel Morris; Natalie Naudus; Preston Norton; Jean Pendziwol; Michelle Quach; Morgan Ryan; Lynsay Sands; L C. Shaw; Lori Nelson Spielman; Vicki Lewis Thompson; Joseph Turkot; Sandra Waugh; Lynn Weingarten; Lori Wilde

Company Director / Literary Agent: Gemma Cooper (**L139**)

Company Director / Literary Agent / Vice President: Victoria Cappello (*L097*)

Literary Agency: The Bent Agency (UK) (**L057**)

Literary Agent / President: Jenny Bent (**L059**)

Literary Agents: Nicola Barr; Claire Draper (**L179**); James Mustelier (**L466**); Zoe Plant (**L507**); John Silbersack; Desiree Wilson (**L655**)

L059 Jenny Bent

Literary Agent; President
United States

queries@thebentagency.com

https://www.thebentagency.com/jenny-bent

Literary Agency: The Bent Agency (**L058**)

ADULT
Fiction > *Novels*
Commercial; Domestic Suspense; Grounded Fantasy; High Concept; Horror; Literary; Romance; Romantic Comedy; Speculative; Upmarket Women's Fiction

Nonfiction > *Nonfiction Books*
Lifestyle; Self Help

YOUNG ADULT > **Fiction** > *Novels*
General, and in particular: Contemporary; Fantasy; Magic; Romantic Comedy; Suspense

Does not want:

> **Fiction** > *Novels*
> Cozy Mysteries; High / Epic Fantasy; Science Fiction

Closed to approaches.

I'm currently looking for literary and commercial fiction and young adult fiction as well as select non-fiction in the areas of self-help and lifestyle. My client list is diverse and I welcome submissions from BIPOC authors.

In adult fiction, I'm looking for high concept, upmarket women's fiction; grounded fantasy; speculative fiction and horror (I particularly love a good ghost story, along the lines of writing by Simone St. James and Jennifer McMahon); and domestic suspense, but the bar is very high in suspense right now so it has to be an extremely creative concept. I also rep

some romance and rom-com, but no other genre fiction: I'm not a good choice for high fantasy, cozy mystery, or sci-fi.

In young adult fiction, I'm pretty open to genre — I love fantasy, rom-coms, suspense, contemporary, almost anything except for sci-fi. I do notice that my YA taste does tend to skew towards older readers, more in a crossover direction.

In general, I tend to prefer plot-driven books to character-driven ones and pacing is very important to me. I also love novels — for adults or young adults — that have an element of magic or fantasy to them or that take me into a world that is new to me, whether real or imaginary. And while I love books to be dark and weird in terms of content, I find that I am more drawn to traditional, rather than experimental, methods of structure and storytelling.

In nonfiction, I am looking for authors with a unique approach and a very large existing platform. I'm not generally the right choice for memoir or narrative non-fiction, but I'm always open to hearing a pitch just in case.

All of the books that I represent speak to the heart in some way: they are linked by genuine emotion, inspiration, and great writing and storytelling. I love books that make me laugh, make me cry, or ideally do both.

Authors: Arvin Ahmadi; Samantha M. Bailey; Gary John Bishop; Tera Lynn Childs; Yangsze Choo; Dhonielle Clayton; Liv Constantine; Spencer Coursen; Susan Crispell; Lisa Doyle; Kerry Douglas Dye; Deborah Falaye; Michael Farquhar; Mina Fears; Delores Fossen; Stephanie Garber; J. T. Geissinger; Seressia Glass; Shannon Greenland; Alexis Henderson; Rita Herron; A. G. Howard; Robert Isaacs; Tiffany D. Jackson; Meredith Jaeger; Elise Kova; Roselle Lim; Julia London; Iman Mahoui; Jo Manning; Barry Martin; Marta McDowell; Luann McLane; Goldy Moldavsky; Laura Morelli; Joel Morris; Natalie Naudus; Preston Norton; Jean Pendziwol; Michelle Quach; Morgan Ryan; Lynsay Sands; L C. Shaw; Lori Nelson Spielman; Vicki Lewis Thompson; Joseph Turkot; Sandra Waugh; Lynn Weingarten; Lori Wilde

L060 Betsy Amster Literary Enterprises

Literary Agency
607 Foothill Blvd #1061, La Canada Flintridge, CA 91012
United States

b.amster.assistant@gmail.com

http://amsterlit.com

Fiction > *Novels*
Literary; Mystery; Thrillers; Upmarket Commercial Fiction; Upmarket Women's Fiction

Nonfiction

Gift Books: General
Nonfiction Books: Biography; Career
Development; Cookery; Gardening; Health;
History; Lifestyle; Medicine; Narrative
Nonfiction; Nutrition; Parenting; Popular
Culture; Psychology; Self Help; Social
Issues; Travel; Women's Issues

How to send: Email
How not to send: Post

A full-service literary agency based in Los
Angeles, California. No romances,
screenplays, poetry, westerns, fantasy, horror,
science fiction, techno thrillers, spy capers,
apocalyptic scenarios, political or religious
arguments, or self-published books. See
website for full guidelines.

Authors: Amy Alkon; Dwight Allen; Will
Allen; Jess J. Araujo; Elaine N. Aron; Sandi
Ault; Lois Barr; Ariel Bernstein; Kim Boyce;
Helene Brenner; Karen Briner; Catheryn J.
Brockett; Karen Burns; Mónica Bustamante;
Joe P. Carr; Steven Carter; Lillian Castillo-
Speed; Robin Chotzinoff; Frank Clifford; Rob
Cohen; David Cundy; Leela Cyd; Margaret
Leslie Davis; Jan DeBlieu; David J. Diamond;
Martha O. Diamond; Phil Doran; Suzanne
Dunaway; Nick Dyer; J. Theron Elkins; Ruth
Andrew Ellenson; Loretta Ellsworth; James P.
Emswiler; Mary Ann Emswiler; Naomi Epel;
Alex Epstein; Karin Esterhammer; Jeannette
Faurot; Tom Fields-Meyer; Joline Godfrey;
Tanya Ward Goodman; Michael I. Goran;
Hindi Greenberg; Ellen Hawley; Marian
Henley; Charney Herst; Leigh Ann Hirschman;
Ariel Horn; Lisa Hunter; Jackie; Melissa
Jacobs; Janet Jaffe; Emily Katz; E. Barrie
Kavasch; Joy Keller; Eileen Kennedy-Moore;
Rachel Tawil Kenyon; Camille Landau; Carol
Lay; Anna Lefler; Margaret Lobenstine; Mark
Lowenthal; Paul Mandelbaum; Ivy Manning;
Melissa Martin; Domenico Minchilli;
Elizabeth Helman Minchilli; Wendy Mogel;
Sharon Montrose; Bonnie Frumkin Morales;
Yolanda Nava; Joy Nicholson; Judith Nies;
Susie Norris; Christopher Noxon; Lynette
Padwa; Neela Paniz; Kishani Perera; Cash
Peters; Barry Prizant; Winifred Reilly; Andrea
Richards; Eileen Roth; Adam Sappington;
Marjorie Barton Savage; Anthony Schmitz;
M.D. Edward Schneider; Kyle Schuneman;
George Shannon; Nancy Spiller; Allison Mia
Starcher; Louise Steinman; Bill Stern; Terry
Theise; Christina Baglivi Tinglof; Linda Venis;
MPH Emily Ventura; Marisel Vera; Elizabeth
Verdick; John Vorhaus; Hannah Voskuil;
Diana Wells; Tiare White; Chris Witt; Karen
Witynski; Steve D. Wolf; David Wollock;
Dawn Young

Literary Agent: Betsy Amster

L061 Tina Betts
Literary Agent; Company Director
United Kingdom

https://www.andrewmann.co.uk/agents
Literary Agency: Andrew Mann Ltd

ADULT
  Fiction > *Novels*: Commercial

  Nonfiction > *Nonfiction Books*

  Scripts
    Radio Scripts; *TV Scripts*
CHILDREN'S > **Fiction** > *Novels*

Closed to approaches.

List includes quality commercial fiction, as
well as some non-fiction and children's titles.

Also represents a small list of dramatists for
television and radio.

L062 Beverley Slopen Literary Agency
Literary Agency
131 Bloor St. W., Suite 711, Toronto, M5S
1S3
Canada
Tel: +1 (416) 964-9598

beverley@slopenagency.ca

https://slopenagency.com

Fiction > *Novels*
  Commercial; Literary

Nonfiction > *Nonfiction Books*

One of Canada's leading literary agents. Based
in Toronto, her list includes serious non-fiction
and literary and commercial fiction.

Literary Agent: Beverley Slopen

L063 The BKS Agency
Literary Agency
Pennine Place, 2A Charing Cross Road,
London, WC2H 0FH
United Kingdom

https://www.thebksagency.com
https://www.facebook.com/thebksagency
https://twitter.com/ThebksAgency

A literary management agency based in
London. Founded in 2018 by three friends,
each of whom has spent over two decades
working across the biggest publishing houses
in London and New York.

Literary Agents: Jason Bartholomew (**L047**);
Joanna Kaliszewska (**L339**); Jessica Killingley
(**L355**); Morwenna Loughman (**L402**); James
Spackman (**L580**)

L064 Blake Friedmann Literary Agency Ltd
Literary Agency
15 Highbury Place, London, N5 1QP
United Kingdom
Tel: +44 (0) 20 7387 0842

info@blakefriedmann.co.uk

http://www.blakefriedmann.co.uk
https://twitter.com/BlakeFriedmann
https://www.instagram.com/
blakefriedmannliteraryagency/

Professional Body: The Association of
Authors' Agents (AAA)

Fiction > *Novels*

Nonfiction > *Nonfiction Books*

Send: Query; Synopsis; Writing sample
How to send: Word file email attachment

Always on the lookout for exciting new work
and welcomes submissions from both
published and debut authors, across many
genres, and from any background.

Associate Agent: Sian Ellis-Martin (**L196**)

Authors: Diane Abbott; Gilbert Adair;
Tatamkhulu Afrika; Mary Akers; Shani
Akilah; Kasim Ali; Ted Allbeury; Dima
Alzayat; Ros Anderson; Graeme Armstrong;
Paul Ashton; Dani Atkins; MiMi Aye; Trezza
Azzopardi; Bolu Babalola; Rue Baldry; Anna
Barrett; Johanna Bell; Tom Bellamy; Jendella
Benson; Meliz Berg; Ian Birch; Rachel
Blackmore; Scarlett Brade; Andy Briggs; Nora
Anne Brown; Erin Bunting; Jo Facer & Erin
Bunting; James Cahill; Ailsa Caine; Natasha
Carthew; Will Carver; Francesca Chang; Norie
Clarke; Julia Cole; Sue Cook; Emma Cowell;
Sara Crowe; Will Dean; Tuyen Do; Michael
Donkor; Jo Facer; Paul Finch; Fiona Ford; Alix
Fox; Sarah Franklin; Roxy Freeman; Jean
Fullerton; Janice Galloway; Gabriella Griffith;
Sarah Hartley; David Haslam; Emma Forsyth
Haslett; Kate Hodges; Michael Hogan; Kerry
Hudson; Leah Hyslop; Tomasz Jedrowski;
Alexandra Jellicoe; Benjamin Johncock; John
Kennedy; Caroline Khoury; Konditor; Sarah
Lee; Kat Lister; Richard Littler; Clayton
Littlewood; Anneliese Mackintosh; Ailbhe
Malone; Lucy Mangan; Amy Mason; Beryl
Matthews; Lia Middleton; Nina-Sophia
Miralles; Emma Mitchell; Sue Moorcroft;
Grace Mortimer; Emer O'Toole; Sara Ochs;
Leeanne O'Donnell; Karen Powell; Rosalind
Powell; Julie Rea; Allie Reynolds; Annie
Robertson; Elliot Ryan; Lora Stimson; Kate
Thompson; Mary Torjussen; Hannah Treave;
John Trenhaile; Jack Urwin; Anne-Marie
Varga; Luca Veste; Pippa Vosper; Helen
Walmsley-Johnson; Andrew Wong

Literary Agent: Juliet Pickering (**L505**)

Literary Agent / Managing Director: Isobel
Dixon (**L170**)

Senior Agent: Kate Burke (**L089**)

L065 Felicity Blunt
Literary Agent
United Kingdom

http://submissions.curtisbrown.co.uk/agents/

Literary Agency: Curtis Brown (**L147**)

Fiction > *Novels*
Domestic Suspense; Historical Fiction; Literary Thrillers; Psychological Suspense; Speculative

Nonfiction > *Nonfiction Books*
Cookery; Food

Send: Full text; Synopsis; Author bio
How to send: Email

"Most simply put I am looking for good stories, compellingly told. The books on my list have one thing in common, the combination of a distinctive voice and a great narrative."

L066 Sidney Boker
Literary Agent
United States

https://inkwellmanagement.com/staff/sidney-boker

Literary Agency: InkWell Management

YOUNG ADULT > **Fiction**
Graphic Novels: General
Novels: Fantasy; Historical Fiction; Science Fiction

Loves to read young adult, fantasy, sci-fi, historical, and graphic novels, and almost anything with a strong female lead.

L067 Camilla Bolton
Senior Agent
United Kingdom

camilla@darleyanderson.com

https://www.darleyanderson.com/our-team
https://twitter.com/CamillaJBolton

Literary Agency: The Darley Anderson Agency

Fiction > *Novels*
Book Club Fiction; Crime; Mystery; Suspense; Thrillers; Women's Fiction

How to send: Email attachment

Looking for accessible and commercial crime, thrillers, mysteries, suspense and women's fiction.

Assistant Agent: Jade Kavanagh (**L346**)

Authors: Emma Bamford; Vicki Bradley; James Carol; Gloria Cook; A J Cross; Jason Dean; Hayley Doyle; C. M. Ewan; G.R. Halliday; Egan Hughes; Emma Kavanagh; T M Logan; Imran Mahmood; L V Matthews; Phoebe Morgan; B.A. Paris; Jo Platt; Mira V. Shah; Rebecca Shaw; KL Slater; Kim Slater; Sean Slater; Catherine Steadman; G X Todd; Tim Weaver

L068 Bookseeker Agency
Literary Agency
United Kingdom

bookseller@blueyonder.co.uk

https://bookseekeragency.com
https://twitter.com/BookseekerAgent

Fiction > *Novels*

Poetry > *Any Poetic Form*

Send: Query; Synopsis; Writing sample
How to send: Email; Post

Handles fiction and (under some circumstances) poetry. No nonfiction. Send query by post or email outlining what you have written and your current projects, along with synopsis and sample chapter (novels).

Literary Agent: Paul Thompson

L069 BookStop Literary Agency, LLC
Literary Agency
P.O. Box 626, Lafayette, CA 94549
United States
Tel: +1 (925) 254-2664

info@bookstopliterary.com

http://www.bookstopliterary.com
https://www.facebook.com/bookstopliterary/
https://www.instagram.com/bookstopliterary/

CHILDREN'S
Fiction
Chapter Books; Graphic Novels; Middle Grade; Novels; Picture Books
Nonfiction > *Nonfiction Books*

YOUNG ADULT > **Fiction** > *Novels*

Handles fiction and nonfiction for children and young adults.

Literary Agents: Minju Chang (**L109**); Karyn Fischer (**L221**); Kendra Marcus (**L420**)

L070 Stefanie Sanchez Von Borstel
Literary Agent
United States

https://www.fullcircleliterary.com/our-agents/stefanie-von-borstel/

Literary Agency: Full Circle Literary, LLC
Professional Bodies: Society of Children's Book Writers and Illustrators (SCBWI); Association of American Literary Agents (AALA)

CHILDREN'S
Fiction > *Middle Grade*
Contemporary; Historical Fiction

Poetry > *Novels in Verse*
Contemporary; History

Closed to approaches.

Looking for middle grade fiction and novels-in-verse (contemporary or historical) with memorable characters and voice. No submissions from white people.

L071 Imogen Bovill
Literary Agent
United Kingdom

Imogen@abnerstein.co.uk

http://abnerstein.co.uk

Literary Agency: Abner Stein

L072 Sarah Bowlin
Senior Agent
Los Angeles
United States

https://aevitascreative.com/agents/
https://querymanager.com/query/
S_Bowlin_queries

Literary Agency: Aevitas

Fiction > *Novels*
General, and in particular: Literary

Nonfiction > *Nonfiction Books*
General, and in particular: Comedy / Humour; Dance; Food History; History; Narrative Nonfiction; Popular Culture; Wine

Closed to approaches.

Focused on bold, diverse voices in fiction and nonfiction. She's especially interested in stories of strong or difficult women and unexpected narratives of place, of identity, and of the shifting ways we see ourselves and each other. She's also interested in food history, wine, and dance.

Authors: Elisa Albert; Wendy Chen; Amanda Churchill; Caroline Corrigan; Meghan Gilliss; Nicky Gonzalez; Jasmin 'Iolani Hakes; Shane Jones; Gene Kwak; Melanie LaBarge; Cory Leadbeater; Ashley Nelson Levy; Ananda Lima; Halimah Marcus; Sabrina Orah Mark; Kelly McClorey; Joanne McNeil; Amelia Morris; Kevin Nguyen; Mary Otis; Janika Oza; Andrew Palmer; Ayşegül Savaş; Elizabeth L. Silver; Lynn Steger Strong; Souvankham Thammavongsa; Vanessa Veselka; Hope Wabuke; Jenny Xie

L073 Bradford Literary Agency
Literary Agency
5694 Mission Center Road # 347, San Diego, CA 92108
United States
Tel: +1 (619) 521-1201

https://bradfordlit.com

ADULT
Fiction > *Novels*
Contemporary Romance; Erotic Romance; Historical Romance; Literary; Mystery; Romance; Romantic Suspense; Supernatural / Paranormal Romance; Thrillers; Upmarket Commercial Fiction; Urban Fantasy; Women's Fiction

Nonfiction > *Nonfiction Books*
Biography; Business; Comedy / Humour; Cookery; Food; History; Memoir;

Parenting; Popular Culture; Relationships; Self Help; Social Issues

CHILDREN'S > Fiction
Novels; Picture Books

How to send: Query Manager

Represents a wide range of fiction and nonfiction. Select a particular agent at the agency to submit to, and submit to only one agent at a time.

Literary Agents: Hannah Andrade (**L022**); Laura Bradford (**L074**); Rebecca Matte (**L428**); Kaitlyn Sanchez (**L546**)

L074 Laura Bradford
Literary Agent
United States

https://bradfordlit.com/about/laura-bradford/
https://querymanager.com/query/laurabradford
http://www.twitter.com/bradfordlit

Literary Agency: Bradford Literary Agency (**L073**)
Professional Bodies: Association of American Literary Agents (AALA); Romance Writers of America (RWA); Society of Children's Book Writers and Illustrators (SCBWI)

ADULT
  Fiction
    Graphic Novels: General
    Novels: Contemporary Romance; Erotic Romance; Historical Fiction; Historical Romance; Mystery; Romance; Romantic Suspense; Speculative; Thrillers; Women's Fiction
  Nonfiction > *Nonfiction Books*

CHILDREN'S > Fiction > *Middle Grade*

YOUNG ADULT > Fiction > *Novels*

How to send: Query Manager

Interested in romance (historical, romantic suspense, category, contemporary, erotic), speculative fiction, women's fiction, mystery, thrillers, young adult, upper middle grade, illustration as well as some select non-fiction.

L075 Karen Brailsford
Consulting Agent
United States

https://aevitascreative.com/agents
https://querymanager.com/query/KarenBrailsford

Literary Agency: Aevitas

Nonfiction > *Nonfiction Books*
  Arts; Biography; Entertainment; Health; Memoir; Spirituality; Wellbeing

Closed to approaches.

Based in Los Angeles and is especially interested in arts and entertainment, memoir, biography, health and wellness, spirituality and works of non-fiction that inspire and shine a light on contemporary conditions.

L076 Maria Brannan
Literary Agent
United Kingdom

maria@greyhoundliterary.co.uk

https://greyhoundliterary.co.uk/agents/maria-brannan

Literary Agency: Greyhound Literary (**L271**)

ADULT > Fiction > *Novels*
  General, and in particular: Book Club Fiction; Commercial; Fantasy; High Concept; Horror; Romance; Romantic Comedy; Soft Science Fiction; Speculative; Thrillers

NEW ADULT > Fiction > *Novels*
  General, and in particular: Book Club Fiction; Commercial; Fantasy; High Concept; Horror; Romance; Romantic Comedy; Soft Science Fiction; Speculative; Thrillers

YOUNG ADULT > Fiction > *Novels*
  General, and in particular: Book Club Fiction; Commercial; Fantasy; High Concept; Horror; Romance; Romantic Comedy; Soft Science Fiction; Speculative; Thrillers

Send: Query; Synopsis; Outline; Writing sample
How to send: Email

Has very wide ranging tastes in fiction and is interested in writing for adult, new adult/crossover and YA readers. She loves character-driven novels with a commercial bent that spark imagination or discussion. In particular she has a passion for genre fiction – especially fantasy with memorable characters and great world-building; horror with a unique concept or perspective; and softer, genre-crossing science fiction. She is also keen on voice-led and emotive reading group fiction; love stories and rom-coms that make you fall for both of leads; unnerving, twisty crime writing; thrillers with a great hook; and anything with a high concept or speculative edge.

L077 Hannah Brattesani
Literary Agent
United States

http://www.friedrichagency.com/about-alternate-2/

Literary Agency: The Friedrich Agency LLC

Fiction > *Novels*
  Arts; Comedy / Humour; Dark; Environment; Food; Horror; Literary; Upmarket

Nonfiction
  Essays: Comedy / Humour
  Nonfiction Books: Comedy / Humour; Environment; Narrative Nonfiction

Send: Query
How to send: In the body of an email

I'd love to see literary novels that use humor in dark and/or interesting ways, playful horror (think Grady Hendrix), smart and funny upmarket fiction, and narrative non-fiction and essay collections that can make me laugh.

L078 The Brattle Agency LLC
Literary Agency
PO Box 380537, Cambridge, MA 02238
United States

submissions@thebrattleagency.com

https://thebrattleagency.com

Fiction
  Graphic Novels: General
  Novels: Literary

Nonfiction > *Nonfiction Books*
  American History; Art History; Culture; European History; Music; Politics; Sport

Closed to approaches.

Accepts submissions only during one-month reading periods. See website for details.

L079 Amy Brewer
Senior Agent
United States

https://www.metamorphosisliteraryagency.com/about
https://querymanager.com/query/1379

Literary Agency: Metamorphosis Literary Agency (**L440**)

Fiction > *Novels*
  General, and in particular: Book Club Fiction; Comedy / Humour; LGBTQIA; Romance; Women's Fiction

Closed to approaches.

For the last few years, she has been learning all she can about social media optimization and platform building in the publishing industry. Her experience in the mental health field and yoga training help her guide and assist clients with stress and anxiety in this highly competitive industry.

L080 The Bright Agency (UK)
Literary Agency
103-105 St John's Hill, London, SW11 1SY
United Kingdom
Tel: +44 (0) 20 7326 9140

mail@thebrightagency.com
literarysubmissions@thebrightagency.com

https://thebrightagency.com
https://thebrightagency.com/uk/submissions/new

Media Company: The Bright Group International Limited

CHILDREN'S

Fiction
Chapter Books; *Graphic Novels*; *Middle Grade*; *Picture Books*
Nonfiction > *Nonfiction Books*

Send: Query; Synopsis; Writing sample
How to send: Email

We love seeing new work, and we'd love to see yours. Talent is exciting, and when you help it grow, it's incredible. We're proud of our ability to discover and establish new artists and authors. We're also proud that we still represent people who were with us when we first opened, and who've truly bloomed over the years. Could you be next?

L081 **The Bright Agency (US)**
Literary Agency
157 – A First Street, C/O – Bright Group US Inc #339, Jersey City, NJ 07302
United States
Tel: +1 (646) 578 6542

mail@thebrightagency.com
literarysubmissions@thebrightagency.com

https://thebrightagency.com
https://thebrightagency.com/us/submissions/new

Media Company: The Bright Group International Limited

CHILDREN'S
Fiction
Chapter Books; *Graphic Novels*; *Middle Grade*; *Picture Books*
Nonfiction > *Nonfiction Books*

Send: Query; Synopsis; Writing sample
How to send: Email

We love seeing new work, and we'd love to see yours. Talent is exciting, and when you help it grow, it's incredible. We're proud of our ability to discover and establish new artists and authors. We're also proud that we still represent people who were with us when we first opened, and who've truly bloomed over the years. Could you be next?

L082 **Savannah Brooks**
Literary Agent
United States

https://www.sblitagent.com
https://ktliterary.com/about/
https://twitter.com/SBLitAgent
https://querymanager.com/query/1346

Literary Agency: KT Literary (**L368**)

ADULT > **Fiction** > *Short Fiction Collections*
Contemporary; Horror; Mystery; Romantic Comedy; Suspense; Thrillers

CHILDREN'S > **Fiction**
Chapter Books; *Middle Grade*; *Picture Books*
YOUNG ADULT
Fiction > *Novels*
Nonfiction > *Nonfiction Books*

Closed to approaches.

Seeking all of kid lit—picture books, chapter books, middle grade, and YA, both fiction and nonfiction—and adult contemporary fiction, romcoms, thrillers/mystery/suspense, and horror.

L083 **Brotherstone Creative Management**
Literary Agency
Mortimer House, 37-41 Mortimer Street, London, W1T 3JH
United Kingdom

submissions@bcm-agency.com
info@bcm-agency.com

http://bcm-agency.com

Professional Body: The Association of Authors' Agents (AAA)

Fiction > *Novels*
Commercial; Literary

Nonfiction > *Nonfiction Books*

Send: Query; Writing sample; Synopsis
How to send: Email

Always on the search for talented new writers. Send query by email. For fiction, include the first three chapters or 50 pages and 2-page synopsis. For nonfiction, include detailed outline and sample chapter. No children's and young adult fiction, sci-fi and fantasy novels or unsolicited short story and poetry collections, or scripts.

Literary Agent: Charlie Brotherstone

L084 **Justin Brouckaert**
Literary Agent
New York
United States

https://aevitascreative.com/agents/
https://querymanager.com/query/justinbrouckaert

Literary Agency: Aevitas

Fiction
Novels: Literary
Short Fiction: Literary

Nonfiction > *Nonfiction Books*
Current Affairs; History; Journalism; Memoir; Narrative Nonfiction; Parenting; Politics; Sport; Travel

Send: Author bio; Outline; Market info; Writing sample
How to send: Query Manager

Actively seeking character-driven and formally inventive literary fiction and memoir, as well as narrative nonfiction in the areas of sports, internet culture, politics and current affairs, parenting, travel, and history. Regardless of genre, he is most passionate about projects that shine a light on underserved and overlooked communities and/or highlight unique

relationships between people and places. He is especially interested in pairing with debut authors and helping them grow their careers.

Authors: Char Adams; Lauren Aguirre; Matthew H. Birkhold; Greg Bluestein; Diane Cardwell; Jesselyn Cook; Susan Crawford; R.S. Deeren; Benoit Denizet-Lewis; William Deverell; Rebekah Diamond; Ali Drucker; Brian Dumaine; Ken Ellingwood; Marisa Franco; Sarah Gearhart; Jeffrey Gettleman; Noah Gittell; Wade Graham; Gabrielle Hartley; Jesse Horwitz; Chris Koslowski; Jacqueline Lewis; Joe Milan; Luma Mufleh; Pamela Pavliscak; Lindsay Powers; Julian Sancton; Amber Share; Meg Vondriska; Evan Waite; Bryan Walsh; Ali Marie Watkins

L085 **Andrea Brown**
President; Literary Agent
United States

andrea@andreabrownlit.com

https://www.andreabrownlit.com/Team/Andrea-Brown

Literary Agency: Andrea Brown Literary Agency, Inc.
Professional Body: Association of American Literary Agents (AALA)

Closed to approaches.

L086 **Browne & Miller Literary Associates**
Literary Agency
United States

mail@browneandmiller.com

https://www.browneandmiller.com
https://www.facebook.com/browneandmiller
https://twitter.com/BrowneandMiller

Fiction > *Novels*: Commercial

Nonfiction > *Nonfiction Books*: Commercial

Closed to approaches.

Handles books for the adult commercial book markets. No children's, young adult, science fiction, fantasy, horror, short stories, poetry, screenplays, or academic works. Send query only by email. No attachments.

Literary Agent: Danielle Egan-Miller

L087 **Chris Bucci**
Senior Agent
New York
United States

https://aevitascreative.com/agents/

Literary Agency: Aevitas

Fiction > *Novels*
Commercial; Historical Fiction; History; Literary; Mystery; Popular Culture; Popular Science; Thrillers

Nonfiction > *Nonfiction Books*

Narrative Nonfiction; Politics; Sport

Send: Author bio; Outline; Market info; Writing sample
How to send: Online submission system

Based in the New York Metropolitan area. Represents a broad range of fiction and nonfiction.

Authors: Amina Akhtar; John Allore; Isa Arsén; Timothy Caulfield; Kendra Coulter; Christine Estima; Kelly J. Ford; Jennifer Heisz; Amy Jones; Jessica McDiarmid; Briana Una McGuckin; Jane McManus; Eliza Nellums; Kelsey Ronan; Kathryn Schmitz; Emily Schultz; Kavin Senapathy; P.J. Vernon.

L088 Danielle Bukowski
Literary Agent
United States

https://www.sll.com/our-team

Literary Agency: Sterling Lord Literistic, Inc. **(L583)**

Fiction > *Novels*

Nonfiction > *Nonfiction Books*

Send: Query; Synopsis; Writing sample
How to send: Online submission system

Represents fiction for adults, from smart bookclub to literary, and select nonfiction, Particularly looking for narratives from writers traditionally excluded from the publishing industry. For fiction, she likes books that balance plot with voice, have a strong sense of place, a unique hook, and are stylistically bold; for nonfiction, she's looking for work grounded in the author's personal interest, rigorously reported and researched, and will expand the reader's view of the world.

L089 Kate Burke
Senior Agent
United Kingdom

kate@blakefriedmann.co.uk

http://blakefriedmann.co.uk/kate-burke
https://twitter.com/kbbooks

Literary Agency: Blake Friedmann Literary Agency Ltd **(L064)**

Fiction > *Novels*
   Book Club Women's Fiction; Contemporary; Crime; Dark; Family; Gothic; High Concept Thrillers; Historical Fiction; Mystery; Thrillers; Women's Fiction

Does not want:

> **Fiction** > *Novels*
> Political Thrillers; Spy Thrillers

Send: Query; Synopsis; Writing sample
How to send: Word file email attachment

My list is made up of everything I like to read – gripping fiction featuring characters you

can't get enough of and whom you don't want to part with at the end of a novel. I love dark stories but also uplifting love stories, too, and I'm keen to find more stories set in unusual or far-flung places. I love to learn more about a place and its inhabitants as I think fiction is all about escapism!

In terms of what I'm looking for: on the crime side, I love dark thrillers that keep me turning the page long into the night and that surprise me with plot twists and interesting narrative structures; crime series featuring new and fresh lead investigators; high-concept thrillers (contemporary or historical) that have a 'what if?' plot structure and say something about our society now or then.

On the historical fiction side, I love stories which combine a great sense of place and time (ideally, post-1800, please) with a mystery. I'm also a huge fan of anything set in a spooky old house so Gothic, atmospheric historical thrillers are also top of my wishlist!

Contemporary-wise, I love novels which have a discussable issue at their heart – and could work well for a heated book club discussion – as well as sweeping family stories about mothers, sisters and daughters (set anywhere in the world).

In case it's helpful to know what I don't represent: non-fiction, children's and young adult books, science fiction, fantasy, spy, conspiracy or political thrillers.

Authors: Dani Atkins; Anna Barrett; Johanna Bell; Scarlett Brade; Andy Briggs; Will Carver; Emma Cowell; Will Dean; Paul Finch; Fiona Ford; Jean Fullerton; John Kennedy; Caroline Khoury; Sarah Lee; Beryl Matthews; Lia Middleton; Sara Ochs; Allie Reynolds; Kate Thompson; Mary Torjussen; Hannah Treave; John Trenhaile; Anne-Marie Varga; Luca Veste

L090 Emelie Burl
Associate Agent
United States

emelie@schulmanagency.com

https://twitter.com/BigKidBookworm
https://www.facebook.com/emelie.s.samuelson
https://www.publishersmarketplace.com/members/Schulman/

Literary Agency: Susan Schulman Literary Agency **(L597)**

ADULT > **Nonfiction** > *Nonfiction Books:* Popular Culture

CHILDREN'S > **Fiction** > *Middle Grade*
   Comedy / Humour; Magic

YOUNG ADULT > **Fiction** > *Novels*
   Comedy / Humour; Magic; Romantic Comedy

Focuses on children's, young adult, and pop culture nonfiction. Likes stories of hope and

humor, rom-coms, strong female leads, and magic of all sorts. Also interested in LGBT+ and BIPOC. Not keen on murder.

L091 Kate Bussert
Literary Agent

Literary Agency: Bret Adams Ltd

L092 C&W (Conville & Walsh)
Literary Agency
Cunard House, 15 Regent Street, London, SW1Y 4LR
United Kingdom
Tel: +44 (0) 20 7393 4200

https://cwagency.co.uk
https://twitter.com/cwagencyuk
https://instagram.com/cwagencyuk

Professional Body: The Association of Authors' Agents (AAA)

ADULT
   Fiction > *Novels*
   Nonfiction > *Nonfiction Books*

CHILDREN'S > **Fiction** > *Novels*

YOUNG ADULT > **Fiction** > *Novels*

Send: Query; Synopsis; Writing sample; Proposal; Author bio; Market info; Outline
How to send: Word file email attachment

See website for agent profiles and submit to one particular agent only. Send submissions by email as Word files only. No postal submissions. For fiction, submit the first three sample chapters of the completed manuscript (or about 50 pages) with a synopsis. For nonfiction, send 30-page proposal. No poetry or scripts, or picture books. See website for full guidelines.

Author / Literary Agent: Catherine Cho **(L120)**

Author Estate: The Estate of Francis Bacon

Authors: Naoko Abe; Shahnaz Ahsan; Nigel Akehurst; Dolly Alderton; Keir Alexander; Piers Alexander; Robin Antalek; Ollie Aplin; Steven Appleby; Will Ashon; Stephen Baker; Lisa Ballantyne; Damian Barr; Tony Barrell; Colin Barrett; Kevin Barry; Neil Bartlett; Brock Bastian; Sara Baume; Richard Beard; Francesca Beauman; Matt Beaumont; Patrick Benson; Mandy Berriman; Josie Bevan; Michael Bhaskar; Vanessa Black; Emma Blackery; Immodesty Blaize; David Bodanis; Lee Bofkin; Simon van Booy; Megan Bradbury; John Bradshaw; Kevin Breathnach; Michael Brooks; Iain Broome; The Wild Swimming Brothers; Dea Brovig; Bill Browder; Tom Burgis; Jo Callaghan; Joanna Cannon; Tim Clare; Maxine Beneba Clarke; Daniel Cole; Caroline Crampton; Marianne Cronin; Fiona Cummins; Howard Cunnell; Lara Dearman; Nathan Filer; Cal Flyn; Julia Forster; Sam Fowles; Ruth Gilligan; Joanna Glen; Colin Grant; Anne Griffin; Guy Gunaratne; Karen Hamilton; Miranda Cowley

Heller; Eileen Horne; Crystal Jeans; Jess Kidd; Olivia Kiernan; Rebecca Ley; Katy Mahood; Shiv Malik; Ramita Navai; Hollie Newton; Christina Patterson; Jenny Quintana; Ben Rawlence; Catherine Riley; Sophy Roberts; Rhik Samadder; David Savill; Holly Seddon; Tali Sharot; Ali Shaw; Kim Sherwood; Natasha Solomons; Tim Spector; M L Stedman; Michelle Sterling; Michelle Thomas; Christie Watson; Adam Weymouth; Tod Wodicka; Jo Browning Wroe

Literary Agents: Susan Armstrong (**L032**); Matilda Ayris; Kate Burton; Alexander Cochran (*L128*); Clare Conville (*L136*); Allison DeFrees; Emma Finn; Carrie Kania; Sophie Lambert (**L371**); Lucy Luck; Richard Pike; Jake Smith-Bosanquet

L093 Linda Camacho
Literary Agent
United States

linda@galltzacker.com
QueryLinda@galltzacker.com

Literary Agency: Gallt & Zacker Literary Agency

Fiction > *Novels*
  Romance; Women's Fiction

Closed to approaches.

L094 Charlie Campbell
Literary Agent
United Kingdom

charlie@greyhoundliterary.co.uk

https://greyhoundliterary.co.uk/agent/charlie-campbell/
https://twitter.com/ScapegoatCC

Literary Agency: Greyhound Literary (**L271**)

ADULT
  Fiction > *Novels*
    Commercial; Crime; Historical Fiction; Literary; Thrillers
  Nonfiction > *Nonfiction Books*
    Comedy / Humour; Commercial; History; Literary; Popular Science; Sport

CHILDREN'S > **Fiction** > *Novels*

Send: Query; Synopsis; Writing sample
How to send: Email

Primarily looking for crime and thrillers, as well as literary and historical fiction. In nonfiction, his interests include sport, popular science, history, humour and business.

Authors: Guy Adams; Tanya Aldred; Becky Alexander; Moeen Ali; Victoria Belim; SJ Bennett; Edward Brooke-Hitching; Theodore Brun; Andy Bull; Jen Campbell; Bonnie Chung; David Collins; Zoë Colville; Duncan Crowe; Iain Dey; Chris Dodd; Adam Fergusson; Jamie Fewery; Rebecca Front; Tom Gabbay; Julian Gough; David Higgins; Will Hill; Thomas W. Hodgkinson; Nicholas Hogg;

Iain Hollingshead; Andrew Hosken; Simon Jones; Paul Levy; Bonnie MacBird; Shingi Mararike; Katie Marsh; Hugh Matheson; Neil McCormick; Anthony McGowan; Barry McKinley; Moin Mir; Anton Mosimann; Rebecca Myers; James Peak; Edvard Radzinsky; Sue Ransom; Amy Raphael; Andrea Stuart; Jo Thompson; Tom Tivnan; Hana Videen; Kate Vigurs; Wendy Wason; Sioned Wiliam; Mike Woodhouse

L095 Vanessa Campos
Literary Agent
United States

Vanessa@d4eo.com

https://www.d4eoliteraryagency.com/p/vanessa-campos.html
https://querymanager.com/query/Vanessa_Reads
https://twitter.com/VanessaShares

Literary Agency: D4EO Literary Agency

Nonfiction > *Nonfiction Books*
  Business; Entrepreneurship; Self Help

Send: Outline; Table of Contents; Writing sample; Marketing Plan
How to send: Query Manager

Looking to help bring more diverse voices to the business, entrepreneurship, and self-help publishing space.

L096 Canterbury Literary Agency
Literary Agency
43 Nunnery Fields, Canterbury, Kent, CT1 3JT
United Kingdom
Tel: +44 (0) 7947 827860

francesca@canterburyliteraryagency.com

http://www.canterburyliteraryagency.com

Fiction > *Novels*

Nonfiction > *Nonfiction Books*
  Autobiography; Biography; Women's Interests

"We are based in the UK, and actively welcome submissions from writers based in the United States and Canada. We sell to publishers in the UK an in the United States and Canada, and we sell translation rights worldwide.

Founded in 2011, we pride ourselves on being a literary agency devoted to the needs of writers. We welcome all kinds of submissions, including fiction, non-fiction, memoirs, collections of short stories and collections of poems. Our aim is to respond to all submissions in no more than two weeks. We will do all we can to give you the best chance of a literary career.

We believe in transparency and friendliness and we realise that, as a writer trying to get your literary career started, you may often feel

the literary world is not very friendly to you; we will be friendly and positive and will do all we can to help you.

Also, we will get back to you. At a time when you are more likely to get an email reply from Charles Dickens than from most literary agencies, we aim to get back to you within two weeks. We reply to ALL emails we receive.

We are very well connected with publishers, we understand what needs to happen with a book to take it from a draft stage to being accepted by a publisher and we spare no effort for our writer clients."

Writers should be aware that there seems to a be a strong connection between this agency and The Conrad Press, a fee-charging publishing service. Listings for both were submitted within 17 minutes of each other at around 1am of the same morning, and their logos are almost identical. The postal address provided for this agency is the same address as was originally provided for The Conrad Press (which has subsequently been changed).

The agency website states that Francesca Garratt carries out editing work for The Conrad Press, and the other agent, Helen Komatsu, is listed as an editor at Conrad Press on her LinkedIn profile.

Oddly, her profile makes no mention of being a literary agent (at this agency or otherwise), despite apparently having been involved with the agency since 2011 and her LinkedIn profile containing changes as recent as 2018, when she became an editor at Conrad Press. The agency website describes her as "a highly experienced writer and literary agent", who "has been involved with the publishing industry for more than twenty years", however her LinkedIn profile lists only PR and marketing roles prior to becoming an editor with Conrad Press in 2018. The majority of that time (over 22 years) was spent in a marketing role working for a PR firm operated by the same person who now runs Conrad Press.

A post-pandemic interview with Helen Komatsu where she discusses her past and present career also fails to make any mention of work as a literary agent (https://www.careershifters.org/success-stories/from-business-owner-to-portfolio-career).

The agency website states that she is a published author, "having written books for the Financial Times organisation, Pearson and Reuters and other well-respected publishing houses", however searches on Amazon return no results for her name. She may, of course, have published under a different name.

Given the close connection between this agency and The Conrad Press, writers should be aware of the possibility that this agency may simply be a front for The Conrad Press, intended to generate customers for their publishing services.

Writers should also note that the agency states that "Our authors prefer us to keep their names confidential". This is highly irregular and raises red flags. Agencies routinely publish lists of their clients and authors appreciate publicity. If the agency has been in operation since 2011 you would expect them to have a number of clients, and the idea that every single one of those clients would want to have their association with this agency kept secret for some reason is both hard to believe, and, if true, suspicious in itself.

In light of these concerns, we would advise against approaching this agency.

Update: *On April 2, 2023, we were contacted by James Essinger, the person who runs Conrad Press, who asked us to include the following clarification: "Helen Komatsu co-authored several books with me some years ago when her name was Helen Wylie. Here is one: https://www.amazon.com/Seven-Deadly-Skills-Competing/dp/1861523742/ref=sr_1_1?crid=3Q3ZPTPTYQ5&keywords=Essinger+Wylie&qid=1680394116&sprefix=essinger+wylie%2Caps%2C173&sr=8-1"*

L097 Victoria Cappello

Literary Agent; Vice President; Company Director
United States

Literary Agency: The Bent Agency (**L058**)

L098 Elise Capron

Literary Agent
United States

https://dijkstraagency.com/agent-page.php?agent_id=Capron
https://querymanager.com/query/DijkstraCapron

Literary Agency: Sandra Dijkstra Literary Agency

Fiction > *Novels*: Literary

Nonfiction > *Nonfiction Books*
Culture; History; Memoir; Narrative Nonfiction; Science

How to send: Query Manager; By referral

Most interested in well-written narrative non-fiction (particularly trade-friendly history, cultural studies, and science) as well as character-driven literary fiction. While she will consider memoir, please note that she is very selective in this genre.

L099 Caroline Sheldon Literary Agency

Literary Agency
71 Hillgate Place, London, W8 7SS

United Kingdom
Tel: +44 (0) 20 7727 9102

info@carolinesheldon.co.uk

https://www.carolinesheldon.co.uk

Professional Body: The Association of Authors' Agents (AAA)

ADULT > **Fiction** > *Novels*

CHILDREN'S > **Fiction**
Board Books; *Chapter Books*; *Early Readers*; *Middle Grade*; *Novels*; *Picture Books*

Send: Query
How to send: Email

Interested in fiction and all types of children's books. Send query by email only, addressed to appropriate agent. Do not send submissions to their individual email addresses.

Literary Agent: Caroline Sheldon

L100 Jamie Carr

Literary Agent
United States

http://www.thebookgroup.com/jamie-carr

Literary Agency: The Book Group

Fiction > *Novels*
Literary; Upmarket Commercial Fiction

Nonfiction > *Nonfiction Books*
Culture; Food; Journalism; Narrative Nonfiction

Send: Query; Writing sample
How to send: In the body of an email

Represents novelists, short story writers, journalists, activists, and food and culture writers. Most interested in adult literary and upmarket commercial fiction and narrative nonfiction, she is drawn to writing that is voice-driven, highly transporting, from unique perspectives and marginalized voices, and that seeks to disrupt or reframe what appears to be known.

Authors: Isabel Banta; Nishant Batsha; Suhaly Bautista-Carolina; Wendy Chin-Tanner; Tiana Clark; Tracy Clark-Flory; Chloe Cole; Ella Dawson; Kimberly Drew; Susie Dumond; Lacey Dunham; Lauren Green; Taylor Hahn; Alex Hoopes; Melissa Larsen; Ashton Lattimore; Esther Levy-Chehebar; Vanessa Lillie; Kristen Martin; Laura McKowen; Abi Morgan; Ava Robinson; Victoria Savanh; Sophia Shalmiyev; Rainesford Stauffer; Elissa Strauss; Noor Tagouri; Rachel Zarrow

L101 Michael Carr

Literary Agent
United States

http://www.veritasliterary.com
https://querymanager.com/query/MichaelCarr

Literary Agency: Veritas Literary Agency

Fiction > *Novels*

Fantasy; Historical Fiction; Science Fiction; Women's Fiction

Nonfiction > *Nonfiction Books*

Send: Query; Writing sample
How to send: Query Manager

L102 Megan Carroll

Literary Agent
United Kingdom

https://www.watsonlittle.com/agent/megan-carroll/
https://twitter.com/MeganACarroll

Literary Agency: Watson, Little Ltd (**L635**)

ADULT
Fiction > *Novels*
Nonfiction > *Nonfiction Books*

CHILDREN'S
Fiction > *Middle Grade*
Nonfiction > *Nonfiction Books*

YOUNG ADULT > **Fiction** > *Novels*

Send: Query; Synopsis; Writing sample
How to send: Word file email attachment
How not to send: PDF file email attachment

Looking for writers in a variety of areas, and from a wide range of backgrounds – she is particularly keen to hear from Black, Asian, and LGBTQIA+ writers. Her main areas of focus this year are adult fiction and non-fiction, as well as non-fiction for 7+, and MG and YA fiction.

Authors: Luci Adams; Tom Adams; Rose Alexander; Faima Bakar; Louise Soraya Black; Laura Chamberlain; Sophie Claire; Sarah J. Coleman; Tara Costello; Bryony Cousins; Alex Day; Marianne Eloise; Lauren Ford; Tessa Gibbs; Natasha Holmes; Hayley Hoskins; Elias Jahshan; Hiba Noor Khan; Lindiwe Maqhubela; Erin Murgatroyd; Fiona O'Brien; Ben Pechey; Rhian Parry; Will Richard; Alan Robinson; Kohinoor Sahota; Jeremy Williams; Alex Woolhouse

L103 Rebecca Carter

Literary Agent
United Kingdom

https://rebeccacarterliteraryagent.wordpress.com/
https://twitter.com/RebeccasBooks

Literary Agency: Rebecca Carter Literary (**L519**)

ADULT
Fiction > *Novels*
Crime; Experimental

Nonfiction > *Nonfiction Books*
Biography; Creative Nonfiction; Cultural Commentary; Design; Environment; History; Memoir; Politics; Social Commentary; Technology; Travel

CHILDREN'S

Fiction > *Novels*
Nonfiction > *Nonfiction Books*

L104 Claire Cartey
Literary Agent
United Kingdom

claire@holroydecartey.com

https://www.holroydecartey.com/about.html
https://www.holroydecartey.com/submissions.html

Literary Agency: Holroyde Cartey

CHILDREN'S
 Fiction
  Novels; *Picture Books*
 Nonfiction > *Nonfiction Books*

Send: Synopsis; Full text
How to send: Email attachment

I have worked in children's publishing for over twenty years as Art Director at Hodder Children's Books and in design for Random House. I am looking for author and illustrator proposals for picture books, young fiction and non-fiction. In illustration I'm also looking for creative brand building potential in markets outside of publishing.

L105 Robert Caskie
Literary Agent
United Kingdom

robert@robertcaskie.com
submissions@robertcaskie.com

https://www.robertcaskie.com
https://twitter.com/rcaskie1

Literary Agency: Robert Caskie Ltd

Fiction > *Novels*
 Book Club Fiction; Commercial; Literary

Nonfiction > *Nonfiction Books*
 Memoir; Narrative Nonfiction; Nature; Politics; Social Issues

Send: Query; Writing sample; Proposal
How to send: Email

Interested in fiction and nonfiction writing that stimulates debate, comments on the world around us, and invokes an emotional response. Currently closed to fiction submissions, but still welcomes nonfiction submissions.

L106 Cecily Ware Literary Agents
Literary Agency
30 Elsiedene Road, London, N21 2RP
United Kingdom
Tel: +44 (0) 20 7359 3787

info@cecilyware.com

http://www.cecilyware.com

Scripts
 Radio Scripts; *TV Scripts*

Send: Full text; Author bio
How to send: Word file email attachment; PDF file email attachment; Final Draft email attachment

Handles television and radio writers and producers. No books or theatre scripts.

Literary Agents: Carol Reyes; Warren Sherman

L107 Jemiscoe Chambers-Black
Associate Agent
Los Angeles
United States

jemiscoe@andreabrownlit.com

https://www.andreabrownlit.com/agents.html
https://twitter.com/Jemiscoe
https://querymanager.com/query/Jemiscoe

Literary Agency: Andrea Brown Literary Agency, Inc.

ADULT > **Fiction** > *Novels*
 Comedy / Humour; Cozy Mysteries; Crime; LGBTQIA; Literary; Low Fantasy; Psychological Thrillers; Romance; Urban Fantasy

CHILDREN'S > **Fiction**
 Graphic Novels: General
 Middle Grade: Adventure; Comedy / Humour; Contemporary; Culture; Fantasy; Folklore, Myths, and Legends; Ghost Stories; Horror; LGBTQIA; Magical Realism; Mystery; Supernatural / Paranormal
YOUNG ADULT > **Fiction** > *Novels*
 Contemporary; Fantasy; Ghost Stories; Horror; LGBTQIA; Mystery; Romance; Romantic Comedy; Supernatural / Paranormal

Send: Author bio; Query; Synopsis; Writing sample; Pitch; Market info
How to send: Query Manager

Currently building her client list in the middle grade, YA, and adult categories. She is also interested in considering illustrators and author-illustrators.

L108 Sonali Chanchani
Literary Agent
United States

sonali@foliolit.com

https://www.foliolit.com/agents-1/sonali-chanchani

Literary Agency: Folio Literary Management, LLC
Professional Body: Association of American Literary Agents (AALA)

Fiction > *Novels*
 Book Club Fiction; Coming of Age; Family; Friends; Literary Mystery; Literary; Speculative; Thrillers; Women's Fiction

Nonfiction > *Nonfiction Books*

Culture; Ethnic Groups; Gender; Investigative Journalism; Narrative Nonfiction; Politics; Social Class; Social Justice; Society

Send: Query; Writing sample
How to send: In the body of an email

In fiction, she is looking for literary fiction and book club fiction with a strong, distinctive voice. She's particularly interested in smart, funny coming of age novels; braided narratives of friendship or family; literary mysteries; and atmospheric stories with a speculative or fabulist twist. She loves novels that subvert dominant cultural narratives and engage with themes of identity, belonging, community, inheritance, and diaspora. In nonfiction, she is looking for narratives and collections that illuminate some aspect of our society or culture with an eye towards social justice. She is especially drawn to investigative journalism and deeply researched narratives that advance our current conversations about race, class, gender, and politics.

L109 Minju Chang
Literary Agent
United States

Literary Agency: BookStop Literary Agency, LLC **(L069)**

CHILDREN'S
 Fiction
  Chapter Books; *Graphic Novels*; *Middle Grade*; *Picture Books*
 Nonfiction > *Nonfiction Books*

YOUNG ADULT > **Fiction** > *Novels*

How to send: By referral

Represents both fiction and nonfiction in all children's book categories: picture books, chapter books, middle-grade, graphic novels and YA. She also represents illustrators and is on the hunt for author-illustrators.

L110 Nicola Chang
Literary Agent
United Kingdom

nicolasubmissions@davidhigham.co.uk

https://www.davidhigham.co.uk/agents-dh/nicola-chang/

Literary Agency: David Higham Associates Ltd **(L159)**

Fiction > *Novels*

Nonfiction > *Nonfiction Books*
 Cookery; Cultural Criticism; Culture; Food; Memoir; Narrative Nonfiction; Philosophy; Politics; Psychology; Revisionist History; Society

Poetry > *Any Poetic Form*

Closed to approaches.

Represents writers of fiction and non-fiction as well as a small list of poets. She is an editorially-focused agent and is passionate about working with writers closely to develop their proposals and manuscripts for submission to publishers.

Authors: Arenike Adebajo; Ore Agbaje-Williams; Sara Ahmed; Rosanna Amaka; Iman Amrani; Raymond Antrobus; Yemisí Aríbisálà; Gina María Balibrera; Amman Brar; Symeon Brown; Judith Bryan; Stephen Buoro; Vanessa Chan; Jacqueline Crooks; Tsitsi Dangarembga; Subhadra Das; Melissa Franklin; Nikita Gill; Emma Glass; Will Harris; Alex Holder; Angela Hui; Keith Jarrett; Bhanu Kapil; Lara Lee; Huw Lemmey; Momtaza Mehri; Anna Metcalfe; Emma-Lee Moss; Mark Mukasa; James Conor Patterson; Riaz Phillips; Alake Pilgrim; Leone Ross; Saba Sams; Lisa Smith; Varaidzo; Christian Weaver; Mandy Yin

L111 Edwina de Charnace
Literary Agent
United Kingdom

https://mmbcreative.com/agents/edwina-de-charnace/

Literary Agency: MMB Creative (**L452**)

Fiction > *Novels*
Domestic Suspense; East Asia; Literary

Nonfiction > *Nonfiction Books*
East Asia; Memoir; Narrative Nonfiction; Self Help

Send: Query; Author bio; Synopsis; Writing sample
How to send: Email

She loves stories centring on relationships and group dynamics and will read anything promising answers to the question of belonging (a start will do). Has a soft spot for writing from or about East Asia.

L112 Chase Literary Agency
Literary Agency
11 Broadway, Suite 1010, New York, NY 10004
United States
Tel: +1 (212) 477-5100

farley@chaseliterary.com

https://chaseliterary.com
https://twitter.com/FarleyChase
https://www.publishersmarketplace.com/members/farleychase/

Fiction
Graphic Novels: General
Novels: Commercial; Contemporary; Fantasy; High Concept; Historical Fiction; Horror; Literary
Nonfiction
Illustrated Books: Arts; Photography

Nonfiction Books: Biography; Business; Comedy / Humour; Current Affairs; History; Journalism; Memoir; Nature; Science; Self Help

Send: Query; Writing sample
How to send: Email

In fiction I'm looking for literary or commercial projects in either contemporary, historical, or fantasy settings. I'm open to anything with a strong sense of place, voice, and, especially, character and plot. I agree with Lorrie Moore who wrote 'We don't often know what intimate life consists of until novels tell us.' If you have a high-concept, character-driven fantasy, sci-fi, or horror novel please try me.

In nonfiction I'm keen to see memoir, natural history, science, current affairs, journalism, history, humor, and biography. Original business and self-help books stemming from expertise are also of serious interest.

I'm interested in visually-driven, Illustrated and graphic books. Whether they involve photography, comics, illustrations, or art, I'm taken by creative storytelling with visual elements, four color or black and white.

Literary Agent: Farley Chase (**L113**)

L113 Farley Chase
Literary Agent
United States

https://chaseliterary.com
https://aalitagents.org/author/farleychase/
https://www.linkedin.com/in/farley-chase-76b3b832/
https://twitter.com/FarleyChase

Literary Agency: Chase Literary Agency (**L112**)
Professional Body: Association of American Literary Agents (AALA)

L114 Mic Cheetham
Literary Agent
United Kingdom

Mic@miccheetham.co.uk

Literary Agency: Mic Cheetham Literary Agency (**L441**)

L115 Elyse Cheney
Literary Agent
United States

https://www.cheneyagency.com/elyse-cheney

Literary Agency: The Cheney Agency

L116 Jennifer Chevais
Assistant Agent
Canada

https://www.therightsfactory.com/Agents/Jennifer-Chevais/

https://querymanager.com/query/JChevais
https://twitter.com/jchevais

Literary Agency: The Rights Factory

Fiction
Graphic Novels: General
Novels: General, and in particular: Fantasy; Horror; Science Fiction; Thrillers; Upmarket
Nonfiction > *Nonfiction Books*
General, and in particular: Memoir

Does not want:

Nonfiction > *Nonfiction Books*: Warfare

How to send: Query Manager

Currently building her list of authors specialising in fantasy, science fiction, and horror, but she also has a soft spot for thrillers, upmarket fiction, memoir, graphic novels, and many more.

Authors: Tal Cohen; Eleanor Cooney; Drew Dotson; Greta Kelly; Richard A. Kirk; A. A. Livingston; Dan Livingston; Dan Malossi; Rachelle Meyer; Damascus Mincemeyer; Markus Redmond; Emma Sachsse; Mark David Smith; Lauren Roedy Vaughn

L117 Patrick Child
Literary Agent
United Kingdom

Literary Agency: Independent Talent Group Ltd (**L317**)

L118 Jamie Weiss Chilton
Senior Agent
United States

jamie@andreabrownlit.com

https://www.andreabrownlit.com/Team/Jamie-Weiss-Chilton
http://twitter.com/jwchilton

Literary Agency: Andrea Brown Literary Agency, Inc.

CHILDREN'S > **Fiction**
Middle Grade: Realistic; Science Fiction; Speculative; Thrillers
Picture Books: General

YOUNG ADULT > **Fiction** > *Novels*
Realistic; Science Fiction; Speculative; Thrillers

Closed to approaches.

Represents children's books in all categories, with a focus on preschool, picture books, novelty, and real-world-based middle grade and YA. Genre interests include thrillers, science fiction, and speculative fiction.

L119 Danielle Chiotti
Literary Agent
United States

danielle.submission@gmail.com

https://www.upstartcrowliterary.com/agents/danielle-chiotti

Literary Agency: Upstart Crow Literary

ADULT
  Fiction > *Novels*
    Literary; Upmarket Commercial Fiction

  Nonfiction > *Nonfiction Books*
    Comedy / Humour; Cookery; Current Affairs; Food; Lifestyle; Memoir; Narrative Nonfiction; Relationships; Wine

CHILDREN'S > **Fiction** > *Middle Grade*

YOUNG ADULT > **Fiction** > *Novels*

Closed to approaches.

For adult fiction, she is seeking upmarket commercial fiction and literary fiction. She prefers books that explore deep emotional relationships in an interesting or unusual way.

For middle grade and YA: She is actively seeking fresh young adult and middle grade fiction across all genres. She is drawn toward gorgeous writing and strong, flawed characters. Her dream project for young readers is one that challenges and inspires, with a compelling voice that will make her stay up all night reading.

For nonfiction: she is looking for compelling, voice-driven projects that shed a humorous or thought-provoking light on a previously unknown topic in the areas of narrative nonfiction/memoir, lifestyle, relationships, humor, current events, food, wine, and cooking.

L120 Catherine Cho
Literary Agent; Author
United Kingdom

https://www.paperliterary.com/submissions-catherine/
https://twitter.com/catkcho

Literary Agencies: Paper Literary (**L488**); C&W (Conville & Walsh) (**L092**)
Literary Agent: Sophie Lambert (**L371**)

ADULT
  Fiction > *Novels*
    Book Club Fiction; Family; Folklore, Myths, and Legends; High Concept; Historical Fiction; Literary; Magical Realism; Multicultural; Relationships; Speculative; Suspense; Thrillers

  Nonfiction > *Nonfiction Books*
    Entrepreneurship; History; Memoir; Narrative Nonfiction; Psychology; Science

YOUNG ADULT > **Fiction** > *Novels*: Fantasy

Send: Query; Synopsis; Writing sample

Originally from Kentucky. After a background in law and public affairs, she began her publishing career in New York at Folio Literary Management before moving to London.

L121 Erica Christensen
Senior Agent
United States

https://www.metamorphosisliteraryagency.com/about
https://querymanager.com/query/ericachristensen
https://twitter.com/literaryerica

Literary Agency: Metamorphosis Literary Agency (**L440**)

ADULT > **Fiction** > *Novels*
  Romance; Thrillers

YOUNG ADULT > **Fiction** > *Novels*
  Contemporary; Romance

Does not want:

> **ADULT** > **Fiction** > *Novels*
>   Historical Romance; Supernatural / Paranormal Romance
>
> **YOUNG ADULT** > **Fiction** > *Novels*
>   Historical Romance; Supernatural / Paranormal Romance

How to send: Query Manager

Only open to SUBSIDIARY RIGHTS queries for established Romance and Thriller authors (Self-Published/Indie and Traditional) who retain the subsidiary rights (audio, foreign, gaming, film/tv) for their book(s). The book(s) must have a minimum of 50 reviews. Please include your Amazon author page and Goodreads page in the Bio section.

L122 Jennifer Christie
Literary Agent
United Kingdom

http://www.grahammawchristie.com/about1.html

Literary Agency: Graham Maw Christie Literary Agency (**L263**)

Nonfiction > *Nonfiction Books*
  Business; Comedy / Humour; Memoir; Philosophy; Popular Science

Send: Outline; Author bio; Market info; Writing sample
How to send: Email

Interests are wide ranging, from popular science, philosophy and humour to business and memoir.

L123 The Chudney Agency
Literary Agency
72 North State Road, Suite 501, Briarcliff Manor, NY 10510
United States
Tel: +1 (201) 758-8739
Fax: +1 (201) 758-8739

steven@thechudneyagency.com

http://www.thechudneyagency.com

ADULT
  Fiction > *Novels*
    General, and in particular: Gender; Historical Fiction; LGBTQIA; Middle East; Mystery; Sexuality; Thrillers; Women's Fiction

  Nonfiction
    Gift Books: General
    Illustrated Books: General
    Nonfiction Books: Comedy / Humour

CHILDREN'S > **Fiction**
  Chapter Books: General, and in particular: Comedy / Humour; Coming of Age; Contemporary; Culture; Gender; Historical Fiction; Literary; Mystery; Spirituality
  Middle Grade: General, and in particular: Comedy / Humour; Coming of Age; Contemporary; Culture; Gender; Historical Fiction; Literary; Mystery; Spirituality
  Picture Books: General

TEEN > **Fiction** > *Novels*
  General, and in particular: Comedy / Humour; Coming of Age; Contemporary; Culture; Gender; Historical Fiction; Literary; Mystery; Spirituality

How to send: By referral

Specialises in children's and teen books, but will also consider adult fiction. Closed for queries and submissions – except for those by professional referral. These can be by fellow agents, industry colleagues, and current clients.

Authors: Jessica Alexander; Mary Jane Beaufrand; Tess Hilmo; Kristen Landon

Literary Agent: Steven Chudney

L124 Kayla Cichello
Literary Agent
United States

kayla.submission@gmail.com

https://www.upstartcrowliterary.com/agents/kayla-cichelloa
https://twitter.com/SeriousKayla

Literary Agency: Upstart Crow Literary

CHILDREN'S > **Fiction**
  Middle Grade: General
  Picture Books: Comedy / Humour

YOUNG ADULT > **Fiction** > *Novels*
  Commercial; Dark Humour; Literary; Magical Realism; Mystery; Romance; Romantic Comedy; Suspense

How to send: Email
How not to send: Post

Seeking everything from heartfelt or humorous picture books (she has a soft spot for animal protagonists) to dynamic, unpredictable YA (she loves a good murder mystery or a clever rom-com).

L125 Ginger Clark

Literary Agent
United States

submissions@GingerClarkLiterary.com

https://gingerclarkliterary.com/About
https://gingerclarkliterary.com/Submissions

Literary Agency: Ginger Clark Literary (**L249**)

ADULT > **Fiction** > *Novels*
Fantasy; Horror; Romance; Science Fiction;
Women's Fiction

CHILDREN'S
Fiction > *Middle Grade*
Nonfiction > *Middle Grade*

YOUNG ADULT
Fiction > *Novels*
Nonfiction > *Nonfiction Books*

Send: Query
How to send: Email

Has a special focus on science fiction, fantasy,
horror, romance, and women's fiction. For
children's works, she represents young adult
and middle grade fiction and nonfiction in all
genres. Emailed queries are strongly preferred.

L126 Caro Clarke

Literary Agent
United Kingdom

submissions@portobelloliterary.co.uk

https://www.portobelloliterary.co.uk

Literary Agency: Portobello Literary (**L509**)

Fiction > *Novels*
Crime; Fantasy; Literary; Speculative

Nonfiction
Essays: General
Nonfiction Books: Cookery; Culture; Food;
Intersectional Feminism; LGBTQIA;
Memoir; Narrative Nonfiction; Nature;
Popular Science; Travel

Send: Synopsis; Author bio; Writing sample
How to send: Email
How not to send: Post

I am actively building a list of authors writing
fiction and non-fiction. I have very broad taste
in fiction and I'm attracted to excellent writing,
clever plots, unusual settings and complex
characters. I love all types of stories from niche
literary novels, to speculative fiction and
fantasy, gripping crime and novels with wide
appeal. I am partial to fiction that transports
you, steals your heart and makes you think. On
the non-fiction side, I'm looking for narrative
non-fiction, memoir, popular science, big
ideas, travel, culture, essays, queer culture and
intersectional feminism. I'm also interested in
food writing and cookbooks. I have a particular
soft spot for nature writing of any type. What I
look for in non-fiction are fascinating topics, a
unique perspective or one that disrupts the
status quo and an engaging voice. Most of all,

I'm looking for writers who are passionate
about the topic of their book.

Authors: Polly Atkin; Fiona Black; Gill
Booles; Rachel Charlton-Dailey; Mona Dash;
Samantha Dooey-Miles; Harry Josephine
Giles; CL Hellisen; Russell Jones; Aefa
Mulholland; JC Niala; Andrés N. Ordorica;
Wendy Pratt; Adam Ramsay; Christina Riley;
Elspeth Wilson

L127 Catherine Clarke

Literary Agent; Managing Director
United Kingdom

https://felicitybryan.com/fba-agent/catherine-
clarke/

Literary Agency: Felicity Bryan Associates
(**L211**)

ADULT > **Nonfiction** > *Nonfiction Books*
Biography; History; Memoir; Nature;
Philosophy

CHILDREN'S > **Fiction** > *Novels*

I have been building a list of adult non-fiction
and children's fiction writers since 2001. In
non-fiction, I particularly love history and
philosophy and biography, especially from
authors who have the academic credentials or
expertise but also have the ambition and vision
and writerly skill to make us see their subjects
in a new light, or to overturn received wisdom.
I also love outstanding nature writing with a
dash of compelling memoir.

Authors: Samira Ahmed; David Almond;
Karen Armstrong; Lucy Ash; Rachel Aspden;
James Attlee; Katya Balen; James Barr; David
Barrie; Rosamund Bartlett; John Barton; John
Batchelor; Erica Benner; Nic Bennett; Claire
Bertschinger; Paul Betts; Michael Bird; Simon
Blackburn; Elleke Boehmer; Stella Botchway;
John Bowker; Christopher Brickell; Susan
Brigden; Irena Brignull; Adam Brookes;
Matthew Burton; John Charmley; Nick Chater;
Morten H. Christiansen; Liza Cody; Artemis
Cooper; Sarah Courtauld; Cath Crowley; Chloe
Daykin; John Dickie; Jenny Downham; Tobias
Druitt; Natasha Farrant; Edmund Fawcett;
Catherine Fletcher; CJ Flood; Pauline Francis;
Peter Frankopan; Lawrence Freedman; Clare
Furniss; Sally Gardner; Robert Gildea;
Jonathan Glover; Chris Gosden; A.C.
Grayling; Barbara Graziosi; Thomas Halliday;
Julie Hearn; Peter Heather; Gavin Hewitt;
Penelope Hobhouse; Alex Howard; Alice
Hunt; Kathryn Hurlock; Belinda Jack; Lauren
St John; Colin Jones; Vijay Joshi; Liz Kessler;
Katherine Langrish; Lucy Lethbridge; John
Lister-Kaye; Jonathan Loh; Diarmaid
Macculloch; Laurie Maguire; John Man; Toby
Matthiesen; James Mcdougall; Sophia
Mcdougall; Chris Mcgrath; Kate Mcloughlin;
Martin Meredith; Tom Moorhouse; Katy
Moran; Natasha Narayan; James Naughtie;
Linda Newbery; TN Ninan; Adjoa Osei;
Richard Ovenden; Joanne Owen; Roger

Pearson; Thomas Penn; Andrew Pettegree;
Jonathan Phillips; Annabel Pitcher; Rachel
Polonsky; Andrew Prentice; Sue Prideaux;
Diane Purkiss; Josephine Quinn; Owen Rees;
Julian Richards; Thomas Rid; Ritchie
Robertson; Eugene Rogan; Meg Rosoff; Miri
Rubin; Ulinka Rublack; Alec Ryrie; Joseph
Sassoon; Paul Seabright; Alom Shaha; Liam
Shaw; Matthew Skelton; Emma Smith; Lexi
Stadlen; Marc Stears; Andrew Strong; Roy
Strong; Julie Summers; Krystal Sutherland;
Lydia Syson; Eleanor Updale; Christopher
Vick; Charles Walton; Arthur Der Weduwen;
Jonathan Weil; Anna Whitelock; Tim
Whitmarsh; K.J. Whittaker; Lisa Williamson;
Michael Wood; Lucy Wooding; Lucy Worsley;
Jessica Wärnberg

L128 Alexander Cochran

Literary Agent
United Kingdom

Literary Agency: C&W (Conville & Walsh)
(**L092**)

Closed to approaches.

L129 Colwill & Peddle

Literary Agency
London
United Kingdom

https://www.colwillandpeddle.com
http://instagram.com/colwillandpeddle
https://twitter.com/colwillpeddle

Professional Body: The Association of
Authors' Agents (AAA)

Literary Agents: Charlotte Colwill (**L130**); Kay
Peddle (**L493**)

L130 Charlotte Colwill

Literary Agent
United Kingdom

Charlotte@colwillandpeddle.com
submissions@colwillandpeddle.com

https://www.colwillandpeddle.com/about

Literary Agency: Colwill & Peddle (**L129**)

ADULT > **Fiction** > *Novels*
General, and in particular: Comedy /
Humour; Historical Fiction; Literary Horror;
Literary; Romance; Science Fiction

CHILDREN'S
Fiction > *Novels*

Nonfiction
Middle Grade: Real Life Stories
Nonfiction Books: General

YOUNG ADULT
Fiction > *Novels*
Contemporary; Fantasy; High Concept

Nonfiction > *Nonfiction Books*: Real Life
Stories

Send: Query; Synopsis; Writing sample; Author bio; Market info; Outline

Looking for adult fiction and children's fiction and non-fiction.

Always looking for fiction with a unique voice and compelling story, with something new to say. Loves unusual perspectives, dark twists and sharp writing. Particularly on the lookout for smart romance with an edge, page-turning historical dramas, literary horror or science fiction with a contemporary resonance and literary fiction that is funny and moving, with a brand new hook.

In children's books she is open to both fiction and non-fiction for all ages, from picture books to Young Adult. At the moment she is really looking for a funny and engaging author/illustrator with a fresh new series for young readers (5+), middle grade fiction with a new hook, brilliant world-building and characters we haven't seen before, and in YA she's looking for homegrown fantasy fiction, high concept contemporary stories and books about unusual relationships. In children's non-fiction she'd love to see books that tackle curriculum subjects in a brand new and super engaging way, and real life stories for middle grade and YA readers.

L131 Chris Combemale
Associate Agent
United States

https://www.sll.com/our-team

Literary Agency: Sterling Lord Literistic, Inc. (**L583**)

Fiction > *Novels*
Literary; Upmarket Commercial Fiction

Nonfiction
Essays: Economics; Food; Popular Science; Technology
Nonfiction Books: Economics; Food; Memoir; Popular Science; Technology

Send: Query; Synopsis; Proposal; Writing sample
How to send: Online submission system

Looking for a broad range of literary fiction and commercial fiction with an unexpected hook, from psychological suspense to speculative and fantasy. In non-fiction he is interested in memoir, essay, and expert-driven projects across subject areas with special attention to technology, food, pop-science, economics, and any book that asks big questions about forces of change.

L132 Andrea Comparato
Literary Agent
United States

andrea@inscriptionsliterary.com

https://inscriptionsliterary.com/our-agents/
https://www.publishersmarketplace.com/

members/inscriplit/
https://querymanager.com/query/InscriptionsLit_Query

Literary Agency: Inscriptions Literary Agency (**L318**)

ADULT
Fiction > *Novels*
Mystery; Suspense

Nonfiction > *Nonfiction Books:* Memoir

CHILDREN'S
Fiction
Middle Grade; Picture Books
Scripts > *Film Scripts*

How to send: Query Manager

L133 Cristina Concepcion
Literary Agent; Foreign Rights Manager
United States

dca@doncongdon.com

Literary Agency: Don Congdon Associates, Inc. (**L175**)

Fiction > *Novels*

Nonfiction > *Nonfiction Books*
Current Affairs; Narrative Nonfiction

How to send: Email

Represents writers of adult fiction, history, current events and narrative non-fiction.

L134 Concord Theatricals
Literary Agency; Book Publisher
250 W. 57th Street, 6th Floor, New York, NY 10107-0102
United States
Tel: +1 (866) 979-0447

info@concordtheatricals.com

https://www.concordtheatricals.com/

Scripts > *Theatre Scripts*

Closed to approaches.

Publishes plays and represents writers of plays. Deals in well-known plays from Broadway and London's West End.

L135 Claire Paterson Conrad
Literary Agent
United Kingdom

http://www.janklowandnesbit.co.uk/node/671

Literary Agency: Janklow & Nesbit UK Ltd (**L324**)

Fiction > *Novels*

Nonfiction > *Nonfiction Books*
Biology; Creative Nonfiction; Environment; Nature; Popular Science

Send: Query; Synopsis; Writing sample; Outline
How to send: Email
How not to send: Post

Keen to represent more books about the natural world and our co-existence with it (whether that be popular science, biology, ecology or nature writing); books that celebrate women in science; books that help us understand the world and bring change; and creative nonfiction that blends genres. In fiction, gravitates towards atmospheric, character-driven novels that are rooted to a strong sense of place.

L136 Clare Conville
Literary Agent
United Kingdom

Literary Agency: C&W (Conville & Walsh) (**L092**)

Closed to approaches.

L137 Clare Coombes
Literary Agent
United Kingdom

https://www.liverpool-literary.agency/about

Literary Agency: The Liverpool Literary Agency (**L396**)

Fiction > *Novels*
General, and in particular: Crime; Historical Fiction; Psychological Thrillers; Women's Fiction

Closed to approaches.

Would love to see historical fiction, crime fiction, psychological thrillers and women's fiction, but as a new agent, she is open to all great writing with a strong hook in any area (excluding non-fiction, children's and YA).

L138 Coombs Moylett & Maclean Literary Agency
Literary Agency
120 New Kings Road, London, SW6 4LZ
United Kingdom

info@cmm.agency

https://cmm.agency
https://www.instagram.com/cmmlitagency/
https://www.facebook.com/cmmlitagency/

Professional Body: The Association of Authors' Agents (AAA)

ADULT
Fiction > *Novels*
Chick Lit; Commercial; Contemporary; Crime; Historical Fiction; Horror; Literary; Mystery; Suspense; Thrillers; Women's Fiction

Nonfiction > *Nonfiction Books*
General, and in particular: Biography; Crime; Current Affairs; Environment; Food; History; How To; Lifestyle; Narrative Nonfiction; Politics; Popular Science; Self Help

YOUNG ADULT > **Fiction** > *Novels*

Closed to approaches.

Send query with synopsis and first three chapters via online form. No submissions by email, fax or by post. No poetry, plays or scripts for film and TV. Whole books and postal submissions will not be read.

Literary Agents: Zoe Apostolides; Elena Langtry (**L377**); Jamie Maclean (**L413**); Lisa Moylett (**L462**)

L139 Gemma Cooper
Literary Agent; Company Director
United States

http://www.thebentagency.com/gemma-cooper

Literary Agency: The Bent Agency (**L058**)

CHILDREN'S
Fiction
Chapter Books; *Graphic Novels*; *Illustrated Books*; *Middle Grade*
Nonfiction > *Nonfiction Books*
History; Science

YOUNG ADULT
Fiction > *Novels*
Contemporary; Family; Friends; High Concept; Magic; Romantic Comedy; Supernatural / Paranormal Romance

Nonfiction > *Nonfiction Books*

Does not want:

> **YOUNG ADULT** > **Fiction** > *Novels*: High / Epic Fantasy

Represents authors and author / illustrators who write chapter books, middle-grade, and young adult fiction and nonfiction, as well as select webcomic adaptations. No adult fiction or nonfiction, or children's picture books, other than by existing clients.

L140 Maggie Cooper
Literary Agent
Boston, MA
United States

https://aevitascreative.com/agents/
https://querymanager.com/query/cooper

Literary Agency: Aevitas

Fiction > *Novels*
Feminist Romance; Historical Fiction; LGBTQIA; Literary

Nonfiction > *Nonfiction Books*
Cookery; Food

Closed to approaches.

Represents imaginative, genre-bending literary fiction; capacious historical novels; beautifully told queer stories; and smart, feminist romance. Her other loves include unclassifiable book projects, food and cookbooks, and work by writers traditionally underrepresented in mainstream publishing.

Authors: Emma Ahlqvist; Will Betke-Brunswick; Zoë Bossiere; Rita Zoey Chin; Marisa Crane; Carla Fernandez; JR Ford; Vanessa Ford; Andrew J. Graff; Rebecca Kling; Hali Lee; Rue Mapp; Jessica Martin; Katie Mitchell; Carolyn Prusa; Margie Sarsfield; Nina Sharma; Jack Shoulder; Mark Small; Julia Ridley Smith; June Thomas

L141 Peter Cox
Literary Agent
United Kingdom

Literary Agency: Redhammer (**L520**)

L142 Becca Crandall
Literary Agent
United States

becca@carolynjenksagency.com

https://www.carolynjenksagency.com/agent/BECCA-CRANDALL

Literary Agency: Carolyn Jenks Agency

ADULT
Fiction
Graphic Novels; *Novels*
Nonfiction > *Nonfiction Books*

CHILDREN'S > **Fiction**
Middle Grade; *Picture Books*
YOUNG ADULT > **Fiction** > *Novels*

Closed to approaches.

L143 Claudia Cross
Literary Agent; Partner
United States

https://www.foliolit.com/agents-1/claudia-cross

Literary Agency: Folio Literary Management, LLC

Closed to approaches.

L144 Cull & Co. Ltd
Literary Agency
United Kingdom

tom@cullandco.com

https://cullandco.com
https://www.facebook.com/cullandco/
https://www.youtube.com/channel/UCp8AcbMXQ7UenhgFxX4XM6g

Professional Body: The Association of Authors' Agents (AAA)

Nonfiction > *Nonfiction Books*
Biography; Crime; Memoir; Military; Narrative Nonfiction; Politics; Sport; Travel

Send: Synopsis; Writing sample; Author bio
How to send: Email

Handles full-length fiction and nonfiction for adults only. No children's picture books,

poetry, plays or musical theatre. Primarily looking for authors from the UK and Ireland writing in English. Occasionally considers international writers but you must make it clear when submitting why you are looking for a literary agent in the UK.

L145 Mary Cummings
Literary Agent
United States

Literary Agency: Great River Literary (**L268**)
Professional Bodies: Association of American Literary Agents (AALA); Society of Children's Book Writers and Illustrators (SCBWI)

L146 Sabhbh Curran
Literary Agent
United Kingdom

sabhbh.curran@curtisbrown.co.uk

http://submissions.curtisbrown.co.uk/agents/

Literary Agency: Curtis Brown (**L147**)

Fiction > *Novels*
Book Club Fiction; Dark; Historical Fiction; Literary; Psychological Suspense

Nonfiction > *Nonfiction Books*
Art History; Arts; Current Affairs; Fashion; Food; History; Mind, Body, Spirit; Narrative Nonfiction; Popular Culture; Popular Science; Psychology; Travel

Send: Query; Synopsis; Writing sample; Proposal
How to send: Email

I am on the hunt for literary, book club fiction and psychological suspense fiction. What I look for is well-crafted and stylish prose, complex characterisations and probably at least a hint of darkness: obsessive friendships and relationships; loneliness; trauma; dysfunctional families; the strangeness of urban life. I'm also drawn to beautifully written, researched and evoked historical fiction.

In non-fiction, I'm particularly keen to hear from chefs, mixologists and food writers but I am also interested in narrative non-fiction, history, travel writing, current affairs, popular science, psychology, MBS, fashion and popular culture. I would like to hear from non-fiction writers (especially journalists and activists) who speak to a younger audience. I have a real soft spot for anything related to art or art history, whatever the genre.

L147 Curtis Brown
Literary Agency
Cunard House, 15 Regent Street, London, SW1Y 4LR
United Kingdom
Tel: +44 (0) 20 7393 4400

info@curtisbrown.co.uk

https://www.curtisbrown.co.uk
http://submissions.curtisbrown.co.uk/

Professional Body: The Association of
Authors' Agents (AAA)
Literary Agency: United Talent Agency (UTA)

ADULT
Fiction > *Novels*
General, and in particular: Commercial
Women's Fiction; Crime; Erotic; Historical
Fiction; Horror; Literary; Memoir;
Romance; Thrillers

Nonfiction > *Nonfiction Books*

Scripts
Film Scripts; TV Scripts; Theatre Scripts

CHILDREN'S > **Fiction**
Early Readers: General
Middle Grade: General, and in
particular: Fantasy; Science Fiction
Picture Books: General

YOUNG ADULT > **Fiction** > *Novels*
General, and in particular: Fantasy; Science
Fiction

Send: Query; Synopsis; Writing sample
How to send: Online submission system; Email

Costs: Offers services that writers have to pay
for. Offers writing courses.

Renowned and long established London
agency. Handles general fiction and nonfiction,
and scripts. Also represents directors,
designers, and presenters. No longer accepts
submissions by post – submissions must be
made using online submissions manager or by
email, depending on individual agent
preference. Also offers services such as writing
courses for which authors are charged.

Literary Agent / President: Jonathan Lloyd
(**L399**)

Literary Agents: Davinia Andrew-Lynch
(*L024*); Felicity Blunt (**L065**); Sabhbh Curran
(**L146**); Jonny Geller; Alice Lutyens; Lucy
Morris; Cathryn Summerhayes; Gordon Wise

L148 Curtis Brown (Australia) Pty Ltd
Literary Agency
Australia

submission@curtisbrown.com.au

https://www.curtisbrown.com.au

Professional Body: Australian Literary Agents'
Association (ALAA)

Fiction > *Novels*

Nonfiction > *Nonfiction Books*

How to send: Email
How not to send: Post

Accepts submission from within Australia and
New Zealand only, during March, June, and
October. No fantasy, sci-fi, stage/screenplays,
poetry, self-help books, children's picture

books, early reader books, young adult books,
comic books, short stories, cookbooks,
educational, corporate books or translations.
Send query by email with synopsis up to two
pages and first three chapters. See website for
full guidelines.

Literary Agents: Clare Forster; Grace Heifetz;
Fiona Inglis; Pippa Masson; Tara Wynne

L149 John Cusick
Literary Agent; Vice President
United States

https://www.publishersmarketplace.com/
members/JohnC/
https://twitter.com/johnmcusick

Literary Agencies: Folio Literary Management,
LLC; Folio Jr.

ADULT > **Fiction** > *Novels*
Fantasy; Horror; Science Fiction; Suspense;
Thrillers

CHILDREN'S > **Fiction** > *Middle Grade*
Comedy / Humour; Contemporary; Fantasy;
Science Fiction; Speculative

YOUNG ADULT > **Fiction** > *Novels*
Comedy / Humour; Contemporary; Fantasy;
Science Fiction; Speculative

Closed to approaches.

Authors: Courtney Alameda; Kayla Cagan;
Josephine Cameron; Anna Carey; Linda
Cheng; Marina Cohen; Paula Garner; Joan He;
Christian McKay Heidicker; Sailor J; James
Kennedy; Jeramey Kraatz; Kristen Lippert-
Martin; Julie Murphy; Abdi Nazemian; Jordan
Reeves; Caitlin Schneiderhan; Laura
Sebastian; Quinn Sosna-Spear; Sharon Biggs
Waller; Don Zolidis

L150 Cyle Young Literary Elite
Literary Agency
United States

https://cyleyoung.com
https://www.facebook.com/cyle61?fref=ts
https://twitter.com/cyleyoung

Author / Junior Agent: Del Duduit

Author / Literary Agent: Cyle Young

Junior Agent: Megan Burkhart

Literary Agent: Tessa Emily Hall

L151 Cynthia Cannell Literary Agency
Literary Agency
United States

info@cannellagency.com

https://cannellagency.com
https://twitter.com/cynthiacan
https://www.facebook.com/
CynthiaCannellLiteraryAgency/
https://www.linkedin.com/company/cynthia-
cannell-literary-agency/about/

Professional Body: Association of American
Literary Agents (AALA)

Fiction > *Novels*

Nonfiction > *Nonfiction Books*
Biography; Contemporary; Memoir; Personal
Development; Spirituality

Closed to approaches.

Full-service literary agency based in New
York. Represents fiction, memoir, biography,
self-improvement, spirituality, and nonfiction
on contemporary issues. No screenplays,
children's books, illustrated books, cookbooks,
romance, category mystery, or science fiction.
Send query by email only, including brief
description of the project, relevant biographical
information, and any publishing credits. No
attachments or submissions by post. Response
not guaranteed.

Literary Agent: Cynthia Cannell

L152 Dana Newman Literary, LLC
Literary Agency
1800 Avenue of the Stars, 12th Floor, Los
Angeles, CA 90067
United States

dananewmanliterary@gmail.com

https://www.dananewman.com
https://twitter.com/DanaNewman
https://www.linkedin.com/in/dananewman/
https://www.instagram.com/danamnewman/

Fiction > *Novels*
Literary; Suspense; Thrillers; Upmarket

Nonfiction > *Nonfiction Books*
Biography; Business; Current Affairs;
Fitness; Health; History; Literary; Memoir;
Mind, Body, Spirit; Narrative Nonfiction;
Parenting; Popular Culture; Psychology;
Social Issues; Sport; Technology; Wellbeing;
Women's Interests

Send: Query; Outline; Author bio
How to send: Email

We are interested in practical nonfiction
(business, health and wellness,
mind/body/spirit, psychology, parenting,
technology) by authors with smart, unique
perspectives and established platforms who are
committed to actively marketing and
promoting their books.

We love compelling, inspiring narrative
nonfiction in the areas of memoir, biography,
history, pop culture, current affairs/women's
interest, social trends, and sports/fitness. A
favorite genre is literary nonfiction: true
stories, well told, that read like a novel you
can't put down.

On the fiction side we consider a select amount
of literary fiction, upmarket fiction, and
suspense/thriller. We look for character-driven

stories written in a distinctive voice that are emotionally truthful.

Submissions are accepted via email only.

Literary Agent: Dana Newman

L153 Melissa Danaczko
Literary Agent
United States

Literary Agency: Stuart Krichevsky Literary Agency, Inc. (**L596**)

L154 Margaret Danko
Literary Agent
United States

https://www.irenegoodman.com/margaret-danko
https://querymanager.com/query/margaretdanko

Literary Agency: Irene Goodman Literary Agency (IGLA)

ADULT
  Fiction > *Novels*
    Contemporary; Historical Fiction; Literary; Magical Realism; Romantic Comedy; Suspense; Upmarket

  Nonfiction > *Nonfiction Books*
    Comedy / Humour; Cookery; Crime; Environment; Health; Lifestyle; Mental Health; New Age; Popular Science; Spirituality; Wellbeing

YOUNG ADULT > **Fiction** > *Novels*: Fantasy

Closed to approaches.

Actively looking for attention-grabbing voices especially historical fiction with a dash of magical realism, literary and upmarket suspense and horror, spooky contemporary and fantasy YA, narratives with a deep sense of place and history, quirky and heartwarming family stories, and rom-coms full of charm and whimsy. She is also interested in nonfiction in the areas of humor, lifestyle, new age and general spirituality, popular science especially in environmental and human sciences, mental health/wellness, true crime that challenges established conventions, and select cooking projects with an emphasis on new takes on tradition, especially within the Latine diaspora. She does not represent Middle Grade or picture books.

L155 Jon Michael Darga
Literary Agent
New York
United States

https://aevitascreative.com/agents/
https://querymanager.com/query/jonmichaeldarga

Literary Agency: Aevitas

ADULT
  Fiction > *Novels*: Commercial

  Nonfiction > *Nonfiction Books*
    Biography; Cookery; History; Photography; Popular Culture

YOUNG
ADULT > **Fiction** > *Novels*: Commercial

Send: Author bio; Outline; Pitch; Market info; Writing sample
How to send: Online submission system

Represents both nonfiction and fiction. He is most interested in voice-driven pop culture writing and histories that re-cast the narrative by emphasizing unexpected or unheard voices.

Authors: Matt Abdoo; Zac Bissonnette; Sydney Bucksbaum; Tony Chin-Quee; Angel Luis Colón; Melissa Croce; Ashley Cullins; Sarah Horowitz; Patty Lin; Violet Lumani; Hugo Huerta Marin; Ann Marks; Shane McBride; Tarek El Moussa; James Park; Erik Piepenburg; Lynette Rice; Geena Rocero; Maurice "Mopreme" Shakur; Ashley Spencer; Jason Sperling; Jesse Szewczyk; Amy Watson; Rusty Williams; Angel Di Zhang

L156 Darhansoff & Verrill Literary Agents
Literary Agency
275 Fair Street, Suite 17D, Kingston NY, 12401
United States
Tel: +1 (917) 305-1300

submissions@dvagency.com
info@dvagency.com

https://www.dvagency.com

ADULT
  Fiction > *Novels*
  Nonfiction > *Nonfiction Books*

YOUNG ADULT > **Fiction** > *Novels*

Send: Query; Writing sample
How to send: In the body of an email
How not to send: Post

Response only if interested. If no response within eight weeks, assume rejection.

Foreign Rights Director / Literary Agent: Eric Amling (**L020**)

Literary Agents: Liz Darhansoff; Michele Mortimer (**L459**)

L157 Darley Anderson Children's
Literary Agency
Unit 19, Matrix Studios, 91 Peterborough Road, London, SW6 3BU
United Kingdom
Tel: +44 (0) 20 7386 2674

childrens@darleyanderson.com

http://www.darleyandersonchildrens.com
http://twitter.com/DA_Childrens

Professional Body: The Association of Authors' Agents (AAA)

CHILDREN'S
  Fiction
    Chapter Books; *Middle Grade*; *Picture Books*
  Nonfiction > *Nonfiction Books*

YOUNG ADULT > **Fiction** > *Novels*

Send: Query; Synopsis; Writing sample; Author bio; Pitch
How to send: Word file email attachment; PDF file email attachment
How not to send: Post

Always on the look out for exciting, inspiring and original novels for both Young Adult and Middle-Grade readers, chapter books, picture books, and nonfiction.

Literary Agent: Clare Wallace (**L631**)

L158 David Godwin Associates
Literary Agency
2nd Floor, 40 Rosebery Avenue, Clerkenwell, London, EC1R 4RX
United Kingdom
Tel: +44 (0) 20 7240 9992

submissions@davidgodwinassociates.co.uk

http://www.davidgodwinassociates.com

Professional Body: The Association of Authors' Agents (AAA)

Fiction > *Novels*

Nonfiction > *Nonfiction Books*

Send: Query; Synopsis; Writing sample
How to send: Email

Handles a range of nonfiction and fiction. Send query by email with synopsis and first 30 pages. No poetry. No picture books, except for existing clients.

Literary Agent: David Godwin

L159 David Higham Associates Ltd
Literary Agency
6th Floor, Waverley House, 7-12 Noel Street, London, W1F 8GQ
United Kingdom
Tel: +44 (0) 20 7434 5900
Fax: +44 (0) 20 7437 1072

reception@davidhigham.co.uk
submissions@davidhigham.co.uk
childrenssubmissions@davidhigham.co.uk

http://www.davidhigham.co.uk

Professional Body: The Association of Authors' Agents (AAA)

Agency Assistant: Sara Langham

Assistant Agent: David Evans (**L201**)

Authors: Rachel Abbott; J. R. Ackerley; Richard Adams; Arenike Adebajo; Ore Agbaje-Williams; Katie Agnew; Sara Ahmed;

Kat Ailes; Naomi Alderman; Tracy Alexander; Elizabeth Alker; Rachael Allen; Jason Allen-Paisant; Alan Allport; Nuar Alsadir; Geraint Anderson; Kelly Andrew; Abi Andrews; Carol Anshaw; Erica Sugo Anyadike; Michael Arditti; Edward Ardizzone; Noga Arikha; Michael Arlen; Thomas Asbridge; Jenn Ashworth; Jennifer Atkins; Julian Baggini; Harriet Baker; Tina Baker; Gina María Balibrera; Katy Balls; Antonia Barber; Lindsey Barcham; Nigel Barley; Robert Barnard; Suzanne Barton; Kaushik Basu; Yvonne Battle-Felton; Belinda Bauer; Felix Bazalgette; Ella Beech; Laura Beers; Hannah Begbie; Annie Bell; Aimee Bender; Margot Bennett; Joe Berger; Sarah Bernstein; Elizabeth Berridge; Tessa Bickers; Rebecca Birrell; James Bloodworth; Edmund Blunden; Margaret Boden; Jonathan Boff; Tim Bowler; Maria Bradford; E. R. Braithwaite; Mikki Brammer; Lauren Bravo; Carys Bray; Neville Braybrooke; Kevin Brazil; Theresa Breslin; Kevin Brockmeier; Glen Brown; Martin Brown; Hester Browne; Janet Browne; Mike Brownlow; Jessica Bruder; Rukky Brume; Martin Brunt; Arthur Bryant; Ella Bucknall; Anthony Burgess; Mark Burnell; Rob Burnett; Sheila Burnford; Nick Butterworth; Eliza Barry Callahan; Paco Calvo; John Carey; John Dickson Carr; Jess Cartner-Morley; Anne-Marie Casey; Barbara Castle; Charles Causley; Kathryn Cave; Aditya Chakrabortty; Vanessa Chan; Jason Chapman; Eve Chase; James Hadley Chase; Seerut K. Chawla; Camilla Chester; Emma Chichester Clark; Arthur C. Clarke; Lady Mary Clive; J. M. Coetzee; Kathleen Collins; Sophie Collins; Charlie Connelly; Alan Connor; Peter Cook; Trish Cooke; Emily S. Cooper; Natasha Cooper; Bernard Cornwell; Jamie Costello; Chris Cove-Smith; Cressida Cowell; Jason Cowley; Nick Crumpton; John Cunliffe; James Curtis; Roald Dahl; David Daiches; Tsitsi Dangarembga; Nicola Davies; Susie Day; Lizzie Dearden; Tish Delaney; R. F. Delderfield; Kady MacDonald Denton; Lucy Diamond; Morgan Dick; Lucy Dillamore; Lucy Dillon; Jonathan Dimbleby; Berlie Doherty; Naoise Dolan; Sareeta Domingo; Kelly Doust; Alicia Drake; Bobby Duffy; Sarah Duguid; Ruth Eastham; Mark Easton; Ellie Eaton; David Edmonds; Eve Edwards; Kerry Egan; Jonathan Emmett; Gavin Esler; Maz Evans; Rowan Evans; Seb Falk; Eleanor Farjeon; J. Jefferson Farjeon; Ben Faulks; Felipe Fernández-Armesto; Elizabeth Ferrars; Ophelia Field; Anne Fine; Cordelia Fine; Pip Finkemeyer; Nicholas Fisk; Pauline Fisk; Theodora Fitzgibbon; Corina Fletcher; Margot Fonteyn; Ford Madox Ford; Karen Joy Fowler; Catherine Fox; Matthew Frank; Melissa Franklin; P. M. Freestone; Tom de Freston; Stephen Fry; Mavis Gallant; Jane Gardam; Eve Garnett; Susan Gates; Jonathan Gathorne-Hardy; Ryan Gattis; Jamila Gavin; Jessica George; Adèle Geras; Susannah Gibson; Andrew Gimson; Guinevere Glasfurd;

Ralph Glasser; Victoria Glendinning; Julia Golding; Elizabeth Goudge; Caroline Graham; Holly Gramazio; Marlowe Granados; Ryan Graudin; Saska Graville; Dominic Green; Linda Green; Peter Green; Graham Greene; Richard Greene; John Gribbin; Geoffrey Grigson; Jane Grigson; Dennis Grube; Candy Guard; David Guss; Araminta Hall; Jo Hamya; Penny Hancock; Isabel Hardman; Sophie Harman; Candida Harper; Tim Harper; Ali Harris; Oliver Harris; Alice Hattrick; Paula Hawkins; Mo Hayder; Lottie Hazell; Oli Hazzard; Claire Marie Healy; Lisa Heathfield; Emma Henderson; James Herbert; Mick Herron; Deborah Hewitt; Rosie Hewlett; Sarah Hilary; Chris Hirst; Russell Hoban; Eric Hobsbawm; Gavannda Hodge; Leigh Hodgkinson; Jesse Hodgson; Paul Hoffman; Dianne Hofmeyr; Edward Hogan; Phil Hogan; Anna Hoghton; Ian Holding; Euny Hong; Meredith Hooper; Simon Hopkinson; Trevor Horn; Tansy Hoskins; Lucy Hounsom; Yuji Huang; Tristan Hughes; Masud Husain; William Hussey; Will Iredale; Julian Jackson; Julia Jarman; Milly Johnson; Rebecca May Johnson; Diana Wynne Jones; Owen Jones; Anthony Joseph; Alan Judd; Jessie Keane; Anna Keay; John Keay; Anna Kemp; Laura Kemp; Paul Kennedy; Barbara Keys; Sulmaan Wasif Khan; Rachel Khoo; Claire King; Clive King; Binnie Kirshenbaum; Halik Kochanski; Jay Kristoff; Fifi Kuo; Emily LaBarge; Stephen Lacey; David Lammy; Hugh Laurie; Eleanor Lavender; Natalie Lawrence; Elisabeth Leake; Kate Leaver; Jeremy Lee; Noby Leong; Beth Lewis; Daniel Light; Penelope Lively; Saci Lloyd; Jo Lodge; Joanna Lumley; Richard Lumsden; Kesia Lupo; Dame Vera Lynn; Sophie Mackintosh; Usma Malik; Kathryn Mannix; Sarfraz Manzoor; Greil Marcus; Kathryn Maris; Jan Mark; Ellie Marney; Patrick Marnham; David Marquand; Helen Marten; Simon Mason; Sadie Matthews; Evan Mawdsley; Peter May; Rufaro Faith Mazarura; Helen McCarthy; Geraldine McCaughrean; Elizabeth McCracken; Val McDermid; Iain McGilchrist; Elizabeth McKenzie; Tom McLaughlin; Thomas McMullan; Jean McNeil; Rosanna Mclaughlin; Anna Metcalfe; Ed Miliband; Louise Millar; Kei Miller; Gwen Millward; Myfanwy Millward; Kate Milner; Sarah Mitchell; Tony Mitton; Victoria Moore; Kate Morton; Emma-Lee Moss; Laura Mucha; Fraser Nelson; Jenny Nimmo; Johan Norberg; David Nott; Sigrid Nunez; Peter Oborne; Yewande Omotoso; Laurie Owens; Susan Owens; Deborah O'Donoghue; C. S. Pacat; Sandeep Parmar; Helen Parr; James Conor Patterson; Harry Pearson; Eleanor Penny; Gilles Peterson; Kate Reed Petty; Liz Pichon; Alake Pilgrim; Courtney Pine; Christina Pishiris; Anthony Powell; Shannon Pufahl; Sadiah Qureshi; Amol Rajan; Madhvi Ramani; Hanna Randall; Catherine Rayner; Jacqui Rayner; Gwyneth Rees; Katy Regan; Hannah Regel; Chris Renwick; Steve Richards; Fiona

Roberton; Lucy Robinson; Helen Roche; Claudia Roden; Jane Rogoyska; Rachel Rooney; Leone Ross; Rupert Russell; Saba Sams; Jane Sanderson; Noo Saro-Wiwa; Kathryn Scanlan; Izabella Scott; Alice Sebold; Antonia Senior; Miranda Seymour; Rachel Shabi; Nick Sharratt; Penelope Shuttle; Sujit Sivasundaram; Alexander McCall Smith; Lisa Smith; Mark B. Smith; Mary South; Kristina Spohr; Hilary Spurling; Devi Sridhar; Jessica Stanley; Joss Stirling; Peter Stott; Hew Strachan; Jeremy Strong; Nicola Sturgeon; Tasha Sylva; Sally Symes; Vanessa Tait; Dizz Tate; Lulu Taylor; Sureka Thanenthiran-Dharuman; Dylan Thomas; Frances Thomas; Simon Thurley; Phil Tinline; Theresa Tomlinson; Lynne Truss; Ann Turnbull; Simon Tyler; Jack Underwood; Rosamund Urwin; Varaidzo; Yanis Varoufakis; Sarah Vaughan; Stephanie Victoire; Martin Waddell; Lucy Wadham; Alice Walker; Joanna Walsh; Melanie Walsh; Rosie Walsh; Stephen Walsh; Minette Walters; Vanessa Walters; Miranda Ward; Bernard Wasserstein; Holly Watt; Christian Weaver; Sam Wetherell; Phil Whitaker; Elizabeth Wilhide; Gina Wilson; Jacqueline Wilson; Jon Wilson; David Wojtowycz; Hope Wolf; Carolyn Woods; Mandy Yin; Kate Zambreno

Chair / Literary Agent: Anthony Goff (**L258**)

Company Director / Literary Agent: Veronique Baxter (**L052**)

Literary Agents: Nicola Chang (**L110**); Elise Dillsworth (**L169**); Jemima Forrester (**L227**); Georgia Glover (**L255**); Andrew Gordon (**L262**); Lizzy Kremer (**L365**); Harriet Moore (**L453**); Caroline Walsh (**L632**); Jessica Woollard (**L663**)

L160 David Luxton Associates

Literary Agency
United Kingdom

admin@davidluxtonassociates.co.uk

https://www.davidluxtonassociates.co.uk
https://twitter.com/DLuxAssociates
https://www.instagram.com/davidluxtonassociates/

Professional Body: The Association of Authors' Agents (AAA)

Nonfiction > *Nonfiction Books*
Food; Investigative Journalism; Lifestyle; Music; Nature; Photography; Sport

Send: Query; Synopsis; Writing sample; Author bio
How to send: Email
How not to send: Post

Specialises in nonfiction, including sport, celebrity biography, business & leadership, food-writing, nature-writing and lifestyle. No scripts or screenplays.

Literary Agents: David Luxton (**L405**); Nick Walters (**L634**); Rebecca Winfield (**L657**)

L161 Bonnie Davis
Literary Agent

Literary Agency: Bret Adams Ltd

L162 Liza Dawson
Senior Agent; President
United States

queryliza@lizadawsonassociates.com

https://www.lizadawsonassociates.com/liza-dawson

Literary Agency: Liza Dawson Associates
(**L397**)
Professional Bodies: The Authors Guild;
Mystery Writers of America (MWA)

Fiction > *Novels*
Book Club Fiction; Contemporary; Historical
Fiction; Literary; Mystery; Social Class; Spy
Thrilllers; Thrillers

Nonfiction > *Nonfiction Books*
Comedy / Humour; Culture; Environment;
Ethnic Groups; Finance; Memoir; Narrative
History; Politics; US Southern States;
Women's Issues

Closed to approaches.

She specializes in: Smart, plot-driven
bestselling fiction. Memorable, confidently-
written, literary fiction. Page-turning thrillers
that teach you about spycraft, foreign intrigue
or an unusual career. Mysteries – featuring
brainy detectives. Literary fiction for book
clubs. Breakout historical novels. In
nonfiction, she is drawn to cross-cultural and
women's issues written by experts. She is
looking for narrative history, memoirs about
women and men who have escaped from
closed, repressive societies and books by
journalists and poets who are trying to make
sense of exotic locations, race, the
environment, Wall Street, Washington, and the
South. Humor and tenderness are a plus, and
she has a weakness for cartoonists and quirky
humor.

Authors: Annie Barrows; Marie Bostwick; Bob
Brier; Stella Cameron; Robyn Carr; Ross Gay;
Susan Hasler; Julia Lee; Victoria Christopher
Murray; Tawni O'Dell; Jean Sasson

L163 Liza DeBlock
Literary Agent
United Kingdom

submissions@mushens-entertainment.com

https://www.mushens-entertainment.com/liza-deblock

Literary Agency: Mushens Entertainment

Fiction > *Novels*
Grounded Fantasy; Historical Fiction;
Literary; Thrillers; Upmarket

Nonfiction > *Nonfiction Books*
Cookery; Popular Science; Social History

Send: Query; Synopsis; Writing sample
How to send: Email

Looking for both fiction and non fiction. For
fiction, she is interested in adult only. She is
looking for historical fiction, literary and
upmarket, grounded fantasy (no sci-fi), and
thriller.

On the non fiction side, she is looking for
books that teach her something new or reframe
a topic from an alternative point of view. This
can include cookery, pop science, and social
history.

Authors: Sally Abe; Natalie Chandler; Sally
El-Arifi; Jane Hennigan; Eleanor Houghton;
Carys Jones; Hayley Nolan; Stacey Thomas;
Pim Wangtechawat

L164 The Dench Arnold
Agency
Literary Agency
United Kingdom
Tel: +44 (0) 20 7437 4551
Fax: +44 (0) 20 7437 4551

fiona@den.charnold.com

https://www.dencharnold.com
https://www.instagram.com/
dencharnold_agency/
https://twitter.com/DenchArnold

Scripts
Film Scripts; *TV Scripts*

Send: Query; Author bio; Synopsis
How to send: Email

Send query with CV and synopsis by email
only. Represents writers, directors and heads of
department (directors of photography,
production designers, costume designers,
editors and make-up designers).

Authors: Joe Ainsworth; Maurice Bessman;
Giles Borg; William Borthwick; Peter Briggs;
Karen Brown; Peter Chelsom; Rob Churchill;
David Conolly; Hannah Davies; Jim Davies;
Eric Deacon; Adrian Dunbar; Chris Fallon;
Susanne Farrell; Matthew Faulk; Lucy
Flannery; Ellis Freeman; Liam Gavin;
Nicholas Gibbs; Steve Gough; Robert
Hammond; James Handel; Michael Harvey; Jo
Ho; David Lg Hughes; Julian Kemp; Malcolm
Kohll; Anna Kythreotis; Sarah Lambert;
Dominic Macdonald; Steve Mcateer; Alan
Mcdonald; Kevin Molony; Courttia Newland;
Matthew Newman; Omid Nooshin; Paul
Parkes; Junior Rhone; Dave Simpson; Mark
Skeet; Mark Stay; Francesca Tatini; Stewart
Thomson; Alan Whiting; Terry Winsor; Kate
Wood

Literary Agents: Michelle Arnold; Elizabeth
Dench; Matthew Dench

L165 Dado Derviskadic
Literary Agent
United States
Tel: +1 (212) 400-1494

dado@foliolitmanagement.com

http://foliolit.com/dado-derviskadic

Literary Agency: Folio Literary Management,
LLC

Nonfiction > *Nonfiction Books*
Art History; Biography; Cookery; Cultural
History; Fashion; Films; Food; Health;
Motivational Self-Help; Nutrition;
Philosophy; Popular Culture; Popular
Science; Psychology; Religion; Spirituality;
Sub-Culture

Send: Query; Writing sample; Proposal
How to send: In the body of an email

I am primarily interested in: cultural history;
biography; art history; film; religion and
spirituality; psychology; philosophy; pop
science and motivational self-help; health and
nutrition; pop culture and subcultures; fashion;
and food narrative and cookbooks.

L166 Allison Devereux
Literary Agent
United States

https://www.cheneyagency.com/allison-devereux

Literary Agency: The Cheney Agency

L167 DHH Literary Agency Ltd
Literary Agency
23-27 Cecil Court, London, WC2N 4EZ
United Kingdom
Tel: +44 (0) 20 3990 2452

enquiries@dhhliteraryagency.com

http://www.dhhliteraryagency.com

Professional Body: The Association of
Authors' Agents (AAA)

ADULT
Fiction > *Novels*
Nonfiction > *Nonfiction Books*

CHILDREN'S > **Fiction** > *Novels*

YOUNG ADULT > **Fiction** > *Novels*

Send: Query
Don't send: Full text

Accepts submissions by email only. No postal
submissions. See website for specific agent
interests and email addresses and approach one
agent only. Do not send submissions to generic
"enquiries" email address.

Associate Agent: Tom Drake Lee (**L383**)

Authors: Foluso Agbaje; Kishan Devani BEM;
Graham Bartlett; Louise Beech; R.C.
Bridgestock; Tom Brown; Paul Burston;
Andrea Carter; Paul Fraser Collard; Howard
Colyer; James Conway; M.W. Craven; John

Curran; Libby Cutts; Heather Darwent; Becca Day; Michael Delahaye; A. A. Dhand; Suzie Edge; Stephen Edger; David Fennell; Fishlove; Essie Fox; Anita Frank; Erin Green; Katy Harrison; Lisa Hilton; Valerie Jack; Ragnar Jonasson; Jón Atli Jónasson; Katrín Júlíusdóttir; Anthony Kavanagh; Diana Kessler; Caroline Lamond; Michael Leggo; S.V. Leonard; Kathy Lette; Sean Lusk; Adrian Magson; Chris McDonald; Brian McGilloway; Emma Medrano; Rachel Meller; Jean Menzies; Janie Millman; Elizabeth S. Moore; Noel O'Reilly; Valerie O'Riordan; Vikki Patis; Anthony J. Quinn; Reagan Lee Ray; Becky Rhush; Nicole Robinson; Leon Romero-Montalvo; Iain Rowan; Robert Rutherford; Talia Samuels; Victoria Selman; Richard Stirling; Annie Taylor; Jo Thomas; Rebecca Thorne; Amanda Tuke; Ola Tundun; Ronnie Turner; L.C. Tyler; A. J. West; Clare Whitfield; Kathleen Whyman; Eva Björg Ægisdottir

Company Director / Literary Agent: Emily Glenister (**L253**)

Literary Agent / Managing Director: David H. Headley (**L300**)

Literary Agents: Broo Doherty; Harry Illingworth

L168 Sandra Dijkstra
Literary Agent
United States

https://www.dijkstraagency.com/sandra-dijkstra.php
https://querymanager.com/query/DijkstraCapron

Literary Agency: Sandra Dijkstra Literary Agency

Fiction > *Novels*
Commercial; Literary

Nonfiction > *Nonfiction Books*
Business; Current Affairs; History; Politics; Religion; Science

How to send: By referral

Agent to authors in the arenas of nonfiction (including history, politics, current affairs, business, and science), and quality fiction which crosses over between literary and commercial, her mission is to champion authors whose books make a difference.

L169 Elise Dillsworth
Literary Agent
United Kingdom

elise@elisedillsworthagency.com

https://www.davidhigham.co.uk/agents-dh/elise-dillsworth/

Literary Agencies: Elise Dillsworth Agency (EDA); David Higham Associates Ltd (**L159**)

Fiction > *Novels*

General, and in particular: International; Literary

Nonfiction > *Nonfiction Books*
General, and in particular: International; Literary

Represents literary and general fiction and nonfiction, with a keen aim to reflect writing that is international.

Authors: Erica Sugo Anyadike; Yvonne Battle-Felton; Maria Bradford; Anthony Joseph; Noby Leong; Usma Malik; Yewande Omotoso; Courtney Pine; Hanna Randall; Noo Saro-Wiwa; Stephanie Victoire

L170 Isobel Dixon
Literary Agent; Managing Director
United Kingdom

isobeldixon@blakefriedmann.co.uk

http://blakefriedmann.co.uk/isobel-dixon
https://twitter.com/isobeldixon

Literary Agency: Blake Friedmann Literary Agency Ltd (**L064**)

Fiction > *Novels*
Contemporary; Crime; Historical Fiction; Literary; Thrillers

Nonfiction > *Nonfiction Books*
Biography; Memoir; Narrative History

Closed to approaches.

Interests are wide-ranging and her clients' work includes contemporary, historical and literary fiction, crime and thrillers, memoir, biography and narrative history.

Authors: James Cahill; Tomasz Jedrowski

L171 Saffron Dodd
Literary Agent
United Kingdom

submissions@ashliterary.com

https://ashliterary.com/#saffronwishlist
https://querymanager.com/query/saffronashliterary

Literary Agency: ASH Literary (**L035**)

CHILDREN'S > **Fiction** > *Middle Grade*
Adventure; Contemporary; Fantasy; Magic

YOUNG ADULT > **Fiction** > *Novels*
Fantasy; Mystery; Romantic Comedy; Thrillers

Send: Query; Synopsis; Writing sample
How to send: Query Manager; Email

I'm looking for fully realised, immersive, and creative worlds with standout characters. I love middle-grade fantasy and I'm looking for something filled with adventure, magic, and intrigue, with a strong and distinct voice. In contemporary middle-grade, I'm looking for witty and sharp protagonists with something to say and an interesting perspective on the world. In YA, I lean towards fantasy but would

also love a solid mystery thriller or a shenanigan filled rom-com that does or says something new. I'm also keen to see stories set in the UK during the transitional period between sixth form/college and university. Above all, I'm keen to see work from historically excluded and underrepresented writers in the UK.

L172 Trevor Dolby
Literary Agent
United Kingdom

https://aevitascreative.com/agents/#agent-7410

Literary Agency: Aevitas Creative Management (ACM) UK (**L008**)

Nonfiction > *Nonfiction Books*
Biography; Comedy / Humour; Memoir; Military History; Narrative History; Nature; Popular Culture; Popular Science

Closed to approaches.

Looking for popular science with a clear relevance to everyday life, narrative history, military history, humour, biography, popular culture, natural history and great memoirs by passionate people whose lives have been well lived.

L173 Adriana Dominguez
Senior Agent
United States

https://aevitascreative.com/agents/
https://querymanager.com/query/2243

Literary Agency: Aevitas

ADULT > **Nonfiction** > *Nonfiction Books*: Narrative Nonfiction

CHILDREN'S
Fiction
Middle Grade; Picture Books
Nonfiction > *Nonfiction Books*

How to send: Query Manager

Interested in illustrators with fresh, unmistakable styles, platform-driven narrative nonfiction from children to adult, and select children's fiction from picture books to middle grade.

Authors: Jacqueline Alcántara; Ana Aranda; Andrés López; Angela Cervantes; Daniel Fishel; John Parra; Juliet Menéndez; Lucía Franco; Marcelo Verdad; Maria Hinojosa; Claudia Guadalupe Martinez; Maya Wei-Haas; Gerardo Ivan Morales; Emma Otheguy; Katheryn Russell-Brown; Madrid Santos; David Smith; Tania de Regil; Janelle Washington

L174 Don Buchwald and Associates
Literary Agency
United States

info@buchwald.com

https://www.buchwald.com
https://twitter.com/buchwaldtalent
https://www.facebook.com/buchwaldtalent
https://www.instagram.com/buchwaldtalent

Professional Body: Writers Guild of America (WGA)

Scripts
Film Scripts; *TV Scripts*; *Theatre Scripts*

Closed to approaches.

Does not accept unsolicited submissions of any kind.

L175 Don Congdon Associates, Inc.
Literary Agency
88 Pine Street, Suite 730, New York, NY 10005
United States
Tel: +1 (212) 645-1229

dca@doncongdon.com

https://doncongdon.com

Professional Body: Association of American Literary Agents (AALA)

Fiction > *Novels*

Nonfiction > *Nonfiction Books*

Send: Query; Synopsis; Writing sample
How to send: Email; Query Manager

Send query by email (no attachments) or by Query Manager, per agent preference. Include one-page synopsis, relevant background info, and first chapter, all within the body of the email if submitting by email. Include the word "Query" in the subject line. See website for full guidelines. No unsolicited MSS.

Foreign Rights Manager / Literary Agent: Cristina Concepcion (**L133**)

Literary Agents: Michael Congdon; Katie Grimm (**L272**); Katie Kotchman (**L364**); Maura Kye-Casella; Susan Ramer (**L518**)

L176 Donald Maass Literary Agency
Literary Agency
1000 Dean Street, Suite 331, Brooklyn, NY 11238
United States
Tel: +1 (212) 727-8383

info@maassagency.com

http://www.maassagency.com

Professional Body: Association of American Literary Agents (AALA)

ADULT
Fiction > *Novels*
Nonfiction > *Nonfiction Books*

YOUNG ADULT > **Fiction** > *Novels*

Send: Query; Synopsis; Writing sample
How to send: Email
How not to send: Post; Phone; Social Media

Welcomes all genres, in particular science fiction, fantasy, mystery, suspense, horror, romance, historical, literary and mainstream novels. Send query to a specific agent, by email, with "query" in the subject line. No queries by post, phone, or social media. See website for individual agent interests and email addresses.

Authors: Saladin Ahmed; Sonya Bateman; Jim Butcher

Literary Agents: Michael Curry; Jennifer Goloboy; Jolene Haley (**L281**); Jennifer Jackson; Kat Kerr; Donald Maass; Cameron McClure; Caitlin McDonald; Kiana Nguyen; Anne Tibbets (**L613**)

Vice President: Katie Shea Boutillier

L177 Dorie Simmonds Agency
Literary Agency
United Kingdom

info@doriesimmonds.com

https://doriesimmonds.com/

Professional Body: The Association of Authors' Agents (AAA)

ADULT
Fiction > *Novels*: Commercial
Nonfiction > *Nonfiction Books*

CHILDREN'S > **Fiction** > *Novels*

Send: Query; Writing sample; Author bio
How to send: PDF file email attachment; Word file email attachment

Send query by email as Word or PDF attachments. Include details on your background and relevant writing experience, and first three chapters or fifty pages. See website for full details.

Literary Agent: Dorie Simmonds

L178 Doug Grad Literary Agency
Literary Agency
156 Prospect Park West, #3L, Brooklyn, NY 11215
United States
Tel: +1 (718) 788-6067

doug.grad@dgliterary.com

http://www.dgliterary.com
https://www.facebook.com/DGLit

Fiction
Graphic Novels: General
Novels: Comedy / Humour; Crime; Historical Fiction; Mystery; Romance; Science Fiction; Thrillers; Westerns; Women's Fiction
Nonfiction
Illustrated Books: Comedy / Humour; Photography

Nonfiction Books: Adventure; Biography; Business; Cars; Comedy / Humour; Cookery; Crime; Dogs; Films; Gardening; Health; History; How To; Journalism; Language; Memoir; Military; Music; Politics; Religion; Self Help; Sport; Theatre; Travel

Send: Query
Don't send: Writing sample
How to send: Email
How not to send: Post; Phone

Send query letter by email. Do not include sample material until requested.

Literary Agent: Doug Grad

L179 Claire Draper
Literary Agent
United States

https://www.thebentagency.com/claire-draper
https://querymanager.com/query/draper_claire

Literary Agency: The Bent Agency (**L058**)

ADULT
Fiction > *Novels*
Feminism; LGBTQIA; Romance

Nonfiction > *Nonfiction Books*
General, and in particular: Arts; Cookery; Crafts; Feminism; Home Improvement; LGBTQIA; Media; Memoir; Parenting; Plants

CHILDREN'S > **Fiction**
Graphic Novels; *Middle Grade*
YOUNG ADULT > **Fiction**
Graphic Novels; *Novels*

How not to send: Query Manager

Prefers to work with queer and BIPOC creators. Likes lighthearted, emotional, hopeful, adventurous reads. Largely genre-agnostic, but prefers books with a fast pace, high stakes, and strong emotional development for the main character(s). Does not want to see books from authors writing identity-based books not of their own identity.

L180 Dunham Literary, Inc.
Literary Agency
United States

query@dunhamlit.com

https://www.dunhamlit.com

ADULT
Fiction > *Novels*

Nonfiction > *Nonfiction Books*: Narrative Nonfiction

CHILDREN'S > **Fiction**
Novels; *Picture Books*

Send: Query; Writing sample
Don't send: Full text
How to send: In the body of an email
How not to send: Post; Fax; Phone; Email attachment; Google Docs shared document

Handles quality fiction and nonfiction for adults and children. Send query by email only. See website for full guidelines. No approaches by post, phone or fax. No email attachments.

Literary Agents: Anjanette Barr (**L046**); Jennie Dunham (**L181**)

L181 Jennie Dunham

Literary Agent
United States

https://www.dunhamlit.com/jennie-dunham.html
https://aalitagents.org/author/jenniedunham/
https://twitter.com/JennieDunhamLit
https://www.linkedin.com/in/jennie-dunham-11028b140/
https://www.facebook.com/JennieDunhamLit
https://www.instagram.com/jenniedunhamlit

Literary Agency: Dunham Literary, Inc. (**L180**)
Professional Bodies: Association of American Literary Agents (AALA); Society of Children's Book Writers and Illustrators (SCBWI)

ADULT
Fiction
Graphic Novels: General
Novels: Comedy / Humour; Historical Fiction; LGBTQIA; Literary; Mystery; Thrillers; Women's Fiction
Nonfiction > *Nonfiction Books*
Biography; Current Affairs; Family; History; Memoir; Narrative Nonfiction; Parenting; Politics; Relationships; Science; Technology

CHILDREN'S > **Fiction**
Middle Grade; *Picture Books*
NEW ADULT
Fiction > *Novels*
Nonfiction > *Nonfiction Books*

YOUNG ADULT > **Fiction** > *Novels*

Send: Query; Writing sample
Don't send: Full text
How to send: In the body of an email
How not to send: Post; Fax; Phone; Email attachment

Represents literary fiction and non-fiction for adults and children.

L182 Neil Dunnicliffe

Literary Agent
United Kingdom

neil@springliterary.com

https://www.springliterary.com/about

Literary Agency: Spring Literary (**L581**)

L183 Dunow, Carlson & Lerner Agency

Literary Agency
27 West 20th Street, Suite 1103, New York, NY 10011

United States
Tel: +1 (212) 645-7606

mail@dclagency.com

https://www.dclagency.com

Professional Body: Association of American Literary Agents (AALA)

ADULT
Fiction > *Novels*
Commercial; Literary

Nonfiction > *Nonfiction Books*

CHILDREN'S > **Fiction**
Chapter Books; *Early Readers*; *Middle Grade*

Send: Query; Writing sample; Self-Addressed Stamped Envelope (SASE)
How to send: In the body of an email; Post
How not to send: Email attachment

Represents literary and commercial fiction, a wide range of nonfiction, and children's literature for all ages. Prefers queries by email, but will also accept queries by post with SASE. No attachments. Does not respond to all email queries.

Author Estates: The Estate of Donald J. Sobol; The Estate of Jim Carroll; The Estate of John Steptoe; The Estate of Joseph Mitchell; The Estate of William Lee Miller

Authors: Nathaniel Adams; Siobhan Adcock; Preston Allen; Mara Altman; Stephen Amidon; Cynthia Anderson; Jessica Applestone; Josh & Jessica Applestone; Richard Aquila; Beth Bacon; Kevin Baker; Nancy Balbirer; Wilton Barnhardt; Jackie Battenfield; Douglas Bauer; Richard Bausch; Aimee Bender; Jennifer Berney; Tanaz Bhathena; Frank Bill; Brandon Bird; George Black; Lea Black; Robin Black; Michael Bobelian; Lorraine Boissoneault; Amy Bonnaffons; Shira Boss; Michelle Bowdler; Sesali Bowen; Svetlana Boym; G.B. Bragg; Benjamin Breen; Elise Broach; Kevin Brockmeier; Mikita Brottman; David W. Brown; Stacia Brown; David Browne; Mónica Bustamante; Hamilton Cain; Katrina Carrasco; Bill Carter; Erika Carter; Adam Cayton-Holland; Climate Central; Bryn Chancellor; Joelle Charbonneau; Noah Charney; Paula Chase; Emily Chenoweth; K Chess; Mark Childress; Christina Chiu; Adam Christopher; Mimi Chubb; Cassandra Rose Clarke; Nigel Cliff; Nancy Coffelt; Jaed Coffin; Cole Cohen; Miriam Cohen; Jaimee Wriston Colbert; Deborah Joy Corey; Paul Cornell; Carrie Courogen; Jeremy Craig; Katherine Crowley; Dave Cullen; Cheyenne Curtis; Mark Dapin; Dame Darcy; Alice Elliott Dark; Michael Dart; Elizabeth Davis; Delilah S. Dawson; Alena Dillon; Heather Dixon; Lawrence Downes; Allyson Downey; Mike Duncan; DK Dyson; Damien Echols; Daniel Ehrenhaft; Rhian Ellis; Katherine Crowley & Kathy Elster; Kathy Elster; Donald J. Sobol Estate; Jim Carroll Estate; John Steptoe Estate; Joseph Mitchell

Estate; Scott O'Dell Estate; William Lee Miller Estate; Marion Ettlinger; Marie Favereau; Stephanie Feldman; Boris Fishman; Emily Flitter; Pia Frey; Seth Fried; Steven Galloway; John Gartner; Amina Gautier; Joshua Gaylord; Valerie Geary; Poppy Gee; Michael Gerber; Alfred Gingold; Owen Gleiberman; Melody Godfred; Brandt Goldstein; Gary Golio; Matthew Goodman; Eli Gottlieb; Temple Grandin; Elizabeth Graver; Casey Gray; Seth Greenland; Gwendolen Gross; Rudy Gutierrez; Kathleen Hale; Lisa Hale; Leah Hampton; Mary Ellen Hannibal; Alyssa Hardy; Windy Lynn Harris; Ethan Hauser; Kevin Hearne; Robert Hellenga; Steve Hendricks; Joe Henry; Becky Hepinstall; George Hodgman; Beatrice Hohenegger; Christopher M. Hood; Erin Hosier; Ilze Hugo; Josie Iselin; Jeremy Jackson; John Hornor Jacobs; Matthew Jobin; Daron Joffe; Noah Z. Jones; David Joy; Frank Wheeler, Jr.; Valerie June; Karen Kane; Hester Kaplan; Jon Keller; Brad Kessler; Christian Kiefer; Andrea Kleine; Taylor Koekkoek; Chrissy Kolaya; Amanda Korman; Gabrielle Korn; Nik Korpon; J. Kasper Kramer; Andrew Krivak; Justin Kuritzkes; Maria Kuznetsova; Johanna Lane; Sarah Langan; Richard Lange; Sarah Laskow; Holly LeCraw; Mirinae Lee; Edan Lepucki; Elizabeth Lesser; Jerry Lee Lewis; Robin Lewis; David Lida; Brad Listi; William Bryant Logan; Jenny Lombard; Leil Lowndes; Joshua Lyon; Robin MacArthur; David Stuart MacLean; Anne Madden; Dennis Mahoney; Tania Malik; Michael Mann; Tanya Marquardt; Debra Marquart; Alex Marshall; Cate Marvin; Suzanne Matson; Abi Maxwell; Matthew McBride; Jill McCorkle; Elizabeth McCracken; Patrick McDonnell; Sean McGinty; Jon McGoran; Will McGrath; Adam McOmber; Bob Mehr; Susan Scarf Merrell; Deborah Meyler; Jenny Milchman; Barnabas Miller; Daphne Miller; Paul Miller; Denise Mina; Celeste Mohammed; T. T. Monday; Gregory Mone; Amanda Montell; Bradford Morrow; Brian Morton; Layne Mosler; Sarah Moss; Ritu Mukerji; Kimberly Shannon Murphy; Debbie Nathan; Ed Nawotka; Greg Neri; Robert Neuwith; Alana Newhouse; Scott O'Connor; Aline Ohanesian; Elizabeth Oness; David Orr; Chad Orzel; Tom Paine; Richard Panek; Michel Paradis; Debra Pascali-Bonaro; Rachel Pastan; Justin Peacock; Jamie Pearlberg; Catherine Pelonero; Tony Perrottet; Annie Rogers, Ph.D.; Chad Orzel, Ph.D.; Max Phillips; Melissa Holbrook Pierson; Nic Pizzolatto; Aimee Pokwatka; Daria Polichetti; Richard Polt; Maggie Pouncey; Jessica Powers; Caroline Preston; Cherie Priest; Mark Prins; D. M. Pulley; Carol Purington; Susan Todd & Carol Purington; Joan Quigley; Mark Rader; Ace Tilton Ratcliff; Susanna Reich; Nelly Reifler; Heidi Reimer; James Renner; Paul Reyes; Robert Riesman; Nicholas Rinaldi; M. L. Rio; Marisa Robinson-Textor; Annie Rogers; Stuart Rojstaczer; Tricia Romano;

Linda Ronstadt; Jane Roper; Alex Rose; Marissa A. Ross; Rebecca Rotert; Shannan Rouss; Katherine Rowland; Lena Roy; David Rubel; Joan Ryan; Richard Sandoval; Marisa de los Santos; Alexis Schaitkin; Kodi Scheer; Patty Schemel; David Schickler; Molly Schiot; Heidi Jon Schmidt; Sally Schmitt; Pat Schories; William Todd Schultz; Kieran Shea; Jeff Shelby; Joshua Wolf Shenk; Jenefer Shute; Marisa Silver; Mohamedou Slahi; Patti Smith; Sherry Smith; Kevin Smokler; Tatjana Soli; Lily Sparks; Shira Spector; Kelli Stanley; Leigh Stein; Javaka Steptoe; Lindsay Stern; Jude Stewart; Susan Straight; Cynthia D'Aprix Sweeney; Vivian Swift; Shannon Takaoka; Liara Tamani; Nick Taylor; David Teague; Tori Telfer; Melanie Thernstrom; Jean Thompson; Richard Todd; Susan Todd; David Tomlinson; Lawrence Turman; James Twitchell; Neil deGrasse Tyson; Robert Utley; Karen Valby; Katherine Vaz; Sarah St. Vincent; Christine Wade; Laura Waldon; Casey Walker; Mark Van de Walle; Margaret Wappler; Elizabeth Weinberg; Jillian Weise; Jan Merete Weiss; Elizabeth Weitzman; Chuck Wendig; Frank Wheeler; Kali White; Kamy Wicoff; Matt Wiegle; Marianne Wiggins; Amy Wilentz; Corban Wilkinson; Tim Wirkus; Mishna Wolff; Hilma Wolitzer; Alisson Wood; Aubrey Wood; Rebecca Woolf; Sara Woster; Kim Wozencraft; Ronald Wright; David Wroblewski; Jeff Yang; David Yoo; Kenji Yoshino; Alia Yunis; Alan Ziegler; Jennifer duBois

Literary Agents: Jennifer Carlson; Arielle Datz; Stacia Decker; Henry Dunow; Erin Hosier; Eleanor Jackson; Julia Kenny; Betsy Lerner; Edward Necarsulmer; Nicki Richesin (**L525**); Yishai Seidman

L184 E. J. McCarthy Agency
Literary Agency
United States

ejmagency@gmail.com

https://twitter.com/ejmccarthy

Nonfiction > *Nonfiction Books*
Biography; History; Memoir; Military History; Sport

Send: Query
How to send: Email

Literary agency from former executive editor with experience at some of the world's largest publishing houses, specialising in military history, politics, history, biography, memoir, media, public policy, and sports.

Literary Agent: E. J. McCarthy

L185 Adam Eaglin
Literary Agent
United States

https://www.cheneyagency.com/adameaglin

Literary Agency: The Cheney Agency

L186 Chelsea Eberly
Literary Agent; Company Director
United States

https://www.greenhouseliterary.com/the-team/chelsea-eberly/
https://twitter.com/chelseberly
https://www.publishersmarketplace.com/members/ChelseaEberly/
https://querymanager.com/query/ChelseaEberly

Literary Agency: The Greenhouse Literary Agency

ADULT > **Fiction** > *Novels*
Book Club Women's Fiction; Upmarket Women's Fiction

CHILDREN'S
Fiction
Graphic Novels: General
Middle Grade: Adventure; Comedy / Humour; Fantasy; Folklore, Myths, and Legends; Magical Realism; Mystery
Picture Books: General

Nonfiction
Nonfiction Books; *Picture Books*
YOUNG ADULT
Fiction
Graphic Novels: Comedy / Humour; Contemporary; Fantasy; Magical Realism; Romance
Novels: Commercial; Fantasy; Feminism; Literary; Mystery; Romance; Social Justice; Thrillers
Nonfiction > *Graphic Nonfiction*
General, and in particular: History

Does not want:

> **CHILDREN'S** > **Fiction** > *Middle Grade*: Horror
>
> **YOUNG ADULT** > **Fiction** > *Novels*: Horror

Send: Query; Author bio; Writing sample; Proposal
How to send: By referral

Represents authors of middle grade, young adult, graphic novels, and women's fiction, as well as illustrators who write picture books.

L187 Eddison Pearson Ltd
Literary Agency
West Hill House, 6 Swain's Lane, London, N6 6QS
United Kingdom
Tel: +44 (0) 20 7700 7763

enquiries@eddisonpearson.com

https://www.eddisonpearson.com
https://linktr.ee/ClarePearson
https://eddisonpearson.tumblr.com/
https://www.linkedin.com/in/clare-pearson-epla
https://twitter.com/ClarePearson_EP

Professional Body: The Association of Authors' Agents (AAA)

CHILDREN'S
Fiction
Novels: Contemporary; Historical Fiction
Picture Books: General

Poetry > *Any Poetic Form*

YOUNG ADULT > **Fiction** > *Novels*

Send: Query; Writing sample
How to send: Email
How not to send: Social Media; Post

A London-based literary agency providing a personal service to a small stable of talented authors, mainly of books for children and young adults. Send query by email only for auto-response containing up-to-date submission guidelines and email address for submissions. No submissions or enquiries by post.

Authors: Valerie Bloom; Michael Catchpool; Sue Heap; Caroline Lawrence; Robert Muchamore; Mary Murphy; Megan Rix

Literary Agent: Clare Pearson

L188 Sam Edenborough
Literary Agent; Foreign Rights Director
United Kingdom

sam@greyhoundliterary.co.uk

https://greyhoundliterary.co.uk/agent/sam-edenborough/
https://twitter.com/SamEdenborough

Literary Agency: Greyhound Literary (**L271**)

Fiction > *Novels*
Cyberpunk; Fantasy; Folklore, Myths, and Legends; Hard Science Fiction; Horror; Speculative; Upmarket

Nonfiction > *Nonfiction Books*
Classical Music; Culture; History; Jazz; Music; Science

Send: Synopsis; Outline; Writing sample
How to send: Email

A life-long reader of speculative fiction. He loves hard SF and cyberpunk that explores the biggest questions about what it means to be human; fantasy with wit, brilliantly deep world-building and characters with an edge. He is interested in upmarket, folkloric or horror-tinged fiction. He is also looking for fiction and non-fiction which engages with landscape or the sea in a profound and original way; books about jazz and classical music and musicians; work by historians and novelists who challenge us to rethink comfortable assumptions about an era or a culture; and writing by scientists who are able to communicate complex ideas to a wide readership with verve.

L189 Max Edwards

Literary Agent
United Kingdom

max@appletreeliterary.co.uk

https://aevitascreative.com/agents/#agent-7412
http://appletreeliterary.co.uk/about/
https://querymanager.com/query/2619

Literary Agency: Aevitas Creative
Management (ACM) UK (**L008**)

Fiction > *Novels*
Commercial; Crime; Fantasy; High Concept;
Science Fiction

Nonfiction > *Nonfiction Books*
History; Journalism; Memoir; Nature

Closed to approaches.

In non-fiction, he is looking for experts telling
a new story for a trade audience; incredible
memoirs and untold histories; journalists
looking to take their stories long-form; and
smart and original ideas. In fiction, he is
looking for commercial and genre novels, and
is a massive fan of novels that mix genres in a
unique way. He's a sucker for high concepts,
smart plots and unique characters – twists and
turns, good (and bad) guys with depth and life.

Authors: William Lee Adams; Theo Barclay;
Ross Barnett; Louise Callaghan; Hannah
Durkin; Lucy Fisher; Johanna Katrin
Fridriksdottir; James Hazel; Alex Hess; David
Hone; Gulchehra Hora; John J. Johnston;
Russell Jones; Snorri Kristjansson; Matt
Lodder; Debora MacKenzie; Oksana Masters;
Laura Mauro; Una McCormack; Keza
McDonald; Juliet E. McKenna; Guy Morpuss;
Luke O'Neill; Jay Owens; Sumit Paul-
Choudhury; Nick Pettigrew; Dominic Pimenta;
Swéta Rana; Joe Tracini; Aliya Whiteley;
James Womack; Jim Worrad; Suzanne Wrack;
Olivia Yallop

L190 Einstein Literary Management

Literary Agency
United States
Tel: +1 (212) 221-8797

submissions@einsteinliterary.com

https://www.einsteinliterary.com
https://twitter.com/Einstein_Lit

ADULT
Fiction > *Novels*
Commercial; Literary

Nonfiction > *Nonfiction Books*
Cookery; Memoir; Narrative Nonfiction

CHILDREN'S > **Fiction** > *Novels*

YOUNG ADULT > **Fiction** > *Novels*

Send: Query; Writing sample
How to send: In the body of an email

Send query by email with first ten double-
spaced pages pasted into the body of the email.

No attachments. See website for details of
individual agents and their interests and
include the name of specific agent you are
submitting to in the subject line. No poetry,
textbooks, or screenplays. No queries by post
or by phone. Response only if interested.

Associate Agent: Paloma Hernando (**L302**)

Literary Agents: Susanna Einstein (**L191**);
Susan Graham (**L265**)

L191 Susanna Einstein

Literary Agent
United States

https://www.einsteinliterary.com/staff/
http://aaronline.org/Sys/PublicProfile/4557347/
417813

Literary Agency: Einstein Literary
Management (**L190**)
Professional Body: Association of American
Literary Agents (AALA)

ADULT
Fiction > *Novels*
Commercial Women's Fiction; Crime;
Upmarket Women's Fiction

Nonfiction > *Nonfiction Books*: Narrative
Nonfiction

CHILDREN'S > **Fiction** > *Middle Grade*

YOUNG ADULT > **Fiction** > *Novels*

Closed to approaches.

Has a particular fondness for crime fiction,
upmarket commercial women's fiction, MG
and YA fiction, and narrative non-fiction. She
likes a good story well told.

L192 Nicole Eisenbraun

Literary Agent
United States

nme@gingerclarkliterary.com

https://gingerclarkliterary.com/About
https://gingerclarkliterary.com/Submissions
http://aaronline.org/Sys/PublicProfile/
51483163/417813

Literary Agency: Ginger Clark Literary (**L249**)
Professional Body: Association of American
Literary Agents (AALA)

CHILDREN'S
Fiction > *Middle Grade*
General, and in particular: Fairy Tales

Nonfiction > *Middle Grade*
History; Popular Culture; Science

YOUNG ADULT
Fiction > *Novels*
General, and in particular: Fairy Tales

Nonfiction > *Nonfiction Books*
History; Popular Culture; Science

Send: Query
How to send: Email

Looking for middle grade and young adult in
all genres, fiction and nonfiction. For fiction,
she is particularly interested in great fairytale
retellings with colorful twists and stories that
tackle difficult subjects in unexpected ways.
For nonfiction, she is looking for books
focusing on science, history, and popular
culture.

L193 Caroline Eisenmann

Senior Agent
United States

ce@goldinlit.com

https://goldinlit.com/agents/

Literary Agency: Frances Goldin Literary
Agency, Inc. (**L231**)
Professional Body: Association of American
Literary Agents (AALA)

Fiction > *Novels*
Literary; Social Issues; Upmarket

Nonfiction
Essays: General
Nonfiction Books: Biography; Cultural
Criticism; History; Literary Memoir; Sub-
Culture

How to send: Email

Particularly drawn to novels that engage with
social issues, stories about obsession, and work
that centers around intimacy and its
discontents. Her nonfiction interests include
deeply reported narratives (especially those
that take the reader into the heart of a
subculture), literary memoir, cultural criticism,
essay collections, and history and biography
with a surprising point of view.

Authors: Kyle Chayka; Ye Chun; Linda Rui
Feng; Amanda Goldblatt; James Gregor; Peter
Kispert; Theresa Levitt; Micah Nemerever;
Jenny Odell; Kate Wagner; Michelle Webster-
Hein

L194 The Ekus Group

Literary Agency
57 North Street, Hatfield, MA 01038
United States
Tel: +1 (413) 247-9325

info@lisaekus.com

https://ekusgroup.com

Nonfiction > *Nonfiction Books*: Cookery

How to send: Online submission system

Handles cookery books only. Submit proposal
through submission system on website.

Literary Agent: Lisa Ekus

L195 Elaine Markson Literary Agency

Literary Agency
116 West 23rd Street, 5th flr, New York, NY

10011
United States

https://www.marksonagency.com

Fiction > *Novels*

Nonfiction > *Nonfiction Books*

Literary Agent: Jeff Gerecke (**L245**)

L196 Sian Ellis-Martin
Associate Agent
United Kingdom

sian@blakefriedmann.co.uk

http://blakefriedmann.co.uk/sianellis-martin
https://twitter.com/sianellismartin

Literary Agency: Blake Friedmann Literary
Agency Ltd (**L064**)

Fiction > *Novels*
Commercial; Contemporary; Crime;
LGBTQIA; Literary; Romance; Romantic
Comedy; Upmarket

Nonfiction > *Nonfiction Books*
Cookery; Food; History; Memoir; Narrative
Nonfiction

Send: Query; Synopsis; Writing sample
How to send: Email attachment

In fiction, I'm looking for contemporary
commercial, upmarket and accessible literary
novels, particularly from authors who are
currently underrepresented in literature. I'm
especially passionate about finding
LGBTQIA+ stories and authors. I'm also
looking for narrative non-fiction and memoir
that reads almost like fiction, history from
different perspectives and books that make
complicated ideas more accessible. I'd love to
find cookery and food books too, particularly
cuisines that are less visible in the book world,
or budget cooking.

Authors: Shani Akilah; Ros Anderson; Rue
Baldry; Leeanne O'Donnell; Karen Powell

L197 Zabé Ellor
Literary Agent
United States

https://www.jdlit.com/zabe-ellor
https://querymanager.com/query/ZabeEllor
https://twitter.com/ZREllor

Literary Agency: The Jennifer DeChiara
Literary Agency

ADULT
Fiction
Graphic Novels: General
Novels: Commercial; Fantasy; Mystery;
Science Fiction; Thrillers; Upmarket
Contemporary Fiction
Nonfiction > *Nonfiction Books*
History; Science

CHILDREN'S > **Fiction**
Graphic Novels: General

Middle Grade: Adventure; Comedy /
Humour; Speculative
YOUNG ADULT > **Fiction**
Graphic Novels: General
Novels: General, and in
particular: Contemporary; Fantasy; Mystery;
Romance; Science Fiction; Thrillers

Closed to approaches.

For fiction, send a query, a 1-2 page synopsis,
and the first 25 pages of your project. For
nonfiction, send a query and a sample chapter.
For graphic novels, send a query with a link to
your portfolio website. I strive to respond to all
queries in 12-14 weeks.

L198 Emily Sweet Associates
Literary Agency
United Kingdom

http://www.emilysweetassociates.com

Professional Body: The Association of
Authors' Agents (AAA)

Types: Fiction; Nonfiction
Subjects: Biography; Commercial; Cookery;
Current Affairs; History; Literary
Markets: Adult

Send: Query
Don't send: Full text

No Young Adult or children's. Query through
form on website in first instance.

Literary Agent: Emily Sweet (**L601**)

L199 Ethan Ellenberg Literary Agency
Literary Agency
United States

agent@ethanellenberg.com

https://ethanellenberg.com

Professional Bodies: Science Fiction and
Fantasy Writers of America (SFWA); Society
of Children's Book Writers and Illustrators
(SCBWI); Romance Writers of America
(RWA); Mystery Writers of America (MWA)

ADULT
Fiction > *Novels*
General, and in particular: Commercial;
Ethnic; Fantasy; Literary; Mystery;
Romance; Science Fiction; Thrillers;
Women's Fiction

Nonfiction > *Nonfiction Books*
General, and in particular: Adventure;
Biography; Cookery; Crime; Current
Affairs; Health; History; Memoir; New
Age; Popular Culture; Psychology;
Science; Spirituality

CHILDREN'S > **Fiction** > *Novels*

Send: Query; Synopsis; Writing sample;
Proposal
How to send: In the body of an email

Send query by email (no attachments; paste
material into the body of the email). For fiction
send synopsis and first 50 pages. For
nonfiction send proposal, author bio, and
sample chapters. For picture books send
complete MS. No poetry, short stories, or
scripts.

We have been in business for over 17 years.
We are a member of the AAR. We accept
unsolicited submissions and, of course, do not
charge reading fees.

Author Estates: The Estate of Bertrice Small;
The Estate of Johnny Quarles

Authors: G.A. Aiken; Jay Allan; Carac Allison;
Amanda Ashley; Claire Avery; Madeline
Baker; Sarah Banks; Jon Bergeron; Patty
Blount; Pat Bowne; Robin Bridges; Leah
Marie Brown; James Cambias; Elaine
Coffman; MaryJanice Davidson; Delilah
Devlin; John Domagalski; Ian Douglas; Bill
Ferris; Candace Fleming; Whitney Gaskell;
Susan Grant; James Hider; Ben Hillman;
Marthe Jocelyn; Aer-ki Jyr; William H. Keith;
Kay Kenyon; Marko Kloos; Travis Langley;
Shelly Laurenston; Georgie Lee; Michael
Livingston; Kevin Luthardt; Gail Z. Martin; Lt.
Col. Matt Martin; Thersa Matsuura; John
McCormack; Karen Miller; Lucy Monroe;
Helen Myers; J. Madison Newsome; Andre
Norton; Christopher Nuttall; Mel Odoam;
Melissa F. Olson; Tim Owens; Cindy Spencer
Pape; Thomas Philpott; Steven Popkes; Paladin
Press; Riptide Publishing; Clay Reynolds;
Matthew Rivett; Eric Rohmann; Peter Sasgen;
Charles Sasser; John Scalzi; Eric Schnabel;
Sharon Shinn; Susan Sizemore; Oz Spies;
Ferret Steinmetz; James Tabor; Dennis E.
Taylor; Kimberly Kaye Terry; Kate Tietje;
Judd Trichter; Margaret Vellez; Wendy
Wagner; Christine Warren; Jennifer Wilde;
Edward Willett; Robert Wolke; Rebecca York

Literary Agent / President: Ethan Ellenberg

Literary Agents: Evan Gregory; Bibi Lewis

L200 The Evan Marshall Agency
Literary Agency
1 Pacio Court, Roseland, NJ 07068-1121
United States
Tel: +1 (973) 287-6216

evan@evanmarshallagency.com

https://www.evanmarshallagency.com

Professional Body: Association of American
Literary Agents (AALA)

Types: Fiction; Nonfiction
Markets: Adult; Young Adult

Closed to approaches.

Represents all genres of adult and young-adult
full-length fiction. New clients by referral
only.

Literary Agent: Evan Marshall

L201 David Evans

Assistant Agent
United Kingdom

davidevans@davidhigham.co.uk

https://www.davidhigham.co.uk/agents-dh/
david-evans/

Literary Agency: David Higham Associates
Ltd (**L159**)
Literary Agent: Andrew Gordon (**L262**)

ACADEMIC > **Nonfiction** > *Nonfiction Books*

ADULT
  Fiction
    Novels: Literary
    Short Fiction: Literary

  Nonfiction > *Nonfiction Books*
    Culture; History; Journalism; Nature;
    Philosophy; Politics; Science

Closed to approaches.

Looking for literary fiction of style and ambition. He admires novelists who create memorable and unsettling voices, and short story writers with a keen sense of the poetic and absurd. In non-fiction, he enjoys projects of rigour, clarity and passion that can make small ideas radiate and big ideas graspable. He is particularly looking for works of academic research or journalistic investigation written for a wide readership, across areas such as culture, philosophy, politics, history, science, nature.

L202 Kate Evans

Literary Agent
United Kingdom
Tel: +44 (0) 20 7344 1047

kevans@pfd.co.uk

https://petersfraserdunlop.com/agent/kate-evans/
https://twitter.com/kateeevans

Literary Agency: Peters Fraser + Dunlop (**L501**)

Fiction > *Novels*
  General, and in particular: Family Saga;
  Literary Suspense; Romance

Nonfiction > *Nonfiction Books*
  Cookery; Economics; Food; History;
  Literary; Memoir; Narrative Nonfiction;
  Nature; Personal Development; Philosophy;
  Politics; Popular Culture; Popular Science;
  Science; Social Issues

Does not want:

> **Fiction** > *Novels*
>   Hard Science Fiction; High / Epic
>   Fantasy

Send: Query; Synopsis; Writing sample;
Proposal; Author bio

How to send: Email
How not to send: Post

I am actively looking for exciting new voices across both fiction and non-fiction.

I'm interested in non-fiction that says something about the way we live- from beautiful narrative non-fiction with a strong voice to passionate manifestos from experts in their fields. Whether it's popular science, big ideas, nature writing, memoir, fresh approaches to history or insightful takes on pop culture, I am drawn to writing that makes social, political, and economic issues accessible and engaging.

I read very widely in fiction but the common thread that runs through most novels I love is a sharply observed take on relationships and strong characters I'll think about long after I've left them on the page. I want a book I can gleefully, greedily consume- that kind of crying in public, ignoring your friends level compulsiveness… but I also want it to be beautifully put together.

I would love to see more literary suspense, a funny-sad family drama and I am forever on the lookout for a great love story.

I am largely genre-agnostic and if you're using genre (crime, horror, speculative) in an interesting way underpinned by exceptional writing I'd love to see it. Having said this, I'm probably not the best agent for hard SFF or YA.

Authors: Ali Abdaal; Nadine Bacchus-Garrick; Heidi Lauth Beasley; Sophie Beresiner; Abigail Bergstrom; Christina Caré; Orsola De Castro; Julia F. Christensen; Olivia Jordan Cornelius; Iona David; Léa Rose Emery; Kate Evans; Richard Fisher; Ione Gamble; Tom Glover; Bre Graham; Malwina Gudowska; Jessica Hamel-Akré; Sarah Haque; Kenya Hunt; Sophie Mort; Jennifer Obidike; Georgina Sturge; Stefanie Sword-Williams; Amelia Tait; Rossalyn Warren; Rose Wilding

L203 Kiya Evans

Assistant Agent
United Kingdom

kiya@mushens-entertainment.com
submissions@mushens-entertainment.com

https://www.mushens-entertainment.com/kiya-evans
https://twitter.com/kiyarosevans

Literary Agency: Mushens Entertainment
Literary Agent: Juliet Mushens (**L465**)

Fiction > *Novels*
  Book Club Fiction; Commercial; Gothic;
  Historical Fiction; LGBTQIA; Literary;
  Psychology; Romantic Comedy; Thrillers;
  Upmarket

Nonfiction > *Nonfiction Books*

Commercial; Literary; Narrative Nonfiction;
Popular History; Psychology; Science

Send: Query; Synopsis; Writing sample;
Proposal

I'm looking for fiction and narrative non-fiction which is commercial, literary, or something that feels like the best of both. Above all, I'm drawn to strong voices, honest, memorable writing, and books which can confidently explore interesting, universal dynamics and experiences.

L204 Stephany Evans

Literary Agent
United States

https://www.pandeliterary.com/about-pandeliterary
https://twitter.com/firerooster
http://aaronline.org/Sys/PublicProfile/2176670/417813

Literary Agency: Ayesha Pande Literary (**L038**)
Professional Bodies: Association of American Literary Agents (AALA); Romance Writers of America (RWA); Mystery Writers of America (MWA); The Agents Round Table (ART)

Fiction > *Novels*
  Commercial; Crime; Literary; Mystery;
  Romance; Thrillers; Upmarket Women's
  Fiction; Women's Fiction

Nonfiction > *Nonfiction Books*
  Fitness; Food and Drink; Health; Lifestyle;
  Memoir; Narrative Nonfiction; Running;
  Spirituality; Sustainable Living; Wellbeing

Closed to approaches.

L205 Samantha Fabien

Literary Agent
United States

https://www.rootliterary.com/agents
https://www.publishersmarketplace.com/members/samfabien/
https://twitter.com/samanthashnh
https://aalitagents.org/author/samanthashnh/
https://querymanager.com/query/samanthafabien

Literary Agency: Root Literary (**L535**)
Professional Body: Association of American Literary Agents (AALA)

ADULT > **Fiction** > *Novels*
  Book Club Fiction; Commercial;
  Contemporary Romance; Diversity; Fantasy;
  High Concept; Horror; Mystery;
  Relationships; Romantic Comedy;
  Speculative; Suspense; Thrillers; Upmarket
  Women's Fiction

CHILDREN'S > **Fiction** > *Middle Grade*
  General, and in particular: Fantasy

YOUNG ADULT > **Fiction** > *Novels*
  General, and in particular: Romance

Closed to approaches.

I live for the rollercoaster of emotions that characters and stories can take me on. Whether I'm swooning or gasping, I want to feel strongly enough about a project that I desperately need to share it with the world.

L206 Fairbank Literary Representation

Literary Agency
21 Lyman Street, Waltham, MA 02452
United States
Tel: +1 (617) 576-0030

queries@fairbankliterary.com

https://fairbankliterary.com
https://www.publishersmarketplace.com/members/SorcheFairbank/
http://www.twitter.com/FairbankLit

ADULT
  Fiction > *Novels*
    International; Literary

  Nonfiction
    Gift Books: General
    Nonfiction Books: Comedy / Humour;
    Crafts; Design; Food; Lifestyle; Memoir;
    Narrative Nonfiction; Popular Culture;
    Wine
CHILDREN'S > **Fiction**
  Middle Grade; *Picture Books*

Send: Query; Writing sample
How to send: In the body of an email; Online contact form; Post
How not to send: Email attachment; Phone

Clients range from first-time authors to international best-sellers, prize winning-journalists to professionals at the top of their fields. Tastes tend toward literary and international fiction; voice-y novels with a strong sense of place; big memoir that goes beyond the me-moir; topical or narrative nonfiction with a strong interest in women's voices, global perspectives, and class and race issues; children's picture books & middle grade from illustrator/artists only; quality lifestyle books (food, wine, and design); pop culture; craft; and gift and humor books. Most likely to pick up works that are of social or cultural significance, newsworthy

Literary Agent: Sorche Elizabeth Fairbank

L207 Delia Berrigan Fakis

Literary Agent
United States

Delia@MartinLit.com

http://www.martinliterarymanagement.com
https://twitter.com/PrimarilyProse

Literary Agency: Martin Literary Management

ADULT
  Fiction > *Novels*
    Commercial; Literary; Mystery

Nonfiction > *Nonfiction Books*
  Business; Crime; Current Affairs; History;
  Leadership; Memoir; Narrative Nonfiction;
  Religion; Spirituality

CHILDREN'S > **Fiction** > *Picture Books*

Send: Query
How to send: Email

Most interested in representing adult nonfiction, but will also consider select fiction and children's picture books.

L208 Leigh Feldman

Literary Agent
United States

Literary Agency: Leigh Feldman Literary
(L385)

L209 The Feldstein Agency

Literary Agency; Editorial Service;
Consultancy
54 Abbey Street, Bangor, Northern Ireland,
BT20 4JB
United Kingdom
Tel: +44 (0) 2891 312485

submissions@thefeldsteinagency.co.uk

https://www.thefeldsteinagency.co.uk
https://twitter.com/feldsteinagency

Fiction > *Novels*

Nonfiction > *Nonfiction Books*

Does not want:

> **Fiction** > *Novels*
>   Fantasy; Historical Fiction; Romance;
>   Science Fiction

Send: Query; Synopsis; Author bio
How to send: Word file email attachment; PDF file email attachment

Costs: Offers services that writers have to pay for. Offers editing, ghostwriting, and consultancy services.

Handles adult fiction and nonfiction only. No children's, young adult, romance, science fiction, fantasy, poetry, scripts, or short stories. Send query by email with 1-2 pages synopsis. No reading fees or evaluation fees. The only instance in which an author would be charged a fee is for ghost-writing.

Consultant / Literary Agent: Paul Feldstein

Editor / Literary Agent: Susan Feldstein

L210 Felicia Eth Literary Representation

Literary Agency
555 Bryant Street, Suite 350, Palo Alto, CA
94301
United States

feliciaeth.literary@gmail.com

https://ethliterary.com

ADULT
  Fiction
    Novels: Historical Fiction; Literary;
    Magical Realism; Multicultural; Suspense
    Short Fiction Collections: General

  Nonfiction > *Nonfiction Books*
    Business; Cookery; Journalism; Memoir;
    Parenting; Popular Culture; Popular
    Science; Psychology; Social Issues; Sport;
    Travel; Women's Issues

YOUNG ADULT > **Fiction** > *Novels*

Send: Query; Author bio; Outline
How to send: Email; Post

Costs: Author covers sundry admin costs.

Send query by email or by post with SASE, including details about yourself and your project. Send sample pages upon invitation only.

Literary Agent: Felicia Eth

L211 Felicity Bryan Associates

Literary Agency
2a North Parade Avenue, Banbury Road,
Oxford, OX2 6LX
United Kingdom
Tel: +44 (0) 1865 513816

submissions@felicitybryan.com

https://felicitybryan.com

Professional Body: The Association of Authors' Agents (AAA)

Fiction > *Novels*

Nonfiction > *Nonfiction Books*

Send: Query; Synopsis; Proposal; Writing sample
How to send: Online submission system
How not to send: Post

As an agency we are always searching for talented new writers. Whether you write beautifully crafted literary fiction, immersive middle-grade novels, or fascinating and informative non-fiction, we would love the opportunity to consider your work. We look for ambitious, confident writing that feels fresh and distinctive, and we welcome voices from all backgrounds. There is no expectation for writers to have existing connections to the publishing industry or a formal creative writing qualification. We take the time to carefully read and review every submission we receive.

Authors: Carlos Acosta; Sally Adee; Samira Ahmed; John Aitchison; David Almond; Karen Armstrong; Lucy Ash; Frances Ashcroft; Rachel Aspden; James Attlee; Modern Baker; Katya Balen; James Barr; David Barrie; Kay Barron; Rosamund Bartlett; John Barton; John Batchelor; Susan Beale; Roderick Beaton; Catherine Belton; Erica Benner; Nic Bennett; Louis De Bernières; Mary Berry; Claire Bertschinger; Paul Betts; Nina Bhadreshwar;

Michael Bird; Tim Birkhead; Simon Blackburn; Elleke Boehmer; Stella Botchway; John Bowker; Christopher Brickell; Susan Brigden; Irena Brignull; Francesca Brill; Rhidian Brook; Adam Brookes; Ursula Buchan; Julia Bueno; Stephen Burke; Matthew Burton; Emma Byrne; Lucy Cavendish; Fernando Cervantes; Sarah Challis; John Charmley; Nick Chater; Simukai Chigudu; Marcus Chown; Morten H. Christiansen; Liza Cody; Jonathan Coe; Will Cohu; Artemis Cooper; T.A. Cotterell; Sarah Courtauld; Cath Crowley; Benjamin Daniels; Chloe Daykin; John Dickie; Jenny Downham; Tobias Druitt; Will Eaves; Reni Eddo-Lodge; Nick Edwards; Natasha Farrant; David Farrier; Edmund Fawcett; James Fearnley; Rebecca Fleet; Catherine Fletcher; CJ Flood; Pauline Francis; Peter Frankopan; Lawrence Freedman; Clare Furniss; Damon Galgut; Sally Gardner; Peter Gatrell; Robert Gildea; Jonathan Glover; Susan Golombok; Kat Gordon; Chris Gosden; A.C. Grayling; Barbara Graziosi; Catherine Hall; Thomas Halliday; James Hamilton; Julie Hearn; Peter Heather; Tim Hecker; Gavin Hewitt; Lindsey Hilsum; Penelope Hobhouse; Anna Hope; Gill Hornby; Richard House; Alex Howard; Alice Hunt; Kathryn Hurlock; Allegra Huston; Belinda Jack; Sarah Jasmon; Joseph Jebelli; Lauren St John; Clare Johnson; Colin Jones; Vijay Joshi; Nick Jubber; Stanley Kenani; Liz Kessler; Amy Key; Liza Klaussmann; Chelsea Kwakye; Katherine Langrish; Grace Lavery; Phyllida Law; Tim Leach; Simon Lelic; Lucy Lethbridge; Suzannah Lipscomb; John Lister-Kaye; Tess Little; Jonathan Loh; Rebecca Lowe; Natasha Lunn; Diarmaid Macculloch; Fiona Maddocks; Laurie Maguire; John Man; Henry Mance; Sarah K Marr; Toby Matthiesen; James Mcdougall; Sophia Mcdougall; Chris Mcgrath; Kate Mcloughlin; Martin Meredith; Tom Moorhouse; Katy Moran; Alistair Morgan; Alan Murrin; Jennifer Nadel; Vanessa Nakate; Tom Nancollas; Natasha Narayan; James Naughtie; Linda Newbery; TN Ninan; Camilla Nord; Jenny Odell; Ore Ogunbiyi; Adjoa Osei; Richard Ovenden; Joanne Owen; Svenja O'donnell; Colm O'gorman; Elsa Panciroli; Iain Pears; Roger Pearson; Thomas Penn; Andrew Pettegree; Jonathan Phillips; Annabel Pitcher; Rachel Polonsky; Nick Potter; Andrew Prentice; Sue Prideaux; Elaine Proctor; Diane Purkiss; Josephine Quinn; Melody Razak; Owen Rees; Alex Reeve; Dan Richards; Julian Richards; Eloise Rickman; Thomas Rid; Alex Riley; Charlotte Lydia Riley; Ritchie Robertson; David Robson; Eugene Rogan; Nicola Rollock; Meg Rosoff; Miri Rubin; Ulinka Rublack; Adam Ruck; Penny Rudge; Edward Russell-Walling; Alec Ryrie; Farhan Samanani; Joseph Sassoon; Paul Seabright; Alom Shaha; Liam Shaw; Matthew Skelton; Emma Smith; Tiffany Watt Smith; Lexi Stadlen; Marc Stears; Miriam Stoppard; Andrew Strong; Roy Strong; Sue Stuart-Smith;

Julie Summers; Krystal Sutherland; Henry Sutton; Katherine Swift; Lydia Syson; Cathy Thomas; Eleanor Updale; Christopher Vick; Edmund De Waal; Martin Walker; Charles Walton; Samantha Walton; Benjamin Wardhaugh; Kirsty Wark; Arthur Der Weduwen; Jonathan Weil; Anna Whitelock; Tim Whitmarsh; K.J. Whittaker; Lisa Williamson; Greg Wise; Michael Wood; Lucy Wooding; Michael Wooldridge; Lucy Worsley; James Wythe; Jessica Wärnberg; Kieran Yates; Lucy Young

Company Directors / Literary Agents: Carrie Plitt (**L508**); Caroline Wood (**L660**)

Literary Agent: Angelique Tran Van Sang (**L548**)

Literary Agent / Managing Director: Catherine Clarke (**L127**)

L212 Hannah Ferguson
Literary Agent
United Kingdom

hannah@hardmanswainson.com
submissions@hardmanswainson.com

https://www.hardmanswainson.com/agent/
hannah-ferguson/
https://twitter.com/AgentFergie

Literary Agency: Hardman & Swainson (**L286**)

Fiction > *Novels*
General, and in particular: Book Club Fiction; Commercial; Crime; Literary; Thrillers; Women's Fiction

Nonfiction > *Nonfiction Books*: Narrative Nonfiction

Send: Query; Synopsis; Full text
How to send: Email

Represents women's fiction, from the more literary to the very commercial. Likes book club reads that really capture a reader's attention or heart. Always on the lookout for great crime and thrillers and interesting non-fiction.

L213 T.S. Ferguson
Literary Agent
United States

http://www.azantianlitagency.com/pages/team-tf.html
https://querymanager.com/query/TSFerguson

Literary Agency: Azantian Literary Agency (**L039**)

CHILDREN'S > **Fiction**
Graphic Novels: General
Middle Grade: General, and in particular: Adventure; Dark; Fairy Tales; Folklore, Myths, and Legends; High Concept; Horror; LGBTQIA
YOUNG ADULT > **Fiction**
Graphic Novels: General

Novels: General, and in particular: Adventure; Dark; Fairy Tales; Folklore, Myths, and Legends; High Concept; Horror; LGBTQIA

Does not want:

> **CHILDREN'S** > **Fiction** > *Middle Grade*
> Hard Science Fiction; Sport
> **YOUNG ADULT** > **Fiction** > *Novels*
> Hard Science Fiction; Sport

How to send: Query Manager

Looking for young adult and middle grade fiction across all genres that combines high-concept, hooky stories with writing and voice that feel standout. An addicting, page-turning quality is always a plus! He has a special place in his heart for dark and edgy stories (including but not limited to horror), fairy tales, mythology, action-adventure, LGBTQ stories, graphic novels, and stories by and about under-represented voices. He is not the best fit for sports-centric stories, high sci-fi, or non-fiction.

L214 Julie Fergusson
Literary Agent
United Kingdom

http://thenorthlitagency.com/our-friends-in-the-north/
https://twitter.com/julie_fergusson

Literary Agency: The North Literary Agency

Fiction > *Novels*
Book Club Fiction; Domestic Suspense; Literary; Psychological Thrillers; Romantic Comedy; Speculative

Closed to approaches.

Looking for fiction across a range of genres, particularly psychological thrillers, domestic suspense, near-future speculative, romcoms, reading group and literary fiction. No submissions from authors who live in North America.

L215 Rochelle Fernandez
Literary Agent
Australia

rochelle@alexadsett.com.au

https://alexadsett.com.au/literary-agency/

Literary Agency: Alex Adsett Literary (**L016**)

Fiction > *Novels*

How to send: Email

Seeking well written manuscripts of any genre with a compelling premise and three dimensional, interesting characters. Based in Sydney, she is passionate about hearing and seeing diverse stories that represent the wonderful multicultural multifaceted society that comprises Australia.

L216 Melanie Figueroa
Literary Agent
United States

https://www.melaniefigueroa.com
https://www.rootliterary.com/agents
https://querymanager.com/query/melaniefigueroa
https://twitter.com/wellmelsbells/
https://www.linkedin.com/in/melaniefigueroa
https://www.instagram.com/wellmelsbells/

Literary Agency: Root Literary (**L535**)
Professional Body: Association of American Literary Agents (AALA)

ADULT > Fiction
  Graphic Novels: General
  Novels: Commercial; Contemporary; Family Saga; Fantasy; Historical Fiction; Horror; LGBTQIA; Literary; Magical Realism; Speculative; Upmarket; Women's Fiction
CHILDREN'S > Fiction > *Middle Grade*
  Contemporary; Fantasy; Historical Fiction; Literary; Mystery; Science Fiction
YOUNG ADULT
  Fiction > *Novels*
    Contemporary; Fantasy; Historical Fiction; Literary; Mystery; Romance; Science Fiction

  Nonfiction > *Nonfiction Books*
    Business; Narrative Nonfiction; Relationships

How to send: Query Manager

I want to work with the kind of stories that both create and sustain life-long readers—books that make me sigh with contentment, learn something new, or take delight in the unexpected. Those stories stay with you, and they're a gift I want to help give readers by lifting up the voices of talented and hard-working creatives.

L217 Fillingham Weston Associates
Literary Agency
20 Mortlake High Street, London, SW14 8JN
United Kingdom
Tel: +44 (0) 20 8748 5594

info@fillinghamweston.com
submissions@fillinghamweston.com

https://www.fillinghamweston.com
https://www.facebook.com/Fillingham-Weston-Associates-117304691662209
https://twitter.com/fwa_litagency
https://www.instagram.com/fillinghamwestonassociates/

ADULT > Scripts
  Film Scripts; *TV Scripts*; *Theatre Scripts*
CHILDREN'S > Scripts
  Film Scripts; *TV Scripts*; *Theatre Scripts*

YOUNG ADULT > Scripts
  Film Scripts; *TV Scripts*; *Theatre Scripts*

Send: Query; Author bio
Don't send: Full text; Writing sample
How to send: Email

Represents writers and directors for stage, film and TV, as well as librettists, lyricists and composers in musical theatre. Does not represent books. See website for full submission guidelines.

Literary Agents: Janet Fillingham; Kate Weston

L218 Alison Finch
Literary Agent
United Kingdom

Literary Agency: JFL Agency (**L327**)

L219 Rebeka Finch
Agency Assistant; Junior Agent
United Kingdom

rebeka@darleyanderson.com

https://www.darleyanderson.com/our-team
https://www.instagram.com/rebeka.finch/

Literary Agency: The Darley Anderson Agency
Literary Agent: Darley Anderson (**L021**)

ADULT > Fiction > *Novels*: Contemporary Romance

NEW ADULT > Fiction > *Novels*
  Contemporary Romance; Fantasy Romance

How to send: Email attachment

Looking for character driven contemporary romances. Also looking for contemporary romantic fiction, specifically for the BookTok hungry new adult/20+. She is also looking for romantasy fiction. (Please note, new adult does not constitute YA fiction).

L220 Stevie Finegan
Literary Agent
United Kingdom

finegan@zenoagency.com

http://zenoagency.com/news/stevie-finegan/
https://twitter.com/StevieFinegan

Literary Agency: Zeno Agency Ltd (**L672**)

ADULT
  Fiction
    Graphic Novels: Feminism; LGBTQIA
    Novels: High / Epic Fantasy; Soft Science Fiction
  Nonfiction > *Nonfiction Books*
    Feminism; Mental Health; Politics; Social Issues
CHILDREN'S > Fiction
  Early Readers; *Middle Grade*; *Picture Books*

Closed to approaches.

Authors: Travis Baldree; Alice Bell; Andrew Cartmel; Mário Coelho; Craig Laurance

Gidney; J.T. Greathouse; Grady Hendrix; Laura Kerseviciute; Sian Lenihan; Anna McNuff; Silvia Moreno-Garcia; Adam Oyebanji; Farrah Riaz; Cassidy Ellis Salter; Katherine Toran; Emily Turner; R.R. Virdi; Angus Watson; Gary Wigglesworth; Jasmine Wigham; Yudhanjaya Wijeratne; Catelyn Wilson

L221 Karyn Fischer
Literary Agent
United States

http://www.bookstopliterary.com/submission.html
https://querymanager.com/query/KarynFischer

Literary Agency: BookStop Literary Agency, LLC (**L069**)

CHILDREN'S > Fiction > *Middle Grade*
  General, and in particular: Contemporary; Dark; Fantasy; Gothic; Historical Fiction; Literary Thrillers
YOUNG ADULT > Fiction > *Novels*
  General, and in particular: Contemporary; Dark; Fantasy; Gothic; Historical Fiction; Literary Thrillers

Closed to approaches.

Particularly drawn to young adult and middle grade novels. Her favorite genres include gothic novels with twisty narratives and dark secrets, historical fiction, literary thrillers, well-drawn fantasy, and heart-tugging contemporary stories. She's looking for anything with memorable characters, an engaging voice, and a tightrope- taut plot.

L222 Bea Fitzgerald
Literary Agent; Author
United Kingdom

beasubmissions@theblairpartnership.com

https://www.theblairpartnership.com/literary-agents/bea-fitzgerald/
https://twitter.com/Bea_a_Bea

Literary Agency: LBA Books Ltd
Literary Agent: Hannah Schofield (**L554**)

Fiction > *Novels*
  Commercial; Upmarket

Nonfiction > *Nonfiction Books*

Send: Pitch; Market info; Author bio; Synopsis; Writing sample
How to send: Word file email attachment; PDF file email attachment

In books, I'm looking for voice-led, propulsive writing in commercial and upmarket fiction and zeitgeisty non-fiction. While I'm a fan of YA, I'm not the right agent for anything younger, though I'll be working with the other agents on these titles for any digital opportunities.

Authors: Essie Dennis; Annabelle Woghiren

L223 Flannery Literary

Literary Agency
United States

jennifer@flanneryliterary.com

https://flanneryliterary.com

CHILDREN'S
 Fiction > *Middle Grade*
 Nonfiction > *Nonfiction Books*

YOUNG ADULT > **Fiction** > *Novels*

Send: Query; Writing sample; Full text
How to send: Email
How not to send: Email attachment

Send query by email, with the word "Query" in the subject line. Include first 5-10 pages of your novel or full picture book text. Deals exclusively in children's and young adults' fiction and nonfiction, including picture books. See website for full guidelines.

Literary Agent: Jennifer Flannery

L224 Diana Flegal

Literary Agent; Editor
United States

https://www.hartlineagency.com/agents-and-authors

Literary Agency: Hartline Literary Agency
(L295)

Fiction > *Novels*
 General, and in particular: Christianity

Nonfiction > *Nonfiction Books*
 General, and in particular: Christianity

A freelance editor and literary coach. Has successfully sold both fiction and nonfiction titles to the Christian and General markets.

Authors: DeAngelo Burse; Nicole Faye Golden; Michael Richard

L225 Fletcher & Company

Literary Agency
United States

info@fletcherandco.com

https://www.fletcherandco.com

Literary Agency: United Talent Agency (UTA)

Fiction > *Novels*
 Commercial; Literary

Nonfiction > *Nonfiction Books*

Send: Query
How to send: Email
How not to send: Phone; Post

Full-service literary agency representing writers of nonfiction and commercial and literary fiction. Send query by email only with brief synopsis and first 5-10 pages of your manuscript / proposal pasted into the body of the email. No attachments. Query only one agent at a time (see website for list of individual agent interests). Response normally in 4-6 weeks. No queries by post.

Literary Agents: Melissa Chinchillo; Christy Fletcher; Gráinne Fox (*L228*); Sarah Fuentes **(L236)**; Veronica Goldstein **(L260)**; Rebecca Gradinger; Lisa Grubka; Eric Lupfer (*L404*); Eve MacSweeney **(L415)**; Peter Steinberg

L226 A for Authors

Literary Agency
73 Hurlingham Road, Bexleyheath, Kent, DA7 5PE
United Kingdom
Tel: +44 (0) 1322 463479

enquiries@aforauthors.co.uk

http://aforauthors.co.uk

Fiction > *Novels*
 Commercial; Literary

Closed to approaches.

Query by email only. Include synopsis and first three chapters (or up to 50 pages) and short author bio. All attachments must be Word format documents. No poetry, fantasy, SF, horror, erotica, or short stories. No submissions by post or by downloadable link.

Literary Agents: Annette Crossland; Bill Goodall

L227 Jemima Forrester

Literary Agent
United Kingdom

jemimaforrester@davidhigham.co.uk

https://www.davidhigham.co.uk/agents-dh/jemima-forrester/

Literary Agency: David Higham Associates Ltd **(L159)**

Fiction > *Novels*
 Commercial; Crime; Feminism; High Concept; Historical Fiction; Literary; Psychological Suspense; Speculative; Thrillers; Upmarket; Women's Fiction

Nonfiction > *Nonfiction Books*
 Comedy / Humour; Cookery; Feminism; Lifestyle; Popular Culture

Send: Query; Synopsis; Writing sample
How to send: Email

Looking for commercial and upmarket fiction, including accessible literary fiction, crime and thrillers, historical, psychological suspense, women's fiction and speculative/high-concept novels. Loves distinctive narrative voices, well-paced plots with a great hook, and complex female characters. In non-fiction, she is looking for innovative lifestyle, cookery and popular-culture projects, unique personal stories and humour.

Authors: Kat Ailes; Tessa Bickers; Mikki Brammer; Lauren Bravo; Rukky Brume; Rob Burnett; Seerut K. Chawla; Lizzie Daykin;

Sarah Daykin; Morgan Dick; Pip Finkemeyer; Jessica George; Penny Hancock; Deborah Hewitt; Rosie Hewlett; Jessie Keane; Kate Leaver; Beth Lewis; Richard Lumsden; Rufaro Faith Mazarura; Deborah O'Donoghue; Christina Pishiris; Tasha Sylva; Sureka Thanenthiran-Dharuman; Minette Walters; Vanessa Walters

L228 Gráinne Fox

Literary Agent
United States

Literary Agency: Fletcher & Company **(L225)**

L229 FRA (Futerman, Rose, & Associates)

Literary Agency
91 St Leonards Road, London, SW14 7BL
United Kingdom
Tel: +44 (0) 20 8255 7755

guy@futermanrose.co.uk

http://www.futermanrose.co.uk

Professional Body: The Association of Authors' Agents (AAA)

Nonfiction > *Nonfiction Books*
 General, and in particular: Entertainment; Media; Music; Politics; Sports Celebrity

Scripts
 Film Scripts; TV Scripts

Send: Query
Don't send: Full text
How to send: Email

Handles nonfiction on practically any subject, but particularly interested in politics, sport, show business and the music industry. Also handles scripts for film and television. No educational textbooks.

For nonfiction, send proposal including chapter breakdown, two or three sample chapters, and any relevant biographical detail.

For scripts, send sample episode or section of the script.

Accepts submissions by post (include SAE of return of work required) or by email with attachments.

See website for full guidelines.

Not currently accepting film and TV scripts.

Authors: Jill Anderson; Larry Barker; Nick Battle; Christian Piers Betley; Tracey Cheetham; Chengde Chen; Kevin Clarke; Lesley Crewe; Richard Digance; Peter Dobbie; Bobby Elliott; Paul Ferris; John French; Susan George; Keith Gillespie; Stephen Griffin; Paul Hendy; Terry Ilott; Sara Khan; Jerry Leider; Sue Lenier; Keith R. Lindsay; Stephen Lowe; Eric MacInnes; Paul Marsden; Paul Marx; Tony McAndrew; Tony McMahon; Sir Vartan Melkonian; Michael Misick; Max Morgan-Witts; Sir Derek Morris; Peter Murphy; Judge

Chris Nicholson; Antonia Owen; Tom Owen; Mary O'Hara; Ciarán O'Keeffe; Miriam O'Reilly; Zoe Paphitis; Liz Rettig; Kenneth G. Ross; Robin Callender Smith; Rt. Hon Iain Duncan Smith; Paul Stinchcombe; Felicity Fair Thompson; Bill Tidy; Mark White; Toyah Willcox; Simon Woodham; Tappy Wright; Allen Zeleski

Literary Agent: Guy Rose

L230 Frances Collin Literary Agent
Literary Agency
PO Box 33, Wayne, PA 19087-0033
United States
Tel: +1 (610) 254-0555
Fax: +1 (610) 254-5029

queries@francescollin.com

http://www.francescollin.com

Fiction > *Novels*
   Fantasy; Historical Fiction; Literary; Science Fiction; Women's Fiction

Nonfiction > *Nonfiction Books*
   Biography; Culture; History; Memoir; Narrative Nonfiction; Nature; Travel

Send: Query
How to send: Email
How not to send: Email attachment; Phone; Fax

Prefers queries by email (no attachments). No queries by phone or fax.

Literary Agent: Frances Collin

L231 Frances Goldin Literary Agency, Inc.
Literary Agency
214 W 29th St., Suite 1006, New York, NY 10001
United States

agency@goldinlit.com

http://www.goldinlit.com

Professional Body: Association of American Literary Agents (AALA)

Types: Fiction; Nonfiction; Poetry; Translations
Formats: Film Scripts
Subjects: Arts; Autobiography; Commercial; Crime; Culture; Current Affairs; Entertainment; History; Legal; Literary; Nature; Philosophy; Politics; Science; Society; Sport; Technology; Thrillers; Travel
Markets: Adult; Children's; Young Adult

Closed to approaches.

Submit to one agent only. See website for specific agent interests and preferred method of approach. No screenplays, romances (or most other genre fiction), and only rarely poetry. No work that is racist, sexist, ageist, homophobic, or pornographic.

Associate Agents: Sulamita Garbuz (**L241**); Jade Wong-Baxter (**L659**)

Authors: Susan Bordo; Monica Byrne; Mandy Catron; Pratap Chatterjee; David Cole; Cliff Conner; Dessa; Ray Douglas; Mark Edmundson; Shelley Fisher Fishkin; Bruce Grierson; Michael Hudson; Lynn Hunt; Margaret Jacob; Steven Jaffe; Barbara Kingsolver; Michelle Kuo; Anna Lappé; Daniel Medwed; Stephanie Mencimer; Rutu Modan; Alexandra Natapoff; Carla Peterson; Sam Polk; Janisse Ray; Gretchen Reynolds; Siva Vaidhyanathan; Mike Wallace; Helene Wecker

Literary Agents: Roz Foster; Ria Julien (**L336**); Alison Lewis (**L388**); Ayla Zuraw-Friedland (**L673**)

President / Senior Agent: Sam Stoloff

Senior Agent: Caroline Eisenmann (**L193**)

Senior Agents / Vice Presidents: Ellen Geiger (**L243**); Matt McGowan (**L433**)

L232 Fraser Ross Associates
Literary Agency
42 Hadfast Road, Cousland, Midlothian, EH22 2NZ
United Kingdom

fraserrossassociates@gmail.com

http://www.fraserross.co.uk

ADULT
   Fiction > *Novels*
   Nonfiction > *Nonfiction Books*

CHILDREN'S > **Fiction** > *Picture Books*

Send: Query; Synopsis; Proposal; Writing sample; Full text
How to send: Email; Post

Send query by email or by post, including CV, the first three chapters and synopsis for fiction, or a one page proposal and the opening chapter and a further two chapter outlines for nonfiction. For picture books, send complete MS, without illustrations. No poetry, playscripts, screenplays, or individual short stories.

Authors: Jo Allan; Sorrel Anderson; Gill Arbuthnott; Tim Archbold; Alice Balfour; Barroux; Jason Beresford; Thomas Bloor; Ella Burfoot; Jill Calder; Simon Chapman; Judy Cumberbatch; Caroline Deacon; Emily Dodd; Lari Don; Christiane Dorion; Nicole Dryburgh; Jane Eagland; Teresa Flavin; Ciara Flood; Hannah Foley; Vivian French; Joe Friedman; Darren Gate; Roy Gill; Edward Hardy; Diana Hendry; Chris Higgins; Barry Hutchison; J D (Julie) Irwin; Cate James; Ann Kelley; Louise Kelly; Tanya Landman; Kate Leiper; Joan Lennon; Joan Lingard; Janis Mackay; L J Macwhirter; Kasia Matyjaszek; Eilidh Muldoon; Erica Mary Orchard; Judy Paterson; Helena Pielichaty; Sue Purkiss; Lynne Rickards; Jamie Rix; Karen Saunders; Dugald

Steer; Chae Strathie; Kate Wakeling; Rosie Wallace

Literary Agents: Lindsey Fraser; Kathryn Ross

L233 Robert Freedman
Literary Agent; President
United States

Literary Agency: Robert A. Freedman Dramatic Agency, Inc.

Scripts > *Theatre Scripts*

L234 Sarah Jane Freymann
Literary Agent
United States

sarah@sarahjanefreymann.com

http://www.sarahjanefreymann.com/?page_id=3872

Literary Agency: Sarah Jane Freymann Literary Agency (**L550**)

ADULT
   Fiction > *Novels*
   Literary; Mainstream

   Nonfiction > *Nonfiction Books*
   Alternative Health; Cookery; Health; Journalism; Lifestyle; Memoir; Men's Issues; Multicultural; Narrative Nonfiction; Nature; Parenting; Psychology; Science; Self Help; Spirituality; Travel; Women's Issues

YOUNG ADULT > **Fiction** > *Novels*

Send: Query; Writing sample
How to send: In the body of an email; Post
How not to send: Email attachment

In nonfiction, interested in spiritual, psychology, self-help, women/men's issues, books by health experts (conventional and alternative), cookbooks, narrative non-fiction, natural science, nature, memoirs, cutting-edge journalism, travel, multicultural issues, parenting, lifestyle. In fiction, interested in sophisticated mainstream and literary fiction with a distinctive voice. Also looking for edgy Young Adult fiction.

L235 Rebecca Friedman
Literary Agent
United States

queries@rfliterary.com

https://rfliterary.com/about/
https://twitter.com/rebeccalitagent

Literary Agency: Rebecca Friedman Literary Agency

ADULT
   Fiction > *Novels*
      Commercial; Contemporary Romance; Literary; Suspense; Women's Fiction

   Nonfiction > *Nonfiction Books*
      Journalism; Memoir

YOUNG ADULT > Fiction > Novels

Send: Query; Writing sample
How to send: Email

Interested in commercial and literary fiction with a focus on literary novels of suspense, women's fiction, contemporary romance, and young adult, as well as journalistic non-fiction and memoir. Most of all, she is looking for great stories told in strong voices.

L236 Sarah Fuentes
Literary Agent
United States

https://www.fletcherandco.com/team/sarah-fuentes/

Literary Agency: Fletcher & Company (**L225**)

Fiction > Novels
Comedy / Humour; Dark; Literary; Relationships; Speculative; Upmarket

Nonfiction > Nonfiction Books
Cultural Criticism; Economics; History; Literary Memoir; Literary; Memoir; Narrative Nonfiction; Nature; Politics; Popular Culture; Popular Science; Science; Social Justice; Technology; Upmarket

Send: Query; Synopsis; Writing sample
How to send: In the body of an email

Represents a range of literary and upmarket fiction and nonfiction, including narrative nonfiction, memoir, cultural criticism, history, and popular science writing.

L237 Eugenie Furniss
Literary Agent

eugeniefurniss@42mp.com

https://www.42mp.com/agents
https://twitter.com/Furniss

Literary Agency: 42 Management and Production

Fiction > Novels
Comedy / Humour; Crime; Historical Fiction

Nonfiction > Nonfiction Books
Biography; Finance; Memoir; Politics; Popular History

Closed to approaches.

Drawn to crime in all its guises and historical fiction. On the nonfiction front seeks biography and popular history, and politics.

L238 Natalie Galustian
Literary Agent
United Kingdom

natalie@greyhoundliterary.co.uk

https://greyhoundliterary.co.uk/agent/natalie-galustian/
https://twitter.com/natgalustian

Literary Agency: Greyhound Literary (**L271**)

Fiction
Novels: Literary
Short Fiction: Literary

Nonfiction
Essays: General
Nonfiction Books: Arts; Biography; Comedy / Humour; Commercial; Cookery; Drama; History; Memoir; Music; Narrative Nonfiction

Send: Query; Synopsis; Writing sample; Outline
How to send: Email
How not to send: Post

Represents narrative and commercial non-fiction as well as literary fiction. She is primarily looking for strong new voices in non-fiction across musical, visual, dramatic and culinary arts, history, memoir, biography, essays and humour, along with some select fiction and short stories of literary quality.

Author Estates: The Estate of Alan Rickman; The Estate of Alfred H. Mendes

Authors: Jennifer Lucy Allan; Jeremy Allen; Bez; Lulah Ellender; Stephen Mallinder; Charlotte Mitchell; David Moats; Andrew Perry; Hamilton Richardson; Lias Saoudi; Matthew Shaw; Michael Smith; Harry Sword; James Thomas; Luke Turner; Robin Turner; Michael Volpe; Liam Patrick Young

L239 Lori Galvin
Senior Agent
Boston
United States

https://aevitascreative.com/agents/
https://querymanager.com/query/QueryLoriGalvin

Literary Agency: Aevitas

Fiction > Novels
Book Club Fiction; Contemporary; Crime; Historical Fiction; Science Fiction; Speculative; Spy Thrilllers; Supernatural / Paranormal Thrillers; Suspense; Thrillers

Nonfiction > Nonfiction Books
Cookery; Crime; Food; Personal Development; Personal Finance

Send: Author bio; Query; Synopsis; Writing sample; Pitch; Market info
How to send: Query Manager

Looking for Crime and Book Club Novels: Thrillers and novels of suspense with great twists or a fresh approach. Supernatural thrillers or thrillers with a hint of (or some) horror. Compassionate novels of crimes or misdemeanours that often provide the reader insight into the human condition. Spy or spy-like novels where the protagonist isn't necessarily a trained spy/investigator. Historical fiction that resonates with today – I welcome dual past/present timelines. Speculative fiction and science fiction that is grounded in the near future. Contemporary fiction that tells stories, not sermons. Resonates with today and aimed at a wide audience. Nonfiction: True crime, Cookbooks and food writing that demonstrate your expertise and for which you have a platform. Personal development, personal finance. No children's books, YA, fantasy, or sci fi that isn't grounded in the near future. Not the best agent for very political or military thrillers or novels.

L240 The Garamond Agency, Inc.
Literary Agency
United States

query@garamondagency.com

https://garamondagency.com
http://www.facebook.com/garamondagency/
https://twitter.com/@garamondagency

Nonfiction > Nonfiction Books
General, and in particular: Business; History; Narrative Nonfiction; Politics; Psychology; Science; Sociology

Does not want:

Nonfiction > Nonfiction Books: Memoir

Send: Query
Don't send: Proposal
How to send: Email
How not to send: Email attachment

Represents only adult, nonfiction projects.

Do not send proposals for children's books, young adult, fiction, poetry, or memoirs.

Query first if you have any questions about whether this is the right agency for your work.

Send email containing a short description of your project before forwarding your proposal. Please send brief queries only. No attachments. Unsolicited attachments will be deleted unread.

Literary Agent: Lisa Adams

L241 Sulamita Garbuz
Associate Agent
United States

sg@goldinlit.com

https://goldinlit.com/agents/

Literary Agency: Frances Goldin Literary Agency, Inc. (**L231**)

Fiction > Novels
Literary; Speculative

Nonfiction > Nonfiction Books
Journalism; Memoir; Narrative Nonfiction; Psychology; Science; Social Justice

How to send: Email

Gravitates primarily towards nonfiction, with an emphasis on books with a social justice bent. Her areas of specialty include narrative nonfiction, memoir, psychology, science, and journalism. She is also looking for character driven literary fiction, and is especially excited by novels that use speculative or dreamlike elements to explore current social dynamics, stories of obsession and women misbehaving, and narratives about immigration and the 2nd generation experience.

L242 Adam Gauntlett

Literary Agent
United Kingdom
Tel: +44 (0) 20 7344 1032

agauntlett@pfd.co.uk

https://petersfraserdunlop.com/agent/adam-gauntlett/
https://twitter.com/albioneye

Literary Agency: Peters Fraser + Dunlop
(L501)

ADULT
   Fiction > *Novels*
      Crime; High Concept; Historical Fiction; Thrillers; Upmarket Commercial Fiction

   Nonfiction > *Nonfiction Books*
      Crime; History; Memoir; Narrative Nonfiction; Popular Science; Psychology

CHILDREN'S > **Fiction** > *Middle Grade*

Send: Query; Synopsis; Writing sample; Proposal; Author bio
How to send: Email
How not to send: Post

Looking for upmarket-commercial fiction, series crime and thrillers, historical fiction, high-concept fiction, middle grade, narrative non-fiction, true crime, memoir, popular science/psychology and serious history. Drawn to strong female leads, original voices, quirky and endearing narrators, and well-executed plot twists.

Authors: Fay Bound Alberti; Dorothy Armstrong; Prof Marc David Baer; Andrew J. Bayliss; Nora Berend; Ed Burstell; Nicola Clark; Jack Cornish; Andrew Craig; Wilfred Emmanuel-Jones; Justine Firnhaber-Baker; Eckart Frahm; Tova Friedman; Ashish Ghadiali; Marina Gibson; Kenneth Harl; Sam Hurcom; Islam Issa; Lloyd Llewellyn-Jones; Monica Mark; Jack Meaning; Helen Molesworth; Anna Motz; Camilla Pang; Suk Pannu; Rupal Patel; Joanne Paul; Charlotte Proudman; Martyn Rady; Jacob Rees-Mogg; Alice Rio; Jane Rosenberg; Georges Simenon; Vanessa Taylor; Lisa Thompson; Charlotte Fox Weber; Adam White; Catherine Wilson; Andy Wood; Neil Woods; David Young; Andrew Zurcher

L243 Ellen Geiger

Senior Agent; Vice President
United States

https://goldinlit.com/agents/

Literary Agency: Frances Goldin Literary Agency, Inc. **(L231)**

Fiction > *Novels*
   Culture; Historical Fiction; Literary Thrillers; Multicultural

Nonfiction > *Nonfiction Books*
   Biography; History; Investigative Journalism; Multicultural; Politics; Psychology; Religion; Social Issues; Women's Issues

Closed to approaches.

Represents a broad range of fiction and non-fiction. She has a lifelong interest in multicultural and social issues embracing change. History, biography, progressive politics, psychology, women's issues, religion and serious investigative journalism are special interests.

In fiction, she loves a good literary thriller, and novels in general that provoke and challenge the status quo, as well as historical and multicultural works. She is drawn to big themes which make a larger point about the culture and times we live in, such as Barbara Kingsolver's Poisonwood Bible. She is not the right agent for New Age, romance, how-to or right-wing politics.

L244 Nicole Geiger

Literary Agent
United States

https://www.fullcircleliterary.com/submissions/
https://querymanager.com/query/NicoleFCL

Literary Agency: Full Circle Literary, LLC

CHILDREN'S > **Fiction** > *Graphic Novels*

Closed to approaches.

Represents graphic novels for middle grade and younger only.

L245 Jeff Gerecke

Literary Agent
United States

gagencyquery@gmail.com
jeff@gagencylit.com
jeff@marksonagency.com

https://www.publishersmarketplace.com/members/jeffg/
http://aaronline.org/Sys/PublicProfile/2176689/417813

Professional Body: Association of American Literary Agents (AALA)
Literary Agencies: The G Agency, LLC; Elaine Markson Literary Agency **(L195)**

Fiction > *Novels*
   General, and in particular: Commercial; Literary; Mystery

Nonfiction > *Nonfiction Books*

Biography; Business; Computers; Finance; History; Military History; Popular Culture; Sport; Technology

Send: Query; Writing sample
How to send: Email attachment

I am interested in commercial and literary fiction, as well as serious non-fiction and pop culture. My focus as an agent has always been on working with writers to shape their work for its greatest commercial potential. I provide lots of editorial advice in sharpening manuscripts and proposals before submission.

L246 Josh Getzler

Literary Agent; Partner
United States

josh@hgliterary.com

https://www.hgliterary.com/josh
https://twitter.com/jgetzler
http://www.publishersmarketplace.com/members/jgetzler/
http://aaronline.org/Sys/PublicProfile/2902758/417813
http://queryme.online/Getzler

Literary Agency: HG Literary **(L305)**
Professional Body: Association of American Literary Agents (AALA)

ADULT
   Fiction > *Novels*
      Historical Fiction; Mystery; Thrillers; Women's Fiction

   Nonfiction > *Nonfiction Books*
      Business; History; Politics

CHILDREN'S > **Fiction** > *Middle Grade*
   Comedy / Humour; Contemporary

Closed to approaches.

L247 Tara Gilbert

Literary Agent
United States

https://taragilbert.com
https://querymanager.com/query/TaraGilbert
https://ktliterary.com/about/
https://www.publishersmarketplace.com/members/tsgilbert/
https://twitter.com/Literary_Tara
https://www.pinterest.com/tarashilohgilbert/
https://www.instagram.com/literary.tara/
https://www.facebook.com/taragilbertlitagent

Literary Agency: KT Literary **(L368)**

ADULT > **Fiction** > *Novels*
   Historical Fantasy; Horror; Low Fantasy; Romance; Speculative; Upmarket

CHILDREN'S > **Fiction** > *Graphic Novels*

YOUNG ADULT > **Fiction** > *Novels*
   Comedy / Humour; Contemporary; Fantasy; Horror; Romance; Romantic Comedy

Closed to approaches.

Their passion is working with LGBTQ+, BIPOC, Neurodiverse, body diverse, and underrepresented authors and illustrators, focusing on fiction and graphic novels for MG, YA, and adults.

L248 Claire Gillespie

Associate Agent
United States

submissions@cheneyagency.com

http://cheneyassoc.com/#scrollto-agents

Fiction > *Novels*
Literary; Upmarket

Nonfiction > *Nonfiction Books*
Cultural Criticism; Memoir

Send: Query; Author bio; Writing sample; Self-Addressed Stamped Envelope (SASE)
How to send: Post; Email

Focuses on literary fiction, memoir, cultural criticism, upmarket fiction, and audio.

L249 Ginger Clark Literary

Literary Agency
554 Boston Post Road, Suite 513, Orange, CT 06477
United States
Tel: +1 (646) 396-0903

info@GingerClarkLiterary.com

https://gingerclarkliterary.com
https://www.instagram.com/clarkliterary/
https://twitter.com/ClarkLiterary

Literary Agents: Ginger Clark (**L125**); Nicole Eisenbraun (**L192**)

L250 Katie Gisondi

Literary Agent
United States

http://www.ldlainc.com/about
https://querymanager.com/query/2696
https://www.manuscriptwishlist.com/mswl-post/katie-gisondi/
https://twitter.com/GisondiKatie

Literary Agency: Laura Dail Literary Agency

ADULT
  Fiction > *Novels*
  Horror; Romance; Romantic Comedy; Thrillers

  Nonfiction > *Nonfiction Books*
  Current Affairs; Disabilities; Drugs; Nature; Popular Culture; Popular Science; Sexuality

CHILDREN'S > **Fiction** > *Middle Grade*
Adventure; Fantasy

YOUNG ADULT > **Fiction** > *Novels*
Fantasy Romance; Fantasy; Folklore, Myths, and Legends; Romance

Does not want:

Fiction > *Novels*
  Political Thrillers; Romantic Thrillers; Spy Thrilllers

Closed to approaches.

Adult: Romance and rom-com; female-led, off-kilter thrillers and horror; nonfiction about drugs, sexuality, current issues, nature, and/or popular science.

Children's: Voicey YA and MG fantasy with adventure, new twists on old tropes, and whimsy. Also swords and ballgowns.

L251 Linda S. Glaz

Author; Literary Agent; Editor; Proofreader
United States

linda@hartlineliterary.com

https://www.hartlineagency.com/agents-and-authors
https://www.facebook.com/linda.glaz
https://twitter.com/LindaGlaz

Literary Agency: Hartline Literary Agency (**L295**)
Professional Body: Advanced Writers and Speakers Association (AWSA)

Fiction > *Novels*
  General, and in particular: Contemporary Romance; Historical Romance; Romance; Romantic Suspense

Nonfiction > *Nonfiction Books*

Looking for nonfiction by experts in their field. In fiction, will consider anything well written, particularly romance, either contemporary, suspense, or historic. No children's or works that include graphic sexuality or profanity.

Authors: Karla Akins; Rick Barry; Kate Breslin; Lance Brown; Raquel Byrnes; J'nell Ciesielski; Ben Conlon; Angela Couch; Susan F. Craft; Rhonda Dragomir; Barbara Ellin Fox; Linda Gilden; Samantha Gomolka; Janet Grunst; Hilary Hamblin; Hilary Hamblin Voni Harris; Voni Harris; Julie Hatch; K Denise Holmberg; Dennis Lambert; A. D. Lawrence; Delores Liesner; Ashley Ludwig; Jessica Manfre; Merliyn Howton Marriott; Cheryl Linn Martin; Joy Massenburge; Dale McElhinney; Donna Mumma; Naomi Musch; Luke Negron; Jessica Nelson Tiffany Nicole; Candice Patterson; Carmen Peone; Karen Prough; DeBora Rachelle; Maria Reed; Cindy Regnier; Kathleen Rouser; Susan Browning Schulz; Colleen Scott; Laura Smith; Donnie Steven; Donnie Stevens; Patti Stockdale; Beth Summitt; Ken Swarner; Tiffany Tajiri; Donn Taylor; Donn Taylor Evelyn Taylor; Evelyn Taylor; Pegg Thomas; Tom Threadgill; Kari Trumbo; Susan L. Tuttle; Jennifer Uhlarik; Hannah Vanderpool; Denise Weimer; Karen Wingate; Maureen Wise; Frank Yates

L252 Gleam Futures

Literary Agency
10 Triton Street, London, NW1 3BF
United Kingdom
Tel: +44 (0) 20 3772 2940

info@gleamfutures.com

https://www.gleamfutures.com
https://www.gleamfutures.com/gleamtitles
https://twitter.com/gleamfutures
https://www.linkedin.com/company/1330612/admin/
https://www.instagram.com/gleamfutures

Fiction > *Novels*

Nonfiction > *Nonfiction Books*

We represent a diverse array of both fiction and non-fiction authors, and take great pride in our record of successfully launching almost 40 books onto the Sunday Times bestseller list.

Authors: Emmanuel Asuquo; Ellie Austin-Williams; Yasmin Benoit; Grace Beverley; Grant Brydon; Andrea Cheong; Max Dickins; Kat Farmer; Amber Fossey; Marvyn Harrison; Mark Lemon; Hana Mahmood; Lauren Mahon; Jay McGuiness; Omari McQueen; Tiwalola Ogunlesi; Tom Parker; Adele Roberts; Becky Smethurst; Sam Stern; Grace Victory; Hana Walker-Brown; Harriet De Winton

L253 Emily Glenister

Literary Agent; Company Director
United Kingdom

eg.submission@dhhliteraryagency.com

http://www.dhhliteraryagency.com/emily-glenister.html
http://www.twitter.com/emily_glenister

Literary Agency: DHH Literary Agency Ltd (**L167**)

Fiction > *Novels*
  Book Club Fiction; Commercial; Crime; Ghost Stories; Historical Fiction; Horror; Magical Realism; Mystery; Psychological Thrillers; Romance; Romantic Comedy

Nonfiction > *Nonfiction Books*
  Autobiography; Biography; Crime; History; Medicine; Memoir; Popular Culture; Women

Does not want:

Fiction > *Novels*: Police Procedural

Send: Synopsis; Writing sample
How to send: Email

Looking for female-led commercial and book club fiction, with a very strong emphasis on diverse / own voices. She loves crime / psychological thrillers and is desperately searching for fresh and unique ideas in this area. She is also on the lookout for smart and quick-witted historical fiction, with a female-focus, and is a fan of a dual timeline narrative, if done well – as well as book club fiction. She is also partial to a little magical realism. Finally, if an original horror novel / ghost story landed in her inbox, she would be utterly delighted as she's a bit of a weirdo and loves to be creeped out. In non-fiction, she is keen to expand her list and is looking in the areas of history (specifically the monarchy, medicine and women), pop culture, biographies / autobiographies / memoir (either from or about those with an established public platform) and most eagerly, true crime – like one of those addictive Netflix documentaries, but in book form. She is not looking for police procedural, screenplays, children's books / YA or Sci-Fi.

Authors: Foluso Agbaje; Louise Beech; Libby Cutts; Heather Darwent; Becca Day; Suzie Edge; Stephen Edger; Katy Harrison; Anthony Kavanagh; Caroline Lamond; S.V. Leonard; Emma Medrano; Jean Menzies; Vikki Patis; Reagan Lee Ray; Reagan Lee Ray; Becky Rhush; Nicole Robinson; Talia Samuels; Annie Taylor; Rebecca Thorne; Ola Tundun; Ronnie Turner; Kathleen Whyman

L254 Global Lion Intellectual Property Management, Inc.

Literary Agency
PO BOX 669238, Pompano Beach, FL 33066
United States
Tel: +1 (754) 222-6948

queriesgloballionmgt@gmail.com

https://globallionmanagement.com
https://www.facebook.com/GlobalLionMgt/
https://twitter.com/globallionmgt
https://www.instagram.com/globallionmgt/

Fiction > *Novels*
Commercial; Fantasy; Science Fiction

Nonfiction > *Nonfiction Books*
Arts; Business; Commercial; Education; Film Industry; Self Help; TV; Technology

Send: Query
How to send: Online submission system

Currently looking for commercial fiction, fantasy, science fiction, and intriguing studies of interesting subjects, art, and "making of" books on the film and television industry. Will not turn down anything with sharp prose, modern takes on classic concepts, a great mystery to solve or intriguing characters.

L255 Georgia Glover

Literary Agent
United Kingdom

https://www.davidhigham.co.uk/agents-dh/georgia-glover/

Literary Agency: David Higham Associates Ltd (**L159**)

Fiction > *Novels*

Nonfiction > *Nonfiction Books*

Looks after an eclectic list of clients, including a large stable of literary estates, working to ensure that the work of these classic writers remains available for new generations to discover and seeking new opportunities to bring back into print those works that are perhaps less well known but no less deserving of attention.

Authors: J. R. Ackerley; Edward Ardizzone; Michael Arlen; Robert Barnard; Margot Bennett; Elizabeth Berridge; Edmund Blunden; E. R. Braithwaite; Neville Braybrooke; Arthur Bryant; Anthony Burgess; Sheila Burnford; John Dickson Carr; Barbara Castle; Charles Causley; James Hadley Chase; Arthur C. Clarke; Lady Mary Clive; Peter Cook; Natasha Cooper; Chris Cove-Smith; James Curtis; David Daiches; R. F. Delderfield; Kelly Doust; Eleanor Farjeon; J. Jefferson Farjeon; Elizabeth Ferrars; Nicholas Fisk; Pauline Fisk; Theodora Fitzgibbon; Margot Fonteyn; Ford Madox Ford; Mavis Gallant; Eve Garnett; Jonathan Gathorne-Hardy; Ralph Glasser; Elizabeth Goudge; Peter Green; Geoffrey Grigson; Jane Grigson

L256 Susannah Godman

Literary Agent
United Kingdom

Literary Agency: Lutyens and Rubinstein

L257 Adria Goetz

Literary Agent
United States

https://ktliterary.com/submissions/
https://querymanager.com/query/adriastreasuretrove
https://adriagoetz.wpcomstaging.com/manuscript-wishlist/

Literary Agency: KT Literary (**L368**)

ADULT > **Fiction** > *Novels*
Cozy Fantasy; Romantic Comedy; Thrillers; Upmarket

CHILDREN'S > **Fiction**
Graphic Novels; *Middle Grade*; *Picture Books*

Closed to approaches.

Seeking picture books (especially by author-illustrators), middle grade fiction, graphic novels, and adult fiction—particularly rom coms, thrillers, upmarket fiction, and cozy fantasy.

L258 Anthony Goff

Literary Agent; Chair
United Kingdom

submissions@davidhigham.co.uk

https://www.davidhigham.co.uk/agents-dh/anthony-goff/

Literary Agency: David Higham Associates Ltd (**L159**)

ADULT
Fiction > *Novels*
Commercial; Literary

Nonfiction > *Nonfiction Books*
Commercial; Literary

CHILDREN'S > **Fiction** > *Novels*

Send: Query; Synopsis; Writing sample

Represents many high-profile and successful authors of literary and commercial fiction and non-fiction, and also several children's writers.

Authors: Carol Anshaw; Jenn Ashworth; Nigel Barley; Aimee Bender; Margaret Boden; Janet Browne; Jessica Bruder; Mark Burnell; J. M. Coetzee; Bernard Cornwell; John Cunliffe; Roald Dahl; Anne Fine; Karen Joy Fowler; Catherine Fox; Stephen Fry; Caroline Graham; Linda Green; Graham Greene; James Herbert; Paul Hoffman; Simon Hopkinson; Alan Judd; Binnie Kirshenbaum; Stephen Lacey; Hugh Laurie; Joanna Lumley; Greil Marcus; David Marquand; Simon Mason; Evan Mawdsley; Peter May; Elizabeth McCracken; Iain McGilchrist; Elizabeth McKenzie; Sigrid Nunez; Kate Reed Petty; Anthony Powell; Shannon Pufahl; Alice Sebold; Miranda Seymour; Nick Sharratt; Hilary Spurling; Hew Strachan; Jeremy Strong; Lynne Truss; Lucy Wadham; Alice Walker; Stephen Walsh; Elizabeth Wilhide

L259 Ellen Goff

Associate Agent
United States

ellen@hgliterary.com

https://www.hgliterary.com/ellen

Literary Agency: HG Literary (**L305**)

CHILDREN'S > **Fiction**
Middle Grade; *Picture Books*
YOUNG ADULT > **Fiction**
Graphic Novels: General
Novels: General, and in particular: Ghost Stories; Gothic; Historical Fiction

List consists of YA writers and illustrators, as well as middle grade and picture book writers. Interested in all genres and formats of YA, especially anything spooky, historical fiction, martial arts, graphic novels, and novels-in-verse. She has a soft spot for Shakespeare as well as southern gothic stories that remind her of her home state of Kentucky.

L260 Veronica Goldstein

Literary Agent
United States

https://www.fletcherandco.com/team/veronica-goldstein/

Literary Agency: Fletcher & Company (**L225**)

Fiction > *Novels*
Autofiction; Contemporary; Culture; Experimental; Literary; Politics; Speculative

Nonfiction in Translation > *Nonfiction Books*
Climate Science; Culture; Economics; Memoir; Narrative Nonfiction; Politics; Social Issues; Technology

Nonfiction > *Nonfiction Books*
Climate Science; Culture; Economics; Memoir; Narrative Nonfiction; Politics; Social Issues; Technology

Send: Query; Synopsis; Writing sample
How to send: In the body of an email

Her list includes contemporary literary fiction and voice-driven narrative nonfiction that probes important social issues.

L261 The Good Literary Agency

Literary Agency
United Kingdom

info@thegoodliteraryagency.org

https://www.thegoodliteraryagency.org
https://twitter.com/thegoodagencyuk

Professional Body: The Association of Authors' Agents (AAA)

ADULT
Fiction > *Novels*
General, and in particular: Cozy Mysteries; Romantic Comedy

Nonfiction > *Nonfiction Books*
General, and in particular: Health; Lifestyle

CHILDREN'S
Fiction > *Novels*
General, and in particular: Supernatural / Paranormal Horror

Nonfiction > *Nonfiction Books*
General, and in particular: Lifestyle

YOUNG ADULT
Fiction > *Novels*
General, and in particular: Magic

Nonfiction > *Nonfiction Books*
General, and in particular: Lifestyle

Send: Query
Don't send: Full text

Focused on discovering, developing and launching the careers of writers of colour, disability, working class, LGBTQ+ and anyone who feels their story is not being told in the mainstream. Writers must be born or resident in Britain. No poetry, plays, or screenplays. Accepts submissions from the 1st to the 21st of each month only. See website for full guidelines and to submit via online form.

L262 Andrew Gordon

Literary Agent
United Kingdom

andrewgordon@davidhigham.co.uk

https://www.davidhigham.co.uk/agents-dh/andrew-gordon/

Literary Agency: David Higham Associates Ltd (**L159**)

ACADEMIC > **Nonfiction** > *Nonfiction Books*: History

ADULT
Fiction > *Novels*
Commercial; Literary

Nonfiction > *Nonfiction Books*
Adventure; Biography; Business; Current Affairs; Economics; Films; History; Memoir; Music; Narrative Nonfiction; Politics; Popular Culture; Popular Science; Psychology; Sport

List is primarily non-fiction. Open to new projects in most genres, especially history, current affairs, biography and memoir, narrative non-fiction, sport, popular culture, popular science and psychology, smart thinking and business books with a strong story. In fiction, likes novels that grab the attention, whether literary or commercial. No YA authors, or science fiction/fantasy.

Assistant Agent: David Evans (**L201**)

Authors: Elizabeth Alker; Alan Allport; Noga Arikha; Thomas Asbridge; Katy Balls; Lindsey Bareham; Kaushik Basu; Laura Beers; James Bloodworth; Jonathan Boff; Martin Brunt; John Carey; Aditya Chakrabortty; Alan Connor; Jason Cowley; Lizzie Dearden; Bobby Duffy; Mark Easton; Gavin Esler; Seb Falk; Felipe Fernández-Armesto; Cordelia Fine; Matthew Frank; Susannah Gibson; Andrew Gimson; Victoria Glendinning; Richard Greene; John Gribbin; Dennis Grube; David Guss; Isabel Hardman; Sophie Harman; Tim Harper; Chris Hirst; Russell Hoban; Eric Hobsbawm; Trevor Horn; Tansy Hoskins; Julian Jackson; Owen Jones; Anna Keay; John Keay; Paul Kennedy; Barbara Keys; Sulmaan Wasif Khan; Halik Kochanski; David Lammy; Elisabeth Leake; Daniel Light; Dame Vera Lynn; Kathryn Mannix; Sarfraz Manzoor; Helen McCarthy; Ed Miliband; Fraser Nelson; Johan Norberg; David Nott; Peter Oborne; Susan Owens; Helen Parr; Harry Pearson; Gilles Peterson; Sadiah Qureshi; Amol Rajan; Chris Renwick; Steve Richards; Helen Roche; Jane Rogoyska; Rupert Russell; Jane Sanderson; Antonia Senior; Rachel Shabi; Sujit Sivasundaram; Mark B. Smith; Kristina Spohr; Devi Sridhar; Peter Stott; Nicola Sturgeon; Dylan Thomas; Simon Thurley; Phil Tinline; Simon Tyler; Rosamund Urwin; Yanis Varoufakis; Bernard Wasserstein; Holly Watt; Sam Wetherell; Phil Whitaker; Jon Wilson; Hope Wolf; Carolyn Woods

L263 Graham Maw Christie Literary Agency

Literary Agency
37 Highbury Place, London, N5 1QP
United Kingdom
Tel: +44 (0) 7971 268342

submissions@grahammawchristie.com

http://www.grahammawchristie.com
https://twitter.com/litagencygmc
https://www.instagram.com/litagencygmc/

Professional Body: The Association of Authors' Agents (AAA)

Nonfiction > *Nonfiction Books*

Send: Query; Outline; Author bio; Market info; Marketing Plan; Writing sample
How to send: Email

No fiction, poetry, or scripts. Send query with one-page summary, a paragraph on the contents of each chapter, your qualifications for writing it, details of your online presence, market analysis, what you could do to help promote your book, and a sample chapter or two.

Literary Agents: Jennifer Christie (**L122**); Jane Graham Maw (**L430**)

L264 Stacey Graham

Literary Agent
United States

stacey@threeseaslit.com

https://www.threeseasagency.com/agents/stacey-graham
http://querymanager.com/Stacey3Seas

Literary Agency: 3 Seas Literary Agency (**L001**)

ADULT
Fiction > *Novels*: Romantic Comedy

Nonfiction > *Nonfiction Books*

CHILDREN'S > **Fiction** > *Middle Grade*
Comedy / Humour; Ghost Stories

How to send: Query Manager

Currently looking to expand her list with snappy Rom-Coms, hilarious/spooky middle grade, and weird nonfiction.

L265 Susan Graham

Literary Agent
United States

https://www.einsteinliterary.com/staff/
http://aaronline.org/Sys/PublicProfile/52451502/417813

Literary Agency: Einstein Literary Management (**L190**)
Professional Body: Association of American Literary Agents (AALA)

ADULT > **Fiction** > *Novels*
General, and in particular: Fantasy; LGBTQIA; Science Fiction

CHILDREN'S > **Fiction** > *Novels*
General, and in particular: Fantasy; LGBTQIA; Science Fiction

YOUNG ADULT
Fiction > *Novels*

General, and in particular: Fantasy; LGBTQIA; Science Fiction

Nonfiction > *Nonfiction Books*

Looking for children's and young adult fiction in all genres, but their favorite books are often science fiction and fantasy, especially written with a queer lens. They also enjoy picture books and represent graphic novels in all age categories and in all genres. They're particularly interested in friendships and sibling narratives, and monster protagonists are always a plus. They're looking for a good nonfiction or two for children or teens but don't know about what. For adult prose, they prefer genre fiction, and monster protagonists are still a plus. Works by and about marginalized voices are welcome and encouraged.

L266 Kara Grajkowski
Literary Agent
United States

threeseasagency.kara@gmail.com

https://www.threeseasagency.com/agents/kara-grajkowski
https://querymanager.com/query/2761

Literary Agency: 3 Seas Literary Agency (**L001**)

CHILDREN'S > *Fiction* > *Novels*: Contemporary

YOUNG ADULT > *Fiction* > *Novels*: Contemporary

Send: Pitch; Writing sample
How to send: Query Manager

Looking for contemporary middle grade fiction; contemporary young adult fiction; and own voices.

L267 Michelle Grajkowski
Literary Agent
United States

michelle@threeseaslit.com

https://www.threeseasagency.com/agents/michelle-grajkowski
http://querymanager.com/Michelle3Seas
http://aaronline.org/Sys/PublicProfile/2176701/417813

Literary Agency: 3 Seas Literary Agency (**L001**)
Professional Body: Association of American Literary Agents (AALA)

ADULT
  Fiction > *Novels*
    Romance; Women's Fiction
  Nonfiction > *Nonfiction Books*

CHILDREN'S > *Fiction* > *Middle Grade*

How to send: Query Manager

Primarily represents romance, women's fiction, young adult and middle grade fiction

along with select nonfiction projects with a terrific message. She is currently looking for fantastic writers with a voice of their own.

Authors: Katie MacAlister; Cathy McDavid; Kerrelyn Sparks; C.L. Wilson

L268 Great River Literary
Literary Agency
United States

greatriverliterary@gmail.com

https://www.greatriverliterary.com

CHILDREN'S
  Fiction
    Board Books; *Chapter Books*; *Middle Grade*; *Picture Books*
  Nonfiction > *Nonfiction Books*: Literary
  Poetry > *Any Poetic Form*

YOUNG ADULT > *Fiction* > *Novels*

How to send: Email
How not to send: Email attachment; Phone; Post

An agency devoted exclusively to representing authors and author/illustrators of books for children and teens.

Literary Agent: Mary Cummings (*L145*)

L269 Greene & Heaton Ltd
Literary Agency
T18, West Wing, Somerset House, Strand, London, WC2R 1LA
United Kingdom

submissions@greeneheaton.co.uk
info@greeneheaton.co.uk

http://www.greeneheaton.co.uk
https://twitter.com/greeneandheaton

Professional Body: The Association of Authors' Agents (AAA)

Fiction > *Novels*

Nonfiction > *Nonfiction Books*

Does not want:

> **CHILDREN'S** > **Fiction** > *Picture Books*

Send: Query; Synopsis; Writing sample
Don't send: Full text
How to send: Email
How not to send: Post

Send query by email only, including synopsis and three chapters or approximately 50 pages. No submissions by post. No response unless interested. Handles all types of fiction and nonfiction, but no scripts or children's picture books.

Author Estates: The Estate of Julia Darling; The Estate of Sarah Gainham

Authors: Juliana Adelman; Amen Alonge; Anthony Anaxagorou; Lucy Ashe; Michelle Bang; Raffaella Barker; Charlotte Bauer; Emily Bootle; Lucy Brazier; Bridget; Lynne Bryan; Zoe Burgess; Jason Byrne; Tom Campbell; Charles Cockell; Pam Corbin; Russell Davies; Anna Davis; Rachel Dawson; Rageshri Dhairyawan; Patrick Drake; Kim Duke; Lily Dunn; Suzannah Dunn; Jeremy Duns; Jonn Elledge; Gabriela Evangelou; Lucia Evangelou; Olaf Falafel; Hugh Fearnley-Whittingstall; Jane Fearnley-Whittingstall; Christopher Fitz-Simon; Felix Flicker; Christophe Galfard; Chandra Ganguly; Helen Giltrow; Francis Gimblett; Molly Greeley; Jake Hall; Julie Hayward; Stuart Heritage; Kit Heyam; Kat Hill; Julian Hitch; Beatrice Hitchman; Julia Hollander; Wayne Holloway-Smith; Andrew Holmes; Alex Hourston; Sarah Housley; David Howard; Daisy J. Hung; Charles Jennings; Joan; D.B. John; Sam Johnson-Schlee; Keith Kahn-Harris; Fiona Keating; Vedashree Khambete-Sharma; Gabrielle Kimm; Esme King; Max Kinnings; David Kirk; Rikke Schmidt Kjærgaard; Rebecca Dinerstein Knight; Joseph Knox; Sonya Kudei; Manon Lagrève; William Leith; Dan Lepard; Robert Lewis; Eric Lindstrom; Kieran Long; Dorian Lynskey; L. A. MacRae; Carina Maggar; Ruth Mancini; Rob Manuel; Anna Sulan Masing; Jolyon Maugham; James McGee; Gill Meller; Thomasina Miers; Lottie Moggach; Cathy Newman; Mary-Ann Ochota; Ciara Ohartghaile; Christopher Osborn; Iain Overton; John O'Connell; Nicolas Padamsee; Pete Paphides; Anna Parker; Jyoti Patel; Neel Patel; Marie Phillips; Tom Phillips; Shivi Ramoutar; Richard Reed; Ana Reyes; Sam Rice; C. J. Sansom; Marcus du Sautoy; Indyana Schneider; Alev Scott; Eddie Scott; Rebecca Seal; Paul Keers: Sediment; Laura Shepherd-Robinson; Mimi Spencer; Polly Stewart; Count Arthur Strong; Jacqueline Sutherland; Andrew Taylor; Georgie Tilney; Ian Vince; John Vincent; Adam Wagner; Jennie Walker; Sarai Walker; Andrew Webb; Ione Wells; Robyn Wilder; Will Wiles; Jason Wilson; Susie Yang; Erin Young; Robyn Young; Andrew Ziminski

Literary Agents: Holly Faulks; Carol Heaton; Imogen Morrell (**L457**); Judith Murray; Antony Topping; Laura Williams; Claudia Young (**L669**)

L270 Katie Greenstreet
Literary Agent
United Kingdom

submissions@paperliterary.com

Literary Agency: Paper Literary (**L488**)

Fiction > *Novels*
  Book Club Fiction; Commercial; Family; Historical Fiction; Literary Suspense; Psychological Suspense; Romance; Upmarket

Nonfiction > *Nonfiction Books*: Memoir

I'm building a list of quality commercial and upmarket/book club fiction, with a select number of memoirs and non-fiction projects also in the mix.

L271 Greyhound Literary

Literary Agency
United Kingdom

info@cclagents.com

https://greyhoundliterary.co.uk

Professional Body: The Association of Authors' Agents (AAA)

ADULT
  Fiction > *Novels*
    Commercial; Literary

  Nonfiction > *Nonfiction Books*
    General, and in particular: Biography; Comedy / Humour; Cookery; History; Lifestyle; Memoir; Music; Politics; Sport; Wellbeing

CHILDREN'S
  Fiction > *Novels*
  Nonfiction > *Nonfiction Books*

Send: Query; Synopsis; Writing sample
How to send: Email

Author Estates: The Estate of Alan Rickman; The Estate of Alfred H. Mendes

Authors: Guy Adams; Tanya Aldred; Becky Alexander; Moeen Ali; Jennifer Lucy Allan; Jeremy Allen; Tobi Asare; Carol Atherton; Victoria Belim; Juliet Bell; SJ Bennett; Bez; Leona Nichole Black; Owen Booth; Luce Brett; Edward Brooke-Hitching; Theodore Brun; Andy Bull; Jen Campbell; Bonnie Chung; David Collins; Zoë Colville; Duncan Crowe; Iain Dey; Chris Dodd; Lulah Ellender; Kirsty Eyre; Marchelle Farrell; Adam Fergusson; Jamie Fewery; A P Firdaus; Liz Fraser; Rebecca Front; Tom Gabbay; Julian Gough; Janet Gover; Sarah Graham; Karen Gurney; Saskia Gwinn; Ed Hawkins; David Higgins; Maisie Hill; Will Hill; Thomas W. Hodgkinson; Nicholas Hogg; Michael Holding; Iain Hollingshead; Andrew Hosken; Michael Hutchinson; Heidi James; Ginger Jones; Simon Jones; Jennifer Lane; Carlie Lee; Paul Levy; Fiona Longmuir; Michelle Lovric; Bonnie MacBird; Stephen Mallinder; Shingi Mararike; Katie Marsh; Amanda Mason; Hugh Matheson; Alison May; Neil McCormick; Anthony McGowan; Barry McKinley; Moin Mir; Charlotte Mitchell; David Moats; Paul Morgan-Bentley; Anton Mosimann; Rebecca Myers; James Peak; Andrew Perry; Edvard Radzinsky; Amy Ransom; Sue Ransom; Amy Raphael; Hamilton Richardson; Susan Richardson; Rebecca Rogers; Lias Saoudi; Rebecca Schiller; Clare Seal; Matthew Shaw; Sarah Shephard; Ally Sinclair; Michael Smith; Tatton Spiller; Andrea Stuart; Harry Sword; James Thomas; Jo Thompson; Tom Tivnan;

Luke Turner; Robin Turner; Hana Videen; Kate Vigurs; Michael Volpe; Wendy Wason; Jen Wight; Sioned Wiliam; Penny Wincer; Mike Woodhouse; Liam Patrick Young

Chair: Patrick Janson-Smith

Foreign Rights Director / Literary Agent: Sam Edenborough (**L188**)

Literary Agents: Charlotte Atyeo (**L036**); Maria Brannan (**L076**); Charlie Campbell (**L094**); Natalie Galustian (**L238**); Dotti Irving (**L320**); Philip Gwyn Jones (**L334**); Julia Silk (**L570**)

L272 Katie Grimm

Literary Agent
United States

http://doncongdon.com/agents.shtml#agent-03
https://querymanager.com/query/KGRIMM

Literary Agency: Don Congdon Associates, Inc. (**L175**)

ADULT
  Fiction
    Graphic Novels: General
    Novels: Historical Fiction; Literary; Mystery; Speculative; Upmarket Women's Fiction
    Short Fiction Collections: General

  Nonfiction > *Nonfiction Books*
    History; Memoir; Narrative Nonfiction; Science; Social Issues

YOUNG ADULT > **Fiction** > *Novels*
  Contemporary; High Concept; Speculative

How to send: Query Manager

She represents vivid literary fiction (be it voicey, historical, speculative, or mysterious), up-market women's fiction, cohesive short story collections, and graphic novels. In young adult, she loves compelling and heartbreaking contemporary novels and speculative high-concepts rooted in science and history. In middle grade, she enjoys novels with a heartfelt, timeless quality, and stories that explore the magic of our world or those imagined. For non-fiction, she is looking for memoirs and narratives that explore greater social issues, dark and weird times in human history, the personal impact of science, and any off-beat topic explored through an academic lens.

L273 Loren R. Grossman

Literary Agent
United States
Tel: +1 (310) 314-2113
Fax: +1 (310) 450-0181

lrg@ix.netcom.com

https://paulslevinelit.com/loren-r-grossman/

Literary Agency: Paul S. Levine Literary Agency (**L492**)

Nonfiction > *Nonfiction Books*

Archaeology; Architecture; Arts; Autobiography; Education; Gardening; Genealogy; Health; Legal; Medicine; Science; Sociology; Technology

Send: Query
How to send: Email; Post

Send one-page query, preferably by email (though snail mail is acceptable). No query-related phone calls.

L274 Pam Gruber

Literary Agent
United States

pam.queries@irenegoodman.com

https://www.irenegoodman.com/pam-gruber
https://www.instagram.com/pjgruber/
https://twitter.com/Pamlet606

Literary Agency: Irene Goodman Literary Agency (IGLA)

ADULT
  Fiction > *Novels*
    Coming of Age; Commercial; Fantasy; Literary; Magical Realism; Romantic Comedy; Speculative

  Nonfiction > *Nonfiction Books*

CHILDREN'S > **Fiction**
  Graphic Novels: General
  Middle Grade: Coming of Age; Commercial; Fantasy; Literary; Magical Realism; Romantic Comedy; Speculative
YOUNG ADULT > **Fiction**
  Graphic Novels: General
  Novels: Coming of Age; Commercial; Fantasy; Literary; Magical Realism; Romantic Comedy; Speculative

How to send: Email

Looking for adult, young adult, and middle grade fiction with literary voices and commercial hooks. She is particularly interested in layered fantasy, speculative fiction, fantastical realism, rom-coms, and coming-of-age stories with a twist. She is also open to middle grade and YA graphic novels, as well as select narrative non-fiction on lesser-known subjects. She would not be the best fit for prescriptive non-fiction, anthologies, potty humor, paranormal, or erotica.

L275 Hattie Grunewald

Literary Agent
United Kingdom

hattiesubmissions@theblairpartnership.com

https://www.theblairpartnership.com/literary-agents/hattie-grunewald/
https://twitter.com/hatteatime

Literary Agency: The Blair Partnership

Fiction > *Novels*
  Book Club Fiction; Commercial; Crime; Historical Fiction; Thrillers; Upmarket

Nonfiction > *Nonfiction Books*
Lifestyle; Mental Health; Personal Development

Send: Pitch; Market info; Synopsis; Writing sample
How to send: Email

Represents commercial and upmarket fiction, including women's fiction, crime and thriller, historical and book club fiction. Also represents some non-fiction in the areas of lifestyle and personal development.

Authors: Jassa Ahluwalia; Danny Altmann; Amy Beashel; Emma J. Bell; Ryan Collett; Lizzy Dent; Rebecca Denton; Roxane Dhand; Clare Empson; Sue Fortin; Mark Freeman; Alice Gendron; Marina Gerner; Lucy V. Hay; Peter Komolafe; Alex Lassoued; Liam Livings; Niki Mackay; Ruthy Mason; Luna McNamara; Gez Medinger; Catherine Miller; Rob Perry; Celine Saintclare; Anbara Salam; Lauren Sharkey; Jennifer Stone; Sarah Stovell; Nancy Tucker; Sophie Walker; Steve White; Ed Winters; Emma Woodhouse; Stephanie Yeboah; Lola Young

L276 Robert Guinsler

Senior Agent
United States

https://www.sll.com/our-team

Literary Agency: Sterling Lord Literistic, Inc. (**L583**)

Nonfiction > *Nonfiction Books*

Send: Query; Synopsis; Writing sample
How to send: Online submission system

His general curiosity in all things has allowed him the opportunity to represent a wide variety of prize-winning and New York Times bestselling nonfiction authors and projects. Most every avenue of the nonfiction spectrum can be found on his list. As well, he has been a champion of LGBTQ+ voices his entire career.

L277 Masha Gunic

Associate Agent
United States

http://www.azantianlitagency.com/pages/team-mg.html
https://querymanager.com/query/MashaGunic

Literary Agency: Azantian Literary Agency (**L039**)

CHILDREN'S > **Fiction** > *Middle Grade*
Adventure; Comedy / Humour; Contemporary; Fantasy; Historical Fiction; Horror

YOUNG ADULT > **Fiction** > *Novels*
Commercial; Contemporary; Fantasy; High Concept; Historical Fiction; Literary; Magical Realism; Mystery; Science Fiction; Space Opera; Thrillers

How to send: Query Manager

Represents middle grade and young adult novels.

L278 Gurman Agency, LLC

Literary Agency
United States
Tel: +1 (212) 749-4618

assistant@gurmanagency.com

http://www.gurmanagency.com

Professional Body: Writers Guild of America (WGA)

Scripts > *Theatre Scripts*

How to send: By referral

Represents playwrights, directors, choreographers, composers and lyricists. New clients by referral only, so prospective clients should seek a referral rather than querying. No queries accepted.

Literary Agent: Susan Gurman (*L279*)

L279 Susan Gurman

Literary Agent
United States

Literary Agency: Gurman Agency, LLC (**L278**)

L280 Serene Hakim

Literary Agent
United States

https://www.pandeliterary.com/about-pandeliterary
https://twitter.com/serenemaria
http://aaronline.org/Sys/PublicProfile/52119398/417813

Literary Agency: Ayesha Pande Literary (**L038**)
Professional Body: Association of American Literary Agents (AALA)

ADULT > **Fiction** > *Novels*
Culture; International; Literary

CHILDREN'S > **Fiction** > *Middle Grade*: Fantasy

YOUNG ADULT > **Fiction** > *Novels*
Contemporary; Culture; International

Closed to approaches.

Represents authors in a variety of genres, from MG fantasy to adult literary fiction to contemporary YA. Particularly interested in both YA and adult fiction that has international themes, highlights a variety of cultures, and focuses on underrepresented and/or marginalized voices. At the moment, she is mostly focusing on YA/MG and taking on adult writers more selectively. Specifically, she's looking for writing that explores different meanings of identity, home, and family, and in general would love to find more Middle Eastern writers.

L281 Jolene Haley

Literary Agent
United States

https://www.jolenehaley.com
http://maassagency.com/jolene-haley/
https://querymanager.com/query/QueryJolene
https://twitter.com/JoleneHaley
https://www.instagram.com/jolenehaleybooks/

Literary Agency: Donald Maass Literary Agency (**L176**)

ADULT
Fiction > *Novels*
Cozy Mysteries; Crime; Ghost Stories; Mystery; Romantic Comedy; Romantic Suspense

Nonfiction > *Nonfiction Books*
Crime; Magic; Mind, Body, Spirit; Spirituality; Witchcraft

CHILDREN'S > **Fiction** > *Middle Grade*
Adventure; Comedy / Humour; Contemporary; Family; Horror; Magic; Magical Realism; Mystery

YOUNG ADULT > **Fiction** > *Novels*
Adventure; Coming of Age; Contemporary; Folklore, Myths, and Legends; Ghost Stories; Horror; Magical Realism; Mystery; Romance; Tarot; Thrillers; Witches

Closed to approaches.

Has been in the publishing industry since 2012 on both the publisher and agency sides in editorial, marketing, publicity, contracts, and agent positions.

L282 The Hanbury Agency

Literary Agency
Suite 103, 88 Lower Marsh, London, SE1 7AB
United Kingdom

enquiries@hanburyagency.com

http://www.hanburyagency.com
https://www.facebook.com/HanburyAgency/
https://twitter.com/hanburyagency
https://www.instagram.com/the_hanbury_agency/

Professional Body: The Association of Authors' Agents (AAA)

Fiction > *Novels*

Nonfiction > *Nonfiction Books*
Current Affairs; History; Popular Culture

Closed to approaches.

Closed to submissions as at August 2019. Check website for current status.

No film scripts, plays, poetry, books for children, self-help. Not accepting fantasy, science fiction, or misery memoirs. Send query by post with brief synopsis, first 30 pages (roughly), and your email address and phone number. No submissions by email. Do not include SAE, as no material is returned.

Response not guaranteed, so assume rejection if no reply after 8 weeks.

Authors: George Alagiah; Simon Callow; Jane Glover; Bernard Hare; Imran Khan; Judith Lennox; Katie Price

Literary Agent: Margaret Hanbury

L283 Hannah Sheppard Literary Agency

Literary Agency
United Kingdom

https://hs-la.com
https://twitter.com/hannah_litagent
https://instagram.com/hannah_litagent
https://www.facebook.com/hannahsheppard.editor

ADULT
  Fiction > *Novels*
    Crime Thrilllers; Family; Fantasy Romance; Friends; High Concept; Horror; Speculative Romance; Speculative; Thrillers

  Nonfiction > *Nonfiction Books*
    Feminism; Narrative Nonfiction

CHILDREN'S > **Fiction**
  Graphic Novels: General
  Middle Grade: Comedy / Humour; Fantasy Romance; Ghost Stories; Horror; Romance
YOUNG ADULT > **Fiction** > *Graphic Novels*

Send: Query; Synopsis; Writing sample
How to send: Online submission system

I represent both adult and children's fiction (as well as a small amount of non-fiction) and, more than anything, I want to be entertained by a great story while caring deeply about your characters. In general, I love bold, distinctive voices, intriguing stories with a strong hook and flawed characters with something to learn. I want characters who are truly diverse – let's be inclusive, body positive and joyful in our representation. I also like big, mind-bending ideas and combinations of genres that feel fresh and create something new...

Literary Agent: Hannah Sheppard (*L568*)

L284 Carrie Hannigan

Literary Agent; Partner
United States

carrie@hgliterary.com

https://www.hgliterary.com/carrie
http://queryme.online/Hannigan

Literary Agency: HG Literary (**L305**)
Professional Body: Association of American Literary Agents (AALA)

ADULT > **Nonfiction** > *Nonfiction Books*

CHILDREN'S
  Fiction
    Graphic Novels: General

Novels: Comedy / Humour; Contemporary; Fantasy
Nonfiction > *Nonfiction Books*

Closed to approaches.

L285 Stephanie Hansen

Senior Agent
United States

https://www.metamorphosisliteraryagency.com/about
https://querymanager.com/query/Query_Metamorphosis

Literary Agency: Metamorphosis Literary Agency (**L440**)
Professional Body: Association of American Literary Agents (AALA)

ADULT
  Fiction > *Novels*: Thrillers

  Nonfiction > *Nonfiction Books*

YOUNG ADULT > **Fiction** > *Novels*
  Contemporary; Thrillers

How to send: Query Manager

Represents authors with their debut novels and New York Times-bestsellers and has brokered deals with small presses, mid-size publishers, major publishing houses, foreign publishers, audio producers, gaming app companies, reading app companies, and film producers. Looks for Thrillers (YA & Adult); YA contemporary with unexpected antagonists; Prose that flows as smoothly as poetry; Unforgettable plot twists; Well-rounded characters; and Non-fiction with heart.

L286 Hardman & Swainson

Literary Agency
S106, New Wing, Somerset House, Strand, London, WC2R 1LA
United Kingdom
Tel: +44 (0) 20 3701 7449

submissions@hardmanswainson.com

https://www.hardmanswainson.com
https://twitter.com/HardmanSwainson

Professional Body: The Association of Authors' Agents (AAA)

Send: Query; Proposal; Writing sample; Full text
How to send: Email

Agency launched June 2012 by former colleagues at an established agency. Welcomes submissions of fiction and nonfiction. See website for full submission guidelines.

Authors: Jennifer Barclay; Lilly Bartlett; Jackie Bateman; Alex Bell; Anna Bell; Jon Bounds; Oggy Boytchev; Paul Braddon; Cathy Bramley; Elizabeth Brooks; Isabelle Broom; Mark Broomfield; Tracy Buchanan; Meg Cabot; Elisabeth Carpenter; Simon Cheshire; Adrienne Chinn; Abby Clements; Helen Cox; Jeremy Craddock; Sara Crowe; Joshua

Cunningham; Emma Darwin; Stuart David; Sharron Davies; Daniel M. Davis; Caroline Davison; Lisa Dickenson; Miranda Dickinson; Sarah Ditum; Carol Donaldson; Charlotte Duckworth; Simon David Eden; Rachel Edwards; Miranda Emmerson; Miguel Farias; Helen Fields; Eugene Finkel; Rosie Fiore; Carrie Hope Fletcher; Giovanna Fletcher; Nicola Ford; Harry Freedman; Michele Gorman; James Gould-Bourn; Vanessa Greene; Kirsty Greenwood; Alastair Gunn; Tom Higham; Michael Jecks; Dinah Jefferies; Oskar Cox Jensen; Stuart Johnstone; Ishani Kar-Purkayastha; Elaine Kasket; Beth Kempton; Holly Kingston; Lucy Lawrie; Peter Laws; Christine Lehnen; Malinda Lo; Craig Lord; Alice Loxton; David B. Lyons; Kevin Macneil; Katie Marsh; S R Masters; Cressida Mclaughlin; Ali Mcnamara; Susy Mcphee; Siobhan Miller; Kr Moorhead; Martina Murphy; Julien Musolino; Helen Naylor; Nigel Packer; Lauren Price; Philip C Quaintrell; Martina Reilly; Charlotte Rixon; Caroline Roberts; Gareth Roberts; Patrick Roberts; Nick Russell-Pavier; Susanna Rustin; Nikola Scott; Catherine Simpson; Emma Slade; Danny Smith; Karen Ingala Smith; Victoria Smith; Gareth Southwell; Elisabeth Spencer; Hollie Starling; Fiona Sussman; Eliska Tanzer; Sarah Tierney; Liz Trenow; Sarah Turner; Rebecca Wait; B P Walter; Louise Walters; Victoria Walters; Sue Watson; Alison White; Catherine Wikholm; Samantha Wilson; Laura Ziepe

Literary Agents: Hannah Ferguson (**L212**); Caroline Hardman (**L287**); Joanna Swainson (**L600**)

L287 Caroline Hardman

Literary Agent
United Kingdom

submissions@hardmanswainson.com
caroline@hardmanswainson.com

http://www.hardmanswainson.com/agents/caroline-hardman/

Literary Agency: Hardman & Swainson (**L286**)

Fiction > *Novels*
  Book Club Fiction; Crime; Historical Fiction; Literary; Thrillers; Upmarket Commercial Fiction

Nonfiction > *Nonfiction Books*
  Current Affairs; Feminism; Health; Human Biology; Lifestyle; Medicine; Memoir; Narrative Nonfiction; Personal Development; Popular Science; Psychology; Wellbeing

Send: Synopsis; Full text
How to send: Email

Direct submissions to the agent, but send to the submissions email address, not her individual email address.

Authors: Katie Allen; Jennifer Barclay; Lilly Bartlett; Tracy Buchanan; Elisabeth Carpenter; HS Chandler; Emma Christie; Sharron Davies;

Daniel M. Davis; Sarah Ditum; Andrew Doig; Charlotte Duckworth; Miranda Emmerson; Miguel Farias; Louise Fein; Helen Fields; Eugene Finkel; Eliese Colette Goldbach; Michele Gorman; Paula Greenlees; Alastair Gunn; Dinah Jefferies; Helen Joyce; Ishani Kar-Purkayastha; Elaine Kasket; Beth Kempton; Craig Lord; Alice Loxton; Martina Murphy; Helen Naylor; Jenni Nuttall; Julia Parry; Laura Pashby; Vanessa Potter; Martina Reilly; Charlotte Rixon; Gareth Roberts; Susanna Rustin; Nikola Scott; Joanne Sefton; Karen Ingala Smith; Victoria Smith; Miss South; Elisabeth Spencer; Kathleen Stock; John Tregoning; Liz Trenow; Rebecca Wait; Alison White; Catherine Wikholm; Ryan Wilson; Eleanor Wood

L288 Jessica Hare

Literary Agent
United Kingdom

jhare@theagency.co.uk

https://theagency.co.uk/the-agents/jessica-hare/
https://twitter.com/jcchare
https://instagram.com/jcchare

Literary Agency: The Agency (London) Ltd (**L009**)

L289 Esmond Harmsworth

Literary Agent; President
United States

https://aevitascreative.com/agents/
https://querymanager.com/query/
Esmond_Harmsworth_Submissions

Literary Agency: Aevitas

Fiction > *Novels*
Crime; Historical Fiction; Horror; Literary; Mystery; Suspense; Thrillers

Nonfiction > *Nonfiction Books*
Business; Culture; History; Politics; Psychology; Science

Closed to approaches.

Represents serious nonfiction books on topics such as politics, psychology, culture, business, history and science. For fiction, he represents literary fiction, mystery and crime, thriller, suspense and horror, and historical novels.

Authors: Ron Adner; Aaron Ahuvia; Devery Anderson; Erin Arvedlund; Dave Balter; Justin L. Barrett; Jean-Louis Barsoux; Christian Bason; Ann Bauer; David Benjamin; Jedediah Berry; Lucy Blake; Didier Bonnet; Giacomo Bono; Lisa Borders; Cyril Bouquet; Gary Braver; Carolyn S. Briggs; Debra Bruno; Majka Burhardt; Tara Button; Jonathan Byrnes; Shawn Casemore; Paola Cecchi-Dimegli; Ulrik Christensen; Joshua Cohen; James Cullen; David Dabscheck; Niraj Dawar; Sandeep Dayal; Jeremy DeSilva; Brian Deer; Dan DiMicco; Barry C. Dorn; Ilana Edelstein; Elisabeth Elo; Robert Emmons; Katherine C.

Epstein; Mark Esposito; David Farbman; Keith Ferrazzi; Noah Fleming; Chad E. Foster; Rebecca Frankel; Seth Freeman; Jeffrey Froh; Samuel W. Gailey; Jeff Gothelf; Ronnie Greene; Olaf Groth; Sunetra Gupta; Lise Haines; Chris Hamby; George Harrar; Joseph M. Henderson; Michelle Hoover; John Horn; Erich Joachimsthaler; Jon Katzenbach; Fred Kiel; Kasley Killam; Kim Kleman; David Komlos; Andrew Lam; Adam Lashinsky; Clifton Leaf; Junheng Li; Josh Linkner; Barbara K. Lipska; Tim Lomas; Courtney Lynch; Sean Lynch; Dario Maestripieri; David Magee; Leonard J. Marcus; Robert Martin; Grace Dane Mazur; Elaine McArdle; Jeffrey D. McCausland; Claire McDougall; Keith McFarland; Eric J. McNulty; Christopher Michaelson; Paddy Miller; Angie Morgan; Nick Morgan; Jim Morris; Mark Nitzberg; Howard Nusbaum; Barry O'Reilly; Angela V. Paccione; Patricia Park; Deborah Plummer; Dan Pope; Sebastian Purcell; Anne Raeff; Amanda Ripley; Sara Roahen; Barbara Roberts; Victoria L. Roberts; Craig Ross; John J. Ross; David Rothkopf; Paul Rudnick; Laurie Ruettimann; Craig Russell; SHRM; Scott Sampson; R. Keith Sawyer; Bradley Schurman; Josh Seiden; Jens Martin Skibsted; Marc Solomon; Mathew Sweezey; Sarah Stewart Taylor; Jennifer Tosti-Kharas; Terence Tse; Michael Veltri; Marga Vicedo; Tom Vossler; Michael Wade; Tony Wagner; John Wass; Luc Wathieu; Holly Watt; Thomas Wedell-Wedellsborg; Dan Willingham; Everett Worthington; Tomoko Yokoi; Hester Young; Sergey Young; Howard Yu; Dan Zehr

L290 Harold Ober Associates, Inc.

Literary Agency
286 Madison Avenue, 10th Floor, New York, NY 10017
United States
Tel: +1 (212) 759-8600

contact@haroldober.com

https://www.haroldober.com

Fiction > *Novels*

Nonfiction > *Nonfiction Books*

Closed to approaches.

Describes itself as one of the most storied and celebrated literary agencies in the country, representing some of the most iconic authors of the 20th Century.

Literary Agency: Richard Curtis Associates, Inc. (**L524**)

L291 Logan Harper

Literary Agent
United States

https://www.janerotrosen.com/agents

Literary Agency: Jane Rotrosen Agency

Fiction > *Novels*
Book Club Fiction; Crime; Domestic Suspense; Horror; Literary; Mystery; Psychological Thrillers; Upmarket; Women's Fiction

Send: Query
How to send: Online contact form

Seeking a variety of character-driven fiction and is particularly drawn to women's fiction, book club fiction, psychological thrillers, domestic suspense, horror, mystery/crime, upmarket and literary fiction. She is always eager to read and champion underrepresented voices and perspectives.

L292 Erin Harris

Literary Agent; Vice President
United States

eharris@foliolitmanagement.com

https://www.publishersmarketplace.com/members/eharris/
https://twitter.com/ErinHarrisFolio

Literary Agency: Folio Literary Management, LLC
Professional Body: Association of American Literary Agents (AALA)

ADULT

Fiction > *Novels*
Alternative History; Book Club Fiction; Contemporary; Fabulism; Fairy Tales; Family Saga; Folklore, Myths, and Legends; High Concept; Historical Fiction; Horror; Literary Mystery; Literary; Science Fiction; Suspense

Nonfiction > *Nonfiction Books*
High Concept; Memoir; Narrative Nonfiction

Poetry > *Poetry Collections*

YOUNG ADULT > **Fiction** > *Novels*
Contemporary; High Concept; Magic; Speculative; Suspense

Send: Query; Writing sample
How to send: In the body of an email

Passionate about books that interrogate our collective and personal histories with heart and intelligence; characters that make us feel and stories that make us think, even as they keep us feverishly turning pages; and book club and literary fiction that is high concept, whether it be contemporary, historical, or genre-bending (i.e. an accessible, elevated dash of fabulism, sci-fi, horror, suspense, alt. history, etc.)

L293 Jim Hart

Literary Agent
United States

jim@hartlineliterary.com

https://www.hartlineagency.com/agents-and-authors

Literary Agency: Hartline Literary Agency
(**L295**)

Fiction > *Novels*
Amish Romance; Contemporary Romance;
Historical Romance; Romance; Romantic
Suspense; Science Fiction; Speculative;
Suspense; Thrillers; Women's Fiction

Nonfiction > *Nonfiction Books*
Business; Christian Living; Leadership;
Parenting; Self Help; Social Issues

Send: Query; Proposal
How to send: Email attachment

Serves both Christian and general markets.
Currently most interested in non-fiction on the
topics of Christian living, church growth,
leadership, business, social issues, parenting,
and some self-help. Non-fiction writers will
need to show a strong platform in their area of
expertise. He is not looking at memoirs or
devotionals at this time.

Also looking at select fiction in these
categories: suspense/thrillers, romance
(contemporary, historical, suspense, Amish),
women's fiction, and some speculative and sci-
fi. Fiction writers should possess a strong and
growing platform. He is not looking at
children's or middle-grade fiction at this time.

Not looking at proposals for books that have
been previously self-published. Please do not
send proposals for books that include graphic
language and sex.

Authors: Mark Baker; Chaim Bentorah; Robin
Bertram; Shanna Brickell; Terri Clark;
Jacqueline Gillam Fairchild; William P.
Farley; Malinda Fuller; Heidi Gaul; PJ Gover;
John Gray; Brandy Heineman; Chaka Heinz;
Kim Taylor Henry; Bill Higgs; Dena Hobbs;
Jason Hobbs; Vivian Hyatt; Dalton Jantzen;
Vicki Jantzen; Gary Keel; Troy Kennedy;
Anita Knight Kuhnley; R.J. Larson; Joseph
Max Lewis; Kathi Macias; Vicki McCollum;
Stephenia McGee; Jairo de Oliveira; Kevin
Ott; Ava Pennington; R.K. Pillai; Leigh
Powers; Daniel Rhee; Penny Richards; Mary
Selzer; Laurel Shaler; Marc Sikma; Adam
Smith; Richard Spillman; John Stange; Buck
Storm; Leah Weber; Hope Welborn; Susan
Kimmel Wright; Beth Ann Ziarnik

L294 Joyce A. Hart
Literary Agent; President
United States

joyce@hartlineliterary.com

http://hartlineliteraryagency.blogspot.com

Literary Agency: Hartline Literary Agency
(**L295**)

Fiction > *Novels*: Inspirational

Closed to approaches.

Over 35 years of experience marketing and
promoting books. A pioneer of selling high
quality fiction to the inspirational market.

Authors: Christy Barritt; Lorraine Beatty;
Molly Noble Bull; Peggy Byers; Daniel Carl;
Michael Carl; Dorothy Clark; Ace Collins;
Dawn Crandall; Lena Nelson Dooley; Birdie
Etchison; Suzanne Woods Fisher; Lisa
Godfrees; Jeenie Gordon; Anne Greene;
Pamela Griffin; Eleanor Gustafson; Ann
Guyer; Lisa Harris; Sandra M. Hart; Rebecca
Jepson; Melanie M. Jeschke; Mary Johnson;
Jane Kirkpatrick; Zoe M. McCarthy; Rebekah
Montgomery; Pola Marie Muzyka; Darrel
Nelson; Melissa Ohden; Susan Titus Osborne;
Carrie Fancett Pagels; Sam D. Pakan; Susan J.
Reinhardt; Rita A. Schulte; Stacie Ruth
Stoelting; Ward Tanneberg; Diana Taylor;
Margorie Vawter; Jacqueline Wheelock;
Nancy Willich; Courtney Young

L295 Hartline Literary Agency
Literary Agency
United States
Tel: +1 (412) 829-2483

http://www.hartlineliterary.com

Fiction > *Novels*

Nonfiction > *Nonfiction Books*

Costs: Offers services that writers have to pay
for.

Specialises in Christian bookseller market, and
particularly interested in adult fiction,
nutritional, business, devotional, and self-help.
No short fiction, screenplays, scripts, poetry,
magazine articles, science fiction, fantasy,
extraordinary violence, unnecessary profanity,
gratuitous sexuality, or material that conflicts
with the Christian worldview. Probably not the
right agency for literary fiction, either. See
website for detailed submission guidelines.

Note that this agency also offers literary
services, which may be considered a conflict of
interests.

Author / Editor / Literary Agent: Patricia
Riddle-Gaddis (**L527**)

Author / Editor / Literary Agent / Proofreader:
Linda S. Glaz (**L251**)

Author / Literary Agent: Cyle Young

Authors: Karla Akins; Mark Baker; Rick
Barry; Chaim Bentorah; Robin Bertram; Kate
Breslin; Shanna Brickell; Lance Brown;
DeAngelo Burse; Raquel Byrnes; J'nell
Ciesielski; Terri Clark; David E. Clarke; Karen
Condit; Ben Conlon; Angela Couch; Susan F.
Craft; Rhonda Dragomir; Jacqueline Gillam
Fairchild; William P. Farley; Barbara Ellin
Fox; Malinda Fuller; Heidi Gaul; Linda
Gilden; Nicole Faye Golden; Samantha
Gomolka; PJ Gover; John Gray; Janet Grunst;
Hilary Hamblin Voni Harris; Julie Hatch;
Brandy Heineman; Chaka Heinz; Kim Taylor

Henry; Bill Higgs; Dena Hobbs; Jason Hobbs;
K Denise Holmberg; Vivian Hyatt; Dalton
Jantzen; Vicki Jantzen; Gary Keel; Troy
Kennedy; Anita Knight Kuhnley; Dennis
Lambert; R.J. Larson; Julie Lavender; A. D.
Lawrence; Joseph Max Lewis; Delores
Liesner; Ashley Ludwig; Kathi Macias; Jessica
Manfre; Merliyn Howton Marriott; Cheryl
Linn Martin; Joy Massenburge; Vicki
McCollum; Dale McElhinney; Stephenia
McGee; Donna Mumma; Naomi Musch; Luke
Negron; Jessica Nelson Tiffany Nicole; Jairo
de Oliveira; Kevin Ott; Candice Patterson; Ava
Pennington; Carmen Peone; R.K. Pillai; Leigh
Powers; Karen Prough; DeBora Rachelle;
Maria Reed; Cindy Regnier; Daniel Rhee;
Michael Richard; Penny Richards; Kathleen
Rouser; Susan Browning Schulz; Colleen
Scott; Mary Selzer; Laurel Shaler; Marc
Sikma; Adam Smith; Laura Smith; Richard
Spillman; Debbie Sprinkle; John Stange;
Donnie Steven; Donnie Stevens; Patti
Stockdale; Buck Storm; Beth Summitt; Ken
Swarner; Tiffany Tajiri; Donn Taylor Evelyn
Taylor; Pegg Thomas; Tom Threadgill; Kari
Trumbo; Susan L. Tuttle; Jennifer Uhlarik;
Hannah Vanderpool; Leah Weber; Denise
Weimer; Karen Wingate; Maureen Wise;
Susan Kimmel Wright; Frank Yates

Editor / Literary Agent: Diana Flegal (**L224**)

Literary Agent: Jim Hart (**L293**)

Literary Agent / President: Joyce A. Hart
(**L294**)

L296 Hilary Harwell
Literary Agent
United States

https://ktliterary.com/submissions/
https://www.manuscriptwishlist.com/mswl-
post/hilary-harwell/
https://querymanager.com/query/
HilaryHarwell

Literary Agency: KT Literary (**L368**)

CHILDREN'S > **Fiction**
*Chapter Books; Graphic Novels; Middle
Grade; Picture Books*
YOUNG ADULT > **Fiction** > *Novels*

Closed to approaches.

Seeking picture books, chapter books, graphic
novels, middle grade and young adult fiction.

L297 Jack Haug
Associate Agent
United States

Literary Agency: Aevitas

L298 Susan Hawk
Literary Agent
United States

susanhawk.submission@gmail.com

http://www.upstartcrowliterary.com/agent/
susan-hawk/
https://twitter.com/@susanhawk

Literary Agency: Upstart Crow Literary

CHILDREN'S
Fiction
Chapter Books; Middle Grade; Picture Books
Nonfiction > *Nonfiction Books*

TEEN > **Fiction** > *Novels*

YOUNG ADULT > **Fiction** > *Novels*

Closed to approaches.

Represents work for children and teens only: picture books, chapter books, middle grade, and young adult, along with some non-fiction for young readers. She doesn't represent adult projects.

L299 Molly Ker Hawn
Literary Agent; Managing Director
United Kingdom

hawnqueries@thebentagency.com

http://www.thebentagency.com/molly-ker-hawn
http://www.twitter.com/mollykh
https://www.publishersmarketplace.com/members/mkhawn

Literary Agency: The Bent Agency (UK) (**L057**)

CHILDREN'S
Fiction
Graphic Novels; Middle Grade
Nonfiction > *Nonfiction Books*

YOUNG ADULT > **Fiction**
Graphic Novels; Novels

Closed to approaches.

I'm looking for middle grade and young adult fiction and graphic novels that are inventive, well-crafted, and rich with emotion. I'm also interested in non-fiction for readers ages 8–18. I like wit, but not snark; I prefer books that lean more toward literary than commercial, but of course, my perfect book neatly bridges the two. The fiction on my list all has a strong sense of authentic place, whether real or imaginary; I'm not the right agent for books with animal protagonists. Except maybe cats.

L300 David H. Headley
Literary Agent; Managing Director
United Kingdom

submission@dhhliteraryagency.com

http://www.dhhliteraryagency.com/david-h-headley.html
https://twitter.com/davidhheadley

Literary Agency: DHH Literary Agency Ltd (**L167**)

Fiction > *Novels*

General, and in particular: Crime; High Concept; Suspense; Thrillers

Nonfiction > *Nonfiction Books*
Biography; Food; History; Memoir; Politics; Popular Culture; Science

Send: Query; Synopsis; Writing sample
How to send: Email

Actively looking for: character-driven debuts and epic sweeping stories with big universal themes. Issue-driven crime and thrillers, high concepts and fear-inducing suspense. Thought-provoking stories, original narrative voices, uplifting fiction and emotional journeys – "stories that I don't want to end". Also accepts non-fiction submissions, from memoir, biography and history to politics, science, popular culture and food.

Authors: Kishan Devani BEM; Graham Bartlett; R.C. Bridgestock; Tom Brown; Paul Burston; Andrea Carter; Paul Fraser Collard; James Conway; M.W. Craven; John Curran; A. A. Dhand; David Fennell; Fishlove; Essie Fox; Anita Frank; Erin Green; Lisa Hilton; Ragnar Jonasson; Katrín Júlíusdóttir; Sean Lusk; Adrian Magson; Chris McDonald; Brian McGilloway; Janie Millman; Elizabeth S. Moore; Noel O'Reilly; Anthony J. Quinn; Robert Rutherford; Victoria Selman; Jo Thomas; L.C. Tyler; A. J. West; Clare Whitfield; Eva Björg Ægisdottir

L301 Chelsea Hensley
Associate Agent
United States

https://www.chelseahensley.com
https://ktliterary.com/agents
https://www.chelseahensley.com/mswl
https://querymanager.com/query/Chelseahensley

Literary Agency: KT Literary (**L368**)

ADULT > **Fiction** > *Novels*
Fantasy; Supernatural / Paranormal Horror

CHILDREN'S > **Fiction** > *Middle Grade*
Adventure; Fairy Tales; Fantasy; Folklore, Myths, and Legends; Historical Fiction; Mystery

YOUNG ADULT > **Fiction** > *Novels*
Contemporary Fantasy; Contemporary; Dark; Dystopian Fiction; Fantasy; High / Epic Fantasy; Historical Fiction; Mystery; Romance; Science Fiction; Thrillers

Closed to approaches.

In general, here are some of the things I love to see in a manuscript: Intricate plots and complex emotional arcs; Whipsmart protagonists who aren't afraid to get their hands dirty. There's nothing I love more than a main character who throws themselves into the thick of things and doesn't look back; Female friendship, partnerships, rivalries, and everything in between are high up on my

wishlist. Girls, girls, girls basically. I prefer narratives to be female driven, and I'd love to see more F/F romantic pairings; I'm a big fan of spies, assassins, thieves and other rogue-ish characters; I love, love, love heists; and I'd love to see some great antiheroes or characters embarking on redemption arcs.

L302 Paloma Hernando
Associate Agent
United States

submissions@einsteinliterary.com

https://www.einsteinliterary.com/staff/
https://twitter.com/AgentPaloma

Literary Agency: Einstein Literary Management (**L190**)

ADULT
Fiction
Graphic Novels: High / Epic Fantasy; LGBTQIA; Magic; Romance; Science Fiction
Novels: High / Epic Fantasy; LGBTQIA; Magic; Romance; Science Fiction
Nonfiction > *Nonfiction Books*
General, and in particular: History; Media

CHILDREN'S
Fiction > *Middle Grade*: Comedy / Humour

Nonfiction > *Nonfiction Books*
General, and in particular: History; Media

YOUNG ADULT > **Fiction**
Graphic Novels: High / Epic Fantasy; LGBTQIA; Magic; Romance; Science Fiction
Novels: High / Epic Fantasy; LGBTQIA; Magic; Romance; Science Fiction

Send: Query; Writing sample
How to send: In the body of an email
How not to send: Email attachment

Her favorite books often have a bit of magic in them, and she loves being able to dive into any world, real or invented, presented on the page. She is looking for both graphic novels and prose fiction for YA or adult, including more mature stories, particularly ones that deal with difficult emotions and nuanced characters. She loves romance, particularly queer romance, science fiction that feels fresh, high fantasy, and middle grade with a good sense of humor. She is interested in non-fiction for all ages, especially anything that digs into media analysis or an event in history. She loves a story with a strong voice and solid construction.

L303 Danny Hertz
Literary Agent
United States

Literary Agency: The Cheney Agency

L304 Lane Heymont
President; Literary Agent
United States

https://www.thetobiasagency.com/lane-heymont
https://querymanager.com/query/1291
http://aaronline.org/Sys/PublicProfile/27203936/417813

Literary Agency: The Tobias Literary Agency (**L614**)
Professional Body: Association of American Literary Agents (AALA)

ADULT
  Fiction > *Novels*
    Commercial; Horror

  Nonfiction > *Nonfiction Books*
    Celebrity; Culture; History; Popular Culture; Science

YOUNG ADULT > **Fiction** > *Novels*: Horror

Send: Author bio; Query; Market info; Writing sample
How to send: Query Manager

Represents a broad range of commercial fiction and serious nonfiction. In fiction, he is especially interested in projects broadly defined as horror. This includes select young adult horror. He is always looking for projects by underrepresented voices both in horror, fiction in general, and nonfiction. In nonfiction, he focuses on the sciences, cultural studies, history, pop-culture, and celebrity projects.

L305 HG Literary
Literary Agency
6 West 18TH Street, Suite 7R, New York, NY 10011
United States

https://www.hgliterary.com
https://twitter.com/hgliterary
http://instagram.com/hgliterary

Associate Agents: Jon Cobb; Ellen Goff (**L259**)

Literary Agent / Vice President: Soumeya Bendimerad Roberts (**L531**)

Literary Agents: Victoria Wells Arms (**L031**); Julia Kardon (**L341**); Rhea Lyons (**L407**)

Literary Agents / Partners: Josh Getzler (**L246**); Carrie Hannigan (**L284**)

L306 Victoria Hobbs
Literary Agent
United Kingdom

https://amheath.com/agents/victoria-hobbs/
http://twitter.com/victoriajhobbs

Literary Agency: A.M. Heath & Company Limited, Author's Agents (**L002**)

Fiction > *Novels*
  General, and in particular: Crime; Thrillers

Nonfiction > *Nonfiction Books*
  General, and in particular: Cookery; Food; Health; Narrative Nonfiction; Nature; Politics

Agency Assistant: Jessica Lee

L307 Jodie Hodges
Literary Agent
United Kingdom
Tel: +44 (0) 20 3214 0891

jhodges@unitedagents.co.uk

https://www.unitedagents.co.uk/jhodgesunitedagentscouk
http://twitter.com/jodiehodges31

Literary Agency: United Agents (**L619**)

CHILDREN'S > **Fiction**
  Comics: General
  Graphic Novels: General
  Middle Grade: Adventure; Comedy / Humour; Domestic; Fantasy; Historical Fiction
  Picture Books: General

Send: Query; Synopsis; Writing sample; Full text
How to send: Email attachment
How not to send: Post

I'll always be keen to see classic storytelling for 8-12s be it an adventure, a fantasy, historical, domestic, a comedy. Anything and everything to appeal to the both the voracious child reader I was and those children for whom books aren't an everyday part of life. Additionally, I'm always searching for children's book illustrators or writer/illustrators who know their own style and are attuned to the children's book market. I also represent creators of comics and graphic novels for children and very happy to see more.

Associate Agent: Molly Jamieson (**L323**)

Literary Agent: Emily Talbot (**L605**)

L308 Scott Hoffman
Literary Agent; Partner
United States

shoffman@foliolitmanagement.com

https://www.foliolit.com/agents-1/scott-hoffman

Literary Agency: Folio Literary Management, LLC

Nonfiction > *Nonfiction Books*
  Business; Fitness; Health; History; Psychology; Social Issues; Wellbeing

Closed to approaches.

Send query by email with first ten pages. Assume rejection if no response within six weeks.

L309 Penny Holroyde
Literary Agent
United Kingdom

penny@holroydecartey.com

https://www.holroydecartey.com/about.html
https://www.holroydecartey.com/submissions.html

Literary Agency: Holroyde Cartey

CHILDREN'S
  Fiction
    Board Books; Chapter Books; Early Readers; Middle Grade; Picture Books
  Nonfiction > *Nonfiction Books*

Send: Synopsis; Full text
How to send: Email attachment

I've worked in publishing for nearly thirty years at publishers Walker Books in the UK and Candlewick Press in the US and then as an agent with Caroline Sheldon. I have a particular love for the picture book but am looking for authors and illustrators working across fiction and non-fiction for all ages.

L310 Vanessa Holt
Literary Agent
United Kingdom

v.holt791@btinternet.com

Literary Agency: Vanessa Holt Ltd (**L623**)

L311 Sarah Hornsley
Literary Agent
United Kingdom

shornsley@pfd.co.uk

https://petersfraserdunlop.com/agent/sarah-hornsley/
https://twitter.com/SarahHornsley

Literary Agency: Peters Fraser + Dunlop (**L501**)

Fiction > *Novels*
  Book Club Fiction; Commercial; Crime; High Concept; Historical Fiction; Romantic Comedy; Thrillers; Upmarket

Closed to approaches.

Represents authors across commercial and upmarket / reading group fiction and is actively looking for new writers. She is drawn to high concept hooks with brilliant writing and compulsive plots, and is on the lookout for original and unputdownable crime and thrillers, complex relatable female characters, sweeping love stories, hooky modern rom coms and historical fiction. She loves novels that start conversations and characters who stay with you long after you've turned the last page. She is looking for new clients across all genres. If you've written a book with fantastic characters and a well-paced plot, then she may well be the agent for you!

Authors: Claire Ackroyd; Ciara Attwell; Olivia Beirne; Roxie Cooper; Philippa East; Anstey Harris; Emma Heatherington; Emily Houghton; Becky Hunter; Lynsey James; Fionnuala Kearney; Gina Lamanna; Jo Lovett; Ali Pantony; Polly Phillips; Jessica Ryn; Emily Stone; Tim Sullivan; Russ Thomas; Rachel Ward; Helen Whitaker; S.M. Wilson

L312 Millie Hoskins

Associate Agent
United Kingdom

https://www.unitedagents.co.uk/
mhoskinsunitedagentscouk

Literary Agency: United Agents (**L619**)

Fiction > *Novels*
  Commercial; Historical Fiction; Literary; Thrillers; Upmarket; Women's Fiction

Nonfiction > *Nonfiction Books*
  Memoir; Narrative Nonfiction

Send: Synopsis; Writing sample; Proposal
How to send: Email

On the lookout for exciting debut authors of both commercial and literary upmarket fiction of any genre (excluding SFF), with a particular focus on women's fiction, thrillers and historical fiction. Especially interested in finding more great zeitgeist novels for our generation and discovering new experiences and places through people's writing. With regards to non-fiction, largely drawn to memoirs and narrative non-fiction with a distinct writing style, an incredible story, or an underrepresented voice or topic.

Authors: Amrou Al-Kadhi; Hina Belitz; LMK Berry; Sophie Ellis Bextor; Quentin Blake; Maggie Brookes; Emma Campbell; Brian Catling; Jessie Cave; Leah Cowan; JP Delaney; Rebecca Gibb; Susannah Hoffman; Alison Irvine; Lenka Janiurek; Katie Kirby; James McNicholas; Coco Mellors; Michelle Morgan; Bobby Palmer; Philip Pullman; Talulah Riley; LJ Ross; Kate Saunders; Mika Simmons

L313 Valerie Hoskins

Literary Agent
United Kingdom

Literary Agency: Valerie Hoskins Associates

L314 Clare Hulton

Literary Agent
United Kingdom

Literary Agency: Clare Hulton Literary Agency

L315 Annie Hwang

Literary Agent
United States

https://twitter.com/AnnieAHwang
https://www.publishersmarketplace.com/
members/hwangan/

Literary Agency: Ayesha Pande Literary (**L038**)

Fiction > *Novels*: Literary

Nonfiction > *Nonfiction Books*: Narrative Nonfiction

Poetry > *Poetry Collections*

Send: Pitch; Author bio; Synopsis; Writing sample
How to send: Online submission system

Primarily represents voice-driven literary fiction that plays with genre, though she also takes on nonfiction and poetry on occasion. In particular, she is drawn to what she likes to think of as "literary fiction with teeth"— ambitious novels that are daring in their approach that also grapple with the complexities of the world with nuance and finesse.

L316 ILA (Intercontinental Literary Agency)

Literary Agency
10 Waterloo Court, Theed Street, London, SE1 8ST
United Kingdom
Tel: +44 (0) 20 7379 6611

ila@ila-agency.co.uk

http://www.ila-agency.co.uk

Professional Body: The Association of Authors' Agents (AAA)

ADULT
  Fiction in Translation > *Novels*
  Nonfiction in Translation > *Nonfiction Books*

CHILDREN'S > **Fiction in Translation** > *Novels*

Closed to approaches.

Handles translation rights only for, among others, the authors of LAW Ltd, London; Harold Matson Co. Inc., New York; PFD, London. Submissions accepted via client agencies and publishers only – no submissions from writers seeking agents.

Company Director / Literary Agent:
Clementine Ahearne (**L012**)

Literary Agents: Nicki Kennedy; Jenny Robson; Katherine West

L317 Independent Talent Group Ltd

Literary Agency
40 Whitfield Street, London, W1T 2RH
United Kingdom
Tel: +44 (0) 20 7636 6565

writersubmissions@independenttalent.com

http://www.independenttalent.com

Scripts

Film Scripts; Radio Scripts; TV Scripts; Theatre Scripts

Send: Author bio
How to send: By referral

Specialises in scripts and works in association with agencies in Los Angeles and New York.

Author: Hazel Kyle

Literary Agents: Oliver Azis; Anwar Chentoufi; Patrick Child (*L117*); Francesca Devas; Alec Drysdale; Humphrey Elles-Hill; Olivia Gray; Duncan Heath; Greg Hunt; Jago Irwin; Georgia Kanner; Paul Lyon-Maris; Michael McCoy; Jennie Miller; Ikenna Obiekwe; Will Peterson; Lyndsey Posner; Sue Rodgers; Laura Rourke; Alex Rusher; Paul Stevens; Jessica Stewart; Jessica Sykes; Jack Thomas; Sarah Williams; Hugo Young

L318 Inscriptions Literary Agency

Literary Agency
United States
Tel: +1 (636) 633-7846

https://inscriptionsliterary.com
https://querymanager.com/query/
InscriptionsLit_Query

ADULT
  Fiction > *Novels*
  General, and in particular: Christian Romance; Contemporary Romance; Hardboiled Crime; Mystery; Science Fiction; Suspense

  Nonfiction > *Nonfiction Books*
  Christianity; Crime; Memoir

  Scripts > *Film Scripts*

CHILDREN'S > **Fiction**
  Middle Grade; Picture Books

Does not want:

> **CHILDREN'S** > **Fiction** > *Middle Grade*
> Dark Magic; Gender Issues; Science Fiction; Voodoo; Witchcraft

Send: Query; Synopsis; Writing sample; Full text; Pitch
How to send: Query Manager; Email

A boutique literary agency which offers representation services to authors who are both published and pre-published. Our mission is to form strong partnerships with our clients and build long-term relationships that extend from writing the first draft through the entire length of the author's career.

What is a boutique literary agency? A small, but mighty agency that has less than 12 agents. We specialize in quality, not quantity. We limit the amount of clients we take on, in order to give each client our full attention.

We are not looking for books containing: political agenda, controversies, AI content, alternative religion books, books labeled "Christian" that do not follow the standards of the Bible, Sci-Fi-Christian, illustrated children's books.

We are not looking for: Erotic, board books, baby or toddler books, lyrical books, SEL books, or topics in children's books that contradict basic Christian standards. We believe Christian values should always be portrayed in Children's fiction.

Submit literary submissions via QueryManager. Submit pitches for screenplay representation by email.

Literary Agent: Andrea Comparato (**L132**)

L319 Lucy Irvine
Literary Agent
United Kingdom
Tel: +44 (0) 20 7344 1087

lirvine@pfd.co.uk

https://petersfraserdunlop.com/agent/lucy-irvine/

Literary Agency: Peters Fraser + Dunlop (**L501**)

ADULT > **Fiction** > *Novels*
Fantasy; Science Fiction

CHILDREN'S > **Fiction**
Chapter Books: General
Early Readers: General
Middle Grade: General, and in particular: Adventure; Commercial; Folklore, Myths, and Legends
Picture Books: General, and in particular: Comedy / Humour
YOUNG ADULT > **Fiction** > *Novels*
Fantasy; Historical Fiction; Romance; Science Fiction; Thrillers

Does not want:

> Fiction > *Novels*: Grimdark

Send: Query; Synopsis; Writing sample; Proposal; Author bio
How to send: Email

My taste is generally very broad; I represent anything that falls under the Childrens umbrella, from picture books to YA, as well as Science Fiction and Fantasy in the Adult market.

I'm being very selective with the picture books I take on at the moment, but am particularly looking here for funny stories with returnable potential and unexpected twists on popular themes.

My taste in middle-grade books veers towards the commercial; I'm drawn to quick-paced, adventurous narratives with series potential. I love stories set in worlds that pull you in and stay with you long after you've finished reading, and am particularly keen to see original worldbuilding and hooky, plot driven narratives. I would love to find something in the vein of Maria Kuznair's The Ship of Shadows or B.B. Alston's Amari and the Night Brothers. I'm also very drawn to reimagined folktales, myths, and legends, especially from voices traditionally less represented within publishing. Some middle-grade books I grew up on and adored include The Roman Mysteries, the Chronicles of Ancient Darkness, and the Percy Jackson series.

On the YA side, I love all kinds of genre fiction, from fantasy to historical to romance to thriller. I'm drawn to romances with a twist, and am particularly looking here for diverse voices and protagonists. SFF wise I'm keen to see original world-building, and love anything that genre bends or offers a fresh take on traditional themes. A few YA books I've recently loved include Hani and Ishu's Guide to Fake Dating, The Upper World, and (belatedly!) Aristotle and Dante Discover the Secrets of the Universe. I am a perpetual fan of enemies/rivals to lovers, fake-dating, found-family, unexpected friendships, and platonic love stories.

Adult wise, I accept submissions in anything that falls under the SFF umbrella, from urban to epic fantasy, from space opera to steampunk, but am not the right person for anything too grimdark, or anything with graphic sexual violence. I would love to find something with the ambition and wit of Gideon the Ninth, or the scope and narrative-weaving of The Priory of the Orange Tree.

I am always looking for diverse writers and protagonists across race, sexuality, gender, and disability.

Across the board, I'd love to find stories with casts of characters that make me feel as much as the Stranger Things characters make me feel (which is, to say, a lot).

I try to respond to queries within eight weeks of submission, however, if you've had no response by then please assume it's a rejection.

Authors: Sunita Chawdhary; Katie Dale; Judith Eagle; Ava Eldred; Rowan Foxwood; Tessa Gearing; William Goldsmith; Norma Gregory; Lindsay Hirst; Lexy Hudson; Lis Jardine; Aneesa Marufu; Daphne Olive; Simji Park; Anna Quirke; Emily Randall; Laila Rifaat; Ali Stegert; Sam Stewart; Sarah Street; Gail Upchurch; Catherine Ward; Alison Weatherby; Melissa Welliver

L320 Dotti Irving
Literary Agent
United Kingdom

dotti@greyhoundliterary.co.uk

https://greyhoundliterary.co.uk/agents/dotti-irving

Literary Agency: Greyhound Literary (**L271**)

Nonfiction > *Nonfiction Books*: Narrative Nonfiction

Send: Query; Synopsis; Writing sample
How to send: Email

Primarily interested in narrative non-fiction, in books that tell a story that rings true and speaks to a wider world.

L321 Rachel Jacobson
Literary Agent
United States

https://aliveliterary.com/about/

Literary Agency: Alive Literary Agency (**L018**)

Nonfiction > *Nonfiction Books*

How to send: By referral

Enjoys helping authors hone their ideas, tap into their generative creativity, and share their message—because she wholeheartedly believes books can be a positive force for good in the world.

L322 The James Fitzgerald Agency
Literary Agency
PO Box 940, 70 Irish Road, Ranchos de Taos, NM 87557
United States
Tel: +1 (575) 758-2687

submissions@jfitzagency.com

https://jfitzagency.com

ADULT
  Fiction > *Novels*
    Crime; Popular Culture

  Nonfiction
    Illustrated Books: Popular Culture
    Nonfiction Books: Adventure; Biography; Crime; Films; Food; History; Memoir; Music; Popular Culture; Religion; Socio-Political; Spirituality; Sport; TV
CHILDREN'S > **Fiction** > *Novels*

YOUNG ADULT > **Fiction** > *Novels*

Send: Full text; Synopsis; Author bio; Market info
How to send: Email attachment

Primarily represents books reflecting the popular culture of the day, in fiction, nonfiction, graphic and packaged books. No poetry or screenplays. All information must be submitted in English, even if the manuscript is in another language. See website for detailed submission guidelines.

Editorial Assistant: Anna Tatelman

L323 Molly Jamieson

Associate Agent
United Kingdom
Tel: +44 (0) 20 3214 0973

mjamieson@unitedagents.co.uk

https://www.unitedagents.co.uk/
mjamiesonunitedagentscouk

Literary Agency: United Agents (**L619**)
Literary Agent: Jodie Hodges (**L307**)

ADULT > **Fiction** > *Novels*
Commercial; Fantasy; Romance; Science
Fiction

CHILDREN'S > **Fiction** > *Novels*
Fantasy; Science Fiction

Send: Query; Synopsis; Writing sample
How to send: Email

Has a particular interest in scifi and fantasy
across both adult and children's books. She
loves anything with high stakes, characters you
would follow anywhere, big stories, expansive
worldbuilding, breathless romance, and threads
of adventure running throughout. She is also
looking for commercial romantic fiction in all
shapes and forms. She has a real soft spot for
classic tropes, a great sense of humour, and
anything with a clear pitch that makes you sit
up and take notice, but in the end it all comes
down to chemistry. Please send a cover letter,
synopsis, and first three chapters by email.

Author Estates: The Estate of Algernon
Blackwood; The Estate of Rafael Sabatini

Authors: Jackson P. Brown; John Chalmers;
Olivia Collard; Guy Haley; Hannah-Marie
Holwell; Arden Jones; Sandra Marrs; Christine
Modafferi; Aimee Oliver; Melissa Powell

L324 Janklow & Nesbit UK Ltd

Literary Agency
66-67 Newman Street, Fitzrovia, London,
W1T 3EQ
United Kingdom
Tel: +44 (0) 20 7243 2975

submissions@janklow.co.uk

http://www.janklowandnesbit.co.uk
https://twitter.com/JanklowUK

Professional Body: The Association of
Authors' Agents (AAA)

ADULT
Fiction > *Novels*
General, and in particular: Commercial;
Literary

Nonfiction > *Nonfiction Books*

CHILDREN'S > **Fiction** > *Novels*

YOUNG ADULT > **Fiction** > *Novels*

Send: Query; Synopsis; Writing sample
How to send: Email

Send query by email, including informative
covering letter providing background about

yourself and your writing; first three chapters /
approx. 50 pages; a brief synopsis for fiction,
or a full outline for nonfiction.

Literary Agents: Claire Paterson Conrad
(**L135**); Will Francis

L325 The Jeff Herman Agency, LLC

Literary Agency
PO Box 1522, Stockbridge, MA 01262
United States
Tel: +1 (413) 298-0077

submissions@jeffherman.com
Jeff@Jeffherman.com

https://jeffherman.com

Nonfiction
Nonfiction Books: Business; Crime; Health;
History; How To; Memoir; Multicultural;
Narrative Nonfiction; Parenting; Psychology;
Self Help; Spirituality
Reference: General

Send: Query; Pitch
Don't send: Proposal; Full text
How to send: Email; Post

Send query by post with SASE. With few
exceptions, handles nonfiction only, with
particular interest in the genres given above.
No scripts or unsolicited MSS.

Literary Agents: Deborah Levine Herman; Jeff
Herman

L326 JetReid Literary Agency

Literary Agency
151 1st Ave #257, New York, NY 10003
United States

http://www.jetreidliterary.com

Authors: Robin Becker; Bill Cameron; Gary
Corby; Phillip DePoy; Stephanie Evans;
Kennedy Foster; Lee Goodman; Dana Haynes;
Patrick Lee; Thomas Lippman; Jeff Marks;
Warren Richey; Terry Shames; Jeff Somers;
Robert Stubblefield; Deb Vlock

Literary Agent: Janet Reid

L327 JFL Agency

Literary Agency
48 Charlotte Street, London, W1T 2NS
United Kingdom
Tel: +44 (0) 20 3137 8182

representation@jflagency.com
agents@jflagency.com

http://www.jflagency.com

Scripts
Film Scripts; *Radio Scripts*; *TV Scripts*;
Theatre Scripts

Send: Query
How to send: Email

Handles scripts only (for television, film,
theatre and radio). Considers approaches from

established writers with broadcast experience,
but only accepts submissions from new writers
during specific periods – consult website for
details.

Authors: Humphrey Barclay; Liam Beirne;
Adam Bostock-Smith; Tim Brooke-Taylor; Ian
Brown; Grant Cathro; Paul Charlton; Gabby
Hutchinson Crouch; Bill Dare; Tim Dawson;
Martin Day; Ed Dyson; Polly Eden; Jan
Etherington; Sinéad Fagan; Anji Loman Field;
Phil Ford; Patrick Gallagher; Ted Gannon;
Lisa Gifford; Rob Gittins; Ben Harris; James
Hendrie; Wayne Jackman; Tony Lee; Richard
Leslie Lewis; Jane Marlow; Jonathan Morris;
Cardy O'Donnell; Jim Pullin; Jackie Robb;
Graeme Rooney; Gary Russell; David Semple;
James Serafinowicz; Pete Sinclair; Paul Smith;
Fraser Steele

Literary Agents: Alison Finch (**L218**); Dominic
Lord (**L400**); Gary Wild (**L649**)

L328 Jo Unwin Literary Agency

Literary Agency
Somerset House, West Wing, London, WC2R
1LA
United Kingdom
Tel: +44 (0) 20 7257 9599

info@jounwin.co.uk
submissions@jounwin.co.uk

http://www.jounwin.co.uk

Professional Body: The Association of
Authors' Agents (AAA)

ADULT
Fiction > *Novels*
Nonfiction > *Nonfiction Books*

CHILDREN'S > **Fiction** > *Novels*

YOUNG ADULT > **Fiction** > *Novels*

How to send: Email

Handles literary fiction, commercial women's
fiction, comic writing, narrative nonfiction,
Young Adult fiction and fiction for children
aged 9+. No poetry, picture books, or
screenplays, except for existing clients.
Accepts submissions by email. Mainly
represents authors from the UK and Ireland,
and sometimes Australia and New Zealand.
Only represents US authors in very exceptional
circumstances. See website for full guidelines.

Authors: Heather Akumiah; Zoe Beaty; Soraya
Bouazzaoui; Wibke Brueggemann; Fran
Bushe; Darren Chetty; Eliza Clark; Ellie
Clements; Lucy Cuthew; Caleb Femi; Mark
Grist; Jade LB; Janelle McCurdy; Jack
Meggitt-Phillips; Catriona Morton; Gary
Panton; Gianna Pollero; Bethany Rutter;
Angharad Walker

Literary Agents: Donna Greaves; Rachel Mann
(**L419**); Milly Reilly; Jo Unwin (*L621*)

L329 Joelle Delbourgo Associates, Inc.

Literary Agency
101 Park St., Montclair, Montclair, NJ 07042
United States
Tel: +1 (973) 773-0836

submissions@delbourgo.com

https://www.delbourgo.com

ADULT

Fiction > *Novels*
Commercial; Fantasy; Literary; Mystery; Science Fiction; Thrillers; Women's Fiction

Nonfiction
Nonfiction Books: Biography; Cookery; Current Affairs; Food; Health; History; Memoir; Mind, Body, Spirit; Narrative Nonfiction; Parenting; Popular Culture; Psychology; Science
Reference: Popular

CHILDREN'S

Fiction
Middle Grade; Picture Books
Nonfiction > *Middle Grade*

YOUNG ADULT > **Fiction** > *Novels*

Send: Query; Writing sample; Synopsis
How to send: Email
How not to send: Phone

Costs: Author covers sundry admin costs.

A boutique literary agency based in the greater New York City area. We represent a wide range of authors writing for the adult trade market, from creative nonfiction to expert-driven nonfiction, commercial fiction to literary fiction, as well as middle grade fiction and nonfiction.

Authors: Tanya Acker; P. David Allen; Jennifer Lynn Alvarez; Heather Anastasiu; Lisa Anselmo; Thomas Armstrong; Sara Au; Frances Bartkowski; Audrey Bellezza; Waitman Beorn; Suzanne Bohan; Lynn Kiele Bonasia; Michele Borba; Robert Bornstein; Elizabeth Reid Boyd; Nora Bradbury-Haehl; Anne Greenwood Brown; Gay Browne; Ariel Burger; Susan Campbell; Craig Carlson; Paul Carter; Jill Castle; Debbie Cenziper; Rachael Cerrotti; Marj Charlier; John Christianson; Tara L. Clark; Gay Courter; Nancy Cowan; Katherine Scott Crawford; Michelle Dempsey-Multack; Karla Dougherty; Nancy Dreyfus; Rosa Kwon Easton; Charity Elder; Chris Farrell; Marilyn Fedewa; Michael Feuer; Laura Berman Fortgang; Susan Forward; Philip Freeman; Terry Gaspard; John Gaudet; Susan Gilbert-Collins; Ann E. Grant; Jonathon Grayson; Brenda Greene; Beth A. Grosshans; Julie L. Hall; Emily Harding; Kate Harding; Laura Hartema; Kristi Hedges; Holly Herrick; Roy Hoffman; Helaina Hovitz; Erik Forrest Jackson; Grace Jung; Theresa Kaminski; Rachelle Katz; Joseph Kelly; Stephen Kelly; Brynne S. Kennedy; Nancy Kennedy; Hilary Kinavey; Sean Kingsley; Willem Kuyken; Mary Languirand; Missy Chase Lapine; Claire Lerner; Irene S. Levine; Alexandra Levitt; Lisa L. Lewis; Mary Ann Little; Geralyn Lucas; Lauren Mackler; Juliet Madison; Kerstin March; David J. Marsh; Chuck Martin; Lama Marut; Carol Masciola; Roy Meals; Cristina Nehring; Nicola Nice; Jennifer O'Callaghan; Emily J. O'Dell; Colleen O'Grady; Jim Obergefell; Elaine Neil Orr; Lindsey J. Palmer; Theresa Payton; Michelle Pearce; Scott Peeples; Julia Pimsleur; Gleb Raygorodetsky; Eliza Redgold; Michael Reichert; James Renner; Ashley Rhodes-Courter; Paige Rien; Alexandra Rimer; Jillian Roberts; Tatsha Robertson; Lisa Romeo; Marilyn Simon Rothstein; Dale Russakoff; Michael Sadowski; Karla Salinari; Roberta Sandenbergh; Sue Scheff; Elisa A. Schmitz; Melissa Schorr; Ellen E. Schultz; Sara Sherbill; Heather Shumaker; Alexandra Silber; Pamela Slim; Joanna Sliwa; Christopher A. Snyder; Laura Sobiech; Julie M. Stamm; Peter L. Stavinoha; Maryon Stewart; Nancy Rubin Stuart; Dana Sturtevant; Deborah J. Swiss; Jeff Sypeck; Ericka Sóuter; John Temple; Christopher Van Tilburg; M.D. Usher; Julie Valerie; Rebecca Lynn Viera; Michael Volpatt; Caroline Welch; Susan Wels; Elizabeth White; Elizabeth "Barry" White; Kristin M. White; Barrie Wilson; Ben H. Winters; Jon Wuebben; Gabra Zackman; Peter Zheutlin; Gabe Zichermann

Literary Agents: Carrie Cantor; Joelle Delbourgo; Jacqueline Flynn

L330 Johnson & Alcock

Literary Agency
West Wing, Somerset House, Strand, London, WC2R 1LA
United Kingdom
Tel: +44 (0) 20 7251 0125

http://www.johnsonandalcock.co.uk

Professional Body: The Association of Authors' Agents (AAA)

Send: Query; Synopsis; Writing sample
How to send: Email attachment
How not to send: Post

Send query by email to specific agent. Response only if interested. Include synopsis and first three chapters (approximately 50 pages).

Company Directors / Literary Agents: Andrew Hewson; Ed Wilson (**L656**)

Literary Agent / Managing Director: Anna Power (**L511**)

Literary Agents: Michael Alcock (**L014**); Charlotte Seymour (**L564**)

L331 Jonathan Clowes Ltd

Literary Agency
United Kingdom
Tel: +44 (0) 20 7722 7674

admin@jonathanclowes.co.uk

https://www.jonathanclowes.co.uk

Professional Body: The Association of Authors' Agents (AAA)

Fiction > *Novels*

Nonfiction > *Nonfiction Books*

Send: Query; Synopsis; Writing sample
How to send: Email
How not to send: Post

Send query with synopsis and three chapters (or equivalent sample) by email.

Authors: Frances Bingham; Jonas Claesson; Simon Critchley; Maureen Duffy; Ewan Fernie; Brian Freemantle; Miles Gibson; Rana Haddad; Francesca Hornak; David Llewellyn; Kirsten MacGillivray; Mohamed Mesrati; Kirsten Norrie; David Quantick; Gruff Rhys; Toby Vieira; Barbara Voors

Literary Agents: Ann Evans; Nemonie Craven Roderick

L332 Jonathan Pegg Literary Agency

Literary Agency
c/o Workshop, 47 Southgate Street, Winchester, SO23 9EH
United Kingdom
Tel: +44 (0) 1962 656101

submissions@jonathanpegg.com
info@jonathanpegg.com

https://jonathanpegg.com

Professional Body: The Association of Authors' Agents (AAA)

Fiction > *Novels*
Historical Fiction; Literary; Suspense; Thrillers; Upmarket

Nonfiction
Gift Books: Comedy / Humour
Nonfiction Books: Biography; Business; Comedy / Humour; Current Affairs; History; Lifestyle; Memoir; Nature; Popular Psychology; Popular Science

Send: Query; Synopsis; Author bio; Market info; Writing sample
How to send: Email

Aims to read every submission and respond within a month, but cannot guarantee to do so in all cases.

Literary Agent: Jonathan Pegg

L333 Barbara Jones

Literary Agent
United States

bjquery@skagency.com

http://skagency.com/submission-guidelines/

Literary Agency: Stuart Krichevsky Literary Agency, Inc. (**L596**)

How to send: Email

L334 Philip Gwyn Jones
Literary Agent
United Kingdom

https://greyhoundliterary.co.uk/agents/philip-gwyn-jones
https://twitter.com/PGJPublishing

Literary Agency: Greyhound Literary (**L271**)

Fiction > *Novels*

Thirty-three years of experience as an editor and publisher, just over half of them in corporate publishing and just under half in independent publishing.

L335 Julie Crisp Literary Agency
Literary Agency; Editorial Service
United Kingdom

juliecrisp@gmail.com

http://www.juliecrisp.co.uk
https://querymanager.com/query/2079

Professional Body: The Association of Authors' Agents (AAA)

Fiction > *Novels*
  Crime; Fantasy; Historical Fiction; Science Fiction; Speculative Horror; Thrillers

Closed to approaches.

Costs: Offers services that writers have to pay for.

Open to submissions and looking forward to considering any fantasy, science fiction, historical, bookclub, crime/thrillers. Would be particularly pleased to consider diverse and own voices novels.

Authors: E. J. Beaton; Heather Child; John Gwynne; Sam Hawke; Lucy Kissick; Devin Madson; Den Patrick; C. T. Rwizi; Nick Setchfield; Kell Woods

L336 Ria Julien
Literary Agent
United States

rj@goldinlit.com

https://francesgoldinliteraryagency.submittable.com/submit

Literary Agency: Frances Goldin Literary Agency, Inc. (**L231**)

How to send: Submittable

L337 Ella Diamond Kahn
Literary Agent
United Kingdom

http://dkwlitagency.co.uk/agents/
https://twitter.com/elladkahn

Literary Agency: Diamond Kahn and Woods (DKW) Literary Agency Ltd

ADULT
  Fiction > *Novels*
    Contemporary; Crime; Historical Fiction; Speculative; Upmarket

  Nonfiction > *Nonfiction Books*

CHILDREN'S > **Fiction** > *Middle Grade*

YOUNG ADULT > **Fiction** > *Novels*

Closed to approaches.

Represents upmarket contemporary and historical fiction, crime fiction, speculative fiction, and some non-fiction. She also represents a wide range of children's fiction for the 9-12 and YA age groups. She is passionate about finding and championing new voices, including those traditionally under-represented in publishing.

L338 Jody Kahn
Literary Agent
United States

jkahn@bromasite.com

http://brandthochman.com/agents

Literary Agency: Brandt & Hochman Literary Agents, Inc.

Fiction > *Novels*
  Comedy / Humour; Culture; Literary; Upmarket

Nonfiction > *Nonfiction Books*
  Culture; Food; History; Journalism; Literary Memoir; Narrative Nonfiction; Social Justice; Sport

Send: Query
How to send: Email

L339 Joanna Kaliszewska
Literary Agent
United Kingdom

https://www.thebksagency.com/about
https://www.thebksagency.com/submissions

Literary Agency: The BKS Agency (**L063**)

Fiction > *Novels*
  General, and in particular: Book Club Fiction; Crime; Literary; Thrillers; Upmarket Commercial Fiction

Looking for all types of fiction but particularly interested in reading group, upmarket commercial, literary, crime and thriller.

L340 Kane Literary Agency
Literary Agency
United Kingdom

submissions@kaneliteraryagency.com
getintouch@kaneliteraryagency.com

https://www.kaneliteraryagency.com
https://www.facebook.com/kaneliteraryagency/
https://twitter.com/YasminKane3
https://www.instagram.com/YasminKane3/

Professional Body: The Association of Authors' Agents (AAA)

Fiction > *Novels*
  Crime; Domestic Thriller; Noir; Police Procedural; Psychological Thrillers; Thrillers

Send: Query; Synopsis; Writing sample; Pitch; Market info
How to send: Email

Currently only looking for: crime fiction, thrillers, police procedurals, psychological thrillers, and domestic thrillers. Bring on the noir!

Authors: Simon Arrowsmith; J Y Bee; Isabelle Brizee; Louise Cliffe-Minns; Sarah Harris; Vicki Howie; Zoe Marriott; Andrew Murray; Emily Nagle; Marisa Noelle

Literary Agent: Yasmin Standen

L341 Julia Kardon
Literary Agent
United States

julia@hgliterary.com

https://www.hgliterary.com/julia
https://twitter.com/jlkardon
https://querymanager.com/query/JuliaKardon

Literary Agency: HG Literary (**L305**)

Fiction > *Novels*
  Literary; Upmarket

Nonfiction > *Nonfiction Books*
  History; Journalism; Memoir; Narrative Nonfiction

How to send: Query Manager

She is interested primarily in literary and upmarket fiction and memoir, and especially stories grappling with racial, religious, sexual or national identity, narrative nonfiction, journalism, and history. She does not represent thrillers, any children's literature or books about spirituality or Christianity.

L342 Maryann Karinch
Literary Agent
United States

mak@rudyagency.com

http://rudyagency.com

Fiction > *Novels*
  Adventure; Crime; Historical Fiction; Mystery; Thrillers

Nonfiction > *Nonfiction Books*
  General, and in particular: Business; Health; History; Investigative Journalism; Medicine; Sport

Send: Query
Don't send: Proposal; Full text
How to send: Email

Wants to see non-fiction projects from authors who are experts in their field, and that could be any field—business, investigative journalism, sports, history, health and medicine. Genre fiction is preferred. Grab her with your storytelling on the first page.

L343 Michelle Kass

Literary Agent
United Kingdom

Literary Agency: Michelle Kass Associates (**L444**)

L344 Kate Barker Literary, TV, & Film Agency

Literary Agency
London,
United Kingdom
Tel: +44 (0) 20 7688 1638

kate@katebarker.net

https://www.katebarker.net

Professional Body: The Association of Authors' Agents (AAA)

Fiction > *Novels*
Book Club Fiction; Commercial; Contemporary; High Concept; Historical Fiction; Literary

Nonfiction > *Nonfiction Books*
History; Lifestyle; Memoir; Nature; Popular Psychology; Science; Wellbeing

Send: Query; Writing sample
How to send: Online submission system

I'm looking for commercial, literary and reading group novels: my taste in fiction is broad. I like strong stories, interesting settings (contemporary or historical) and high concept novels. I especially love books that make me cry. Please note that I do not represent science fiction, fantasy or books for children. Work in those genres will not be read. Non-fiction: I'm looking for smart thinking, history, memoir, popular psychology and science, nature writing, lifestyle and wellbeing. Big ideas and subjects that get people talking. I particularly enjoy helping experts translate their work for a general audience.

Literary Agent: Kate Barker

L345 Kate Nash Literary Agency

Literary Agency
United Kingdom

https://katenashlit.co.uk
https://www.facebook.com/
KateNashLiteraryAgency/
https://twitter.com/katenashagent
https://www.youtube.com/channel/
UCAugaYbUoZXD7wldntZ8DwQ

Professional Body: The Association of Authors' Agents (AAA)

ADULT
  Fiction > *Novels*

Nonfiction > *Nonfiction Books*: Commercial

CHILDREN'S > **Fiction** > *Middle Grade*

YOUNG ADULT > **Fiction** > *Novels*

Send: Query; Synopsis; Writing sample; Pitch; Author bio
How to send: Online submission system

Open to approaches from both new and established authors. Represents general and genre fiction and popular nonfiction. No poetry, drama, or genre SFF. Send query via online submission form with synopsis and first chapter (fiction) or up to three chapters (nonfiction) pasted into the body of the email (no attachments).

Agency Assistant: Bethany Ferguson

Assistant Agent: Saskia Leach (**L381**)

Literary Agent: Kate Nash

Literary Agent / Managing Director: Justin Nash (**L468**)

L346 Jade Kavanagh

Assistant Agent
United Kingdom

https://www.darleyanderson.com/our-team

Literary Agency: The Darley Anderson Agency
Senior Agent: Camilla Bolton (**L067**)

Author: Holly Craig

L347 Simon Kavanagh

Literary Agent
United Kingdom

Simon@miccheetham.co.uk

Literary Agency: Mic Cheetham Literary Agency (**L441**)

L348 Taylor Martindale Kean

Literary Agent
United States

https://www.fullcircleliterary.com/our-agents/
taylor-martindale-kean/
https://querymanager.com/query/TaylorFCL

Literary Agency: Full Circle Literary, LLC

CHILDREN'S > **Fiction** > *Middle Grade*
General, and in particular: Contemporary; Fantasy; Historical Fiction; Literary; Magical Realism

YOUNG ADULT > **Fiction** > *Novels*
General, and in particular: Fantasy; Magical Realism

How to send: Query Manager

She is looking for young adult fiction and literary middle grade fiction, across all genres. She is interested in finding unique and unforgettable voices in contemporary, fantasy, historical and magical realism novels. She is looking for books that demand to be read. More than anything, she is looking for diverse,

character-driven stories that bring their worlds vividly to life, and voices that are honest, original and interesting.

L349 Keane Kataria Literary Agency

Literary Agency
United Kingdom

info@keanekataria.co.uk

https://www.keanekataria.co.uk/submissions/

Fiction > *Novels*
Book Club Fiction; Commercial Women's Fiction; Contemporary; Cozy Mysteries; Historical Fiction; Romance; Saga

Send: Query; Synopsis; Writing sample
How to send: PDF file email attachment

Currently accepting submissions in the crime, domestic noir and commercial women's fiction genres. No thrillers, science fiction, fantasy or children's books. Send query by email only with synopsis and first three chapters. Attachments in PDF format only.

Literary Agents: Kiran Kataria; Sara Keane

L350 Sara O' Keeffe

Literary Agent
United Kingdom

https://www.saraokeeffe.co.uk
https://www.acvitascreative.com/agent/sara-
okeeffe
https://querymanager.com/query/
SaraOK_QueryForm
https://www.instagram.com/sarabookcrazy/
https://twitter.com/okeeffe05

Literary Agency: Acvitas Creative Management (ACM) UK (**L008**)

Fiction > *Novels*
Book Club Fiction; Crime; Ireland; Science Fiction; Thrillers; Upmarket; Women's Fiction

How to send: Query Manager

Has worked with major brand names in crime, science fiction and has a passion for Irish writing. Currently looking in particular for sophisticated thrillers and upmarket "book club" reads.

L351 Frances Kelly

Literary Agent
United Kingdom

Literary Agency: Frances Kelly Agency

L352 Eli Keren

Associate Agent
United Kingdom
Tel: +44 (0) 20 3214 0775

ekeren@unitedagents.co.uk

https://www.unitedagents.co.uk/
ekerenunitedagentscouk
https://twitter.com/EliArieh

Literary Agency: United Agents (**L619**)
Literary Agent: Sarah Ballard (**L043**)

Fiction > *Novels*
Commercial; Crime; Domestic Suspense;
Historical Fiction; LGBTQIA; Literary;
Magical Realism; Mystery; Speculative;
Thrillers; Upmarket

Nonfiction > *Nonfiction Books*
General, and in particular: Cultural History;
LGBTQIA; Popular Science

Closed to approaches.

In non-fiction, I am particularly interested in
expert-led smart and engaging popular science.
My own background is in chemistry, but I'm
fairly omnivorous and happy to look at any
non-fiction that grips me, be that science,
cultural history or something unexpected. I
enjoy books by writers completely obsessed
with a niche subject who are skilled enough
communicators to make the rest of the world
fall in love with their passion too, whatever
that passion might be. I am interested in any
book that will change the world for the better.
I'm probably not the right agent for books on
religion or spirituality.

In fiction, I mostly work with commercial and
upmarket fiction, not so much with the very
literary. In commercial fiction, I'm interested
in crime/thriller and domestic suspense with a
strong hook and addictive storytelling. I love
mysteries and whodunnits, and am also open to
uplifting general fiction. I'm happy to look at
historical fiction with a contemporary outlook.
Towards the more literary side, I'm looking for
books with plot and pace that set out to achieve
something, change the way I see the world,
challenge me and subvert my expectations. I
don't typically work with science-fiction or
fantasy, but am open to some grounded
speculative fiction and magical realism. I don't
work with holocaust novels.

I do not represent authors for children's and
YA literature.

Authors: Marieke Bigg; Sarah Burton; Huho
Greenhalgh; Ioan Marc Jones; Johanna Lukate;
David Miles; Jem Poster; Claire Seeber; Sam
White

L353 Kathleen Kerr
Literary Agent
United States

Literary Agency: Alive Literary Agency
(**L018**)

L354 Ki Agency Ltd
Literary Agency
Studio 105, Screenworks, 22 Highbury Grove,
London, N5 2EF

United Kingdom
Tel: +44 (0) 20 3214 8287

https://ki-agency.co.uk

Professional Bodies: The Association of
Authors' Agents (AAA); Personal Managers'
Association (PMA); Writers' Guild of Great
Britain (WGGB)

Fiction > *Novels*

Nonfiction > *Nonfiction Books*
Leadership; Personal Coaching; Personal
Development

Scripts
Film Scripts; *TV Scripts*; *Theatre Scripts*

Send: Synopsis; Writing sample
How to send: Email attachment

Represents novelists and scriptwriters in all
media. No children's or poetry, or submissions
from writers in the US or Canada. Send
synopsis and first three chapters / first 50 pages
by email. See website for individual agent
interests.

Authors: John Allison; Fiona Barnett; Simon
Bestwick; Linda Carey; Louise Carey; Mike
Carey; Lucy Chalice; Kate Charlesworth;
Amber Chen; Daniel Church; Helena Coggan;
Daniel Depp; Joanne Drayton; Diane Duane;
Matthew Feldman; Kitty Ferguson; Marianne
Gordon; Stark Holborn; Shaun Hutson; Luke
Kondor; Ryan Love; Laura Madeleine; Sarah
McManus; Robin Norwood; Marie O'Regan;
Anne Perry; Adam Roberts; Phoenicia
Rogerson; Angela Slatter; Gillian Spraggs;
Jesse Stuart; Becky Ward; Catherine Webb

Literary Agent: Meg Davis

L355 Jessica Killingley
Literary Agent
United Kingdom

https://www.thebksagency.com/about
https://www.thebksagency.com/submissions

Literary Agency: The BKS Agency (**L063**)

Fiction > *Novels*
Dark Humour; Fantasy; High Concept;
Science Fiction

Nonfiction > *Nonfiction Books*
Business; Personal Development; Self Help

Send: Query; Outline; Author bio
How to send: Online submission system

Looking for self help, personal development,
business and smart thinking. A strong personal
brand, a great platform and a clear vision for
the future a must! Additionally, I'm really
interested in projects and authors related to
neurodivergence (I have ADHD). I am also
currently open for original, high-concept adult
SFF – ideally with some dark humour thrown
in for good measure.

L356 Natalie Kimber
Literary Agent
Canada

Literary Agency: The Rights Factory

ADULT
Fiction
Graphic Novels: General
Novels: Adventure; Commercial; Cookery;
Historical Fiction; Literary; Science Fiction
Nonfiction > *Nonfiction Books*
Creative Nonfiction; Memoir; Popular
Culture; Science; Spirituality; Sustainable
Living

YOUNG ADULT > **Fiction** > *Novels*: Boy
Books

Closed to approaches.

L357 Kimberley Cameron & Associates
Literary Agency
1550 Tiburon Blvd #704, Tiberon, CA 94920
United States

info@kimberleycameron.com

https://www.kimberleycameron.com
https://www.facebook.com/
kimberleycameronandassociates
https://twitter.com/K_C_Associates
https://www.instagram.com/kcandaliterary/

Fiction > *Novels*

Nonfiction > *Nonfiction Books*

How to send: Query Manager

See website for specific agent interests and
submit to most suitable agent through their
online submission system.

Literary Agents: Lisa Abellera; Kimberley
Cameron; Amy Cloughley; Elizabeth Kracht;
Dorian Maffei; Mary C. Moore

L358 Robert Kirby
Literary Agent; Company Director
United Kingdom

https://www.unitedagents.co.uk/
rkirbyunitedagentscouk

Literary Agency: United Agents (**L619**)

Fiction > *Novels*
Adventure; Commercial; Speculative

Nonfiction > *Nonfiction Books*
Cultural History; Environment; Psychology;
Science

Send: Synopsis; Writing sample
How to send: Email
How not to send: Post

I have an interest in science, psychology,
cultural history and environmental issues. I
enjoy gripping adventure fiction, speculative
fiction and emotionally driven commercial
fiction. Submissions should be sent to my
assistant by via email, with a synopsis and first

three chapters. Please do not send submissions via the post.

Associate Agent: Kate Walsh (**L633**)

L359 Kelly Knatchbull
Literary Agent; Company Director
United Kingdom

Literary Agency: Sayle Screen Ltd

L360 Kneerim & Williams
Literary Agency
88 Broad St, Suite 503, Boston, MA 02110
United States

submissions@kwlit.com

https://kwlit.com
https://twitter.com/KWLitAgency

Professional Body: Association of American Literary Agents (AALA)

Fiction > *Novels*

Nonfiction > *Nonfiction Books*

Send: Query; Synopsis; Author bio; Writing sample
How to send: In the body of an email
How not to send: Post; Phone

Send query by email with synopsis, brief bio, and 10-20 pages of initial sample material in the body of the email. No attachments or queries by post or by phone. See website for full guidelines.

Literary Agents: Lucy Cleland; Katherine Flynn; Carol Franco; Elaine Rogers; Carolyn Savarese; Matthew Valentinas; Ike Williams

L361 Knight Features
Literary Agency
Trident Business Centre, 89 Bickersteth Road, London, SW17 9SH
United Kingdom

https://www.knightfeatures.com

Nonfiction > *Nonfiction Books*
  Business; Communication; Military

Send: Query; Synopsis; Writing sample; Market info
How to send: Online submission system

Send query with synopsis and three sample chapters. Include information on whether you envisage the book being illustrated, and details of the target market, the level at which it might be pitched, and the likely readership. Include information about any works in the same field which might be seen as competition for your book, or give some indication of how yours differs from these.

Company Directors: Samantha Ferris; Gaby Martin

Managing Director: Andrew Knight

L362 Charlotte Knight
Literary Agent
United Kingdom

http://www.knighthallagency.com/about-us/who-we-are/

Literary Agency: Knight Hall Agency

Author: Angharad Elen

L363 Martin Knight
Literary Agent
United Kingdom

Literary Agency: Knight Hall Agency

L364 Katie Kotchman
Literary Agent
United States

https://doncongdon.com/agents
https://querymanager.com/query/Kkotchman
https://aalitagents.org/author/kkotchman/
https://twitter.com/kkotchman

Literary Agency: Don Congdon Associates, Inc. (**L175**)
Professional Body: Association of American Literary Agents (AALA)

Fiction > *Novels*
  American Midwest; Literary; Women's Fiction

Nonfiction > *Nonfiction Books*
  American Midwest; Business; Culture; Memoir; Motivational Self-Help; Narrative Nonfiction; Popular Culture; Popular Science; Psychology; Social Issues

How to send: Query Manager

In non-fiction, she specializes in narrative non-fiction (particularly memoir, popular science, pop culture, and social/cultural issues), business (all areas), and self-help that focuses on success, motivation, and psychology. She is actively seeking new nonfiction clients with built-in platforms from whom she can learn something new. In fiction, she's interested in representing women's fiction and literary fiction. In all areas, she's particularly interested in characters who struggle with dualities of nature and/or culture, as the topics of cognitive dissonance and those who straddle two different worlds fascinate her. She has soft spots for the Midwest, family secrets, and a good underdog story.

L365 Lizzy Kremer
Literary Agent
United Kingdom

lizzymanuscripts@davidhigham.co.uk

https://www.davidhigham.co.uk/agents-dh/lizzy-kremer/
https://publishingforhumans.com/
https://twitter.com/lizzykremer

Literary Agency: David Higham Associates Ltd (**L159**)

Fiction > *Novels*
  Commercial; Literary

Nonfiction > *Nonfiction Books*

Send: Query; Synopsis; Writing sample
How to send: Email

Represents commercial and literary fiction and non-fiction. She was President of the Association of Authors' Agents from January 2018-2020 and was named the British Book Industry Awards 2016 Agent of the Year in May 2016. Always keen to discover compelling new voices in commercial and literary fiction.

Authors: Rachel Abbott; Julian Baggini; Annie Bell; Hester Browne; Jess Cartner-Morley; Anne-Marie Casey; Eve Chase; Charlie Connelly; Tish Delaney; Lucy Diamond; Lucy Dillon; Sareeta Domingo; Alicia Drake; Sarah Duguid; Kerry Egan; Ophelia Field; Ryan Gattis; Saska Graville; Dominic Green; Araminta Hall; Ali Harris; Paula Hawkins; Mick Herron; Gavanndra Hodge; Euny Hong; Yuji Huang; Milly Johnson; Laura Kemp; Rachel Khoo; Jeremy Lee; Penelope Lively; Sadie Matthews; Val McDermid; Louise Millar; Victoria Moore; Kate Morton; Laurie Owens; Katy Regan; Lucy Robinson; Claudia Roden; Jessica Stanley; Lulu Taylor; Sarah Vaughan; Rosie Walsh

L366 Mary Krienke
Literary Agent
United States

https://www.sll.com/our-team

Literary Agency: Sterling Lord Literistic, Inc. (**L583**)

Fiction > *Novels*
  Literary; Upmarket

Nonfiction > *Nonfiction Books*
  Culture; Health; Sexuality

Send: Query; Synopsis; Writing sample
How to send: Online submission system

Represents literary and upmarket fiction, voice-driven nonfiction, and memoir. She is particularly drawn to nonfiction that speaks to something essential and of-the-moment, especially work that engages with themes of culture, identity, sexuality, and health.

L367 Kruger Cowne
Literary Agency
Unit 7C, Chelsea Wharf, 15 Lots Road, London, SW10 0QJ
United Kingdom
Tel: +44 (0) 20 8103 1089

hello@krugercowne.com

https://www.krugercowne.com
https://twitter.com/krugercowne
https://www.instagram.com/krugercowne/
https://www.facebook.com/krugercowne
https://www.linkedin.com/company/kruger-

cowne
https://www.youtube.com/user/
KrugerCowneTalent

Professional Body: The Association of
Authors' Agents (AAA)

Nonfiction > *Nonfiction Books*
General, and in particular: Celebrity;
Entrepreneurship; Futurism; Journalism

How to send: Email

A talent management agency, with an
extremely strong literary arm.

The majority of the works handled by the
agency fall into the category of celebrity
nonfiction. However, also regularly work with
journalists, entrepreneurs and influencers on
projects, with a speciality in polemics, and
speculative works on the future.

Authors: Akala; Steven Bartlett; Boris Becker;
Kelly Holmes; Lia Leendertz; Jennifer
Medhurst; Jack Monroe; Christine Morgan;
Selene Nelson; John Simpson; Nicholas Boys
Smith; Dave Stewart

L368 KT Literary
Literary Agency
United States

queries@ktliterary.com

https://ktliterary.com
https://twitter.com/ktliterary
https://www.instagram.com/ktliterary/

ADULT > **Fiction** > *Novels*

CHILDREN'S > **Fiction** > *Middle Grade*

YOUNG ADULT > **Fiction** > *Novels*

Send: Query
How to send: Query Manager; Email
How not to send: Post; Social Media

Please see each individual agent's bio for
instructions on how to best query them. If
QueryManager provides an accessibility issue,
send an email addressed to the specific agent in
question. No snail mail queries or pitches via
social media.

Associate Agent: Chelsea Hensley (**L301**)

Literary Agents: Savannah Brooks (**L082**);
Tara Gilbert (**L247**); Adria Goetz (**L257**);
Hilary Harwell (**L296**); Renee Nyen (*L479*);
Jas Perry (*L499*); Kelly Van Sant (**L549**);
Arley Sorg (**L579**); Kari Sutherland (**L598**);
Laurel Symonds (**L603**); Kate Testerman
(*L610*)

Senior Agent / Vice President: Sara Megibow
(*L436*)

L369 The Labyrinth Literary Agency
Literary Agency
India

submissions@labyrinthagency.com

http://www.labyrinthagency.com
https://www.instagram.com/labyrinthagency/
https://twitter.com/LabyrinthAgency
https://twitter.com/LabyrinthAgency

Fiction > *Novels*

Nonfiction > *Nonfiction Books*

Send: Synopsis; Writing sample; Author bio
How to send: Email

Costs: Offers services that writers have to pay
for. Offers editorial and advice services to
authors with whom they do not have a business
relationship.

Literary Agent: Anish Chandy

L370 Natalie Lakosil
Literary Agent
United States

https://www.adventuresinagentland.com
https://www.irenegoodman.com/natalie-lakosil
https://twitter.com/Natalie_Lakosil
http://www.manuscriptwishlist.com/mswl-post/natalic-lakosil/
https://querymanager.com/query/natlak

Literary Agency: Irene Goodman Literary
Agency (IGLA)

ADULT
Fiction > *Novels*
Cozy Mysteries; Crime; Thrillers;
Upmarket Women's Fiction; Upmarket

Nonfiction > *Nonfiction Books*
Business; Parenting; Psychology; Science;
Self Help

CHILDREN'S
Fiction
Chapter Books; *Middle Grade*; *Picture Books*
Nonfiction
Gift Books: General
Nonfiction Books: Biography; Comedy /
Humour; Feminism; New Age; Social
Issues
YOUNG ADULT > **Fiction** > *Novels*

Closed to approaches.

Represents adult nonfiction, adult cozy
mystery/crime, female-driven thrillers,
upmarket women's/general fiction, illustrators,
and all ages (picture book, chapter book, MG,
YA) of children's literature, both fiction and
nonfiction.

Assistant Agent / Junior Agent: Antoinette Van
Sluytman (**L576**)

L371 Sophie Lambert
Literary Agent
United Kingdom
Tel: +44 (0) 20 7393 4200

sophie.lambert@cwagency.co.uk

https://cwagency.co.uk/agent/sophie-lambert

Literary Agency: C&W (Conville & Walsh)
(**L092**)

Fiction > *Novels*
Commercial; Crime; Literary; Thrillers

Nonfiction > *Nonfiction Books*
Anthropology; Arts; Environment; Food;
History; Memoir; Narrative Nonfiction;
Nature; Travel

Send: Query; Synopsis; Writing sample;
Proposal
How to send: Word file email attachment

I love fiction which is voice driven and
introduces readers to different perspectives and
singular narrators, as well as beautifully
written literary fiction which has a strong sense
of place, and commercial crime and thrillers
which keep the reader on the edge of their seats
and continually surprise and excite me. Where
nonfiction is concerned I am drawn to narrative
nonfiction which straddles genre and I'm
especially interested in nature writing, travel,
history, anthropology, art and the environment.
I represent lots of memoir, as well as books by
experts in their field and specialists. I would
love to find a gorgeous, all-consuming love
story, or a food writer who matches Bill
Burford or Anthony Bourdain. Essentially, I'm
looking for an exquisite writer to take me by
the hand and show me a different way to see
the world, whether that's through fiction or
nonfiction.

Author / Literary Agent: Catherine Cho (**L120**)

Authors: Lisa Ballantyne; Brock Bastian; Josie
Bevan; Michael Bhaskar; Megan Bradbury;
Tom Burgis; Tim Clare; Caroline Crampton;
Fiona Cummins; Howard Cunnell; Lara
Dearman; Nathan Filer; Cal Flyn; Julia Forster;
Sam Fowles; Ruth Gilligan; Colin Grant; Guy
Gunaratne; Karen Hamilton; Eileen Horne;
Rebecca Ley; Katy Mahood; Shiv Malik;
Ramita Navai; Hollie Newton; Christina
Patterson; Jenny Quintana; Ben Rawlence;
Catherine Riley; Sophy Roberts; Rhik
Samadder; David Savill; Holly Seddon; Tali
Sharot; Tim Spector; Michelle Sterling;
Michelle Thomas; Christie Watson; Adam
Weymouth; Tod Wodicka

L372 Sarah Landis
Literary Agent
United States

https://www.sll.com/our-team

Literary Agency: Sterling Lord Literistic, Inc.
(**L583**)

ADULT > **Fiction** > *Novels*
Fantasy; High Concept; Speculative;
Thrillers

CHILDREN'S > **Fiction** > *Middle Grade*
Fantasy; High Concept; Speculative;
Thrillers

Send: Query; Synopsis; Writing sample
How to send: Online submission system

Represents a wide range of fiction from middle grade to adult. She is particularly drawn to high-concept plots, big hooks, speculative fiction, twisty thrillers, novels with a strong emotional core, and sweeping fantasy. She is always on the lookout for new talent and narrative risk-takers.

L373 Lina Langlee

Literary Agent
United Kingdom

http://thenorthlitagency.com/our-friends-in-the-north/
https://twitter.com/LinaLanglee

Literary Agency: The North Literary Agency

ADULT
  Fiction > *Novels*
    General, and in particular: Commercial; Crime; Fantasy; High Concept; Horror; Literary; Romance; Science Fiction; Speculative; Thrillers

  Nonfiction > *Nonfiction Books*

CHILDREN'S > **Fiction** > *Middle Grade*

YOUNG ADULT > **Fiction** > *Novels*

Closed to approaches.

Looking for books across genres: commercial/high concept fiction with a great hook (be that romance, crime, thriller or general fiction), accessible literary fiction, and intriguing speculative fiction, SFF & horror. Also looking for fun, fantastical, and moving Middle Grade, and "big emotion" Young Adult across genres. In terms of non-fiction, she is interested either in "the small made big" or "the big made small": specialists that can make really niche subjects accessible and interesting to a wider market, or deeply personal accounts of the big issues we might all one day tackle. Actively welcomes authors from all backgrounds and would like to see more diverse stories and voices. She is less keen on political or gangland thrillers. As a general rule, she would not offer representation to US-based authors since they are better served by US-based agents, except in the very rare situation where their story ought to originate from the UK.

L374 Becca Langton

Literary Agent
United Kingdom

https://www.darleyanderson.com/our-team

Literary Agency: The Darley Anderson Agency

CHILDREN'S > **Fiction**
  Graphic Novels: General
  Middle Grade: General, and in particular: Adventure
TEEN > **Fiction** > *Novels*

YOUNG ADULT > **Fiction** > *Novels*
  General, and in particular: Contemporary; Fantasy; LGBTQIA; Romantic Comedy

Closed to approaches.

Looking for new stories in all shapes and sizes, from middle grade and graphic novel to teen and YA fiction. Reads widely but loves books with compelling voices, twists and brave new ideas. In YA she would love to see some Queer fantasy, rom-coms with plenty of 'com' and contemporary stories told from a new perspective. For younger readers she love/hates the books that make her cry and is on the search for characters that stay with her long after the final page. High-stakes adventure stories are welcome as are graphic novels and books that make you want to read just one more chapter…

Author: Faith Williams Schesventer

L375 Linda Langton

Literary Agent
United States

https://langtonsinternational.com/langtons-international/about-us/
https://www.linkedin.com/in/lindalangton

Literary Agency: Langtons International (**L376**)

L376 Langtons International

Literary Agency
United States

llangton@earthlink.net
langtonsinternational@gmail.com

https://langtonsinternational.com
https://www.facebook.com/LangtonsInternationalAgency

Fiction > *Novels*
  Literary; Mystery; Thrillers; Women's Fiction

Nonfiction > *Nonfiction Books*
  Business; Crime; Memoir; Self Help

Literary agency based in New York, specializing in business, self-help, memoir, and true crime, as well as mystery, thrillers, women's and literary fiction.

Literary Agent: Linda Langton (**L375**)

L377 Elena Langtry

Literary Agent
United Kingdom

https://cmm.agency/about-us.php

Literary Agency: Coombs Moylett & Maclean Literary Agency (**L138**)

Fiction > *Novels*
  Commercial Women's Fiction; Psychological Thrillers

Nonfiction > *Nonfiction Books*
  Crime; Popular Science

How to send: Online submission system

L378 Jennifer Laughran

Senior Agent
United States

jennL@andreabrownlit.com

https://www.jenniferlaughran.com
https://www.andreabrownlit.com/Team/Jennifer-Laughran
http://twitter.com/literaticat
http://www.instagram.com/literaticat
https://querymanager.com/JenniferLaughran
https://www.publishersmarketplace.com/members/jennla/
https://www.manuscriptwishlist.com/mswl-post/jennifer-laughran/

Literary Agency: Andrea Brown Literary Agency, Inc.
Professional Body: Association of American Literary Agents (AALA)

CHILDREN'S > **Fiction** > *Middle Grade*

YOUNG ADULT > **Fiction** > *Novels*

Send: Query; Author bio; Writing sample
How to send: Query Manager

Always on the lookout for sparkling YA and middle grade fiction with unusual and unforgettable characters and vivid settings, she is drawn to nearly all kinds of books, whether realistic comedies or richly imagined magical adventures. However, the common thread in her favorite stories is an offbeat world-view.

L379 Laxfield Literary Associates

Literary Agency
United Kingdom

submissions@laxfieldliterary.com

https://laxfieldliterary.com

Professional Body: The Association of Authors' Agents (AAA)

Fiction > *Novels*
  Commercial; Literary

Nonfiction > *Nonfiction Books*
  Creative Nonfiction; Memoir; Nature; Travel

Does not want:

  Fiction > *Novels*: Fantasy

Send: Query; Synopsis; Writing sample; Author bio; Outline
How to send: Word file email attachment

We are looking for fiction and non-fiction of the highest quality. We are keen to receive literary and commercial fiction. We are also looking for non-fiction, particularly creative non-fiction, travel writing, memoir and nature writing. We do not represent poetry, plays, children's books or YA.

L380 Sarah Lazin

Literary Agent
United States

https://www.aevitascreative.com/agent/sarah-lazin
http://lazinbooks.com/about-us/

Literary Agencies: Sarah Lazin Books; Aevitas

Nonfiction
  Nonfiction Books: Biography; Current Affairs; Health; History; Journalism; Memoir; Parenting; Politics; Popular Culture; Social Issues
  Reference: General

How to send: By referral

Represents a range of nonfiction writers working in fields such as popular culture, biography, history, politics, journalism, memoir, parenting, health, practical nonfiction, contemporary affairs, social issues, and general reference. She accepts submissions through referral only.

Authors: Michael Azerrad; Patricia Romanowski Bashe; Michael Benson; Will Birch; Jenny Blake; Bill Brewster; Frank Broughton; Kate Brown; E. Jean Carroll; Ted Chapin; Robert Christgau; Broughton Coburn; Charles R. Cross; Charles Daniels; Anthony DeCurtis; Ani DiFranco; Banning Eyre; Jim Farber; Alison Fernsterstock; Ben Fong-Torres; Georgia Freedman; Elysa Gardner; Richard Gehr; Nelson George; Robin Green; Charlie Harding; Elizabeth Hess; Jewly Hight; Janet Hopson; Bill Ivey; Lucretia Tye Jasmine; Booker T. Jones; Laura Joplin; Jason King; Michael Lang; Bernie Lierow; Diane Lierow; Kurt Loder; Kim MacQuarrie; Evelyn McDonnell; Kembrew McLeod; Dennis McNally; Paula Mejia; Joan Morgan; Daniel Nadel; Robert K. Oermann; Patricia Pearson; Ann Powers; Mark Seliger; Sylvie Simmons; Nate Sloan; John Szwed; Jessica Vitkus; Elijah Wald

L381 Saskia Leach

Assistant Agent
United Kingdom

https://katenashlit.co.uk/people/
https://twitter.com/saskialeach_

Literary Agency: Kate Nash Literary Agency **(L345)**

Fiction > *Novels*

Send: Query; Pitch; Author bio; Synopsis; Writing sample
How to send: In the body of an email

Enjoys reading a wide range of genres and is fascinated by stories written from multiple perspectives. She also loves books which feature complex and dynamic characters.

L382 Shannon Lechon

Associate Agent
United States

http://www.azantianlitagency.com/pages/team-sl.html
https://querymanager.com/query/shannonlechon

Literary Agency: Azantian Literary Agency **(L039)**

ADULT
  Fiction > *Novels*
    Fantasy Romance; Fantasy; Folklore, Myths, and Legends; Horror; Literary; Mystery; Science Fantasy; Social Issues; Speculative; Thrillers

  Nonfiction
    Graphic Nonfiction: Mental Health
    Nonfiction Books: Medicine; Memoir; Mental Health
CHILDREN'S > **Fiction**
  Graphic Novels: General
  Middle Grade: Comedy / Humour; Horror; Mystery; Speculative
YOUNG ADULT > **Fiction**
  Graphic Novels: Fantasy
  Novels: Dark; Fantasy; Gothic; Horror; Mystery; Science Fiction; Speculative; Thrillers

Closed to approaches.

Interested in experimental styles and unreliable narrators. Intense platonic interpersonal bonds are a particular favorite of hers. She likes underexplored magic systems and fantasy that doesn't care if you understand it or not.

L383 Tom Drake Lee

Associate Agent
United Kingdom

tdl.submission@dhhliteraryagency.com

http://www.dhhliteraryagency.com/tom-drake-lee.html
http://twitter.com/tomdrakelee

Literary Agency: DHH Literary Agency Ltd **(L167)**

Fiction > *Novels*
  Commercial; Literary

Nonfiction > *Nonfiction Books*
  History; Memoir; Nature; Popular Science

Closed to approaches.

Looking for commercial literary and genre fiction which tells stories and illuminates the human condition; fiction which has compelling plot, narrative and characters.

Also looking for non-fiction which tells us more about the world around us; nature writing, popular science, history and memoir.

No screenplays, short story / novellas, children's books / YA or Sci-Fi/Fantasy.

Authors: Howard Colyer; Michael Delahaye; Valerie Jack; Diana Kessler; Michael Leggo; Rachel Meller; Valerie O'Riordan; Leon Romero-Montalvo; Iain Rowan; Richard Stirling; Amanda Tuke

L384 Jordan Lees

Literary Agent
United Kingdom

jordansubmissions@theblairpartnership.com

https://www.theblairpartnership.com/literary-agents/jordan-lees/

Literary Agency: The Blair Partnership

ADULT
  Fiction > *Novels*
    Commercial; Crime; Dark; Detective Fiction; High Concept; Literary; Speculative; Thrillers; Upmarket

  Nonfiction > *Nonfiction Books*
    General, and in particular: Crime

CHILDREN'S > **Fiction** > *Middle Grade*
    General, and in particular: Crime; Detective Fiction; Fantasy; Horror; Science Fiction

Does not want:

  Fiction > *Novels*: Spy Thrillers

Send: Synopsis; Writing sample; Pitch; Market info
How to send: Email

I primarily represent crime and thrillers, upmarket/literary fiction and some children's, as well as true crime and non-fiction written by journalists and experts in their respective fields. I'm typically drawn to writing with an upmarket edge, and I'm open to anything high-concept, speculative or which blends one genre with another.

Authors: Alwia Al-Hassan; Bana Alabed; JJ Arcanjo; Daniel Broadstock; Tom Carlisle; Dawn Coulter-Cruttenden; Helena Duggan; Emma Farrarons; William Friend; Jo Furniss; Toby Gutteridge; Elle Hardy; Oli Hyatt; Ruth Kelly; Scott Kershaw; Kieran Larwood; The Urban Legend; John Lutz; Dan Malakin; Major Scotty Mills; Markus Motum; Rogba Payne; Daisy Pearce; Stephen Ronson; Babita Sharma; Tom Spencer; P. A. Staff

L385 Leigh Feldman Literary

Literary Agency
United States

query@lfliterary.com
assistant@lfliterary.com

https://www.lfliterary.com

ADULT
  Fiction > *Novels*
    Historical Fiction; Literary

  Nonfiction > *Nonfiction Books*
    Memoir; Narrative Nonfiction

YOUNG
ADULT > **Fiction** > *Novels*: Contemporary

Send: Query; Writing sample; Proposal
How to send: Email

Particularly interested in historical fiction, contemporary YA, literary fiction, memoir, and narrative nonfiction. No adult and YA paranormal, fantasy, science fiction, romance, thrillers, mysteries, or picture books. Send query by email with first ten pages or proposal. Only makes personal response if interested.

Literary Agent: Leigh Feldman (*L208*)

L386 **Paul S. Levine**
Literary Agent
United States

paul@paulslevinelit.com

Literary Agency: Paul S. Levine Literary Agency (**L492**)

L387 **Sarah Levitt**
Literary Agent
New York
United States

https://aevitascreative.com/agents/
https://querymanager.com/query/2585

Literary Agency: Aevitas

Fiction > *Novels*: Literary

Nonfiction > *Nonfiction Books*
Comedy / Humour; History; Journalism; Memoir; Narrative Nonfiction; Popular Culture; Popular Science

Send: Author bio; Outline; Market info; Writing sample
How to send: Online submission system

Most interested in narrative nonfiction in the areas of popular science, big ideas, history, humor, pop culture, memoir, and reportage, in addition to voice-driven literary fiction with a bold plot and fresh, imaginative characters. She's excited by strong female and underrepresented voices, the strange and speculative, and projects that ignite cultural conversation.

Authors: Ruha Benjamin; Laura Bliss; Marc Bojanowski; Elizabeth Brooks; Adam Chandler; Bloomberg CityLab; Daniel M. Davis; Sarah Ditum; Baz Dreisinger; Sarah Duenwald; Mieke Eerkens; Claire Evans; Becky Ferreira; Marion Gibson; Annette Giesecke; Eliese Colette Goldbach; Elyse Graham; Wade Graham; Ayanna Howard; Tung-Hui Hu; Saru Jayaraman; Nancy McSharry Jensen; Robin Wall Kimmerer; Doma Mahmoud; Sara Majka; Antonia Malchik; Maggie Mertens; Ann Morgan; Laine Nooney; Jenni Nuttall; Abigail Pogrebin; Letty Cottin Pogrebin; Amelia Possanza; Elizabeth Preston; Steve Ramirez; Ashanté Reese; Charlotte Rixon; Anjali Sachdeva; Suzanne Scanlon; Kathleen Sheppard; Lauren Shields;

Ly Ky Tran; Phuc Tran; Sarah Turner; Sarah Vallance; Lizzie Wade; Peter von Ziegesar

L388 **Alison Lewis**
Literary Agent
United States

atl@goldinlit.com

https://www.goldinlit.com/alison-lewis
https://twitter.com/atatelewis

Literary Agency: Frances Goldin Literary Agency, Inc. (**L231**)

Fiction > *Novels*: Literary

Nonfiction > *Nonfiction Books*
Cultural Criticism; History; Journalism; Literary Memoir; Science

Send: Query; Writing sample; Proposal
How to send: Email

Represents a wide range of nonfiction, spanning journalism, cultural criticism, history, science, literary memoir, and essays, as well as select literary fiction. She is particularly drawn to writers with a distinctive voice and perspective, a sense of social or political imagination and responsibility, scholars and researchers who can translate their expertise for a wide readership, and writers pushing the boundaries of form, preconceived ideas, and histories of representation in literature.

L389 **Kayla Lightner**
Literary Agent
United States

https://www.pandeliterary.com/our-team-pandeliterary
https://www.manuscriptwishlist.com/mswl-post/kayla-lightner/
https://twitter.com/LightnerKayla
https://www.linkedin.com/in/kayla-lightner-362406ab/

Literary Agency: Ayesha Pande Literary (**L038**)
Professional Body: Association of American Literary Agents (AALA)

Fiction > *Novels*
Book Club Fiction; Family Saga; Literary; Magical Realism; Upmarket

Nonfiction > *Nonfiction Books*
Arts; Business; Crime; Current Affairs; Ethnic Groups; History; Internet Culture; Internet; Memoir; Mental Health; Narrative Nonfiction; Popular Culture; Social Class; Technology

Closed to approaches.

I love discovering diverse and fresh new perspectives across adult literary + upmarket fiction and non-fiction. I'm particularly a fan of authors with singular voices that masterfully straddle the line between story-telling and teaching readers something new (about

themselves, their communities, or the world we live in).

L390 **Limelight Management**
Literary Agency
10 Filmer Mews, 75 Filmer Road, London, SW6 7BZ
United Kingdom
Tel: +44 (0) 20 7384 9950

mail@limelightmanagement.com

https://www.limelightmanagement.com
https://www.facebook.com/pages/Limelight-Celebrity-Management-Ltd/399328580099859?fref=ts
https://twitter.com/Fionalimelight
https://www.youtube.com/channel/UCCmxquRk_blKqjR8jKRryFA
https://instagram.com/limelightcelebritymanagement/
https://www.linkedin.com/company-beta/11219861/

Professional Body: The Association of Authors' Agents (AAA)

Fiction > *Novels*
Commercial Women's Fiction; Crime; Historical Fiction; Mystery; Suspense; Thrillers

Nonfiction > *Nonfiction Books*
Arts; Autobiography; Biography; Business; Cookery; Crafts; Health; Nature; Popular Science; Sport; Travel

Send: Query; Synopsis; Writing sample; Author bio
How to send: Email

Always looking for exciting new authors. Send query by email with the word "Submission" in the subject line and synopsis and first three chapters as Word or Open Document attachments. Also include market info, and details of your professional life and writing ambitions. Film and TV scripts for existing clients only. See website for full guidelines.

Literary Agent / Managing Director: Fiona Lindsay (*L393*)

L391 **Linda Seifert Management**
Literary Agency
United Kingdom
Tel: +44 (0) 20 3327 1180

contact@lindaseifert.com

http://www.lindaseifert.com

Professional Body: Personal Managers' Association (PMA)

ADULT > **Scripts**
Film Scripts; *TV Scripts*
CHILDREN'S > **Scripts**
Film Scripts; *TV Scripts*

Closed to approaches.

Costs: Author covers sundry admin costs.

A London-based management company representing screenwriters and directors for film and television. Our outstanding client list ranges from the highly established to the new and exciting emerging talent of tomorrow. Represents UK-based writers and directors only.

Literary Agent: Edward Hughes

L392 Lindsay Literary Agency
Literary Agency
United Kingdom
Tel: +44 (0) 1420 831430

info@lindsayliteraryagency.co.uk

http://www.lindsayliteraryagency.co.uk
https://twitter.com/lindsaylit

Professional Body: The Association of Authors' Agents (AAA)

CHILDREN'S > Fiction
  Middle Grade; Picture Books
YOUNG ADULT > Fiction > *Novels*

Send: Query; Author bio; Pitch; Synopsis; Writing sample
How to send: Email

Send query by email only, including single-page synopsis and first three chapters. For picture books send complete ms. No submissions by post.

Authors: Helen Brandom; Pamela Butchart; Sital Gorasia Chapman; Christina Collins; Jim Daly; Donna David; Keighley Douglas; Rachel Emily; Louise Finch; Sam Gayton; Ruth Hatfield; Larry Hayes; Sharon Hopwood; Peter Jones; Jay Joseph; Titania Krimpas; Mike Lancaster; Beth O'Brien; Giles Paley-Phillips; Kate Peridot; Josh Silver; Daniel Tawse; Sharon Tregenza; Rachel Valentine; Sue Wallman; Jacqueline Whitehart; Joe Wilson

Literary Agent: Becky Bagnell

L393 Fiona Lindsay
Literary Agent; Managing Director
United Kingdom

Literary Agency: Limelight Management (**L390**)

L394 Laurie Liss
Literary Agent; Executive Vice President
United States

https://www.sll.com/our-team
http://aaronline.org/Sys/PublicProfile/2176754/417813

Literary Agency: Sterling Lord Literistic, Inc. (**L583**)
Professional Body: Association of American Literary Agents (AALA)

Fiction > *Novels*

Nonfiction > *Nonfiction Books*

Send: Query; Synopsis; Writing sample
How to send: Online submission system

L395 Literary Management Group, Inc.
Literary Agency
150 Young Way, Richmond Hill, GA 31324
United States
Tel: +1 (615) 812-4445

BruceBarbour@
LiteraryManagementGroup.com

https://literarymanagementgroup.com/

Nonfiction > *Nonfiction Books*
  Biography; Business; Lifestyle; Religion

Send: Query; Writing sample
How to send: Word file email attachment
How not to send: PDF file email attachment

Handles Christian books (defined as books which are consistent with the historical, orthodox teachings of the Christian fathers). Handles adult nonfiction only. No children's or illustrated books, poetry, memoirs, YA Fiction or text/academic books. Download proposal from website then complete and send with sample chapters.

Literary Agent: Bruce R. Barbour

L396 The Liverpool Literary Agency
Literary Agency
Liverpool
United Kingdom

submissions@liverpool-literary.agency

https://www.liverpool-literary.agency/
https://twitter.com/LiverpoolLit
https://www.instagram.com/
liverpool_literary_agency/

Professional Body: The Association of Authors' Agents (AAA)

ADULT > Fiction > *Novels*

YOUNG ADULT > Fiction > *Novels*
  Dystopian Fiction; Fantasy; Post-Apocalyptic; Science Fiction; Steampunk; Urban Fantasy

Closed to approaches.

Costs: Offers services that writers have to pay for. Also offers editorial services.

Literary agency based in Liverpool, focusing on helping writers from Northern England break into the publishing industry.

Associate Agent / Editor: Laura Bennett (**L056**)

Literary Agent: Clare Coombes (**L137**)

L397 Liza Dawson Associates
Literary Agency
121 West 27th Street, Suite 1201, New York, NY 10001
United States

lwu@lizadawson.com

https://www.lizadawsonassociates.com
https://twitter.com/LizaDawsonAssoc

Professional Body: Association of American Literary Agents (AALA)

Fiction > *Novels*

Nonfiction > *Nonfiction Books*

See website for specific agent interests and query appropriate agent directly. Specific agent submission guidelines and contact details are available on website.

Authors: Annie Barrows; Marie Bostwick; Bob Brier; Stella Cameron; Robyn Carr; Ross Gay; Susan Hasler; Scott Hawkins; Julia Lee; Victoria Christopher Murray; Tawni O'Dell; Jean Sasson; Marybeth Whalen

Junior Agent: Lauren Bajek (**L041**)

Literary Agents: Rachel Beck; Caitlin Blasdell; Hannah Bowman; Caitie Flum; Tom Miller

President / Senior Agent: Liza Dawson (**L162**)

L398 The LKG Agency
Literary Agency
134 West 83rd Street, 3rd Floor, New York, NY 10024
United States

mgya@lkgagency.com
query@lkgagency.com

http://lkgagency.com

CHILDREN'S
  Fiction > *Middle Grade*
    General, and in particular: Contemporary; High / Epic Fantasy; Magical Realism; Science Fiction; Thrillers
  Nonfiction > *Nonfiction Books*
YOUNG ADULT > Fiction > *Novels*

Does not want:

> **CHILDREN'S > Fiction >** *Middle Grade:* Horror

Send: Query; Synopsis; Writing sample
How to send: Email

Specializes in middle grade and young adult fiction. Within children's, is primarily drawn to contemporary and magical realism but is open to high fantasy, sci-fi, thriller, almost everything except maybe horror.

Literary Agent: Lauren Galit

L399 Jonathan Lloyd
Literary Agent; President
United Kingdom

Literary Agency: Curtis Brown (**L147**)

Fiction > *Novels*

Nonfiction > *Nonfiction Books*

Send: Query; Synopsis; Writing sample
How to send: Online submission system

Represents a number of best-selling fiction authors who feature in the Guardian Top 100 annual list and he also has a wide range of non-fiction clients and well known autobiographers, from politicians to celebrities.

L400 Dominic Lord
Literary Agent
United Kingdom

Literary Agency: JFL Agency (**L327**)

L401 Lotus Lane Literary
Literary Agency
United States

contact@lotuslit.com

https://lotuslit.com

Fiction > *Novels*

Nonfiction > *Nonfiction Books*

Closed to approaches.

Independent literary agency based in New Jersey, representing a diverse list of debut and seasoned authors. Handles adult fiction and nonfiction, and sells rights to the US, UK, Europe, and India.

Literary Agent: Priya Doraswamy

L402 Morwenna Loughman
Literary Agent
United Kingdom

https://www.thebksagency.com/about

Literary Agency: The BKS Agency (**L063**)

Fiction > *Novels*

Nonfiction > *Nonfiction Books*
Cookery; Lifestyle; Narrative Nonfiction; Popular Psychology; Popular Science

How to send: Online submission system

I am looking for narrative non-fiction, particularly across smart thinking, pop-science and pop-psychology – as well as lifestyle and cookery. I'm open to all types of fiction.

L403 Amberley Lowis
Literary Agent
15 Lyne Crescent, London, E17 5HY
United Kingdom

amberley@thevineyagency.com

http://thevineyagency.com/about.html

Literary Agency: The Viney Agency (**L626**)

ADULT
Fiction > *Novels*
Book Club Fiction; Commercial; Literary

Nonfiction > *Nonfiction Books*

Biography; Cookery; Memoir; Narrative Nonfiction

CHILDREN'S > **Fiction** > *Novels*

YOUNG ADULT > **Fiction** > *Novels*

Send: Query; Synopsis; Writing sample
How to send: Post

I'm actively building my list and looking for debut commercial, reading group and literary fiction. I love beautifully crafted, evocative and original storytelling. I am also very interested in a broad range of lively and original non-fiction, particularly in the areas of narrative non-fiction, biography, memoir and cookery. I am also developing a children's and young adult fiction list.

L404 Eric Lupfer
Literary Agent
United States

Literary Agency: Fletcher & Company (**L225**)

L405 David Luxton
Literary Agent
United Kingdom

https://www.davidluxtonassociates.co.uk/the-agency/

Literary Agency: David Luxton Associates (**L160**)

Nonfiction > *Nonfiction Books*
Food; Music; Politics; Sport

Principal interests are in the fields of sport, music, food-writing and politics and he represents a diverse range of authors including countless high-profile sports personalities.

L406 Rebecca Lyon
Literary Agent
United Kingdom

https://www.sheilland.com/about

Literary Agency: Sheil Land Associates Ltd (**L567**)

Scripts
Film Scripts; *TV Scripts*; *Theatre Scripts*

L407 Rhea Lyons
Literary Agent
United States

rhea@hgliterary.com

https://www.hgliterary.com/rhea

Literary Agency: HG Literary (**L305**)

ADULT
Fiction
Graphic Novels: General
Novels: Commercial; Fantasy; Horror; Literary; Science Fiction
Nonfiction > *Nonfiction Books*
Journalism; Narrative Nonfiction

CHILDREN'S > **Nonfiction** > *Nonfiction Books*

Closed to approaches.

Looking to represent writers of fiction, nonfiction, and graphic novelists who want to confront and destroy the status quo. For fiction, she is looking for anything that could be deemed literary/commercial crossover with a speculative bend, as well as science fiction and fantasy -- both true to the genre as well as genre-busting -- told in an accessible, entertaining voice. She likes horror but more on the cerebral end, less on the gory end (slashers are a no). For nonfiction, she is looking for narrative nonfiction and journalistic deep-dives into a single subject, particular location, or that examines a moment in history from an underrepresented, international, or little-known point of view. For children's books, she is especially interested in nonfiction that inspires learning and creativity for all ages.

L408 Emily MacDonald
Literary Agent
United Kingdom

emilymacdonald@42mp.com

https://www.42mp.com/agents
https://twitter.com/Ebh_mac

Literary Agency: 42 Management and Production

Fiction > *Novels*
Literary; Upmarket

Nonfiction > *Nonfiction Books*
History; Memoir; Narrative Nonfiction; Nature; Regional; Scotland; Social Commentary

Closed to approaches.

Looking for literary fiction, narrative nonfiction with an investigative twist, and untold true stories, either personal or historical. Also interested in Scottish and regional voices with stories to tell.

L409 Laura Macdougall
Literary Agent
United Kingdom

LMacdougall@unitedagents.co.uk

https://www.unitedagents.co.uk/lmacdougallunitedagentscouk
https://twitter.com/L_Macdougall
https://www.instagram.com/lmac_84/?hl=en
https://www.pinterest.co.uk/lmvmacdougall/

Literary Agency: United Agents (**L619**)

Fiction > *Novels*
Book Club Fiction; Commercial; Historical Fiction; LGBTQIA; Literary; Romance; Saga

Nonfiction
Illustrated Books: General

Nonfiction Books: Gardening; History; LGBTQIA; Narrative Nonfiction; Nature; Parenting; Philosophy; Politics; Science; Scotland

Send: Synopsis; Writing sample; Proposal
How to send: Email

I represent a diverse spectrum of commercial fiction – saga, romance, historical, book club and 'up-lit' – and literary fiction, ranging from the quirky to the daring and experimental. I've always been a big fan of historical fiction and also have a soft spot for novels that explore the complexities of relationships and family life.

My non-fiction list is equally varied, spanning illustrated books to parenting titles, history, popular philosophy and gardening. I also represent a fascinating wealth of narrative non-fiction, from Scottish nature writing to death, hormones, materials science, politics, manufacturing and the recent history of gay bars. A writer who can successfully communicate their passion, whether that's about something niche or obscure or a global phenomenon, will always be of interest to me.

As a queer woman, I represent a large number of LGBTQ writers and I'm particularly keen to hear from those who also identify as LGBTQ and who are exploring the full spectrum of LGBTQ lives in their writing.

L410 MacGregor & Luedeke

Literary Agency
PO Box 1316, Manzanita, OR 97130
United States
Tel: +1 (503) 389-4803

submissions@macgregorliterary.com

http://www.macgregorandluedeke.com
https://twitter.com/MacGregorLit

Fiction > *Novels*
 Christianity; Literary; Romance

Nonfiction > *Nonfiction Books*
 Crime; Memoir; Self Help; Spirituality

Send: Query; Market info; Author bio; Writing sample
Don't send: Full text
How to send: Email

Costs: Author covers sundry admin costs.

The company has focused on specific niche markets — memoir, spirituality, self-help books, Christian and literary fiction, true crime, romance, as well as some specialty projects.

Authors: Don Brown; Davis Bunn; Rashawn Copeland; Sheila Gregoire; Rachel Hauck; James Byron Huggins; Steve Jackson; Jessica Kate; Rachel Linden; Holly Lorincz; Evelyn Lozada; Scott Parazynski; Jay Payleitner; Tom Satterly; Kimberly Stuart; David Thomas; Vincent Zandri

Literary Agent / President: Chip MacGregor

Literary Agent / Vice President: Amanda Luedeke

L411 Kate Mack

Literary Agent; Vice President; Company Director
United States

https://www.aevitascreative.com/agent/kate-mack

Literary Agency: Aevitas

Nonfiction
 Illustrated Books: General
 Nonfiction Books: Culture; Fashion; History; Music

Closed to approaches.

She is most interested in cultural history, fashion, music, illustrated books for adults, strong female voices, and stories that give a voice to a person or community that's historically been silenced or ostracized.

Authors: Joana Avillez; Robyn Crawford; Liza Donnelly; America Ferrera; Patricia Field; Katy Fishell; Lucretia Tye Jasmine; Betsey Johnson; Sam Kashner; Rookie Magazine; Ian Purkayastha; Kate Schelter; Ramin Setoodeh; Amber Share; Kate Sidley; Kevin West; Alden Wicker

L412 Joanna MacKenzie

Literary Agent
United States

https://nelsonagency.com/joanna-mackenzie/
https://www.publishersmarketplace.com/members/JoannaMacKenzie/
https://twitter.com/joannamackenzie
https://www.facebook.com/joanna.topor.mackenzie

Literary Agency: Nelson Literary Agency, LLC (**L472**)

Fiction > *Novels*
 Commercial; Family; Friends; Mystery; Speculative; Thrillers; Women's Fiction

Send: Author bio; Query; Writing sample
How to send: By referral

Interested in high-concept, twisty, unputdownable stories with a strong voice in the areas of women's fiction, thriller, and speculative; timely commercial fiction in which the personal intersects with the world at large, and/or that explores toxic friendships and complex, challenging family dynamics; Heartfelt and timeless stories that you want to re-read about identity, unlikely friendships, reinvention, second acts, and women finding their voices and power, especially with touches of magic or speculative; Voicey, confident, atmospheric mysteries set in close-knit communities; creepy islands and Midwest-set are a plus. Always looking for stories about the immigrant experience.

Authors: Brooke Abrams; Kate Baer; Ali Brady; Lina Chern; Shana Galen; John Galligan; Jill Grunenwald; Alison Hammer; Sarah Zachrich Jeng; Sierra Kincade; Karen Koh; Gillian Libby; Amanda Marbais; Jonathan Messinger; Meghan Scott Molin; Katrina Monroe; Lyndsay Rush; Kristen Simmons; Jennifer Springsteen; Stacy Stokes; Joy Sullivan; Chrysler Szarlan; Ben Tanzer; Kathleen West

L413 Jamie Maclean

Literary Agent
United Kingdom

https://cmm.agency/about-us.php

Literary Agency: Coombs Moylett & Maclean Literary Agency (**L138**)

Fiction > *Novels*
 Erotic; Historical Crime; Mystery; Thrillers

Nonfiction > *Nonfiction Books*
 Gender Politics; How To; Lifestyle; Relationships

Send: Synopsis; Writing sample
How to send: Online submission system

Specialises in both fiction and nonfiction and is particularly interested in sexual politics, relationship, lifestyle how-to's, erotica, thrillers, whodunit and historical crime.

L414 Lauren MacLeod

Senior Agent
United States

https://www.aevitascreative.com/agent/lauren-macleod
https://www.strothmanagency.com/about
https://querymanager.com/query/LMacLeod
https://twitter.com/Lauren_MacLeod
http://aaronline.org/Sys/PublicProfile/12259463/417813

Literary Agencies: Aevitas; The Strothman Agency (**L593**)
Professional Body: Association of American Literary Agents (AALA)

ADULT > **Nonfiction** > *Nonfiction Books*
 Cookery; Crime; Food; History; Memoir; Narrative Nonfiction; Popular Culture

CHILDREN'S > **Fiction** > *Middle Grade*

YOUNG ADULT > **Fiction** > *Novels*

Send: Query
How to send: Email; Query Manager; By referral

Only accepting nonfiction queries for food writing, cookbooks, true crime, and pop culture without a referral. If you have a memoir, narrative nonfiction, or YA or MG fiction project and have been referred by a friend or client, make contact directly.

Authors: Hélène Boudreau; Helene Dunbar; Rogelio Garcia; Kenny Gilbert; Tyler Gillespie; Ron Goldberg; Steven Hale; Allison

Horrocks; Sashi Kaufman; Claire and Alan Linic; Mary Mahoney; Nicole Maines; Jodi Meadows; Andrea Mosqueda; Frederick Douglass Opie; Erik Rebain; Beck Rourke-Mooney; Aminah Mae Safi; Alora Young

L415 Eve MacSweeney
Literary Agent
United States

https://www.fletcherandco.com/team/eve-macsweeney/

Literary Agency: Fletcher & Company (**L225**)

Fiction > *Novels*: Literary

Nonfiction > *Nonfiction Books*: Narrative Nonfiction

Developing narrative non-fiction and literary fiction titles that speak to her interest in emotionally driven stories, singular voices, and compelling social issues, particularly as they concern the lives of women.

L416 Neeti Madan
Senior Agent
United States

https://www.sll.com/our-team

Literary Agency: Sterling Lord Literistic, Inc. (**L583**)

Fiction > *Novels*

Nonfiction > *Nonfiction Books*
  Journalism; Lifestyle; Memoir; Popular Culture

Send: Query; Synopsis; Writing sample
How to send: Online submission system

Her books run the gamut from the commercial to the cerebral. A true generalist, she is drawn to thoughtful writing on intriguing and important subjects, including memoir, journalism, popular culture, lifestyle, and the occasional novel. She is on the lookout for the types of books she loves as a reader—writing that breaks through barriers and elevates underrepresented voices, page-turners that keep her up until 3 AM, and irreverent books that makes her laugh.

Associate Agent: Maria Bell (**L054**)

L417 Madeleine Milburn Literary, TV & Film Agency
Literary Agency
The Factory, 1 Park Hill, London, SW4 9NS
United Kingdom
Tel: +44 (0) 20 7499 7550

submissions@madeleinemilburn.com
childrens@madeleinemilburn.com
info@madeleinemilburn.com

https://madeleinemilburn.co.uk
https://twitter.com/MMLitAgency
https://www.instagram.com/madeleinemilburn/?hl=en

https://www.facebook.com/MadeleineMilburnLiteraryAgency

Professional Body: The Association of Authors' Agents (AAA)

ADULT
  Fiction > *Novels*
  Nonfiction > *Nonfiction Books*

CHILDREN'S
  Fiction > *Novels*
  Nonfiction > *Nonfiction Books*

NEW ADULT
  Fiction > *Novels*
  Nonfiction > *Nonfiction Books*

TEEN
  Fiction > *Novels*
  Nonfiction > *Nonfiction Books*

YOUNG ADULT
  Fiction > *Novels*
  Nonfiction > *Nonfiction Books*

Send: Query; Synopsis; Pitch; Market info; Writing sample
How to send: Online submission system
How not to send: Post; Email

Represents award-winning and bestselling authors of adult and children's fiction and non-fiction. Submit via online submissions system. No submissions by post or by email.

Associate Agents: Maddy Belton (**L055**); Rachel Yeoh (**L667**)

Chief Executive Officer / Literary Agent: Madeleine Milburn (**L447**)

Literary Agents: Emma Bal (**L042**); Olivia Maidment (**L418**); Hannah Todd (**L615**)

Managing Director: Giles Milburn

Senior Agent: Chloe Seager (**L558**)

L418 Olivia Maidment
Literary Agent
United Kingdom

submissions@madeleinemilburn.com

https://www.madeleinemilburn.co.uk/agents/olivia-maidment/
https://twitter.com/liv_maidment

Literary Agency: Madeleine Milburn Literary, TV & Film Agency (**L417**)

Fiction > *Novels*
  Book Club Fiction; Contemporary; Culture; Family Saga; High Concept; Historical Fiction; Literary; Magical Realism; Politics; Social Issues; Speculative; Upmarket

Nonfiction > *Nonfiction Books*: Narrative Nonfiction

Send: Synopsis; Writing sample
How to send: Email
How not to send: Post

Looking for literary, upmarket, and book club fiction; contemporary and historical fiction;

narrative non-fiction; human stories; sweeping narratives; urgent themes; identity driven narratives; social, cultural, political themes; speculative fiction; magical realism; multi-generational; high concept stories; big ideas; thought provoking narratives.

L419 Rachel Mann
Literary Agent
United Kingdom

http://www.jounwin.co.uk/rachel-mann/

Literary Agency: Jo Unwin Literary Agency (**L328**)

ADULT
  Fiction > *Novels*
    Commercial; Literary

  Nonfiction > *Nonfiction Books*
    Comedy / Humour; Lifestyle

CHILDREN'S
  Fiction > *Middle Grade*
    Commercial; High Concept

  Nonfiction > *Nonfiction Books*
    Comedy / Humour; Lifestyle

YOUNG ADULT > **Fiction** > *Novels*

Does not want:

> **CHILDREN'S** > **Fiction** > *Picture Books*

In all cases I want compelling voices, unpatronizing writing and vivid, complex characters. International settings and traditions, unconventional narratives, and radical social commentary will always get my attention. I'm particularly interested in writers from underrepresented backgrounds writing across genres for both adults and children, especially those writing joyful and uplifting work, or darkly funny stories.

I want to see work that engages with the very urgent need for action on our climate and environment, and the ways in which this is affecting our individual and collective psyches.

I represent the full spectrum of 'commercial' through to 'literary' fiction for adults. I'd love to see strong hooks, compelling voices and rich world-building, often with both humour and darkness.

At the moment, I'm very much on the look-out for both contemporary and high-concept middle-grade, and stories that present gentler forms of masculinity than those previously seen in this area of the market. I'm interested in ambitious and cinematic YA novels, and new takes on existing tropes and genres.

Authors: Heather Akumiah; Zoe Beaty; Soraya Bouazzaoui; Wibke Brueggemann; Fran Bushe; Darren Chetty; Eliza Clark; Ellie Clements; Lucy Cuthew; Caleb Femi; Mark Grist; Jade LB; Janelle McCurdy; Jack

Meggitt-Phillips; Catriona Morton; Gary Panton; Gianna Pollero; Bethany Rutter; Angharad Walker

L420 Kendra Marcus

Literary Agent
United States

http://www.bookstopliterary.com/submission.html

Literary Agency: BookStop Literary Agency, LLC (**L069**)

CHILDREN'S
Fiction
Novels: General
Picture Books: Comedy / Humour

Nonfiction > *Nonfiction Books*
General, and in particular: History; Science

How to send: By referral

Gravitates toward quirky and funny picture books, fiction with unforgettable characters and stories that will bring her to tears. Unusual non-fiction, especially science presented in new ways and little gems of history are also her cup of tea. Stories with Hispanic or Latino characters are always welcome, and she is thrilled to find accomplished illustrators with a fresh style who can tell a strong story in pictures to accompany a text.

L421 Marjacq Scripts Ltd

Literary Agency
The Space, 235 High Holborn, London, WC1V 7DN
United Kingdom
Tel: +44 (0) 20 7935 9499

enquiries@marjacq.com

http://www.marjacq.com
https://twitter.com/marjacqscripts

Professional Body: The Association of Authors' Agents (AAA)

ADULT
Fiction > *Novels*

Nonfiction > *Nonfiction Books*

Scripts
Film Scripts; *TV Scripts*
CHILDREN'S
Fiction > *Novels*
Nonfiction > *Nonfiction Books*

Send: Query
Don't send: Full text
How to send: Email
How not to send: Post

Accepts submissions by email only. For books, send query with synopsis and first 50 pages. For scripts, send short treatment and entire screenplay. Send only Word or PDF documents less than 2MB. Do not paste work into the body of the email. See website for full details. No children's picture books, poetry, plays or musical theatre.

Authors: Tanya Atapattu; Holly Baxter; Alexandra K Benedict; Daisy Buchanan; Cecil Cameron; James Campbell; Angela Clarke; Mathew Clayton; Fiona Collins; Caroline Corcoran; Isabel Costello; Hannah Dolby; Francesca Dorricott; Lilly Ebert; Dov Forman; Eve Harris; Louise Hulland; Catriona Innes; Harriet Johnson; Amy Jones; Eve Makis; Andrea Mara; Francesca May; Claire McGowan; Emma Orchard; Adam Pearson; Fiona Perrin; Alice Peterson; Das Petrou; Rachel Phipps; Carmen Reid; Samantha Renke; Lee Ridley; Diana Rosie; Frances Ryan; Jennifer Savin; Hema Sukumar; Lucy Vine; James Wallman; Roz Watkins; Eva Woods

Literary Agents: Diana Beaumont (**L053**); Leah Middleton (**L445**); Philip Patterson; Imogen Pelham (*L494*); Catherine Pellegrino; Sandra Sawicka (*L551*)

L422 Mildred Marmur

Literary Agent
United States

Literary Agency: Mildred Marmur Associates, Ltd. (**L448**)

L423 Jill Marr

Literary Agent
United States

https://www.dijkstraagency.com/agent-page.php?agent_id=Marr
https://querymanager.com/query/JillMarr

Literary Agency: Sandra Dijkstra Literary Agency

Fiction > *Novels*
Commercial; Fantasy; Folklore, Myths, and Legends; Food; Gothic; Historical Fiction; Horror; Magical Realism; Mystery; Psychological Suspense; Romance; Romantic Comedy; Speculative; Thrillers; Upmarket

Nonfiction > *Nonfiction Books*
Comedy / Humour; Crime; Current Affairs; Health; History; Memoir; Music; Narrative Nonfiction; Nutrition; Politics; Popular Culture; Science; Social Commentary; Sport

How to send: Query Manager

Looking for fiction and non-fiction by unrepresented voices, BIPOC and Latinx writers, disabled persons, and people identifying as LGBTQ+, among others. She is interested in commercial and upmarket fiction, with an emphasis on mysteries, thrillers, Gothic, horror, romance, fantasy, speculative fiction, and historical fiction. She loves food-centric novels, no matter what the genre. She is looking to find more rom coms with a fresh voice, perspective and a strong hook. When it comes to suspense she likes it dark and psychological. Her tastes lean more in the vein of The Silent Patient, The Lost Apothecary or

Mexican Gothic than Private Investigator and CIA stories. And she almost never takes on military or Western projects. However she is a sucker for novels with grounded magical realism, and is always looking for a new take on mythology or folklore. She is also looking for non-fiction by authors with a big, timely, smart message. She'd like to see work that does a deep dive into subcultures and social commentary as well as historical projects that look at big picture issues. She is looking for non-fiction projects in the areas of current events, true crime, science, history, narrative non-fiction, sports, politics, health and nutrition, pop culture, humor, music, and very select memoir.

L424 The Marsh Agency

Literary Agency
50 Albemarle Street, London, W1S 4BD
United Kingdom
Tel: +44 (0) 20 7493 4361

http://www.marsh-agency.co.uk

Professional Body: The Association of Authors' Agents (AAA)

Types: Fiction; Nonfiction
Subjects: Literary
Markets: Adult; Young Adult

Closed to approaches.

Not currently accepting unsolicited mss as at March 2018. Most new clients come through recommendations.

Authors: Jill Bays; Ian Dear; Ed Halliwell; Tendai Huchu; Sam Kriss; Anita Nair; Alan Palmer; Allyson Pollock; Alfred Price; Gillian Riley; Richard Seymour; Christine Shaw

Literary Agent: Susie Nicklin

L425 Jen Marshall

Literary Agent
New York
United States

https://www.aevitascreative.com/agent/jen-marshall
https://querymanager.com/query/JenMarshall
https://twitter.com/jenmarshall3

Literary Agency: Aevitas

ADULT
Fiction
Graphic Novels: General
Novels: Adventure; Commercial; Crime; Drama; Horror; Literary; Popular Culture; Romance
Nonfiction > *Nonfiction Books*
Arts; Business; Crime; Design; Fashion; Health; History; Investigative Journalism; Mathematics; Narrative Nonfiction; Popular Culture; Science; Social Justice; Technology

CHILDREN'S > **Fiction** > *Novels*

Closed to approaches.

Represents acclaimed and bestselling narrative nonfiction projects. Also represents select literary and commercial fiction projects. Areas of interest in nonfiction are wide-ranging: investigative journalism, untold histories, fashion and design, social justice, true crime, tech, business, science, cities, and pop culture. In fiction, she primarily seeks literary and commercial works for adults.

Authors: Natasha S. Barrett; Elena Brower; Maggie Bullock; Windy Chien; Hopwood DePree; Danielle Dreilinger; Neil Gross; Ericka Hart; Gabrielle Hartley; Katherine Sharp Landdeck; Marisa Meltzer; Jenny Minton; Vanessa O'Brien; Joe Pompeo; Gene Pressman; Paul Pringle; Nancy Jo Sales; Kate Schapira; Chris Smalls; Keziah Weir.

L426 Olivia Martin
Associate Agent
United Kingdom
Tel: +44 (0) 20 3214 0778

omartin@unitedagents.co.uk

https://www.unitedagents.co.uk/omartinunitedagentscouk

Literary Agency: United Agents (**L619**)
Literary Agent: Charles Walker (**L629**)

Authors: Anjana Appachana; Neil Ely; Lloyd Eyre-Morgan; Max Tobin

L427 Maria Massie
Literary Agent
United States

Literary Agency: Massie & McQuilkin

Fiction > *Novels*: Literary

Nonfiction > *Nonfiction Books*
    Memoir; Narrative Nonfiction

Send: Query; Author bio; Writing sample
How to send: In the body of an email

Brings over two decades' worth of experience in representing authors and helping to make sure that they can be read around the world.

L428 Rebecca Matte
Literary Agent
United States

https://bradfordlit.com/about/rebecca-matte/
https://querymanager.com/query/RMatte
https://www.manuscriptwishlist.com/mswl-post/rebecca-matte/
https://twitter.com/rebeccalmatte

Literary Agency: Bradford Literary Agency (**L073**)

ADULT > **Fiction** > *Novels*
    Disabilities; Fantasy Romance; Fantasy; Queer Romance; Romance; Science Fiction

YOUNG ADULT > **Fiction** > *Novels*
    Disabilities; Fantasy Romance; Fantasy; Queer Romance; Romance; Science Fiction

Closed to approaches.

Loves adult and YA science fiction/fantasy and queer romance. But no matter the setting—be it a far off kingdom beset by magic or around the corner in Brooklyn—she seeks out books that feature diverse, complex characters in deeply rooted relationships, platonic and romantic. A well-crafted romance will make her heart sing, while a beautifully detailed friendship will elevate any book to an instant favorite. She also gravitates towards inherently hopeful stories of self-discovery and reinvention at all ages, particularly those that center questions of gender and sexuality. She tries to bring magic to every moment of life, and loves books that do the same.

L429 Jennifer Mattson
Literary Agent
United States

jmatt@andreabrownlit.com

https://www.andreabrownlit.com/Team/Jennifer-Mattson
http://twitter.com/jannmatt
http://instagram.com/jennmattson
https://www.publishersmarketplace.com/members/JenMatt/
https://www.manuscriptwishlist.com/mswl-post/jennifer-mattson/
https://querymanager.com/query/JenniferMattson

Literary Agency: Andrea Brown Literary Agency, Inc.

CHILDREN'S > **Fiction** > *Middle Grade*

YOUNG ADULT > **Fiction** > *Novels*

How to send: Query Manager

Represents authors, illustrators, and author-illustrators who bring a distinct point of view to their work, and who tell stories with multiple layers. In middle grade and YA both, her heart beats faster for stories that cascade from a mind-expanding premise. She also loves survival stories and losing herself in Dickensian sagas (WOLVES OF WILLOUGHBY CHASE!), and enjoys watching characters puzzle their way through problems. She has a special soft spot for middle grade about resilient kids sorting out the messiness of life.

L430 Jane Graham Maw
Literary Agent
United Kingdom

submissions@grahammawchristie.com

https://www.grahammawchristie.com/about

Literary Agency: Graham Maw Christie Literary Agency (**L263**)

Nonfiction > *Nonfiction Books*
    General, and in particular: Activism; Memoir; Narrative Nonfiction; Psychology

Send: Outline; Author bio; Market info; Writing sample; Proposal; Pitch
How to send: Email

For general non-fiction she seeks out activists, psychologists, creatives, change-makers and thought-leaders. On the narrative/memoir side she is looking for beautifully crafted books that take the reader somewhere new – a time, a place, or an experience, while managing to be universally appealing. The topics her authors write about are often aligned to the changes readers are seeking post-pandemic.

L431 Juliana McBride
Literary Agent
United States

https://rfliterary.com/about/
https://querymanager.com/query/JulianaMcBride
https://twitter.com/julianaotabot
https://www.instagram.com/julianalovesbooks/
https://www.manuscriptwishlist.com/mswl-post/juliana-mcbride/

Literary Agency: Rebecca Friedman Literary Agency

ADULT > **Fiction** > *Novels*
    Commercial; Literary

CHILDREN'S > **Fiction** > *Middle Grade*
    Contemporary; Relationships; Speculative

YOUNG ADULT > **Fiction** > *Novels*

How to send: Submittable

Loves commercial and literary fiction, young adult novels, and middle grade novels; mostly grounded contemporary stories with a speculative element, and honest stories that explore relationships and make her laugh.

L432 McCormick Literary
Literary Agency
United States
Tel: +1 (212) 691-9726

queries@mccormicklit.com

http://mccormicklit.com

ADULT

    Fiction > *Novels*
        Commercial; Literary

    Nonfiction > *Nonfiction Books*
        Arts; Biography; Cookery; Cultural History; Memoir; Narrative Nonfiction; Politics

YOUNG ADULT > **Fiction** > *Novels*

Send: Query; Author bio; Writing sample
How to send: Email
How not to send: Email attachment

Send queries by email with short bio and ten sample pages, indicating in the subject line which agent you are querying (see website for individual agent interests). No attachments. Response only if interested.

Literary Agents: Bridget McCarthy; David McCormick; Edward Orloff; Pilar Queen

L433 Matt McGowan
Senior Agent; Vice President
United States

mm@goldinlit.com

Literary Agency: Frances Goldin Literary Agency, Inc. (**L231**)

Fiction > *Novels*: Literary

Nonfiction
Essays: General
Nonfiction Books: Biography; Crime; Culture; Food; Football / Soccer; History; Journalism; Memoir; Narrative Nonfiction; Politics; Popular Culture; Popular Science; Sport; Sub-Culture; Travel

How to send: Email

Looking for emotionally, intellectually, and formally adventurous work of all kinds and is particularly interested in writers who believe nonfiction can be as artful as fiction. Queries for essays; literary fiction (strong but difficult characters, examinations of place, sub-cultures, and/or recent history or time periods); researched narrative nonfiction; journalism; politics; history; memoir; biography; cultural studies; popular culture & science; sports (particularly soccer); travel, crime, food, literary graphic work (especially NF), are all welcome.

L434 Eunice McMullen
Literary Agent
United Kingdom

Literary Agency: Eunice McMullen Children's Literary Agent Ltd

L435 Rob McQuilkin
Literary Agent
United States

info@mmqlit.com

https://www.mmqlit.com/about/

Literary Agency: Massie & McQuilkin

Fiction > *Novels*

Nonfiction > *Nonfiction Books*
Cultural Criticism; History; Memoir

Poetry > *Poetry Collections*

Send: Query; Author bio; Writing sample
How to send: Email

Specializes in fiction, memoir, history, cultural criticism, and poetry.

L436 Sara Megibow
Vice President; Senior Agent
United States

Literary Agency: KT Literary (**L368**)

Closed to approaches.

L437 Jane von Mehren
Literary Agent; Senior Partner
United States

https://aevitascreative.com/agents/

Literary Agency: Aevitas

Fiction > *Novels*
Book Club Fiction; Historical Fiction; Literary

Nonfiction > *Nonfiction Books*
Business; History; Memoir; Popular Culture; Science

Send: Query; Author bio; Market info; Writing sample
How to send: Online submission system

Interested in narratives in the areas of business, history, memoir, popular culture and science, books that help us live our best lives, literary, book club, and historical fiction.

Authors: Ruthie Ackerman; Alan Andres; Daniel Barbarisi; Jené Ray Barranco; Christine Melanie Benson; Janet Benton; Dan Bouk; Susan Bratton; Jared Brock; Anne Brusatte; Stephen Brusatte; Maggie Bullock; Nicole Centeno; Carrie Classon; Stacey Colino; Tyler Cowen; David Daley; Carey Davidson; Peter J. Dean; Maddy Dychtwald; Linda T. Elkins-Tanton; Carla Fernandez; Emily Jane Fox; Ramin Ganeshram; Bob Garfield; David Gilkey; Sabrina Greenlee; Daniel Gross; Mauro Guillén; Minrose Gwin; Heather Hirsch; Jessica Iannotta; Kendra James; Claire Jimenez; Jordan Kassalow; Eliza Kingsford; Linda Kay Klein; Erica Komisar; Alison Kosik; Jennifer Krause; Shannon Lee; Adam Valen Levinson; Pamela Lilly; Heather K. Lloyd; John Long; Humble Lukanga; Andrea Marcum; Christopher Marquis; Ama Marston; Stephanie Marston; Leigh Marz; Kevin Morris; Paul Napper; Raul Palma; Richard Parker; Marilyn Paul; Dr. Deborah Plummer; Gene Pressman; Nathan Raab; National Public Radio; Anthony Rao; Travis Rieder; Travis N. Rieder; Jodi Rogers; Francine Russo; Robin Ryan; Jonathan Santlofer; Tom Selleck; Molly D. Shepard; Robert Stone; Susan Stryker; Shanna Swan; Anne Bahr Thompson; Allie Ticktin; Michael Veltri; Wanda Wallace; Caroline Webb; Glen Weldon; Rob Wesson; Kelvin Wong; Clive D. Wynne; Justin Zorn

L438 Isabel Mendia
Associate Agent
United States

https://www.cheneyagency.com/isabel-mendia

Literary Agency: The Cheney Agency

Nonfiction > *Nonfiction Books*
Cultural Criticism; History; Narrative Journalism; Politics

Send: Query; Self-Addressed Stamped Envelope (SASE)
How to send: Post; Email

Interested in representing a range of nonfiction, including cultural criticism, narrative reportage, politics, and history.

L439 Meridian Artists
Literary Agency
43 Britain Street, Suite A02, Toronto, Ontario M5A 1R7
Canada
Tel: +1 (416) 961-2777

info@meridianartists.com

https://www.meridianartists.com

Fiction > *Novels*

Nonfiction > *Nonfiction Books*

Scripts
Film Scripts; *TV Scripts*

Send: Synopsis; Author bio; Writing sample
How to send: Online submission system

Offers premier full-service entertainment industry representation with principal offices in Toronto and Los Angeles. An established leader in the representation and management of Talent, Screenwriters, Directors, Authors, and Key Creatives.

L440 Metamorphosis Literary Agency
Literary Agency
United States

info@metamorphosisliteraryagency.com

https://www.metamorphosisliteraryagency.com
https://www.facebook.com/metamorphosislitagent
https://twitter.com/MetamorphLitAg
https://www.linkedin.com/company/metamorphosis-literary-agency
https://www.instagram.com/metamorphosis_literary_agency/

ADULT
Fiction > *Novels*
Nonfiction > *Nonfiction Books*

YOUNG ADULT > **Fiction** > *Novels*

Send: Query; Author bio; Writing sample; Synopsis
How to send: Query Manager

Costs: Author covers sundry admin costs.

Our mission is to help authors become traditionally published. We represent well-crafted commercial fiction and nonfiction. We work with authors to ensure that every book is in the best presentable form. Our publishing connections come from experience, numerous conferences, hard work, and genuine care.

Authors: Suleena Bibra; Kelly Cain; Natalie Cammaratta; Ashley M. Coleman; Stephanie Eding; Caroline Flynn; Charlee James; Karen Lynch; LaRonda Gardner Middlemiss; Janice Milusich; Anitra Rowe Schulte; Samara

Shanker; Angela Shanté; Bruce Smith; Laura Snider; Heather Grace Stewart; Shannon Stults

Junior Agent: Caroline Trussell (**L616**)

Senior Agents: Amy Brewer (**L079**); Erica Christensen (**L121**); Stephanie Hansen (**L285**); Jessica Reino (**L522**); Katie Salvo (**L545**)

L441 Mic Cheetham Literary Agency
Literary Agency
62 Grafton Way, London, W1T 5DW
United Kingdom
Tel: +44 (0) 20 3976 7713

submissions@miccheetham.co.uk

https://miccheetham.com

Fiction > *Novels*

Nonfiction > *Nonfiction Books*

Closed to approaches.

Agency with a deliberately small list. Only takes on two or three new writers each year. New writers are advised to acquaint themselves with the work of the writers currently represented by the agency before submitting their own work.

Authors: Carol Birch; Nm Browne; Pat Cadigan; Alan Campbell; Gregory Doran; Barbara Ewing; Ian Green; M John Harrison; Alice James; Ken MacLeod; Paul Mcauley; China Miéville; Sharon Penman; Antony Sher; Adrian Tchaikovsky

Literary Agents: Mic Cheetham (**L114**); Simon Kavanagh (**L347**)

L442 Caroline Michel
Literary Agent; Chief Executive Officer
United Kingdom
Tel: +44 (0) 20 7344 1000

cmichelsubmissions@pfd.co.uk

https://petersfraserdunlop.com/agent/caroline-michel/

Literary Agency: Peters Fraser + Dunlop (**L501**)

Fiction > *Novels*

Nonfiction > *Nonfiction Books*
  Biography; History; Science

Send: Query; Synopsis; Writing sample; Proposal; Author bio
How to send: Email
How not to send: Post

Loves everything and anything. She is endlessly curious about people's ideas, what's going on in the world and how to understand it, whether it's through history, fiction, biography, science. She is an eternal optimist and loves working with people who believe that everything is possible.

Authors: Jamie Bartlett; Camila Batmanghelidjh; Elaine Bedell; Simon Booker;

Peter Bowles; Rosie Boycott; Pattie Boyd; Melvyn Bragg; Jonathan Bryan; Michael Caine; Emma Calder; Tamsin Calidas; Mark Carney; Augustus Casely-Hayford; Mavis Cheek; Helen Chislett; Rita Clifton; Sebastian Coe; Georgia Coleridge; Natalia Conroy; Chi-chi Nwanoku

L443 Micheline Steinberg Associates
Literary Agency
Suite 315, ScreenWorks, 22 Highbury Grove, London, N5 2ER
United Kingdom

info@steinplays.com

http://www.steinplays.com
https://twitter.com/steinbergassocs

Scripts
  Film Scripts; *Radio Scripts*; *TV Scripts*; *Theatre Scripts*

Send: Query
How to send: By referral

We're a mid-size agency in which all the agents have background in theatre and related media. We work closely with writers and the industry, developing writers work, managing their careers, and negotiating all rights. We also have affiliations with book agents and agents overseas including in the USA. Please note that we do not accept unsolicited submissions without a letter of recommendation from an industry professional. All unsolicited material will be deleted unread. Does not consider books.

Literary Agents: Jazz Adamson; Micheline Steinberg

L444 Michelle Kass Associates
Literary Agency
85 Charing Cross Road, London, WC2H 0AA
United Kingdom
Tel: +44 (0) 20 7439 1624

office@michellekass.co.uk

http://www.michellekass.co.uk

Professional Body: The Association of Authors' Agents (AAA)

Fiction > *Novels*
  Commercial; Literary

Scripts
  Film Scripts; *TV Scripts*

How to send: Phone

Represents authors, dramatists/screenwriters, and screenwriters based in the UK and Ireland. Call before submitting.

Literary Agent: Michelle Kass (*L343*)

L445 Leah Middleton
Literary Agent
United Kingdom

leah@marjacq.com

http://www.marjacq.com/leah-middleton.html

Literary Agency: Marjacq Scripts Ltd (**L421**)

Scripts
  Film Scripts: General, and in particular: Comedy / Humour
  TV Scripts: General, and in particular: Comedy / Humour

Closed to approaches.

Represents book to screen and screenwriters.

L446 Natasha Mihell
Associate Agent
Canada

https://www.therightsfactory.com/Agents/Natasha-Mihell
https://querymanager.com/query/natashatrf

Literary Agency: The Rights Factory

ADULT
  Fiction > *Novels*
    Fantasy; Historical Fiction; Literary; Science Fiction

  Nonfiction
    Graphic Nonfiction: History
    Nonfiction Books: Memoir

CHILDREN'S
  Fiction
    Middle Grade: Allegory; Cyberpunk; Fantasy; Historical Fiction; Horror
    Picture Books: Magic

  Nonfiction > *Picture Books*

YOUNG ADULT
  Fiction > *Novels*
    Fantasy; Historical Fiction; Literary; Science Fiction

  Nonfiction
    Graphic Nonfiction: History
    Nonfiction Books: Memoir

Closed to approaches.

Loves stories that sing, move, and shimmer, and most especially, those that are fearless in speaking their truths. She is a great fan of conceptual depth and courage (in characters and in writing), and will consider any story (Adult, YA, MG, and PB; fiction and nonfiction) that has clear heart and vision. She is always keen to support voices from the 2SLGBTQQIA+, BIPOC, #ownvoices, disabled and neurodiverse communities.

Authors: Sylvie Cathrall; Joe Frye; C.C. Graystone; Taryn Herlich; Nicholas Pullen; Ana Toumine; Vani Varshney; Fatemeh Zarei

L447 Madeleine Milburn
Literary Agent; Chief Executive Officer
United Kingdom

https://madeleinemilburn.co.uk/team-member/
madeleine-milburn/
https://twitter.com/agentmilburn

Literary Agency: Madeleine Milburn Literary,
TV & Film Agency (**L417**)

Fiction > *Novels*
General, and in particular: Book Club
Fiction; Commercial; Crime; Family Saga;
Historical Fiction; Literary; Romantic
Mystery; Suspense; Thrillers; Upmarket

Send: Query; Pitch; Market info; Author bio;
Synopsis; Writing sample
How to send: Email
How not to send: Post

Open to submissions from writers based in the
UK and internationally, with strong ties in
Canada and the US, and looking for upmarket
and accessible literary fiction with a strong
hook, compelling characters and propulsive
storytelling. I'm looking to build on the crime
and thriller side of my list with a big new
suspense, and also looking for an epic multi-
generational family drama, or a powerful love
story with a mystery at its heart.

L448 Mildred Marmur
Associates, Ltd.
Literary Agency
2005 Palmer Avenue, Suite 127, Larchmont,
NY 10538
United States

https://aaronline.wildapricot.org/Sys/
PublicProfile/2176773/417813

Fiction > *Novels*

Nonfiction > *Nonfiction Books*

Literary agent based in Larchmont, New York.

Literary Agent: Mildred Marmur (*L422*)

L449 Jessica Mileo
Literary Agent
United States

submissions@inkwellmanagement.com

https://inkwellmanagement.com/staff/jessica-
mileo

Literary Agency: InkWell Management

ADULT
Fiction > *Novels*
Book Club Fiction; Commercial; High
Concept; Romantic Comedy; Women's
Fiction

Nonfiction > *Nonfiction Books*
Narrative Nonfiction; Prescriptive
Nonfiction

CHILDREN'S > **Fiction**
Graphic Novels; *Novels*

Send: Query; Writing sample
How to send: Email

Primarily focuses on children's books,
children's graphic novels, women's fiction,
rom-coms, commercial/book club fiction, and
select prescriptive and narrative nonfiction.
The projects she works with are high concept,
commercial, and have a juicy hook. She is
always looking for books that are from points
of view of underrepresented folks in books and
media, such as BIPOC and/or LGBTQIA+.

L450 Miles Stott Children's
Literary Agency
Literary Agency
East Hook Farm, Lower Quay Road, Hook,
Haverfordwest, Pembrokeshire, SA62 4LR
United Kingdom
Tel: +44 (0) 7855 252043

fictionsubs@milesstottagency.co.uk
picturebooksubs@milesstottagency.co.uk

https://www.milesstottagency.co.uk
https://www.facebook.com/pages/Miles-Stott-
Childrens-Literary-Agency/311096870669
https://twitter.com/MilesStott
https://www.instagram.com/milesstottagency/

Professional Body: The Association of
Authors' Agents (AAA)

CHILDREN'S
Fiction
Middle Grade; *Novels*; *Picture Books*
Nonfiction > *Nonfiction Books*

YOUNG ADULT > **Fiction** > *Novels*

Closed to approaches.

Handles Board books, Picture books, Novelty
Books, Young fiction, Middle grade fiction,
YA fiction, and Non-fiction. No poetry,
musical works, or educational texts. For fiction
send query with synopsis and first three
chapters. For picture book submissions, send
query by email only, with short covering letter,
details about you and your background, and up
to three stories. See website for full guidelines.

Authors: Kip Alizadeh; Kirsty Applebaum;
Atinuke; Dominic Barker; Helen Baugh; Adam
Beer; Rachel Bright; Mark Burgess; Ruth
Doyle; Catherine Emmett; Lu Fraser; Annelise
Gray; Stacy Gregg; Frances Hardinge; Caryl
Hart; Sophie Kirtley; Gill Lewis; Zoë Marriott;
Julia Miranda; Tom Percival; Gareth Peter;
Tom Pollock; Mark Sperring; Amber Stewart;
Leisa Stewart-Sharpe

Literary Agents: Victoria Birkett; Nancy Miles;
Mandy Suhr

L451 Rachel Mills
Literary Agent; Company Director
United Kingdom

rachel@rmliterary.co.uk

https://twitter.com/bookishyogini

Literary Agency: Rachel Mills Literary (**L517**)

Nonfiction > *Nonfiction Books*
Biography; Commercial; Food; Narrative
Nonfiction; Popular Science; Psychology;
Upmarket; Wellbeing

Send: Query; Writing sample
How to send: Email

Very selectively looking for new clients
writing commercial and upmarket non-fiction
and wishing to develop their work into major
global publishing and media brands. Areas of
interest include psychology, popular science,
well-being, narrative non-fiction, biography,
food, sustainability, health, social media and
platform led projects. She looks for projects
which are international and will work on
screen as well as in print.

L452 MMB Creative
Literary Agency
The Old Truman Brewery, 91 Brick Lane,
London, E1 6QL
United Kingdom
Tel: +44 (0) 20 3582 9370
Fax: +44 (0) 20 3582 9377

nonfiction@mmbcreative.com
literaryfiction@mmbcreative.com
historicalfiction@mmbcreative.com
romance@mmbcreative.com
sciencefiction@mmbcreative.com
fantasy@mmbcreative.com
asiansubmissions@mmbcreative.com
horror@mmbcreative.com

https://mmbcreative.com

Professional Body: The Association of
Authors' Agents (AAA)

Fiction > *Novels*
Allegory; Autofiction; Fabulism; Family
Saga; Fantasy; Historical Fiction; Horror;
Literary; Romance; Science Fiction

Nonfiction
Essays: General
Nonfiction Books: Art History;
Autobiography; Economics; History;
Literary Criticism; Literary Memoir;
Memoir; Personal Development; Politics;
Psychology; Science; Self Help; Social
Issues; Society

Send: Query; Synopsis; Author bio; Writing
sample; Market info
How to send: Email

Represents actors, authors, stage and screen
writers, presenters and voice over artists.

Literary Agents: Edwina de Charnace (**L111**);
Ivan Mulcahy; Sallyanne Sweeney

L453 Harriet Moore
Literary Agent
United Kingdom

harrietmoore@davidhigham.co.uk

https://www.davidhigham.co.uk/agents-dh/
harriet-moore/

Literary Agency: David Higham Associates
Ltd (**L159**)

Fiction > *Novels*: Literary

Nonfiction > *Nonfiction Books*
Biography; History; Narrative Nonfiction

Poetry > *Poetry Collections*
Closed to approaches.

Represents literary fiction, narrative nonfiction, and poetry. In fiction, she admires
clarity, energy, emotional candour, intense
interior portraits, close observation, texture,
craft and compression. In non-fiction she is
interested in creative scholarship; intellectual
and artistic endeavour; books which vibrantly
engage with archival work, biography, history,
criticism and private experience. In all forms
she is interested in how writing and visual art
correspond, and a scholarly attention to the
ordinary and everyday.

Authors: Rachael Allen; Jason Allen-Paisant;
Nuar Alsadir; Abi Andrews; Jennifer Atkins;
Harriet Baker; Felix Bazalgette; Sarah
Bernstein; Rebecca Birrell; Kevin Brazil; Ella
Bucknall; Eliza Barry Callahan; Kathleen
Collins; Sophie Collins; Emily S. Cooper;
Naoise Dolan; Alicia Drake; Rowan Evans;
Tom de Freston; Marlowe Granados; Jo
Hamya; Alice Hattrick; Lottie Hazell; Oli
Hazzard; Claire Marie Healy; Rebecca May
Johnson; Emily LaBarge; Sophie Mackintosh;
Kathryn Maris; Helen Marten; Thomas
McMullan; Rosanna Mclaughlin; Kei Miller;
Sandeep Parmar; Eleanor Penny; Hannah
Regel; Kathryn Scanlan; Izabella Scott;
Penelope Shuttle; Mary South; Dizz Tate; Jack
Underwood; Joanna Walsh; Miranda Ward;
Kate Zambreno

L454 Penny Moore
Literary Agent
United States

https://aevitascreative.com/agents/
https://querymanager.com/query/LiteraryPenny

Literary Agency: Aevitas

CHILDREN'S
Fiction
Middle Grade; *Picture Books*
Nonfiction > *Nonfiction Books*

YOUNG ADULT
Fiction > *Novels*
Nonfiction > *Nonfiction Books*

Send: Author bio; Query; Writing sample;
Market info
How to send: Query Manager

Mainly represents children's literature,
including picture books, middle grade, and
young adult. She also has an interest in select
platform nonfiction projects that speak to

younger audiences. Though she's interested in
all genres, she's specifically seeking inventive
works featuring breakout voices and
compelling plot lines that will make young
readers feel seen and heard for the first time.

Authors: Shawn Amos; Akemi Dawn
Bowman; Waka Brown; Auriane Desombre;
Lyla Lee; Sophia Lee; Sangu Mandanna; Maya
Prasad; Nicki Pau Preto; Rona Wang; Jenna
Yoon; Katie Zhao

L455 Tim Moore
Associate Agent

https://www.therightsfactory.com/Agents/Tim-
Moore
https://querymanager.com/query/2396

Literary Agency: The Rights Factory

Fiction > *Novels*
Commercial; Literary

Nonfiction > *Nonfiction Books*
Biography; Business; Comedy / Humour;
Food and Drink; Health; Memoir; Personal
Development; Photography; Self Help;
Wellbeing

How to send: Query Manager

Represents adult non-fiction and fiction. He is
interested in non-fiction which has a clear
platform and fiction which has a distinctive
voice.

L456 Max Moorhead
Junior Agent
United States

http://www.mmqlit.com/about/

Literary Agency: Massie & McQuilkin

L457 Imogen Morrell
Literary Agent
United Kingdom

http://greeneheaton.co.uk/agents/imogen-
morrell/
https://twitter.com/imogen_morrell

Literary Agency: Greene & Heaton Ltd (**L269**)

Fiction > *Novels*
Book Club Fiction; Crime; High Concept;
Historical Fiction; Literary; Politics;
Romance; Romantic Comedy; Society;
Speculative; Thrillers

Nonfiction > *Nonfiction Books*
Cookery; Food; History; Nature; Politics

Send: Query; Synopsis; Writing sample
How to send: Email attachment

Building a list of fiction and non-fiction
authors.

I'm particularly interested in representing
upmarket commercial, accessible literary and
reading group fiction with an edge – a tight
plot, clever writing and even an element of

suspense. I like to be surprised — I want to
read love stories with a twist, workplace
friendships gone wrong, power-based
hierarchies turned on their head, novels where
the characters aren't what they seem.

I'm interested in brilliantly plotted social
thrillers, unconventional love stories, crime
novels with a difference, high concept rom-
coms. My current 'most-wanted' is a playful
take on genre fiction of any kind.

I love historical fiction and I want to read
submissions that use the genre to centre queer
and trans characters, and characters of colour,
within time. I enjoy stories that reframe a well-
trodden narrative arc, with characters or stories
that are typically underrepresented in
publishing.

On the non-fiction side of things, I want to
represent academics, critics and journalists
who are writing their specialist subject for
trade publication, mostly with a strong
narrative or personal element. I'm always
looking for non-fiction that uses one object or
topic to tell history.

Authors: Juliana Adelman; Rachel Dawson;
Kat Hill; Sarah Housley; Daisy J. Hung; Sam
Johnson-Schlee; Fiona Keating; Anna Parker;
Eddie Scott

L458 Natascha Morris
Senior Agent
United States

https://www.thetobiasagency.com/natascha-
morris
https://querymanager.com/query/natascha

Literary Agency: The Tobias Literary Agency
(**L614**)

CHILDREN'S > **Fiction**
Graphic Novels; *Picture Books*
YOUNG ADULT > **Fiction**
Graphic Novels; *Novels*

Closed to approaches.

Primarily looking for picture books, middle
grade graphic novels and young adult across
most genres, including graphic novels. She is
also open to illustrator submissions.

L459 Michele Mortimer
Literary Agent
United States

submissions@dvagency.com

https://www.dvagency.com/aboutus

Literary Agency: Darhansoff & Verrill Literary
Agents (**L156**)

ADULT
Fiction > *Novels*
Crime; Historical Fiction; Horror; Literary;
Mystery; Romance; Thrillers; Upmarket
Women's Fiction

Nonfiction > *Nonfiction Books*

Animals; Crime; Culture; Feminism; Memoir; Music; Narrative Nonfiction; Popular Culture; Sociology; Sport; Wellbeing

YOUNG
ADULT > **Fiction** > *Novels*: Realistic

Send: Query; Writing sample
How to send: In the body of an email

Currently considers literary fiction, historical fiction, sophisticated crime, mystery, thrillers, and horror, upmarket character-rich women's fiction and smart romance, realism-based young adult fiction, and narrative nonfiction. Nonfiction interests include music, sports, wellness, animal welfare, feminism, true crime, sociology, culture both pop and serious, and memoir.

L460 Tasneem Motala
Assistant Agent
Canada

https://www.therightsfactory.com/submissions
https://querymanager.com/query/2005

Literary Agency: The Rights Factory

ADULT > **Fiction**
Graphic Novels; *Novels*; *Short Fiction Collections*
YOUNG ADULT > **Fiction**
Graphic Novels; *Novels*; *Short Fiction Collections*

Closed to approaches.

No submissions from white people.

L461 Movable Type Management
Literary Agency
244 Madison Avenue, Suite 334, New York, NY 10016
United States
Tel: +1 (646) 431-6134

Submission@MovableTM.com

https://www.movabletm.com

Fiction > *Novels*: Commercial

Nonfiction > *Nonfiction Books*: Commercial

How to send: Email

Looking for authors of high quality commercial fiction and nonfiction with archetypal themes, stories, and characters, especially if they have strong film/TV potential. Response only if interested.

Literary Agent: Adam Chromy

L462 Lisa Moylett
Literary Agent
United Kingdom

https://cmm.agency/about-us.php
http://twitter.com/MoylettLisa

Literary Agency: Coombs Moylett & Maclean Literary Agency (**L138**)

Fiction > *Novels*
Commercial Women's Fiction; Crime; Ireland; Northern Ireland; Psychological Thrillers

Nonfiction > *Nonfiction Books*
Politics; Popular Science

Send: Synopsis; Writing sample
How to send: Online submission system
How not to send: Email

Represents an eclectic list of authors and writers and is currently looking for well-written, commercial women's fiction.

L463 Karen Murgolo
Literary Agent
United States

https://www.aevitascreative.com/agent/karen-murgolo
https://querymanager.com/query/KarenMurgoloQueries

Literary Agency: Aevitas

Nonfiction > *Nonfiction Books*
Cookery; Health; Memoir; Narrative Nonfiction; Psychology; Science; Spirituality; Wellbeing

Send: Pitch; Author bio; Outline; Market info; Writing sample
How to send: Query Manager

Interested in authoritative health, wellness, science and psychology, spirituality, inspirational (or just really fun) memoirs; original cookbooks, and narratives that illuminate a compelling subject or start a conversation.

Authors: Cathy Barrow; Whitney Casares; Judith Choate; Chelsey Goodan; Illyanna Maisonet; Lauretta Malloy; LeeAnet Noble; Brittany Piper; Mike Sapiro; Terry Sargent; Kevin Tracey; Brigid Washington; Veronica Webb

L464 Nate Muscato
Literary Agent
New York
United States

https://aevitascreative.com/agents/

Literary Agency: Aevitas

Fiction > *Novels*
Fantasy; Literary; Science Fiction

Nonfiction > *Nonfiction Books*
Arts; Education; Politics; Popular Culture; Sociology; Technology

Send: Author bio; Outline; Pitch; Market info; Writing sample
How to send: Online submission system

Drawn to nonfiction that illuminates the past and present—from arts and pop culture to

education, politics, sociology, and technology—and envisions more just and equitable futures. He is also interested in select genre fiction with literary trappings, sci-fi/fantasy stories that leap into new worlds yet reveal something radical about our own.

Authors: Pamela Anderson; Carl Sferrazza Anthony; Samara Bay; Elizabeth Beller; Joshua Bennett; Charles Blow; Patricia Bosworth; Holly Brubach; Jim Carrey; Kimberlé Crenshaw; Hugh Eakin; Arline T. Geronimus; John Giorno; Karl Taro Greenfeld; Bob Greifeld; Michael Grynbaum; David Hallberg; Linda Hirshman; Charlayne Hunter-Gault; Elise Jordan; Henry Louis Gates Jr.; Amy Larocca; Andrew McCarthy; Adam Moss; Mary Norris; Mark Oppenheimer; Holly Peterson; Gerald Posner; Peter Rader; James Reginato; Karin Roffman; James Romm; Mark Ronson; Thaddeus Russell; Alexandra Sacks; Elizabeth Samet; Michael Schulman; Erich Schwartzel; Elizabeth Shackelford; Colin Spoelman; Greg Steinmetz; Craig Unger; Dana Vachon; Darren Walker; Jesse Wegman; Genevieve West; Casey Wilson; Linda Yablonsky

L465 Juliet Mushens
Literary Agent
United Kingdom

submissions@mushens-entertainment.com

https://www.mushens-entertainment.com/juliet-mushens
https://twitter.com/mushenska

Literary Agency: Mushens Entertainment

Fiction > *Novels*
Book Club Fiction; Crime; Fantasy; Gothic; High Concept; Historical Fiction; Psychology; Science Fiction; Thrillers

Send: Query; Synopsis; Writing sample
How to send: Email

Looking for: crime, thriller, reading group fiction, gothic novels, historical fiction, and SFF. Do not send her: picture-books, MG, non-fiction, novellas, short stories/short story collections, screenplays, poetry collections or erotica. Please do not send her unfinished books. Unless she has specifically asked to see it, do not send her revised versions of earlier manuscripts she has rejected. Do not send her novels which her colleagues have rejected.

Assistant Agent: Kiya Evans (**L203**)

Authors: Claire Alexander; Aliya Ali-Afzal; Luke Allnutt; Marie-Claire Amuah; Sussie Anie; Krystle Zara Appiah; Ross Armstrong; Stephen Aryan; Joanna Barnard; Jessica Bull; Jessie Burton; Mary Chamberlain; Katy Colins; Polly Crosby; Sarah Day; Abigail Dean; LM Dillsworth; Claire Douglas; Saara El-Arifi; Fiona Erskine; Maria Farrer; Robert Gold; Kate Gray; Jack Guinness; Francesca Haig; Stacey Halls; Lou Morgan / Maggie

Harcourt; Elodie Harper; Sophie Haydock; Debbie Howells; Theresa Howes; Ali Imdad; Liz De Jager; Hannah Kaner; Katie Khan; L.R. Lam; Ali Land; Lia Louis; Katie Lowe; Chris MacDonald; Taran Matharu; Anna Mazzola; Amy McCulloch; Elvin James Mensah; Jo Monroe; Hester Musson; Peter Newman; Louise O'Neill; Richard Osman; James Oswald; Buki Papillon; Nell Pattison; Laura Purcell; Andrew Reid; Laure Van Rensburg; Jennifer Saint; Vanessa Savage; Boris Starling; Andrea Stewart; Susan Stokes-Chapman; Rob Temple; Liz Tipping; Rajasree Variyar; Sonia Velton; Gray Williams; Jen Williams; Nick Clark Windo

L466 James Mustelier

Literary Agent
United States

http://www.thebentagency.com/james-mustelier
https://querymanager.com/query/1908

Literary Agency: The Bent Agency (**L058**)

ADULT
  Fiction > *Novels*
    Alternative History; Commercial; Dark Humour; Fantasy; Horror; Literary; Mystery; Science Fiction; Speculative

  Nonfiction > *Nonfiction Books*
    Commercial; Literary

CHILDREN'S > **Fiction** > *Middle Grade*
    Fairy Tales; Folklore, Myths, and Legends; High / Epic Fantasy; Historical Fiction; Science Fiction

YOUNG ADULT > **Fiction** > *Novels*
    Fairy Tales; Folklore, Myths, and Legends; High / Epic Fantasy; Historical Fiction; Science Fiction

Does not want:

  Fiction > *Novels*
    High / Epic Fantasy; Space Opera

Closed to approaches.

L467 Jen Nadol

Associate Agent
United States

Jen.Nadol@theunteragency.com

http://theunteragency.com

Literary Agency: The Unter Agency (**L620**)

Send: Pitch
How to send: Email

L468 Justin Nash

Literary Agent; Managing Director
United Kingdom

https://katenashlit.co.uk/people/
https://twitter.com/JustinNashLit

Literary Agency: Kate Nash Literary Agency (**L345**)

Fiction > *Novels*
    Book Club Fiction; Crime; Fantasy; Folklore, Myths, and Legends; Historical Fiction; Science Fiction; Thrillers

Nonfiction > *Nonfiction Books*
    General, and in particular: Classics / Ancient World; History; Medieval; Military; Travel

Looking for thrillers and crime fiction of all types; book club and historical fiction that moves me and makes me think (including novels featuring fantasy/mythology) and SF. In non-fiction, books which open up the conversation and take me on a journey.

L469 Natasha Kern Literary Agency

Literary Agency
United States

http://natashakernliterary.com

Fiction > *Novels*

Closed to approaches.

Closed to queries from unpublished writers. Focusses on developing the careers of established writers. Will continue to accept referrals through current clients or editors, and through conferences.

Authors: Tamera Alexander; Nikki Arana; Nina Bangs; Angela Benson; Cheryl Bolen; Maggie Brendan

Literary Agent: Natasha Kern

L470 Abigail Nathan

Literary Agent
Sydney
Australia

https://alexadsett.com.au/literary-agency/
https://querymanager.com/query/AbigailNathanQueries

Literary Agency: Alex Adsett Literary (**L016**)

ADULT > **Fiction** > *Novels*
    General, and in particular: Crime; Fantasy; Horror; Romance; Science Fiction; Supernatural / Paranormal; Thrillers

CHILDREN'S > **Fiction** > *Middle Grade*
    General, and in particular: Crime; Fantasy; Horror; Romance; Science Fiction; Supernatural / Paranormal; Thrillers

YOUNG ADULT > **Fiction** > *Novels*
    General, and in particular: Crime; Fantasy; Horror; Romance; Science Fiction; Supernatural / Paranormal; Thrillers

Send: Query; Author bio; Synopsis
How to send: Query Manager

Looking for engaging plots and convincing characters. Something that will keep her turning the pages and that will stay with her after she's finished reading. There are some

rules and conventions it pays to follow, but something a bit weird or slightly (or very) unexpected will pique her interest, and characters that touch a nerve or worlds that make us question the status quo are always welcome. Above all, she's looking for great stories, told well – fiction in general and all things genre: sci-fi, fantasy, paranormal, horror, crime, thriller, romance (and any combination of those), for adult, YA or middle grade.

L471 Rachel Neely

Literary Agent
United Kingdom

submissions@mushens-entertainment.com

https://www.mushens-entertainment.com/rachel-neely

Literary Agency: Mushens Entertainment

Fiction > *Novels*
    Book Club Fiction; Crime; Historical Fiction; Literary; Thrillers

Send: Query; Synopsis; Writing sample
How to send: Email

I'm looking for unforgettable and thought-provoking fiction, the kind that leaves your mind racing uncontrollably, hours after turning the last page. Whether commercial or literary, or something in between, I want authors who can match a distinctive voice with an equally compelling plot. I generally prefer darker stories; my favourite books often centre characters with tragic fates, dark pasts or buried trauma. I would also particularly like to find authors from underrepresented groups, who often bring a fresh perspective to well-worn story arcs or reflect experiences that are shared by many but, as of yet, underexplored in fiction.

L472 Nelson Literary Agency, LLC

Literary Agency
1732 Wazee Street, Suite 207, Denver, CO 80202
United States
Tel: +1 (303) 292-2805

info@nelsonagency.com

https://nelsonagency.com

Professional Body: Association of American Literary Agents (AALA)

ADULT > **Fiction** > *Novels*

CHILDREN'S > **Fiction**
    Middle Grade; Picture Books
YOUNG ADULT > **Fiction** > *Novels*

Send: Query; Author bio; Writing sample
How to send: Query Manager

View individual agent interests and submit to one agent only.

Authors: Brooke Abrams; Kate Baer; L. Biehler; Jillian Boehme; Ali Brady; Lina Chern; Kristen Ciccarelli; Jessi Cole; Lisa Duffy; Doug Engstrom; Reese Eschmann; Shana Galen; John Galligan; Florence Gonsalves; Jill Grunenwald; Alison Hammer; Sarah Zachrich Jeng; Becca Jones; Chloe Jory; Ausma Zehanat Khan; Sierra Kincade; Karen Koh; Gillian Libby; Maryann Jacob Macias; Amanda Marbais; Jonathan Messinger; Meghan Scott Molin; Katrina Monroe; Vanessa Montalban; Rosaria Munda; Jennifer Nissley; Lynette Noni; James Persichetti; Celesta Rimington; Laura Brooke Robson; Lyndsay Rush; Ehsaneh Sadr; Jeff Seymour; Kristen Simmons; Lisa Springer; Jennifer Springsteen; Stacy Stokes; Joy Sullivan; Chrysler Szarlan; Ben Tanzer; Jordyn Taylor; Kathleen West

Literary Agents: Joanna MacKenzie (**L412**); Kristin Nelson (**L473**)

L473 Kristin Nelson

Literary Agent
United States

https://nelsonagency.com/kristin-nelson/
https://twitter.com/agentkristinNLA
https://querymanager.com/query/1350

Literary Agency: Nelson Literary Agency, LLC (**L472**)
Professional Body: Association of American Literary Agents (AALA)

ADULT > **Fiction** > *Novels*
  Commercial; Fantasy; High Concept; Historical Fiction; Literary; Science Fiction; Speculative; Thrillers

YOUNG ADULT > **Fiction** > *Novels*

Send: Author bio; Query; Writing sample
How to send: Query Manager

My goal as an agent is simple: I want every client of mine to make a living solely from writing and 90% of my authors do without help from any other source of income.

L474 Mariah Nichols

Literary Agent
United States

https://www.mariahlovesliterary.com
https://www.d4eoliteraryagency.com/p/mariah-nichols.html
https://twitter.com/litagentmariah

Literary Agency: D4EO Literary Agency

ADULT
  Fiction > *Novels*
    Contemporary Romance; Psychological Thrillers; Romantic Comedy; Women's Fiction

  Nonfiction > *Nonfiction Books*
    Cookery; Diversity; How To; Lifestyle; Mental Health; Romance; Self Help

YOUNG ADULT > **Fiction** > *Novels*

Contemporary Romance; Science Fiction; Supernatural / Paranormal Romance; Thrillers

Closed to approaches.

Interested in upmarket and commercial adult fiction focusing on women's fiction, psychological thrillers, and contemporary romance/rom-coms, along with representing young adult fiction with genres including science fiction, paranormal romance, thrillers, and contemporary romance. She is also wanting to represent nonfiction in categories such as cookbooks, memoirs, self-help, lifestyle, and how-to. Stories that showcase diversity and highlight mental health or special needs is something that she would especially like to see.

L475 Nick Turner Management Ltd

Literary Agency
United Kingdom
Tel: +44 (0) 20 3723 8833

nick@nickturnermanagement.com

http://nickturnermanagement.com
https://uk.linkedin.com/in/nicolas-turner-2a84a1103
https://twitter.com/NickTurnerMgmt

ADULT > **Scripts**
  Film Scripts; *Radio Scripts*; *TV Scripts*
CHILDREN'S > **Scripts** > *TV Scripts*

How to send: By referral

Creative talent agency representing a broad mix of writers, directors and producers working across feature-film, television drama, comedy, children's, continuing-drama and radio. No unsolicited submissions. New clients come through producer or personal recommendations only.

Literary Agents: Phil Adie (**L006**); Nick Turner (*L617*)

L476 Erin Niumata

Literary Agent; Senior Vice President
United States
Tel: +1 (212) 400-1494

erin@foliolit.com

https://www.foliolit.com/agents-1/erin-niumata
https://www.instagram.com/ecniumata/?hl=en
https://twitter.com/ecniumata?ref_src=twsrc%5Egoogle%7Ctwcamp%5Eserp%7Ctwgr%5Eauthor

Literary Agency: Folio Literary Management, LLC

Fiction > *Novels*
  Book Club Fiction; Commercial Women's Fiction; Commercial; Historical Fiction; Mystery; Romance; Romantic Comedy; Thrillers; Women's Fiction

Nonfiction > *Nonfiction Books*

Commercial; Cookery; Memoir; Narrative Nonfiction; Prescriptive Nonfiction

Closed to approaches.

Looking for commercial nonfiction, from prescriptive and practical to narrative and memoir, as well as a select list of fiction including mysteries, rom-coms, and commercial women's fiction.

L477 Laura Nolan

Literary Agent; Senior Partner
United States

https://aevitascreative.com/agents/

Literary Agency: Aevitas
Professional Body: Association of American Literary Agents (AALA)

Nonfiction > *Nonfiction Books*
  Celebrity; Culture; Investigative Journalism; Medicine; Music; Performing Arts; Psychology; Sub-Culture

Send: Query; Writing sample
How to send: Online submission system

Represents investigative journalists, thought leaders, doctors, psychologists, musicians, and celebrities who inspire, entertain, educate and are striving to upend the culture. Seeks clients who are asking the "big" questions, exploring fascinating sub-cultures, and are paradigm-shifters in their fields, as well as performing artists who are successful in one medium but whose talents and passion translate into narrative.

Authors: Aaron Ayscough; Michael Azerrad; Sara Bareilles; Hunter Biden; Jill Blakeway; Kenneth Bock; Mariann Edgar Budde; Gesine Bullock-Prado; David Burtka; Scott Carney; Ratha Chaupoly; Ben Daitz; Dagmara Dominczyk; Madeleine Dore; Charlotte Druckman; Aria Finger; John Fogerty; Ben Folds; Holly George-Warren; Rhiannon Giddens; Danny Goldberg; Andrea Gutiérrez-Glik; Neil Patrick Harris; Josiah Hesse; Bonnie J. Kaplan; Angela Jia Kim; Laura Krantz; Carson Kressley; Leah Lagos; Christine Lahti; Jennifer Lapidus; Alan Light; Anita Lo; Danica McKellar; Sara C. Mednick; Allison Moorer; Mandy Morris; Meagan B Murphy; Einat Nathan; Sabina Nawaz; Oliver Niño; David Peisner; Wendell Pierce; Matt Pinfield; Nicole Ponseca; Elizabeth Poynor; Eric Prum; Julia J. Rucklidge; Anneli Rufus; Erika Schickel; Joseph Shuldiner; Rachel Signer; Julie Smolyansky; Gayla Trail; Miguel Trinidad; Nia Vardalos; Lynx Vilden; Martha Wainwright; Tionne Watkins; Elettra Wiedemann; Josh Williams; Vern Yip; Kristal Zook; Alan Zweibel

L478 Northbank Talent Management
Literary Agency
United Kingdom
Tel: +44 (0) 20 3973 0836

info@northbanktalent.com
fiction@northbanktalent.com
nonfiction@northbanktalent.com
childrens@northbanktalent.com

https://www.northbanktalent.com
https://twitter.com/NorthbankTalent
https://www.facebook.com/northbanktalent/
https://www.instagram.com/northbanktalent
https://www.linkedin.com/company/
northbank-talent-management/
https://www.youtube.com/channel/
UCKEAHOg6Y2G3NOy146k9y4A?view_as=
subscriber

Professional Body: The Association of
Authors' Agents (AAA)

ADULT
  Fiction > *Novels*
  Nonfiction > *Nonfiction Books*

YOUNG ADULT > **Fiction** > *Novels*

Send: Query; Synopsis; Writing sample
How to send: Email

Literary and talent agency based in central
London. Actively seeking new clients. Send
query by email with synopsis and first three
chapters as Word or Open Document
attachments to appropriate email address.

L479 Renee Nyen
Literary Agent
United States

Literary Agency: KT Literary (**L368**)

Closed to approaches.

L480 Lee O'Brien
Literary Agent
United States

Lee.queries@irenegoodman.com

https://www.irenegoodman.com/lee-obrien

Literary Agency: Irene Goodman Literary
Agency (IGLA)

Fiction > *Novels*
  LGBTQIA; Magic; Romance

Closed to approaches.

Across all age categories, they're looking for
books with clear stakes and an immersive
world, as well as anything with lots of
atmosphere, magic, monsters, intrigue, or a
plot full of twists and turns. They're actively
seeking underrepresented voices, and they
have a particular soft spot for queer romance
(whether it's an epic love story or a first
crush), ace rep, and trans kids with swords.

L481 Faith O'Grady
Literary Agent
108 Upper Leeson Street, Dublin 4
Ireland
Tel: + 353 1 637 5000
Fax: + 353 1 667 1256

info@lisarichards.ie

http://lisarichards.ie/writers#.YAgtljlxdaS

Literary Agency: The Lisa Richards Agency

ADULT
  Fiction > *Novels*

  Nonfiction > *Nonfiction Books*
  Biography; Comedy / Humour; History;
  Lifestyle; Memoir; Motorsports; Narrative
  Nonfiction; Popular Culture; Self Help

CHILDREN'S > **Fiction**
  Chapter Books; Middle Grade

Does not want:

> **ADULT**
>   **Fiction** > *Novels*
>   Horror; Science Fiction
>
>   **Scripts**
>   *Film Scripts; TV Scripts*
> **CHILDREN'S** > **Fiction** > *Picture
> Books*

Send: Query; Writing sample; Self-Addressed
Stamped Envelope (SASE); Proposal
How to send: Email

If sending fiction, please limit your submission
to the first three or four chapters. If sending
non-fiction, please send a detailed proposal
about your book, a sample chapter and a cover
letter. Every effort will be made to respond to
submissions within 3 months of receipt.

L482 Niamh O'Grady
Literary Agent
United Kingdom

https://www.thesohoagency.co.uk/agent/
niamh-ogrady

Literary Agency: The Soho Agency

Fiction > *Novels*
  Book Club Fiction; Comedy / Humour;
  Family; Literary; Relationships

Nonfiction > *Nonfiction Books*
  Comedy / Humour; Narrative Nonfiction

Send: Query; Synopsis; Writing sample
How to send: Email attachment

Actively looking for accessible literary and
reading-group fiction, and narrative nonfiction. She is drawn to books with heart and
humour, thought-provoking writing and
distinctive, compelling voices. She particularly
loves novels that explore family and
relationships and wants to read stories that
leave an emotional impact, with characters that
stay with her long after the final page. She is

keen to find new Irish and Northern writing
talent.

L483 Kristin van Ogtrop
Literary Agent
United States

https://inkwellmanagement.com/staff/kristin-
van-ogtrop

Literary Agency: InkWell Management

Fiction > *Novels*: Literary

Nonfiction
  Illustrated Books: General
  Nonfiction Books: Lifestyle; Memoir;
  Prescriptive Nonfiction

Represents lifestyle, illustrated books,
prescriptive nonfiction, literary fiction and
memoir.

L484 Mark Orsini
Literary Agent; Partner
United States

Literary Agency: Bret Adams Ltd

L485 Kristin Ostby
Literary Agent
United States

https://www.greenhouseliterary.com/the-team/
kristin-ostby/
https://querymanager.com/query/kristinostby

Literary Agency: The Greenhouse Literary
Agency

ADULT > **Fiction** > *Novels*
  Mystery; Upmarket

CHILDREN'S
  Fiction
    Chapter Books: Comedy / Humour
    Graphic Novels: General
    Middle Grade: Adventure; Comedy /
    Humour; Contemporary; Cozy Mysteries;
    Friends; Historical Fiction; Light Fantasy;
    Mystery; Supernatural / Paranormal;
    Thrillers
    Picture Books: General

  Poetry > *Novels in Verse*

YOUNG ADULT > **Fiction** > *Novels*
  Comedy / Humour; Contemporary; Cozy
  Mysteries; Friends; Historical Fiction;
  Historical Romance; Light Fantasy; Mystery;
  Romance; Speculative Romance;
  Supernatural / Paranormal; Thrillers

How to send: Query Manager

Represents authors of middle grade and young
adult fiction, as well as picture book
author/illustrators. She is primarily seeking
voice- and character-driven contemporary
middle-grade and young adult fiction, with a
focus on BIPOC creators.

L486 Bruce Ostler
Literary Agent; Partner
United States

Literary Agency: Bret Adams Ltd

L487 Ayesha Pande
Literary Agent
United States

https://www.pandeliterary.com/about-pandeliterary
https://twitter.com/agent_ayesha
http://aaronline.org/Sys/PublicProfile/2455085/417813

Literary Agency: Ayesha Pande Literary (**L038**)
Professional Bodies: Association of American Literary Agents (AALA); The Agents Round Table (ART)

ADULT
Fiction > *Novels*: Literary

Nonfiction > *Nonfiction Books*
Biography; Cultural Commentary; History; Memoir; Narrative Nonfiction

YOUNG ADULT > **Fiction** > *Novels*

Closed to approaches.

While her interests are wide-ranging and eclectic, she works mostly with literary fiction, narrative nonfiction across a broad range of topics including history and cultural commentary, memoir and biography, and the occasional work of young adult fiction. She is drawn to distinctive voices with a compelling point of view and memorable characters.

L488 Paper Literary
Literary Agency
United Kingdom

submissions@paperliterary.com

https://www.paperliterary.com
https://twitter.com/paperliterary
https://www.instagram.com/PaperLiterary/?hl=en

Professional Body: The Association of Authors' Agents (AAA)

Founded in 2021, with a vision of building author careers. Approach is built on a commitment to storytelling and maximizing every opportunity for our clients.

Author / Literary Agent: Catherine Cho (**L120**)

Literary Agent: Katie Greenstreet (**L270**)

L489 Paradigm Talent and Literary Agency
Literary Agency
810 Seventh Avenue, Suite 205, New York, NY 10019
United States
Tel: +1 (212) 897-6400
Fax: +1 (310) 288-2000

books@paradigmagency.com

https://www.paradigmagency.com

Fiction > *Novels*

Nonfiction > *Nonfiction Books*

Scripts
Film Scripts; *TV Scripts*; *Theatre Scripts*

Send: Query; Writing sample
How to send: In the body of an email

Talent and literary agency with offices in Los Angeles, New York, and London. Represents books in all areas and genres, as well as scriptwriters for film, TV, and theatre.

L490 Elana Roth Parker
Literary Agent
United States

http://www.ldlainc.com/submissions/
http://www.manuscriptwishlist.com/mswl-post/elana-roth-parker/
https://querymanager.com/query/queryelana
http://aaronline.org/Sys/PublicProfile/43775067/417813

Literary Agency: Laura Dail Literary Agency
Professional Body: Association of American Literary Agents (AALA)

ADULT > **Fiction** > *Novels*
Commercial; Contemporary; Mystery; Romance; Romantic Comedy; Thrillers; Upmarket Women's Fiction

CHILDREN'S > **Fiction** > *Middle Grade*
Adventure; Comedy / Humour; High / Epic Fantasy; High Concept

YOUNG ADULT > **Fiction** > *Novels*
Adventure; Comedy / Humour; Commercial; High Concept; Romance

Send: Query; Pitch; Synopsis; Author bio
How to send: Query Manager

Handles middle grade and young adult fiction. Closed to picture book submissions.

L491 Marina De Pass
Literary Agent
United Kingdom

https://www.thesohoagency.co.uk/agent/marina-de-pass
https://twitter.com/marinadepass

Literary Agency: The Soho Agency

Fiction > *Novels*
General, and in particular: Book Club Fiction; Commercial; Cookery; Food; Horoscopes; Literary; Mystery; Romance; Tarot; Upmarket Thrillers; Upmarket

Nonfiction > *Nonfiction Books*: Narrative Nonfiction

Does not want:

> **Fiction** > *Novels*: Science Fiction

Send: Query; Synopsis; Writing sample
How to send: Email attachment

Building a list of upmarket commercial, reading group and accessible literary fiction – and is actively looking to take on clients in this area. She is looking for strong hooks, compelling writing and unforgettable characters. Among other things, she is drawn to books that feature: mysteries; heatwaves and/or raging storms; plot twists; hotels; secrets simmering under the surface; dramatic landscapes, a vivid sense of place; an unusual structure; characters who are not what they seem; cults; against-the-odds survival; dry humour; a light dusting of myths and folklore; chemistry that leaps off the page; love triangles, family tensions, heady affairs and forbidden romances – relationships under pressure, essentially.

L492 Paul S. Levine Literary Agency
Literary Agency
1054 Superba Avenue, Venice, CA 90291-3940
United States
Tel: +1 (310) 450-6711
Fax: +1 (310) 450-0181

paul@paulslevine.com

https://paulslevinelit.com

ADULT
Fiction
Graphic Novels: General
Novels: Adventure; Legal; Mainstream; Mystery; Politics; Romance; Thrillers; Women's Fiction
Nonfiction > *Nonfiction Books*
Archaeology; Architecture; Arts; Autobiography; Business; Contemporary; Education; Gardening; Genealogy; Health; How To; Legal; Medicine; Mind, Body, Spirit; Politics; Popular Culture; Relationships; Science; Self Help; Sociology; Sport; Technology

CHILDREN'S
Fiction
Graphic Novels; *Novels*
Nonfiction > *Nonfiction Books*

YOUNG ADULT
Fiction
Graphic Novels; *Novels*
Nonfiction > *Nonfiction Books*

Send: Query
How to send: Email; Post
How not to send: Phone

Send query by email, or by post with SASE. No phone calls.

Literary Agents: Loren R. Grossman (**L273**); Paul S. Levine (**L386**)

L493 Kay Peddle

Literary Agent
United Kingdom

Kay@colwillandpeddle.com
submissions@colwillandpeddle.com

https://www.colwillandpeddle.com/about

Literary Agency: Colwill & Peddle (**L129**)

Nonfiction > *Nonfiction Books*
Cookery; Current Affairs; Food; History;
Journalism; Literary Memoir; Narrative
Nonfiction; Nature; Politics; Popular
Science; Social Justice; Travel

Closed to approaches.

Looking for books that spark discussion, that
have the potential to change opinions and
reveal hidden aspects of a familiar story.
Interested in narrative nonfiction; literary
memoir; cookery and food writing; travel
writing; nature writing; journalism with a
social justice angle; politics; current affairs;
history and popular science.

L494 Imogen Pelham

Literary Agent
United Kingdom

Literary Agency: Marjacq Scripts Ltd (**L421**)

Closed to approaches.

L495 Perez Literary & Entertainment

Literary Agency
49 Greek Street, London, W1D 4EG
United Kingdom
Tel: +44 (0) 20 7193 4792

assist@perezliterary

https://www.perezliterary.com
http://querymanager.com/KristinaPerez
https://www.instagram.com/perezliterary/
https://twitter.com/perez_literary
https://www.linkedin.com/company/
perezliterary/
https://www.facebook.com/perezliterary

Professional Body: The Association of
Authors' Agents (AAA)

ADULT
Fiction > *Novels*
Book Club Fiction; Commercial; Crime;
Thrillers; Upmarket

Nonfiction > *Nonfiction Books*
Biography; Cultural History; Current
Affairs; Feminism; Popular Science

YOUNG ADULT > **Fiction** > *Novels*
Fantasy; Romance

Send: Query; Writing sample
How to send: Query Manager
How not to send: Email

A full-service agency dedicated to storytelling
in all of its forms. We believe in the power of
words to open minds and change lives. In
today's fast moving marketplace, we are on the
constant lookout for opportunities in both
traditional and non-traditional media. We are
committed to empowering our clients and
helping them to formulate the best strategies to
achieve their storytelling goals.

Authors: Alexia Casale; Shauna Clinning;
Sharon Emmerichs; Marina Evans; Jennifer
Wolf Kam; Erin Rose Kim; S. K. Meekings;
Kim Mykura; Troy Tassier; Vincent Tirado;
Amy Trueblood; Khadijah VanBrakle; Johanna
van Veen; Stephen Vines; Cristin Williams;
Josh Winning; Kelly deVos

Literary Agent / Managing Director: Kristina
Perez (**L496**)

L496 Kristina Perez

Literary Agent; Managing Director
United Kingdom

https://www.perezliterary.com/about-us/the-
team/
http://querymanager.com/KristinaPerez
https://twitter.com/kperezagent

Literary Agency: Perez Literary &
Entertainment (**L495**)

ADULT
Fiction > *Novels*
Book Club Fiction; Commercial; Crime;
Thrillers; Upmarket

Nonfiction > *Nonfiction Books*
Biography; Cultural History; Current
Affairs; Feminism; Popular Science

YOUNG ADULT > **Fiction** > *Novels*
Fantasy; Romance

Send: Query; Writing sample
How to send: Query Manager

Being both an agent and an author allows her
to fully guide her clients through every step of
the publishing process. She loves launching
debut authors' careers as well as working with
mid-career authors looking for new challenges.
She sees each client relationship as a true
partnership in which they develop the right
strategy for a client's career together. Author
care is paramount and she prides herself on
using her multifaceted understanding of the
industry to help her clients achieve their goals.
She is eager to work with writers from around
the globe.

Authors: Alexia Casale; Shauna Clinning;
Sharon Emmerichs; Marina Evans; Jennifer
Wolf Kam; Erin Rose Kim; S. K. Meekings;
Kim Mykura; Martin Purbrick; Troy Tassier;
Vincent Tirado; Amy Trueblood; Amy True /
Amy Trueblood; Khadija L. VanBrakle;
Khadijah VanBrakle; Johanna van Veen;
Stephen Vines; Cristin Williams; Josh
Winning; Kelly deVos

L497 Martha Perotto-Wills

Associate Agent
United Kingdom

http://www.thebentagency.com/martha-
perotto-wills
https://twitter.com/martha_again

Literary Agency: The Bent Agency (UK)
(**L057**)

ADULT
Fiction > *Novels*
Fantasy; Horror; Literary; Science Fiction

Nonfiction > *Nonfiction Books*

CHILDREN'S > **Fiction** > *Middle Grade*

YOUNG ADULT > **Fiction** > *Novels*

Closed to approaches.

Representing authors of adult literary fiction
and sci-fi/fantasy/horror, as well as select adult
non-fiction and middle-grade and young adult
fiction. Particularly enjoys authorial
confidence; unexpected, singular narrative
voices; good, stylish sentences; humour/wit;
knotty interpersonal relationships; and
transportive writing that immerse the reader in
a fully-formed world, whether fantastical,
geographical, or emotional.

L498 Perry Literary

Literary Agency
211 South Ridge Street, Suite 2, Rye Brook,
NY 10573
United States

jperry@perryliterary.com

https://www.perryliterary.com

Nonfiction > *Nonfiction Books*
Business; Cookery; Crime; Journalism;
Memoir; Narrative Nonfiction; Parenting;
Popular Culture; Psychology; Science; Self
Help; Sociology; Sport; Technology

How to send: Email

Send query by email with first ten pages in the
body of the email (or full manuscript for
picture books). No attachments. See website
for full guidelines.

Literary Agent: Joseph Perry

L499 Jas Perry

Literary Agent

Literary Agency: KT Literary (**L368**)

Closed to approaches.

L500 Carrie Pestritto

Literary Agent
United States

http://www.ldlainc.com/about
http://aaronline.org/Sys/PublicProfile/
53765008/417813
http://twitter.com/literarycarrie
https://literarycarrie.wixsite.com/blog

http://www.manuscriptwishlist.com/mswl-post/carrie-pestritto/

Literary Agency: Laura Dail Literary Agency
Professional Body: Association of American Literary Agents (AALA)

ADULT
Fiction > *Novels*
Chick Lit; Commercial; Cozy Mysteries; Historical Fiction; Literary; Mystery; Romance; Thrillers; Upmarket Women's Fiction

Nonfiction > *Nonfiction Books*
Biography; Memoir; Narrative Nonfiction

CHILDREN'S > **Fiction** > *Middle Grade*
Commercial; High Concept

YOUNG ADULT > **Fiction** > *Novels*
Contemporary; Fantasy; Historical Fiction; Horror; Mystery; Thrillers

Closed to approaches.

Loves the thrill of finding new authors with strong, unique voices and working closely with her clients. Always strives to help create books that will introduce readers to new worlds and is drawn in by relatable characters, meticulous world-building, and unusual, compelling premises.

L501 **Peters Fraser + Dunlop**
Literary Agency
55 New Oxford Street, London, WC1A 1BS
United Kingdom
Tel: +44 (0) 20 7344 1000
Fax: +44 (0) 20 7836 9539

info@pfd.co.uk

https://petersfraserdunlop.com
https://twitter.com/pfdagents
https://www.instagram.com/pfdagents/

Professional Body: The Association of Authors' Agents (AAA)

Fiction > *Novels*

Nonfiction > *Nonfiction Books*

Scripts
Film Scripts; *Radio Scripts*; *TV Scripts*

Send: Query; Synopsis; Writing sample
How to send: Email

One of the longest-established literary and talent agencies in London. We develop industry-leading work in the fields of literature, film, television, radio, audio, public speaking, digital platforms and journalism.

Authors: Ali Abdaal; Claire Ackroyd; Tufayel Ahmed; Fay Bound Alberti; Dorothy Armstrong; Ciara Attwell; Nadine Bacchus-Garrick; Prof Marc David Baer; Iain Ballantyne; Jamie Bartlett; Camila Batmanghelidjh; Andrew J. Bayliss; Heidi Lauth Beasley; Elaine Bedell; Olivia Beirne; Nora Berend; Sophie Beresiner; Abigail Bergstrom; Lesley Blanch; Tom Blass; Brian Blessed; Simon Booker; Peter Bowles; Rosie Boycott; Pattie Boyd; Melvyn Bragg; Kevin Brennan; Whitney Brown; Jonathan Bryan; Jacqueline Bublitz; Ed Burstell; Michael Caine; Emma Calder; Tamsin Calidas; Leland Carlson; Mark Carney; Christina Caré; Augustus Casely-Hayford; Orsola De Castro; Angela Chadwick; Kimberley Chambers; Sunita Chawdhary; Mavis Cheek; Helen Chislett; Julia F. Christensen; Nicola Clark; Rita Clifton; Sebastian Coe; Georgia Coleridge; Richard Coles; Natalia Conroy; Brendan Cooper; Roxie Cooper; Olivia Jordan Cornelius; Jack Cornish; Virginia Cowles; Andrew Craig; Katie Dale; Sara Dallin; Iona David; Len Deighton; Pepsi Demacque-Crockett; Naomi Devlin; Martin Dorey; Jon Dunn; Roxy Dunn; Judith Eagle; Philippa East; Ava Eldred; Léa Rose Emery; Wilfred Emmanuel-Jones; Kate Evans; Justine Firnhaber-Baker; Richard Fisher; Caroline Fleming; Rowan Foxwood; Eckart Frahm; Will Francis; Tova Friedman; Ione Gamble; Tessa Gearing; Irina Georgescu; Ashish Ghadiali; Marina Gibson; Caro Giles; Romy Gill; Tom Glover; William Goldsmith; Jean G Goodhind; Jonathan Gornall; Bre Graham; Delayed Gratification; Annie Gray; Norma Gregory; Malwina Gudowska; Simon Halfon; Eddie Hall; Ben Halls; Jessica Hamel-Akré; Tony Hannan; Sarah Haque; Kenneth Harl; Anstey Harris; Dawn Harris; Josephine Hart; Angela Hartnett; Emma Heatherington; Lindsay Hirst; James Hogg; Becky Holmes; Emily Houghton; Lexy Hudson; Kenya Hunt; Becky Hunter; Sam Hurcom; Islam Issa; Lynsey James; Lis Jardine; Fionnuala Kearney; Shilo Kino; Amari Koryang; Gina Lamanna; Lizzie Lane; Lloyd Llewellyn-Jones; Jo Lovett; Jack Lowe; Monica Mark; Aneesa Marufu; Graham Masterton; Peter Mayle; Kira Mcpherson; Jack Meaning; Stanley Middleton; Helen Molesworth; Sophie Mort; Nicholas Mosley; Anna Motz; Gary Numan; Chi-chi Nwanoku; Okechukwu Nzelu; Jennifer Obidike; Daphne Olive; Jonathan Page; Chris Paling; Camilla Pang; Suk Pannu; Ali Pantony; David Papineau; Simji Park; Rupal Patel; Joanne Paul; Jo Pavey; Lesley Pearse; Polly Phillips; James Plunkett; Charlotte Proudman; Anna Quirke; Martyn Rady; Emily Randall; Hermione Ranfurly; Nigel Reed; Jacob Rees-Mogg; Andrew Ridgeley; Laila Rifaat; Alice Rio; Debora Robertson; Jane Rosenberg; Noble Rot; Neil 'Razor' Ruddock; Romla Ryan; Jessica Ryn; Roger Scruton; Rupert Shortt; Georges Simenon; Susannah Stapleton; Ali Stegert; Sam Stewart; Emily Stone; Sarah Street; Georgina Sturge; Tim Sullivan; Stefanie Sword-Williams; Amelia Tait; Colin Taylor; Vanessa Taylor; Russ Thomas; Lisa Thompson; Caroline Tremlett; Miles Tripp; Gail Upchurch; Catherine Ward; Rachel Ward; Valentine Warner; Rossalyn Warren; Alison Weatherby; Charlotte Fox Weber; Melissa Welliver; Emma J. Wells; Helen Whitaker; Adam White; Rose Wilding; Catherine Wilson; S.M. Wilson; Andy Wood; Neil Woods; Keren Woodward; Jacqueline Yallop; David Young; Andrew Zurcher

Chief Executive Officer / Literary Agent: Caroline Michel (**L442**)

Literary Agents: Kate Evans (**L202**); Adam Gauntlett (**L242**); Sarah Hornsley (**L311**); Lucy Irvine (**L319**); Annabel Merullo; Silvia Molteni; Michael Sissons and Fiona Petheram; Elizabeth Sheinkman; Cara Lee Simpson (**L574**); Jonathan Sissons; Rebecca Wearmouth

Senior Agent: Tim Bates (**L048**)

L502 **Rachel Petty**
Literary Agent
United Kingdom

rachelsubmissions@theblairpartnership.com

https://www.theblairpartnership.com/literary-agents/rachel-petty/
https://twitter.com/Rachel_petty_

Literary Agency: The Blair Partnership

CHILDREN'S
Fiction
Chapter Books; *Early Readers*; *Middle Grade*; *Picture Books*
Nonfiction > *Nonfiction Books*

YOUNG ADULT
Fiction > *Novels*
Contemporary Romance; Diverse Romance; Fantasy; High Concept; Horror; Romance; Speculative; Thrillers

Nonfiction > *Nonfiction Books*

How to send: Email

Represents children's fiction and non-fiction, from picture books up to YA and crossover. Looking for ambitious storytelling, a bold approach to structure and voice and a fresh take on genre, and particularly interested in submissions from author/illustrators and people from underrepresented and marginalised communities. Looking for ROMANCE as the primary focus in anything YA – and would really like high concept, diverse contemporary YA romance of the sort that will launch a thousand ships. Likes horror and thrillers (or a combination of both, especially with a twist), hooky YA fantasy/speculative (but only with excellent world building with a simple, clever pitch), hilarious middle grade, bold graphic picture books, and anything that has the potential to jump off the page and onto the screen.

Authors: Susanna H Cunningham; Hazel Gardner; Erica Gomez; Megan Hopkins; Rose Lihou; Margaret McDonald; Alexander Slater; Kari Trogen

L503 Beth Phelan

Literary Agent
United States

QueryBeth@galltzacker.com
beth@galltzacker.com

https://www.galltzacker.com/submissions.html
https://querymanager.com/query/querybeth

Literary Agency: Gallt & Zacker Literary Agency

CHILDREN'S
  Fiction > *Middle Grade*
    Contemporary; Fantasy

  Nonfiction > *Middle Grade*

YOUNG ADULT
  Fiction > *Novels*
    Contemporary; Fantasy

  Nonfiction > *Nonfiction Books*

How to send: By referral; Conferences

Gravitates toward stories and characters that inspire, and anything with a touch of humor and the bittersweet. She is very interested in powerful and unique storytelling, offbeat contemporary fiction, immersive fantasy, and profoundly resonant voices.

L504 Ariana Philips

Literary Agent
United States

https://www.jvnla.com/our-team.php
https://twitter.com/ArianaPhilips

Literary Agency: The Jean V. Naggar Literary Agency

ADULT
  Fiction > *Novels*
    Commercial; Family Saga; Historical Fiction; Literary; Romantic Comedy; Upmarket Women's Fiction

  Nonfiction
    Gift Books: General
    Illustrated Books: General
    Nonfiction Books: Comedy / Humour; Cookery; Crime; Food; Lifestyle; Literary Memoir; Narrative Nonfiction; Popular Culture; Popular History; Prescriptive Nonfiction; Science; Social Issues; Sport; Travel

CHILDREN'S > **Fiction** > *Middle Grade*
  Adventure; Magic; Mystery

YOUNG ADULT > **Fiction** > *Novels*
  Contemporary; Romantic Comedy

Send: Query; Author bio
How to send: Online submission system

Loves to find new talent and work with her clients to develop strong proposals and manuscripts. She enjoys being the author's advocate, often being their first editor, business manager, and trusted confidante. Her personal agenting philosophy is to take on an author for the duration of their career and help guide

them through the ever-changing publishing landscape. She is actively building her client list while also handling audio, permissions, and electronic rights for the agency.

L505 Juliet Pickering

Literary Agent
United Kingdom

juliet@blakefriedmann.co.uk

http://blakefriedmann.co.uk/juliet-pickering
https://twitter.com/julietpickering

Literary Agency: Blake Friedmann Literary Agency Ltd (**L064**)

Fiction > *Novels*
  Book Club Fiction; Commercial; Literary

Nonfiction > *Nonfiction Books*
  Cookery; Food; Memoir; Popular Culture; Social History

Closed to approaches.

Alongside literary, book club and commercial fiction, I represent non-fiction writers across the board, including memoir, pop culture, social history, writing on issues of race, gender and class, and cookery and food.

Authors: Diane Abbott; Kasim Ali; Dima Alzayat; Graeme Armstrong; MiMi Aye; Trezza Azzopardi; Bolu Babalola; Tom Bellamy; Jendella Benson; Meliz Berg; Ian Birch; Rachel Blackmore; Nora Anne Brown; Erin Bunting; Jo Facer & Erin Bunting; Ailsa Caine; Natasha Carthew; Francesca Chang; Norie Clarke; Julia Cole; Sue Cook; Sara Crowe; Tuyen Do; Michael Donkor; Jo Facer; Alix Fox; Sarah Franklin; Roxy Freeman; Janice Galloway; Gabriella Griffith; Sarah Hartley; David Haslam; Emma Forsyth Haslett; Kate Hodges; Michael Hogan; Kerry Hudson; Leah Hyslop; Alexandra Jellicoe; Benjamin Johncock; Konditor; Kat Lister; Richard Littler; Clayton Littlewood; Anneliese Mackintosh; Ailbhe Malone; Lucy Mangan; Amy Mason; Nina-Sophia Miralles; Emma Mitchell; Sue Moorcroft; Grace Mortimer; Emer O'Toole; Rosalind Powell; Julie Rea; Annie Robertson; Elliot Ryan; Lora Stimson; Jack Urwin; Pippa Vosper; Helen Walmsley-Johnson; Andrew Wong

L506 Gideon Pine

Literary Agent
United States

submissions@inkwellmanagement.com

https://inkwellmanagement.com/staff/gideon-pine

Literary Agency: InkWell Management

Fiction > *Novels*
  Horror; Literary; Mystery; Thrillers

Nonfiction > *Nonfiction Books*
  Crime; Health; History; Investigative Journalism; Narrative Nonfiction; Wellbeing

Send: Query; Writing sample
How to send: In the body of an email

Interested in representing writers in the nonfiction space with a focus on historical narrative nonfiction, true crime, health and wellness, and long form investigative journalism. He is also looking for voice-driven debut novels, including but not limited to the following genres: thriller, mystery, horror, or literary fiction.

L507 Zoe Plant

Literary Agent
United States

plantqueries@thebentagency.com

http://www.thebentagency.com/zoe-plant
https://www.twitter.com/zoeplant89

Literary Agency: The Bent Agency (**L058**)

ADULT > **Fiction** > *Novels*
  Commercial; Fantasy; Gothic; High Concept; Horror; Mystery; Science Fiction; Speculative; Thrillers

CHILDREN'S > **Fiction** > *Middle Grade*
  General, and in particular: Commercial

YOUNG ADULT > **Fiction** > *Novels*
  General, and in particular: Commercial; Horror; Magic; Science Fiction; Speculative; Thrillers

Closed to approaches.

I am looking for middle-grade and young adult fiction across all genres, as well as adult science fiction, fantasy, horror and speculative fiction. Across the board, my tastes lean towards commercial, entertaining, accessible books that also have something to say about the world. I am particularly interested in seeing submissions from writers from traditionally underrepresented backgrounds.

L508 Carrie Plitt

Literary Agent; Company Director
United Kingdom

https://felicitybryan.com/fba-agent/carrie-plitt/

Literary Agency: Felicity Bryan Associates (**L211**)

Fiction
  Novels: Book Club Fiction; Coming of Age; Family; Friends; Literary; Romance
  Short Fiction Collections: General

Nonfiction > *Nonfiction Books*
  History; Investigative Journalism; Memoir; Narrative Essays; Narrative Nonfiction; Nature; Popular Psychology; Popular Science; Social Issues; Travel

Send: Query; Synopsis; Proposal
How to send: Online submission system

I am actively building a list of non-fiction and fiction. In non-fiction, I love to represent expert authors who are passionate about their subject, who have something new to say, and who can convey their argument in a clear and invigorating manner. I have a particular interest in books about the issues our society faces today, narrative non-fiction, investigative journalism, popular science, popular psychology, big ideas, nature writing, history and travel. I also love book-length essays or cohesive essay collections, and memoirs that explore wider themes like freedom or education. In fiction, the books I represent range from the very literary to those you might read in a book club. Besides excellent writing, I am often drawn to emotionally complex novels; coming of age stories; sprawling narratives about love, friendship or families; and stories that capture the zeitgeist in some way – even when they are set in the past. I love a good short story collection, especially if the stories are linked together.

Authors: Sally Adee; John Aitchison; Frances Ashcroft; Roderick Beaton; Catherine Belton; Tim Birkhead; Ursula Buchan; Julia Bueno; Emma Byrne; Fernando Cervantes; Simukai Chigudu; Marcus Chown; Will Eaves; Reni Eddo-Lodge; David Farrier; Peter Gatrell; Susan Golombok; James Hamilton; Tim Hecker; Lindsey Hilsum; Sarah Jasmon; Joseph Jebelli; Clare Johnson; Nick Jubber; Chelsea Kwakye; Grace Lavery; Suzannah Lipscomb; Tess Little; Rebecca Lowe; Natasha Lunn; Fiona Maddocks; Henry Mance; Vanessa Nakate; Tom Nancollas; Camilla Nord; Jenny Odell; Ore Ogunbiyi; Elsa Panciroli; Alex Reeve; Dan Richards; Eloise Rickman; Alex Riley; Charlotte Lydia Riley; David Robson; Nicola Rollock; Farhan Samanani; Tiffany Watt Smith; Miriam Stoppard; Cathy Thomas; Samantha Walton; Benjamin Wardhaugh; Michael Wooldridge; Kieran Yates

L509 Portobello Literary

Literary Agency
United Kingdom

info@portobelloliterary.co.uk
submissions@portobelloliterary.co.uk

https://www.portobelloliterary.co.uk
https://twitter.com/portyliterary
https://instagram.com/portyliterary

Professional Body: The Association of Authors' Agents (AAA)

Fiction > *Novels*

Nonfiction > *Nonfiction Books*

Send: Synopsis; Author bio; Writing sample
How to send: Email
How not to send: Post

Literary agency based in Edinburgh.

Authors: Polly Atkin; Fiona Black; Gill Booles; Jenny Chamarette; Rachel Charlton-Dailey; Mona Dash; Samantha Dooey-Miles; Harry Josephine Giles; CL Hellisen; Russell

Jones; Louise Kenward; Wenying Li; Aefa Mulholland; JC Niala; Andrés N. Ordorica; Wendy Pratt; Adam Ramsay; Christina Riley; Elspeth Wilson

Literary Agent: Caro Clarke (**L126**)

L510 Marcy Posner
Literary Agent; Senior Vice President
United States

marcy@foliolit.com

https://www.foliolit.com/agents-1/marcy-posner
https://querymanager.com/query/marcyposner

Literary Agency: Folio Literary Management, LLC

ADULT
  Fiction > *Novels*
    Historical Fiction; Mystery; Psychological Suspense; Thrillers; Women's Fiction

  Nonfiction > *Nonfiction Books*
    Culture; Environment; Journalism; Narrative Nonfiction; Nature; Psychology; Social Issues; Women's Issues

CHILDREN'S > **Fiction** > *Middle Grade*
  Contemporary; Fantasy; Historical Fiction; Mystery; Science Fiction

YOUNG ADULT > **Fiction** > *Novels*
  Contemporary; Historical Fiction; Mystery; Romance

How to send: Query Manager
How not to send: Email

Looking for Thrillers, Psychological suspense, Historical fiction, Women's fiction, Mystery, YA (contemporary, historical, romance, mystery), Middle grade (contemporary, SFF, historical, mystery, Narrative non-fiction, Cultural/social issues, Journalism, Nature and ecology, Psychology and Women's issues. No longer accepts queries through email. Submit through online submission system only.

Authors: Christi Clancy; Christina Clancy; Lexie Elliott; Jacqueline Kelly; Erika J. Kendrick; Michael McGarrity; Sheri Reynolds; Rebecca Stafford; Rachel J. Webster; Patricia Wood

L511 Anna Power
Literary Agent; Managing Director
Bloomsbury House, 74-77 Great Russell Street, London, WC1B 3DA
United Kingdom

anna@johnsonandalcock.co.uk

http://www.johnsonandalcock.co.uk/anna-power
https://twitter.com/APowerAgent

Literary Agency: Johnson & Alcock (**L330**)

Fiction
  Graphic Novels: General

Novels: Book Club Fiction; Crime; Historical Fiction; Literary; Psychological Suspense
Nonfiction > *Nonfiction Books*
Cultural Criticism; Current Affairs; Food; History; Memoir; Popular Science; Psychology

Send: Query; Synopsis; Writing sample
How to send: Email attachment
How not to send: Post

In fiction, she is looking for voice-driven literary novels, book club and historical fiction, and psychological suspense and crime. Whatever the genre, she enjoys distinctive and compelling writing and worldbuilding that transports the reader. She is drawn especially to a moral dilemma, warm, human stories about families and relationships, and contemporary fiction with strong talking points, and which may be dark and funny. She is also keen to see graphic novels which appeal to a crossover readership.

In non-fiction, she invites submissions of history, memoir, current affairs, cultural criticism, popular science, psychology and food writing; anything that communicates an author's passion in an inventive and inspiring way. She particularly enjoys books by experts with new and surprising takes on subjects that change the way we think about the world.

L512 Marta Praeger
Literary Agent
United States

Literary Agency: Robert A. Freedman Dramatic Agency, Inc.

Scripts > *Theatre Scripts*

L513 Tanusri Prasanna
Literary Agent
United States

tpsubmissions@defliterary.com

https://www.defliterary.com/agent/tanusri-prasanna/

Literary Agency: DeFiore and Company

ADULT
  Fiction > *Novels*: Diversity

  Nonfiction > *Nonfiction Books*
    Memoir; Narrative Nonfiction; Social Justice

CHILDREN'S
  Fiction
    Middle Grade: Coming of Age; Contemporary; School; Suspense
    Picture Books: General

  Nonfiction
    Middle Grade; *Picture Books*
YOUNG ADULT
  Fiction > *Novels*
    Coming of Age; Contemporary; School; Suspense

Nonfiction > *Nonfiction Books*

Send: Pitch; Author bio; Synopsis; Full text
How to send: Email

Looks for accessible and wide-reaching, narrative nonfiction set against themes in social justice and representation, as well as memoirs and select fiction featuring diverse perspectives, contexts, and even storytelling styles. In the YA and middle-grade spaces, Drawn to contemporary coming-of-age stories, charming and relatable romances, ambitious world-building fantasies, and well-plotted, voice-driven suspense. She's also a big fan of stories set in schools or interesting neighborhoods told from fresh viewpoints. For picture books, her list includes both meaningful, lyrical, stories as well as ones that bring alive the wonder and complexity of our world with humor and heart. She's also interested in nonfiction that excites the imagination and curiosity of young readers.

Send a concise pitch, short bio, and a two-page synopsis if querying YA/MG fiction. For picture books, include the entire text in the body of your email. If querying an illustrated project, provide sample illustrations and links to your website / Instagram page.

L514 **Amanda Preston**
Literary Agent
United Kingdom

amandasubmissions@lbabooks.com

http://www.lbabooks.com/agent/amanda-preston/

Literary Agency: LBA Books Ltd

ADULT
Fiction > *Novels*
Book Club Fiction; Commercial; Crime; High Concept Thrillers; Historical Fiction; Romance

Nonfiction > *Nonfiction Books*
Contemporary; Crime; Environment; History; Memoir; Narrative Nonfiction; Nature; Psychology; Science; Wellbeing

YOUNG ADULT > **Fiction** > *Novels*
Contemporary; Historical Fiction; Speculative

Closed to approaches.

Represents a wide range of best-selling and award-winning authors across fiction and non-fiction. On the hunt for a high-concept thriller which is character and plot driven, but also has a discussable issue at its heart. Would also love a novel where the location is as integral to the plot as the crime. Would love a new crime series. On the hunt for a glorious book club love story that is doing something a bit different and special. For nonfiction, would love more true crime. It can be contemporary or historical, an unsolved case or a different perspective on a well known case. Not looking

for any child-related crime stories. Looking for narrative non-fiction predominately in science, the environment, psychology, nature writing, well-being and memoir.

Authors: Emily Adlam; Jaimie Admans; Sarah Alderson; Dominique Antiglio; Kerry Barrett; A.L. Bird; Darcie Boleyn; Christina Bradley; Catherine Brookes; Jo Carnegie; Lucie Cave; Rebecca Chance; Emma Cooper; Susie Donkin; Hannah Doyle; Katherine Dyson; Kate Hackworthy; Natalie Heaton; Holly Jade; Jane Jesmond; Lesley Kara; Simon Kernick; Emily Kerr; Ella King; Amy Lavelle; Georgina Lees; Freda Lightfoot; Jane Linfoot; Fiona Lucas; Rachael Lucas; Dee MacDonald; Ian Marber; Colin McDowell; Lisa Medved; L. C. North; Angelique Panagos; Catherine Piddington; Anna Pointer; Gillian Richmond; Natali Simmonds; Tom Simons; Johanna Spiers; Zara Stoneley; Heidi Swain; Karen Swan; Sophie Tanner; Jonathan Trigell; Anna Turns; Claire Wade; Kate Wells; Kate Winter; Dalton Wong

L515 **Arthur B. Pulitzer**
Literary Agent
United States

Literary Agency: Arthur B Pulitzer Agency (**L033**)

L516 **Rufus Purdy**
Literary Agent
United Kingdom

Literary Agency: The Two Piers Literary Agency (**L618**)

L517 **Rachel Mills Literary**
Literary Agency
M27, South Wing, Somerset House, Strand, London, WC2R 1LA
United Kingdom

submissions@rmliterary.co.uk

https://www.rachelmillsliterary.co.uk
https://twitter.com/bookishyogini
https://www.instagram.com/rachelmillsliterary/

Professional Body: The Association of Authors' Agents (AAA)

How to send: Email

As an agency we are particularly interested in female voices, and in showcasing talent which deserves to be heard, regardless of age or background. We seek to work with authors whose careers we can help build over the long term, across multiple projects.

Company Director / Literary Agent: Rachel Mills (**L451**)

Literary Agent: Nelle Andrew (**L023**)

L518 **Susan Ramer**
Literary Agent
United States

dca@doncongdon.com

https://doncongdon.com/agents

Literary Agency: Don Congdon Associates, Inc. (**L175**)

Fiction > *Novels*
Book Club Fiction; Contemporary; Literary; Upmarket

Nonfiction > *Nonfiction Books*
Arts; Cultural History; Fashion; Food; Literary Memoir; Music; Narrative Nonfiction; Popular Culture; Social History; Women's Issues

How to send: Email

Looks for literary fiction, upmarket 'book club' fiction (contemporary and historical, American in particular), and narrative non-fiction. Is drawn to an authentic voice, unforgettable characters with an edge, and an unfamiliar, well-crafted story that is emotional in unpredictable ways. For non-fiction, her interests include social history, cultural history, smart pop culture (fashion, food, art, music), women's issues, politics, health/diet/fitness, and literary memoir with a distinctive theme. She particularly likes a narrative that combines a personal thread with reporting and analysis of a broader social or cultural issue. In everything, she appreciates a sense of humor, especially when it's on the dark side. No queries in the following categories: romance, sci-fi, fantasy, espionage, mysteries, politics, health/diet/fitness, self-help sports or children's (young adult, middle grade or picture book); and she does not represent screenplays.

L519 **Rebecca Carter Literary**
Literary Agency
United Kingdom

info@rebeccacarterliterary.com

https://www.rebeccacarterliterary.com

Professional Body: The Association of Authors' Agents (AAA)

Literary Agent: Rebecca Carter (**L103**)

L520 **Redhammer**
Literary Agency
United Kingdom

https://redhammer.info
https://www.facebook.com/RealLitopia
https://twitter.com/Litopia
https://www.linkedin.com/in/petecox/
https://studio.youtube.com/channel/UCmbrM2ciaxb4hHQFfnSeOpg

Fiction > *Novels*

Nonfiction > *Nonfiction Books*

Send: Pitch; Writing sample
How to send: Online submission system

Runs weekly pop-up submission sessions where you can watch your submission being discussed.

Literary Agent: Peter Cox (*L141*)

L521 Regina Ryan Books
Literary Agency
United States

queries@reginaryanbooks.com

https://www.reginaryanbooks.com

Professional Body: Association of American Literary Agents (AALA)

Nonfiction
Nonfiction Books: Architecture; Birds; Business; Cookery; Crime; Diet; Environment; Gardening; Health; History; Leisure; Lifestyle; Narrative Nonfiction; Nature; Parenting; Politics; Psychology; Science; Spirituality; Sport; Sustainable Living; Travel; Wellbeing; Women's Issues
Reference: Popular

Does not want:

Nonfiction > *Nonfiction Books*: Religion

Send: Query; Proposal; Writing sample; Full text; Author bio; Market info; Marketing Plan
How to send: Word file email attachment

Costs: Offers services that writers have to pay for. Offers publishing consultation services and book packaging and production (print and electronic).

We are a Manhattan-based boutique literary agency primarily representing adult nonfiction. We also offer publishing consultation services and book packaging and production (print and electronic).

We are always looking for new and exciting books in our areas of interest, including well-written narrative nonfiction, architecture, history, politics, natural history (especially birds), true crime, science (especially the brain), the environment, women's issues, parenting, cooking, psychology, health, wellness, diet, business, non-religious contemporary spirituality, lifestyle, sustainability, popular reference, and leisure activities including sports, narrative travel, and gardening. We represent books that have something new to say, are well-written and that will, if possible, make the world a better place.

Authors: Ben Austro; Randi Minetor; Doug Whynott

Literary Agent: Regina Ryan

L522 Jessica Reino
Senior Agent
United States

https://www.
metamorphosisliteraryagency.com/about

https://querymanager.com/query/JessicaReino
https://twitter.com/jnrlitauthor

Literary Agency: Metamorphosis Literary Agency (**L440**)

ADULT
Fiction > *Novels*
General, and in particular: Contemporary Romance; Fantasy; Legal Thrillers; Mystery; Psychological Thrillers; Suspense; Women's Fiction

Nonfiction > *Nonfiction Books*
Comedy / Humour; Health; Parenting; Popular Culture; Sport

CHILDREN'S > **Fiction** > *Middle Grade*
General, and in particular: Horror

YOUNG ADULT > **Fiction** > *Novels*
Contemporary; Fantasy; Horror; Magical Realism; Romance; Science Fiction; Supernatural / Paranormal

Closed to approaches.

Looking for manuscripts that are well-written with a strong voice in order to make that emotional connection. Seeking MG, YA, Adult and nonfiction projects.

L523 Laura Rennert
Executive Agent
United States

ljrennert@mac.com

http://www.litagentlaurarennert.com
https://www.andreabrownlit.com/Team/Laura-Rennert
https://www.publishersmarketplace.com/members/LauraRennert/
https://www.manuscriptwishlist.com/mswl-post/laura-rennert/
https://querymanager.com/query/LauraRennert

Literary Agency: Andrea Brown Literary Agency, Inc.

ADULT > **Fiction**
Graphic Novels: General
Novels: Commercial; Fantasy; Folklore, Myths, and Legends; Gothic; Historical Fiction; Horror; Literary; Police Procedural; Science Fiction; Social Issues; Speculative; Thrillers
CHILDREN'S > **Fiction**
Chapter Books; *Middle Grade*; *Picture Books*
YOUNG ADULT > **Fiction** > *Novels*

Send: Query; Author bio; Writing sample
How to send: Email

Specializes in all categories of children's books, from picture books to young adult. On the adult side, she represents literary-commercial fiction, thrillers, horror, sci-fi/fantasy, speculative fiction, and select historical fiction. Her sweet spot in the market is literary voice and commercial conception.

L524 Richard Curtis Associates, Inc.
Literary Agency
286 Madison Avenue, 10th Floor, New York, NY 10017
United States
Tel: +1 (212) 759-8600

curtisagency@haroldober.com
contact@haroldober.com

https://www.haroldober.com/richard-curtis

Literary Agency: Harold Ober Associates, Inc. (**L290**)
Professional Body: Association of American Literary Agents (AALA)

Fiction > *Novels*

Nonfiction > *Nonfiction Books*

Closed to approaches.

Acquired in January 2022. Continues to administer advance, royalty and other payments for the thousands of backlist titles brought to readers since the agency was founded in 1979.

Literary Agent: Richard Curtis

L525 Nicki Richesin
Literary Agent
United States

https://www.dclagency.com

Literary Agency: Dunow, Carlson & Lerner Agency (**L183**)

ADULT > **Fiction** > *Novels*
Literary; Upmarket
YOUNG ADULT
Fiction > *Novels*

Nonfiction > *Nonfiction Books*
Biography; Cookery; Diversity; Feminism; Films; Investigative Journalism; Memoir; Music; Popular Culture; TV

Represents literary and upmarket fiction, and young adult fiction. She also focuses on nonfiction including investigative journalism, pop culture (especially film/TV and music), biography, cooking, and memoir that makes an impact and becomes part of a larger cultural conversation. She is particularly interested in discovering underrepresented voices from around the world exploring identity, feminism, and social diversity.

L526 Rick Richter
Literary Agent; Senior Partner
United States

https://aevitascreative.com/agents/
https://querymanager.com/query/RickRichter

Literary Agency: Aevitas

ADULT
Fiction > *Novels*

Commercial; Horror; Psychological Thrillers

Nonfiction > *Nonfiction Books*
Celebrity Memoir; Crime; Food; History; Memoir; Music; Narrative Nonfiction; Politics; Popular Culture; Religion; Science; Self Help; Social Justice; Sports Celebrity

CHILDREN'S
Fiction
Chapter Books; *Early Readers*; *Middle Grade*; *Picture Books*
Nonfiction
Early Readers; *Middle Grade*; *Picture Books*
YOUNG ADULT
Fiction > *Novels*
Nonfiction > *Nonfiction Books*

Send: Author bio; Market info; Writing sample
How to send: Online submission system

Areas of interest include self-help, pop culture, memoir, history, thriller, true crime, political and social issues, narrative food writing, and faith. He has deep experience and interest in children's books.

Authors: John Bainbridge; Rob Barnett; Mary Jane Begin; Sheryl Berk; Tom Booth; Marcus Brotherton; Kyle Buchanan; Andrew Bustamante; Marc and Angel Chernoff; Pan Cooke; Amanda Craig; Geoff Edgers; Michael Emberley; Jeremy Enger; JR and Vanessa Ford; Michael and Ava Gardner; Dan Goldman; Margaret Greanais; Andy Greene; Erik Gude; Peter Guralnick; Madeline Pendleton Hansen; Michael Hendrix; James Hibberd; Barry Jackson; Jeffrey H. Jackson; Alan Katz; Erin Kimmerle; Rebecca Kling; William J. Kole; Deb Miller Landau; Neil Lane; Kim Mager; Aaron Mahnke; Amanda Marrone; SSG Travis Mills; Malcolm Mitchell; Real Sports Entertainment Network; Chris and Emily Norton; Cate Osborn; Panos Panay; Shawn Peters; Greg Presto; Jessica Radloff; Michael Relth; David Ricciardi; Geo Rutherford; Hannah Selinger; Tim Sommer; Isaiah Stephens; Melanie Sumrow; Leah Tinari; Neil Tomba; Sheree Tomba; Allison Varnes; Sara Vladic; Molly Webster; Paige Wetzel; Sean Fay Wolfe

L527 Patricia Riddle-Gaddis
Author; Literary Agent; Editor
United States

patricia@hartlineliterary.com

https://www.hartlineagency.com/agents-and-authors

Literary Agency: Hartline Literary Agency (**L295**)

ADULT
Fiction > *Novels*
Cozy Mysteries; Romance

Nonfiction > *Nonfiction Books*

YOUNG ADULT > **Fiction** > *Novels*

Interested in obtaining sweet romance, cozy mysteries, and young adult categories. (think Princess Diaries and a modern Nancy Drew.) She will also consider a range of nonfiction.

L528 Louise Ripley-Duggan
Literary Agent
United Kingdom

https://www.theseus.agency/team

Literary Agency: The Theseus Agency (**L611**)

L529 Rebecca Ritchie
Literary Agent
United Kingdom

https://amheath.com/agents/rebecca-ritchie/
https://twitter.com/Becky_Ritchie1

Literary Agency: A.M. Heath & Company Limited, Author's Agents (**L002**)

Fiction > *Novels*
Book Club Fiction; Comedy / Humour; Commercial; Contemporary Women's Fiction; Crime; High Concept; Historical Fiction; Police Procedural; Psychological Suspense; Romance; Saga; Thrillers

Nonfiction > *Nonfiction Books*
Cookery; Health; Travel; Wellbeing

L530 Robert Smith Literary Agency Ltd
Literary Agency
12 Bridge Wharf, 156 Caledonian Road, London, N1 9UU
United Kingdom
Tel: +44 (0) 20 8504 0024

robert@robertsmithliteraryagency.com

https://www.robertsmithliteraryagency.com

Professional Body: The Association of Authors' Agents (AAA)

Nonfiction > *Nonfiction Books*
Autobiography; Biography; Comedy / Humour; Crime; Current Affairs; Fitness; Health; History; Inspirational; Language; Military; Personal Development; Popular Culture; Real Life Stories; Warfare

Send: Query; Outline; Author bio; Synopsis; Writing sample; Market info; Self-Addressed Stamped Envelope (SASE)
How to send: Post; Email

Email or post a covering letter, briefly describing the book you want to write and why you are well qualified to be its author. Do not submit proposals for novels, academic books, poetry, children's books, religious books or film / TV scripts.

Authors: Arthur Aldridge; Sarbjit Kaur Athwal; Richard Anthony Baker; Delia Balmer; Juliet Barnes; Amanda Barrie; John Baxter; William Beadle; Robert Beasley; Peta

Bee; Paul Begg; John Bennett; Kevin Booth; Ralph Bulger; James Carnac; John Casson; Gary Chapman; Shirley Charters; John Clarke; Robert Clarke; Carol Clerk; Martyn Compton; Michelle Compton; Judy Cook; Les Cummings; Clive Driscoll; Rosie Dunn; Georgie Edwards; Russell Edwards; Kate Elysia; Stewart P. Evans; Penny Farmer; Martin Fido; Sarah Flower; Freddie Foreman; Helen Foster; Becci Fox; Astrid Franse; Stephen Fulcher; Alison Goldie; Charlotte Green; Christopher Green; Allan Grice; Christine Hamilton; Andrew Hansford; James Haspiel; Chris Hutchins; Rosalinda Hutton; Albert Jack; Naomi Jacobs; Muriel Jakubait; Nikola James; Sarah Jones; Christine Keeler; Anita Kelsey; Siobhan Kennedy-McGuinness; Heidi Kingstone; Brian Kirby; Tim Kirby; John Knight; Ronnie Knight; Reg Kray; Roberta Kray; Tony Lambrianou; Carol Ann Lee; John Lee; Angela Levin; Chris Lightbown; Seth Linder; David R. L. Litchfield; Mary Long; Tony Long; Jean MacColl; Gretel Mahoney; Maurice Mayne; Lenny McLean; Ann Ming; Paddy Monaghan; James Moore; Michelle Morgan; Caroline Morris; Zana Morris; Rochelle Morton; Alan Moss; Bobbie Neate; Paul Nero; Kim Noble; Laurie O'Leary; Marnie Palmer; Theo Paphitas; Gordon Rayner; Mike Reid; Frances Reilly; Lyn Rigby; William D. Rubinstein; Mark Ryan; Sarah Schenker; Nathan Shapow; Alexander Sinclair; Keith Skinner; David Slattery-Christy; Len Smith; Rita Smith; Allan Starkie; Jayne Sterne; Cameron Stewart; Neil R. Storey; Claudia Strachan; Bob Taylor; Christopher Warwick; Monica Weller; Natalie Welsh; Wynne Weston-Davies; Karl Williams; Peter Wilton; Robert Winnett; Joanne Zorian-Lynn

Literary Agents: Anne Smith; Robert Smith

L531 Soumeya Bendimerad Roberts
Literary Agent; Vice President
United States

soumeya@hgliterary.com

https://www.hgliterary.com/soumeya
https://querymanager.com/query/SBR
https://www.publishersmarketplace.com/members/SoumeyaRoberts/

Literary Agency: HG Literary (**L305**)
Professional Body: Association of American Literary Agents (AALA)

ADULT
Fiction > *Novels*
Literary; Postcolonialism; Upmarket

Nonfiction > *Nonfiction Books*
Crafts; Design; Lifestyle; Memoir; Narrative Nonfiction; Personal Essays

CHILDREN'S > **Fiction** > *Middle Grade:* Realistic

YOUNG

ADULT > **Fiction** > *Novels*: Realistic

Send: Query; Synopsis; Writing sample
How to send: Query Manager

Represents award-winning and best-selling authors in literary and upmarket fiction, narrative non-fiction, and memoir. She also represents select, quality realistic middle-grade and young-adult authors, in addition to a curated list across creative fields including design, craft, and lifestyle. She seeks observant writing that illuminates dynamic relationships between complex but sympathetic characters, unconventional settings and subcultures, and controlled experiments with form. She is particularly, but not exclusively, interested in work that investigates or reflects on the post-colonial world, marginalized and liminal spaces, and narratives by people of color. In non-fiction, she is primarily looking for idea-driven or voice-forward memoirs, personal essay collections, and narrative non-fiction of all stripes.

L532 Quressa Robinson

Literary Agent
United States

https://querymanager.com/query/1066
https://www.publishersmarketplace.com/members/QuressaRobinson/
https://twitter.com/qnrisawesome

Literary Agency: Folio Literary Management, LLC

ADULT

Fiction > *Novels*
Fantasy; Science Fiction

Nonfiction > *Nonfiction Books*
Commercial; Literary Memoir; Literary; Narrative Nonfiction; Popular Science; Westerns

CHILDREN'S > **Fiction** > *Middle Grade*
Contemporary; Fantasy; Literary; Science Fiction

YOUNG ADULT > **Fiction** > *Novels*
Contemporary; Fantasy; Romantic Comedy; Science Fiction

Closed to approaches.

Looking for:

Modern-day blue stockings, BIPOC fangirls/fanboys, #blackgirlmagic, #carefreeblackgirls, #blackboyjoy, LGBTQ+, BIPOC falling in love, neuroatypical / neurodivergent, and disabled BIPOCs as leads.

Middle Grade (contemporary, literary, and SF/F). Cute, quirky, charming, and fun. Along the lines of Kiki's Delivery Service, Spirited Away, The Girl that Drank the Moon, the Pandava series, Hurricane Child.

Young adult (contemporary, Rom Coms, and SF/F) *I have TONS of SF/F on my current list so I am extremely selective with this genre*

Adult SF/F with strong genre-bending/crossover appeal. (Think the All Souls Trilogy by Deborah Harkness, The Night Circus by Erin Morgenstern, and The Age of Miracles by Karen Thompson Walker. I'm also a fan of Anne Bishop and Naomi Novik. More recent books that I've loved: Trail of Lightning, The Ten Thousand Doors of January, and Empire of Sand.)

Passion projects in narrative nonfiction with a strong literary voice and commercial appeal (Wild by Cheryl Strayed, Black Man in a White Coat by Damon Tweedy, When Breath Becomes Air by Paul Kalanithi). Would love to see non-whitewashed cowboy stories; pop science by women, specifically women of color; and literary, voice-driven memoir with commercial appeal.

#ownvoices and marginalized authors in all genres mentioned above. Inclusive narratives in all genres.

L533 Rochelle Stevens & Co.

Literary Agency
2 Terretts Place, Upper Street, London, N1 1QZ
United Kingdom
Tel: +44 (0) 20 7359 3900

info@rochellestevens.com

http://www.rochellestevens.com
http://twitter.com/TerrettsPlace
http://www.rochellestevens.com/submissions/#

Scripts
Film Scripts; *Radio Scripts*; *TV Scripts*; *Theatre Scripts*

Send: Query; Author bio
How to send: By referral

Handles script writers for film, television, theatre, and radio. No longer handles writers of fiction, nonfiction, or children's books. See website for full submission guidelines.

Literary Agents: Frances Arnold; Rochelle Stevens

L534 Jennifer Rofe

Senior Agent
United States

jennifer@andreabrownlit.com

https://www.andreabrownlit.com/Team/Jennifer-Rof%C3%A9
http://twitter.com/jenrofe
http://instagram.com/jenrofe
https://www.publishersmarketplace.com/members/jenrofe/
https://www.manuscriptwishlist.com/mswl-post/jennifer-rofe/
http://queryme.online/jenrofe

Literary Agency: Andrea Brown Literary Agency, Inc.

CHILDREN'S > **Fiction**
Chapter Books: General
Middle Grade: General, and in particular: Commercial; Contemporary; Fantasy; Historical Fiction; Literary; Magic
Picture Books: General

Send: Query; Author bio; Writing sample
How to send: Query Manager

Always seeking distinct voices and richly developed characters. Middle grade has long been her soft spot and she's open to all genres in this category—literary, commercial, contemporary, magical, fantastical, historical, and everything in between. She especially appreciates stories that make her both laugh and cry, and that offer an unexpected view into the pre-teen experience. In picture books, she likes funny, character-driven projects; beautifully imagined and written stories; and milestone moments with a twist.

Currently only accepting queries for Author-Illustrators, Illustrators, and Middle Grade writers. Not currently accepting picture book text authors. (However, if you write in multiple spaces, query for one of the listed spaces and mention your other areas of interest.)

L535 Root Literary

Literary Agency
United States

info@rootliterary.com
submissions@rootliterary.com

https://www.rootliterary.com
https://www.instagram.com/rootliterary/
https://twitter.com/RootLiterary
https://www.pinterest.com/rootliterary/_created/

We're a boutique, future-focused literary agency, representing award-winning, bestselling, and up-and-coming authors, illustrators, and graphic novelists. We're committed to helping our clients confidently define and redefine their vision of success while they build a lasting body of work and a meaningful career, and we do so by advocating, empowering, educating, negotiating, problem-solving, and revenue-generating in innovative ways to support our clients' creative work.

Literary Agents: Kurestin Armada (**L030**); Samantha Fabien (**L205**); Melanie Figueroa (**L216**)

L536 The Rosenberg Group

Literary Agency
United States

http://www.rosenberggroup.com
https://querymanager.com/query/QueryManagerRosenbergGroup

Professional Body: Association of American Literary Agents (AALA)

ACADEMIC > **Nonfiction** > *Nonfiction Books*

ADULT
Fiction > *Novels*
Romance; Women's Fiction

Nonfiction > *Nonfiction Books*
General, and in particular: Apiculture (Beekeeping); History; Psychology; Wine

How to send: Query Manager

Represents romance and women's fiction for an adult audience, nonfiction, and college textbooks.

Literary Agent: Barbara Collins Rosenberg (*L537*)

L537 **Barbara Collins Rosenberg**
Literary Agent
United States

Literary Agency: The Rosenberg Group (**L536**)

L538 **Whitney Ross**
Literary Agent
United States

Literary Agency: Irene Goodman Literary Agency (IGLA)

L539 **Stefanie Rossitto**
Literary Agent
United States

https://www.thetobiasagency.com/stefanie-rossitto
https://querymanager.com/query/1927

Literary Agency: The Tobias Literary Agency (**L614**)

Fiction > *Novels*
Historical Fiction; Historical Romance; Medieval; Romance

How to send: Query Manager

Currently looking for historical fiction, and funny, witty, modern romances. She also enjoys anything and everything medieval as well as exciting historical romances and/or fiction based on real characters.

L540 **Rupert Crew Ltd**
Literary Agency
Southgate, 7 Linden Avenue, Dorchester, Dorset, DT1 1EJ
United Kingdom
Tel: +44 (0) 1305 260335

info@rupertcrew.co.uk

http://www.rupertcrew.co.uk

Fiction > *Novels*

Nonfiction > *Nonfiction Books*

Closed to approaches.

Closed to submissions as at July 2023. Check website for current status.

Send query with SAE, synopsis, and first two or three consecutive chapters. International representation, handling volume and subsidiary rights in fiction and nonfiction properties. No Short Stories, Science Fiction, Fantasy, Horror, Poetry or original scripts for Theatre, Television and Film. Email address for correspondence only. No response by post and no return of material with insufficient return postage.

Literary Agent: Caroline Montgomery

L541 **The Ruppin Agency**
Literary Agency
London,
United Kingdom

submissions@ruppinagency.com

https://www.ruppinagency.com/
https://twitter.com/ruppinagency

Fiction > *Novels*
Commercial; Crime; Historical Fiction; Literary; Mystery; Thrillers

Nonfiction > *Nonfiction Books*
Memoir; Narrative Nonfiction; Nature; Science; Social Issues

Closed to approaches.

Literary agency set up by a former bookseller, offering writers a new perspective on finding the right publisher for their work. Keen to find writers with something to say about society today and particularly looking for storylines that showcase voices and communities that have tended to be overlooked by the publishing world, although that should deter no-one from sending their writing. No poetry, children's, young adult, graphic novels, plays and film scripts, self-help or lifestyle (including cookery, gardening, or interiors), religious or other esoteric titles, illustrated, academic, business or professional titles.

Literary Agent: Jonathan Ruppin

L542 **Kathleen Rushall**
Senior Agent
United States

kathleen@andreabrownlit.com

https://www.kathleenrushall.com
https://www.andreabrownlit.com/Team/Kathleen-Rushall
https://www.facebook.com/kathleen.rushall.5/
https://www.publishersmarketplace.com/members/KatRushall/
https://www.manuscriptwishlist.com/mswl-post/kathleen-rushall/

Literary Agency: Andrea Brown Literary Agency, Inc.

CHILDREN'S > **Fiction**

Middle Grade: Animals; Astrology; Contemporary; Environment; Family Saga; Ghosts; High Concept; Magic; Romance; Social Justice; Tarot; Witches
Picture Books: Animals; Astrology; Environment; Ghosts; Social Justice; Tarot; Witches

YOUNG ADULT > **Fiction** > *Novels*

Closed to approaches.

Represents a wide range of children's literature. She represents NYT bestselling and award-winning authors. She's drawn to environmental and social justice themes, particularly for the youngest set. She loves animals and books about their welfare and science. She's always interested in picture books that inspire emotional intelligence, self-awareness, and empathy.

L543 **Laetitia Rutherford**
Literary Agent
United Kingdom

https://www.watsonlittle.com/agent/laetitia-rutherford/
http://www.twitter.com/laetitialit

Literary Agency: Watson, Little Ltd (**L635**)

Fiction > *Novels*
Africa; Crime; High Concept; Legal Thrillers; Literary; Upmarket

Nonfiction > *Nonfiction Books*
Contemporary; Culture; Environment; Gender; Nature; Parenting; Sexuality

Send: Query; Synopsis; Writing sample
How to send: Email

I represent a broad and diverse list of authors, ranging across Fiction and contemporary Non Fiction, and including literary prizewinners and commercial bestsellers. In Fiction, my special areas are Literary, Upmarket Fiction and Crime.

Author Estate: The Estate of Akemi Tanaka

Authors: Rebecca Abrams; R.G. Adams; Lucy Ayrton; Jenny Blackhurst; Emile Chabal; Ajay Chowdhury; Cynthia Clark; Vivianne Crowley; Jeremy Daldry; Rose Diell; Rebecca Elliott; JM Hewitt; Samson Kambalu; Holan Liang; Lindiwe Maqhubela; Alex Marwood; Diana McCaulay; Thabi Moeketsi; Tamsin Omond; Matt Rendell; Richard Owain Roberts; Anika Scott; Hannah Silva; Zoe Somerville; Shane Spall; Geeta Vara; Vincent Vincent; Jeremy Williams

L544 **Jim Rutman**
Vice President; Literary Agent
United States

https://www.sll.com/our-team
http://aaronline.org/Sys/PublicProfile/4090054/417813

Literary Agency: Sterling Lord Literistic, Inc. (**L583**)

Professional Body: Association of American Literary Agents (AALA)

Fiction > *Novels*

Nonfiction > *Nonfiction Books*
Culture; History

Send: Query; Synopsis; Writing sample
How to send: Online submission system

Represents formally adventurous and stylistically diverse authors of fiction as well as a variety of journalists and critics whose non-fiction work examines an array of cultural and historical subjects.

L545 Katie Salvo
Senior Agent
United States

https://www.
metamorphosisliteraryagency.com/about
https://querymanager.com/query/KatieSalvo
https://www.
metamorphosisliteraryagency.com/submissions

Literary Agency: Metamorphosis Literary Agency (**L440**)

ADULT
Fiction > *Novels*
LGBTQIA; Romance; Women's Fiction

Nonfiction > *Nonfiction Books*
Biography; History; LGBTQIA

CHILDREN'S > **Fiction** > *Middle Grade*

YOUNG ADULT > **Fiction** > *Novels*

How to send: Query Manager

Has a background in literary criticism, philosophy, political theory, and history. She is particularly interested in representing women's fiction, romance, children's books, middle grade, young adult, LGBTQ+, and historical biography.

L546 Kaitlyn Sanchez
Literary Agent
United States

https://bradfordlit.com/kaitlyn-sanchez/
https://querymanager.com/query/2049
https://twitter.com/KaitlynLeann17

Literary Agency: Bradford Literary Agency (**L073**)

CHILDREN'S
Fiction
Graphic Novels: General
Middle Grade: Adventure; Comedy / Humour; Coming of Age; Friends; Magic
Picture Books: General

Nonfiction > *Nonfiction Books*

YOUNG ADULT > **Fiction**
Graphic Novels: General
Novels: Adventure; Comedy / Humour; Coming of Age; Friends; Magic

Closed to approaches.

Looking for children's books (picture books through YA) in all categories, including graphic novels, nonfiction, and illustration. She is incredibly eclectic in her tastes, with a great affinity for emotional stories as well as funny stories. Always looking for diversity in all forms, including but not limited to BIPOC, neurodiversity, and LGBTQ+. Loves working with artists, so she's always on the lookout for great illustrators, author-illustrators, and graphic novelists. Generally leans PG and PG-13 for most submissions, though some intensity here and there is fine.

L547 Rayhane Sanders
Literary Agent
United States

http://www.mmqlit.com/about/

Literary Agency: Massie & McQuilkin
Professional Body: Association of American Literary Agents (AALA)

Fiction
Graphic Novels: General
Novels: Book Club Fiction; Historical Fiction; Literary; Upmarket
Short Fiction Collections: General

Nonfiction
Essays: General
Nonfiction Books: Memoir; Narrative Nonfiction

Does not want:

> **YOUNG ADULT** > **Fiction** > *Novels*: Speculative

Closed to approaches.

Represents and is on the lookout for literary and historical fiction, upmarket book-club fiction, comic novels, short story collections, propulsive narrative nonfiction, essay collections, and memoir. She likes projects that are voice-centered and site-specific, whether that be a place, profession, culture, or subculture. Though quality of writing is the most important factor, she is particularly interested in fresh voices telling fresh stories we haven't heard before and is fond of immigrant stories and stories concerned with race, sexuality, cross-cultural themes, and notions of identity.

L548 Angelique Tran Van Sang
Literary Agent
United Kingdom

Literary Agency: Felicity Bryan Associates (**L211**)

Fiction > *Novels*: Literary

Nonfiction > *Nonfiction Books*
Arts; History; Literature; Memoir; Narrative Nonfiction; Philosophy; Politics

Send: Query; Synopsis; Writing sample
How to send: Online submission system

Actively building a list of authors of literary fiction and narrative non-fiction. Interested in essays and longform narratives that have a distinctive voice. Also partial to an exquisitely written memoir, ideally one that weaves in art, literature, history, politics or philosophy.

Author: Amy Key

L549 Kelly Van Sant
Literary Agent
United States

https://www.penandparsley.com
https://querymanager.com/query/kellyvansant
https://www.manuscriptwishlist.com/mswl-post/kelly-van-sant/

Literary Agency: KT Literary (**L368**)

CHILDREN'S > **Fiction** > *Middle Grade*

YOUNG ADULT > **Fiction** > *Novels*

How to send: Query Manager

Seeks young adult and middle grade fiction, with a particular interest in projects by marginalized creators.

L550 Sarah Jane Freymann Literary Agency
Literary Agency
United States

Submissions@SarahJaneFreymann.com

http://www.sarahjanefreymann.com

ADULT
Fiction > *Novels*
Commercial; Literary

Nonfiction > *Nonfiction Books*
Cookery; Design; Journalism; Lifestyle; Memoir; Narrative Nonfiction; Self Help; Spirituality

YOUNG ADULT > **Fiction** > *Novels*

Send: Query; Writing sample
How to send: In the body of an email; Post

Strongly prefers to receive queries by email. Include pitch letter and first ten pages pasted into the body of the email (no attachments). If approaching by post, include SASE or email address for response.

Literary Agents: Sarah Jane Freymann (**L234**); Steve Schwartz (**L555**)

L551 Sandra Sawicka
Literary Agent
United Kingdom

Literary Agency: Marjacq Scripts Ltd (**L421**)

Closed to approaches.

L552 The Sayle Literary Agency
Literary Agency
1 Petersfield, Cambridge, CB1 1BB
United Kingdom
Tel: +44 (0) 1223 303035

info@sayleliteraryagency.com

http://www.sayleliteraryagency.com

Fiction > *Novels*

Nonfiction > *Nonfiction Books*

Closed to approaches.

Established in 1896, we are an independent, full-service literary agency dedicated to representing the finest writers and experts in their fields. We work with experienced editors and publishers and in collaboration with dedicated co-agents to give these writers the best chance of success in a highly competitive and international industry.

Literary Agent: Rachel Calder

L553 Rory Scarfe
Literary Agent; Company Director
United Kingdom

https://www.theblairpartnership.com/literary-agents/rory-scarfe/

Literary Agency: The Blair Partnership

ADULT
 Fiction > *Novels*: Commercial

 Nonfiction > *Nonfiction Books*: Commercial

 Scripts
  Film Scripts; *TV Scripts*
CHILDREN'S
 Fiction > *Novels*
 Nonfiction > *Nonfiction Books*

Closed to approaches.

Represents clients across commercial fiction, children's fiction and non-fiction, as well as screenwriters and brands.

Authors: Marina Abramović; Matt Allen; Jane Asher; Rafael Behr; Gary Bell; Ronen Bergman; David Bolchover; Michael Calvin; Sir Ronald Cohen; Laura Dodsworth; Owen Eastwood; Henry Fraser; John Fury; Paris Fury; Tyson Fury; Pippa Grange; Catherine Green; Maria Hatzistefanis; Jordan Henderson; Amelia Henley; Leigh Hosy-Pickett; Chris Hoy; James Inverne; Louise Jensen; Joanne Lake; Frank Lampard; Liz Lawler; Lee Lawrence; Arizona Leger; Aseem Malhotra; Joe Marler; Mercy Muroki; Shabnam Nasimi; Maajid Nawaz; Michal Oshman; Justine Pattison; Adam Peaty; Trevor Phillips; Nirmal Purja; Duncan Roe; Terry Ronald; Dan Saunders; Babita Sharma; Jon Smith; Jon Sopel; Dean Stott; Jessica Taylor; Pete Townshend; John Volanthen; Tom Watson; Brian Wood; Nadhim Zahawi

L554 Hannah Schofield
Literary Agent
United Kingdom

hannahsubmissions@lbabooks.com

http://www.lbabooks.com/agent/hannah-schofield/

Literary Agency: LBA Books Ltd

ADULT
 Fiction > *Novels*
  Book Club Fiction; Commercial; Fantasy Romance; Historical Fiction; Romantic Comedy; Suspense; Thrillers; Women's Fiction

 Nonfiction > *Nonfiction Books*
  Crime; History; Memoir; Narrative Nonfiction; Personal Development; Social History

YOUNG ADULT > **Fiction** > *Novels*

How to send: Email

Represents a broad list of commercial and reading-group fiction, and select non-fiction.

Author / Literary Agent: Bea Fitzgerald (**L222**)

Authors: Emad Ahmed; Chris Bridges; Amanda Brooke; Charlotte Butterfield; Sam Caporn; Catherine Chang; Erin Connor; Kim Donovan; Elizabeth Drummond; Chloe Duckworth; Lucy Goacher; Isabella Harcourt; Anam Iqbal; Jenni Keer; Amy Lavelle; Nicole Louie; Marina McCarron; Heather Mottershead; Ellie Pilcher; Ande Pliego; Heidi Shertok; Celia Silvani; Tania Tay; David Turner; Catherine Walsh

L555 Steve Schwartz
Literary Agent
United States

http://www.sarahjanefreymann.com/?page_id=3872

Literary Agency: Sarah Jane Freymann Literary Agency (**L550**)

Fiction > *Novels*
 Crime; Historical Fiction; Popular; Thrillers

Nonfiction > *Nonfiction Books*
 Business; Comedy / Humour; Current Affairs; Psychology; Self Help; Sport; Travel

Send: Query; Writing sample
How to send: In the body of an email

Interested in popular fiction (crime, thrillers, and historical novels), world and national affairs, business books, self-help, psychology, humor, sports and travel.

L556 The Science Factory
Literary Agency
Scheideweg 34C, Hamburg, 20253
Germany
Tel: + 49 40 4327 4959; +44 (0) 20 7193 7296 (Skype)

info@sciencefactory.co.uk

https://www.sciencefactory.co.uk
https://twitter.com/sciencefactory

ACADEMIC > **Nonfiction** > *Nonfiction Books*
 General, and in particular: Health; History; Mathematics; Medicine; Nature; Philosophy; Science; Technology

ADULT > **Nonfiction** > *Nonfiction Books*
 General, and in particular: Health; History; Mathematics; Medicine; Nature; Philosophy; Science; Technology

Send: Query; Writing sample
Don't send: Full text
How to send: Email

Specialises in science, technology, medicine, and natural history, but will also consider other areas of nonfiction. Novelists handled only occasionally, and if there is some special relevance to the agency (e.g. a thriller about scientists, or a novel of ideas). See website for full submission guidelines.

Literary Agents: Jeff Shreve; Tisse Takagi; Peter Tallack

L557 Rosemary Scoular
Literary Agent
United Kingdom

https://www.unitedagents.co.uk/rscoularunitedagentscouk

Literary Agency: United Agents (**L619**)

Nonfiction > *Nonfiction Books*
 Adventure; Arts; Food; History; Investigative Journalism; Memoir; Nature; Politics; Popular Science; Travel

Focuses on nonfiction, from food writing to history, popular science and nature, travel and adventure, politics and investigative journalism, the arts and memoir of all kinds.

L558 Chloe Seager
Senior Agent
United Kingdom

https://madeleinemilburn.co.uk/team-member/19023/

Literary Agency: Madeleine Milburn Literary, TV & Film Agency (**L417**)

CHILDREN'S
 Fiction > *Middle Grade*
 Nonfiction > *Middle Grade*

TEEN > **Fiction** > *Novels*

YOUNG ADULT
 Fiction > *Novels*
 Nonfiction > *Nonfiction Books*

Send: Query; Pitch; Market info; Author bio; Synopsis; Writing sample
How to send: Email
How not to send: Post

Actively looking for: Middle Grade age 7 and up; clean teen; young adult; non-fiction MG and YA.

L559 Sean McCarthy Literary Agency

Literary Agency
United States

submissions@mccarthylit.com

https://www.mccarthylit.com

CHILDREN'S > **Fiction**
Board Books; *Chapter Books*; *Early Readers*; *Middle Grade*; *Picture Books*

Send: Query; Synopsis; Author bio; Writing sample
How to send: Email

Accepts submissions across all genres and age ranges in children's books. Send query by email with a description of your book, author bio, and literary or relevant professional credits, and first three chapters (or roughly 25 pages) for novels, or complete ms if your work is a picture book. No picture books over 1,000 words. Response in 6-8 weeks.

Literary Agent: Sean McCarthy

L560 Sebes & Bisseling

Literary Agency
United Kingdom

https://sebesbisseling.co.uk

Fiction > *Novels*

Nonfiction > *Nonfiction Books*

Does not want:

Fiction > *Novels*
Fantasy; Horror; Romance; Science Fiction

Send: Query; Synopsis; Writing sample

London branch of a literary agency with offices in Amsterdam and Stockholm. Represents authors in the US, UK and in translation, for their book, digital and screen adaptation rights. Welcomes submissions from authors writing in English across all genres, except fantasy, scifi, horror, romance, poetry, YA, middle grade and picture books.

L561 Dani Segelbaum

Literary Agent
United States

dani@carolmannagency.com

https://www.carolmannagency.com/dani-segelbaum
https://www.instagram.com/danisegelbaum/
https://twitter.com/DaniSegelbaum

Literary Agency: Carol Mann Agency

Fiction > *Novels*

Historical Fiction; Literary; Romantic Comedy; Upmarket; Women's Fiction

Nonfiction > *Nonfiction Books*
Cookery; Current Affairs; Lifestyle; Memoir; Narrative Nonfiction; Politics; Popular Culture; Women's Issues

Send: Query; Author bio; Writing sample; Synopsis; Proposal
How to send: In the body of an email
How not to send: Email attachment; Post

Interested in both fiction and non-fiction. Is seeking non-fiction titles with an emphasis on politics, women's issues, popular culture, and current events. Also loves memoir, narrative non-fiction, lifestyle, and cookbooks. In fiction, she is looking for literary and upmarket adult fiction including debut, historical, rom-coms, and women's fiction. In both fiction and non-fiction, she hopes to work with authors from diverse backgrounds to tell stories that are important to them. She loves compelling narrators and is drawn to writing that is voice-driven, highly transporting, and features unique perspectives and marginalized voices.

L562 Selectric Artists

Literary Agency
9 Union Square #123, Southbury, CT 06488
United States
Tel: +1 (347) 668-5426

query@selectricartists.com

https://www.selectricartists.com

ADULT
Fiction
Graphic Novels: General
Novels: Commercial; Science Fiction; Thrillers
Nonfiction
Graphic Nonfiction: General
Nonfiction Books: Memoir; Narrative Nonfiction
YOUNG ADULT > **Fiction** > *Novels*
Fantasy; Science Fiction

Send: Query; Full text
How to send: Email

Send query by email with your manuscript attached as a .doc, .pdf, or .pages file. Put the word "query" in the subject line. No queries by phone. Response only if interested.

Literary Agent: Christopher Schelling

L563 Maria Cardona Serra

Literary Agent
Spain

https://www.aevitascreative.com/agent/maria-cardona-serra
https://querymanager.com/query/MariaCardona_Queries

Literary Agency: Aevitas Creative Management (ACM) UK (**L008**)

Fiction > *Novels*

Literary; Romance; Upmarket Crime; Upmarket

Nonfiction > *Nonfiction Books*
Narrative Nonfiction; Women's Issues

Closed to approaches.

Focuses in upmarket and literary fiction by authors who write in English and Spanish. Maria is an editorially minded agent that works closely with her authors with a long-term career plan. She is passionate about international voices and is used to working with authors that live in different corners of the world. She reads broadly yet is particularly drawn by character-driven, heart-wrenching fiction, modern love stories, and genre-bending upmarket crime. She is always looking for that perfect line that makes her thrill, paying special attention to the voice on the page and is always up for a surprise in a manuscript, looking for stories she hasn't read before. She is also interested in narrative non-fiction about women's experiences.

Authors: Safia El Aaddam; Ayesha Harruna Attah; Federico Axat; Lucía Baskaran; Meaghan Beatley; Lucía Benavides; Maame Blue; Rijula Das; Avni Doshi; Guillermo Erades; Eudald Espluga; Sujatha Fernandes; Beatriz Flamini; Javier Fuentes; Karen Havelin; Sunnah Khan; Natalia Litvinova; Lucía Alba Martínez; Elena Medel; Elizabeth Morris; Irene Muchemi-Ndiritu; Maria Nicolau; Mariane Pearl; Claudia Polo; Alana S. Portero; Zara Raheem; Devika Rege; Yaffa S. Santos; Marta Sanz; Shubhangi Swarup; María Sánchez; Cristina Sánchez-Andrade; Begoña Gómez Urzaiz

L564 Charlotte Seymour

Literary Agent
United Kingdom

charlotte@johnsonandalcock.co.uk

http://www.johnsonandalcock.co.uk/charlotte-seymour

Literary Agency: Johnson & Alcock (**L330**)

Fiction > *Novels*
Book Club Fiction; Crime; Literary; Suspense; Thrillers

Nonfiction > *Nonfiction Books*
Arts; Cookery; Cultural History; Food; Journalism; Nature; Popular Science; Social History

Send: Query; Synopsis; Writing sample
How to send: Email

In fiction, looks for book club and literary fiction as well as outstanding character – and voice-driven crime, thriller and suspense. She loves writing that crosses boundaries, whether geographic or linguistic or in bringing a twist to a genre.

In non-fiction, she is interested in accessible, engaging writing on a range of subjects including popular science, social and cultural history, reportage, nature, the arts, food and cookery. She especially loves hybrid books, for example, when in a memoir, the personal is interwoven with a bigger story or subject.

L565 Lauren Sharp
Literary Agent
United States

https://aevitascreative.com/agents/

Literary Agency: Aevitas

Nonfiction > *Nonfiction Books*
Current Affairs; History; Narrative Nonfiction; Politics; Science

Represents nonfiction in the areas of politics, history, current affairs, narrative nonfiction, and science.

Authors: Amanda Becker; Carrie Lane; Maya Wei-Haas; Jagadish Shukla; Glen Weldon; Payam Zamani

L566 The Shaw Agency
Literary Agency
United Kingdom

https://www.theshawagency.co.uk

ADULT
Fiction > *Novels*
Commercial; Literary

Nonfiction > *Nonfiction Books*
Lifestyle; Narrative Nonfiction; Wellbeing

CHILDREN'S
Fiction > *Novels*
Nonfiction > *Nonfiction Books*

TEEN > **Fiction** > *Novels*

Send: Query; Pitch; Synopsis; Writing sample
Don't send: Full text
How to send: Online contact form

Handles literary and commercial fiction, fact and fiction books for children (6+) and teenagers/young adults, and narrative non-fiction. Send query through online form with one-page synopsis, first 10 pages, and email address for response. See website for full guidelines.

Literary Agent: Kate Shaw

L567 Sheil Land Associates Ltd
Literary Agency
RM 9-25, LABS House, 15-19 Bloomsbury Way, London, WC1A 2TH
United Kingdom
Tel: +44 (0) 20 7405 9351
Fax: +44 (0) 20 7831 2127

submissions@sheiland.co.uk

https://www.sheiland.com
https://twitter.com/sheiland

ADULT

Fiction > *Novels*
Book Club Fiction; Commercial Women's Fiction; Contemporary; Crime; Family Saga; Fantasy; Ghost Stories; Historical Fiction; Horror; Literary; Mystery; Romance; Science Fiction; Thrillers

Nonfiction
Gift Books: Comedy / Humour
Nonfiction Books: Biography; Cookery; Gardening; Lifestyle; Memoir; Mind, Body, Spirit; Personal Development; Politics; Popular Science; Psychology; Travel
Scripts
Film Scripts; *TV Scripts*; *Theatre Scripts*
CHILDREN'S
Fiction > *Novels*

Scripts
Animation Scripts; *TV Scripts*
YOUNG ADULT > **Fiction** > *Novels*

Send: Query
Don't send: Full text
How to send: Email

A long-established literary, theatrical and film agency. Welcomes approaches from new clients of all backgrounds, whether they have been published already or are first time writers. Looks for literary fiction, commercial fiction and non-fiction. Also represents celebrities and journalists with a story to tell.

Authors: Peter Ackroyd; Melvyn Bragg; Susan Hill; David Lister; Catherine Robertson; Jonathan Steele

Literary Agents: Gaia Banks (**L045**); Piers Blofeld; Ian Drury; Lucy Fawcett; Sonia Land; Rebecca Lyon (**L406**)

L568 Hannah Sheppard
Literary Agent
United Kingdom

Literary Agency: Hannah Sheppard Literary Agency (**L283**)

L569 Michael Signorelli
Literary Agent
United States

https://aevitascreative.com/agents/
https://querymanager.com/query/2593

Literary Agency: Aevitas

Fiction > *Novels*
Commercial; Literary

Nonfiction > *Nonfiction Books*
Culture; Current Affairs; History; Memoir; Politics; Science; Sport; Technology

Send: Pitch; Market info; Writing sample
How to send: Query Manager

Represents literary and commercial fiction as well as nonfiction in cultural history, current affairs, memoir, politics, science, sports, and technology.

Authors: Mark Arsenault; Anne Soon Choi; Brandi Collins-Dexter; Matthew Davis; Joan Donovan; Emily Dreyfuss; Abby Ellin; Justin Evans; Morgan Falconer; Alex Cody Foster; Jared Fox; Meryl Frank; Brian Friedberg; J. Weston Phippen; Nancy Kress; Robert Lanza; Oksana Masters; Kelly Richmond Pope; Benjamin Reeves; Kevin Sites; Adam Philip Stern; Deanne Stillman; CeCe Telfer; Michelle Theall

L570 Julia Silk
Literary Agent
United Kingdom

julia@greyhoundliterary.co.uk

https://greyhoundliterary.co.uk/agent/julia-silk/
https://twitter.com/juliasreading
https://www.instagram.com/juliasreading/
https://www.pinterest.co.uk/juliasreadingbo/my-favourite-books/

Literary Agency: Greyhound Literary (**L271**)

Fiction > *Novels*
Commercial; Contemporary; Crime; Historical Fiction; Literary; Upmarket Thrillers; Upmarket

Nonfiction > *Nonfiction Books*
Health; Journalism; Narrative Nonfiction; Wellbeing

Send: Query; Writing sample
How to send: Email

Particularly looking for crime with a series character, upmarket thrillers, and a compelling historical novel with a strong voice. She is also always looking for upmarket contemporary commercial/accessible literary fiction with equal attention paid to concept, voice, character and plot. In narrative non-fiction she is also keen to hear from journalists and experts illuminating new stories and previously unexplored subjects, and on the practical side she represents a number of writers in health and wellbeing and is interested in original evidence-based proposals in this area from experts with a strong platform.

Authors: Tobi Asare; Juliet Bell; Leona Nichole Black; Owen Booth; Luce Brett; Kirsty Eyre; Marchelle Farrell; A P Firdaus; Liz Fraser; Janet Gover; Sarah Graham; Karen Gurney; Maisie Hill; Heidi James; Ginger Jones; Carlie Lee; Fiona Longmuir; Amanda Mason; Alison May; Paul Morgan-Bentley; Amy Ransom; Rebecca Rogers; Rebecca Schiller; Clare Seal; Ally Sinclair; Penny Wincer

L571 Janet Silver
Literary Agent; Senior Partner
United States

https://aevitascreative.com/agents/

Literary Agency: Aevitas

Fiction > *Novels*: Literary

Nonfiction > *Nonfiction Books*: Creative Nonfiction

Poetry > *Poetry Collections*

Closed to approaches.

Represents a roster of bestselling and award-winning authors of literary fiction, creative nonfiction, and poetry.

Authors: Saher Alam; Samina Ali; Dur E Aziz Amna; Kendra Atleework; Michael Byers; Christopher Castellani; Michael Collier; Jonathan Crowl; Vievee Francis; Christa Fraser; Omer Friedlander; Linda Gregerson; Jennifer Grotz; Brooks Hansen; Angela Hopkins; Sativa January; Menachem Kaiser; Dana Kletter; Alyssa Knickerbocker; Chaney Kwak; Samuel Leader; Tom Macher; Anthony Marra; Amanda Rose Martinez; Spencer Matheson; Mark Mayer; Anna Mazhirov; Matthew Neill Null; D. Wystan Owen; Matthew Pockrus; Hanna Pylväinen; Ladette Randolph; Humaira Awais Shahid; Alan Shapiro; Safiya Sinclair; Emily Strasser; Cheryl Strayed; Mecca Jamilah Sullivan; Monique Truong; Zachary Tyler Vickers; Devon Walker-Figueroa; Yara Zgheib

L572 Lydia Silver
Literary Agent
United Kingdom

https://www.darleyanderson.com/our-team
https://twitter.com/LydiaRSilver

Literary Agency: The Darley Anderson Agency

CHILDREN'S
Fiction
  Chapter Books; *Middle Grade*; *Picture Books*
Nonfiction
  Chapter Books; *Middle Grade*; *Picture Books*
TEEN
Fiction > *Novels*
Nonfiction > *Nonfiction Books*

YOUNG ADULT
Fiction > *Novels*
Nonfiction > *Nonfiction Books*

Send: Query; Synopsis; Writing sample
How to send: Word file email attachment; PDF file email attachment; Post

Represents clients across all age groups, including picture book, chapter book, middle grade and YA, and has a particular focus on non-fiction. Reads and considers widely, and among other things she is looking for snort-inducing stories for younger readers, clever and contemporary teenage and YA fiction, and non-fiction projects that take big ideas and make them easily navigable, accessible and fun. She loves working editorially with writers and is always on the lookout for new talent.

Authors: Maria Motunrayo Adebisi; Gina Blaxill; Sarah Bowie; Mark Bradley; Danielle

Brown; Lanisha Butterfield; Lucy Tandon Copp; Ryan Hammond; Alice Harman; Joyce Efia Harmer; Mina Ikemoto; Catherine Jacob; Amie Jordan; Hannah Moffatt; Rachel Morrisroe; Eva Wong Nava; Laura Noakes; Lisa Richardson; Ellie Robinson; Nick Sheridan; Rashmi Sirdeshpande; Mimi Thebo

L573 Tanera Simons
Literary Agent
United Kingdom

tanera@darleyanderson.com

https://www.darleyanderson.com/our-team
https://twitter.com/tanera_simons

Literary Agency: The Darley Anderson Agency

Fiction > *Novels*
  Book Club Fiction; Commercial; Historical Fiction; Romance; Romantic Comedy

How to send: Email attachment
How not to send: Post

Looking for romantic comedies, sweeping love stories, accessible book club fiction, historical/timeslip, and general commercial fiction.

Authors: Mandy Baggot; Sara Bragg; Laura Carter; Claire Frost; Mary Hargreaves; Sandie Jones; Beth O'Leary; Sally Page; Kate G. Smith; Emma Steele; Sophie White; Ally Zetterberg

L574 Cara Lee Simpson
Literary Agent
United Kingdom

clsimpson@pfd.co.uk

https://petersfraserdunlop.com/agent/cara-lee-simpson/

Literary Agency: Peters Fraser + Dunlop (**L501**)

Fiction > *Novels*
  Book Club Fiction; Ethnic Groups; Gender Politics; Literary; Mental Health; Relationships; Sexuality; Social Class

Send: Query; Synopsis; Writing sample; Proposal; Author bio
How to send: Email

I am particularly on the lookout for voice-driven fiction with unusual and absorbing protagonists, books with an interesting structure, and fiction that crosses genre in new and unexpected ways. I lean towards books that are accessible to a wide readership while remaining beautifully written, especially if the writing is suspenseful or quirky. I am always interested in stories that explore gender politics, race, class, sexuality, mental health, and those which offer a profound look at relationship dynamics.

Authors: Tufayel Ahmed; Jacqueline Bublitz; Angela Chadwick; Roxy Dunn; Ben Halls;

Shilo Kino; Kira Mcpherson; Okechukwu Nzelu; Jonathan Page

L575 Skylark Literary
Literary Agency
19 Parkway, Weybridge, Surrey, KT13 9HD
United Kingdom
Tel: +44 (0) 20 8144 7440

submissions@skylark-literary.com
info@skylark-literary.com

http://www.skylark-literary.com
https://twitter.com/SkylarkLit
http://www.facebook.com/skylarkliteraryltd

Professional Body: The Association of Authors' Agents (AAA)

CHILDREN'S > **Fiction**
  Chapter Books; *Early Readers*; *Middle Grade*
YOUNG ADULT > **Fiction** > *Novels*

Send: Full text; Synopsis
How to send: Word file email attachment

Handles fiction for children, from chapter books for emerging readers up to young adult / crossover titles. No picture books. Send query by email with one-page synopsis and full ms. No postal submissions.

Literary Agents: Amber J. Caravéo; Joanna Moult

L576 Antoinette Van Sluytman
Junior Agent; Assistant Agent
United States

https://www.irenegoodman.com/antoinette-van-sluytman
https://aalitagents.org/author/antoinette-van-sluytman/
https://twitter.com/antoinight
https://www.instagram.com/toni_vansluy
https://www.linkedin.com/in/antoinette-van-sluytman-83b5a423a/

Literary Agency: Irene Goodman Literary Agency (IGLA)
Literary Agent: Natalie Lakosil (**L370**)
Professional Body: Association of American Literary Agents (AALA)

ADULT > **Fiction**
  Graphic Novels: General
  Novels: Adventure; Dark Fantasy; High / Epic Fantasy; Historical Fiction; Horror; Science Fiction; Speculative
YOUNG ADULT > **Fiction**
  Graphic Novels; *Novels*

Closed to approaches.

Interested in all genres of speculative fiction, specifically cosmic horror, dark fantasy, epic fantasy, sci-fi, in addition to historical fiction. Antoinette maintains special interest in adult projects but is also open to select YA and graphic novels. In general she loves lyrical prose that challenges narrative conventions, ambitiously immersive worlds inspired by different cultures, morally gray and dysfunctional but lovable characters with fun dynamics, and new takes on old tropes. She is drawn to atmospheric and lyrical prose and complex philosophical/psychological themes across all genres. Some general themes she enjoys are adventures, antiheroines, quirky concepts you might find in an anime, dark fantasy, and anticolonialism. In historical fiction she's interested in finding stories inspired by non-western mythologies or about the untold stories of female heroines around the world.

L577 Jennifer March Soloway
Literary Agent
United States

soloway@andreabrownlit.com

https://querymanager.com/query/JenniferMarchSoloway
https://twitter.com/marchsoloway

Literary Agency: Andrea Brown Literary Agency, Inc.

ADULT > Fiction > *Novels*
Commercial; Crime; Literary; Psychological Suspense

CHILDREN'S > Fiction
Middle Grade: Adventure; Comedy / Humour; Contemporary; Fantasy; Ghost Stories; Mystery; Realistic
Picture Books: General, and in particular: Comedy / Humour
YOUNG ADULT > Fiction > *Novels*
Family; Literary; Mental Health; Psychological Horror; Relationships; Romance; Sexuality; Suspense; Thrillers

Send: Query
How to send: Email; By referral

Represents authors and illustrators of picture book, middle grade, and YA stories, and is actively building her list. Although she specializes in children's literature, she also represents adult fiction, both literary and commercial, particularly crime and psychological suspense projects.

Currently accepting queries by referral only.

L578 Kelly Sonnack
Senior Agent
United States

https://www.andreabrownlit.com/agents.html
https://twitter.com/KSonnack

Literary Agency: Andrea Brown Literary Agency, Inc.

CHILDREN'S > Fiction > *Picture Books*

YOUNG ADULT > Fiction
Graphic Novels; *Novels*

How to send: By referral

L579 Arley Sorg
Literary Agent
United States

https://arleysorg.com
https://ktliterary.com/submissions/
https://querymanager.com/query/QueryArley

Literary Agency: KT Literary (**L368**)

Fiction > *Novels*
Environment; Fantasy; Horror; Literary; Science Fiction; Speculative

How to send: Query Manager

Primarily interested in adult speculative titles, including science fiction, fantasy, and horror with speculative/fantastic elements, literary speculative fiction, and climate fiction.

L580 James Spackman
Literary Agent
United Kingdom

https://www.thebksagency.com/about
https://www.thebksagency.com/submissions

Literary Agency: The BKS Agency (**L063**)

Fiction > *Graphic Novels*

Nonfiction
Graphic Nonfiction: General
Nonfiction Books: Culture; Music; Sport

Send: Query; Outline; Author bio
How to send: Online submission system

Looking for sport, music, culture and smart thinking.

L581 Spring Literary
Literary Agency
United Kingdom

submissions@springliterary.com

https://www.springliterary.com
https://twitter.com/springliterary
https://www.instagram.com/springliterary

CHILDREN'S > Fiction > *Picture Books*

YOUNG ADULT
Fiction > *Novels*
Nonfiction > *Nonfiction Books*

Send: Query; Synopsis; Writing sample; Author bio; Full text
How to send: Email

Specialises in children's and YA writing and illustration. Works with all the major publishing houses, plus entertainment companies, to ensure the best match for each book, author and illustrator.

Literary Agent: Neil Dunnicliffe (**L182**)

L582 Stephanie Tade Literary Agency
Literary Agency
United States

https://www.stephanietadeagency.com

Nonfiction > *Nonfiction Books*: Mind, Body, Spirit

Send: Query
How to send: Online contact form

A full service literary agency with a focus on nonfiction, particularly in the categories of physical, psychological, and spiritual well-being.

Literary Agent: Stephanie Tade

L583 Sterling Lord Literistic, Inc.
Literary Agency
594 Broadway, New York, NY 10012
United States
Tel: +1 (212) 780-6050
Fax: +1 (212) 780-6095

info@sll.com

https://www.sll.com

Send: Query; Synopsis; Writing sample
How to send: Online submission system

Select one agent to query and approach via online form on website.

Associate Agents: Maria Bell (**L054**); Chris Combemale (**L131**)

Chair / Literary Agent: Peter Matson

Executive Vice President / Literary Agent: Laurie Liss (**L394**)

Foreign Rights Director: Szilvia Molnar

Literary Agent / President: Philippa Brophy

Literary Agent / Vice President: Jim Rutman (**L544**)

Literary Agents: Elizabeth Bewley; Danielle Bukowski (**L088**); Jessica Friedman; Mary Krienke (**L366**); Sarah Landis (**L372**); Jenny Stephens

Senior Agents: Robert Guinsler (**L276**); Neeti Madan (**L416**)

L584 Sternig & Byrne Literary Agency
Literary Agency
2370 S. 107th Street, Apt 4, Milwaukee, Wisconsin 53227-2036
United States
Tel: +1 (414) 328-8034

jackbyrne@hotmail.com

https://sternig-byrne-agency.com

Professional Bodies: Science Fiction and Fantasy Writers of America (SFWA); Mystery Writers of America (MWA)

Fiction > *Novels*
Fantasy; Science Fiction

Closed to approaches.

Send brief query by post or email in first instance (if sending by email send in the body of the mail, do not send attachments). Will request further materials if interested. Currently only considering science fiction and fantasy. Preference given to writers with a publishing history.

Authors: Katherine Addison; John Haefele; Lael Littke; Kelly McCullough; Sarah Monette; Moira Moore; Jo Walton; David Michael Williams; John C. Wright

Literary Agent: Jack Byrne

L585 Stephanie Stevens
Literary Agent
United States

stephanieat3seas@gmail.com

https://www.threeseasagency.com/agents/stephanie-stevens
https://querymanager.com/query/2732

Literary Agency: 3 Seas Literary Agency
(L001)

Fiction > *Novels*
  Mystery; Romance; Thrillers; Women's Fiction

How to send: Query Manager

Loves working with mystery, thriller, women's fiction, and romance authors especially when the story involves an unexpected twist.

L586 Douglas Stewart
Literary Agent; Vice President
United States

https://www.sll.com/our-team

Literary Agency: Sterling Lord Literistic, Inc. **(L583)**

ADULT
  Fiction > *Novels*
    Commercial; Literary

  Nonfiction > *Nonfiction Books*: Narrative Nonfiction

CHILDREN'S
  Fiction > *Novels*

  Nonfiction > *Nonfiction Books*: Narrative Nonfiction

YOUNG ADULT
  Fiction > *Novels*

  Nonfiction > *Nonfiction Books*: Narrative Nonfiction

Send: Query; Synopsis; Writing sample
How to send: Online submission system

List consists of fiction and narrative nonfiction for all ages, from the innovatively literary to the unabashedly commercial, and includes multiple million-copy bestsellers and award-winners.

Associate Agent: Maria Bell **(L054)**

L587 Geoffrey Stone
Literary Agent
United States

gstone@rudyagency.com

http://rudyagency.com/

Nonfiction > *Nonfiction Books*
  Christian Living; Cookery; History; Sport

Send: Query
How to send: Email

Looking for proposals and manuscripts on history, sports, cooking, personal stories, and Christian living, and is open to a wide range of non-fiction and fiction that align with those interests.

L588 Strachan Literary Agency
Literary Agency
P.O. Box 2091, Annapolis, MD 21404
United States

Query@StrachanLit.com

http://www.strachanlit.com

Types: Fiction; Nonfiction
Subjects: Autobiography; Comedy / Humour; Commercial; Cookery; Crime; Gardening; Health; Lifestyle; Literary; Mystery; Personal Development; Religion; Suspense; Thrillers; Travel; Women's Interests
Markets: Adult; Children's; Young Adult

Closed to approaches.

Send query through online form on website, providing a brief description of your book as well as your biographical information and writing credits or professional experience. No samples or mss unless requested. No picture books, genre fiction, poetry, or screenplays.

Literary Agents: Laura Strachan; Marisa Zeppieri

L589 The Stringer Literary Agency LLC
Literary Agency
PO Box 111255, Naples, FL 34108
United States

https://www.stringerlit.com
https://www.instagram.com/stringerlit/
https://www.pinterest.com/stringerlit/
https://www.facebook.com/StringerLit
https://twitter.com/MarleneStringer

Professional Bodies: Association of American Literary Agents (AALA); Mystery Writers of America (MWA); Society of Children's Book Writers and Illustrators (SCBWI); The Authors Guild; Women's Fiction Writers Association (WFWA)

ADULT > **Fiction** > *Novels*

CHILDREN'S > **Fiction**
  Middle Grade; Picture Books
YOUNG ADULT > **Fiction** > *Novels*

Send: Query; Synopsis; Pitch; Outline; Author bio; Writing sample
How to send: Query Manager

A full-service literary agency specializing in commercial fiction since 2008.

Authors: Melissa Amateis; Caroline L. Bayley; Emily Bleeker; Marta Bliese; Anna Bradley; Emily Cavanagh; Don Dixon; Charlie Donlea; Pat Esden; Alyxandra Harvey; Erica Hayes; Charlie N Holmberg; Suzanne Johnson; Kristin Kisska; Kallie Lane; Caitlin McFarland; Liane Merciel; Sophie Munday; Melanie Novak; Liz Perrine; Molly Pierce; Emily Rittel-King; Alexandra Rushe; Luanne G. Smith; Kate Pawson Studer; Andrea Thalasinos; Tessa Wegert; Bethany Wiggins; Clare Zeschky

Literary Agents: Shari Maurer; Marlene Stringer **(L590)**

L590 Marlene Stringer
Literary Agent
United States

http://aaronline.org/Sys/PublicProfile/5108942/417813
https://querymanager.com/query/StringerLit

Literary Agency: The Stringer Literary Agency LLC **(L589)**

ADULT
  Fiction > *Novels*
    Book Club Fiction; Commercial; Contemporary; Crime; Fantasy; Historical Fiction; Literary; Romance; Suspense; Thrillers; Upmarket; Women's Fiction

  Nonfiction > *Nonfiction Books*: Narrative Nonfiction

CHILDREN'S > **Fiction** > *Middle Grade*

YOUNG ADULT > **Fiction** > *Novels*
  Contemporary; Fantasy

Does not want:

  Fiction > *Novels*: High / Epic Fantasy

Send: Author bio; Query; Synopsis; Writing sample; Pitch; Market info
How to send: By referral; Conferences

L591 Amy Strong
Assistant Agent
United Kingdom

https://lbabooks.com/agents/amy-strong

Literary Agency: LBA Books Ltd

Fiction > *Novels*
  Fairy Tales; Fantasy; Folklore, Myths, and Legends

Closed to approaches.

I am an avid reader with an eclectic taste in fiction. But my go-to genre is fantasy. I especially love books that draw on fairy tales or folklore – even better if they approach classic stories with a new twist.

L592 Catharine Strong
Associate Agent
United States

Literary Agency: Aevitas

L593 The Strothman Agency
Literary Agency
Box 255, Newcastle, ME 04553
United States

strothmanagency@gmail.com
info@strothmanagency.com

https://www.strothmanagency.com/
https://twitter.com/StrothmanAgency
https://www.facebook.com/StrothmanAgency/

Send: Query
How to send: Email; Query Manager
How not to send: Email attachment; Post

Only accepts electronic submissions. Physical query letters will be recycled unopened. Accepts referrals by email. Queries without referral must approach through Query Manager. Do not send entire manuscripts or attachments unless requested. All unrequested attachments will be deleted unread. Does not accept or respond to queries via fax or telephone.

Literary Agent / Partner: Wendy Strothman (**L594**)

Senior Agent: Lauren MacLeod (**L414**)

L594 Wendy Strothman
Literary Agent; Partner
United States

https://www.aevitascreative.com/agent/wendy-strothman
https://www.strothmanagency.com/about
https://querymanager.com/query/WStrothman
http://aaronline.org/Sys/PublicProfile/2176866/417813

Literary Agencies: Aevitas; The Strothman Agency (**L593**)
Professional Body: Association of American Literary Agents (AALA)

Nonfiction > *Nonfiction Books*
Current Affairs; History; Narrative Journalism; Narrative Nonfiction; Nature; Science

Closed to approaches.

Looking for books that matter, books that change the way we think about things we take for granted, that tell stories that readers can't forget, and advance scholarship and knowledge. History, narrative nonfiction, narrative journalism, science and nature, and current affairs.

Accepts referrals by email; otherwise approach through Query Manager.

Authors: Alan Allport; Michelle Wilde Anderson; Tonio Andrade; Christian G. Appy; Deborah N. Archer; Ray Arsenault; Shadi Bartsch; Alice Baumgartner; Sian Beilock; David W. Blight; Nikolas Bowie; Mark Philip Bradley; Thanassis Cambanis; Peter Canellos; Tess Chakkalakal; Chip Colwell; Elena Conis; Peter Conti-Brown; Catherine Conybeare; Darcie DeAngelo; Gloria Dickie; Laurent DuBois; Scott V. Edwards; Caitlin Fitz; Richard T. Ford; Joanne B. Freeman; James K. Galbraith; Michael Graetz; Linda Greenhouse; Martha Hodes; David Hollinger; Yunte Huang; Pacifique Irankunda; Gene Jarrett; Daniel Brock Johnson; Mara Kardas-Nelson; Kenn Kaufman; Thomas Forrest Kelly; David Kertzer; Barbara Keys; Anthony Kronman; Carlton F. W. Larson; Daniel Lewis; Joseph Manning; W. Caleb McDaniel; Catherine McNeur; Alain Mikhail; Tony Molho; Eric Moskowitz; Benjamin Nathans; Amy Ellis Nutt; Bennett Parten; Steven Pincus; Benjamin Reiss; Daphna Renan; Judith Resnik; Alison F. Richard; Seth Rockman; Anne Ruderman; Benjamin Taylor; Shane White

L595 Hannah Strouth
Assistant Agent
United States

https://www.janerotrosen.com/agents

Literary Agency: Jane Rotrosen Agency
Literary Agents: Andrea Cirillo; Kathy Schneider

Fiction > *Novels*
Contemporary; Historical Fiction; Literary; Romantic Comedy; Upmarket

Send: Query; Author bio; Synopsis; Writing sample
How to send: Online contact form

Helps maintain the lists of two agents, while keeping her sights set on growing her own list. She is constantly diving into historical fiction, contemporary rom-coms, and upmarket / literary fiction.

L596 Stuart Krichevsky Literary Agency, Inc.
Literary Agency
118 East 28th Street, Suite 908, New York, NY 10016
United States
Tel: +1 (212) 725-5288
Fax: +1 (212) 725-5275

query@skagency.com

http://skagency.com

ADULT
Fiction > *Novels*
Nonfiction > *Nonfiction Books*

YOUNG ADULT
Fiction > *Novels*
Nonfiction > *Nonfiction Books*

Send: Query; Writing sample
How to send: In the body of an email

Send query by email with first few pages of your manuscript (up to 10) pasted into body of the email (no attachments). See website for complete submission guidelines and appropriate submission addresses for each agent.

Authors: Roxanna Asgarian; Ahmed Badr; Emily Bloom; Katherine Blunt; Lyndsie Bourgon; Hannah Brencher; Emily Chammah; Angela Chen; Carla Ciccone; Georgia Cloepfil; Caren Cooper; Helen Donahue; Hope Ewing; Victoria Facelli; Chelsea Fairless; Kathryn Finney; Kit Fox; Katie Fricas; Lauren Garroni; Olivia Gatwood; Jessica Goudeau; Rose Hackman; Anita Hannig; Sarah Jaffe; Rachel McCarthy James; Ruth Joffre; R. Dean Johnson; Sophie Lucido Johnson; Megan Kimble; Audrea Lim; Catherine Lo; Michael Loynd; Jennifer Lunden; Peter Mercurio; José Olivarez; Madeline Ostrander; Robin Page; Soraya Palmer; Amy Peterson; Karen Pinchin; Shelley Puhak; Lydia Reeder; Victoria Reihana; Nadim Roberts; A. Brad Schwartz; Margot Lee Shetterly; David Shih; Brie Spangler; Rachel Swaby; Sofi Thanhauser; Kaitlyn Tiffany; Carson Vaughan; Sarah Vogel; Kimberley Welman; Christina Wilcox; Nina Willner; Bernice Yeung; Tom Zeller; Sara Zin

Literary Agents: Melissa Danaczko (*L153*); Barbara Jones (**L333**); Stuart Krichevsky; David Patterson; Aemilia Phillips; Hannah Schwartz; Laura Usselman (**L622**); Mackenzie Brady Watson (**L636**); Chandler Wickers (**L648**)

L597 Susan Schulman Literary Agency
Literary Agency
454 West 44th Street, New York, NY 10036
United States
Tel: +1 (212) 713-1633

Susan@Schulmanagency.com

https://twitter.com/SusanSchulman

Professional Body: Association of American Literary Agents (AALA)

Fiction > *Novels*
General, and in particular: Commercial; Literary; Women's Fiction

Nonfiction > *Nonfiction Books*
Creativity; Economics; Finance; Health; History; Legal; Memoir; Mind, Body, Spirit; Politics; Psychology; Social Issues; Writing

Send: Query; Synopsis; Writing sample; Author bio
How to send: Email

Handles commercial and literary fiction and non-fiction, specifically narrative memoir, politics, economics, social issues, history, urban planning, finance, law, health, psychology, body/mind/sprit, and creativity and writing.

Associate Agent: Emelie Burl (**L090**)

Literary Agent: Susan Schulman

L598 Kari Sutherland
Literary Agent
United States

https://ktliterary.com/about/
https://querymanager.com/query/
Kari_Sutherland_Query_Form
https://twitter.com/KariSutherland

Literary Agency: KT Literary (**L368**)

ADULT > **Fiction** > *Novels*
Gothic; International; Magic; Psychology; Saga; Suspense; Upmarket Women's Fiction

CHILDREN'S
Fiction
Chapter Books: General
Graphic Novels: General
Middle Grade: Adventure; Contemporary Romance; Drama; Environment; Fantasy; Social Justice; Social Media; Suspense; Technology
Picture Books: General

Nonfiction > *Nonfiction Books*
Beauty; Environment; Health; History; Information Science; Science

YOUNG ADULT > **Fiction**
Graphic Novels: General
Novels: Adventure; Contemporary Romance; Drama; Environment; Fantasy; Social Justice; Social Media; Suspense; Technology

Closed to approaches.

Open to genres from picture books through adult. Most interested in finding stories full of heart; ones that carry readers to faraway places or deep into a character's mind; action-packed page-turners that surprise her; dark dramas with touches of humor; and, above all, a voice that leaps off the page. She is actively seeking diverse voices across all genres.

L599 Alice Sutherland-Hawes
Literary Agent
United Kingdom

https://www.ashliterary.com/#about

Literary Agency: ASH Literary (**L035**)

Closed to approaches.

Authors: Dina Al-Sabawi; HF Brownfield; Ryan Crawford; Alex Falase-Koya; Abimbola Fashola; Kereen Getten; Gina Gonzales; Sarah Guillory; Ravena Guron; Radiya Hafiza; Anika Hussain; Jennifer Iacopelli; Nansubuga Isdahl; Richard Mercado; Yasmine Naghdi; Samuel Pollen; Ryan Robinson; Elizabeth Rounding; Cynthia So; Chitra Soundar; Claire Tomasi; Ryan Rose Vinson-Jacobs; Adelle Yeung

L600 Joanna Swainson
Literary Agent
United Kingdom

submissions@hardmanswainson.com

http://www.hardmanswainson.com/agents/
joanna-swainson/
https://twitter.com/JoannaSwainson

Literary Agency: Hardman & Swainson (**L286**)

Fiction > *Novels*
Comedy / Humour; Commercial; Contemporary; Crime; Folk Horror; Ghost Stories; Historical Fiction; Horror; Literary; Speculative; Thrillers

Nonfiction > *Nonfiction Books*
Memoir; Narrative Nonfiction; Nature; Popular History; Science

Send: Synopsis; Full text
How to send: Email
How not to send: Post

Authors: Jon Bounds; Oggy Boytchev; Paul Braddon; Elizabeth Brooks; Mark Broomfield; Adrienne Chinn; Helen Cox; Jeremy Craddock; Sara Crowe; Emma Darwin; Stuart David; Caroline Davison; Carol Donaldson; Simon David Eden; Rachel Edwards; Nicola Ford; Harry Freedman; James Gould-Bourn; Tom Higham; Michael Jecks; Oskar Cox Jensen; Stuart Johnstone; Lucy Lawrie; Peter Laws; David B. Lyons; Kevin Macneil; S R Masters; Lauren Price; Philip C Quaintrell; Patrick Roberts; Nick Russell-Pavier; Catherine Simpson; Danny Smith; Hollie Starling; Eliska Tanzer; Sarah Tierney; B P Walter; Samantha Wilson

L601 Emily Sweet
Literary Agent
United Kingdom

https://www.emilysweetassociates.com
https://www.aevitascreative.com/agent/emily-sweet

Literary Agencies: Emily Sweet Associates (**L198**); Aevitas Creative Management (ACM) UK (**L008**)

Nonfiction > *Nonfiction Books*
Biography; Cookery; Current Affairs; Food and Drink; History; Lifestyle; Memoir

Send: Query; Synopsis
How to send: Online contact form

Particularly looks for exciting, original and useful cookery and lifestyle books, as well as innovative storytelling in the areas of history, memoir, biography, current affairs and topical non-fiction.

Authors: Nicky Corbishley; Anja Dunk; Nicola Lamb; Mitch Lane; Su Scott

L602 SYLA – Susan Yearwood Literary Agency
Literary Agency
2 Knebworth House, Londesborough Road, Stoke Newington, London, N16 8RL
United Kingdom
Tel: +44 (0) 20 7503 0954

submissions@susanyearwoodagency.com

https://susanyearwoodagency.com

Professional Body: The Association of Authors' Agents (AAA)

ADULT
Fiction > *Novels*
Nonfiction > *Nonfiction Books*

CHILDREN'S > **Fiction** > *Novels*

YOUNG ADULT > **Fiction** > *Novels*

Send: Query; Author bio; Writing sample; Synopsis
How to send: Email attachment

Send query by email, including synopsis and first thirty pages as Word or PDF attachment.

Authors: Rebecca Adams; Catherine Balavage; Lucy Basey; Katie Brewer; Angela Cairns; Fran Clark; Sarah Dobbs; Selina Flavius; Kimberley Glover; Liz Kolbeck; Prajwal Parajuly; Fil Reid; Sarupa Shah; Jacqueline Shaw; Sarah Shoesmith; Mahalia Smith; Suzanne Snow; Sarah Stephenson; Kerry Young

Literary Agent: Susan Yearwood (**L666**)

L603 Laurel Symonds
Literary Agent
United States

https://ktliterary.com/about/
https://www.manuscriptwishlist.com/mswl-post/laurel-symonds/
https://twitter.com/laurelsymonds
https://www.facebook.com/laurelsymondsagent
https://www.linkedin.com/in/laurelsymonds/

Literary Agency: KT Literary (**L368**)

CHILDREN'S
Fiction
Graphic Novels: General
Middle Grade: General, and in particular: Contemporary; Fantasy; Historical Fiction; Literary
Picture Books: General

Nonfiction > *Nonfiction Books*
General, and in particular: Engineering; History; Mathematics; Science; Technology

YOUNG ADULT
Fiction
Graphic Novels: General
Novels: General, and in particular: Commercial; Contemporary; Fantasy; Historical Fiction

Nonfiction > *Nonfiction Books*
General, and in particular: Engineering;
History; Mathematics; Science;
Technology

Closed to approaches.

I represent young adult and middle grade
fiction, and I have a special interest in
contemporary, historical fiction, and genre-
blending fantasy. I look for engaging voices,
commercial hooks, and immersive worlds. My
YA tastes are pretty commercial but my middle
grade tastes can skew more literary, and I'm
especially interested in middle grade that might
lend itself to illustration.

I also represent picture books, graphic novels,
and other illustrated work, and I am open to
new clients who are both authors and
illustrators. My tastes are diverse, ranging from
sophisticated to quirky to gently humorous. I
especially appreciate a smart use of color and
perspective.

Additionally, I represent select nonfiction for
children and young adults, especially projects
about STEM or history with age-appropriate
hooks and series potential.

L604 Marin Takikawa
Associate Agent
United States

mtakikawa@friedrichagency.com

http://www.friedrichagency.com/marin
https://twitter.com/marintakikawa

Literary Agency: The Friedrich Agency LLC

ADULT
Fiction > *Novels*
Family; Literary Suspense; Literary;
Magic; Speculative; Upmarket

Nonfiction > *Nonfiction Books*
Memoir; Narrative Nonfiction;
Postcolonialism

YOUNG ADULT > **Fiction** > *Novels*
Family; Literary Suspense; Literary; Magic;
Romantic Comedy; Speculative; Upmarket

Send: Query
Don't send: Writing sample
How to send: In the body of an email
How not to send: Email attachment

For adult fiction, I'm looking for character-
driven upmarket and literary fiction. In
particular, I'm always driven by the need to
understand people and discover the various
kinks that aren't visible from the surface—
what drives them? What do they desire most
but can't get? I'm particularly enamored by
genre-bending works, fiction with a
speculative or magical bent, literary suspense,
narratives about complex family relationships,
and those that subvert forms of power,
specifically neocolonialist ones. My tastes in
YA are similar, although with more focus on
speculative concepts and maybe surprisingly,

contemporary rom-coms. In nonfiction, I
gravitate toward memoirs that balance personal
narratives with engaging and insightful
research and/or cultural analysis. I'm also
looking for narrative nonfiction that is resistant
and radical in nature, that questions why we
have the institutions, ideas, and systems we
have in place. I often think about the legacies
of colonialism, how it haunts and perpetuates
in various forms in the modern age (such as the
environment and in capitalism), but also about
collective action and its sense of possibilities
and what the future could look like. I'd love to
hear from you if your work is in this space.

L605 Emily Talbot
Literary Agent
United Kingdom

etalbot@unitedagents.co.uk

https://www.unitedagents.co.uk/
etalbotunitedagentscouk

Literary Agency: United Agents (**L619**)
Literary Agent: Jodie Hodges (**L307**)

ADULT > **Nonfiction** > *Nonfiction Books*

CHILDREN'S > **Fiction**
Middle Grade; *Picture Books*
YOUNG ADULT > **Fiction** > *Novels*

Send: Query; Synopsis; Writing sample

Represents hildren's illustrators and authors of
picture books, middle grade, YA and nonfiction.

Authors: Aysha Awwad; Susanna Bailey;
Abigail Balfe; Alex Barrow; Becky Baur;
Gabby Dawnay; Sophie Deen; Chloe
Douglass; Ed Eaves; Alison Guile; James
Harris; Sam Hearn; Benjamin Hughes; James
Lent; Rebecca Lewis-Oakes; Maggie Li; Roger
McGough; Becka Moor; Polly Owen; Keith
Robinson; Andy Sagar; Jion Sheibani; Qian
Shi; Georgina Stevens; Barry Timms;
Jacqueline Tucker; Kael Tudor; Lucy Unwin;
Maddy Vian; Lucia Vinti

L606 Trisha Telep
Associate Agent
Canada

https://www.therightsfactory.com/Agents/
Trisha-Telep

Literary Agency: The Rights Factory

Closed to approaches.

L607 The Tennyson Agency
Literary Agency
109 Tennyson Avenue, New Malden, Surrey,
KT3 6NA
United Kingdom
Tel: +44 (0) 20 8543 5939

agency@tenagy.co.uk

http://www.tenagy.co.uk

Types: Scripts
Formats: Film Scripts; Radio Scripts; TV
Scripts; Theatre Scripts
Subjects: Drama
Markets: Adult

Closed to approaches.

Mainly deals in scripts for film, TV, theatre,
and radio, along with related material on an ad-
hoc basis. Handles writers in the European
Union only. Send query with CV and outline of
work. Prefers queries by email. No nonfiction,
poetry, short stories, science fiction and
fantasy or children's writing, or unsolicited
MSS.

L608 Teresa Chris Literary Agency Ltd
Literary Agency
43 Musard Road, London, W6 8NR
United Kingdom
Tel: +44 (0) 20 7386 0633

teresachris@litagency.co.uk

http://www.teresachrisliteraryagency.co.uk

Professional Body: The Association of
Authors' Agents (AAA)

Fiction > *Novels*
Commercial Women's Fiction; Commercial;
Crime; Literary

Does not want:

Fiction > *Novels*
Fantasy; Horror; Science Fiction

Send: Query; Synopsis; Writing sample
How to send: Email

Welcomes submissions. Send submissions by
email only, with first three chapters, and one-
page synopsis. Specialises in crime fiction and
commercial women's fiction. No poetry, short
stories, fantasy, science fiction, horror, or
children's fiction.

Authors: Stephanie Austin; Lily Baxter; Ginny
Bell; M A Bennett; Victoria Blake; Stephen
Booth; Benita Brown; Rory Clements; Julie
Cohen; Dilly Court; Martin Davies; Ellie
Dean; Linda Finlay; Marina Fiorato; Emily
Freud; Kate Furnivall; Annie Groves; Clare
Harvey; Debby Holt; Hunter; Corrie Jackson;
Jim Kelly; Danuta Kot; Linscott; Tamara
McKinley; Jane McMorland; Charlotte
Parsons; Stuart Pawson; Caro Peacock/Gillian;
Nicola Pryce; Eileen Ramsay; Kate Rhodes;
Mary-Jane Riley; Caroline Scott; Marsali
Taylor; Jane Wenham-Jones

L609 Paige Terlip
Literary Agent
United States

paige@andreabrownlit.com

https://www.andreabrownlit.com/agents.html
https://twitter.com/pterlip
https://www.instagram.com/pterlip/

Literary Agency: Andrea Brown Literary Agency, Inc.

ADULT
Fiction > *Novels*
Cozy Mysteries; Fantasy; High Concept; Magic; Psychological Suspense; Science Fiction; Thrillers; Upmarket

Nonfiction > *Nonfiction Books*
Mind, Body, Spirit; Narrative Nonfiction; Self Help

CHILDREN'S > **Fiction**
Chapter Books; Middle Grade; Picture Books
YOUNG ADULT > **Fiction** > *Novels*
High Concept; Magic

Send: Author bio; Query; Writing sample; Pitch; Market info
How to send: Query Manager

Represents all categories of children's books from picture books to young adult, as well as select adult fiction and nonfiction. She is also actively building her list of illustrators and is especially looking for author-illustrators and graphic novel illustrators.

L610 Kate Testerman
Literary Agent
United States

Literary Agency: KT Literary (**L368**)

Closed to approaches.

L611 The Theseus Agency
Literary Agency
29 Rosslyn Hill, London, NW3 5UJ
United Kingdom

info@theseus.agency

https://www.theseus.agency

Fiction > *Novels*

Nonfiction > *Nonfiction Books*

We help brands and writers pin-point, protect, and harness what makes them matter to the wider world.

We manage rights, brand and dealmaking. And we do it for any idea that lives in the public imagination, whether it started life as a book or script, a product, or a person.

By bringing together management, representation, and strategy, we balance long-term goals and short-term opportunities. We map plans for the future, while seeking out and striking innovative deals in the present, knowing that each is integral to the other.

Literary Agent: Louise Ripley-Duggan (**L528**)

L612 Sydnie Thornton
Literary Agent
United States

sydnie.queries@irenegoodman.com

https://www.irenegoodman.com/sydnie-thornton

Literary Agency: Irene Goodman Literary Agency (IGLA)

ADULT > **Fiction** > *Novels*
Contemporary Fantasy; Historical Fiction

YOUNG ADULT > **Fiction** > *Novels*
General, and in particular: Contemporary; Fantasy; Historical Fiction; Literary; Upmarket Thrillers

How to send: Email

Interested in YA across all genres: fantasy, historical fiction, contemporary that leans literary, as well as thrillers with upmarket qualities and distinctive characterization. As for the adult side, she is actively looking for transportive, complex historical fiction and whimsical contemporary fantasy. Regardless of genre, she's very likely to connect with manuscripts that bridge the YA/Adult divide. She's also eager to champion any book that prominently features disability representation.

L613 Anne Tibbets
Literary Agent
United States

http://maassagency.com/anne-tibbets/
https://querymanager.com/query/AnneTibbets

Literary Agency: Donald Maass Literary Agency (**L176**)

ADULT > **Fiction** > *Novels*
Adventure; Contemporary; Diversity; Feminism; Historical Fiction; Horror; LGBTQIA; Mystery; Police Procedural; Psychological Horror; Romance; Romantic Suspense; Thrillers; Women's Fiction

YOUNG ADULT > **Fiction** > *Novels*
Diversity; Feminism; Historical Fiction; LGBTQIA; Thrillers

Closed to approaches.

Represents adult and young adult commercial genre, primarily thrillers, mysteries, science fiction, fantasy, horror, and historical women's fiction.

L614 The Tobias Literary Agency
Literary Agency
United States

https://www.thetobiasagency.com
https://twitter.com/TheTobiasAgency
https://www.facebook.com/TobiasLiteraryAgency
https://www.instagram.com/thetobiasliteraryagency/

Specializes in all Intellectual Property matters in the publishing industry, from the seed of an idea to the day a book hits the shelves. A full-service literary agency headquartered in New York City with satellite offices in Boston, Nashville, and soon-to-be Los Angeles. Represents established and debut authors.

Literary Agent: Stefanie Rossitto (**L539**)

Literary Agent / President: Lane Heymont (**L304**)

Senior Agent: Natascha Morris (**L458**)

L615 Hannah Todd
Literary Agent
United Kingdom

submissions@madeleinemilburn.com

https://madeleinemilburn.co.uk/team-member/hannah-todd/

Literary Agency: Madeleine Milburn Literary, TV & Film Agency (**L417**)

Fiction > *Novels*
20th Century; Commercial; Cozy Mysteries; Crime; Historical Fiction; LGBTQIA; Police Procedural; Romance; Romantic Comedy; Saga; Thrillers; Women's Fiction

Send: Query; Pitch; Market info; Synopsis; Writing sample
How to send: Email attachment
How not to send: Post

Actively looking for: commercial fiction across all genres including women's fiction; police procedurals; clever thrillers; cosy crime; romantic comedies; accessible historical fiction focusing on 20th century and including dual timeline novels; sagas; emotional issues-led fiction. If you can make her laugh, cry or fall in love then you're onto a winner!

L616 Caroline Trussell
Junior Agent
United States

https://www.metamorphosisliteraryagency.com/about
https://querymanager.com/query/2782
https://twitter.com/carolinejtrulit

Literary Agency: Metamorphosis Literary Agency (**L440**)

ADULT > **Fiction** > *Novels*
Cozy Mysteries; Fantasy; Magical Realism; Psychological Thrillers; Romance; Romantic Comedy; Thrillers; Urban Fantasy

CHILDREN'S > **Fiction** > *Middle Grade*

Closed to approaches.

Passionate about finding writers with unique voices and points of view and is looking for steamy romances, out of this world fantasies, and YA and MG that touch on vital topics that can't be ignored.

L617 Nick Turner
Literary Agent
United Kingdom

Literary Agency: Nick Turner Management Ltd
(**L475**)

L618 The Two Piers Literary Agency
Literary Agency
Brighton
United Kingdom

hello@twopiersagency.com

https://twopiersagency.com
https://twitter.com/TwoPiersAgency
https://www.facebook.com/TwoPiersAgency
https://www.instagram.com/twopiersagency/

ADULT
  Fiction > *Novels*
  Nonfiction > *Nonfiction Books*

CHILDREN'S > **Fiction** > *Middle Grade*

YOUNG ADULT > **Fiction** > *Novels*

Closed to approaches.

Costs: Offers services that writers have to pay for. Sister company provides online novel-writing course.

Literary agency based in Brighton, which represents writers from all over the world and sells their work into the UK, US and international territories. An editorially focused agency that works closely with authors to produce manuscripts that are as strong as they can possibly be before submitting them to publishers.

Literary Agent: Rufus Purdy (*L516*)

L619 United Agents
Literary Agency
12-26 Lexington Street, London, W1F 0LE
United Kingdom
Tel: +44 (0) 20 3214 0800
Fax: +44 (0) 20 3214 0802

info@unitedagents.co.uk

https://www.unitedagents.co.uk
https://twitter.com/UnitedAgents
https://www.instagram.com/unitedagents/

Professional Body: The Association of Authors' Agents (AAA)

Fiction > *Novels*

Nonfiction > *Nonfiction Books*

Send: Query; Pitch; Market info; Synopsis; Writing sample
How to send: Email
How not to send: Post

Do not approach the book department generally. Consult website and view details of each agent before selecting a specific agent to approach personally. Accepts submissions by email only. Submissions by post will not be returned or responded to.

Associate Agents: Seren Adams (**L005**); Millie Hoskins (**L312**); Molly Jamieson (**L323**); Eli Keren (**L352**); Olivia Martin (**L426**); Kate Walsh (**L633**)

Author Estates: The Estate of Dornford Yates; The Estate of Maurice Baring OBE; The Estate of Algernon Blackwood; The Estate of Rafael Sabatini

Authors: Amrou Al-Kadhi; Laura Albert; Rosie Alison; Nina Allan; Esme Allman; Karin Altenberg; Jessica Anthony; Anjana Appachana; Oana Aristide; Aysha Awwad; Sarah Bagshaw; Susanna Bailey; Adam Baker; Joan Bakewell; Abigail Balfe; Tia Bannon; Alex Barrow; Nivedita Barve; Becky Baur; Deborah Bee; Hina Belitz; Alan Bennett; Stephen Bernard; LMK Berry; Sophie Ellis Bextor; Jennifer Otter Bickerdike; Marieke Bigg; Mark Blacklock; Quentin Blake; Stefan Merrill Block; James Bloom; Ezekiel Boone; Akwasi Brenya-Mensa; Melitta Breznik; Molly Brodak; Maggie Brookes; Christopher Brookmyre; Jackson P. Brown; Sylvia Brownrigg; Robin Bunce; John Burnside; Sarah Burton; Justin Butcher; Jen Calleja; Emma Campbell; Robin Carhart-Harris; Brian Catling; Carl Cattermole; Jessie Cave; John Chalmers; Alex Alvina Chamberland; Clare Chambers; Roland Chambers; Tom Chivers; Emma Cline; Amanda Coe; Olivia Collard; Mick Collins; Sean Patrick Cooper; Wendy Cope; Oliver Cotton; Marion Coutts; Leah Cowan; Geoff Cox; Al Crow; Dan Cruickshank; Lauren Aimee Curtis; Rosie Dastgir; Richard Davidson; Carys Davies; Russell Davies; Gabby Dawnay; Jill Dawson; Tim Dee; Sophie Deen; JP Delaney; Sam Diamond; Christie Dickason; Susannah Dickey; Minoo Dinshaw; Paddy Docherty; Chloe Douglass; Olivia Douglass; Miranda Doyle; Alicia Duffy; Dennis Duncan; Nic Dunlop; Douglas Dunn; Elanor Dymott; Tim Dynevor; Ben Eastham; Ed Eaves; Christy Edwall; Lucie Elven; Neil Ely; Chris England; Hermione Eyre; Lloyd Eyre-Morgan; James Fenton; Toby Ferris; Rakaya Fetuga; Tim Finch; Ronan Fitzgerald; William Fowler; Amaryllis Gacioppo; Rivka Galchen; William Ghosh; Rebecca Gibb; Maria Giron; Sue Glover; Rebecca Gowers; Ysenda Maxtone Graham; Huho Greenhalgh; Charlotte Grimshaw; Camilla Grudova; Alison Guile; Jeff Gulvin; Tessa Hadley; Guy Haley; Lili Hamlyn; Lynsey Hanley; Robert Hardman; James Harris; David Harsent; Jack Hartnell; Samantha Harvey; Will Hayward; Sam Hearn; Colin Heber-Percy; Sheila Heti; Ben Hinshaw; Susannah Hoffman; Michael Hofmann; Richard Holloway; Hannah-Marie Holwell; Joseph Hone; Benjamin Hughes; Caoilinn Hughes; Catherine Humble; Mark Hussey; Nicholas Hytner; Ashley Inglis; Alison Irvine; William Irvine; Mick Jackson; Blair James; Liza St. James; Lenka Janiurek; Annaleese Jochems; Arden Jones; Ioan Marc Jones; Matthew Jukes; Peter Stephan Jungk; Ammar Kalia; Line Kallmayer; Francesca Kay; I. J. Kay; Tobias Kelly; Katharine Kilalea; Ana Kinsella; Katie Kirby; Max Kirsten; Clement Knox; Laura Kounine; Nakul Krishna; Richard Lambert; James Larkin; James Lasdun; David Lawrence; Paul Lay; Jessica Lea; Mike Leigh; James Lent; Louise Levene; Rebecca Lewis-Oakes; Nell Leyshon; Maggie Li; Samara Linton; Molly Lipson; Victor Lodato; Benoît Loiseau; Tom Lubbock; Johanna Lukate; Anna Mackmin; Caroline Maclean; Deirdre Madden; Michelle Magorian; Aileen Maguire; Jonathan Maitland; Emily St. John Mandel; Sandra Marrs; Adam Mars-Jones; Philip Marsden; Andrew Martin; Nicholas Martin; Megan Marz; Anita Mason; Laura Maw; Simon Mawer; Nicola McCartney; Patrick McGinley; Roger McGough; Daisy McNally; James McNicholas; Jamal Mehmood; Coco Mellors; Livi Michael; David Miles; Christine Modafferi; Peter Moffat; Dominique Moloney; Sinéad Mooney; Becka Moor; Michelle Morgan; Jan Morris; Blake Morrison; Ottessa Moshfegh; Sarah Moss; John Mullan; Chris Mullin; Nicholas Murray; Malik Al Nasir; Anna Neima; Luke Neima; Caleb Azumah Nelson; Anthea Nicholson; Trevor Norton; Alissa Nutting; Redmond O'Hanlon; Timothy Ogene; Nat Ogle; Aimee Oliver; David Olusoga; Alice Oswald; Polly Owen; Bobby Palmer; William Palmer; Anna Chapman Parker; Tim Parks; Ambrose Parry; Ian Pattison; Ruth Pavey; Rebecca Perry; Helen Pike; Joanna Pocock; Jem Poster; Miranda Pountney; Melissa Powell; Philip Pullman; Karina Lickorish Quinn; Julya Rabinowich; Natasha Randall; Victoria Redel; Harris Reed; Gemma Reeves; Ruth Rendell; Talulah Riley; Sam Riviere; Michael Symmons Roberts; Michèle Roberts; Laura Robertson; Keith Robinson; Juno Roche; Jane Rogers; Michael Rosen; Olivia Rosenthall; LJ Ross; Alan Rossi; James Rourke; Saumya Roy; Taylor-Dior Rumble; Thomas Rutter; Andy Sagar; Michael Salu; Kate Saunders; Lina Scheynius; Claire Seeber; Jenn Shapland; Jion Sheibani; Qian Shi; Mika Simmons; Tracey Slaughter; Laura Southgate; Olivia Spring; Alexander Starritt; Wendell Steavenson; Georgina Stevens; Sean Stoker; Alexander Stuart; Jordan Sullivan; Alain Claude Sulzer; David Szalay; George Szirtes; Georgina Terry; Alessandra Thom; Emily Thomas; Barry Timms; Max Tobin; Jacqueline Tucker; Kael Tudor; Peter Turnbull; Ryan Turner; Zakia Uddin; Lucy Unwin; Kenechi Uzor; Maddy Vian; James Vincent; Lucia Vinti; Francesca Wade; Tom Wainwright; Lauren Wallach; Stephen Walsh; Natasha Walter; James Walvin; Eva Warrick; Lyall Watson; Ralf Webb; Gavin Weightman; Kate West; Sam White; Derek Wilson; Gaby Wood; Rohullah Yakobi; Matthew Yorke; An Yu; Zinovy Zinik; Tirdad Zolghadr

Company Director / Literary Agent: Robert Kirby (**L358**)

Literary Agents: Sarah Ballard (**L043**); Caroline Dawnay; Ariella Feiner; Jim Gill; Jodie Hodges (**L307**); Laura Macdougall (**L409**); Zoe Ross; Sophie Scard; Rosemary Scoular (**L557**); Emily Talbot (**L605**); Charles Walker (**L629**); Anna Webber (**L639**)

L620 The Unter Agency

Literary Agency
141 Parkway Road, Suite 10, Bronxville, NY 10708
United States
Tel: +1 (212) 401-4068

Jennifer@theunteragency.com

http://www.theunteragency.com
https://twitter.com/JenniferUnter
https://www.linkedin.com/in/jennifer-unter-6b379a45/

ADULT
  Fiction > *Novels*

  Nonfiction > *Nonfiction Books*
    General, and in particular: Adventure; Biography; Cookery; Crime; Environment; Fitness; Food; Health; Memoir; Nature; Politics; Popular Culture; Travel

CHILDREN'S > **Fiction**
  Middle Grade; Picture Books
YOUNG ADULT > **Fiction** > *Novels*

Send: Query
How to send: Email

Interested in quality fiction and general nonfiction, particularly memoir, food/cooking, nature/environment, biography, pop culture, travel/adventure, true crime, politics and health/fitness. Also all types of children's literature (picture books, middle grade, and young adult). Send query letter by email. If no response within three months, assume rejection.

Associate Agent: Jen Nadol (**L467**)

Literary Agent: Jennifer Unter

L621 Jo Unwin

Literary Agent
United Kingdom

Literary Agency: Jo Unwin Literary Agency (**L328**)

L622 Laura Usselman

Literary Agent
United States

http://skagency.com/agents/laura-usselman/

Literary Agency: Stuart Krichevsky Literary Agency, Inc. (**L596**)

Fiction > *Novels*

Nonfiction > *Nonfiction Books*
  General, and in particular: Memoir

Closed to approaches.

Represents adult fiction and nonfiction. Her fiction interests include character-centered fiction of all stripes, from the formally strange to the family saga. For nonfiction, she is interested in thoughtful narrative nonfiction for younger readers, restlessly curious idea books, and voice-driven memoir.

Authors: Emily Bloom; Katherine Blunt; Emily Chammah; Angela Chen; Carla Ciccone; Georgia Cloepfil; Victoria Facelli; Sarah Jaffe; Rachel McCarthy James; Ruth Joffre; Peter Mercurio; Madeline Ostrander; Robin Page; Soraya Palmer; Nadim Roberts; A. Brad Schwartz; David Shih; Sofi Thanhauser; Kaitlyn Tiffany

L623 Vanessa Holt Ltd

Literary Agency
1422/4 London Road, Leigh On Sea, Essex, SS9 2UL
United Kingdom

v.holt791@btinternet.com

https://find-and-update.company-information. service.gov.uk/company/02391626

Professional Body: The Association of Authors' Agents (AAA)

Fiction > *Novels*

Nonfiction > *Nonfiction Books*

Literary Agent: Vanessa Holt (**L310**)

L624 The Vines Agency, Inc.

Literary Agency
320 7th Avenue, Suite 178, Brooklyn, NY 11215
United States
Tel: +1 (212) 777-5522
Fax: +1 (718) 228-4536

http://www.vinesagency.com

Professional Bodies: The Authors Guild; Writers Guild of America (WGA)

Fiction > *Novels*
  Commercial; Historical Fiction; Literary; Mystery; Science Fiction

Nonfiction > *Nonfiction Books*: Commercial

Closed to approaches.

This agency is closed to new clients and is no longer accepting query letters or submissions.

Authors: Laura Doyle; Shawne Johnson; Bernice McFadden; Christine Moriarty; Don Winslow; Moon Unit Zappa

Literary Agent: James C. Vines (*L625*)

L625 James C. Vines

Literary Agent
United States

Literary Agency: The Vines Agency, Inc. (**L624**)

L626 The Viney Agency

Literary Agency
64 New Cavendish Street, London, W1G 8TB
United Kingdom

https://www.thevineyagency.com

Professional Body: The Association of Authors' Agents (AAA)

ADULT
  Fiction > *Novels*

  Nonfiction > *Nonfiction Books*
    Biography; Narrative Nonfiction

CHILDREN'S > **Fiction** > *Novels*

Send: Query; Synopsis; Writing sample
How to send: Email

A London-based literary agency founded in 2008. The agency represents a diverse range of authors primarily handling their book deals with publishers worldwide, and providing a full range of services including selling film and TV options to broadcasters and production companies. Represents over 100 authors, writing across many genres, including adult and children's fiction and a wide variety of narrative nonfiction and biography.

Company Director / Literary Agent: Charlie Viney (**L627**)

Literary Agent: Amberley Lowis (**L403**)

L627 Charlie Viney

Literary Agent; Company Director
21 Dartmouth Park Avenue, London, NW5 1JL
United Kingdom

https://www.thevineyagency.com/about

Literary Agency: The Viney Agency (**L626**)

Fiction > *Novels*

Nonfiction > *Nonfiction Books*

I have been a literary agent since 2002 and founded the agency in 2008. The agency represents a diverse range of clients writing across a wide range of subjects. I first started in the book trade as a bookseller and then enjoyed a twenty-five-year career in general trade publishing, mostly working in international sales and marketing, later becoming a board director at a major British publishing house. Being a literary agent combines my love of books and an enjoyment of business while enabling me to work very closely with our wonderful authors and manage their careers across all media.

L628 Andrea Walker

Literary Agent
United States

https://querymanager.com/query/1702
https://twitter.com/andreaewalker

ADULT > **Fiction**
  Graphic Novels: General

Novels: Thrillers

CHILDREN'S > Fiction
Middle Grade: Contemporary; Fantasy;
Historical Fiction; Literary; Mystery; Science
Fiction
Picture Books: General

YOUNG ADULT > Fiction > *Novels*
Contemporary; Fantasy; Historical Fiction;
Literary; Mystery; Romance; Science Fiction

Closed to approaches.

I am actively building my client list looking for
author and illustrators of picture books, middle
grade, young adult, and adult.

L629 Charles Walker
Literary Agent
United Kingdom
Tel: +44 (0) 20 3214 0874

cwalker@unitedagents.co.uk

https://www.unitedagents.co.uk/
cwalkerunitedagentscouk

Literary Agency: United Agents (**L619**)

Fiction > *Novels*
Crime; Historical Fiction; Literary; Science
Fiction

Nonfiction > *Nonfiction Books*
History; Memoir

Send: Query; Synopsis; Writing sample
How to send: Email

In nonfiction deals mainly in history and
memoir. In fiction, leans toward literary
fiction, although it can contain historical and
crime and very occasionally sci-fi. Send query
by email to assistant.

Associate Agent: Olivia Martin (**L426**)

Authors: Sarah Bagshaw; Adam Baker; Alan
Bennett; James Bloom; Christopher
Brookmyre; Justin Butcher; Mick Collins;
Wendy Cope; Oliver Cotton; Geoff Cox; Dan
Cruickshank; Richard Davidson; Russell
Davies; Paddy Docherty; Alicia Duffy;
Douglas Dunn; Tim Dynevor; Chris England;
Sue Glover; Robert Hardman; David Harsent;
Colin Heber-Percy; Mark Hussey; Ashley
Inglis; Richard Lambert; James Larkin; David
Lawrence; Paul Lay; Jessica Lea; Mike Leigh;
Michelle Magorian; Jonathan Maitland;
Nicholas Martin; Anita Mason; Simon Mawer;
Nicola McCartney; Patrick McGinley; Roger
McGough; Livi Michael; Peter Moffat;
Dominique Moloney; Blake Morrison; Chris
Mullin; Nicholas Murray; Malik Al Nasir;
Redmond O'Hanlon; David Olusoga; William
Palmer; Ruth Rendell; Michèle Roberts; Jane
Rogers; Michael Rosen; James Rourke;
Alexander Stuart; Peter Turnbull; James
Walvin; Lyall Watson; Gavin Weightman;
Derek Wilson; Matthew Yorke

L630 The Wallace Literary Agency
Literary Agency
United States

contact@wallaceliteraryagency.com

http://www.wallaceliteraryagency.com

Literary Agencies: Robin Straus Agency, Inc.;
Andrew Nurnberg Associates, Ltd

L631 Clare Wallace
Literary Agent
United Kingdom

https://www.darleyandersonchildrens.com/
about-us
https://twitter.com/LitAgentClare

Literary Agencies: The Darley Anderson
Agency; Darley Anderson Children's (**L157**)

ADULT > Fiction > *Novels*: Commercial
Women's Fiction

CHILDREN'S > Fiction
Middle Grade; *Picture Books*
TEEN > Fiction > *Novels*

YOUNG ADULT > Fiction > *Novels*

Scouting for new authors of picture books,
middle grade, teenage, YA and illustrators.
Also represents a boutique list of commercial
and accessible literary women's fiction but is
closed to new submissions.

Assistant Agent: Chloe Davis

Authors: Honor Cargill-Martin; Sophie
Cousens; Tom Ellen; Alex Evelyn; Kerry
Fisher; Martyn Ford; Polly Ho-Yen; Nathanael
Lessore; Ayaan Mohamud; Phaedra Patrick;
Beth Reekles; Pat Sowa; Deirdre Sullivan;
Samantha Tonge

L632 Caroline Walsh
Literary Agent
United Kingdom

https://www.davidhigham.co.uk/agents-dh/
caroline-walsh/

Literary Agency: David Higham Associates
Ltd (**L159**)

ADULT
 Fiction > *Novels*
 Nonfiction > *Nonfiction Books*

CHILDREN'S > Fiction
 Chapter Books; *Novels*; *Picture Books*

Client list is made up predominantly of
children's writers and illustrators, many of
them award-winners and bestsellers. In
addition she handles some adult fiction and
non-fiction and is always on the look-out for
original contemporary writing and talented
author/illustrators.

Authors: Kelly Andrew; Antonia Barber;
Suzanne Barton; Ella Beech; Joe Berger; Tim
Bowler; Theresa Breslin; Martin Brown; Mike

Brownlow; Kathryn Cave; Jason Chapman;
Emma Chichester Clark; Trish Cooke; Susie
Day; Kady MacDonald Denton; Lucy
Dillamore; Ruth Eastham; Eve Edwards;
Jonathan Emmett; Ben Faulks; Corina
Fletcher; P. M. Freestone; Jane Gardam; Susan
Gates; Adèle Geras; Julia Golding; Ryan
Graudin; Candida Harper; Leigh Hodgkinson;
Jesse Hodgson; Dianne Hofmeyr; Anna
Hoghton; Meredith Hooper; Julia Jarman;
Anna Kemp; Clive King; Jay Kristoff; Fifi
Kuo; Eleanor Lavender; Jo Lodge; Jan Mark;
Ellie Marney; Tom McLaughlin; Gwen
Millward; Myfanwy Millward; Kate Milner;
Tony Mitton; Laura Mucha; Jenny Nimmo; C.
S. Pacat; Liz Pichon; Madhvi Ramani;
Catherine Rayner; Jacqui Rayner; Gwyneth
Rees; Fiona Roberton; Rachel Rooney;
Alexander McCall Smith; Joss Stirling; Sally
Symes; Vanessa Tait; Frances Thomas;
Theresa Tomlinson; Ann Turnbull; Martin
Waddell; Melanie Walsh; Gina Wilson;
Jacqueline Wilson; David Wojtowycz

L633 Kate Walsh
Associate Agent
United Kingdom
Tel: +44 (0) 20 3214 0884

kwalsh@unitedagents.co.uk

https://www.unitedagents.co.uk/
kwalshunitedagentscouk

Literary Agency: United Agents (**L619**)
Literary Agent / Company Director: Robert
Kirby (**L358**)

Nonfiction > *Nonfiction Books*
20th Century; Commercial; Current Affairs;
History; Music; Popular Science

Send: Query; Synopsis; Writing sample
How to send: Email

Actively building her list. She's on the lookout
mainly (although not exclusively) for
commercial non-fiction, with a particular
interest in music titles, history and broad-
spectrum popular science, and anything that
feels like a fresh and original way of looking at
the world. She is especially drawn to 20th and
21st century affairs, and welcomes anything
from anyone willing to speculate on what
comes next.

Authors: Jennifer Otter Bickerdike; Christie
Dickason; Nic Dunlop; Jeff Gulvin; Will
Hayward; Matthew Jukes; Max Kirsten; Harris
Reed; Tom Wainwright; Rohullah Yakobi

L634 Nick Walters
Literary Agent
United Kingdom

nick@davidluxtonassociates.co.uk

https://www.davidluxtonassociates.co.uk/the-
agency/

Literary Agency: David Luxton Associates (**L160**)

Nonfiction > *Nonfiction Books*
Commercial; Leadership; Lifestyle; Self Help; Sport

Send: Synopsis; Writing sample; Author bio
How to send: Email

Agent and Rights Manager. Principle interests are in the fields of sport, true crime, current affairs, lifestyle and self-help.

L635 Watson, Little Ltd

Literary Agency
Suite 315, ScreenWorks, 22 Highbury Grove, London, N5 2ER
United Kingdom
Tel: +44 (0) 20 7388 7529

office@watsonlittle.com
submissions@watsonlittle.com

https://www.watsonlittle.com
https://twitter.com/watsonlittle

Professional Body: The Association of Authors' Agents (AAA)

ADULT
Fiction > *Novels*
Nonfiction > *Nonfiction Books*

CHILDREN'S
Fiction > *Novels*
Nonfiction > *Nonfiction Books*

Send: Query; Author bio; Writing sample; Market info; Outline
How to send: Word file email attachment; PDF file email attachment; In the body of an email
How not to send: Post

Send query by email only with outline in the body of the email, and synopsis and sample material as Word document attachments (or PDF attachments, if illustrated), addressed to a specific agent. See website for full guidelines and details of specific agents. No scripts, poetry, or unsolicited MSS.

Author Estate: The Estate of Akemi Tanaka

Authors: Rebecca Abrams; Luci Adams; Tom Adams; Rose Alexander; Faima Bakar; Louise Soraya Black; Laura Chamberlain; Sophie Claire; Sarah J. Coleman; Tara Costello; Bryony Cousins; Alex Day; Rose Diell; Marianne Eloise; Lauren Ford; Tessa Gibbs; Natasha Holmes; Hayley Hoskins; Elias Jahshan; Hiba Noor Khan; Lindiwe Maqhubela; Diana McCaulay; Erin Murgatroyd; Fiona O'Brien; Ben Pechey; Rhian Parry; Will Richard; Richard Owain Roberts; Alan Robinson; Kohinoor Sahota; Hannah Silva; Jeremy Williams; Alex Woolhouse

Literary Agents: Megan Carroll (**L102**); Mandy Little; Laetitia Rutherford (**L543**); James Wills (*L654*); Donald Winchester

L636 Mackenzie Brady Watson

Literary Agent
United States

mbwquery@skagency.com

http://skagency.com/agents/mackenzie-brady-watson/

Literary Agency: Stuart Krichevsky Literary Agency, Inc. (**L596**)

ADULT > **Nonfiction** > *Nonfiction Books*
Business; Food; Investigative Journalism; Memoir; Narrative Nonfiction; Science; Sociology

YOUNG ADULT > **Fiction** > *Novels*

Focuses on narrative non-fiction for all ages and select Young Adult fiction. As a former genetics lab technician, she has a great passion for science books, especially if they are historically driven or revolutionize current theory, as well as sociology, investigative journalism, food writing, memoir, and business books. She particularly appreciates work that sheds light on marginalized experiences and helps contribute to the cultural conversation.

Authors: Roxanna Asgarian; Ahmed Badr; Lyndsie Bourgon; Hannah Brencher; Angela Chen; Caren Cooper; Helen Donahue; Hope Ewing; Chelsea Fairless; Kathryn Finney; Kit Fox; Katie Fricas; Lauren Garroni; Olivia Gatwood; Jessica Goudeau; Rose Hackman; Anita Hannig; Sarah Jaffe; R. Dean Johnson; Sophie Lucido Johnson; Megan Kimble; Audrea Lim; Catherine Lo; Michael Loynd; Jennifer Lunden; José Olivarez; Amy Peterson; Karen Pinchin; Shelley Puhak; Lydia Reeder; Victoria Reihana; Margot Lee Shetterly; Brie Spangler; Rachel Swaby; Carson Vaughan; Sarah Vogel; Kimberley Welman; Christina Wilcox; Nina Willner; Bernice Yeung; Tom Zeller; Sara Zin

L637 Rebecca Watson

Literary Agent
United Kingdom

Literary Agency: Valerie Hoskins Associates

L638 Jessica Watterson

Literary Agent
United States

https://www.dijkstraagency.com/agent-page.php?agent_id=Watterson
https://querymanager.com/query/jessicawatterson

Literary Agency: Sandra Dijkstra Literary Agency

ADULT > **Fiction** > *Novels*
Cozy Mysteries; Romance; Women's Fiction

CHILDREN'S
Fiction > *Picture Books*

Nonfiction > *Nonfiction Books*: Popular Culture

YOUNG ADULT > **Fiction** > *Novels*
Contemporary; Romance

Send: Query; Synopsis; Writing sample
How to send: Query Manager

Most interested in all genres of romance. Also loves women's fiction and is open to select Cozy Mysteries. In Young Adult, will consider just about anything in the contemporary sphere, particularly with some romance. Will also consider author-illustrated books and nonfiction on Pop Culture by authors who have established platforms.

L639 Anna Webber

Literary Agent
United Kingdom
Tel: +44 (0) 20 3214 0876

awebber@unitedagents.co.uk

https://www.unitedagents.co.uk/awebberunitedagentscouk
https://twitter.com/acewebber

Literary Agency: United Agents (**L619**)

Fiction > *Novels*

Nonfiction > *Nonfiction Books*: Literary

Poetry > *Any Poetic Form*

Send: Synopsis; Writing sample; Proposal

Represents both fiction and non-fiction, with a special focus on literary fiction and voice-driven non-fiction. She is open for submissions, but can only take on a small number of new clients per year.

Associate Agent: Seren Adams (**L005**)

Authors: Laura Albert; Rosie Alison; Nina Allan; Karin Altenberg; Jessica Anthony; Deborah Bee; Mark Blacklock; Stefan Merrill Block; Ezekiel Boone; Melitta Breznik; Molly Brodak; Sylvia Brownrigg; John Burnside; Robin Carhart-Harris; Carl Cattermole; Roland Chambers; Emma Cline; Amanda Coe; Marion Coutts; Rosie Dastgir; Carys Davies; Tim Dee; Miranda Doyle; Dennis Duncan; Elanor Dymott; Ben Eastham; Christy Edwall; Hermione Eyre; James Fenton; Toby Ferris; William Fowler; Rivka Galchen; William Ghosh; Rebecca Gowers; Samantha Harvey; Sheila Heti; Ben Hinshaw; Michael Hofmann; Joseph Hone; Caoilinn Hughes; Nicholas Hytner; William Irvine; Mick Jackson; Peter Stephan Jungk; Francesca Kay; I. J. Kay; Katharine Kilalea; James Lasdun; Louise Levene; Nell Leyshon; Victor Lodato; Tom Lubbock; Anna Mackmin; Caroline Maclean; Deirdre Madden; Emily St. John Mandel; Adam Mars-Jones; Philip Marsden; Andrew Martin; Daisy McNally; Ottessa Moshfegh; Sarah Moss; John Mullan; Anthea Nicholson; Trevor Norton; Alissa Nutting; Nat Ogle; Alice Oswald; Tim Parks; Ian Pattison; Helen Pike; Miranda Pountney; Julya Rabinowich; Natasha Randall; Victoria Redel; Sam Riviere; Michael Symmons Roberts; Jenn Shapland; Alexander

Starritt; Wendell Steavenson; Alain Claude Sulzer; David Szalay; George Szirtes; Natasha Walter; Gaby Wood; An Yu; Zinovy Zinik; Tirdad Zolghadr

L640 Alexandra Weiss
Associate Agent
United States

http://www.azantianlitagency.com/pages/team-awe.html
https://querymanager.com/query/AlexandraWeiss

Literary Agency: Azantian Literary Agency (L039)

ADULT > Nonfiction
Gift Books: General
Nonfiction Books: Environment; Mental Health; Science; Space
CHILDREN'S
Fiction
Graphic Novels; *Picture Books*
Nonfiction
Chapter Books: General
Middle Grade: Adventure; Contemporary; Magic; Science Fiction; Time Travel
Picture Books: General

YOUNG ADULT > Fiction
Graphic Novels: General
Novels: Coming of Age; Contemporary; Folklore, Myths, and Legends; Low Fantasy; Magical Realism; Romantic Comedy; Soft Science Fiction

How to send: Query Manager

Represents fiction and nonfiction picture books, middle grade, young adult, graphic novels, and select adult nonfiction.

L641 Karmen Wells
Literary Agent
Canada

karmen@therightsfactory.com

https://www.therightsfactory.com/Agents/Karmen-Wells
https://twitter.com/KarmenEdits

Literary Agency: The Rights Factory

Fiction > Novels
Comedy / Humour; Coming of Age; Commercial; Drama; Dystopian Fiction; High Concept; Horror; LGBTQIA; Literary; Popular Culture; Science Fiction

Nonfiction > Nonfiction Books: Narrative Nonfiction

Send: Query; Pitch; Author bio; Writing sample
How to send: Email

Looking for published or to-be-published books to represent to producers for film or TV adaptation.

Authors: Daniel Barnett; Kelly Florence; Rhonda J. Garcia; Jessica Guess; Meg Hafdahl; Tim Meyer

L642 Jennifer Weltz
Literary Agent
United States

Literary Agency: The Jean V. Naggar Literary Agency

Closed to approaches.

L643 Erin Casey Westin
Literary Agent
United States

https://querymanager.com/query/erincaseywestin
https://twitter.com/erincaseywestin

Literary Agency: Gallt & Zacker Literary Agency

CHILDREN'S > Fiction
Middle Grade; *Picture Books*
YOUNG ADULT
Fiction
Graphic Novels; *Novels*
Nonfiction > Nonfiction Books

Closed to approaches.

Open to queries from the 1st to the 7th of every month.

L644 Michaela Whatnall
Literary Agent
United States

mwhatnall@dystel.com

https://www.dystel.com/michaela-whatnall
https://querymanager.com/query/michaelawhatnall
https://twitter.com/mwhatnall

Literary Agency: Dystel, Goderich & Bourret LLC

ADULT
Fiction
Graphic Novels: General
Novels: Contemporary; Grounded Fantasy; Historical Fiction; Speculative; Upmarket
Nonfiction > Nonfiction Books: Narrative Nonfiction

CHILDREN'S
Fiction
Graphic Novels; *Middle Grade*; *Picture Books*
Nonfiction > Nonfiction Books: Narrative Nonfiction

YOUNG ADULT > Fiction
Graphic Novels: General
Novels: General, and in particular: Adventure; Contemporary; Fantasy; Historical Fiction; Horror; Romantic Comedy; Science Fiction

How to send: Query Manager

Strong interest in children's literature, particularly middle grade and young adult fiction of all genres, including contemporary, fantasy, science fiction, historical, adventure, horror, and rom-com. In the adult fiction space, they are particularly seeking contemporary, speculative, and historical upmarket fiction, as well as character-driven, grounded fantasy. They are also open to select narrative nonfiction for both children and adults, graphic novels, and picture books.

L645 Maria Whelan
Literary Agent
United States

http://www.inkwellmanagement.com/staff/maria-whelan

Literary Agency: InkWell Management

Fiction > Novels
Comedy / Humour; Commercial; Culture; Literary; Magical Realism; Speculative; Upmarket Women's Fiction

Nonfiction > Nonfiction Books
General, and in particular: Cultural Commentary; Society

Send: Query; Writing sample
How to send: In the body of an email

Enjoys literary fiction, magical realism, upmarket women's fiction and humor, as well as non-fiction, revolving around peculiar topics especially overlooked facets of society.

L646 Whispering Buffalo Literary Agency
Literary Agency
97 Chesson Road, London, W14 9QS
United Kingdom
Tel: +44 (0) 20 7385 4655

info@whisperingbuffalo.com

https://www.whisperingbuffalo.com

ADULT
Fiction > Novels
Commercial; Literary
Nonfiction > Nonfiction Books: Commercial

CHILDREN'S > Fiction > Novels

YOUNG ADULT > Fiction > Novels

Send: Query; Author bio; Synopsis; Writing sample; Proposal
How to send: Word file email attachment

Represents a growing stable of storytellers including individuals with a high media profile in a variety of fields. The agency is building its list and welcomes unsolicited submissions.

Literary Agent: Mariam Keen

L647 Alice Whitwham
Literary Agent
United States

https://www.cheneyagency.com/alice-whitwham

Literary Agency: The Cheney Agency

L648 Chandler Wickers
Literary Agent
United States

cw@skagency.com

http://skagency.com/agents/chandler-wickers/

Literary Agency: Stuart Krichevsky Literary Agency, Inc. (**L596**)

Fiction > *Novels*
Coming of Age; Family Saga; Literary; Upmarket

Nonfiction > *Nonfiction Books*
Adventure; History; Journalism; Popular Culture; Technology; Warfare

Send: Query; Writing sample; Proposal
How to send: In the body of an email
How not to send: Email attachment

Interested in representing adult fiction and non-fiction.

She is drawn to voice-driven literary and upmarket fiction with a strong sense of place, novels featuring darkly funny narrators, flawed protagonists, coming of age stories, and family sagas. She's especially excited about writing that plays with form, stories that explore visceral experiences of body and mind, and characters grappling with philosophical questions about faith and desire.

In non-fiction, she looks for novelistic journalism, comprehensive histories, war reporting, wilderness adventures, and journeys to the edges of the Earth. As a San Francisco native and Brooklyn transplant she is keen on stories that intersect tech and pop culture, converge scholarly with personal narratives, and those that demystify a subculture or reveal an underbelly.

L649 Gary Wild
Literary Agent
United Kingdom

Literary Agency: JFL Agency (**L327**)

L650 Alice Williams
Literary Agent
United Kingdom

alice@alicewilliamsliterary.co.uk

https://twitter.com/alicelovesbooks
https://www.instagram.com/agentalicewilliams/

Literary Agency: Alice Williams Literary (**L017**)

L651 Sarah Williams
Literary Agent
United Kingdom

sarah@sophiehicksagency.com
williamsoffice@sophiehicksagency.com

http://www.sophiehicksagency.com/sarahwilliams

Literary Agency: Sophie Hicks Agency

Fiction > *Novels*
Commercial; Family Saga; Literary; Romance; Thrillers

Nonfiction > *Nonfiction Books*
Memoir; Nature; Science; Travel

Send: Synopsis; Writing sample; Outline

She is always on the lookout for creative, engaging storytellers and is currently hoping to hear from writers of narrative non-fiction of most types – memoir, travel, nature, science, and explorations of the intricacies of the human experience. In fiction, she would love to find a surprising and excellently plotted multi-generational family story, and is perpetually hoping for a sweeping love story with colliding geographies. A twisty thriller is always welcome.

Authors: Omar Al-Khayatt; Sarah Bannan; Lee Boyce; William Butler-Adams; Helen Chandler-Wilde; Carl Cox; Sarah Crosby; Michaela Dunbar; Ruth Fitzmaurice; Kate Ford; Lewis Hine; Shahroo Izadi; Signe Johansen; Sophie Monks Kaufman; Jesse McClure; Phil McNulty; Andrew Meehan; Claire Nelson; Katie Treggiden; Claire Walsh; Tom Whipple; Jim White

L652 Jo Williamson
Literary Agent
United Kingdom

jo@antonyharwood.com

http://antonyharwood.com/jo-williamson/

Literary Agency: Antony Harwood Limited (**L029**)

CHILDREN'S > **Fiction**
Middle Grade: Adventure
Picture Books: General

YOUNG ADULT > **Fiction** > *Novels*

L653 Kathryn Willms
Literary Agent
Canada

kathryn@therightsfactory.com

https://www.therightsfactory.com/Agents/Kathryn-Willms
https://querymanager.com/query/2039

Literary Agency: The Rights Factory

Nonfiction > *Nonfiction Books*
Culture; Environment; Food and Drink; History; Lifestyle; Narrative Nonfiction; Nature; Psychology; Social Justice

Send: Query; Author bio; Writing sample
How to send: Query Manager; Email attachment

Currently focused on building her nonfiction list in culture, social justice, psychology, history, nature/environmentalism, lifestyle, and food and beverage. She is not currently acquiring conventional memoirs (although books exploring a topic that incorporate a personal story are very welcome).

Authors: Chloe Ackerman; Lisa Brahin; Lynda Calvert; Meghan Chayka; Lana Hall; Alyssa Huizing; Andrew Mayeda; Michelle McIvor; Riley E. Moynes; Nancy Pearson; Karen Pierce; Laura Pratt; Banuta Rubess; Jaime Weinman; Zed Zha

L654 James Wills
Literary Agent
United Kingdom

Literary Agency: Watson, Little Ltd (**L635**)

Closed to approaches.

L655 Desiree Wilson
Literary Agent
United States

https://www.thebentagency.com/desiree-wilson
https://querymanager.com/query/dwilson
https://desir.ee/submissions/
https://twitter.com/swindlesoiree

Literary Agency: The Bent Agency (**L058**)

ADULT
Fiction
Graphic Novels: Contemporary; Fantasy; Horror; Magical Realism; Science Fiction; Speculative
Novels: Contemporary; Fantasy; Horror; Magical Realism; Romantic Comedy; Science Fiction; Speculative; Thrillers; Upmarket
Short Fiction: General

Nonfiction > *Nonfiction Books*: Narrative Nonfiction

CHILDREN'S
Fiction
Graphic Novels: General
Middle Grade: Gender; Horror; Mental Health
Nonfiction > *Middle Grade*
Engineering; History; Mathematics; Science; Technology

YOUNG ADULT > **Fiction**
Graphic Novels: High Concept; Relationships
Novels: Fairy Tales; Fantasy; High Concept; Horror; LGBTQIA; Romance; Romantic Comedy; Science Fiction; Urban Fantasy

Does not want:

Fiction > *Novels*: Hard Science Fiction

Closed to approaches.

I represent upper middle grade, YA, and adult genre fiction, especially horror (and kid-horror), high-concept fantasy, speculative fiction, magical realism, and accessible or near-future science fiction. I am also looking for select middle grade nonfiction about history or STEM.

L656 Ed Wilson

Literary Agent; Company Director
United Kingdom
Tel: +44 (0) 20 7251 0125

ed@johnsonandalcock.co.uk

http://www.johnsonandalcock.co.uk/ed-wilson
https://twitter.com/literarywhore

Literary Agency: Johnson & Alcock (**L330**)

Fiction
Graphic Novels: General
Novels: Commercial; Crime; Experimental; Fantasy; High Concept; Literary; Science Fiction; Speculative; Thrillers
Nonfiction > *Nonfiction Books*
History; Nature; Politics; Popular Culture; Sport

Send: Query; Synopsis; Writing sample
How to send: Email attachment

In fiction, he looks for anything with originality and style, both literary and commercial: books with an imaginative setting, strong narrative voice, and compelling premise. He has an active SFF list, with mutliple award-winning and nominated authors, and is always on the lookout for new writers. He's open to all forms of high concept writing, intelligent crime and thrillers, and books that transcend genre. Ed is not currently taking on any new YA or children's authors, and does not represent play or film scripts.

His non-fiction tastes cover a wide range: from serious politics and sweeping narrative history, to sport, natural history and popular culture. He loves intelligent and original graphic novels and infographics, and anything that tackles well-known subjects in an interesting and quirky way.

L657 Rebecca Winfield

Literary Agent
United Kingdom

https://www.davidluxtonassociates.co.uk/the-agency/

Literary Agency: David Luxton Associates (**L160**)

Nonfiction
Nonfiction Books: History; Memoir; Travel
Reference: Popular Reference

Send: Synopsis; Writing sample; Author bio
How to send: Email
How not to send: Post

L658 Caryn Wiseman

Executive Agent
United States

https://www.andreabrownlit.com/agents.html
https://querymanager.com/query/CarynWiseman
https://www.facebook.com/caryn.wiseman
https://twitter.com/CarynWiseman

Literary Agency: Andrea Brown Literary Agency, Inc.

CHILDREN'S
Fiction
Chapter Books: General, and in particular: Diversity; Social Justice
Graphic Novels: General, and in particular: Diversity; Social Justice
Middle Grade: General, and in particular: Diversity; Social Justice
Picture Books: General, and in particular: Diversity; Social Justice
Nonfiction
Nonfiction Books: General, and in particular: Diversity; Social Justice
Picture Books: General, and in particular: Biography; Diversity; Social Justice
YOUNG ADULT
Fiction > *Novels*
General, and in particular: Diversity; Romance; Social Justice

Nonfiction > *Nonfiction Books*
General, and in particular: Diversity; Social Justice

Send: Author bio; Query; Writing sample; Pitch; Market info
How to send: Query Manager

Drawn to contemporary YA and middle grade with a strong voice, multifaceted characters, complex relationships, beautiful writing, and a well-developed hook. Great world-building is essential, whether it's a real time and place that becomes almost a character in a book, or a light fantasy element in a unique story that's grounded in reality. Zombies, horror, and high fantasy will, most likely, never appeal. She is particularly interested in books for children and teens that explore themes of diversity and social justice. She would be thrilled to see more books by underrepresented authors that deeply explore their culture, as well as books in which the ethnicity of the character is not the issue. She adores a swoon-worthy, layered romance; a funny or poignant middle grade novel with a hook that makes it stand out from the crowd would hold great appeal; and she's partial to lyrical, non-institutional picture book biographies and character-driven, not-too-sweet picture book fiction, particularly by author-illustrators.

L659 Jade Wong-Baxter

Associate Agent
United States

jwb@goldinlit.com

https://goldinlit.com/contact/

Literary Agency: Frances Goldin Literary Agency, Inc. (**L231**)

Fiction > *Novels*
Literary; Magical Realism; Upmarket

Nonfiction > *Nonfiction Books*
Cultural Criticism; History; Memoir; Narrative Nonfiction; Popular Culture

Send: Query; Writing sample
How to send: Email

L660 Caroline Wood

Literary Agent; Company Director
United Kingdom

https://felicitybryan.com/fba-agent/caroline-wood/

Literary Agency: Felicity Bryan Associates (**L211**)

Fiction > *Novels*
Commercial; Family; Literary; Relationships

Nonfiction > *Nonfiction Books*
Cookery; Memoir

I represent prize-winning literary fiction and well written commercial fiction. I am actively looking for original, character driven debuts. I love books that transport me to a different time or place, books that have a secret or mystery at the heart of them, books about family and relationships, books that leave me with something to ponder. My authors have won the Booker Prize, the Costa Novel and First Novel Awards, the Commonwealth Writers' Prize, the Prix Médicis Etranger, the Desmond Elliot Prize and the Betty Trask. I greatly enjoy the editing process and work closely with my authors to make their books the best they can be. In non-fiction, I represent primarily cookery and memoirs. I also sell book to film/TV rights for a number of my authors.

Authors: Carlos Acosta; Modern Baker; Kay Barron; Susan Beale; Louis De Bernières; Mary Berry; Nina Bhadreshwar; Francesca Brill; Rhidian Brook; Stephen Burke; Lucy Cavendish; Sarah Challis; Jonathan Coe; Will Cohu; T.A. Cotterell; Benjamin Daniels; Nick Edwards; James Fearnley; Rebecca Fleet; Damon Galgut; Kat Gordon; Catherine Hall; Anna Hope; Gill Hornby; Richard House; Allegra Huston; Stanley Kenani; Liza Klaussmann; Phyllida Law; Tim Leach; Simon Lelic; Sarah K Marr; Alistair Morgan; Alan Murrin; Jennifer Nadel; Svenja O'donnell; Colm O'gorman; Iain Pears; Nick Potter; Elaine Proctor; Melody Razak; Adam Ruck; Penny Rudge; Edward Russell-Walling; Sue Stuart-Smith; Henry Sutton; Katherine Swift;

Edmund De Waal; Martin Walker; Kirsty Wark; Greg Wise; James Wythe; Lucy Young

L661 James Woodhouse

Literary Agent
United Kingdom

enquiries@tiborjones.com

http://www.tiborjones.com/about/

Literary Agency: Tibor Jones & Associates

Fiction > *Novels*
   Africa; Commercial; Literary

Send: Query; Synopsis; Writing sample

Passionate about stories from Africa, but his interests range from strong commercial crime fiction to high-end literary work.

L662 Bryony Woods

Literary Agent
United Kingdom

submissions.bryony@dkwlitagency.co.uk

http://dkwlitagency.co.uk/agents/
https://twitter.com/BryonyWoods

Literary Agency: Diamond Kahn and Woods (DKW) Literary Agency Ltd

ADULT
   Fiction > *Novels*
      General, and in particular: Commercial; Dark Magic; Fairy Tales; Fantasy; Friends; Literary; Romance; Science Fiction; Upmarket Contemporary Fiction

   Nonfiction
      Essays: General
      Nonfiction Books: Memoir

CHILDREN'S > **Fiction** > *Middle Grade*

YOUNG ADULT > **Fiction** > *Novels*

Does not want:

> **Fiction** > *Novels*
>   Crime; Psychological Thrillers

Send: Query; Writing sample; Synopsis
How to send: Email attachment

My reading taste is fairly eclectic, and covers commercial to literary and everything in between.

At the moment I'd particularly love to find some beautifully written, upmarket contemporary novels; books about friendships and platonic love; thought-provoking sci-fi or richly imagined fantasy worlds; brilliant, sweeping love stories on an epic canvas; found families, or novels about finding love in unexpected places; anything that truly makes me laugh; fairy tales, or anything darkly magical; books that surprise me; books that will break my heart; books that are full of hope.

I tend to avoid anything particularly gritty or depressing, so crime novels or harrowing psychological thrillers are likely to be a no. I also don't represent children's picture books, or poetry collections. The non-fiction side of my list is small, but I have been known to fall for a beautiful memoir or a moving collection of essays.

L663 Jessica Woollard

Literary Agent
United Kingdom

jessicawoollard@davidhigham.co.uk

https://www.davidhigham.co.uk/agents-dh/jessica-woollard/

Literary Agency: David Higham Associates Ltd (**L159**)

Fiction > *Novels*: Literary

Nonfiction > *Nonfiction Books*
   Activism; Africa; Culture; Current Affairs; Environment; Gender; Japan; Memoir; Middle East; Narrative Nonfiction; Nature; Science; South-East Asia

Represents a diverse range of international literary fiction and narrative non-fiction. South East Asia, Japan, Africa and the Middle East are areas of particular interest; she lived in Mumbai for five years. She's long worked with memoir, perhaps it's the new novel, and books that explore multiple genres; science, natural history, gender, landscape, cultural and current affairs and the way these subjects impact on our daily lives, poetic, awake, activist, environmentally aware writing.

Authors: Paco Calvo; Masud Husain; Natalie Lawrence

L664 Wordserve Literary

Literary Agency
United States

admin@wordserveliterary.com

http://www.wordserveliterary.com
http://wordservewatercooler.com
https://twitter.com/WordServeLit
http://www.facebook.com/WordServeLiterary

ADULT
   Fiction > *Novels*
      Christianity; Historical Fiction; Legal; Literary; Mainstream; Romance; Supernatural / Paranormal; Suspense; Women's Fiction

   Nonfiction > *Nonfiction Books*
      Biography; Christianity; Current Affairs; Family; Finance; Health; History; Memoir; Military; Popular Culture; Psychology; Self Help; Women's Issues

CHILDREN'S > **Fiction**
   Middle Grade; *Novels*
YOUNG ADULT > **Fiction** > *Novels*

Send: Query; Writing sample
How to send: In the body of an email
How not to send: Email attachment

Represents books for the general and Christian markets. Nonfiction 40,000 – 100,000 words; fiction 60,000-120,000 words. No gift books, poetry, short stories, screenplays, children's picture books, science fiction or fantasy for any age. Email approaches only. See website for detailed submission guidelines. Submissions that disregard the submission guidelines may themselves be disregarded.

Literary Agents: Keely Boeving; Sarah Joy Freese; Nick Harrison; Greg Johnson

L665 Writer's Side

Literary Agency; Editorial Service
8 Chanan Singh Park, Delhi Cantt, New Delhi, 110010
India

kanishka500@gmail.com
kanishka@writersside.com

http://www.writersside.com

Fiction > *Novels*
   General, and in particular: Commercial; Literary

Nonfiction > *Nonfiction Books*
   General, and in particular: Business; Narrative Nonfiction

Send: Synopsis; Author bio; Writing sample
How to send: Word file email attachment

Costs: Offers services that writers have to pay for.

Describes itself as the number one literary agency in South Asia. Represents authors from India and abroad. Particularly interested in debut writing from India, Pakistan, Sri Lanka and Bangladesh. Also offers editorial services, but this is held separate from the literary agency and customers of the editorial service will not be represented by the agency.

Literary Agent: Kanishka Gupta

L666 Susan Yearwood

Literary Agent
United Kingdom

submissions@susanyearwoodagency.com

https://susanyearwoodagency.com

Literary Agency: SYLA – Susan Yearwood Literary Agency (**L602**)

ADULT
   Fiction > *Novels*
      Book Club Fiction; Commercial; Crime; Romance; Saga; Thrillers

   Nonfiction > *Nonfiction Books*
      General, and in particular: Business; Cookery; Finance; Lifestyle; Self Help; Wellbeing

CHILDREN'S > **Fiction** > *Middle Grade*

TEEN > **Fiction** > *Novels*

YOUNG ADULT > **Fiction** > *Novels*

Send: Query; Author bio; Writing sample; Synopsis
How to send: Email attachment

Looks for book club fiction, commercial fiction including romance and saga, genre fiction i.e. crime/thriller, children's aged 9+ and teen/young adult novels as well as non-fiction, particularly business and finance, self-help and well-being, and lifestyle, including cookery.

Authors: Rebecca Adams; Catherine Balavage; Lucy Basey; Katie Brewer; Angela Cairns; Fran Clark; Sarah Dobbs; Selina Flavius; Kimberley Glover; Liz Kolbeck; Prajwal Parajuly; Fil Reid; Sarupa Shah; Jacqueline Shaw; Mahalia Smith; Suzanne Snow; Sarah Stephenson; Kerry Young

L667 **Rachel Yeoh**
Associate Agent
United Kingdom

submissions@madeleinemilburn.com

https://madeleinemilburn.co.uk/team-member/rachel-yeoh/

Literary Agency: Madeleine Milburn Literary, TV & Film Agency (**L417**)

Fiction > *Novels*
Autofiction; Book Club Fiction; Literary; Magical Realism; Nature; Philosophy; Politics; Postcolonialism; Social Commentary; Upmarket

Nonfiction > *Nonfiction Books*: Memoir

Send: Query; Pitch; Market info; Author bio
How to send: Email

Actively looking for: literary, upmarket, book club, autobiographical fiction, political perspectives, social critiques, postcolonial literature, magical realism, nature writing, philosophical themes, classical retellings, character-driven stories, topical issues, narrative memoir, global voices, diaspora.

I am looking for global voices in literary, upmarket and book club fiction that tell compelling stories reflective of the human experience, as well as autobiographical fiction and narrative non-fiction.

L668 **YMU Books**
Literary Agency
180 Great Portland Street, London, W1W 5QZ
United Kingdom

https://www.ymugroup.com
https://books.ymugroup.com

Nonfiction > *Nonfiction Books*
Celebrity; Commercial

Closed to approaches.

A market-leading literary agency in premium brand and platform representation, working with writers and creators who excel in their genres.

Authors: Francis Bourgeois; Rosie Day; Jane Dunn; Paloma Faith; Cherry Healey; Cat Sims; Jemma Solomon

L669 **Claudia Young**
Literary Agent
United Kingdom

http://greeneheaton.co.uk/agents/claudia-young/
https://twitter.com/ClaudiaL_Young

Literary Agency: Greene & Heaton Ltd (**L269**)

Fiction > *Novels*
Contemporary; Crime; Historical Fiction; Literary; Thrillers

Nonfiction > *Nonfiction Books*
Comedy / Humour; Cookery; Food Journalism; Travel

Interested in all types of writing, in particular cooking and food journalism, comedy and travel writing. Loves literary fiction, contemporary as well as historical novels, crime fiction and thrillers.

Authors: Sam Akbar; Anthony Anaxagorou; Ros Atkinson; Jordan Bourke; Aine Carlin; Matt Chapple; Martha Collison; Jack Cooke; Kevan Davis; Kim Duke; Gabriela Evangelou; Lucia Evangelou; Ella Frears; Francis Gimblett; Lewis Goodall; Peter Harper; Alice Hart; Wayne Holloway-Smith; Lizzie King; Vanessa King; Jenny Lee; Eleanor Maidment; Janina Matthewson; Ciara Ohartghaile; Val Payne; Alice Procter; Rejina Pyo; James Ramsden; Rosie Ramsden; Charlie Ryrie; Kat Sadler; Viviane Schwarz; Tim Sebastian; Dale Shaw; Rachel de Thample; Georgie Tilney; Regina Wong

L670 **Lane Zachary**
Literary Agent
United States

lane@mmqlit.com

http://www.mmqlit.com/about/
http://www.mmqlit.com/contact/

Literary Agency: Massie & McQuilkin

Fiction > *Novels*

Nonfiction > *Nonfiction Books*

Send: Query
How to send: Email

Looking for books of nonfiction and fiction that are beautifully crafted and have the capacity to change the way in which we see and live in the world. Response only if interested. If no response within 6 weeks, assume rejection.

L671 **Marietta B. Zacker**
Literary Agent
United States

https://www.galltzacker.com/submissions.html
https://querymanager.com/query/querymarietta

Literary Agency: Gallt & Zacker Literary Agency

CHILDREN'S > **Fiction**
Middle Grade; Picture Books
YOUNG ADULT
Fiction
Graphic Novels; Novels
Nonfiction > *Nonfiction Books*

Closed to approaches.

Open to queries from the 1st to the 7th of every month.

L672 **Zeno Agency Ltd**
Literary Agency
Primrose Hill Business Centre, 110 Gloucester Avenue, London, NW1 8HX
United Kingdom
Tel: +44 (0) 20 7096 0927

info@zenoagency.com

http://zenoagency.com

Professional Body: The Association of Authors' Agents (AAA)

ADULT > **Fiction** > *Novels*
Crime; Fantasy; Horror; Science Fiction; Thrillers; Women's Fiction

YOUNG ADULT > **Fiction** > *Novels*

London-based literary agency specialising in Science Fiction, Fantasy, and Horror, but expanding into other areas such as crime, thrillers, women's fiction, and young adult fiction. Adult fiction must be at least 75,000 words and children's fiction should be at least 50,000 words. Send query by email with synopsis up to two pages, and first three chapters (or approximately 50 double-spaced pages) as attachments in .docx or .pdf format. No submissions by post.

Authors: Travis Baldree; Alice Bell; Andrew Cartmel; Mário Coelho; Craig Laurance Gidney; J.T. Greathouse; Grady Hendrix; Laura Kerseviciute; Sian Lenihan; Anna McNuff; Silvia Moreno-Garcia; Adam Oyebanji; Martin Purbrick; Farrah Riaz; Cassidy Ellis Salter; Katherine Toran; Amy True / Amy Trueblood; Emily Turner; R.R. Virdi; Angus Watson; Gary Wigglesworth; Jasmine Wigham; Yudhanjaya Wijeratne; Catelyn Wilson

Literary Agents: John Berlyne; Stevie Finegan (**L220**)

L673 **Ayla Zuraw-Friedland**
Literary Agent
United States

azf@goldinlit.com

https://www.goldinlit.com/ayla-zuraw-friedland
https://twitter.com/kaylasansk

Literary Agency: Frances Goldin Literary Agency, Inc. (**L231**)

Fiction
  Graphic Novels: General

Novels: Literary

Nonfiction > *Nonfiction Books*
  Arts; LGBTQIA; Social Class; Technology

Poetry > *Poetry Collections*

Send: Query; Writing sample
How to send: Email

Interested in literary fiction and nonfiction that inspect big questions about queer identity, class, community, and art and technology through a personal lens, as well as poetry and a limited number of graphic or hybrid projects.

Magazines

For the most up-to-date listings of these and hundreds of other magazines, visit https://www.firstwriter.com/magazines

To claim your free access to the site, please see the back of this book.

M001 The 2River View
Online Magazine
Santa Rosa, CA 95404
United States

Be1ong@2river.org

https://www.2river.org
https://2river.submittable.com/submit

Poetry > *Any Poetic Form*

Send: Full text
How to send: Submittable

Costs: A fee is charged upon submission. $3 reading fee per submission.

Considers unpublished poems only. Submit via online submission system. See website for more details.

Editor-in-Chief: Richard Long

M002 30 North
Magazine
United States

https://30northliterarymagazine.com

Fiction > *Short Fiction*: Literary

Nonfiction > *Short Nonfiction*: Creative Nonfiction

Poetry > *Any Poetic Form*

Closed to approaches.

Publishes previously unpublished poetry, fiction, creative non-fiction, and art by undergraduate writers and artists. Submit via online submission system.

M003 32 Poems
Magazine
Washington & Jefferson College, Department of English, 60 S. Lincoln Street, Washington, PA 15301
United States

submissions@32poems.com

http://32poems.com

Nonfiction > *Reviews*: Poetry as a Subject

Poetry > *Any Poetic Form*

Send: Full text
How to send: Submittable; Duosuma

Costs: A fee is charged for online submissions. $3 fee for online submissions.

Publishes poems and reviews of recent poetry collections. Submit via online submission systems. Will re-open to postal submissions in January 2022.

Editor: George David Clark

Managing Editor: Elisabeth Clark

M004 34th Parallel
Magazine
United States

editorial@34thParallel.net

https://34thparallel.net

Fiction > *Short Fiction*: Literary

Nonfiction
　Articles: Journalism
　Essays: Creative Nonfiction

Poetry > *Any Poetic Form*

Send: Full text

Costs: A fee is charged upon submission. $14.50 fee includes download of latest digital edition.

Publishes fiction, creative nonfiction, essays, scripts, poetry, and artwork. Submit via online submission system.

M005 417 Magazine
Magazine
Whitaker Publishing, 2111 S. Eastgate Ave., Springfield, MO 65809
United States
Tel: +1 (417) 883-7417

https://www.417mag.com
http://facebook.com/417mag
http://instagram.com/417mag
http://twitter.com/417mag
http://pinterest.com/417magazine
https://www.linkedin.com/company/whitaker-publishing

Nonfiction > *Articles*
　Food; Lifestyle; Missouri; Outdoor Activities

Publishes material of local interest to southwest Missouri only. Potential contributors are advised to study the magazine before approaching.

M006 5-7-5 Haiku Journal
Online Magazine
United Kingdom

https://575haikujournal.wordpress.com/

Book Publisher / Magazine Publisher: Atlantean Publishing (**P044**)

Poetry
　Haibun; *Haiku*; *Senryu*; *Tanka*

Send: Full text
How to send: In the body of an email

Publishes Haiku (and related forms such as senryu and scifaiku). Plus, Haiku Sequences, Haibun and Tanka.

M007 AARP The Magazine
Magazine
c/o Editorial Submissions, 601 E St. NW, Washington, DC 20049
United States

pubspitches@aarp.org

https://www.aarp.org/magazine/

Nonfiction
　Articles: General, and in particular: Fitness; Food; Health; Investments; Nutrition; Personal Finance; Relationships; Travel
　Essays: Personal Essays

Send: Query
Don't send: Full text
How to send: Email

Magazine for those over 50. Rarely uses unsolicited ideas but will review those submitted in accordance with the guidelines on the website.

M008 About Place Journal
Magazine
PO Box 24, Black Earth, WI 53515-0424
United States

blackearthinstitute@gmail.com

https://aboutplacejournal.org

Fiction > *Short Fiction*: Literary

Nonfiction
　Essays: General
　Short Nonfiction: Creative Nonfiction

Poetry > *Any Poetic Form*

Closed to approaches.

Publishes poetry, fiction, and essays / creative nonfiction. Accepts submissions during specific submission windows. See website for details and for themes.

M009 The Account
Online Magazine
United States

poetryprosethought@gmail.com

https://theaccountmagazine.com
https://
theaccountajournalofpoetryprosethought.
submittable.com/submit
https://twitter.com/TheAccountMag
https://www.facebook.com/
TheAccountAJournalOfPoetryProseAndThoug
ht

Fiction > *Short Fiction*

Nonfiction > *Short Nonfiction*: Creative Nonfiction

Poetry > *Any Poetic Form*

Send: Full text

Accepts poetry, fiction, and creative nonfiction. Send 3-5 poems, essays up to 6,000 words, or fiction between 1,000 and 6,000 words, through online submission system. Each piece of work must be accompanied by an account between 150 and 500 words, giving voice to the artist's approach.

Editors: Brianna Noll, Poetry Editor; Jennifer Hawe, Nonfiction Editor; M. Milks, Fiction Editor; Tyler Mills, Editor-in-Chief; Christina Stoddard, Managing Editor/ Publicist

M010 Accountancy Age
Magazine
United Kingdom

https://www.accountancyage.com
https://www.twitter.com/accountancyage/
https://www.linkedin.com/groups?gid=
2352548

PROFESSIONAL > **Nonfiction** > *Articles*
  Accounting; Business; Finance

Weekly magazine publishing articles on accountancy, business, and the financial world.

Editor: Aaran Fronda

M011 Accountancy Daily
Online Magazine
240 Blackfriars Road, London, SE1 8NW
United Kingdom

accountancynews@croneri.co.uk

https://www.accountancydaily.co
https://twitter.com/accountancylive

Book Publisher: Croner-i Limited (**P146**)

PROFESSIONAL > **Nonfiction** > *News*
  Accounting; Business; Finance

Specialises in technical analysis, news and comment on tax, accounting and audit for the accounting profession working across practice and business.

M012 AdventureBox
Magazine
United Kingdom

contact@bayard-magazines.co.uk

https://bayard-magazines.co.uk/collections/all-products/products/adventurebox-magazine

Magazine Publisher: Bayard Magazines

CHILDREN'S > **Fiction** > *Early Readers*: Adventure

Magazine that aims to keep kids hooked on reading. This title was made for kids who have just begun to read independently. The distinctive format helps kids feel grown up and that they've arrived at the next step in their reading journey.

M013 Africa Poetry Magazine
Online Magazine
101-5170 Dunster Road, Suite 108, Nanaimo, BC, V9T 6M4
Canada
Tel: +1 (250) 667-7748

info@waxpoetryart.com

http://waxpoetryart.com/africa/

Magazine Publisher: Wax Poetry and Art Network

Poetry > *Any Poetic Form*
  General, and in particular: Africa

How to send: Email

Accepts poetry submissions from poets living in Africa. Read the Submissions page and follow the guidelines to submit.

M014 African American Review
Magazine
United States

aileen.keenan@slu.edu

https://afamreview.org
https://twitter.com/afamreview

Book Publisher: The Johns Hopkins University Press (**P297**)

Fiction > *Short Fiction*: African American

Nonfiction
  Essays: African American; Arts; Culture; Films; Literature; Theatre; Visual Culture
  Interviews: African American
  Reviews: African American; Books
Poetry > *Any Poetic Form*: African American

How to send: Online submission system

Publishes insightful essays on African American literature, theatre, film, the visual

arts, and culture; "Forgotten Manuscript" features; interviews; poetry; fiction; and book reviews.

Editor: Aileen Keenan

M015 Agni
Magazine
Boston University, 236 Bay State Road, Boston, MA 02215
United States

agni@bu.edu

https://agnionline.bu.edu
https://twitter.com/AGNIMagazine
https://facebook.com/agnimag

Fiction > *Short Fiction*

Nonfiction > *Essays*

Poetry > *Any Poetic Form*

Closed to approaches.

Costs: A fee is charged upon submission. $3 submission fee.

Submit one story, one essay, or up to five poems, and wait for reply before sending more. Accepts submissions by post with SASE or via online submission system. No submissions by email. Open to submissions between September 1 and December 15; and between February 15 and May 31.

Editor: Sven Birkerts

M016 Agricultural History
Magazine
Kennesaw State University, Dept. of History and Philosophy, 402 Bartow Ave., Kennesaw, GA 30144
United States

aghistory@kennesaw.edu

https://www.aghistorysociety.org/the-journal
https://read.dukeupress.edu/agricultural-history/pages/Submission_Guidelines
https://mc04.manuscriptcentral.com/aghistory

ACADEMIC > **Nonfiction** > *Articles*
  Agriculture; History

Send: Full text

Publishes articles on all aspects of the history of agriculture and rural life with no geographical or temporal limits. Submit via online submission system. See website for full guidelines.

Editor: Albert Way

M017 Air & Space Quarterly
Magazine
United States

https://airandspace.si.edu/air-and-space-quarterly

Magazine Publisher / Book Publisher: Smithsonian Institution

Nonfiction > *Articles*
Aviation; Military Aviation; Space

Magazine exploring topics in aviation and space, from the earliest moments of flight to today.

M018 Alaska Quarterly Review
Magazine
United States

https://aqreview.org
https://alaskaquarterlyreview.submittable.com/submit
https://www.facebook.com/AlaskaQuarterlyReview/
https://www.youtube.com/channel/UCvtOaG2FJ7tuEs8Vsd-rbFQ
https://twitter.com/AQReview

Fiction
Novel Excerpts: Experimental; Traditional
Novellas: Experimental; Traditional
Short Fiction: Experimental; Traditional
Nonfiction > *Short Nonfiction*
Experimental; Literary; Traditional

Poetry > *Any Poetic Form*
Experimental; Traditional

Scripts > *Theatre Scripts*
Drama; Experimental; Traditional

Closed to approaches.

Costs: A fee is charged upon submission. $3 submission fee.

The editors invite submissions of fiction, short plays, poetry, photo essays, and literary nonfiction in traditional and experimental styles.

M019 Aleph
Magazine
The Sidney M. Edelstein Center, The Hebrew University of Jerusalem, Givat Ram, 91904 Jerusalem
Israel
Tel: +972.2.658.56
Fax: +972.2.658.67.09

edelstein.aleph@mail.huji.ac.il

https://iupress.org/journals/aleph/

ACADEMIC > **Nonfiction** > *Essays*
History; Judaism; Science

Send: Full text

Magazine devoted to the exploration of the interface between Judaism and science in history.

Editors: Resianne Fontaine; Reimund Leicht

M020 Alfred Hitchcock Mystery Magazine
Magazine
6 Prowitt Street, Norwalk, CT 06855
United States

https://www.alfredhitchcockmysterymagazine.com

Fiction > *Short Fiction*
Courtroom Dramas; Crime; Mystery; Police Procedural; Suspense

How to send: Online submission system

Interested in nearly every kind of mystery: stories of detection of the classic kind, police procedurals, private eye tales, suspense, courtroom dramas, stories of espionage, and so on. Only requirement is that the story be about a crime (or the threat or fear of one).

Editor: Linda Landrigan

M021 Allegro Poetry Magazine
Online Magazine
United Kingdom

https://www.allegropoetry.org

Poetry > *Any Poetic Form*: Contemporary

Send: Full text; Author bio
How to send: In the body of an email

Biannual online poetry magazine. Accepts poetry submissions up to 40 lines by email between June 1 and July 31, and between December 1 and January 31. Each year the March issue is a general issue, and the September issue is a themed one.

M022 Alternatives Journal
Magazine
PO Box 26016 College PO, Kitchener ON N2G 0A4
Canada
Tel: +1 (519) 578-2327

https://www.alternativesjournal.ca
http://twitter.com/AlternativesJ
https://www.youtube.com/user/alternativesjournal
https://www.facebook.com/AlternativesJ

Nonfiction > *Articles*
Environment; Sustainable Living

Publishes features, articles, and news on environmental action and ideas.

M023 American Book Review
Magazine
United States
Tel: +1 (361) 248-8245

americanbookreview@gmail.com

https://www.americanbookreview.org
https://www.facebook.com/AmBookRev
https://www.youtube.com/user/AmericanBookReview

Book Publisher: University of Nebraska Press

Nonfiction > *Reviews*
Cultural Criticism; Fiction as a Subject; Literary Criticism; Poetry as a Subject

Closed to approaches.

Specializes in reviews of frequently neglected works of fiction, poetry, and literary and cultural criticism from small, regional, university, ethnic, avant-garde, and women's presses. In nonfiction, reviews important books of criticism, biographies, and cultural studies. No reviews of "how-to" or "self-help" books. Would consider a review of innovative children's literature, but not usually part of the preferred content. Prefers books that have been published in the past six months, but will review books that have been published in the past year. No unsolicited reviews.

M024 American Heritage
Online Magazine
United States

https://www.americanheritage.com
https://www.facebook.com/ameriheritage/
https://twitter.com/AmeriHeritage

Nonfiction > *Articles*
American History; Culture; Travel; United States

Magazine of American history, travel, food and culture. Originally a print magazine, now an online magazine as of 2017.

Editor: Richard Snow

M025 Amethyst Review
Online Magazine
United Kingdom

editor@amethystmagazine.org
Sarah.Poet@gmail.com

https://amethystmagazine.org
https://www.facebook.com/AmethystReview/

Fiction > *Short Fiction*: Spirituality

Nonfiction > *Short Nonfiction*: Spirituality

Poetry > *Any Poetic Form*: Spirituality

Send: Full text; Author bio
How to send: Word file email attachment; In the body of an email

Publishes work that engages in some way with spirituality or the sacred. Submit up to five poems (of any length) and / or prose pieces of up to 2,000 words. Simultaneous submissions if notification of acceptance elsewhere is provided. No previously published work. Send submissions by email with author bio of around 50 words. See website for full guidelines.

Editor: Sarah Law

M026 And Magazine
Magazine
India

https://andmagazine824063762.wordpress.com

Fiction > *Short Fiction*: Literary

Nonfiction > *Articles*

Poetry > *Any Poetic Form*

Send your best work poems, article, essay, paper, artwork in MS word file and images in jpeg format by email.

All the accepted accepted works will be published with ISBN No. and will available in major bookstores worldwide.

M027 Angela Poetry Magazine
Online Magazine
Wax Poetry and Art, Attn: Angela Poetry Magazine, 101-5170 Dunster Road, Suite 108, Nanaimo, BC, V9T 6M4,
Canada
Tel: +1 (250) 667-7748

info@waxpoetryart.com

http://waxpoetryart.com/angela/

Magazine Publisher: Wax Poetry and Art Network

Poetry > *Any Poetic Form*: Contemporary

How to send: Email

Accepts poetry submissions from everyone on Earth and orbiting spacecraft. Publishes poems that are curious, humorous, and generally on the lighter side of life. Read the Submissions page and follow the guidelines to submit.

M028 The Antigonish Review
Magazine
PO Box 5000, Antigonish, Nova Scotia, B2G 2W5
Canada
Tel: +1 (902) 867-3962
Fax: +1 (902) 867-5563

tar@stfx.ca

https://antigonishreview.com
https://twitter.com/antigonishrevie
https://www.facebook.com/The-Antigonish-Review-332083480162513/
https://www.linkedin.com/in/the-antigonish-review-7602052a

Fiction in Translation > *Short Fiction*: Literary

Fiction > *Short Fiction*: Literary

Nonfiction > *Essays*
   Creative Nonfiction; Culture; History; Memoir; Sport; Travel

Poetry in Translation > *Any Poetic Form*

Poetry > *Any Poetic Form*

Send: Full text
How to send: Submittable
How not to send: Post; Email

Costs: A fee is charged upon submission. $5 for prose; $3 for poetry.

Submit via online portal only. Submit no more than 2-3 poems (or 3-4 pages of poetry) and submit no more till a response is received. Considers poetry on any subject written from

any point of view and in any form. For fiction, send only one story at a time. Also publishes poetry and prose translated into English from other languages (be sure to indicate source language). Also considers critical articles and essays that are fresh, vigorous, and free from jargon. Welcomes creative nonfiction. No email submissions, postal submissions, or simultaneous submissions.

M029 The Antioch Review
Magazine
One Morgan Place, Yellow Springs, OH 45387
United States
Tel: +1 (937) 769-1365

review@antiochcollege.edu

http://review.antiochcollege.org

Fiction > *Short Fiction*

Nonfiction
   Essays: General
   Reviews: Literature

Poetry > *Any Poetic Form*

Closed to approaches.

Send MS with SASE for return. Strongly encourages potential contributors to buy a sample copy and peruse the magazine before submitting. Considers fiction from September 1 to May 31 only, and accepts poetry from September 1 to April 30 only. Do not mix poetry and prose submissions in the same envelope. No email submissions or unsolicited book reviews.

M030 The Architectural Review
Magazine
15 Bouverie Street, London, EC4Y 8DP
United Kingdom
Tel: +44 (0) 20 3953 2000

https://www.architectural-review.com

Magazine Publisher: EMAP Publishing

PROFESSIONAL > **Nonfiction** > *Articles*
   Architecture; Design

Magazine of architecture and design aimed at professionals.

Editor: Paul Finch

M031 Art Monthly
Magazine
Peveril Garden Studios, 140 Great Dover Street, London, SE1 4GW
United Kingdom
Tel: +44 (0) 20 7240 0389

info@artmonthly.co.uk

http://www.artmonthly.co.uk
https://www.twitter.com/artmonthly
https://www.facebook.com/artmonthly
https://instagram.com/art_monthly_uk

Nonfiction

Articles: Arts
Interviews: Arts
Reviews: Arts

Magazine of contemporary visual art. Publishes in-depth features, interviews with artists, profiles on emerging artists and coverage of major trends and developments by independent critics.

M032 Art Papers
Magazine
PO Box 5748, Atlanta, GA 31107
United States
Tel: +1 (404) 588-1837
Fax: +1 (678) 999-7002

editor@artpapers.org
info@artpapers.org

https://www.artpapers.org
https://www.facebook.com/artpapers
https://twitter.com/artpapers
https://www.instagram.com/artpapers/

Nonfiction > *Articles*
   Arts; Contemporary; Culture

The independent critical voice covering contemporary art and culture in the world today.

M033 Art Quarterly
Magazine
PO Box 4387, Chippenham, SN15 9NY
United Kingdom
Tel: +44 (0) 20 3757 9772

artquarterly@artfund.org

https://www.artfund.org/about-us/art-quarterly

Nonfiction > *Articles*: Arts

Arts magazine publishing features on artists, galleries and museums.

M034 Art Times Journal
Online Magazine
PO Box 730, Mount Marion, NY 12456
United States
Tel: +1 (914) 246-6944
Fax: +1 (914) 246-6944

info@arttimesjournal.com

https://www.arttimesjournal.com
http://www.youtube.com/user/arttimes
https://facebook.com/ArtTimesJournal
https://twitter.com/ARTTIMESjournal
https://www.instagram.com/arttimesjournal/

Fiction > *Short Fiction*: Literary

Nonfiction > *Articles*
   Arts; Culture

Poetry > *Any Poetic Form*

Send: Full text
How to send: Email

Formerly a print journal, online-only since 2016. Publishes articles on arts and culture, literary fiction, poetry, and opinion pieces relating to creativity and the arts. Send submissions by email. See website for full guidelines.

M035 The Artist
Magazine
The Maltings, West Street, Bourne, Lincolnshire, PE10 9PH
United Kingdom
Tel: +44 (0) 1580 763673

https://www.painters-online.co.uk
https://www.facebook.com/paintersonline
https://twitter.com/artpublishing
https://www.instagram.com/paintersonline/
https://www.pinterest.co.uk/paintersonline/

Magazine Publisher: Warners Group Publications

Nonfiction > *Articles*: Arts

Written by artists for artists, since 1931, this magazine has inspired generations of passionate, practising artists from experienced amateur up to professionals, with practical painting and drawing articles and projects, designed to improve painting technique.

Editor: Sally Bulgin

M036 ARTmosterrific
Online Magazine
19 Ila-Orangun Street, Ketu
Nigeria
Tel: 08164187014

dhadarms@gmail.com
Prose@artmosterrific.com
Editor@artmosterrific.com
Poetry@artmosterrific.com

https://artmosterrific.com
https://facebook.com/artmosterrific
https://twitter.com/artmosterrific
https://instagram.com/_artmosterrific
https://duotrope.com/listing/31866/artmosterrific-magazine

Fiction > *Short Fiction*

Nonfiction > *Essays*
Contemporary; Personal Essays

Poetry > *Any Poetic Form*

Closed to approaches.

An online platform and community by and for African undergraduates. It runs on five sections, all different and independent from one another: Virtual residence where 3 college writers are mentored to complete a book of art; the African Prize for Undergraduates awarded every year to an African undergraduate; the Biannual Chapbook that works as an anthology, exploring thematic issues in society, the Online Issue/Mag (Prose, Poetry, Essay, Photography), and the Community (with webinars, Book Chat, Bookstore, Physical Conference, etc). Check our submission page

for detailed information on each section, and feel free to subscribe to our newsletter.

Editorial Calendar

Issue Submission (January — February)

Virtual Residence (March — April)

Chapbook Submission (May — June)

Funso Oris Prize / African Prize For Undergraduates (June — July)

ISSUE SUBMISSION (August — September)

CHAPBOOK SUBMISSION (October — November)

Dates and time for community programmes, such as the book chat, webinar, undergraduate-led auditorium conference, are subject to factors.

A literary publication that features fiction, poetry, creative nonfiction, and photography for everything that makes you sleep, keeps you awake, breaks your heart and repairs it. Everything that rusts and unrusts you. Send us your flaws and strengths, awesome and bizarre, brilliant and outrageous. However, please note that while we accept all submissions, we are especially on the lookout for works by African undergraduates. Send us your terrific work anyways!

M037 Asimov's Science Fiction
Magazine
United States

asimovs@dellmagazines.com

https://www.asimovs.com
http://asimovs.magazinesubmissions.com/

Magazine Publisher: Dell Magazines

Fiction > *Short Fiction*
Fantasy; Science Fiction; Slipstream; Surreal

Poetry > *Any Poetic Form*
Fantasy; Science Fiction; Slipstream; Surreal

Does not want:

> **Fiction** > *Short Fiction*: Sword and Sorcery

How to send: Online submission system; Post

Seeks serious, character-orientated science fiction and (borderline) fantasy, slipstream, and surreal. The characters should always be the main focus, rather than the science. Humour will be considered. No simultaneous submissions, sword-and-sorcery, horror, explicit sex, violence, or works written, developed, or assisted by AI.

M038 Astronomy Now
Magazine
United Kingdom

https://astronomynow.com

Nonfiction
Articles: Astronomy
News: Astronomy

The UK's biggest astronomy magazine. Since 1987 it has been essential reading for astronomers in the UK and around the world. Each month, the magazine contains features, reviews, news and practical guides on all aspects of astronomy, from the latest scientific discoveries to advice for those discovering the night sky for the first time.

M039 Atlanta Magazine
Magazine
5901-A Peachtree Dunwoody Rd NE, Suite 350, Atlanta, GA 30328
United States
Tel: +1 (404) 527-5500

https://www.atlantamagazine.com
https://www.facebook.com/atlantamag
http://instagram.com/atlantamagazine
https://www.linkedin.com/company/atlantamagazine
https://twitter.com/atlantamagazine

Nonfiction
Articles: Arts; Atlanta; Culture; Design; Food and Drink; Gardening; Health; Lifestyle; Property / Real Estate; Travel; Wellbeing
News: Atlanta

Send: Query
How to send: Email

We focus on Atlanta and the metro region. We're looking for stories that haven't been told before, that help us see the city, the state, the region, and ourselves in new ways.

M040 Atlanta Review
Magazine
Suite 333, 686 Cherry St. NW, Atlanta, GA 30332-0161
United States

atlantareview@gatech.edu

http://atlantareview.com
https://atlantareview.submittable.com/submit
https://twitter.com/ATLReview
https://www.facebook.com/atlantareview
https://www.instagram.com/atlantareviewpojo/

Poetry > *Any Poetic Form*

Closed to approaches.

Costs: A fee is charged for online submissions. $3. Also runs competitions for which a fee is charged.

Accepts submissions of poetry between January 1 and June 1, and between September 15 and December 1. Submit online ($3 submission fee) or by post with SASE. Also runs competitions.

M041 Atlantic Northeast
Magazine
United States

https://atlanticnortheastmag.com
https://www.instagram.com/atlanticnemag/
https://twitter.com/AtlanticNEMag

Fiction > *Short Fiction*
  Atlantic Northeast; Culture; History

Nonfiction > *Short Nonfiction*
  Atlantic Northeast; Creative Nonfiction;
  Culture; History

Closed to approaches.

A magazine dedicated to exploring the history, culture, and spirit of the Northeastern United States and Canada.

M042 Atrium
Online Magazine
Worcestershire
United Kingdom

https://atriumpoetry.com
https://www.facebook.com/AtriumPoetry
https://twitter.com/Atrium_Poetry

Poetry > *Any Poetic Form*

Closed to approaches.

A poetry webzine based in Worcestershire, UK. A new poem is published twice a week, on Tuesdays and Fridays. Aims to publish poems that allow readers to think, feel and see things in a new way.

M043 Auroras & Blossoms PoArtMo Anthology
Online Magazine
United Kingdom

submissions@abpositiveart.com

https://abpositiveart.com
https://www.facebook.com/abpositiveart
https://twitter.com/ab_positiveart
https://www.youtube.com/channel/UCkAh-EnwcJbd865SEXJQsEw

ADULT
  Fiction > *Short Fiction*
  Nonfiction > *Essays*

TEEN
  Fiction > *Short Fiction*
  Nonfiction > *Essays*

Send: Query; Author bio; Writing sample
How to send: Email

Annual anthology sold in ebook format.

Editors / Poets: David Ellis; Cendrine Marrouat

M044 Authentic Shorts
Online Magazine
United Kingdom

enquiries@integrity-media.co.uk

http://integrity-media.co.uk

Book Publisher: Integrity Media (**P287**)

Send: Query; Outline; Full text
How to send: Email

An online platform for publishing short stories. We are open minded with regard to the subject of short stories and will consider submissions across all genres.

There is no perfect length for a short story, only the author can decide, but we would expect them to be no more than 7,000 to 8,000 words. This will allow them to be adaptable for online publication, either as a serialisation or under small collections of aligned works.

M045 Aviation News
Magazine
United Kingdom

https://www.key.aero/aviationnews

Magazine Publisher: Key Publishing

Nonfiction
  Articles: Aviation
  News: Aviation

Publishes news and features related to aviation, including military, civil, business, historical, contemporary, aircraft, airports, and equipment.

Editor: Jamie Ewan

M046 Awen
Magazine
Atlantean Publishing, 4 Pierrot Steps, 71 Kursaal Way, Southend-on-Sea, Essex, SS1 2UY
United Kingdom

atlanteanpublishing@hotmail.com

http://atlanteanpublishing.wikia.com/wiki/Awen
https://atlanteanpublishing.wordpress.com/guidelines/

Book Publisher / Magazine Publisher:
Atlantean Publishing (**P044**)

Fiction > *Short Fiction*

Poetry > *Any Poetic Form*

How to send: Email; Post

Now normally eight A4 sides in length, it contains poetry and short prose fiction and has appeared four times a year since 2013. Submit by post or by email.

Editor: David-John Tyrer

M047 Babybug
Magazine
United States

https://cricketmedia.com
https://cricketmedia.com/babybug-submission-guidelines/
https://cricketmag.submittable.com/submit

Magazine Publisher: Cricket Media, Inc.

CHILDREN'S
  Fiction > *Short Fiction*
  Nonfiction > *Short Nonfiction*
  Poetry > *Any Poetic Form*

Send: Full text

Publishes poetry, stories, and nonfiction (including activities and parent–child interaction) for children aged 6 months to 3 years. Stories should be up to six short sentences; poems should be rhythmic and rhyming and up to eight lines long.

M048 Backcountry Magazine
Magazine
60 Main Street, PO Box 190, Jeffersonville, VT 05464
United States
Tel: +1 (802) 644-6606

https://backcountrymagazine.com

Nonfiction > *Articles*
  Skiing; Snowboarding

Send: Query
How to send: Email

Magazine of skiing and snowboarding. Send query by email.

Editor-in-Chief: Betsy Manero

M049 Bacopa Literary Review
Magazine
United States

https://writersalliance.org/bacopa-literary-review/

Fiction > *Short Fiction*: Literary

Nonfiction > *Short Nonfiction*: Creative Nonfiction

Poetry > *Any Poetic Form*

Closed to approaches.

Annual print journal publishing short stories, creative nonfiction, poetry, and prose poetry. Accepts submissions only through free annual contest.

M050 The Baffler
Magazine
234 5th Avenue, New York, NY 10001
United States
Tel: +1 (212) 390-1569

https://thebaffler.com
https://www.facebook.com/TheBafflerMagazine/
https://twitter.com/thebafflermag

Fiction > *Short Fiction*
  Comedy / Humour; Politics; Satire

Nonfiction > *Articles*
  Culture; Left Wing Politics

Poetry > *Any Poetic Form*

Send: Pitch
How to send: Online submission system

Describes itself as "America's leading voice of interesting and unexpected left-wing political criticism, cultural analysis, short stories, poems and art". Submit pitch using online form on website.

M051 Balance

Magazine
Wells Lawrence House, 126 Back Church Lane, London, E1 1FH
United Kingdom
Tel: +44 (0) 3451 232399
Fax: +44 (0) 20 7424 1001

helpline@diabetes.org.uk

https://www.diabetes.org.uk/balance

Nonfiction
 Articles: Diabetes; Exercise; Health; Recipes
 News: Diabetes

News articles and features of interest to people with diabetes.

M052 Bandit Fiction

Online Magazine
United Kingdom

https://banditfiction.com
https://www.facebook.com/banditfiction/
https://twitter.com/BanditFiction
https://www.instagram.com/banditfiction/
https://open.spotify.com/show/
4roZtA65SdavXAwfflm1eE

Fiction > *Short Fiction*

Poetry > *Any Poetic Form*

Entirely not-for-profit and run by a team of passionate volunteers, our community is a place where writers can grow, learn, engage and further themselves in whichever ways they wish. We're always seeking out new avenues to engage readers, from releasing podcasts to working with literary awards, and love to engage our audiences as we move in new and exciting directions. We publish short fiction and poetry direct to our website, free to read.

M053 Banipal

Magazine
1 Gough Square, London, EC4A 3DE
United Kingdom

editor@banipal.co.uk

http://www.banipal.co.uk
https://www.facebook.com/BanipalMagazine/
https://twitter.com/banipalmagazine

Fiction in Translation > *Short Fiction*

Nonfiction
 Interviews: Writing
 Reviews: Books

Poetry in Translation > *Any Poetic Form*

Send: Query
How to send: Email; Post

Contemporary Arab authors in English translations. Publishes new and established writers, and diverse material including translations, poetry, short stories, novel excerpts, profiles, interviews, appreciations, book reviews, reports of literary festivals, conferences, and prizes. Welcomes submissions by post, but queries only by email. Unsolicited email submissions with attachments will be automatically deleted. Response in 3-6 months.

M054 Bard

Magazine
Atlantean Publishing, 4 Pierrot Steps, 71 Kursaal Way, Southend-on-Sea, Essex, SS1 2UY
United Kingdom

atlanteanpublishing@hotmail.com

http://atlanteanpublishing.wikia.com/wiki/Bard
https://atlanteanpublishing.wordpress.com
https://www.facebook.com/groups/
169974286448031/

Book Publisher / Magazine Publisher:
Atlantean Publishing (**P044**)

Poetry > *Any Poetic Form*

Send: Full text; Self-Addressed Stamped Envelope (SASE)
How to send: Post; Email

Flyer-style broadsheet of poetry released roughly monthly and available for free to subscribers of the publisher's magazines. Occasionally runs themed issues but generally open to any and all poetry. See website for full submission guidelines.

M055 Barren Magazine

Magazine
United States

info@barrenmagazine.com
poetry@barrenmagazine.com
fiction@barrenmagazine.com
flashcnf@barrenmagazine.com
creativenonfiction@barrenmagazine.com

https://barrenmagazine.com
http://twitter.com/BarrenMagazine
http://facebook.com/BarrenMagazine
http://instagram.com/barrenmagazine

Fiction > *Short Fiction*

Nonfiction > *Nonfiction Books*: Creative Nonfiction

Poetry > *Any Poetic Form*

Closed to approaches.

An Alt.Lit Introspective.

A literary publication that features fiction, poetry, creative nonfiction, and photography for hard truths, long stares, and gritty lenses.

We revel in the shadow-spaces that make up the human condition, and aim to find antitheses to that which defines us: light in darkness; beauty in ugliness; peace in disarray. We invite you to explore it with us.

Editor: Jason D. Ramsey

M056 BBC Countryfile Magazine

Magazine
Eagle House, Bristol, BS1 4ST
United Kingdom
Tel: +44 (0) 1173 147399

editor@countryfile.com

http://www.countryfile.com

Nonfiction > *Articles*
 Countryside; Nature

Send: Query
Don't send: Full text

Magazine on British countryside and rural life. Send queries with ideas by email. No unsolicited mss.

Editor: Fergus Collins

M057 BBC Doctor Who Magazine

Print Magazine
United Kingdom

dwm@panini.co.uk

https://doctorwhomagazine.com

Magazine Publisher: Panini UK

CHILDREN'S > **Nonfiction** > *Articles*
 Science Fiction; TV

Magazine for fans of Doctor Who, aged 6-12.

M058 BBC Science Focus

Magazine
Eagle House, Colston Avenue, Bristol, BS1 4ST
United Kingdom
Tel: +44 (0) 1173 008755

editorialenquiries@sciencefocus.com

https://www.sciencefocus.com
https://www.facebook.com/sciencefocus
https://twitter.com/sciencefocus
https://www.instagram.com/bbcsciencefocus
http://uk.pinterest.com/ScienceFocus
https://www.youtube.com/channel/
UCS0P18FM3wfcKIS7Asy6cUQ

Magazine Publisher: Immediate Media Co.

Nonfiction
 Articles: Science
 News: Science

Send: Query
Don't send: Full text
How to send: Email

Publishes news and articles on science and technology. Accepts queries for articles only. Do not send completed articles. Does not accept submissions of news items.

M059 The Beano

Magazine
185 Fleet Street, London, EC4A 2HS
United Kingdom
Tel: +44 (0) 20 7400 1030

hello@beano.com

https://www.beano.com

Newspaper Publisher / Magazine Publisher:
DC Thomson Media

CHILDREN'S > *Fiction* > *Cartoons*: Comedy / Humour

Publishes comic strips for children aged 6-12.

M060 The Bear Deluxe Magazine

Magazine
820 N. River Street, Suite 112, Portland, OR 97227
United States
Tel: +1 (971) 235-2734

thebear@orlo.org
beardeluxe@orlo.org

https://orlo.org
https://www.facebook.com/pages/Bear-Deluxe-Magazine/115925931775159
https://twitter.com/orlobear

Fiction > *Short Fiction*

Nonfiction > *Articles*
   Arts; Culture; Environment

Poetry > *Any Poetic Form*

Send: Full text
How to send: Email

Magazine of the arts, culture and environment. Send submissions by email.

Editor: Tom Webb

M061 Bella

Magazine
The Lantern, 75 Hampstead Road, London, NW1 2PL
United Kingdom

Bella.Hotline@bauermedia.co.uk

https://www.bellamagazine.co.uk
https://twitter.com/#!/bellamagazineUK
http://facebook.com/bellamagazineUK
https://www.instagram.com/bellamagazineuk/

Magazine Publisher: Bauer Media Group

Nonfiction > *Articles*
   Celebrity; Diet; Fashion; Real Life Stories; Travel

Send: Query
How to send: Email

Human interest magazine for women, publishing articles on celebs, diet, style, travel, and real-life stories. Send query by email.

M062 Belmont Story Review

Magazine
United States

belmontstoryreview@gmail.com

https://belmontstoryreview.wixsite.com/website
https://belmontstoryreview.submittable.com/submit

Fiction > *Short Fiction*

Nonfiction > *Short Nonfiction*: Creative Nonfiction

Poetry > *Any Poetic Form*

Closed to approaches.

Established in 2016, the magazine aims to surprise and delight readers through an eclectic mix of storytelling which includes fiction, personal essay, poetry, songwriting, drama, graphic narrative, and photography; as well as creative reportage, including coverage of music, film, creativity and collaboration, and the intersection of faith and culture. "Faith" is not a specific religious perspective but a broad idea of faith is important for all selected publications.

We seek to publish new and established writers passionate about their craft, fearlessly encountering difficult ideas, seeking to explore human experience in all its broken blessedness.

M063 Beloit Fiction Journal

Magazine
Box 11, Beloit College, 700 College Street, Beloit, WI 53511
United States

https://www.beloit.edu/fiction-journal/
https://beloitfictionjournal.submittable.com/submit

Fiction > *Short Fiction*: Literary

Closed to approaches.

Costs: A fee is charged upon submission. $3 per submission.

Open to literary fiction on any subject or theme, up to 13,000 words. Also accepts flash fiction. Showcases new writers as well as established writers. Simultaneous submissions are accepted.

M064 Best of British

Magazine
2nd Floor, Saunders House, 52-53 The Mall, Ealing, W5 3TA
United Kingdom

https://www.bestofbritishmag.co.uk
https://www.facebook.com/bestbritishmag/
https://twitter.com/bestofbritishuk

Magazine Publisher: Diamond Publishing

Nonfiction > *Articles*
   History; Nostalgia; United Kingdom

Describes itself as "the UK's premier nostalgia magazine", covering every aspect of life from the 1930s to today.

M065 Better Homes and Gardens

Magazine
United States

bhgeditor@meredith.com

https://www.bhg.com
https://www.facebook.com/mybhg/
https://twitter.com/bhg/
https://www.pinterest.com/bhg/
https://www.instagram.com/betterhomesandgardens/

Magazine Publisher: Dotdash Meredith

Nonfiction > *Articles*
   Cookery; Gardening; Home Improvement; Recipes

The fourth best-selling magazine in the United States. Publishes articles on gardening, home improvement, cleaning and organizing, and cooking and recipes.

M066 Better Than Starbucks

Magazine
PO Box 673, Mayo, FL 32066
United States
Tel: +1 (561) 719-8627

betterthanstarbucks2@gmail.com

https://www.betterthanstarbucks.org

ADULT
   Fiction > *Short Fiction*

   Nonfiction > *Short Nonfiction*: Creative Nonfiction

   Poetry in Translation > *Any Poetic Form*

   Poetry
      Any Poetic Form: Africa; Comedy / Humour; International
      Experimental Poetry: General
      Formal Poetry: General
      Free Verse: General
      Haiku: General
      Prose Poetry: General

CHILDREN'S > *Poetry* > *Any Poetic Form*

Closed to approaches.

Publishes African Poetry, International Poetry, Prose Poetry, Forms as well as Formal Poetry, Poetry Translations, Experimental Poetry and poetry for children. Encourages sentiment in poetry. Also publishes Fiction, Flash Fiction, Micro Fiction and Creative Nonfiction. Submitted opinion pieces will be considered.

Editor: Vera Ignatowitsch

M067 BFS Horizons
Magazine
United Kingdom

bfshorizons@britishfantasysociety.org
poetry@britishfantasysociety.org

https://www.britishfantasysociety.org/bfs-horizons/

Association: The British Fantasy Society

Fiction > *Short Fiction*
  Fantasy; Horror; Science Fiction; Sword and Sorcery

Poetry > *Any Poetic Form*
  Fantasy; Horror; Science Fiction; Sword and Sorcery

Send: Full text; Author bio
How to send: Word file email attachment; In the body of an email

Biannual fantasy journal of fiction and poetry, published in print and ebook formats. Features a mix of work from new and established writers. Mainly looking for stories of up to 5000 words, but will consider more. Authors don't have to be British, but prefers if stories have a thread linking it to these isles. Definition of 'fantasy' is broad, encapsulating weird fiction, swords and sorcery, science fiction and all varieties of horror. Accepts poetry in any form, up to 36 lines. Not keen on seeing rhyming poetry in iambic pentameter, but would be interested in sonnets, Villanelles, Rondeaus, or other forms. Lengthy poems or sagas will be considered, but should be submitted according to the guidelines for fiction. See website for full guidelines.

M068 BFS Journal
Magazine
United Kingdom

bfsjournal@britishfantasysociety.org

https://www.britishfantasysociety.org/
https://www.britishfantasysociety.org/bfs-journal/
https://twitter.com/BritFantasySoc

Association: The British Fantasy Society

ACADEMIC > **Nonfiction** > *Articles*: Fantasy

ADULT > **Nonfiction**
  Articles: Fantasy
  Interviews: Fantasy
  Reviews: Fantasy

How to send: Email

Fantasy journal devoted to non-fiction: interviews, academic articles, reviews and features.

M069 Bike Magazine
Magazine
United Kingdom

https://www.bikemagazine.co.uk
https://www.facebook.com/bikemagazineUK
https://twitter.com/BikeMagazine

Magazine Publisher: Bauer Media Group

Nonfiction > *Articles*: Motorbikes

Your definitive guide to the world of motorcycling. Every issue features incredible motorcycling travel stories from our team and readers with amazing adventures and epic photography. Plus there's expert opinion on all the new motorcycles available in the UK, giving you all the details you need to choose your next bike.

M070 Birds & Blooms
Magazine
1610 North 2nd Street, Suite 102, Milwaukee, WI 53212
United States

customercare@birdsandblooms.com

https://www.birdsandblooms.com
https://www.facebook.com/BirdsBlooms
https://twitter.com/birdsblooms
https://www.pinterest.com/birdsblooms/
https://www.instagram.com/birdsblooms/

Nonfiction > *Articles*
  Birds; Gardening

Send: Full text
How to send: Online submission system

Magazine for backyard / bird enthusiasts, covering how to improve your garden and attract birds. Conversational tone.

M071 Black Belt
Magazine
United States

https://blackbeltmag.com
https://www.instagram.com/blackbeltmag/
https://twitter.com/black_belt_mag
https://www.facebook.com/BlackBeltMagazine/
https://www.linkedin.com/company/black-belt-magazine/

Nonfiction > *Articles*: Martial Arts

Magazine on martial arts for the experienced and inexperienced alike.

Editor-in-Chief: Robert Young

M072 Black Moon Magazine
Online Magazine
United States

blackmoonmageditors@gmail.com

http://www.blackmoonmag.com
https://www.facebook.com/BlackMoonMagazine
https://www.instagram.com/black.moon.mag/
https://twitter.com/Black_Moon_Mag

Fiction > *Short Fiction*

Nonfiction
  Interviews: Literature
  Reviews: Books

Poetry > *Any Poetic Form*

Send: Full text; Query; Author bio
How to send: Email attachment

Submit up to three short stories between 1,000 and 8,000 words, or up to five poems of up to five pages each. Also accepts book reviews and interviews with professionals in the writing community for online publication.

M073 Black Static
Magazine
United Kingdom

blackstatic@ttapress.com

http://ttapress.com/blackstatic/

Magazine Publisher / Book Publisher: TTA Press (**P527**)

Fiction > *Short Fiction*
  Dark; Horror

Closed to approaches.

Always open to unsolicited submissions of new dark/horror stories up to a maximum of 10,000 words.

Editor: Andy Cox

M074 Black Warrior Review
Magazine
United States

blackwarriorreview@gmail.com
fiction.bwr@gmail.com
poetry.bwr@gmail.com
nonfiction.bwr@gmail.com

https://bwr.ua.edu
https://www.facebook.com/pages/Black-Warrior-Review/335215809212
https://twitter.com/BlackWarriorRev

Fiction
  Cartoons: General
  Short Fiction: General, and in particular: Experimental
Nonfiction
  Graphic Nonfiction; *Short Nonfiction*
Poetry
  Any Poetic Form; *Visual Poetry*

How to send: Submittable; Email

Costs: A fee is charged upon submission. $3. Black, indigenous, and incarcerated writers may submit by email for free.

Accepts short stories and nonfiction up to 7,000 words, or submit up to five poems up to 10 pages total. Accepts work that takes risk or is experimental, in lieu of convention and/or grammatical cleanliness. Seeks nonfiction pieces outside western traditions; pieces that defy any such categorization. Welcomes submissions of striking visual narratives (think: graphic novel or memoir in short form).

Online Magazine: Boyfriend Village (**M080**)

M075 Blue Collar Review
Magazine
PO 11417, Norfolk, VA 23517
United States

red-ink@earthlink.net

https://www.partisanpress.org

Book Publisher: Partisan Press (**P401**)

Fiction > *Short Fiction*: Working Class

Nonfiction
 Essays: Culture; Working Class
 Reviews: General

Poetry > *Any Poetic Form*: Working Class

Send: Full text; Self-Addressed Stamped
Envelope (SASE)

Magazine that aims to "expand and promote a
progressive working class vision of culture that
inspires us and that moves us forward as a
class". Submit up to five poems or short
stories, essays, or reviews up to 1,000 words
by post with SASE for response.

M076 Blue Earth Review
Magazine
230 Armstrong Hall, Minnesota State
University, Mankato, Mankato, MN 56001
United States

blueearthreview@gmail.com

https://blueearthreview.mnsu.edu
https://www.facebook.com/
thebluearthreview/
https://twitter.com/BlueEarthReview

Fiction > *Short Fiction*

Nonfiction
 Essays: Personal Essays
 Short Nonfiction: Creative Nonfiction;
Memoir
Poetry > *Any Poetic Form*

Send: Full text
How to send: Submittable

Publishes fiction, creative nonfiction and
poetry. Interested in creative nonfiction
(memoir and personal essay) with
contemporary themes. No literary criticism.
Submit up to five poems at a time.

M077 Bluegrass Unlimited
Magazine
311 W 2nd St, Owensboro, KY 42301
United States
Tel: +1 (800) 258-4727

https://www.bluegrassunlimited.com
https://www.facebook.com/
BluegrassUnlimited/
https://www.instagram.com/
bluegrassunlimited/
https://twitter.com/bgunlimitedmag

https://www.youtube.com/channel/
UCxNYVomNcDI-5mrOy3KgoHA

Nonfiction
 Articles: Bluegrass
 Interviews: Bluegrass
 News: Bluegrass
 Reviews: Bluegrass

A print magazine that has been dedicated to the
furtherance of bluegrass music for over 50
years.

Managing Editor: Dan Miller

M078 Booklaunch
Magazine
12 Wellfield Avenue, London, N10 2EA,
United Kingdom

book@booklaunch.london

https://www.booklaunch.london
https://www.facebook.com/booklaunch.
london/
https://twitter.com/booklaunch_ldn
https://www.youtube.com/channel/
UCNQfRhWa8DdObMJ9xxxvveA/videos
https://www.instagram.com/
booklaunchlondon/

Fiction > *Novel Excerpts*

Nonfiction > *Book Extracts*

Poetry > *Book Extracts*

Does not want:

> **Fiction** > *Novel Excerpts*
> Erotic; Fantasy; Gothic; Romance;
> Suspense; Westerns
>
> **Nonfiction** > *Nonfiction Books*
> Hobbies; How To; Leisure; New Age;
> Self Help; Spirituality

Send: Full text
How to send: PDF file email attachment

Costs: A fee is charged for publication.

Carries extracts from new and newish books.
Its editorial balance is largely towards nonfiction but also accepts novels and poetry. (See
past issues on website.) Tabloid format with
space for approx 1,600 words per page. Does
not run extracts at less than a page. Charges for
inclusion. Has the largest print run of any
books magazine in the UK. Page rate a fifth of
that of rival publications. Uploads and archives
every print edition. Helps its authors to record
audio tracks to its YouTube channel. Contact
by email for ratecard.

M079 The Bookseller
Magazine
47 Bermondsey Street, London, SE1 3XT
United Kingdom
Tel: +44 (0) 20 7403 1818

https://www.thebookseller.com
http://twitter.com/thebookseller

http://www.facebook.com/
TheBooksellerMagazine
http://www.linkedin.com/company/the-
bookseller-magazine
https://www.instagram.com/_thebookseller/
https://www.youtube.com/channel/
UCF5SoBkJKDO9CXtmr1eGW9Q

Magazine Publisher: The Stage Media
Company Ltd

PROFESSIONAL > **Nonfiction** > *Articles*
 Book Publishing; Books

Magazine for the book business covering
publishing, the book trade, retail, and libraries,
publishing trade news and features.

M080 Boyfriend Village
Online Magazine
United States

https://bwr.ua.edu/about-boyfriend-village/

Magazine: Black Warrior Review (**M074**)

Fiction > *Short Fiction*

Nonfiction > *Short Nonfiction*

Poetry > *Any Poetic Form*

Closed to approaches.

Costs: A fee is charged upon submission. $3.

There is one submission category for all
genres. Accepts fiction, poetry, nonfiction,
hybrid, visual and multimedia art, as well as
sound collage, video, games, and more.

M081 Brick
Magazine
P.O. Box 609, STN P, Toronto, ON, M5S 2Y4
Canada

info@brickmag.com

https://brickmag.com/
https://brickmag.submittable.com/submit
https://twitter.com/brickMAG
https://facebook.com/brickmagazine
https://instagram.com/brickliterary

Nonfiction
 Essays: Arts; City and Town Planning;
Dance; Food; History; Literature; Music;
Photography; Science; Sport; Travel; Writing
 Interviews: Arts; Literature; Performing Arts
 Short Nonfiction: Literary; Memoir

Closed to approaches.

Send entire submission in first instance. Please
read magazine before submitting. Accepts
unsolicited nonfiction submissions on a variety
of subjects during April and October each year.
No unsolicited fiction or poetry.

M082 Britain Magazine
Magazine
The Chelsea Magazine Company, Jubilee
House, 2 Jubilee Place, London, SW3 3QW

United Kingdom
Tel: +44 (0) 20 7349 3700

editor@britain-magazine.co.uk

https://www.britain-magazine.com
https://www.facebook.com/BritainMagazine/
https://www.instagram.com/britain_magazine/
https://twitter.com/BritainMagazine

Magazine Publisher: The Chelsea Magazine
Company

Nonfiction > *Articles*
  Culture; History; Nature; Royalty; Travel;
  United Kingdom

Magazine of UK travel, culture, heritage and
style, and the go-to publication for visitors
fascinated by British history. Each issue is
packed with tales of kings and queens, heroes
and villains and the stories behind British
castles, cathedrals, stately homes and gardens,
countryside, and coastline.

M083 Brush Talks
Magazine
United States

editor@brushtalks.com

http://www.brushtalks.com
https://twitter.com/BrushTalks

Nonfiction > *Essays*
  Arts; China; Culture; History; Memoir;
  Narrative Nonfiction; Science; Technology;
  Travel

Poetry in Translation > *Any Poetic
Form*: China

Poetry > *Any Poetic Form*: China

Send: Full text
How to send: Email attachment

A journal of creative nonfiction, photography,
and poetry related to China. Articles can take
many forms: general essays, travel essays,
profiles, memoir, and narrative nonfiction. We
seek submissions about places, people, history,
culture, the arts, science and technology —
anything related to China that is well written,
creative, and true (we do not publish fiction).
Rolling submissions, no fee. Please visit our
website for more information and read the
guidelines before submitting.

M084 Business London
Magazine
210 Dundas St., Suite 201, London, ON N6A
5J3
Canada

https://lfpress.com/category/business-london/

Media Company: The London Free Press

PROFESSIONAL > **Nonfiction** > *Articles*: B
usiness

Business magazine for southwestern Ontario.

Managing Editor: Madisyn Latham

M085 Business Traveller
Magazine
10 John Street, London, WC1N 2EB
United Kingdom
Tel: +44 (0) 20 7821 2700

editorial@businesstraveller.com
enquiries@panaceapublishing.com

https://www.businesstraveller.com
https://www.linkedin.com/groups/2136397
https://www.facebook.com/BusinessTraveller
https://www.twitter.com/BTUK
https://www.instagram.com/
businesstravelleruk/

Nonfiction > *Articles*
  Business; Travel

The leading magazine around the world for the
frequent corporate traveller. A consumer
publication, it is aimed at entertaining business
travellers, saving them money and making
their travelling life easier. Each edition is
packed with editorial on the latest news about
airlines, airports, hotels and car rental.

Editor: Tom Otley

M086 Buttered Toast
Magazine
United States

https://www.toadhalleditions.ink/buttered-toast

*Book Publisher / Self Publishing Service /
Magazine Publisher*: Toad Hall Editions
(P517)

CHILDREN'S
  Fiction > *Short Fiction*

  Nonfiction
    Essays: General
    Short Nonfiction: Creative Nonfiction

  Poetry > *Any Poetic Form*

Annual journal publishing work by and for
young people up to 18 years old.

M087 Cahoodaloodaling
Magazine
United States

cahoodaloodaling@gmail.com

https://cahoodaloodaling.com
https://cahoodaloodaling.submittable.com/
submit

Fiction > *Short Fiction*

Nonfiction
  Articles: Publishing; Writing
  Essays: Publishing; Writing
  Interviews: General
  Reviews: Books

Poetry > *Any Poetic Form*

Closed to approaches.

Themed triannual journal, publishing poetry,
fiction, and articles and essays that are either
about writing and publishing, or match the

current submission call. See website for
upcoming themes, and to submit via online
submission system. If you would like your
book reviewing, query by email with a brief
sample.

Editor: Raquel Thorne

M088 Cambridgeshire Pride
Magazine
United Kingdom
Tel: +44 (0) 1733 242312

info@pridepublications.co.uk

http://www.pridepublications.co.uk
https://sites.google.com/view/
pridepublications/home/cambridgeshire-pride

Magazine Publisher: Pride Publications

Nonfiction
  Articles: Business; Cambridgeshire;
  Education; Fashion; Fishing; Food;
  Gardening; Lifestyle; Music; Travel; Wine
  News: Cambridgeshire
  Reviews: Books

Interested in news and features relating to the
Cambridgeshire UK area in particular.

Editor: Carol Lawless

M089 Campaign
Magazine
Bridge House, 69 London Road, Twickenham,
TW1 3SP
United Kingdom

https://www.campaignlive.co.uk
https://www.facebook.com/campaignmag/
https://twitter.com/campaignmag
https://www.linkedin.com/groups/3614115/
https://www.instagram.com/
campaignmagazine/
https://www.youtube.com/CampaignLiveTV

Magazine Publisher: Haymarket Media Group

PROFESSIONAL > **Nonfiction**
  Articles: Advertising; Business; Marketing;
  Media
  News: Advertising; Business; Marketing;
  Media

Describes itself as the world's leading business
media brand serving the marketing, advertising
and media communities.

Editor: Claire Beale

Editor-in-Chief: Gideon Spanier

M090 Car Mechanics
Magazine
The Granary, Downs Court, Yalding Hill,
Yalding, Maidstone, Kent, ME18 6AL
United Kingdom
Tel: +44 (0) 1959 543747

https://shop.kelsey.co.uk/subscription/CME

Magazine Publisher: Kelsey Media

ADULT > **Nonfiction** > *Articles*
Cars; Engineering

PROFESSIONAL > **Nonfiction** > *Articles*
Cars; Engineering

The UK's only magazine with essential advice on maintaining and repairing popular makes and models of car. If you fancy yourself as a home mechanic, then this is an invaluable motoring resource that appeals to both the DIY car enthusiast and the more experienced motor trade professional.

Editor: Peter Simpson

M091 The Casket of Fictional Delights

Online Magazine
United Kingdom

https://thecasket.co.uk
https://www.facebook.com/casketfiction/
https://twitter.com/casketfiction
https://uk.pinterest.com/thecasket/

Fiction > *Short Fiction*

Send: Full text
How to send: By referral

Online magazine publishing flash fiction and short stories. Submissions by invitation and recommendation only.

Editor: Joanna Sterling

M092 CBeebies Art

Magazine
United Kingdom

https://www.immediate.co.uk/brands/cbeebies-art/

Magazine Publisher: Immediate Media Co.

CHILDREN'S > **Nonfiction** > *Articles*
Arts; Crafts

Packed with hours of craft fun, mini-makers can learn a new art skill every month from collaging, painting, printing, constructing, sticker art and more. With an amazing craft kit to make, plus plenty of art tips to follow and space for crafty kids to make their own creative choices too!

Editor: Hollie Fisher

Publisher: Alex Coates-Newman

M093 Cemetery Dance

Magazine
132-B Industry Lane, Unit 7, Forest Hill, MD 21050
United States
Tel: +1 (410) 588-5901
Fax: +1 (410) 588-5904

info@cemeterydance.com

https://www.cemeterydance.com/
https://www.cemeterydance.com/cemetery-dance-magazine.html

Fiction > *Short Fiction*
Dark; Horror; Mystery; Suspense

Nonfiction
Articles: Dark; Horror; Mystery; Suspense
Interviews: Dark; Horror; Mystery; Suspense
News: Dark; Horror; Mystery; Suspense
Reviews: Dark; Horror; Mystery; Suspense

Closed to approaches.

Publishes horror, dark mystery, crime, and suspense stories which are powerful, emotional, pacy, and original.

Editor: Richard Chizmar

M094 Chapman

Magazine
4 Broughton Place, Edinburgh, EH1 3RX
United Kingdom
Tel: +44 (0) 131 557 2207

chapman-pub@blueyonder.co.uk

http://www.chapman-pub.co.uk

Book Publisher: Chapman Publishing (**P114**)

Fiction > *Short Fiction*: Literary

Nonfiction > *Articles*: Literary Criticism

Poetry > *Any Poetic Form*

Send: Full text; Self-Addressed Stamped Envelope (SASE)
How to send: Post
How not to send: Email

Describes itself as Scotland's leading literary magazine, publishing new creative writing: poetry, fiction, discussion of cultural affairs, theatre, reviews and the arts in general, plus critical essays. It publishes international as well as Scottish writers and is a dynamic force for artistic and cultural change and development. Always open to new writers and ideas.

Fiction may be of any length, but average is around 3,000 words. Send one piece at a time. Poetry submissions should contain between four and ten poems. Single poems are not usually published.

Articles and reviews are usually commissioned and ideas should be discussed with the editor in advance.

All submissions must include an SAE or IRCs or email address for response. No submissions by email.

M095 Charleston Style and Design Magazine

Magazine
United States

https://www.charlestonstyleanddesign.com
https://www.facebook.com/Charleston-Style-Design-Magazine-108903839161607/
https://www.instagram.com/chasstyleanddesign/

https://twitter.com/CharlestonSDMa1
https://www.pinterest.com/charlestonsdmag/

Nonfiction > *Articles*
Architecture; Arts; Design; Fashion; Food; Lifestyle; Travel; Wine

Design and lifestyle magazine for the Lowcountry, covering architects, designers and builders, home projects, lifestyle trends, restaurants, wines, fashions, art galleries, and travel destinations.

Editor: Mary Love

M096 CharlottesvilleFamily

Magazine
4282 Ivy Rd, Charlottesville, VA 22901
United States
Tel: +1 (434) 984-4714

jennifer@ivylifeandstylemedia.com

http://www.charlottesvillefamily.com
https://www.facebook.com/CharlottesvilleFamily
https://twitter.com/ChvilleFamily
https://www.linkedin.com/company/ivylifeandstylemedia/

Magazine Publisher: Ivy Life & Style Media

Nonfiction > *Articles*
Albemarle; Charlottesville; Education; Health; Leisure; Lifestyle; Parenting

Send: Query

An award-winning quarterly magazine dedicated to serving families in Virginia's Charlottesville-Albemarle area with engaging feature stories on parenting, education, health and recreation as well as useful resources designed to help "Make Parenting Easier & Growing Up Fun."

M097 Chautauqua Literary Journal

Magazine
United States

chautauquajournal@gmail.com

https://chautauquajournal.wixsite.com/website
https://chautauqua.submittable.com/submit
https://www.instagram.com/chautauquajournal/
https://www.facebook.com/chautauqualiteraryjournal/
https://twitter.com/chautauqualit
http://chautauqualit.tumblr.com/

Fiction > *Short Fiction*

Nonfiction > *Short Nonfiction*: Creative Nonfiction

Poetry > *Any Poetic Form*

Closed to approaches.

Costs: A fee is charged upon submission. $2 submission fee.

Welcomes unsolicited submissions of poetry, flash, fiction, and creative nonfiction from February 15 to March 15 and from September 1 to September 30.

M098 Cheshire Life

Magazine
United Kingdom

Magazine Publisher: Great British Life

M099 The Cincinnati Review

Magazine
PO Box 210069, Cincinnati, Ohio 45221-0069
United States

editors@cincinnatireview.com

https://www.cincinnatireview.com/
https://facebook.com/CincinnatiReview
https://twitter.com/CincinnReview
https://www.youtube.com/channel/
UCbDPomwAnBAddHtuKKh4HqA

Fiction in Translation > *Short Fiction*: Literary

Fiction > *Short Fiction*: Literary

Nonfiction > *Short Nonfiction*
Creative Nonfiction; Literary

Poetry in Translation > *Any Poetic Form*

Poetry > *Any Poetic Form*

Scripts
Film Scripts; *Theatre Scripts*

How to send: Online submission system

Submit up to ten pages of poetry, up to forty pages of double-spaced fiction, or up to twenty pages of double-spaced literary nonfiction during September, December, or May.. Accepts micro submissions year-round, except when accepting contest submissions.

Editors: Michael Griffith; Kristen Iversen; Rebecca Lindenberg

M100 Climbing

Magazine
United States

https://www.climbing.com
https://www.facebook.com/climbingmagazine
https://twitter.com/climbingmag
https://www.youtube.com/user/
ClimbingMagazine
https://www.instagram.com/climbingmagazine

Magazine Publisher: Outside Interactive Inc.

Nonfiction > *Articles*: Climbing

Climbing photography and writing magazine.

M101 Coal City Review

Magazine
English Department, University of Kansas,
Lawrence KS, 66045
United States

https://coalcity.org
http://www.facebook.com/
CoalCityReviewAndPress/
http://twitter.com/CoalCityReview
http://instagram.com/coalcityreview

Book Publisher / Magazine Publisher: Coal City Press (**P133**)

Fiction > *Short Fiction*

Poetry > *Any Poetic Form*

Send: Full text; Self-Addressed Stamped Envelope (SASE)
How to send: Post
How not to send: Email

Publishes poetry, short stories, and flash fiction. Send up to 6 poems, or one story up to 4,000 words, per year. Submissions by post only, with SASE for reply.

Editor: Brian Daldorph

M102 Cocoa Girl

Print Magazine
United Kingdom

admin@thecocoadream.com

https://www.cocoagirl.com
https://www.instagram.com/cocoagirlmag/

Magazine Publisher: Cocoa Publishing

CHILDREN'S
Nonfiction
Articles: Black People; Culture
Interviews: Black People; Culture
Poetry > *Any Poetic Form*
Black People; Culture

How to send: Email

Magazine for Black girls. This magazine gives Black children a voice whilst educating the community about the Black culture. Filled with inspiring and empowering content for children aged 7-11 years old. Particularly looking for children aged 7-11 to contribute as writers, poets, artists, and young journalists.

M103 The Coil

Online Magazine
United States

https://medium.com/the-coil
https://twitter.com/CoilMag
https://alternatingcurrent.submittable.com/submit

Book Publisher: Alternating Current Press (**P021**)

Fiction
Novel Excerpts: General
Short Fiction: Literary

Nonfiction
Essays; *Interviews*; *Reviews*
Poetry > *Any Poetic Form*
General, and in particular: History

How to send: Submittable

Independent online literary magazine.

M104 Coin News

Magazine
8 Oaktree Place, Manaton Close, Matford Business Park, Exeter, Devon, EX2 8WA
United Kingdom
Tel: +44 (0) 1404 46972

info@tokenpublishing.com

https://www.tokenpublishing.com

Magazine Publisher: Token Publishing

Nonfiction > *Articles*: Numismatics (Coin / Currency Collecting)

Magazine covering coin collecting.

M105 Cola

Print Magazine
United States

https://www.colaliteraryreview.com
https://colaliteraryreview.submittable.com/
submit
https://twitter.com/ColaLitReview

Fiction > *Short Fiction*: Literary

Poetry > *Any Poetic Form*

Closed to approaches.

Costs: A fee is charged upon submission in some cases. $3 submission fee during spring submission period. Autumn submissions are free.

Annual print journal edited by graduate students. Publishes poetry and fiction. Submit 3-5 poems or pieces of flash fiction up to 1,000 words, or a longer short story up to 8,000 words (1,000 words to 5,000 words preferred), via online submission system. See website for full guidelines.

M106 The Comics Journal

Magazine
7563 Lake City Way NE, Seattle, WA 98115
United States

editorial@tcj.com

http://tcj.com

Book Publisher: Fantagraphics

Nonfiction > *Articles*: Comic Books

Send: Pitch
How to send: Email

Journal covering comics as an art form. Send pitch by email with subject line "Submission Inquiry".

M107 Commando

Magazine
185 Fleet Street, London, EC4A 2HS
United Kingdom

generalenquiries@commandomag.com

https://www.commandocomics.com
https://www.facebook.com/Commando-
Comics-168688426504994

Newspaper Publisher / Magazine Publisher:
DC Thomson Media

ADULT > **Fiction** > *Cartoons*
Adventure; Warfare

CHILDREN'S > **Fiction** > *Cartoons*
Adventure; Warfare

YOUNG ADULT > **Fiction** > *Cartoons*
Adventure; Warfare

Publishes stories of action and adventure set in times of war, told in graphic novel format. May be wars of the modern age or ancient wars, or even occasionally wars of the future.

M108 Commonweal
Magazine
475 Riverside Drive, Room 244, New York, NY 10115
United States
Tel: +1 (212) 662-4200

editors@commonwealmagazine.org

https://www.commonwealmagazine.org
https://www.facebook.com/
commonwealmagazine
https://twitter.com/commonwealmag

Nonfiction > *Articles*
Culture; Politics; Religion

Poetry > *Any Poetic Form*

How to send: Submittable

Journal of opinion edited by Catholic lay people. Publishes articles on religion, literature, and the arts. More interested in articles which examine the links between "worldly" concerns and religious beliefs than churchy or devotional pieces. Also publishes poetry.

M109 Computing
Magazine
New London House, 172 Drury Lane, London, WC2B 5QR
United Kingdom
Tel: +44 (0) 20 7484 9744

stuart.sumner@incisivemedia.com

https://www.computing.co.uk
https://www.youtube.com/playlist?list=
PL2k5gwH-
ELDedgZlV4iYGTMJKMvzSLKEA
https://twitter.com/computing_news
https://www.linkedin.com/showcase/
computing--/
https://www.facebook.com/ComputingUK

Magazine Publisher: Incisive Media

PROFESSIONAL > **Nonfiction**
Articles: Computers
News: Computers

Publishes news and articles for IT professionals.

Editor: Bryan Glick

M110 Concho River Review
Magazine
United States

http://www.conchoriverreview.org
https://www.facebook.com/conchoriverreview

Fiction > *Short Fiction*

Nonfiction
Essays: General
Reviews: Books
Short Nonfiction: Creative Nonfiction

Poetry > *Any Poetic Form*

Closed to approaches.

Costs: A fee is charged upon submission. $3 per submission.

Published biannually, welcomes submissions of high-quality fiction, nonfiction, poetry, and book reviews year-round.

Accepts only original work that has not been published previously.

Accepts submissions from writers residing outside the United States, however, international contributors should provide a domestic address to which a contributor's copy can be mailed.

M111 Conjunctions
Magazine
21 East 10th St., #3E, New York, NY 10003
United States

conjunctions@bard.edu

http://www.conjunctions.com
https://conjunctions.submittable.com/submit
http://www.facebook.com/pages/Conjunctions/
133404885505
https://www.instagram.com/_conjunctions/
https://twitter.com/_conjunctions

Fiction > *Short Fiction*: Literary

Nonfiction > *Short Nonfiction*: Creative Nonfiction

Poetry > *Any Poetic Form*

Closed to approaches.

Publishes short and long form fiction, poetry, and creative nonfiction. No academic essays or book reviews. Do not query or send samples – submit complete ms by post with SASE (year-round) or using online submission system (during specific online submission windows in autumn and winter). See website for full guidelines.

Editor: Bradford Morrow

Online Magazine: Conjunctions Online
(**M112**)

M112 Conjunctions Online
Online Magazine
21 E 10th Street, #3E, New York, NY 10003
United States

http://www.conjunctions.com/online/
https://conjunctions.submittable.com/submit
http://www.facebook.com/pages/Conjunctions/
133404885505
https://www.instagram.com/_conjunctions/
https://twitter.com/_conjunctions

Magazine: Conjunctions (**M111**)

Fiction > *Short Fiction*

Nonfiction > *Short Nonfiction*: Creative Nonfiction

Poetry > *Any Poetic Form*

Closed to approaches.

Weekly online magazine. No thematic restrictions. Postal submissions are accepted year-round, but online submissions are open only during specific windows.

M113 Conscience
Magazine
United States

conscience@catholicsforchoice.org

https://www.catholicsforchoice.org/
conscience-magazine/about/
https://twitter.com/Catholic4Choice
https://www.facebook.com/CatholicsforChoice

Nonfiction > *Articles*
Christianity; Feminism; Gender; Politics; Sexuality; Social Issues

How to send: Email

Magazine offers in-depth, cutting-edge coverage of vital contemporary issues, including reproductive rights, sexuality and gender, feminism, the religious right, church and state issues and US politics. Send submissions by email.

M114 The Conversation (UK)
Online Magazine
Shropshire House (4th Floor), 11-20 Capper Street, London, WC1E 6JA
United Kingdom

uk-support@theconversation.com

https://theconversation.com
https://www.facebook.com/ConversationUK
https://twitter.com/ConversationUK
https://www.instagram.com/
theconversationdotcom
https://www.linkedin.com/company/the-
conversation-uk
https://newsie.social/@TheConversationUK

Nonfiction
Articles: Arts; Business; Culture; Economics; Education; Environment; Health; Politics; Science; Society; Technology

News: Arts; Business; Culture; Economics; Education; Environment; Health; Politics; Science; Society; Technology

How to send: Online submission system

Online magazine describing itself as "the world's leading publisher of research-based news and analysis... a unique collaboration between academics and journalists." Publishes news and articles researchers and academics currently employed by a university or research institution. This includes PhD students under supervision, but nor Masters students.

M115 Cornwall Life
Magazine

Magazine Publisher: Archant

M116 The Corridor of Uncertainty
Magazine
United Kingdom

clarky@corridorofuncertainty.com

https://www.corridorofuncertainty.com
https://twitter.com/clarkyfanzine
https://www.facebook.com/groups/10963081916

Nonfiction > *Articles*: Cricket

Unofficial England cricket fanzine.

Editor: James Buttler

M117 Cotswold Life
Magazine
United Kingdom

https://www.greatbritishlife.co.uk/magazines/cotswold/

Magazine Publisher: Great British Life

Nonfiction > *Articles*
Arts; Cotswolds; Countryside; Fashion; Food and Drink; Gardening; History; Interior Design; Property / Real Estate

Publishes articles on Cotswold property, interiors, gardens, arts, heritage, fashion, food & drink and countryside matters.

M118 Country Living
Magazine
House of Hearst, 30 Panton Street, London, SW1Y 4AJ
United Kingdom

https://www.countryliving.com
https://www.facebook.com/countrylivinguk
https://twitter.com/countrylivinguk
https://www.pinterest.com/UKcountryliving/
https://www.instagram.com/countrylivinguk/

Magazine Publisher: Hearst Magazines UK

Nonfiction > *Articles*

Country Lifestyle; Countryside; Crafts; Gardening; Houses; Nature; Recipes; Travel; Wellbeing

Magazine for people who love the country, whether they live in it or not. Includes articles on the countryside, wildlife, conservation, gardens, houses, rural life, etc.

M119 Country Smallholding
Magazine
The Granary, Downs Court, Yalding Hill, Yalding, Kent, ME18 6AL
United Kingdom
Tel: +44 (0) 7725 829575

https://www.countrysmallholding.com/

Magazine Publisher: Kelsey Media

Nonfiction > *Articles*
Country Lifestyle; Countryside; Gardening; Self-Sufficiency; Smallholdings

Magazine for smallholders, small farmers and landowners, and those interested in both rural and urban self-sufficiency.

M120 Crab Orchard Review
Magazine
United States

https://craborchardreview.siu.edu
https://craborchardreview.submittable.com/submit

Fiction > *Short Fiction*

Nonfiction > *Essays*

Poetry > *Any Poetic Form*

Closed to approaches.

Closed to submissions for the foreseeable future following the death of the editor in December 2019. Check website for current status.

M121 Crannog Magazine
Magazine
47 Dominick, St Lower, Galway, H91 X0AP
Ireland

hello@crannogmagazine.com

https://crannogmagazine.com
https://twitter.com/crannogm
https://www.facebook.com/crannogmagazine/

Book Publisher / Magazine Publisher: Wordsonthestreet (**P595**)

Fiction > *Short Fiction*: Literary

Poetry > *Any Poetic Form*

Send: Full text; Author bio
How to send: Online submission system
How not to send: Post

Costs: A purchase is required. Authors who have not previously been published in the magazine must purchase the current issue before submitting.

A literary magazine publishing fiction and poetry only. No reviews or nonfiction. Published twice yearly in March and September. Accepts submissions in May and November. Authors who have been previously published in the magazine are required to purchase a copy of the current issue (or take out a subscription); for authors who have not been previously published in the magazine this is a requirement. Send up to one story or up to three poems via online submission system.

M122 Crazyhorse / Swamp Pink
Magazine
Department of English, College of Charleston, 66 George Street, Charleston, SC 29424
United States
Tel: +1 (843) 953-4470

crazyhorse@cofc.edu

https://crazyhorse.cofc.edu
https://www.facebook.com/CrazyhorseLiteraryJournal
https://twitter.com/crazyhorselitjo

Fiction > *Short Fiction*

Nonfiction > *Short Nonfiction*: Creative Nonfiction

Poetry > *Any Poetic Form*

Closed to approaches.

Costs: A fee is charged upon submission. $3.00.

Publishes fiction, poetry, and nonfiction on a semi-monthly basis. Aims to publish exceptional work from writers at all stages of their careers. Particularly interested in submissions from writers of color and writers from marginalized and underrepresented communities. Submissions of fiction and nonfiction can be up to 7,500 words in length. Has published exceptional work that falls outside this range, but it is an unusual occurrence. For poetry, submit a set of 3-6 poems.

M123 Cream City Review
Magazine
Department of English, University of Wisconsin-Milwaukee, P.O. Box 413, Milwaukee, WI 53201
United States

poetry@creamcityreview.org
fiction@creamcityreview.org
nonfiction@creamcityreview.org
art@creamcityreview.org
io@creamcityreview.org

https://uwm.edu/creamcityreview/
https://www.facebook.com/creamcityreview/
https://twitter.com/creamcityreview
https://www.instagram.com/cream_city_review/

Fiction > *Short Fiction*

Nonfiction > *Short Nonfiction*: Creative Nonfiction

Poetry > *Any Poetic Form*

Closed to approaches.

Send prose up to 20 pages, or up to five poems of any length. Open to submissions January 1 to April 1 and August 1 to November 1.

M124 Creative Nonfiction

Magazine
5877 Commerce Street, Pittsburgh, PA 15206
United States
Tel: +1 (412) 404-2975
Fax: +1 412-345-3767

information@creativenonfiction.org

https://creativenonfiction.org
https://creativenonfiction.submittable.com/submit/
https://www.facebook.com/creativenonfiction
https://twitter.com/cnfonline
https://instagram.com/creativenonfiction/

Nonfiction > *Essays*
  Creative Nonfiction; Memoir; Personal Essays

Closed to approaches.

Publishes all types of creative nonfiction, from immersion reportage to lyric essay to memoir and personal essays. See website for specific submission calls and their topics, or submit a pitch for a column year-round.

M125 Creem

Magazine
United States

editor@creem.com
info@creem.com

https://www.creem.com
https://instagram.com/creemmag
https://twitter.com/creemmag

Nonfiction
  Articles: Rock Music
  Reviews: Rock Music

How to send: Email

Revival of the magazine that describes itself as "America's only rock n' roll magazine".

M126 Crimewave

Magazine
United Kingdom

http://www.ttapress.com/crimewave/

Magazine Publisher / Book Publisher: TTA Press (**P527**)

Fiction > *Short Fiction*
  Crime; Mystery

Closed to approaches.

Publishes crime and mystery short stories. See website for complete guidelines.

Editor: Andy Cox

M127 Critical Quarterly

Magazine
Newbury, Crediton, Devon, EX17 5HA
United Kingdom

CRIQ@wiley.com
CQpoetry@gmail.com
CQcriticism@gmail.com

http://onlinelibrary.wiley.com/journal/10.1111/(ISSN)1467-8705

Book Publisher: John Wiley & Sons, Inc.

Fiction > *Short Fiction*

Nonfiction > *Essays*
  Culture; Literary Criticism

Poetry > *Any Poetic Form*

How to send: Online submission system

Internationally renowned for its unique blend of literary criticism, cultural studies, poetry and fiction. The journal addresses the whole range of cultural forms so that discussions of, for example, cinema and television can appear alongside analyses of the accepted literary canon. It is a necessary condition of debate in these areas that it should involve as many and as varied voices as possible, and the journal welcomes submissions from new researchers and writers as well as more established contributors.

Editor: Colin MacCabe

M128 Cruising World

Magazine
517 N. Virginia Ave, Winter Park, FL 32789
United States
Tel: +1 (407) 628-4802

editor@cruisingworld.com

https://www.cruisingworld.com
https://www.facebook.com/cruisingworld/
https://twitter.com/cruisingworld/
https://www.instagram.com/cruisingworldmag/
https://www.youtube.com/c/cruisingworld

Media Company: Bonnier Corporation

Nonfiction > *Articles*
  Boats; Sailing

Send: Full text; Author bio
How to send: Word file email attachment

Magazine for owners of sailboats between 20 and 50 feet in length. Authors should familiarise themselves with the magazine before approaching.

M129 Crystal Magazine

Magazine
3 Bowness Avenue, Prenton, Birkenhead, CH43 0SD
United Kingdom
Tel: +44 (0) 1516 089736 / +44 (0) 7769 790676

christinecrystal@hotmail.com

http://www.christinecrystal.blogspot.com

Fiction > *Short Fiction*
  Adventure; Comedy / Humour; Fantasy; Horror; Mystery; Romance; Science Fiction; Suspense; Thrillers; Westerns

Nonfiction
  Articles: Comedy / Humour; Literature; Nature; Travel
  News: General

Poetry > *Any Poetic Form*

Send: Full text
How to send: Email

An A4, 40-page, spiral-bound, print only bi-monthly. With colour images.

The magazine is intended for subscribers. They will receive six issues a year. (£21) Non-subscribers may send in work and purchase the issue it appears in for £3.50. This is the same price a subscriber would pay for one issue.

Contents: stories, poems and articles.

Also accepting fillers and very long stories which could be turned into serials.

Usually pages of letters and an opportunity to share writing achievements and anything of interest to writers.

There are yearly Surprise Competitions with very low entry fee (£1.23) and small surprise gifts. There are pictures of previous prizes and winning entries on the website. Surprise Competitions are open to all.

The Surprise Competition for this year is 'Open Article' – any subject, any length.

There is a Feedback page on the website.

Editor: Christine Carr

M130 CutBank

Magazine
University of Montana, English Dept, LA 133, Missoula, MT 59812
United States

editor.cutbank@gmail.com
cutbankonline@gmail.com
cutbankreview@gmail.com

http://www.cutbankonline.org
https://cutbank.submittable.com/submit
https://twitter.com/cutbankonline
http://instagram.com/cutbankmag
https://www.facebook.com/cutbanklitmag/

Fiction > *Short Fiction*

Nonfiction > *Short Nonfiction*: Creative Nonfiction

Poetry > *Any Poetic Form*

Closed to approaches.

Costs: A fee is charged upon submission. $5 reading fee.

Accepts poetry, fiction, creative nonfiction, and visual art submissions. Please only submit online; paper submissions will be recycled.

M131 Cyphers
Magazine
3 Selskar Terrace, Ranelagh, Dublin 6, D06 DW66
Ireland

letters@cyphers.ie

https://www.cyphers.ie

Fiction in Translation > *Short Fiction*

Fiction > *Short Fiction*

Poetry in Translation > *Any Poetic Form*

Poetry > *Any Poetic Form*

Send: Full text
How to send: Post
How not to send: Email

Publishes poetry and fiction in English and Irish, from Ireland and around the world. Translations are welcome. No unsolicited critical articles. Submissions by post only. Attachments sent by email will be deleted. See website for full guidelines.

M132 Dalesman
Magazine
The Gatehouse, Skipton Castle, Skipton, North Yorkshire, BD23 1AL
United Kingdom
Tel: +44 (0) 1756 701381

https://www.dalesman.co.uk
https://www.facebook.com/yorkshire.dalesman
https://twitter.com/The_Dalesman
https://www.youtube.com/user/TheYorkshireDalesman
https://www.instagram.com/dalesmanmagazine/

Book Publisher / Magazine Publisher:
Dalesman Publishing Co. Ltd

Nonfiction > *Articles:* Yorkshire

Magazine publishing material of Yorkshire interest.

Editor: Mick Smith

M133 Dancing Times
Magazine
82 St John Street, London, EC1M 4JN
United Kingdom
Tel: +44 (0) 20 3773 6557

editorial@dancing-times.co.uk

https://www.facebook.com/1dancingtimes/
https://twitter.com/dancingtimes

Nonfiction
Articles: Dance
News: Dance
Reviews: Dance

Monthly magazine of dance, publishing features, news, and review.

M134 The Dark Horse
Magazine
PO Box 8351, Irvine, KA12 2DD
United Kingdom

https://www.thedarkhorsemagazine.com
https://www.facebook.com/The-Dark-Horse-Magazine-184043168311270/
https://twitter.com/thedarkhorsemag

Poetry > *Any Poetic Form*

Send: Full text; Self-Addressed Stamped Envelope (SASE)
How to send: Post
How not to send: Email

International literary magazine committed to British, Irish and American poetry. Send submissions by post only, to UK or US editorial addresses. No simultaneous submissions. See website for full guidelines.

Editor: Gerry Cambridge

M135 The Dawntreader
Magazine
24 Forest Houses, Halwill, Beaworthy, Devon, EX21 5UU
United Kingdom

dawnidp@indigodreams.co.uk

https://www.indigodreams.co.uk/magazines

Book Publisher: Indigo Dreams Publishing (**P283**)

Fiction > *Short Fiction*
Environment; Folklore, Myths, and Legends; Mysticism; Nature; Spirituality

Nonfiction > *Articles*
Environment; Folklore, Myths, and Legends; Mysticism; Nature; Spirituality

Poetry > *Any Poetic Form*
Environment; Folklore, Myths, and Legends; Mysticism; Nature; Spirituality

Send: Full text
How to send: Email attachment

A quarterly publication specialising in myth, legend; in the landscape, nature; spirituality and love; the mystic, the environment. Submit up to five poems, and prose, articles, and local legends up to 1,000 words.

Editor: Ronnie Goodyer

M136 Deep Overstock Magazine
Magazine
United States

submissions@deepoverstock.com

https://deepoverstock.com/issues/
https://deepoverstock.com/submission-guidelines/

Book Publisher / Magazine Publisher: Deep Overstock Publishing (**P157**)

Fiction > *Short Fiction*

Send: Full text; Author bio
How to send: In the body of an email

Accepts fiction. Issues are themed. Check website for current theme. Prefers fiction to be under 6,000 words. Submissions over 3,000 words may not be considered. Submit one or two pieces of fiction per theme, or up to three if they are each under 1,000 words. Send up to seven poems per theme.

M137 Derbyshire Life
Magazine
United Kingdom

Magazine Publisher: Great British Life

M138 Descent
Magazine
PO Box 297, Kendal, LA9 9GQ
United Kingdom
Tel: +44 (0) 7354 794240

info@descentmagazine.co.uk

https://www.descentmagazine.co.uk
https://twitter.com/CavingMagazine
https://www.facebook.com/profile.php?id=100083468112084
https://www.instagram.com/descentcavingmagazine/

Magazine Publisher: Stalactite Publishing

Nonfiction > *Articles:* Caving and Potholing

Send: Query
How to send: Email; Post

Magazine written by cavers, for cavers. Contact with ideas prior to submission.

Editor: Chris Howes

M139 Devon Life
Magazine
United Kingdom

https://www.greatbritishlife.co.uk/magazines/devon/

Magazine Publisher: Great British Life

Nonfiction > *Articles*
Arts; Countryside; Devon; Events; Food and Drink; History; Houses; Lifestyle; Travel; Walking

Celebrates all that is great about Devon. The people, the places, the food and drink spots, the walks, the countryside, the history, the beaches, the homes, the events, the arts scene…produced by those with inside knowledge of the best and brightest Devon has to offer.

M140 Diver
Magazine
216 East Esplanade St., North Vancouver, BC,

V7L 1A3
Canada
Tel: +1 (604) 988-0711

mail@divermag.com

https://divermag.com
https://www.facebook.com/divermagazine

Nonfiction > *Articles*: Scuba Diving

North America's longest established scuba diving magazine.

M141 Dogs Monthly
Magazine
The Old Print House, 62 The High Street, Chobham, Surrey, GU24 8AA
United Kingdom
Tel: +44 (0) 1276 402599

https://dogsmonthly.co.uk
https://www.facebook.com/DogsMonthly
https://www.instagram.com/
dogsmonthlymagazine/
https://twitter.com/dogsmonthly

Nonfiction > *Articles*: Dogs

Send: Query
How to send: Online contact form; Phone; Post

Magazine for dog enthusiasts publishing articles on breeds, topical news, and features. Contact through form on website, or by phone or post in first instance.

M142 Dorset
Magazine
United Kingdom

Magazine Publisher: Great British Life

M143 Dorset Magazine
Magazine

Magazine Publisher: Archant

M144 Dream Catcher
Magazine
109 Wensley Drive, Leeds, LS7 2LU
United Kingdom

https://www.dreamcatchermagazine.co.uk

Fiction > *Short Fiction*

Nonfiction > *Interviews*

Poetry > *Any Poetic Form*

Send: Full text
How to send: Post

Send submissions by post, following guidelines on website. No electronic submissions.

M145 Early American Life
Magazine
Firelands Media Group LLC, Post Office Box 221230, Shaker Heights, OH 44122-0996
United States

queries@firelandsmedia.com

https://www.ealonline.com

Magazine Publisher: Firelands Media Group LLC

Nonfiction > *Articles*
American History; Antiques; Architecture

Send: Query
How to send: Email

Magazine aimed at people with an interest in the style of the period 1600-1840 in America, and its use in their modern homes and lives. Covers architecture, antiques, etc. Will consider unsolicited mss but prefers initial queries by email.

M146 The Economist
Magazine
The Adelphi, 1-11 John Adam Street, London, WC2N 6HT
United Kingdom

https://www.economist.com
https://www.facebook.com/theeconomist
https://www.instagram.com/theeconomist
https://www.twitter.com/theeconomist
https://www.linkedin.com/company/the-economist
https://www.youtube.com/user/
economistmagazine

Nonfiction
Articles: Business; Current Affairs; Finance; Politics
News: Business; Current Affairs; Finance; Politics

Magazine covering economics, business, finance, politics, and current affairs.

M147 Ecotone
Magazine
Department of Creative Writing, University of North Carolina Wilmington, 601 South College Road, Wilmington, NC 28403-5938
United States

ecotone@uncw.edu

https://ecotonemagazine.org

Fiction > *Short Fiction*

Nonfiction > *Short Nonfiction*

Poetry > *Any Poetic Form*

Send: Full text

Publishes work from a wide range of voices. Particularly interested in hearing from writers historically underrepresented in literary publishing and in place-based contexts: people of colour, Indigenous people, people with disabilities, gender-nonconforming people, LGBTQIA+, women, and others. Check website for specific reading periods and submit prose up to 30 double-spaced pages or 3-5 poems by post with SAE or using online

system ($3 charge). No hard copy submissions from outside the US.

Editor: David Gessner

M148 El Portal
Magazine
United States

el.portal@enmu.edu

https://elportaljournal.com
https://elportal.submittable.com/submit
https://twitter.com/elportaljournal

Fiction > *Short Fiction*

Nonfiction > *Short Nonfiction*: Creative Nonfiction

Poetry > *Any Poetic Form*

Send: Full text
How to send: Submittable

Accepts submissions of flash fiction up to 500 words, short stories and creative nonfiction up to 4,000 words, or up to five poems.

M149 Electrical Times
Magazine
Purple Media Solutions Ltd, The Old School House, St Stephen's Street, Tonbridge, Kent, TN9 2AD
United Kingdom
Tel: +44 (0) 1732 371579

https://www.electricaltimes.co.uk

Magazine Publisher: Purple Media Solutions

PROFESSIONAL > **Nonfiction** > *Articles*: Electrical Contracting

Magazine for electrical contractors, installers, and designers.

M150 Ellery Queen Mystery Magazine
Magazine
6 Prowitt Street, Norwalk, CT 06855
United States
Tel: +1 (212) 686-7188 x 675

elleryqueenmm@dellmagazines.com

http://www.elleryqueenmysterymagazine.com
https://www.facebook.com/elleryqueenmm
https://twitter.com/eqmm
https://www.instagram.com/elleryqueenmm/
https://somethingisgoingtohappen.net/

Fiction > *Short Fiction*
Crime; Mystery

How to send: Online submission system

Mystery magazine, publishing every kind of mystery short story: psychological suspense; deductive puzzle; private eye case; realistic to imaginative; hard-boiled to "cozies". However, no explicit sex or violence, or true crime. Always seeking original detective stories, and especially happy to review first stories by authors who have never before published fiction professionally (submit to the "Department of First Stories"). No need to send query – unsolicited MSS welcome. Submit through online system (see website for details). Accepts postal submissions only from those with a prior publishing history with the magazine.

M151 Entrepreneur
Magazine
2 Executive Circle, Suite 150, Irvine CA, 92614
United States

https://www.entrepreneur.com/
https://www.facebook.com/EntMagazine
https://twitter.com/entrepreneur
https://www.linkedin.com/company/entrepreneur-media
https://www.pinterest.com/entrepreneurmedia
https://www.instagram.com/entrepreneur/
https://www.youtube.com/user/EntrepreneurOnline

Nonfiction > *Articles*
Business; Entrepreneurship; Finance; How To

Magazine for people who have started and are running their own business, providing news o current trends, practical how-to articles, features on combining work and life, etc. Runs features and several regular columns, as well as an inner magazine on start-ups.

M152 Erotic Review
Online Magazine
United Kingdom

editorial@ermagazine.org

https://eroticreviewmagazine.com
https://www.facebook.com/EroticReviewMag
https://twitter.com/EroticReviewMag
https://www.instagram.com/eroticreview/

Fiction > *Short Fiction*
Erotic; Literary

Nonfiction
Articles: Lifestyle; Literature; Sex; Sexuality
Reviews: Arts; Books; Erotic

Closed to approaches.

Literary lifestyle publication about sex and sexuality aimed at sophisticated, intelligent and mature readers. Print version has been retired and is now online only. Publishes articles, short stories, and reviews. See website for full submission guidelines.

M153 Essex Life
Magazine
United Kingdom

https://www.greatbritishlife.co.uk/magazines/essex/

Magazine Publisher: Great British Life

Nonfiction

Articles: Essex; Fashion; Food and Drink; Gardening; Interior Design; Lifestyle; Nostalgia; Property / Real Estate; Travel; Walking
Interviews: Celebrity; Essex

Magazine publishing material relating to Essex.

M154 Event
Magazine
PO Box 2503, New Westminster, BC, V3L 5B2
Canada
Tel: +1 (604) 527-5293

event@douglascollege.ca

https://www.eventmagazine.ca
https://eventmagazine.submittable.com/submit
https://twitter.com/EVENTmags
https://www.facebook.com/eventmagazine
http://www.youtube.com/channel/UCKuYlH5b3uRaitKO4lCk8zA?feature=watch

Fiction > *Short Fiction*

Nonfiction
Reviews: Books
Short Nonfiction: Creative Nonfiction

Poetry > *Any Poetic Form*

Closed to approaches.

One of Western Canada's longest-running literary magazines. Welcomes submissions in English from around the world during specific submission windows.

M155 Facts & Fiction
Magazine
United Kingdom
Tel: +44 (0) 1773 822829

steel.carpet@tiscali.co.uk

http://www.factsandfiction.co.uk
https://petecastle.co.uk/fandf

Nonfiction
Articles: Storytelling
Interviews: Storytelling
News: Storytelling
Reviews: Storytelling

How to send: Email

The magazine for everyone interested in (oral) storytelling. Not a short story or poetry mag. We deal with storytelling as an oral art form, in many ways as a traditional art form – so articles and other material should reflect that.

Editor: Pete Castle

M156 Fangoria
Magazine
United States

editorial@fangoria.com

https://fangoria.com
https://www.facebook.com/FANGORIA/
https://twitter.com/fangoria
https://www.instagram.com/fangoria
https://www.youtube.com/user/fangoriamagazine

Nonfiction
Articles: Films; Horror
Reviews: Films; Horror

Send: Pitch; Writing sample
How to send: Email

Horror entertainment magazine founded in 1979. Send pitch with writing sample by email.

M157 Fate
Magazine
PO Box 774, Hendersonville, NC 28793
United States
Tel: +1 (828) 702-3032

Phyllis@fatemag.com

https://www.fatemag.com
https://www.youtube.com/channel/UCAjXG-tsjV5VJM-i-afsvqA
https://twitter.com/Fate_Magazine
https://instagram.com/fatemagazine

Nonfiction > *Articles*
Mystery; Science; Supernatural / Paranormal

How to send: Post; Email

Magazine of mysterious and unexplained phenomena.

Editor-in-Chief: Phyllis Galde

M158 Faultline
Magazine
UCI Department of English, 435 Humanities Instructional Building, Irvine, CA 92697-2650
United States
Tel: +1 (949) 824-1573

faultline@uci.edu
ucifaultline@gmail.com

https://faultline.sites.uci.edu/
https://www.facebook.com/uci.faultline
https://twitter.com/faultline_journ

Fiction in Translation > *Short Fiction*

Fiction > *Short Fiction*

Nonfiction in Translation > *Short Nonfiction*: Creative Nonfiction

Nonfiction > *Short Nonfiction*: Creative Nonfiction

Poetry in Translation > *Any Poetic Form*

Poetry > *Any Poetic Form*

Closed to approaches.

Send up to five poems or up to 20 pages of fiction or creative nonfiction, between October 15 and December 15 only.

Fiction Editor: Sara Joyce Robinson

Poetry Editor: Lisa P. Sutton

M159 Fee: Foundation for Economic Education

Online Magazine
1776 Peachtree St. NW, Suite 710S, Atlanta, GA 30309
United States
Tel: +1 (404) 554-9980
Fax: +1 (404) 393-3142

submissions@fee.org

https://fee.org
https://fee.org/submissions

Nonfiction > *Articles*
   Culture; History; Philosophy; Politics

Send: Query; Full text

We welcome compelling, thoughtful articles exploring trends, principles, history, and ideas underlying a free society: private property, the rule of law, voluntary exchange, individual rights, morality, personal character, cultural evolution, self-responsibility, charity, mutual aid, and limitations on power.

M160 Feminist Review

Magazine
c/o Centre for Gender Studies, SOAS University of London, Thornhaugh Street, LONDON, WC1H 0XG
United Kingdom

feministreview@soas.ac.uk

https://journals.sagepub.com/home/fer
https://twitter.com/FeministReview_

Book Publisher / Magazine Publisher: Sage Publications (**P457**)

ACADEMIC > **Nonfiction** > *Articles*: Feminism

Send: Full text
How to send: Online submission system

A peer reviewed, interdisciplinary journal contributing to new agendas for feminism. The journal invites critical reflection on the relationship between materiality and representation, theory and practice, subjectivity and communities, contemporary and historical formations.

M161 Feminist Studies

Magazine
677 Rome Hall, 801 22nd Street, NW, George Washington University, Washington, DC 20052
United States

info@feministstudies.org
submit@feministstudies.org
creative@feministstudies.org
art@feministstudies.org
review@feministstudies.org

http://www.feministstudies.org

ACADEMIC > **Nonfiction** > *Essays*
   Cultural Criticism; Literary Criticism

ADULT
   Fiction > *Short Fiction*: Feminism

   Nonfiction > *Articles*
      Arts; Culture; Feminism

   Poetry > *Any Poetic Form*: Feminism

Closed to approaches.

Feminist journal publishing research and criticism, creative writing, art, essays, and other forms of writing and visual expression. See website for submission guidelines and specific submission email addresses.

M162 Fenland Poetry Journal

Magazine
United Kingdom

fenlandpoetryjournal@gmail.com

https://fenlandpoetryjournal.co.uk

Poetry > *Any Poetic Form*
   Contemporary; Literary

Closed to approaches.

Contemporary poetry journal accepting submissions from anywhere in the world, though particularly encouraged from Fenland. No line limits.

M163 Fiction

Magazine
c/o Department of English, City College of New York, Convent Ave. at 138th Street, New York, NY 10031
United States

fictionmageditors@gmail.com

http://www.fictioninc.com
http://submissions.fictioninc.com/
http://instagram.com/fiction.magazine
https://twitter.com/fictionmag
https://www.facebook.com/fiction.mag/

Fiction > *Short Fiction*: Literary

Closed to approaches.

Accepts short stories, novelettes, and novellas of any length (though staying under 5,000 words is encouraged). Submit by post or using online submission system between October 15 and April 15 only.

M164 The Fiddlehead

Magazine
Campus House, 11 Garland Court, University of New Brunswick, PO Box 4400, Fredericton NB, E3B 5A3
Canada
Tel: +1 (506) 453-3501

fiddlehd@unb.ca

https://thefiddlehead.ca
https://twitter.com/TheFiddlehd
http://www.facebook.com/pages/The-Fiddlehead-Atlantic-Canadas-International-Literary-Journal/174825212565312

Fiction
   Novel Excerpts; *Short Fiction*
Nonfiction > *Short Nonfiction*: Creative Nonfiction

Poetry > *Any Poetic Form*

Closed to approaches.

Publishes poetry, fiction, and creative nonfiction in a variety of styles, including experimental genres. Also publishes excerpts from longer works, and reviews. Submit up to six poems (up to 12 pages total), or a piece of fiction up to 6,000 words. All submissions must be original and unpublished. Prefers submissions through online submission system (January 1 to March 31 and September 15 to November 30 only), but will accept submissions by post all year round. See website for full details.

M165 Firmament

Magazine
United States

support@sublunaryeditions.com

https://sublunaryeditions.com/firmament
https://oleada.io/publication/sublunary-editions

Book Publisher / Magazine Publisher: Sublunary Editions (**P502**)

Fiction > *Short Fiction*

Nonfiction > *Interviews*

Features new writing from around the world, along with in-depth interviews, excerpts from upcoming titles, regular columns, and more.

M166 First For Women

Magazine
270 Sylvan Avenue, Englewood Cliffs, NJ 07632
United States

contactus@firstforwomen.com

https://www.firstforwomen.com
https://www.facebook.com/firstforwomenmag
https://www.instagram.com/firstmag
https://www.pinterest.com/firstforwomen

Nonfiction > *Articles*
   Beauty; Diet; Fashion; Food; Health; Menopause; Personal Finance; Wellbeing

Magazine where active women over 45 come for the tools and inspiration they need to look good, feel great, and enjoy every aspect of their lives.

M167 The First Line

Magazine
PO Box 250382, Plano, Texas 75025-0382
United States

submission@thefirstline.com

http://www.thefirstline.com

Fiction > *Short Fiction*

Nonfiction > *Essays*: Literary Criticism

Poetry > *Any Poetic Form*

Send: Full text; Self-Addressed Stamped Envelope (SASE)
How to send: Word file email attachment; Post
How not to send: PDF file email attachment; Google Docs shared document

Prefers submissions by email, but will also accept submissions by post with SASE. Prefers attachments as a Word or Word Perfect file. Stories must begin with the appropriate first line for that issue, as provided on the website. Occasionally accepts poems starting with the specified first line. Also accepts essays on your favourite first line from a book.

M168 Five Points
Magazine
Georgia State University, P.O. Box 3999, Atlanta, GA 30302-3999
United States

http://fivepoints.gsu.edu

Fiction in Translation
  Novel Excerpts: Literary
  Short Fiction: Literary

Fiction > *Short Fiction*: Literary

Nonfiction in Translation > *Essays*

Nonfiction > *Short Nonfiction*
  General, and in particular: Literary

Poetry in Translation > *Any Poetic Form*

Poetry > *Any Poetic Form*

Closed to approaches.

Costs: A fee is charged upon submission.

Welcomes unsolicited submissions of fiction, poetry, flash fiction and nonfiction, and literary nonfiction. Submit through online submission system.

Editor: Megan Sexton

M169 Flaneur
Online Magazine
United Kingdom

editor@flaneur.me.uk

http://www.flaneur.me.uk

Nonfiction > *Articles*
  Arts; Films; Food and Drink; Literature; Music; Politics; Sport; TV; Theatre; Travel

Send: Full text
How to send: In the body of an email

Online magazine of arts, culture, politics, and sport.

Editor: J Powell

M170 Flash: The International Short-Short Story Magazine
Magazine
International Flash Fiction Association, Department of English, University of Chester, Parkgate Road, Chester, CH1 4BJ
United Kingdom

flash.magazine@chester.ac.uk

https://www1.chester.ac.uk/flash-magazine/submissions

Fiction > *Short Fiction*

Send: Full text
How to send: Email

Publishes flash fiction up to 360 words, including the title. Send up to four pieces per issue. Attach submissions to a single email. See website for full submission guidelines.

Editors: Dr Peter Blair; Dr Ashley Chantler

M171 Flyfishing & Tying Journal
Magazine
United States

https://ftjangler.com

Book Publisher / Magazine Publisher: Amato Books (**P023**)

Nonfiction > *Articles*: Fly Fishing

Magazine for both new and veteran anglers, covering flyfishing and fly tying. Magazine is released quarterly, and each issue is appropriate to the given season.

M172 Focus
Magazine
United Kingdom

devhotmail@yahoo.co.uk

https://bsfa.co.uk/focus

Professional Body: BSFA (British Science Fiction Association)

Nonfiction > *Articles*
  Creative Writing; Science Fiction

Send: Query
How to send: Email

Writing magazine, devoted to the craft and practice of writing genre fiction. Publishes articles on writing science fiction. Query by email.

Editor: Dev Agarwal

M173 Folio
Magazine
United States

folio.editors@gmail.com

https://www.american.edu/cas/literature/folio/
https://foliolitjournal.submittable.com/submit
https://www.facebook.com/FolioLitJournal/

https://twitter.com/FolioLitJournal
https://www.linkedin.com/in/folio-literary-journal-a235a8b4
http://folio-lit-journal.tumblr.com/

Fiction > *Short Fiction*: Literary

Nonfiction > *Essays*: Creative Nonfiction

Poetry > *Any Poetic Form*

Closed to approaches.

Accepts submissions of fiction, nonfiction, and poetry on specific themes during specific submission windows. See website for details.

M174 Fortean Times: The Journal of Strange Phenomena
Magazine
Diamond Publishing Ltd, 2nd Floor, Saunders House, 52-53 The Mall, Ealing, W5 3AT
United Kingdom

hello@metropolis.co.uk

http://subscribe.forteantimes.com
https://www.instagram.com/forteantimes/
https://www.facebook.com/ForteanTimes
https://twitter.com/forteantimes

Magazine Publisher: Diamond Publishing

Nonfiction > *Articles*: Supernatural / Paranormal

Publishes accounts of strange phenomena, experiences, curiosities, mysteries, prodigies, and portents. No fiction or poetry.

Editor: David Sutton

M175 The Fortnightly Review
Online Magazine
United Kingdom

info@fortnightlyreview.co.uk

https://fortnightlyreview.co.uk

Fiction > *Short Fiction*

Nonfiction
  Essays; *Reviews*
Poetry > *Any Poetic Form*

Send: Full text
How to send: Email

Online magazine publishing reviews, essays and reportage, fiction, and poetry.

Poetry Editors: Robert Archambeau; Peter Robinson

M176 Foundation: The International Review of Science Fiction
Magazine
28 St John's Road, Guildford, GU2 7UH
United Kingdom

sff@beccon.org

https://www.sf-foundation.org/about-the-sff-journal

Nonfiction
   Articles: Science Fiction
   Reviews: Books; Science Fiction

Describes itself as the essential critical review of science fiction, publishing articles up to 6,000 words and reviews up to 1,500 words.

M177 Fourteen Poems

Print Magazine
United Kingdom

hello@14poems.com

https://www.fourteenpoems.com
https://twitter.com/fourteenpoems
http://instagram.com/14poems

Poetry > *Any Poetic Form*: LGBTQIA

Send: Full text; Author bio
How to send: PDF file email attachment; Word file email attachment

Print magazine published three times a year. Each issue includes work by fourteen LGBTQ+ poets, printing their queer takes on sex, love, race, gender and life in the LGBTQ+ global community.

M178 The Fourth River

Magazine
United States

4thriver@gmail.com

https://www.thefourthriver.com
https://twitter.com/thefourthriver
https://www.instagram.com/thefourthriver/
https://www.facebook.com/TheFourthRiver

Fiction > *Short Fiction*: Literary

Nonfiction > *Short Nonfiction*: Creative Nonfiction

Poetry > *Any Poetic Form*

Closed to approaches.

Costs: A fee is charged upon submission. $2 submission fee.

Print and digital literary magazine publishing creative writing that explores the relationship between humans and their environments, whether natural or man-made. Submit 3-5 poems or prose up to 4,000 words between July 1 and September 1 for print, or December 1 and February 1 for online, via online submission system. No submissions by email.

Online Magazine: Tributaries (**M417**)

M179 Fresh Words – An International Literary Magazine

Print Magazine; Online Magazine
United States

freshwordsmagazine@gmail.com

https://sites.google.com/view/
freshwordsmagazine

Fiction > *Short Fiction*

Nonfiction
   Essays: Literature
   Interviews: General
   Reviews: Books
   Short Nonfiction: Travel

Poetry > *Any Poetic Form*

How to send: Email

We are open for submissions. We invite poems, short stories, essays, plays, diaries, excerpts from books (published or upcoming submitted by author only), book reviews, interviews and travelogues. Please send all submissions by email. See website for full guidelines.

M180 Fugue

Magazine
United States

fugue@uidaho.edu

https://fuguejournal.com
https://twitter.com/FugueJournal
https://www.instagram.com/fugue_journal/
https://www.facebook.com/fuguejournal/

Fiction > *Short Fiction*

Nonfiction
   Essays: General
   Reviews: Books

Poetry > *Any Poetic Form*

Closed to approaches.

Costs: A fee is charged upon submission. $3.

Submit 3 to 5 poems, up to two short shorts, one story, or one essay per submission. Accepts submissions online only, between September 1 and May 1. Submission service charges $3 per submission.

M181 Funeral Business Solutions

Magazine
1809 S Bay St., Eustis, FL 32726-5666
United States
Tel: +1 (352) 242-8111

https://fbsmagazine.com
https://www.facebook.com/profile.php?id=
100088592525602
https://www.linkedin.com/company/
funeralbusinesssolutions/

Magazine Publisher: Radcliffe Media, Inc.

PROFESSIONAL > **Nonfiction**
   Articles: Funeral Industry
   Interviews: Funeral Industry
   News: Funeral Industry
   Reviews: Funeral Industry

Send: Full text
How to send: Email

Different from traditional association magazines or trade journals because it is specially-crafted to bring you the best industry specific business news and solutions that will help you to make effective business decisions for your staff, company, and client families.

Our magazine design and layout is purposefully easy to read and digest in short segments. We know that the average funeral professional has an unpredictable schedule and an effective business magazine gives the reader shorter editorials that get to the point without fluff.

Our writers provide actionable ideas and effective strategies that will help you, the industry professional, run a more profitable business. Issues are published every two months, giving you ample time to digest 8-12 articles, latest industry headlines, the included Funeral Home Success Stories, Vendor Company Spotlights, Industry Book Overviews and more.

Our goal is to never bore you or waste your precious time, so our editors consider each article, press release, and spotlight carefully to make sure it can in some way benefit a funeral director running a business.

At the end of each day, we are primarily a magazine of business solutions for an industry that our publisher, editors, and writers love.

Publisher: Timothy Totten

M182 Funny Times

Magazine
PO Box 18530, Cleveland Heights, OH 44118
United States
Tel: +1 (888) 386-6984

submissions@funnytimes.com
info@funnytimes.com

https://funnytimes.com
https://www.facebook.com/TheFunnyTimes

Fiction
   Cartoons: Business; Comedy / Humour; Current Affairs; Food; Pets; Politics; Relationships; Religion; Technology
   Short Fiction: Business; Comedy / Humour; Current Affairs; Food; Pets; Politics; Relationships; Religion; Technology

Send: Full text; Self-Addressed Stamped Envelope (SASE)
How to send: Email; Post

Send query with SASE and details of previous publishing history (where applicable). Publishes funny stories and cartoons only. No fax or email submissions.

Editor: Raymond Lesser, Susan Wolpert

M183 The Future Fire

Online Magazine
United Kingdom

fiction@futurefire.net
nonfiction@futurefire.net

http://futurefire.net

Fiction in Translation > *Short Fiction*

Fiction > *Short Fiction*
  Crime; Environment; Feminism; LGBTQIA;
  Mystery; Noir; Postcolonialism; Speculative

Nonfiction > *Reviews*
  Arts; Books; Films; Magazines

Poetry in Translation > *Any Poetic Form*

Poetry > *Any Poetic Form*
  Environment; Feminism; LGBTQIA;
  Postcolonialism; Speculative

Send: Full text
How to send: Email attachment

Magazine of social political and speculative cyber fiction. Publishes short stories up to 17,500. Also publishes nonfiction reviews. Accepts email submissions for fiction; for reviews send query by email before submitting material. See website for full submission guidelines.

M184 Garden Answers
Magazine
Bauer Media, Media House, Lynch Wood, PE2 6EA
United Kingdom

https://www.gardenanswersmagazine.co.uk/
https://www.facebook.com/gardenanswers
https://twitter.com/GardenAnswers

Magazine Publisher: Bauer Media Group

Nonfiction > *Articles*: Gardening

A vibrant and inspiring gardening magazine filled with ingenious design ideas and exciting plant combinations guaranteed to make your garden beautiful.

M185 Garden News
Magazine
United Kingdom

https://www.gardennewsmagazine.co.uk
https://www.facebook.com/GardenNewsOfficial
https://twitter.com/GardenNewsmag

Magazine Publisher: Bauer Media Group

Nonfiction > *Articles*: Gardening

Weekly gardening magazine publishing tips, reminders, and expert advice.

Editor: Neil Pope

M186 Gateway
Magazine
Missouri Historical Society, PO Box 775460, St. Louis, MO 63177
United States

https://mohistory.org/publications/gateway/

Nonfiction > *Articles*
  African American; Civil Rights; Culture;
  History; Missouri; Music; Society; Theatre

Magazine covering St. Louis's and Missouri's historical and contemporary cultural, social, and political issues. Particularly interested in articles and essays on preservation and architecture; folk culture and oral history; music and theatre traditions; civil rights and African American history, as well as original poetry, photography, and literature.

Editor: Victoria W. Monks

M187 The Georgia Review
Magazine
706A Main Library, 320 S. Jackson St., The University of Georgia, Athens, GA 30602-9009
United States
Tel: +1 (800) 542-3481

https://thegeorgiareview.com
https://thegeorgiareview.submittable.com/submit
https://www.instagram.com/georgiareview/
https://www.facebook.com/thegeorgiareview/
https://twitter.com/home

Fiction > *Short Fiction*: Literary

Nonfiction
  Essays: General
  Reviews: Books

Poetry > *Any Poetic Form*

Closed to approaches.

Costs: A fee is charged upon submission in some cases. $3 for non-subscribers. Subscribers submit for free.

Publishes literary fiction, poetry (submit 6-10 pages of poetry or one long poem), essays and book reviews. Submissions accepted between August 15 and May 15 only. Submissions received between May 15 and August 15 are returned unread.

M188 German Life
Magazine
PO Box 3000, Denville, NJ 07834-9723
United States
Tel: +1 (866) 867-0251

comments@germanlife.com

https://germanlife.com
http://www.facebook.com/https://www.facebook.com/germanlifemag/

Magazine Publisher: Zeitgeist Publishing

Nonfiction > *Articles*
  Austria; Culture; Germany; Politics; Social
  Commentary; Switzerland

Magazine on German history, culture, and travel, and the way in which Germany and German immigrants have helped shape America.

Editor: Mark Slider

M189 Gertrude
Online Magazine
United States

EditorGertrudePress@gmail.com

https://www.gertrudepress.org

Book Publisher: Gertrude Press (**P213**)

Fiction > *Short Fiction*
  General, and in particular: LGBTQIA

Nonfiction
  Essays: Creative Nonfiction; LGBTQIA
  Short Nonfiction: Creative Nonfiction;
  LGBTQIA; Memoir
Poetry > *Any Poetic Form*
  General, and in particular: LGBTQIA

Closed to approaches.

Costs: A fee is charged upon submission. £3 submission fee.

Online LGBTQA journal publishing fiction, poetry, and creative nonfiction. Subject matter need not be LGBTQA-specific, and writers from all backgrounds are welcomed. Submit fiction or creative nonfiction up to 3,000 words, or up to five poems (no line limit, but under 40 lines preferred), via online submission system. For book reviews and interviews, email editor with proposal. See website for full guidelines.

Editor: Tammy

M190 Ginosko Literary Journal
Magazine
United States

https://ginoskoliteraryjournal.com
https://ginosko.submittable.com/submit/

Fiction > *Short Fiction*

Nonfiction > *Short Nonfiction*: Creative Nonfiction

Poetry > *Any Poetic Form*

Send: Full text
How to send: Submittable

Semi-annual literary journal accepting short fiction, poetry, creative nonfiction, social justice issues, and literary and spiritual insights.

Editor: Robert Cesaretti

M191 Go World Travel Magazine
Online Magazine
United States

submissions@goworldtravel.com

https://www.goworldtravel.com
https://www.facebook.com/Go.World.Travel
https://www.instagram.com/goworldtravelmagazine/
https://pinterest.com/goworldtravel/
https://twitter.com/GoWorldMagazine
https://www.youtube.com/user/GoWorldPublishing

Nonfiction > *Articles*: Travel

How to send: Email

A digital publication for world travelers. We work with journalists around the world, and partner with destination marketing organizations and other tourism and travel businesses to promote travel.

Editor: Heike Schmidt, Senior Editor

M192 Golf Tips
Magazine
iGolf Sports Network LLC, 13800 Panama City Beach PKWY, Suite 106D, #138, Panama City Beach, FL 32407
United States
Tel: +1 (850) 588-1550

ted@igolfsportsnetwork.com

https://www.golftipsmag.com

Nonfiction > *Articles*
   Golf; How To; Travel

Publishes tips, guides, and features on golf.

M193 Good Homes
Magazine
United Kingdom

info@goodhomesmagazine.com

https://www.goodhomesmagazine.com
https://www.facebook.com/GoodHomes
https://uk.pinterest.com/goodhomes/
https://twitter.com/GoodHomesMag
https://www.instagram.com/goodhomesmag/

Magazine Publisher: Media 10

Nonfiction > *Articles*
   Decorating; Interior Design

Magazine of decorating and interior design.

M194 The Good Ski Guide
Magazine
United Kingdom

https://www.goodskiguide.com/
https://www.facebook.com/goodskiguide.official
https://twitter.com/officialGSG
https://www.youtube.com/goodskiguideoffical

Nonfiction > *Articles*
   Skiing; Travel

Magazine of skiing and ski resorts.

M195 Graffiti Magazine
Magazine
United Kingdom

writersinthebrewery@yahoo.co.uk

https://www.facebook.com/pages/Graffiti-Magazine/63653000411

Fiction > *Short Fiction*

Poetry > *Any Poetic Form*

Publishes poetry and prose. Each edition has a short story competition.

M196 Granta
Magazine
12 Addison Avenue, Holland Park, London, W11 4QR
United Kingdom
Tel: +44 (0) 20 7605 1360

editorial@granta.com

https://granta.com

Fiction > *Short Fiction*

Nonfiction > *Short Nonfiction*

Poetry > *Any Poetic Form*

Send: Full text
How to send: Submittable

Costs: A fee is charged upon submission. £3.50 for prose; £2 for poems.

Submit one story or essay, or up to four poems, via online submission system. £3.50 charge for prose submissions; £2 for poems. No specific length limits for prose, but most pieces are between 3,000 and 6,000 words. Unlikely to read anything over 10,000 words.

Editor: Sigrid Rausing

M197 The Great Outdoors (TGO)
Magazine
Kelsey Media Ltd, The Granary, Downs Court, Yalding Hil, Yalding, Kent, ME18 6AL
United Kingdom

carey.davies@kelsey.co.uk

https://www.tgomagazine.co.uk

Magazine Publisher: Kelsey Media

Nonfiction > *Articles*: Walking

Magazine publishing articles on walking and back-packing.

Editor: Carey Davies

M198 Gulf Coast: A Journal of Literature and Fine Arts
Magazine
Department of English, University of Houston, Houston, TX 77204-3013
United States
Tel: +1 (713) 743-3223

gulfcoastea@gmail.com
gcmagreviews@gmail.com

http://www.gulfcoastmag.org
https://www.facebook.com/GulfCoastJournal
https://twitter.com/Gulf_Coast
https://www.instagram.com/gulfcoastjournal/

Fiction in Translation > *Short Fiction*

Fiction > *Short Fiction*

Nonfiction
   Essays: Art Criticism
   Interviews: Literature
   Reviews: Books

Poetry in Translation > *Any Poetic Form*

Poetry > *Any Poetic Form*

How to send: Submittable

Costs: A fee is charged upon submission. $3 submission fee.

Submit up to five poems, or fiction or essays up to 7,000 words, by post or via online submission manager. For other material, send query by email to address on website. $3.00 submission fee. Accepts material September 1 to March 1, annually.

Editor: Luisa Muradyan Tannahill

M199 Gutter Magazine
Magazine
United Kingdom

contactguttermagazine@gmail.com

https://www.guttermag.co.uk/

Fiction > *Short Fiction*
   International; Literary; Scotland

Nonfiction > *Essays*
   Creative Nonfiction; International; Literary; Scotland

Poetry > *Any Poetic Form*
   International; Scotland

Scripts > *Theatre Scripts*
   International; Literary; Scotland

Closed to approaches.

Publishes poetry, short stories, and drama. Publishes work by writers born or living in Scotland alongside international writing. Send up to five poems up to 120 lines total, or prose up to 3,000 words. Submit through online submission system. See website for full guidelines.

Editors: Colin Begg; Kate MacLeary; Laura Waddell

M200 Half Mystic Journal
Print Magazine
United States

hello@halfmystic.com

https://www.halfmystic.com

Book Publisher: Half Mystic Press (**P237**)

Fiction in Translation > *Short Fiction*
   Experimental; Music

Fiction > *Short Fiction*
   Experimental; Music

Nonfiction in Translation > *Short Nonfiction*
   Creative Nonfiction; Experimental; Music

Nonfiction > *Short Nonfiction*
   Creative Nonfiction; Experimental; Music

Poetry in Translation
   Any Poetic Form: Music
   Experimental Poetry: Music

Poetry

Any Poetic Form: Music
Experimental Poetry: Music

Closed to approaches.

Publishes all genres of poetry, prose, creative nonfiction, translations, and experimental work—as long as each piece pertains in some way to music. See website for the theme of the current issue.

M201 Hampshire Life
Magazine
United Kingdom

Magazine Publisher: Great British Life

M202 Hanging Loose
Magazine
PO Box 150608, Brooklyn, NY 11215
United States
Tel: +1 (857) 998-9473

https://www.hangingloosepress.com
https://www.facebook.com/hangingloosepress
https://twitter.com/HangingLooseNY

Fiction > *Short Fiction*

Poetry > *Any Poetic Form*

Send: Full text; Self-Addressed Stamped Envelope (SASE)
How to send: Post
How not to send: Email

Send up to six poems or one story at a time. Potential contributors should familiarise themselves with the magazine before submitting. Includes regular section of High School writers. Send submissions by post with SASE. Allow up to three months for a response.

M203 Harper's Magazine
Magazine
666 Broadway, 11th Floor, New York, NY 10012
United States
Tel: +1 (212) 420-5720

letters@harpers.org
readings@harpers.org

https://harpers.org
https://twitter.com/Harpers
https://www.facebook.com/HarpersMagazine/
https://www.instagram.com/harpersmagazine/

Fiction > *Short Fiction*

Nonfiction
  Articles: Culture; Current Affairs; Environment; Journalism; Politics; Society
  Essays: Culture; Current Affairs; Environment; Politics; Society

Send: Query; Full text; Self-Addressed Stamped Envelope (SASE)
How to send: Post
How not to send: Email

Current affairs magazine publishing topical essays, and fiction. Considers unsolicited fiction MSS, however no unsolicited nonfiction (query in first instance). All queries and submissions must be sent by post.

M204 Harpur Palate
Magazine
Binghamton University, English Department, P.O. Box 6000, Binghamton, NY 13902-6000
United States

harpur.palate@gmail.com

https://harpurpalate.binghamton.edu
https://twitter.com/harpurpalate
https://www.instagram.com/harpurpalate
https://www.facebook.com/harpurpalate
https://harpurpalate.submittable.com/submit

Fiction > *Short Fiction*

Nonfiction > *Short Nonfiction*: Creative Nonfiction

Poetry > *Any Poetic Form*

Closed to approaches.

Submit up to three poems, up to five pages total; fiction up to 4,500 words; creative nonfiction up to 5,500 words; or three pieces of short prose up to 1,000 words each. Submit through online submission system.

M205 Harvard Magazine
Magazine
7 Ware Street, Cambridge, Mass. 02138-4037
United States
Tel: +1 (617) 495-5746
Fax: +1 (617) 495-0324

https://www.harvardmagazine.com
https://www.facebook.com/HarvardMagazine
https://twitter.com/harvardmagazine
https://www.linkedin.com/company/harvard-magazine
https://www.youtube.com/user/HarvardMagazine
https://www.instagram.com/harvardmagazine/

Nonfiction > *Articles*: Harvard

Send: Query
How to send: Email

Magazine for faculty, alumni, and students of the university. Aims to keep alumni connected to the university community, covering the work and thinking being done at the university, and raising contemporary social and political issues and reflecting upon them. Also includes alumni news. Send query to the editor by email.

Editor: John S. Rosenberg

M206 Healthy
Magazine
United Kingdom

healthy@therivergroup.co.uk

https://www.healthy-magazine.co.uk
https://www.facebook.com/HealthyMagazine
https://twitter.com/healthymag
http://instagram.com/healthymagdaily

Magazine Publisher: The River Group

Nonfiction > *Articles*
  Beauty; Fitness; Food; Health; Lifestyle

Magazine of holistic health and lifestyle. Send query by email in first instance.

Editor: Heather Beresford

M207 Hedgerow: A Journal of Small Poems
Print Magazine
United Kingdom

hedgerowsubmission@gmail.com

https://hedgerowhaiku.com
https://www.facebook.com/hedgerowpoems

Fiction > *Short Fiction*

Poetry
  Any Poetic Form; *Haibun*; *Haiga*; *Haiku*; *Prose Poetry*; *Senryu*; *Tanka*

Send: Full text
How to send: In the body of an email

A short-poetry journal dedicated to publishing an eclectic mix of new and established voices across the spectrum of the short poem, with particular attention to the constantly evolving forms of English-language haiku, senryu, tanka, haiga and haibun. Submissions of prose poems, other longer poems and sequences, as well as short stories also welcome. Please note—for consistency, the house style will inform both print and online presentation.

M208 The Helix
Magazine
United States

helixmagazine@gmail.com

https://helixmagazine.org

Fiction > *Short Fiction*

Nonfiction > *Short Nonfiction*

Poetry > *Any Poetic Form*

Closed to approaches.

Publishes fiction, creative nonfiction, poetry, plays, and art. Submit prose up to 3,000 words each, or up to four poems.

Editor: Victoria-Lynn Bell

M209 Here Comes Everyone
Magazine
United Kingdom

https://hcemagazine.com
https://www.facebook.com/HCEmagazine/
https://twitter.com/herecomesevery1

Fiction > *Short Fiction*

Nonfiction > *Articles*

Poetry > *Any Poetic Form*

Closed to approaches.

Biannual literature and arts magazine publishing poetry, fiction, articles, and artwork. Each issue is themed. See website for upcoming themes and to submit.

Editor: Raef Boylan

M210 Hertfordshire Life
Magazine

Magazine Publisher: Archant

M211 Highway News
Magazine
1525 River Road, Marietta, PA 17547
United States
Tel: +1 (717) 426-9977

info@tfcglobal.org

https://tfcglobal.org/highway-news/current-issue/

Nonfiction > *Articles*
Hauliers; Religion

Religious magazine aimed at truck drivers and their families. Publishes testimonials, teachings, and human interest stories that have a foundation in Biblical/Christian values.

M212 History Today
Magazine
2nd Floor, 9 Staple Inn, London, WC1V 7QH
United Kingdom
Tel: +44 (0) 20 3219 7810

submissions@historytoday.com
admin@historytoday.com
enquiries@historytoday.com

https://www.historytoday.com

Nonfiction > *Articles*: History

Send: Query; Author bio
How to send: Email

Historical magazine publishing short articles (up to 1,000 words); mid-length articles (1,300-2,200 words) and feature articles (3,000 to 3,400 words). Send query by email with proposal and details of your career / academic background. See website for full guidelines.

M213 Homes & Antiques
Magazine
United Kingdom

https://www.homesandantiques.com
https://www.facebook.com/homesantiques
http://uk.pinterest.com/homesantiques
https://twitter.com/@homes_antiques
https://www.youtube.com/channel/UChlvNbVVoLcWle1xHnuAZlQ
https://www.instagram.com/homes_antiques

Magazine Publisher: Our Media

Nonfiction > *Articles*
Antiques; Decorating; Interior Design

Magazine of home interest, antiques, and collectibles.

Editor: Angela Linforth

M214 Horse & Rider
Magazine
7500 Alamo Road NW, Albuquerque, NM 87120
United States
Tel: +1 (303) 253-6405

HorseandRider@equinenetwork.com

https://my.horseandrider.com
https://www.facebook.com/HorseandRider
https://www.pinterest.com/hrsrdrmag/
https://www.instagram.com/horseandridermag/
https://twitter.com/Horse_and_Rider

Magazine Publisher: Equine Network

Nonfiction > *Articles*
American West; Horses; Travel

Provides all you need for today's Western horse life. Learn from top professional trainers, clinicians, and horse-keeping experts. Experience Western life. Travel to Western destinations and scenic trails. Your resource to live today's Western horse life.

M215 Hotel Amerika
Magazine
C/O The Department of Creative Writing, Columbia College Chicago, 600 South Michigan Avenue, Chicago, IL 60605
United States
Tel: +1 (312) 369-8175

http://www.hotelamerika.net

Fiction > *Short Fiction*: Literary

Nonfiction > *Essays*

Poetry > *Any Poetic Form*

Closed to approaches.

Costs: A fee is charged upon submission. $3.00.

Submissions will be considered between September 1 and April 1. Materials received after April 1 and before September 1 will not be considered.

Editor: David Lazar

M216 The Hudson Review
Magazine
33 West 67th Street, New York, NY 10023
United States
Tel: +1 (212) 650-0020

info@hudsonreview.com

https://hudsonreview.com
https://www.facebook.com/The-Hudson-Review-134346783271591/
https://twitter.com/TheHudsonReview

Fiction > *Short Fiction*

Nonfiction
Articles: Contemporary Culture
Essays: Arts; Dance; Films; Literary Criticism; Music; Theatre
Reviews: Books

Poetry > *Any Poetic Form*

Send: Full text; Self-Addressed Stamped Envelope (SASE)
How to send: Post; Online submission system

Publishes fiction, poetry, essays, book reviews; criticism of literature, art, theatre, dance, film and music; and articles on contemporary cultural developments.

Accepts certain material at only certain times of year: poetry between April 1 and June 30; fiction between September 1 and November 30; and nonfiction between January 1 and March 31. MSS submitted out of season are returned if adequate return postage is provided only. MSS of subscribers are read year-round.

No specialisation in any particular type of writing – literary quality is the only criteria. Read a sample copy of the magazine for a flavour of the kinds of material published.

No simultaneous submissions. Electronic submissions for fiction only.

M217 Hunger Mountain
Magazine
36 College Street, Montpelier, VT 05602
United States
Tel: +1 (802) 828-8844

hungermtn@vcfa.edu

https://hungermtn.org

Fiction in Translation > *Short Fiction*: Literary

Fiction > *Short Fiction*: Literary

Nonfiction in Translation > *Short Nonfiction*: Creative Nonfiction

Nonfiction > *Short Nonfiction*: Creative Nonfiction

Poetry in Translation > *Any Poetic Form*

Poetry > *Any Poetic Form*

Send: Full text
How to send: Submittable

Costs: A fee is charged upon submission.

Seeks to provide a platform for traditionally silenced voices, to expand representation in literature and to examine culture with a critical eye. Publishes fiction, nonfiction, poetry, hybrid work, and translations of all of these forms. Welcomes work that is genre-less and the traditional genres some magazines shun. Wants more speculative fiction. Doesn't believe in the divide between literary and genre fiction. Wants to read your science fiction, fantasy, magical realism, ecofabulism, irrealism and slipstream. Submit prose up to 8,000 words, or up to three flash pieces, or up to five poems, via online submission system.

Editor: Caroline Mercurio

M218 I-70 Review
Magazine
913 Joseph Drive, Lawrence, KS 66044
United States

i70review@gmail.com

http://i70review.fieldinfoserv.com

Fiction > *Short Fiction*

Poetry > *Any Poetic Form*

Closed to approaches.

Accepts submissions of fiction and flash fiction or 3-5 poems, by email, during the reading period that runs from July 1 to December 31. Accepts simultaneous submissions. See website for full details.

M219 Idaho Review
Magazine
Boise State University, 1910 University Drive, Boise, Idaho 83725
United States

mwieland@boisestate.edu

https://www.idahoreview.org
https://theidahoreview.submittable.com/submit
http://www.facebook.com/10213528569031037
http://twitter.com/idahoreview
http://www.instagram.com/theidahoreview

Fiction > *Short Fiction*: Literary

Nonfiction
  Essays: General
  Short Nonfiction: Creative Nonfiction

Poetry > *Any Poetic Form*

Closed to approaches.

Costs: A fee is charged for online submissions. $3 to submit online.

Annual literary journal publishing poetry and fiction. No specific limit for fiction, but most of the stories accepted are under 25 double-spaced pages. For poetry, submit up to five poems. Reading period runs from September to March (see website for specific dates for this year). Accepts submissions by post with SASE, but prefers submissions through online submission system ($3 fee).

M220 Ideal Home
Magazine
161 Marsh Wall, London, E14 9AP
United Kingdom

ideal_home@futurenet.com

https://www.idealhome.co.uk
https://www.facebook.com/idealhome.co.uk
https://twitter.com/idealhome

https://www.pinterest.co.uk/idealhomemag/
https://www.instagram.com/idealhomeuk/

Magazine Publisher: Future

Nonfiction > *Articles*
  Gardening; Interior Design

Monthly magazine on the home, covering interior design, decoration, furnishing, home improvements, gardening, etc.

M221 Identity Theory
Online Magazine
United States

fiction@identitytheory.com
essays@identitytheory.com
poetry@identitytheory.com

http://www.identitytheory.com
https://identitytheory.submittable.com/submit

Fiction > *Short Fiction*

Nonfiction
  Essays: Lyric Essays; Personal Essays
  Interviews: General
  Short Nonfiction: Creative Nonfiction;
  Memoir
Poetry > *Any Poetic Form*

Send: Full text
How to send: Submittable; Email

Online literary magazine. Send fiction or essays up to 4,000 words through Submittable or through specific email address, or 3-5 unpublished poems in the body of an email.

Editor: Matt Borondy

M222 Image
Magazine
3307 Third Avenue West, Seattle, WA 98119
United States
Tel: +1 (206) 281-2988

Image@imagejournal.org

https://imagejournal.org
http://facebook.com/imagejournal
http://twitter.com/image_journal
https://www.instagram.com/image_journal

Fiction > *Short Fiction*
  Culture; Literary; Religion; Spirituality

Nonfiction > *Essays*
  Arts; Culture; Literature; Religion;
  Spirituality

Poetry > *Any Poetic Form*
  Culture; Religion; Spirituality

Fosters contemporary art and writing that grapple with the mystery of being human by curating, cultivating, convening, and celebrating work that explores religious faith and faces spiritual questions. A vibrant thread in the fabric of culture, contributing to mainstream literary and artistic communities by demonstrating the vitality of contemporary art and literature invigorated by religious faith.

M223 Iman Collective
Online Magazine
Nigeria

imancollectivemag@gmail.com

https://imancollective.wordpress.com

Fiction > *Short Fiction*
  Islam; Literary

Nonfiction > *Short Nonfiction*
  Islam; Literary

Poetry > *Any Poetic Form*
  Islam; Literary

Send: Query
How to send: Email

This is a quarterly magazine publishing Muslim literature in the genres of poetry, fiction, and nonfiction.

M224 Indefinite Space
Magazine
PO Box 40101, Pasadena, CA 91114
United States

indefinitespace@yahoo.com

http://www.indefinitespace.net

Poetry > *Experimental Poetry*

Send: Full text
How to send: Email

Literary journal publishing innovative, imagistic, philosophical, and experimental poetry, drawings, collage, photography and paintings. Reads year round.

M225 Indiana Review
Magazine
Indiana University, Indiana Review Journal, Department of English, Lindley 215, 150 S Woodlawn Ave, Bloomington, IN 47405-7104
United States

inreview@indiana.edu

https://indianareview.org
https://indianareview.submittable.com/submit
https://twitter.com/indianareview
https://www.facebook.com/IndianaReview

Fiction in Translation > *Short Fiction*: Literary

Fiction > *Short Fiction*: Literary

Nonfiction in Translation > *Essays*

Nonfiction > *Essays*

Poetry in Translation > *Any Poetic Form*

Poetry > *Any Poetic Form*

Send: Full text
Don't send: Query
How to send: Submittable

Costs: A fee is charged upon submission. $3 per submission.

Send fiction or nonfiction up 6,000 words or 3-6 poems (up to 12 pages total) per submission, during specific submission windows only (see website for details). No submissions by post or by email – all submissions must be made through online submission manager ($3 fee). See website for full guidelines, and to submit.

M226 InfoWorld
Online Magazine
140 Kendrick Street, Building B, Needham, MA 02494
United States

https://www.infoworld.com
https://www.linkedin.com/company/164364
https://twitter.com/infoworld
https://www.facebook.com/InfoWorld

Magazine Publisher: Foundry

PROFESSIONAL > **Nonfiction** > *Articles*
  Computers; Technology

Closed to approaches.

The leading voice in emerging enterprise technology, is the go-to resource for developers, architects, and business leaders launching next-generation initiatives on scalable cloud platforms, where such future-focused tech as AI/machine learning, big data analytics, and NoSQL databases evolve continuously. Does not publish contributed articles.

Editor: Steve Fox, Editor in Chief

M227 Ink Sweat and Tears
Online Magazine
United Kingdom

submissions@inksweatandtears.co.uk
interns@inksweatandtears.co.uk

https://inksweatandtears.co.uk
https://twitter.com/InkSweatTears
https://www.facebook.com/InkSweatandTears
https://www.instagram.com/insta.inksweatandtears/

Nonfiction > *Reviews*
  Literature; Poetry as a Subject

Poetry
  Any Poetic Form; *Haibun*; *Haiga*; *Haiku*; *Prose Poetry*

Closed to approaches.

UK-based webzine publishing poetry, prose, prose-poetry, word and image pieces, and poetry reviews. Send 4-6 pieces of poetry (or 1-2 short prose/flash fiction works) by email only. Accepts unsolicited reviews of poetry and short story collections. See website for full guidelines.

Editor: Helen Ivory

M228 Inque
Magazine
United Kingdom

info@inquemag.com

https://inquemag.com
http://instagram.com/inquemag
http://twitter.com/inquemagazine

Fiction > *Short Fiction*: Literary

Nonfiction
  Articles: Arts; Literature
  Interviews: Arts; Literature

Annual literary magazine dedicated to extraordinary new writing. Documenting what is going to be an era-defining decade, it will run no advertising, have no web version, and only ever publish 10 issues. Contributors include Margaret Atwood, Max Porter, Joyce Carol Oates, Ocean Vuong, Tom Waits, Ben Lerner, Alexander Chee, Kae Tempest, and more.

M229 Inspire
Magazine
1 Easting Close, Worthing, BN14 8HQ
United Kingdom
Tel: +44 (0) 1903 263354

editor@inspiremagazine.org.uk

https://www.inspiremagazine.org.uk
https://twitter.com/inspirestories
https://www.facebook.com/InspireMagazineUK/

Nonfiction > *Articles*: Christianity

Christian magazine dedicated to telling the good news stories of God at work transforming individuals, churches and communities around the UK and across the world.

Editor: Russ Bravo

M230 InStyle
Magazine
United States
Tel: +1 (800) 274-6200

letters@instylemag.com

https://www.instyle.com
https://www.facebook.com/InStyle
https://twitter.com/InStyle
https://www.pinterest.com/instyle/
https://www.instagram.com/instylemagazine/

Magazine Publisher: Meredith Corporation

Nonfiction
  Articles: Beauty; Celebrity; Fashion; Hairstyles; How To; Lifestyle; Politics; Popular Culture; Social Issues
  News: General

Magazine providing readers with a mix of fashion and beauty advice and celebrity news and lifestyle.

M231 Insurance Age
Online Magazine
Infopro Digital, 133 Houndsditch, London, EC3A 7BX
United Kingdom

Tel: +44 (0) 20 7316 9000
Fax: +44 (0) 20 7681 3401

info@insuranceage.co.uk

https://www.insuranceage.co.uk
https://twitter.com/insuranceage
https://www.linkedin.com/company/insurance-age

PROFESSIONAL > **Nonfiction**
  Articles: Insurance
  News: Insurance

Publishes news and features on the insurance industry.

Editor: Lauren Ingram

M232 International Piano
Magazine
United Kingdom

https://www.markallengroup.com/brands/international-piano/
https://twitter.com/IP_mag
https://www.facebook.com/internationalpiano/
https://www.instagram.com/internationalpianomagazine
https://www.youtube.com/channel/UCOKPU5skkhcvQRjXVkou10Q

Media Company: Mark Allen Group

ACADEMIC > **Nonfiction** > *Articles*: Piano

ADULT > **Nonfiction** > *Articles*: Piano

PROFESSIONAL > **Nonfiction** > *Articles*: Piano

Describes itself as the leading magazine for pianists and piano fans around the world. Wide-ranging reviews and in-depth features meet inspiring practical advice from top performers and teachers in this indispensable guide to the piano in all its forms, published 10 times per year.

Editor: Tim Parry

M233 The Interpreter's House
Online Magazine
United Kingdom

interpretershousesubmissions@gmail.com

https://theinterpretershouse.org

Fiction > *Short Fiction*

Nonfiction
  Essays; *Interviews*; *Reviews*
Poetry > *Any Poetic Form*

Send up to five poems or up to two short stories by email during specific submission windows (see website for details).

Editor: Georgi Gill

M234 Interzone
Magazine
United Kingdom

submissions@interzone.press
editors@interzone.press

https://interzone.press
https://interzone.press/submissions/

Magazine Publisher: MYY Press

Fiction in Translation > *Short Fiction*
Fantasy; Horror; Science Fiction

Fiction > *Short Fiction*
Fantasy; Horror; Science Fiction

Send: Full text
How to send: Email

Publishes fantastika (including science fiction, fantasy, and horror) short stories up to 17,500 words. See website for full guidelines.

Editor / Publisher: Gareth Jelley

M235 Investors Chronicle
Magazine
United Kingdom

https://www.investorschronicle.co.uk
https://www.linkedin.com/showcase/financial-times---investors-chronicle/
https://twitter.com/ichronicle
https://www.instagram.com/investorschronicle/
https://www.facebook.com/InvestorsChronicleOnline

PROFESSIONAL > **Nonfiction** > *Articles*
Business; Finance

Magazine for investors.

Editor: Rosie Carr

M236 Irish Pages
Magazine
129 Ormeau Road, Belfast, BT7 1SH
United Kingdom
Tel: +44 (0) 2890 434800

editor@irishpages.org
sales@irishpages.org
gaeilge@irishpages.org

https://irishpages.org
https://twitter.com/irishpages
https://www.youtube.com/channel/UC08ArKYYmKVUpP5cHfEMz0w

Fiction in Translation > *Short Fiction*

Fiction > *Short Fiction*

Nonfiction in Translation
Essays: General
Short Nonfiction: Autobiography; Creative Nonfiction; History; Literary Journalism; Memoir; Nature; Religion; Science
Nonfiction
Essays: General
Short Nonfiction: Autobiography; Creative Nonfiction; History; Literary Journalism; Memoir; Nature; Religion; Science
Poetry in Translation > *Any Poetic Form*

Poetry > *Any Poetic Form*

Send: Full text
How to send: Post
How not to send: Email

Non-partisan and non-sectarian literary journal publishing writing from the island of Ireland and elsewhere in equal measure. Publishes work in English, and in the Irish Language or Ulster Scots with English translations and glosses. Accepts submissions throughout the year by post only with stamps, coupons or cash for return postage (no self-addressed envelope is needed). See website for more details.

M237 Island
Magazine
PO Box 4703, Hobart TAS 7000
Australia
Tel: +61 (0) 3 6234 1462

admin@islandmag.com

https://islandmag.com
https://island.submittable.com/submit

Fiction > *Short Fiction*

Nonfiction
Articles; Essays
Poetry > *Any Poetic Form*

Closed to approaches.

Welcomes submissions of nonfiction, fiction and poetry from Australia, New Zealand and the Pacific, as well as from Australians living abroad. See website for details and to submit using online submission system.

Online Magazine: Island Online (**M238**)

M238 Island Online
Online Magazine
Australia

admin@islandmag.com
ben@islandmag.com

https://islandmag.com/online
https://island.submittable.com/submit
http://www.facebook.com/islandmagtas
http://instagram.com/islandmagtas
https://twitter.com/IslandMagTas

Magazine: Island (**M237**)

Fiction > *Short Fiction*
Arts; Culture; Environment; Experimental; Literary; Nature; Society

Nonfiction > *Essays*
Arts; Culture; Environment; Nature; Society

Closed to approaches.

Digital publishing platform operated in conjunction with longstanding print magazine.

M239 Janes Defence Weekly
Magazine
United Kingdom
Tel: +44 (0) 20 3997 6594

customer.care@janes.com

https://www.janes.com
https://www.linkedin.com/company/ihs-jane's/
https://www.youtube.com/channel/UCEC1WX1I030Ss6oNk7ynsBA
https://www.facebook.com/JanesIntelligence/

PROFESSIONAL > **Nonfiction**
Articles: Military; Secret Intelligence; Warfare; Weapons
News: Military; Secret Intelligence; Warfare; Weapons

Magazine covering defence topics of worldwide interest. No history.

M240 Jazz Journal
Online Magazine
United Kingdom

editor@jazzjournal.co.uk

https://jazzjournal.co.uk

Nonfiction
Articles: Jazz
News: Jazz
Reviews: Jazz

The oldest English-language magazine dedicated to the coverage of jazz music. Published in print for seven decades and from 2019 as a web-only publication. Provides a rolling jazz news and review service with columns and features added on an ad-hoc, roughly monthly basis. Publishes approximately 70 reviews of newly issued jazz recordings per month.

M241 The Journal
Magazine
38 Pwllcarn Terrace, Blaengarw, Bridgend, CF32 8AS
United Kingdom

asamsmith@hotmail.com

https://thesamsmith.webs.com/

Nonfiction
Interviews: Poetry as a Subject
Reviews: Poetry as a Subject

Poetry in Translation > *Any Poetic Form*

Poetry > *Any Poetic Form*

Send: Full text; Self-Addressed Stamped Envelope (SASE)
How to send: Post

Accepts poems in English, or translations into English (about 6 at a time). Also welcome are interviews with poets, reviews, appreciations or appraisals of current poetry scenes. If a reply is desired within the UK, enclose SAE

Editor: Sam Smith

M242 Kent Life
Magazine
United Kingdom

https://www.greatbritishlife.co.uk/magazines/kent/

Magazine Publisher: Great British Life

Nonfiction > *Articles*
Arts; Celebrity; Countryside; Culture; Food and Drink; Gardening; Houses; Kent; Lifestyle; Local History; Nature; Recipes; Travel; Walking Guides

Every month you'll find within our pages a wealth of fresh ideas on how you can best explore our area's glorious countryside, beautiful coastline, thriving towns and villages and fascinating history. Whether you want to sample great local food and drink, dip into our exciting arts scene or revel in the glorious natural beauty that surrounds us, we've got suggestions galore. You'll hear Kent voices loud and clear, too, of course, with our top-notch writers highlighing the energy and sheer diversity of our community via their stories and interviews, and our columnists adding their unique take on county life. Add to the mix our inspiring monthly features on gorgeous homes and gardens, our town guides, walk suggestions and fascinating stories from local history, and you've got an unmissable monthly blend of ideas, lifestyle, nature and personalities.

M243 The Kenyon Review
Magazine
102 W. Wiggin St., Gambier, OH 43022
United States
Tel: +1 (740) 427-5208
Fax: +1 (740) 427-5417

kenyonreview@kenyon.edu

https://kenyonreview.org

Types: Fiction; Nonfiction; Poetry; Scripts; Translations
Formats: Essays; Reviews; Short Fiction
Subjects: Arts; Literary
Markets: Adult

Closed to approaches.

Submit through online submission system. Send short fiction up to 7,500 words, poetry up to six poems, or plays or excerpts up to 30 pages, with SASE. Translations are also accepted, but author is responsible for permissions. No unsolicited interviews or submissions by email or post.

M244 Kerning
Magazine
United States

hello@toadhalleditions.ink

https://www.toadhalleditions.ink/kerning-a-space-for-words

Book Publisher / Self Publishing Service / Magazine Publisher: Toad Hall Editions
(P517)

Fiction > *Short Fiction*

Nonfiction
Essays: General

Short Nonfiction: Creative Nonfiction

Poetry > *Any Poetic Form*

Closed to approaches.

Costs: Invites donations. Choose to pay $7, $14, or no fee when submitting.

Publishes work by women and gender diverse people only.

M245 Kerrang!
Magazine
90 – 92 Pentonville Road, London, N1 9HS
United Kingdom

feedback@kerrang.com

https://www.kerrang.com
https://www.facebook.com/kerrangmagazine/
https://twitter.com/KerrangMagazine
https://www.instagram.com/kerrangmagazine_/
https://www.youtube.com/user/KerrangPodcast
https://www.tiktok.com/kerrangmagazine_

Magazine Publisher: Wasted Talent

Nonfiction
Articles: Heavy Metal; Music; Punk; Rock Music
News: Heavy Metal; Music; Punk; Rock Music

Weekly rock, metal, and punk magazine.

M246 Kids Alive!
Magazine
The Salvation Army, 101 Newington Causeway, London, SE1 6BN
United Kingdom
Tel: +44 (0) 20 7367 4910

kidsalive@salvationarmy.org.uk

https://www.salvationist.org.uk/media/kidsalive

CHILDREN'S
Fiction > *Cartoons*: Christianity

Nonfiction > *Articles*: Christianity

Christian children's magazine publishing puzzles, comic strips, etc.

Editor: Justin Reeves

M247 The Lake
Online Magazine
United Kingdom

poetry@thelakepoetry.co.uk

http://www.thelakepoetry.co.uk

Poetry > *Any Poetic Form*

Send: Full text; Author bio
How to send: In the body of an email; Word file email attachment

Submit up to five poems within the body of an email or attach one Word document with POETRY SUBMISSION in the Subject line. Please also include a short third person

biography (50 words max.). If you have a publication or personal web site then you can also include a link to the site. I will respond to all submissions within two to three weeks. If after that time you haven't heard from me let me know via email.

M248 Lancashire Life
Magazine
United Kingdom

https://www.lancashirelife.co.uk

Magazine Publisher: Great British Life

Nonfiction > *Articles*
Food and Drink; Lancashire; Property / Real Estate; Travel

Publishes articles, features, and pictures of Lancashire.

M249 Landfall
Magazine
Otago University Press, PO Box 56, Dunedin 9054
New Zealand
Tel: +64 (0) 3 479 4155

editorial@otago.ac.nz
landfall@otago.ac.nz

https://www.otago.ac.nz/press/landfall/index.html
https://www.facebook.com/landfall.journal
https://twitter.com/landfallnz

Fiction > *Short Fiction*: Literary

Nonfiction
Articles: Arts; Culture; New Zealand
Essays: General
Reviews: Books; Local
Poetry > *Any Poetic Form*

Send: Full text
How to send: Email

Publishes literary fiction and essays, poetry, extracts from work in progress, commentary on New Zealand arts and culture, work by visual artists including photographers, and reviews of local books.

M250 Leisure Group Travel
Magazine
United States

Jason@ptmgroups.com

https://leisuregrouptravel.com
https://www.facebook.com/LeisureGroupTravel
https://twitter.com/leisuregroup
https://www.linkedin.com/showcase/leisure-group-travel/

PROFESSIONAL > **Nonfiction** > *Articles*
Business; Travel

How to send: Email; Online contact form

Magazine aimed at group travel buyers. Submit news and press releases that relate to the group travel industry by email or through contact form on website.

M251 Leisure Painter

Magazine
The Maltings, West Street, Bourne, Lincolnshire, PE10 9PH
United Kingdom
Tel: +44 (0) 1778 395174

https://www.painters-online.co.uk

Magazine Publisher: Warners Group Publications

Nonfiction > *Articles:* Painting

Magazine offering artistic inspiration, guidance, tuition and encouragement for beginners and amateur artists. Includes features and step-by-step painting and drawing demonstrations.

M252 Light & Life

Magazine
United States

https://lightandlife.fm
https://twitter.com/lightandlifemag
https://www.facebook.com/lightandlifemagazine
https://www.youtube.com/channel/UCr8nd1V-UnRFTBeCTSPB68A
https://vimeo.com/llcomm
https://www.linkedin.com/company/559925
https://www.flickr.com/photos/llcomm/

Nonfiction > *Articles:* Methodism

Bimonthly magazine that exists to promote thoughtful Christian discipleship from a Wesleyan-Arminian perspective.

Executive Editor: Jeff Finley

M253 Lighthouse

Magazine
United Kingdom

subs.lighthouse@gmail.com
lighthouseprosesubmissions@gmail.com

https://storymachines.co.uk/portfolio/lighthouse/

Fiction > *Short Fiction*

Poetry > *Any Poetic Form*

Closed to approaches.

A literary journal dedicated to publishing new writing and championing new writers. Aims to publish the best short fiction, poetry, and art emerging from the UK scene.

M254 Lincolnshire Life

Magazine
County House, 9 Checkpoint Court, Sadler Road, Lincoln, LN6 3PW
United Kingdom
Tel: +44 (0) 1522 689671

studio@lincolnshirelife.co.uk

https://www.lincolnshirelife.co.uk
http://www.facebook.com/lincolnshirelife
https://twitter.com/lincslife

Nonfiction > *Articles*
Business; Contemporary; Culture; Food; History; Leisure; Lifestyle; Lincolnshire

A monthly magazine devoted to the history, culture and contemporary life of Lincolnshire, England.

M255 Literary Mama

Online Magazine
United States

LMinfo@literarymama.com
LMreviewseditor@gmail.com
LMnonfiction@gmail.com
literarymamafiction@gmail.com
LMliteraryreflections@gmail.com
literarymamapoetry@gmail.com

https://literarymama.com
http://www.facebook.com/litmama
http://twitter.com/literarymama
https://www.instagram.com/literary_mama/

Fiction > *Short Fiction:* Motherhood

Nonfiction
Essays: Creativity; Motherhood; Writing
Reviews: Books; Motherhood
Short Nonfiction: Creative Nonfiction; Motherhood
Poetry > *Any Poetic Form:* Motherhood

Send: Full text; Query
How to send: In the body of an email

Online magazine publishing fiction, poetry, creative nonfiction, and book reviews focusing on mother writers, and the complexities and many faces of motherhood. Accepts submissions in the text of emails only – no snail mail submissions. See website for full submission guidelines. Contact again if no response after three months.

M256 Litro Magazine

Magazine
90 York Way, London, N1 9AG
United Kingdom
Tel: +44 (0) 207 917 2887

editor@litro.co.uk
online@litro.co.uk
podcasts@litro.co.uk

https://www.litro.co.uk
https://www.facebook.com/Litromedia/
https://open.spotify.com/show/78fpfD5ejecJXXdsVHGJqb
https://www.instagram.com/litromedia/
https://twitter.com/litromagazine

Fiction > *Short Fiction*

Nonfiction > *Short Nonfiction*
Literary Journalism; Memoir; Travel

How to send: Submittable
How not to send: Email

Accepts short fiction, flash/micro fiction, nonfiction (memoir, literary journalism, travel narratives, etc), and original artwork (photographs, illustrations, paintings, etc) based on the designated monthly theme. Works translated into English are also welcome. See website for upcoming themes.

M257 The London Magazine

Magazine
Flat 5, 11 Queen's Gate, London, SW7 5EL
United Kingdom
Tel: +44 (0) 20 7584 5977
Fax: +44 (0) 20 7225 3273

editorial@thelondonmagazine.org
admin@thelondonmagazine.org

https://thelondonmagazine.org
https://thelondonmagazine.submittable.com/submit
https://www.facebook.com/thelondonmagazine1732/
https://twitter.com/thelondonmag
https://www.instagram.com/thelondonmagazine/?hl=en

Fiction > *Short Fiction*

Nonfiction > *Short Nonfiction*

Poetry > *Any Poetic Form*

Does not want:

> **Fiction** > *Short Fiction*
> Erotic; Fantasy; Science Fiction

Send: Full text
How to send: Submittable

Send submissions through online submission system or by email. Does not normally publish science fiction or fantasy writing, or erotica. Will consider postal submissions, but prefers submissions electronically. See website for full guidelines.

M258 London Review of Books

Magazine
28 Little Russell Street, London, WC1A 2HN
United Kingdom
Tel: +44 (0) 20 7209 1101

edit@lrb.co.uk

https://www.lrb.co.uk
https://www.facebook.com/LondonReviewOfBooks
https://twitter.com/lrb
https://www.youtube.com/londonreviewofbooks
https://www.instagram.com/londonreviewofbooks/

Nonfiction
Articles: Anthropology; Arts; Biography; Classics / Ancient World; Culture; Economics; History; Legal; Literary

Criticism; Literature; Memoir; Philosophy; Politics; Psychology; Science; Technology
Reviews: General

Poetry > *Any Poetic Form*

Send: Full text; Proposal; Self-Addressed Stamped Envelope (SASE)
How to send: Email; Post

Publishes poems, reviews, reportage, memoir, articles, and blogposts. Send submissions by email or by post (with SAE).

M259 Long Poem Magazine

Magazine
20 Spencer Rise, London, NW5 1AP
United Kingdom

longpoemmagazine@gmail.com

http://longpoemmagazine.org.uk
https://www.facebook.com/groups/longpoemmagazine/
https://twitter.com/LongPoemMag

Nonfiction
Essays: Poetry as a Subject
Reviews: Books

Poetry > *Long Form Poetry*

Closed to approaches.

Magazine dedicated to publishing long poems and sequences. Publishes unpublished poems of at least 75 lines (but no book length poems). Also publishes essays on aspects of the long poem and reviews of books featuring long poems or sequences. Send submissions by email as Word file attachments. Does not accept poems submitted in the body of emails. See website for full guidelines and submission months. Poems submitted outside submission months will be discarded.

M260 Lost Lake Folk Opera Magazine

Print Magazine
United States

https://shipwrecktbooks.press
https://shipwrecktbooks.submittable.com/submit

Book Publisher: Shipwreckt Books Publishing Company (**P477**)

Fiction > *Short Fiction*

Nonfiction > *Essays*

Poetry > *Any Poetic Form*

Scripts > *Theatre Scripts*

Send: Full text; Author bio
How to send: Submittable

Literary magazine published twice annually. Accepts short fiction (1000-6000 wds); one-act and other short plays or scenes (1000-6000 wds); essays and opinion (500-300 wds); poetry (no more than 10 poems or 10 pages).

M261 Louisiana Literature

Magazine
United States

lalit@selu.edu

http://www.louisianaliterature.org
https://twitter.com/LaLiterature
https://louisianaliterature.submittable.com/submit

Fiction > *Short Fiction*: Literary

Nonfiction > *Essays*: Creative Nonfiction

Poetry > *Any Poetic Form*

Send: Full text
How to send: Submittable

Literary journal publishing fiction, poetry, and creative nonfiction. Submit via online system available at the website.

Editor: Dr Jack Bedell

M262 The MacGuffin

Magazine
Schoolcraft College, 18600 Haggerty Road, Livonia, MI 48152
United States
Tel: +1 (734) 462-5327

macguffin@schoolcraft.edu

https://schoolcraft.edu/macguffin
https://themacguffin.submittable.com/submit

Fiction > *Short Fiction*

Nonfiction > *Short Nonfiction*: Creative Nonfiction

Poetry
Any Poetic Form; *Experimental Poetry*; *Free Verse*

Send: Full text
How to send: Submittable

Publishes fiction, creative nonfiction, and poetry. Submit up to five poems or up to two pieces of prose via online submission system.

M263 The Magazine of Fantasy & Science Fiction

Magazine
PO Box 3447, Hoboken, NJ 07030
United States

fsfmag@fandsf.com

http://fandsf.com
https://fandsf.moksha.io/publication/fsf

Fiction > *Short Fiction*
Fantasy; Science Fiction

Send: Full text; Self-Addressed Stamped Envelope (SASE)
How to send: Moksha; Post

We have no formula for fiction, but we like to be surprised by stories, either by the character insights, ideas, plots, or prose. The speculative element may be slight, but it should be present. We prefer character-oriented stories, whether it's fantasy, science fiction, horror, humor, or another genre. We encourage submissions from diverse voices and perspectives, and have published writers from all over the world. Do not query for fiction; submit the entire manuscript. We publish fiction up to 25,000 words in length. Please read the magazine before submitting. A sample copy (print edition) is available for $7.00 in the US and $17.50 elsewhere (to NJ address).

We do not accept simultaneous submissions. Please prepare your submission according to standard guidelines. If you're mailing your manuscript, put your name on each page, and enclose a self-addressed, stamped envelope. Writers are encouraged to submit their work electronically.

We prefer not to see more than one submission from a writer at a time.

Allow 8 weeks for a response.

Payment is 8-12 cents per word on acceptance. We buy first North American and foreign serial rights and an option on anthology rights. All other rights are retained by the author.

Our columns and non-fiction articles are assigned in-house. We do not accept freelance submissions in those areas.

M264 The Malahat Review

Magazine
University of Victoria, McPherson Library, PO Box 1800, Stn CSC, Victoria, BC V8W 3H5
Canada

malahat@uvic.ca

http://www.malahatreview.ca
https://twitter.com/malahatreview

Fiction > *Short Fiction*

Nonfiction
Essays: Personal Essays
Reviews: Books
Short Nonfiction: Biography; Creative Nonfiction; History; Memoir; Narrative Nonfiction; Social Commentary; Travel
Poetry > *Any Poetic Form*

Closed to approaches.

Publishes poetry, short fiction, and creative nonfiction by new and established writers mostly from Canada, reviews of Canadian books, and the best writing from abroad. Submissions from Canadian writers are accepted year-round. Fiction and poetry submissions from international writers only accepted during specific windows.

M265 marie claire

Magazine
United States

marieclairepr@futurenet.com

https://www.marieclaire.com
https://www.facebook.com/MarieClaire

https://twitter.com/marieclaire
https://www.pinterest.com/MarieClaire
https://instagram.com/marieclairemag
https://www.youtube.com/c/MarieClaire

Magazine Publisher: Future

Nonfiction > *Articles*
Beauty; Career Development; Celebrity;
Culture; Fashion; Finance; Fitness; Food and
Drink; Health; Horoscopes; Politics;
Relationships; Sex; Travel; Women's
Interests

Lifestyle magazine aimed at the younger
working woman.

M266 marie claire (UK)
Magazine
Future PLC, 121 – 141 Westbourne Terrace,
Paddington, London, W2 6JR
United Kingdom

https://www.marieclaire.co.uk
https://www.facebook.com/MarieClaireUK/
https://twitter.com/marieclaireuk
https://www.pinterest.co.uk/marieclaireuk/
https://www.instagram.com/marieclaireuk/

Magazine Publisher: Future

Nonfiction > *Articles*
Beauty; Celebrity; Entertainment; Fashion;
Hairstyles; Health; Lifestyle; Relationships;
Sex

Glossy magazine for women.

M267 Marlin
Magazine
517 N. Virginia Ave, Winter Park, FL 32789
United States

editor@marlinmag.com

https://www.marlinmag.com
https://www.facebook.com/marlinmag/
https://twitter.com/MarlinMagazine/
http://instagram.com/marlinmag/
http://www.youtube.com/MarlinMagazine/

Nonfiction > *Articles*
Boats; How To; Offshore Gamefishing;
Travel

Publishes articles, features, and news items
relating to offshore fishing, destinations,
personalities, fishery regulations, the boating
industry and related topics, including how-to
and technical information.

M268 The Massachusetts Review
Magazine
Photo Lab 309, University of Massachusetts,
Amherst, MA 01003
United States
Tel: +1 (413) 545-2689
Fax: +1 (413) 577-0740

massrev@external.umass.edu

http://www.massreview.org
https://www.facebook.com/pages/The-
Massachusetts-Review/40580092594
https://twitter.com/MassReview
http://instagram.com/themassachusettsreview?
ref=badge
http://themassreview.tumblr.com/

Fiction in Translation > *Short
Fiction*: Literary

Fiction > *Short Fiction*: Literary

Nonfiction in Translation > *Essays*
Arts; Current Affairs; Drama; Literature;
Music; Philosophy; Science

Nonfiction
Articles: Arts; Current Affairs; Drama;
Literature; Music; Philosophy; Science
Essays: Arts; Current Affairs; Drama;
Literature; Music; Philosophy; Science
Poetry in Translation > *Any Poetic Form*

Poetry > *Any Poetic Form*

Closed to approaches.

Costs: A fee is charged for online submissions.
$3.

Send one story of up to 25–30 pages or up to
six poems of any length (though rarely
publishes poems of more than 100 lines).
White people may not submit between May 1
and September 30. Others may submit year-
round, and may use email if the online
submission system is closed. White people are
not permitted to submit by email. Articles and
essays of breadth and depth are considered, as
well as discussions of leading writers; of art,
music, and drama; analyses of trends in
literature, science, philosophy, and public
affairs. No plays, reviews of single books, or
submissions by fax or email.

M269 Mayfair Times
Magazine
United Kingdom

https://mayfairtimes.co.uk
https://www.facebook.com/mayfairtimes/
https://twitter.com/MayfairTimes
https://instagram.com/Mayfair.Times

Nonfiction
Articles: Arts; Business; Culture; Fashion;
Finance; Food and Drink; Houses; Lifestyle;
Local; Travel
News: Local

A monthly luxury lifestyle magazine, which
has been serving the people of Mayfair,
Marylebone and St James's for 35 years.

M270 Meetinghouse
Magazine
United States

submissions@meetinghousemag.org

https://www.meetinghousemag.org
https://twitter.com/meethousemag

Fiction > *Short Fiction*

Poetry > *Any Poetic Form*

Closed to approaches.

A literary magazine that provides a space for
diverse voices to speak with one another.
Submit up to two pieces of prose and up to five
poems per submission.

M271 Metropolis Magazine
Magazine
United States
Tel: +1 (212) 934-2800

info@metropolismag.com

https://www.metropolismag.com/
https://www.facebook.com/MetropolisMag
https://metropoliseditorialaccount.
submittable.com/submit
https://twitter.com/MetropolisMag
https://www.linkedin.com/company/
metropolis-magazine
https://www.instagram.com/metropolismag/

Magazine Publisher: Sandow

Nonfiction > *Articles*
Architecture; Arts; City and Town Planning;
Culture; Design; Interior Design; Sustainable
Living; Technology

Send: Pitch
How to send: Submittable

Magazine examining contemporary life
through design: architecture, interior design,
product design, graphic design, crafts,
planning, and preservation.

M272 mg Magazine
Magazine
6520 Platt Ave., Suite 399, West Hills, CA
91307
United States
Tel: +1 (310) 421-1860

https://mgretailer.com

Magazine Publisher: Inc Media

PROFESSIONAL > **Nonfiction**
Articles: Business; Cannabis; Current
Affairs; Farming; Health; Hemp; How To;
Legal; Politics; Science; Technology
Interviews: Business; Cannabis; Current
Affairs; Farming; Health; Hemp; How To;
Legal; Politics; Science; Technology
News: Business; Cannabis; Current Affairs;
Farming; Health; Hemp; How To; Legal;
Politics; Science; Technology

How to send: Email

The resource professionals in the legal
cannabis industry turn to for insight and intel
to help them increase revenues and scale their
businesses. Each glossy monthly issue is filled
with high-concept copy and photographs
covering topics including retail design and
merchandising; advertising; branding and
marketing; law, regulations, and politics;

human resources; products, technology, and finance. Issues typically include two features (3,000 words each), an executive profile (3,000 words), a business profile (1,500 words), a finance column, and a retail design feature, all of which are freelance-written. The associated websites provide freelance-written news, business tips, how-tos, data analysis, business profiles, and other material.

M273 Michigan Quarterly Review
Magazine
3277 Angell Hall, 435 S. State Street, Ann Arbor, MI 48109-1003
United States
Tel: +1 (734) 764-9265

mqr@umich.edu

https://sites.lsa.umich.edu/mqr/
https://mqr.submittable.com/submit

Fiction in Translation > *Short Fiction*

Fiction > *Short Fiction*

Nonfiction
  Articles; *Essays*
Poetry in Translation > *Any Poetic Form*

Poetry > *Any Poetic Form*

Closed to approaches.

Costs: A fee is charged upon submission. $3 submission fee.

An interdisciplinary and international literary journal, combining distinctive voices in poetry, fiction, and nonfiction, as well as works in translation.

Online Magazine: MQR Mixtape (**M282**)

M274 Mid-American Review
Magazine
Department of English, Bowling Green State University, Bowling Green, OH 43403
United States
Tel: +1 (419) 372-2725

mar@bgsu.edu

https://casit.bgsu.edu/midamericanreview/

Fiction in Translation > *Short Fiction*: Literary

Fiction > *Short Fiction*: Literary

Nonfiction
  Essays: General
  Reviews: Books

Poetry in Translation > *Any Poetic Form*

Poetry > *Any Poetic Form*

How to send: Online submission system; Post

Accepts fiction, poetry, translations, and nonfiction (including personal essays, essays on writing, and short reviews). Submit by post with SASE or through online submission system.

M275 Midway Journal
Online Magazine
United States

editors@midwayjournal.com

https://midwayjournal.com
https://www.facebook.com/midway.journal
https://twitter.com/MidwayJournal
https://www.instagram.com/the_midway_journal_/

Fiction > *Short Fiction*

Nonfiction
  Essays: General
  Interviews: General
  Short Nonfiction: Creative Nonfiction

Poetry > *Any Poetic Form*

Send: Full text
How to send: Submittable

Costs: A fee is charged. $2.50 for expedited submissions, available year-round. Free submissions during specific windows only.

Aims to act as a bridge between aesthetics (and coasts), and create an engaging sense of place. Publishes work that aims to complicate and question the boundaries of genre, binary, and perspective. It offers surprises and ways of re-seeing, re-thinking, and re-feeling.

Fiction Editor: Ralph Pennel

Nonfiction Editor: Allie Mariano

Poetry Editor: Mariela Lemus

M276 MiniWorld Magazine
Magazine
The Granary, Downs Court, Yalding Hill, Yalding, Kent, ME18 6AL
United Kingdom
Tel: +44 (0) 1959 543747

https://shop.kelsey.co.uk/miniworld-magazine
http://www.facebook.com/miniworldmagazine
https://twitter.com/MagMiniWorld

Magazine Publisher: Kelsey Media

Nonfiction > *Articles*: Mini Cars

Magazine devoted to the mini, including technical advice, tuning, restoration, social history, maintenance, etc.

M277 Mississippi Review
Magazine
118 College Drive #5144, Hattiesburg, Mississippi 39406-0001
United States
Tel: +1 (601) 266-4321

msreview@usm.edu

http://sites.usm.edu/mississippi-review/

Fiction > *Short Fiction*

Nonfiction > *Essays*

Poetry > *Any Poetic Form*

Costs: A fee is charged upon submission. $16 competition entry fee.

Publishes work submitted to competition only. No unsolicited MSS. See website for competition details.

Editor: Frederick Barthelme

Managing Editor: Rie Fortenberry

M278 The Missouri Review
Magazine
453 McReynolds Hall, University of Missouri, Columbia, MO 65211
United States

question@moreview.com

https://www.missourireview.com
https://www.facebook.com/themissourireview
https://twitter.com/missouri_review
https://www.instagram.com/themissourireview/

Fiction > *Short Fiction*

Nonfiction > *Essays*

Poetry > *Any Poetic Form*

Does not want:

Nonfiction > *Essays*: Literary Criticism

Send: Query; Self-Addressed Stamped Envelope (SASE); Full text
How to send: Post; Online submission system

Costs: A fee is charged for online submissions. $4 submission fee for online submissions.

Publishes poetry, fiction, and essays of general interest. No literary criticism. Submit by post with SASE, or via online system. There is a $4 charge for online submissions.

Editor: Speer Morgan

M279 Modern Poetry in Translation
Magazine
United Kingdom

editor@mptmagazine.com

http://modernpoetryintranslation.com
https://twitter.com/MPTmagazine
https://www.instagram.com/modernpoetryintranslation/

Poetry in Translation > *Any Poetic Form*

Send: Full text
How to send: Submittable

Respected poetry series originally founded by prominent poets in the sixties. New Series continues their editorial policy: translation of good poets by translators who are often themselves poets, fluent in the foreign language, and sometimes working with the original poet. Publishes translations into English only. No original English language poetry. Send submissions via online submission system.

M280 Monomyth

Magazine
Atlantean Publishing, 4 Pierrot Steps, 71 Kursaal Way, Southend-on-Sea, Essex, SS1 2UY
United Kingdom

atlanteanpublishing@hotmail.com

https://atlanteanpublishing.fandom.com/wiki/Monomyth
https://atlanteanpublishing.wordpress.com/guidelines/

Book Publisher / Magazine Publisher: Atlantean Publishing (**P044**)

Fiction > *Short Fiction*

Poetry > *Any Poetic Form*

Send: Full text; Self-Addressed Stamped Envelope (SASE)
How to send: Email; Post

Features mostly short fiction, covering a wide variety of genres but often quirky, offbeat or fantastical. Send submissions by email or by post with SAE / email address for response. See website for full guidelines.

Editor: David-John Tyrer

M281 Moving Worlds: A Journal of Transcultural Writings

Magazine
School of English, University of Leeds, Leeds, LS2 9JT
United Kingdom
Tel: +44 (0) 1133 434792
Fax: +44 (0) 1133 434774

mworlds@leeds.ac.uk

http://www.movingworlds.net
https://twitter.com/Moving_Worlds

ACADEMIC > **Nonfiction** > *Essays*
Culture; Literary Criticism; Literature; Multicultural

ADULT
Fiction in Translation > *Short Fiction*
General, and in particular: Experimental

Fiction > *Short Fiction*
General, and in particular: Experimental

Poetry in Translation > *Any Poetic Form*
General, and in particular: Experimental

Poetry > *Any Poetic Form*
General, and in particular: Experimental

Biannual international magazine for creative work as well as criticism, literary as well as visual texts, writing in scholarly as well as more personal modes, in English and translations into English. It is open to experimentation, and represents work of different kinds and from different cultural traditions. Its central concern is the transcultural.

Editors: Shirley Chew; Stuart Murray

M282 MQR Mixtape

Online Magazine
United States

https://sites.lsa.umich.edu/mqr/mqr-mixtape/
https://mqr.submittable.com/submit

Magazine: Michigan Quarterly Review (**M273**)

Fiction > *Short Fiction*

Poetry > *Any Poetic Form*

Closed to approaches.

Costs: A fee is charged upon submission. $3 submission fee.

An eclectic, online zine guest curated by university graduate students.

M283 Mslexia

Magazine
PO Box 656, Newcastle upon Tyne, NE99 1PZ
United Kingdom
Tel: +44 (0) 1912 048860

postbag@mslexia.co.uk

https://mslexia.co.uk

Fiction > *Short Fiction*

Nonfiction
Articles: Creative Writing
Essays: Creative Writing; Memoir; Personal Essays
Interviews: Creative Writing

Poetry > *Any Poetic Form*

Send: Full text
How to send: Online submission system; Post

By women, for women who write, who want to write, who teach creative writing or who have an interest in women's literature and creativity. Publishes short stories, flash fiction, poetry, memoir and life writing, articles, and interviews.

M284 My Weekly

Magazine
D C Thomson & Co Ltd, My Weekly, 2 Albert Square, Dundee, DD1 1DD
United Kingdom
Tel: +44 (0) 1382 223131

sjohnstone@dcthomson.co.uk
srodger@dcthomson.co.uk
swatson@dcthomson.co.uk

https://www.myweekly.co.uk/
https://www.facebook.com/My-Weekly-199671216711852/
http://twitter.com/My_Weekly
https://www.instagram.com/my_weekly_magazine/

Newspaper Publisher / Magazine Publisher: DC Thomson Media

Fiction > *Short Fiction*

Nonfiction > *Articles*
Beauty; Cookery; Crafts; Fashion; Films; Food and Drink; Gardening; Health; Lifestyle; Personal Finance; Real Life Stories; TV; Travel; Women's Interests

Weekly women's magazine aged at the over-50s, publishing a mix of lifestyle features, true life stories, and fiction.

Editor: S. Johnstone

M285 Mystery Magazine

Magazine
United States

https://www.mysteryweekly.com
https://www.facebook.com/MysteryWeekly
https://twitter.com/MysteryWeekly
https://www.instagram.com/mystery_magazine/
https://www.linkedin.com/in/mystery-magazine-85598110a/

Fiction > *Short Fiction*: Mystery

Send: Full text
How to send: Online submission system

Submit mysteries between 2,500 and 7,500 words through online submission system available on website. No multiple submissions.

M286 Mythaxis Review

Online Magazine; Print Magazine
United States

https://mythaxis.com
https://www.youtube.com/channel/UC4LGvC_n_Fk7jLmoU-KgRag
https://twitter.com/mythaxisreview
https://www.instagram.com/mythaxisreview
https://www.facebook.com/mythaxisreview
https://www.linkedin.com/company/mythaxis-review
https://www.reddit.com/user/Mythaxis/
https://www.crunchbase.com/organization/mythaxis-review

Nonfiction
Articles: Arts; Books; Films; Music; Poetry as a Subject; Technology
Interviews: Arts; Technology

A cutting edge publication that seeks to present art and artists at the axis of curiosity and the energetic core of the creative act. Looks at books, movies, music and more.

M287 Nashville Review

Magazine
United States

thenashvillereview@gmail.com

https://as.vanderbilt.edu/nashvillereview

Fiction in Translation > *Short Fiction*

Fiction
  Comics; *Short Fiction*
Nonfiction in Translation
  Essays: General
  Short Nonfiction: Creative Nonfiction;
  Memoir
Nonfiction
  Essays: General
  Short Nonfiction: Creative Nonfiction;
  Memoir
Poetry in Translation > *Any Poetic Form*

Poetry > *Any Poetic Form*

Send: Query; Author bio; Full text
How to send: Submittable

Submit short stories and novel excerpts up to 8,000 words, or three flash fiction pieces (1,000 words each), 1-3 poems (up to ten pages total), or creative nonfiction including memoir excerpts, essays, imaginative meditations, up to 8,000 words, via online submission system during the two annual reading periods: August and February. Art and comic submissions are accepted year-round. Looking for anything from one-page comics to excerpts from graphic novels, but no single-frame cartoons.

M288 NB Magazine
Magazine
United Kingdom

editor@nbmagazine.co.uk

https://nbmagazine.co.uk

Nonfiction > *Articles*: Book Publishing

Magazine and online platform for book lovers, book clubs and all round bibliophiles. Publishes articles and features on books and the book trade, as well as extracts from books.

M289 Neon
Magazine
United Kingdom

subs@neonmagazine.co.uk

https://www.neonmagazine.co.uk

Fiction > *Short Fiction*
  Dark; Literary; Speculative; Surreal

Poetry
  Any Poetic Form: Dark; Literary; Surreal
  Graphic Poems: Dark; Literary; Surreal

Closed to approaches.

Quarterly online magazine publishing stylised poetry and prose, particularly the new, experimental, and strange. Welcomes genre fiction. Dark material preferred over humour; free verse preferred over rhyme. Send work pasted into the body of an email with a biographical note and the word "Submission" in the subject line.

Editor: Krishan Coupland

M290 The New Accelerator
Online Magazine
United Kingdom

https://newaccelerator.substack.com

Fiction > *Short Fiction*: Science Fiction

Digital science fiction short story anthology. The aim of the anthology is to bring cutting-edge fiction to an eager and discerning global science fiction audience.

M291 New England Review
Magazine
Middlebury College, Middlebury, VT 05753
United States
Tel: +1 (802) 443-5075

nereview@middlebury.edu

https://www.nereview.com
https://newenglandreview.submittable.com/submit
https://www.facebook.com/NewEnglandReviewMiddlebury/
https://twitter.com/nerweb

Fiction
  Novel Excerpts; *Novellas*; *Short Fiction*
Nonfiction in Translation > *Essays*

Nonfiction
  Essays: Personal Essays
  Short Nonfiction: Arts; Cultural Criticism;
  Environment; Films; Literary Criticism;
  Travel
Poetry > *Any Poetic Form*

Scripts > *Theatre Scripts*: Drama

How to send: Submittable; Post

Costs: A fee is charged for online submissions. $3 per submission.

Welcomes submissions in fiction, poetry, nonfiction, drama, and translation. Different submission windows for different categories of work. See website for details.

M292 New Internationalist
Magazine
Old Music Hall, 106-108 Cowley Rd, Oxford, Oxon., OX4 1JE
United Kingdom
Tel: +44 (0) 20 3868 4646

https://newint.org
https://twitter.com/newint
https://www.facebook.com/newint
https://www.instagram.com/newinternationalist

Nonfiction
  Articles: Civil Rights; Environment; Politics;
  Social Issues
  News: Civil Rights; Environment; Politics;
  Social Issues

Closed to approaches.

Independent, non-profit magazine that has been producing in-depth journalism on human rights, politics, and social and environmental justice since 1973.

Editors: Vanessa Baird; Chris Brazier; Dinyar Godrej; David Ransom

M293 New Orleans Review
Online Magazine
United States

noreview@loyno.edu

https://www.neworleansreview.org
https://www.facebook.com/neworleans.review/
https://twitter.com/NOReview

Fiction > *Short Fiction*: Literary

Nonfiction
  Reviews: Literature
  Short Nonfiction: General

Poetry > *Any Poetic Form*

Send: Full text
How to send: Submittable

Costs: A fee is charged upon submission. $3 per submission.

A journal of contemporary literature and culture. Send one story or piece of nonfiction up to 5,000 words, or up to five poems via online submission system.

M294 New Theatre Quarterly
Magazine
United Kingdom

M.Shevtsova@gold.ac.uk

https://www.cambridge.org/core/journals/new-theatre-quarterly

ACADEMIC > **Nonfiction**
  Articles: Theatre
  Interviews: Theatre

Send: Full text
How to send: Email

Provides a lively international forum where theatrical scholarship and practice can meet, and where prevailing assumptions can be subjected to vigorous critical questioning. The journal publishes articles, interviews with practitioners, documentation and reference materials covering all aspects of live theatre.

Editor: Maria Shevtsova

M295 Norfolk & Suffolk Bride
Print Magazine
United Kingdom

https://www.greatbritishlife.co.uk/magazines/bride/

Magazine Publisher: Great British Life

Nonfiction > *Articles*
  Fashion; Norfolk; Suffolk; Weddings

For engaged couples in the region. Filled with inspiration, information and advice, this annual publication is geared towards planning your wedding the local way. From fashion features and expert articles, to real weddings and venue listings,it makes easy work of your wedmin by providing everything you need to plan the perfect day. Glean ideas for your wedding in every aspect and connect with the local suppliers who can bring your vision to life.

M296 Norfolk Magazine
Magazine
United Kingdom

Magazine Publisher: Great British Life

M297 The North
Magazine
The Poetry Business, Campo House, 54 Campo Lane, Sheffield, S1 2EG
United Kingdom
Tel: +44 (0) 1144 384074

office@poetrybusiness.co.uk

https://poetrybusiness.co.uk

Poetry > *Any Poetic Form*: Contemporary

Closed to approaches.

Send up to 6 poems with SASE / return postage. We publish the best of contemporary poetry. No "genre" or derivative poetry. Submitters should be aware of, should preferably have read, the magazine before submitting. See our website for notes on submitting poems. No submissions by email. Overseas submissions may be made through online submission system.

Editors: Ann Sansom; Peter Sansom

M298 Nursery World
Magazine
MA Education, St Jude's Church, Dulwich Road, London, SE24 0PB
United Kingdom

https://www.nurseryworld.co.uk

PROFESSIONAL > **Nonfiction** > *Articles*
Childcare; Preschool

Magazine aimed at professionals dealing with the care of children in nurseries, primary schools, childcare, etc.; nannies and foster parents; and those involved with caring for expectant mothers, babies, and young children.

Editor: Karen Faux

M299 The Oakland Arts Review
Magazine
United States

ouartsreview@oakland.edu

https://oar.submittable.com/submit
http://www.facebook.com/oarjournal
https://twitter.com/OARjournal
http://www.instagram.com/oaklandartsreview/

Fiction

Cartoons: Literary
Graphic Novels: Literary
Short Fiction: Literary

Nonfiction
Graphic Nonfiction: Memoir
Short Nonfiction: Creative Nonfiction

Poetry
Experimental Poetry; *Formal Poetry*; *Free Verse*

Scripts
Film Scripts; *Radio Scripts*; *TV Scripts*; *Theatre Scripts*

Send: Full text
How to send: Submittable

Literary journal publishing work by undergraduates around the world. Publishes fiction between 10 and 15 double spaced pages; creative nonfiction between 7 and 10 double spaced pages; comics of high literary quality; screenwriting; and both free verse and formal poetry (submit 3-5 poems). Submit through online submission system via website.

M300 Obsidian: Literature in the African Diaspora
Magazine
Illinois State University, Williams Hall Annex, Normal, IL 61790
United States

https://obsidianlit.org
https://obsidian.submittable.com/submit

Fiction > *Short Fiction*: African Diaspora

Poetry > *Any Poetic Form*: African Diaspora

Scripts > *Theatre Scripts*: African Diaspora

Send: Full text
How to send: Submittable

Publishes scripts, fiction, and poetry focused on Africa and her Diaspora. See website for submission guidelines and to submit via online submission system.

M301 OK! Magazine
Magazine
One Canada Square, Canary Wharf, London, E14 5AB
United Kingdom
Tel: +44 (0) 20 8612 7000

https://www.ok.co.uk

Magazine Publisher: Reach Magazines Publishing

Nonfiction
Articles: Lifestyle; Women's Interests
Interviews: Celebrity
News: Celebrity

Celebrity magazine, welcoming ideas for features and interviews/pictures of celebrities.

Editor-in-Chief: Caroline Waterston

M302 Old Glory
Magazine
United Kingdom

https://heritagemachines.com
https://www.facebook.com/OldGloryMag/
https://www.kelsey.co.uk/brand/transport-machinery/old-glory/

Magazine Publisher: Kelsey Media

Nonfiction > *Articles*
History; Steam Engines; Steam Power

Publishes articles, features, and news covering industrial and transport heritage in the United Kingdom and overseas, particularly vintage vehicles and the preservation and restoration of steam engines.

Editor: Colin Tyson

M303 Old Red Kimono
Magazine
Georgia Highlands College, 3175 Cedartown Hwy SE, Rome, GA 30161
United States

ORK@highlands.edu

https://sites.highlands.edu/old-red-kimono/

Fiction > *Short Fiction*

Poetry > *Any Poetic Form*

Send: Full text
How to send: Email

Annual student-edited literary magazine. Send 3-5 poems or short stories up to 2,000 words by post or by email. Submissions from contributors outside the university are considered between October and February each year.

Editor: Steven Godfrey

M304 On Spec
Magazine
Canada

onspecmag@gmail.com

https://www.onspec.ca

Fiction > *Short Fiction*
Fantasy; Horror; Science Fiction; Speculative

Poetry > *Any Poetic Form*
Fantasy; Horror; Science Fiction; Speculative

Closed to approaches.

Publishes speculative writing of all kinds, but nothing derivative. Try to avoid what you think are trends.

M305 Orbis International Literary Journal
Magazine
17 Greenhow Avenue, West Kirby, Wirral, CH48 5EL
United Kingdom

carolebaldock@hotmail.com

http://www.orbisjournal.com

Fiction in Translation > *Short Fiction*

Fiction > *Short Fiction*

Nonfiction > *Articles*

Poetry in Translation
  Any Poetic Form; Prose Poetry
Poetry
  Any Poetic Form; Prose Poetry

Send: Query; Full text; Author bio; Self-Addressed Stamped Envelope (SASE)
How to send: Post; International Email
How not to send: Domestic Email; Email attachment

Send four poems or prose up to 1,000 words by post with SASE. No submissions by email, unless from overseas, in which case two submissions maximum and no attachments.

Editor: Carole Baldock

M306 Outside
Magazine
United States

https://www.outsideonline.com
https://www.facebook.com/outsidemagazine
https://twitter.com/outsidemagazine
https://www.instagram.com/outsidemagazine

Magazine Publisher: Outside Interactive Inc.

Nonfiction > *Articles*
  Environment; Fitness; Outdoor Activities; Sport; Travel

Magazine of the outdoors. Covers travel, sports, gear, and fitness, as well as the personalities, the environment, and the style and culture of the outdoors.

M307 Oxford Poetry
Magazine
c/o Partus Press, 266 Banbury Road, Oxford, OX2 7DL
United Kingdom

editors@oxfordpoetry.co.uk
reviews@oxfordpoetry.co.uk

https://www.oxfordpoetry.com
https://www.instagram.com/oxford_poetry
https://www.facebook.com/OxfordPoetryMag/
https://twitter.com/oxfordpoetry

Book Publisher / Magazine Publisher: Partus Press

Nonfiction
  Articles: Literature
  Essays: Literature
  Interviews: Literature
  Reviews: Literature

Poetry in Translation > *Any Poetic Form*

Poetry > *Any Poetic Form*

How to send: Submittable

Costs: A fee is charged upon submission. £3 submission fee.

Publishes poems, interviews, reviews, and essays. Accepts unpublished poems on any theme and of any length during specific biannual submission windows, which are announced on the website. Send up to four poems by email. See website for full details. To suggest a book for review, email the reviews editor.

M308 Oyez Review
Magazine
United States

oyezreview@gmail.com

https://medium.com/oyez-review/
https://www.facebook.com/OyezReview

Fiction > *Short Fiction:* Literary

Nonfiction > *Short Nonfiction:* Creative Nonfiction

Poetry > *Any Poetic Form*

An award-winning literary magazine published annually. There are no restrictions on style, theme, or subject matter. Though we consider it part of our mission to publish undiscovered writers, we also have a strong tradition of publishing some of today's best writers, including Charles Bukowski, James McManus, Carla Panciera, Sandra Kohler, and Saul Bennett.

Editor: Janet Wondra

M309 Pacifica Literary Review
Magazine
Seattle, WA
United States

pacificalitreview@gmail.com

http://www.pacificareview.com
https://pacificaliteraryreview.submittable.com/submit
https://www.facebook.com/PacificaLiteraryReview
https://twitter.com/PacificaReview

Fiction
  Novel Excerpts; Short Fiction
Nonfiction > *Short Nonfiction:* Creative Nonfiction

Poetry > *Any Poetic Form*

Send: Full text
How to send: Submittable

Costs: A fee is charged upon submission. $3 per submission.

Accepts poetry, fiction, and creative nonfiction. Prose should be under 5,000 words. Flash fiction up to 1,000 words. Will consider novel excerpts, but must work as stand alone entities. For poetry and flash fiction submit a maximum of three pieces at a time. Send submissions through online submission system. See website for full guidelines.

Editor: Matt Muth

M310 The Paris Review
Magazine
544 West 27th Street, Floor 3, New York, NY 10001
United States
Tel: +1 (212) 343-1333

queries@theparisreview.org

https://www.theparisreview.org
https://www.facebook.com/parisreview
https://twitter.com/parisreview
http://theparisreview.tumblr.com/

Fiction > *Short Fiction:* Literary

Nonfiction
  Interviews; Short Nonfiction
Poetry > *Any Poetic Form*

How to send: Submittable; Post

Send submissions through online submission system or by post. All submissions must be in English and previously unpublished, though translations are acceptable if accompanied by copy of the original text. Simultaneous submissions accepted as long as immediate notification is given of acceptance elsewhere.

M311 Park Home and Holiday Living
Magazine
The Granary, Downs Court, Yalding Hill, Yalding, Kent, ME18 6AL
United Kingdom
Tel: +44 (0) 1959 541444

phhc.ed@kelsey.co.uk

https://www.parkhomemagazine.co.uk

Magazine Publisher: Kelsey Media

Nonfiction > *Articles*
  Caravans; Holiday Homes; Lifestyle

Magazine for those owning holiday caravans or living in residential park homes.

Editor: Alex Melvin

M312 PC Gamer
Magazine
Quay House, The Ambury, Bath, BA1 1UA
United Kingdom

editors@pcgamer.com

https://www.pcgamer.com
https://steamcommunity.com/groups/pcgamer
https://twitter.com/pcgamer
https://www.facebook.com/pcgamermagazine/
https://www.youtube.com/user/pcgamer

Magazine Publisher: Future

Nonfiction
  Articles: Computer and Video Games; Computers
  News: Computer and Video Games; Computers
  Reviews: Computer and Video Games; Computers

We are the global authority on PC games. We've been covering PC gaming for more than 20 years, and continue that legacy today with worldwide print editions and around-the-clock news, features, esports coverage, hardware testing, and game reviews.

Editor: Alan Dexter

M313 PC Pro

Magazine
Quay House, The Ambury, Bath, BA1 1UA
United Kingdom
Tel: +44 (0) 330 333 9493

customercare@subscribe.pcpro.co.uk

https://subscribe.pcpro.co.uk
https://www.facebook.com/pcpro
https://twitter.com/pcpro

Magazine Publisher: Future

ADULT > **Nonfiction** > *Articles*: Computers

PROFESSIONAL > **Nonfiction** > *Articles*: Computers

IT magazine for professionals in the IT industry and enthusiasts.

M314 Pennine Ink Magazine

Magazine
United Kingdom

g.laura.sheridan@gmail.com

https://pennineink.wordpress.com/submissions-to-pennine-ink/

Fiction > *Short Fiction*

Nonfiction > *Articles*

Poetry > *Any Poetic Form*

Send: Full text
How to send: Email

Publishes poetry, flash fiction, and articles from anywhere in the world. Submit a maximum of three pieces in total.

Editor: Laura Sheridan

M315 Pensacola Magazine

Magazine
21 E. Garden St., Ste. 205, Pensacola, FL 32502
United States
Tel: +1 (850) 433-1166
Fax: +1 (850) 435-9174

info@ballingerpublishing.com

http://www.pensacolamagazine.com
https://www.facebook.com/pensacolamagazine
https://www.instagram.com/pensacola_magazine/

Magazine Publisher: Ballinger Publishing

Nonfiction > *Articles*
Business; Culture; Entertainment; Fashion; Health; Lifestyle; Pensacola

Publishes articles and stories on business, entertainment, culture, fashion, healthcare, lifestyle and other topics important to the Northwest Florida community.

M316 People's Friend Pocket Novels

Magazine
DC Thomson & Co. Ltd, 2 Albert Square, Dundee, DD1 9QJ
United Kingdom

tsteel@dctmedia.co.uk

https://www.thepeoplesfriend.co.uk

Magazine: The People's Friend (**M317**)

Fiction > *Novellas*
Family Saga; Romance

Send: Query; Synopsis; Writing sample
How to send: Email; Post

Publishes romance and family fiction between 37,000 and 39,000 words, aimed at adults aged over 30. Send query by post or by email (preferred) with synopsis and first two chapters in first instance. See website for more information.

Editor: Tracey Steel

M317 The People's Friend

Magazine
DC Thomson & Co. Ltd., 2 Albert Square, Dundee, DD1 9QJ
United Kingdom

peoplesfriend@dcthomson.co.uk

http://www.thepeoplesfriend.co.uk

Newspaper Publisher / Magazine Publisher: DC Thomson Media

Fiction > *Short Fiction*: Women's Fiction

Nonfiction > *Nonfiction Books*
Cookery; Crafts; Lifestyle; Women's Interests

Publishes complete short stories (1,200-3,000 words (4,000 for specials)) and serials, focusing on character development rather than complex plots, plus 10,000-word crime thrillers. Also considers nonfiction from nature to nostalgia and from holidays to hobbies, and poetry. Guidelines available on website.

Magazine: People's Friend Pocket Novels (**M316**)

M318 The Philosopher

Online Magazine
United Kingdom

http://www.the-philosopher.co.uk

Nonfiction > *Articles*: Philosophy

Publishes philosophical articles up to 3,000 words. Articles are considered without discrimination as to subject matter or author. The only criterion is that it must be

philosophical in method. See website for submission guidelines.

Editor: Martin Cohen

M319 The Photographer

Magazine
The British Institute of Professional Photography, The Artistry House, 16 Winckley Square, Preston, PR1 3JJ
United Kingdom
Tel: +44 (0) 1772 367968

admin@bipp.com

https://www.bipp.com

PROFESSIONAL > **Nonfiction** > *Articles*: Photography

Photography magazine for professional photographers.

M320 Pilot

Magazine
United Kingdom

https://www.pilotweb.aero

Magazine Publisher: Kelsey Media

ADULT > **Nonfiction** > *Articles*
Air Travel; Piloting

PROFESSIONAL > **Nonfiction** > *Articles*
Air Travel; Piloting

Send: Full text
How to send: Email

Aimed at private, commercial and would-be flyers, including enthusiasts.

Editor: Philip Whiteman

M321 Pleiades

Magazine
Department of English, Martin 336, University of Central Missouri, 415 E. Clark St., Warrensburg, MO 64093
United States
Tel: +1 (660) 543-4268

pleiadespoetryeditor@gmail.com
pleiadesfictioninquiries@gmail.com
pleiadescnf@gmail.com
pleiadesreviews@gmail.com

https://pleiadesmag.com
https://twitter.com/pleiadesmag
https://www.facebook.com/UCMPleiades
http://websta.me/n/pleiades_magazine
https://www.pinterest.com/pleiadesUCM/

Fiction > *Short Fiction*

Nonfiction
Reviews: Books
Short Nonfiction: Creative Nonfiction

Poetry > *Any Poetic Form*

How to send: Online submission system

Send submissions through online submission system during specific windows only.

M322 Ploughshares

Magazine
Emerson College, 120 Boylston St., Boston,
MA 02116-4624
United States

https://www.pshares.org
http://facebook.com/ploughshares
http://www.pinterest.com/pshares
http://twitter.com/pshares
https://instagram.com/psharesjournal/

Fiction > *Short Fiction*

Nonfiction > *Short Nonfiction*

Poetry > *Any Poetic Form*

Send: Self-Addressed Stamped Envelope
(SASE); Full text
How to send: Online submission system; Post

Costs: A fee is charged for online submissions.
$3 fee for online submissions, except for
subscribers, who may submit for free.

Welcomes unsolicited submissions of fiction,
poetry, and nonfiction during the regular
reading period, which runs from June 1 to
January 15. The literary journal is published
four times a year: mixed issues of poetry and
prose in the Spring and Winter, a prose issue in
the summer, and a longform prose issue in the
Fall, with two of the four issues per year guest-
edited by a different writer of prominence.

Editor: Don Lee

M323 PN Review

Magazine
4th Floor, Alliance House, 30 Cross Street,
Manchester, M2 7AQ
United Kingdom
Tel: +44 (0) 161 834 8730

PNRsubmissions@carcanet.co.uk

https://www.pnreview.co.uk

Nonfiction
Essays: Poetry as a Subject
Reviews: Poetry as a Subject

Poetry > *Any Poetic Form*

Send: Query; Full text
How to send: Email; Post

Poetry may be submitted during the months of
June and December. Subscribers may submit
by email; otherwise submissions should be by
post. Queries for nonfiction submissions may
be sent to the editor at any time, by email.

Editor: Michael Schmidt

M324 Poetry Ireland Review

Magazine
11 Parnell Square East, Dublin 1, D01 ND60
Ireland
Tel: +353 (0)1 6789815
Fax: +353 (0)1 6789782

pir@poetryireland.ie
info@poetryireland.ie

https://www.poetryireland.ie

Nonfiction
Articles: Poetry as a Subject
Reviews: Poetry as a Subject

Poetry > *Any Poetic Form*

Send: Full text; Proposal
How to send: Post; Submittable

Send up to four poems through online
submission system, or by post. Poetry is
accepted from around the world, but must be
previously unpublished. No sexism or racism.
Articles and reviews are generally
commissioned, however proposals are
welcome. No unsolicited reviews or articles.

M325 The Poetry Review

Magazine
The Poetry Society, 22 Betterton Street,
London, WC2H 9BX
United Kingdom
Tel: +44 (0) 20 7420 9880

poetryreview@poetrysociety.org.uk

https://poetrysociety.org.uk/
https://thepoetrysociety.submittable.com/
submit

Nonfiction
Essays: Poetry as a Subject
Reviews: Poetry as a Subject

Poetry in Translation > *Any Poetic Form*

Poetry > *Any Poetic Form*

Send: Full text
How to send: Submittable

Costs: A fee is charged upon submission in
some cases. Non-members pay £2 to submit.

Describes itself as "one of the liveliest and
most influential literary magazines in the
world", and has been associated with the rise
of the New Generation of British poets – Carol
Ann Duffy, Simon Armitage, Glyn Maxwell,
Don Paterson... though its scope extends
beyond the UK, with special issues focusing on
poetries from around the world. Send up to 6
unpublished poems, or literary translations of
poems, through online submission system.

M326 Poetry Wales

Magazine
Suite 6, 4 Derwen Road, Bridgend, CF31 1LH
United Kingdom
Tel: +44 (0) 1656 663018

poetrywalessubmissions@gmail.com
info@poetrywales.co.uk
editor@poetrywales.co.uk

https://poetrywales.co.uk
https://poetrywales.submittable.com/submit
http://twitter.com/poetrywales
http://facebook.com/poetrywales
http://instagram.com/poetrywales

Nonfiction

Articles: Poetry as a Subject
Reviews: Books; Poetry as a Subject
Poetry > *Any Poetic Form*

Closed to approaches.

Publishes poetry, features, and reviews from
Wales and beyond. Submit via online
submission system, or by post. If online form
is not working, use email. Also runs
competitions.

M327 The Political Quarterly

Magazine
Department of Politics, Birkbeck, University of
London, Malet Street, London, WC1E 7HX
United Kingdom

submissions@politicalquarterly.org.uk

https://politicalquarterly.org.uk
https://twitter.com/po_qu
https://www.facebook.com/PoliticalQuarterly

Nonfiction
Articles: Politics
Reviews: Books

How to send: Email

Magazine covering national and international
politics. Accepts unsolicited articles.

M328 Popshot Quarterly

Magazine
United Kingdom

submit@popshotpopshot.com
hello@popshotpopshot.com

https://www.popshotpopshot.com
https://www.facebook.com/popshotmag
https://www.pinterest.com/popshotmag
https://www.instagram.com/popshotmag
https://twitter.com/popshotmag

Fiction > *Short Fiction*: Literary

Poetry > *Any Poetic Form*

Closed to approaches.

Publishes flash fiction, short stories, and poetry
on the theme of the current issue (see website).
Submit by email.

M329 Practical Boat Owner Magazine

Magazine
United Kingdom
Tel: +44 (0) 3303 906467

pbo@futurenet.com

https://www.pbo.co.uk

Magazine Publisher: Future

Nonfiction > *Articles*: Boats

Cruising boats magazine covering both power
and sail. Publishes technical articles on
maintenance, restoration, modifications, etc.

M330 The Practising Midwife
Magazine
Saturn House, Mercury Rise, Altham Industrial Park, Altham, Lancashire, BB5 5BY
United Kingdom

info@all4maternity.com

https://www.all4maternity.com
https://twitter.com/all4maternity
https://www.facebook.com/all4maternity/

PROFESSIONAL > *Nonfiction*
Articles: Midwifery
News: Midwifery

Publishes accessible, authoritative and readable information for midwives, students and other professionals in the maternity services.

Editor-in-Chief: Alys Einion

M331 Present Tense
Print Magazine
United Kingdom

http://www.dahliapublishing.co.uk/present-tense-lit-mag

Book Publisher: Dahlia Books (**P150**)

Fiction > *Short Fiction*

Nonfiction > *Short Nonfiction*: Creative Nonfiction

Poetry > *Any Poetic Form*

Send: Full text
How to send: Online submission system

A literary magazine of new writing. Publishes poetry, flash fiction, short stories, and creative non-fiction with a strong sense of place.

M332 Preservation Magazine
Magazine
600 14th Street NW, Suite 500, Washington, DC 20005
United States
Tel: +1 (202) 588-6013

preservation@savingplaces.org
editorial@savingplaces.org

https://savingplaces.org/preservation-magazine

Nonfiction > *Articles*
History; Travel

Send: Query
How to send: Phone; Email

Magazine publishing material on the preservation of historic buildings and neighbourhoods in the United States.

M333 Pride
Magazine
1 Garrat Lane, London, SW18 4AQ
United Kingdom
Tel: +44 (0) 20 8870 3755

editor@pridemagazine.com

http://pridemagazine.com
http://www.facebook.com/PrideMagazine
http://www.instagram.com/pridemaguk

Nonfiction
Articles: Beauty; Career Development; Entertainment; Fashion; Hairstyles; Health; Lifestyle
News: Ethnic Groups; Social Issues

Magazine aimed at black women. Publishes news, and articles and features on entertainment, hair, beauty, and fashion.

M334 Pulsar Poetry Magazine
Online Magazine
90 Beechwood Drive, Camelford, Cornwall, PL32 9NB
United Kingdom
Tel: +44 (0) 1840 213633

pulsar.ed@btinternet.com

https://www.pulsarpoetry.com

Poetry > *Any Poetic Form*

Send: Full text; Self-Addressed Stamped Envelope (SASE)
How to send: In the body of an email; Domestic Post

The editor's preference is for hard hitting poems that have a message, meaning, and are well written. Not keen on deeply religious poems or de-dah de-dah poems where everything chimes annoyingly like a cheap clock. Please don't send poems about cute and cuddly kittens. Simultaneous submissions are not considered. Postal submissions from within the UK only.

Editor: David Pike

M335 Pushing Out the Boat
Magazine
United Kingdom

info@pushingouttheboat.co.uk

https://www.pushingouttheboat.co.uk

Fiction > *Short Fiction*: Literary

Poetry > *Any Poetic Form*

Scripts > *Theatre Scripts*

Closed to approaches.

Magazine of prose, poetry and visual arts, based in North-East Scotland. Welcomes work in English, Doric or Scots. Submit via online submission system during open reading periods. See website for details.

M336 Qu Literary Magazine
Magazine
United States

qulitmag@queens.edu

http://www.qulitmag.com

Fiction > *Short Fiction*: Literary

Nonfiction > *Essays*

Poetry > *Any Poetic Form*

Scripts
Film Scripts; *TV Scripts*; *Theatre Scripts*

Send: Full text
How to send: Submittable
How not to send: Email

Costs: A fee is charged upon submission. $2.50 per submission.

Literary journal published by a university MFA program. Editorial staff is comprised of current students. Publishes fiction, poetry, essays and script excerpts.

M337 Quail Bell
Magazine
United States

submissions@quailbellmagazine.com

http://www.quailbellmagazine.com

Fiction > *Short Fiction*
Intersectional Feminism; Literary

Nonfiction > *Articles*: Intersectional Feminism

Poetry > *Any Poetic Form*: Intersectional Feminism

Send: Full text
How to send: Email

An intersectional feminist magazine. Send submissions by email. See website for full guidelines.

M338 Rabble Review
Online Magazine
United States

rabblereview420@gmail.com

https://rabblereview.com
https://www.instagram.com/rabble_review/
https://twitter.com/rabble_review

Fiction > *Short Fiction*

Nonfiction > *Essays*
Creative Nonfiction; Cultural Criticism; Current Affairs; Literature; Politics

Poetry > *Any Poetic Form*

How to send: Online submission system

Unapologetically leftist in politics, we recognize the complete abolition of capitalism, coerced labor, and the State as absolute pre-conditions for human and artistic liberation. We want to capture the working class in its full spectrum, that is, we're committed to solidarity among workers of all races, genders, sexual orientations, abilities, and their intersections. By spreading accessible leftist thought, encouraging direct action, and providing a space for revolutionary aesthetics to develop we hope to do our part in the radicalization and ultimate liberation of the working class.

M339 Rabid Oak

Online Magazine
United States

rabidoak@gmail.com

https://rabidoak.com

Fiction > *Short Fiction*

Nonfiction > *Short Nonfiction*

Poetry > *Any Poetic Form*

Send: Full text; Author bio
How to send: Email

Online literary journal. Send up to five poems or two pieces of fiction or nonfiction (up to 1,000 words) in a Word document attachment.

M340 Racecar Engineering

Magazine
The Chelsea Magazine Company, Jubilee House, 2 Jubilee Place, London, SW3 3TQ
United Kingdom
Tel: +44 (0) 20 7349 3700

editorial@racecarengineering.com

https://www.racecar-engineering.com
https://www.facebook.com/
RacecarEngineering/
https://twitter.com/RacecarEngineer

Magazine Publisher: The Chelsea Magazine Company

Nonfiction
Articles: Engineering; Racecars
News: Engineering; Racecars

Publishes news articles and in-depth features on racing cars and related products and technology. No material on road cars or racing drivers.

M341 The Racket

Magazine
United States

theracketreadingseries@gmail.com

https://theracketsf.com

Fiction > *Short Fiction*

Poetry > *Any Poetic Form*

Send: Full text
How to send: Email

Considers submissions that contain work(s) of poetry and/or prose with a total combined word count of 2,000 words or fewer. See website for full guidelines.

M342 Radar Poetry

Magazine
United States

radarpoetry@gmail.com

https://www.radarpoetry.com

Poetry > *Any Poetic Form*

Closed to approaches.

Costs: A fee is charged upon submission. $3.

Electronic journal of poetry and artwork, published quarterly. Interested in the interplay between poetry and visual media. Each issue features pairings of poetry and artwork, selected by the editors. Submit 3-5 original, previously unpublished poems through online submission system. Accepts submissions November 1 to January 1 (free), and March 1 to May 1 ($3) annually.

Editors: Rachel Marie Patterson; Dara-Lyn Shrager

M343 Rail Express

Magazine
United Kingdom

RailExpressEditor@mortons.co.uk

https://www.railexpress.co.uk
https://www.facebook.com/RailExpressMag
https://www.instagram.com/
railexpressmagazine/
https://twitter.com/railexpress

Magazine Publisher: Mortons Media Group

Nonfiction > *Articles*: Railways

Magazine publishing news and features on railways in the UK.

M344 Reach

Magazine
24 Forest Houses, Halwill, Beaworthy, Devon, EX21 5UU
United Kingdom

publishing@indigodreams.co.uk

https://www.indigodreams.co.uk/magazines

Book Publisher: Indigo Dreams Publishing **(P283)**

Poetry > *Any Poetic Form*: Literary

Send: Full text
How to send: Email

Costs: A subscription is required in order to submit.

Currently accepting submissions from subscribers only.

Publishes quality poetry from both experienced and new poets. Formal or free verse, haiku... everything is considered. Submit up to two poems by email. No simultaneous submissions.

Editor: Ronnie Goodyer

M345 The Reader

Magazine
The Mansion House, Calderstones Park, Liverpool, L18 3JB
United Kingdom
Tel: + 44 (0) 1517 292200

https://www.thereader.org.uk
https://www.thereader.org.uk/what-we-do/the-reader-magazine/

https://twitter.com/thereaderorg
https://www.facebook.com/thereaderorg
https://www.instagram.com/thereaderorg/

Nonfiction > *Articles*: Literature

Magazine of charity promoting shared reading through reading aloud groups. No longer publishes original fiction and poetry.

M346 Red Magazine

Magazine
30 Panton Street, London, SW1Y 4AJ
United Kingdom

https://www.redonline.co.uk
https://www.facebook.com/redmagazine/
https://twitter.com/RedMagDaily
https://www.pinterest.co.uk/redmagazine/
https://www.instagram.com/redmagazine/?hl=en
https://www.youtube.com/user/
RedMagazineOnline

Magazine Publisher: Hearst Magazines UK

Nonfiction
Articles: Beauty; Decorating; Fashion; Fitness; Food; Hairstyles; Health; Interior Design; Parenting; Relationships; Sex; Travel; Wellbeing
Interviews: Women's Interests
Reviews: Books; Films; Music; TV

Magazine aimed at women in their thirties.

M347 Redbook Magazine

Online Magazine
300 W. 57th St., New York, NY 10019
United States

https://www.redbookmag.com
https://twitter.com/redbookmag
https://www.youtube.com/c/Redbook?
sub_confirmation=1
https://www.facebook.com/REDBOOK
https://www.instagram.com/redbookmag/
https://www.pinterest.com/redbookmag/

Media Company: Hearst

Nonfiction > *Articles*
Beauty; Design; Family; Fitness; Food and Drink; Friends; Hairstyles; Home Improvement; Lifestyle; Make-Up; Nutrition; Parenting; Pets; Relationships; Sex

Former print magazine now published online only since 2019.

M348 Riptide

Magazine
United Kingdom

riptide@exeter.ac.uk

http://www.riptidejournal.co.uk
https://twitter.com/RiptideJournal
https://www.facebook.com/RiptideJournal/

Fiction > *Short Fiction*: Literary

Closed to approaches.

An Exeter-based literary journal founded in 2006. Publishes new writing by established and emerging writers. Committed to providing a forum for high quality, innovative fiction, expanding the readership of the short story, and enhancing its standing. We aim to include new voices in every issue.

M349 River Hills Traveler

Magazine
212 E Main Street, Neosho, MO 64850
United States
Tel: +1 (417) 451-3798

https://www.riverhillstraveler.com

Nonfiction
Articles: Boats; Camping; Fishing; Hunting; Lifestyle; Missouri; Outdoor Activities; Ozarks
News: Animals; Missouri; Nature; Ozarks; Travel

Magazine covering outdoor sports and nature in the southeast quarter of Missouri, the east and central Ozarks.

Managing Editor: Madeleine Link

Publisher: Jimmy Sexton

M350 River Styx

Online Magazine
3301 Washington Ave, Suite 2C, St. Louis, MO 63103
United States

editor@riverstyx.org

https://www.riverstyx.org
https://riverstyx.submittable.com/submit
https://twitter.com/riverstyxmag/
https://www.facebook.com/
RiverStyxLiteraryMagazine/
https://www.linkedin.com/company/river-styx/
https://www.instagram.com/riverstyxmag/

Fiction > *Short Fiction*

Nonfiction > *Short Nonfiction:* Creative Nonfiction

Poetry > *Any Poetic Form*

Scripts > *Theatre Scripts*

How to send: Submittable
How not to send: Email; Post

Costs: A fee is charged upon submission. $3 submission fee.

A multicultural magazine of poetry, short fiction, creative nonfiction, short plays, and art. Seeks to publish work that is striking in its originality, energy, and craft, from both new and established writers.

M351 Riverbed Review

Online Magazine
Ireland

riverbedreview@gmail.com

https://riverbedreview.wordpress.com
https://www.instagram.com/riverbedreview/
https://twitter.com/RiverbedReview

Fiction > *Short Fiction*
Literary; Rivers

Poetry > *Any Poetic Form:* Rivers

Closed to approaches.

Publishes original and unpublished stories and poems that are set around (or are about) a river — fictional or otherwise. Submissions are accepted from March 16 to May 16; and October 16 to December 16.

M352 Rock & Gem

Magazine
United States

https://www.rockngem.com
https://www.facebook.com/RockandGem/
https://www.instagram.com/
rockandgemmagazine/
https://twitter.com/RandG_official/

Magazine Publisher: EG Media Investments

Nonfiction > *Articles*
Fossils; Gems; How To; Lapidary; Minerals; Rock Collecting / Rockhounding; Rocks

First published in 1971 with the goal of serving the needs and goals of anyone with an interest in rocks, gems, minerals, fossils and general lapidary.

Editor-in-Chief: Pam Freeman

M353 Rugby World

Magazine
Unit 415, Winnersh Triangle, Eskdale Road, Winnersh, RG41 5TU
United Kingdom
Tel: +44 (0) 1225 442244

rugbyworldletters@futurenet.com
sarah.mockford@futurenet.com

https://www.rugbyworld.com
https://www.facebook.com/
rugbyworldmagazine
https://www.youtube.com/user/rugbyworld08
https://twitter.com/rugbyworldmag

Magazine Publisher: Future

Nonfiction
Articles: Rugby
News: Rugby

Send: Query; Author bio; Synopsis

Magazine publishing news and articles related to rugby. Send idea with coverline, headline, and 50-word synopsis, along with brief resume of your experience.

Editor: Sarah Mockford

M354 Rural Builder

Magazine
Shield Wall Media LLC, PO Box 255, Iola, WI 54945
United States

https://ruralbuildermagazine.com

PROFESSIONAL > **Nonfiction**
Articles: Architecture; Building / Construction; Design; How To
News: Architecture; Building / Construction; Design; How To

Magazine for builders and suppliers of primarily low-rise agricultural and small retail and municipal structures in cities with populations under 250,000.

M355 Ruralite

Magazine
5625 NE Elam Young Parkway Suite 100, Hillsboro, OR 97124
United States
Tel: +1 (503) 357-2105

editor@pur.coop
info@pur.coop

https://www.ruralite.com
https://www.facebook.com/Ruralite
https://www.instagram.com/ruralitemag/
https://twitter.com/RuraliteMag
https://vimeo.com/showcase/5668282

Nonfiction > *Articles*
Energy; Lifestyle; Photography; Recipes; Travel

Send: Pitch
How to send: Email

Serves members of publicly owned electric utilities, delivering engaging human-interest features, energy-related content, travel and photography tips, scrumptious recipes, reader submissions and important information about electric service.

M356 SAIL Magazine

Magazine
35 Industrial Park Road, Unit 10, Centerbrook, CT 06409
United States
Fax: +1 (860) 767-1048

sailmail@sailmagazine.com

https://www.sailmagazine.com
https://www.facebook.com/sailmag
https://twitter.com/sailmagazine
https://www.instagram.com/sailmagazine
https://pinterest.com/sailmagazine

Nonfiction > *Articles*
Boats; Sailing

Sailing magazine covering boats, DIY, cruising, racing, equipment, etc.

Editor-in-Chief: Wendy Clarke

M357 Sailing Today

Magazine
The Chelsea Magazine Company, Jubilee House, 2 Jubilee Place, London, SW3 3QW

United Kingdom
Tel: +44 (0) 20 7349 3700

editor@sailingtoday.co.uk

https://www.sailingtoday.co.uk
https://www.facebook.com/sailingtoday/
https://twitter.com/SailingTodayMag
https://www.youtube.com/channel/
UCah1Wlfp86HD0tpbhW1LP1Q

Nonfiction > *Articles*: Sailing

Practical magazine for cruising sailors. Offers a wealth of practical advice and a dynamic mix of in-depth boat, gear and equipment news.

M358 Sainsbury's Magazine
Magazine
United Kingdom

feedback@sainsburysmagazine.co.uk
editor@seven.co.uk

https://www.sainsburysmagazine.co.uk
https://www.instagram.com/sainsburysmag/
https://www.pinterest.com/sainsburysmag/
https://twitter.com/sainsburysmag
https://www.facebook.com/sainsburys/

Magazine Publisher: Seven Publishing

Nonfiction > *Articles*
   Cookery; Food; Lifestyle; Recipes

Focuses mainly on food and cookery.

Editor: Sue Robinson

M359 Sarasvati
Magazine
24 Forest Houses, Halwill, Beaworthy, Devon, EX21 5UU
United Kingdom

dawnidp@indigodreams.co.uk

https://www.indigodreams.co.uk/magazines

Book Publisher: Indigo Dreams Publishing (**P283**)

Fiction > *Short Fiction*

Poetry > *Any Poetic Form*

Closed to approaches.

Showcases poetry and prose. Each contributor will have three to four A5 pages available to their work. Submit up to four poems, or prose up to 1,000 words.

Editor: Dawn Bauling

M360 Savannah Magazine
Magazine
United States
Tel: +1 (912) 652-0293

editor@savannahmagazine.com

https://www.savannahmagazine.com
https://www.facebook.com/SavannahMagazine
https://twitter.com/savmag
https://www.pinterest.com/savmagazine/
https://www.instagram.com/

savannahmagazine/
https://www.youtube.com/user/
SavannahMagazineLive

Nonfiction > *Articles*
   Culture; Food; Health; Houses; Lifestyle; Savannah, GA; Weddings

Send: Query
How to send: Email
How not to send: Phone

Our mission is to celebrate the inimitable Savannah lifestyle and serve the city as thought leaders. We discover and uplift the talented individuals of the city's creative class. With smart, layered, inclusive content, we interpret Savannah's unique cultural identity — and become the change we want to see in the city.

M361 Scifaikuest
Print Magazine; Online Magazine
United States

gatrix65@yahoo.com

https://www.hiraethsffh.com/scifaikuest

Book Publisher / Ebook Publisher / Online Publisher: Hiraeth Books (**P263**)

Nonfiction > *Articles*
   Biography; Creative Writing; Poetry as a Subject

Poetry
   Haibun: Horror; Science Fiction
   Haiku: Horror; Science Fiction
   Senryu: Horror; Science Fiction
   Tanka: Horror; Science Fiction

Send: Full text; Author bio
How to send: Email

Print and online magazine publishing science fiction and horror poetry in forms such as scifaiku, haibun, senryu, and tanka. Also publishes articles. See website for full submission guidelines.

M362 Scintilla
Magazine
United Kingdom

poetry@vaughanassociation.org

http://www.vaughanassociation.org

Fiction > *Short Fiction*
   Contemporary; Metaphysical

Nonfiction > *Essays*
   17th Century; Literature; Metaphysical

Poetry > *Any Poetic Form*
   Contemporary; Metaphysical

Send: Full text
How to send: Email attachment

An international, peer-reviewed journal of literary criticism, prose, and new poetry in the metaphysical tradition.

General Editor: Joseph Sterrett

Poetry Editor: Damian Walford Davies

Prose Editor: Erik Ankerberg

M363 The Scottish Farmer
Magazine
125 Fullarton Drive, Glasgow, G32 8FG
United Kingdom

https://www.thescottishfarmer.co.uk
https://www.facebook.com/scottishfarmer
https://twitter.com/scottishfarmer
https://www.instagram.com/
scottishfarmernewspaper/
https://www.linkedin.com/company/17949188

Magazine Publisher / Newspaper Publisher: Newsquest Media Group

PROFESSIONAL > **Nonfiction**
   Articles: Farming; Scotland
   News: Farming; Scotland

Agricultural magazine publishing news and features on political, personal, and technological developments in farming, as well as rural and craft items. Approach with ideas by email or fax.

Editors: Alasdair Fletcher; Deputy Editor: Ken Fletcher

M364 Scout Life
Magazine
1325 West Walnut Hill Lane, PO Box 152079, Irving, TX 75015-2079
United States
Tel: +1 (866) 584-6589

https://scoutlife.org
https://facebook.com/scoutlifemag
https://twitter.com/scoutlifemag
https://www.instagram.com/boyslifemagazine/
https://www.youtube.com/c/boyslife
https://www.pinterest.com/ScoutLifeMag/

CHILDREN'S > **Nonfiction** > *Articles*
   Comedy / Humour; Games; Hobbies; Leisure; Outdoor Activities

Magazine aimed at young people aged between 6 and 18. Includes games, jokes, contests, giveaways, and articles on hobbies and outdoor activities.

M365 Sea Breezes
Magazine
The Office, Strenaby Farm, Lonan Church Road, Laxey, Isle of Man, IM4 7JX
United Kingdom
Tel: +44 (1624) 863672

sb.enquiries@seabreezes.co.im

https://seabreezes.co.im
https://twitter.com/seabreezesmag
https://www.facebook.com/
seabreezesmagazine/

PROFESSIONAL > **Nonfiction** > *Articles*: Shipping

Monthly magazine devoted to the worldwide shipping industry.

M366 Second Factory
Print Magazine
United States

https://uglyducklingpresse.org/about/
submissions/
https://udp.submittable.com/submit

Book Publisher: Ugly Duckling Presse (**P531**)

Fiction > *Short Fiction*
General, and in particular: Experimental

Nonfiction > *Short Nonfiction*
General, and in particular: Experimental

Poetry > *Any Poetic Form*

Send: Full text; Author bio
How to send: Submittable

Publishes mainly poetry. Fiction and
nonfiction will have a better chance if it is
fairly short (more than 4 pages per contributor
are not usually published) and if it has a fairly
experimental and/or playful nature.
'Traditional' fiction and prose submissions are
not as likely to be accepted, but open to
surprises.

M367 Seventeen
Magazine
300 W. 57th St, 17th Fl. New York, NY 10019
United States

mail@seventeen.com

https://www.seventeen.com
https://www.youtube.com/user/
SeventeenMagazine
https://www.instagram.com/seventeen/
https://www.facebook.com/seventeen/

Magazine Publisher: Hearst Magazines
International

YOUNG ADULT > **Nonfiction** > *Articles*
Beauty; Celebrity; Fashion; Health;
Lifestyle; Politics; Wellbeing

Fashion beauty and lifestyle magazine for
young women in their late teens and early
twenties.

M368 Shenandoah
Magazine
United States

shenandoah@wlu.edu

https://shenandoahliterary.org
https://www.facebook.com/
ShenandoahLiterary
https://www.instagram.com/
shenandoah_literary
https://twitter.com/ShenandoahWLU

Fiction in Translation
Comics; *Novel Excerpts*; *Short Fiction*
Fiction
Comics; *Novel Excerpts*; *Short Fiction*
Nonfiction in Translation
Essays: General

Short Nonfiction: Creative Nonfiction;
Memoir
Nonfiction
Essays: General
Short Nonfiction: Creative Nonfiction;
Memoir
Poetry in Translation > *Any Poetic Form*

Poetry > *Any Poetic Form*

How to send: Submittable

Aims to showcase a wide variety of voices and
perspectives in terms of gender identity, race,
ethnicity, class, age, ability, nationality,
regionality, sexuality, and educational
background. Considers short stories, essays,
excerpts of novels in progress, poems, comics,
and translations of all the above.

M369 Ships Monthly Magazine
Magazine
Kelsey Media, The Granary, Downs Court,
Yalding Hil, Yalding, Kent, ME18 6AL
United Kingdom
Tel: +44 (0) 1959 543747

https://shipsmonthly.com

Magazine Publisher: Kelsey Media

ADULT > **Nonfiction** > *Articles*: Ships

PROFESSIONAL > **Nonfiction** > *Articles*
Shipping; Ships

Magazine aimed at ship enthusiasts and
maritime professionals. Publishes news and
illustrated articles related to all kinds of ships,
including reports on the ferry, cruise, new
building and cargo ship scene as well as navies
across the world.

Editor: Nicholas Leach

M370 Shooter Literary Magazine
Magazine
United Kingdom

submissions.shooterlitmag@gmail.com

https://shooterlitmag.com

Fiction > *Short Fiction*

Nonfiction
Essays: General
Short Nonfiction: Memoir

Poetry > *Any Poetic Form*

Closed to approaches.

Publishes literary fiction, poetry, creative
nonfiction and memoir relating to specific
themes for each issue. See website for current
theme and full submission guidelines.

M371 Shoreline of Infinity
Magazine
United Kingdom

editor@shorelineofinfinity.com

https://www.shorelineofinfinity.com
https://duotrope.com/duosuma/submit/
shoreline-of-infinity-6a37K
https://www.facebook.com/
ShorelineOfInfinity/
https://twitter.com/shoreinf
https://www.youtube.com/channel/
UCm2N3L9V2rvnkS5dCRzttCg
https://www.instagram.com/shoreinf/

Fiction > *Short Fiction*
Fantasy; Science Fiction

Poetry > *Any Poetic Form*: Science Fiction

Closed to approaches.

Science Fiction magazine from Scotland. We
want stories that explore our unknown future.
We want to play around with the big ideas and
the little ones. We want writers to tell us
stories to inspire us, give us hope, provide
some laughs. Or to scare the stuffing out of us.
We want good stories: we want to be
entertained. We want to read how people cope
in our exotic new world, we want to be in their
minds, in their bodies, in their souls.

M372 Shorts Magazine
Online Magazine
United Kingdom

editor.shorts@gmail.com

http://shortsmagazine.com

Fiction > *Short Fiction*

Nonfiction > *Essays*

Poetry > *Any Poetic Form*

Send: Full text; Author bio
How to send: Word file email attachment

Online magazine published four times a year,
and includes short fiction, flash fiction, sci-fi,
life writing, poetry, essays, science, research,
opinion pieces, monologues, drama, top ten
lists, photography, featured artists.

M373 Sierra
Print Magazine; Online Magazine
United States

https://www.sierraclub.org
https://www.sierraclub.org/sierra
https://www.facebook.com/SierraMagazine/
https://www.instagram.com/sierramagazine/
https://twitter.com/sierra_magazine
https://www.pinterest.com/sierramagazine/

Nonfiction
Articles: Adventure; Climate Science;
Culture; Environment; Narrative Nonfiction;
Nature; Social Justice; Sustainable Living;
Travel; Wildlife
Reviews: Books; Films

Send: Query; Pitch
How to send: Online submission system

A quarterly national print and digital magazine
publishing award-winning journalism and

cutting-edge photography, art, and video dedicated to protecting the natural world. Looking for reported stories on a wide range of environmental and social justice issues from writers who can bring to our audience a broad array of perspectives and writing styles.

M374 The Soho Review

Magazine
New York
United States

thesohoreview@gmail.com

https://thesohoreview.com

Fiction
  Cartoons: Comedy / Humour
  Jokes: General
  Short Fiction: Comedy / Humour

Poetry > *Any Poetic Form*: Comedy / Humour

Send: Pitch
How to send: Email

Humor magazine based in New York. Constantly looking for jokes, cartoons, poems, and short stories. Pitch ideas by email.

M375 Somerset Life

Magazine
United Kingdom

https://www.greatbritishlife.co.uk/magazines/somerset/

Magazine Publisher: Great British Life

Nonfiction
  Articles: Food; Gardening; History; Houses; Lifestyle; Somerset; Travel
  Reviews: Restaurants

Magazine that puts the gloss on life in Somerset. Every month it's packed with features about this picturesque part of England – from characters and personalities to heritage and traditions. We turn the focus on our towns and villages, and give comprehensive guides to enjoying life in Somerset – including what's on, restaurant reviews and topical features on major events.

M376 Sonder Magazine

Print Magazine
Dublin
Ireland

sonderlit@gmail.com

https://sonderlit.com
https://www.instagram.com/sonder_lit/
https://twitter.com/MagazineSonder
https://www.facebook.com/sonderlit
https://www.linkedin.com/company/sonder-magazine/
https://www.youtube.com/channel/UCm3GnFrr2QXkz14LeOe7IHA

Fiction > *Short Fiction*

Nonfiction > *Short Nonfiction*: Creative Nonfiction

Closed to approaches.

A Dublin-based print journal, focused on the idea of sonder, the self, and others: that existential feeling you get when you're walking down the street or sitting in the pub and are overcome by the realization that everyone you pass is just out there doing their own thing, thinking their own thoughts and living their own lives. Publishes short stories, flash fiction, and creative non-fiction, all based around the individual and how we interact with each other.

M377 South Carolina Review

Magazine
314 Strode Tower, Clemson, SC 29634
United States
Tel: +1 (864) 656-3151

km@clemson.edu

https://www.clemson.edu/caah/sites/south-carolina-review
https://thesouthcarolinareview.submittable.com/submit

Fiction > *Short Fiction*

Nonfiction
  Essays: General
  Reviews: Books
  Short Nonfiction: Creative Nonfiction

Poetry > *Any Poetic Form*

Closed to approaches.

Publishes fiction and poetry primarily, but will also consider creative nonfiction, scholarly essays, and book reviews.

Editor: Wayne Chapman

M378 Southern Humanities Review

Magazine
9088 Haley Center, Auburn University, Auburn, AL 36849
United States
Tel: +1 (334) 844-9088

shr@auburn.edu

http://www.southernhumanitiesreview.com
https://www.facebook.com/southernhumanitiesreview
https://twitter.com/SouthernHReview
https://www.instagram.com/southernhumanitiesreview/
https://www.youtube.com/channel/UCnywOlZbBtEX7OFYMUMSQsg

Fiction > *Short Fiction*

Nonfiction > *Essays*
  Creative Nonfiction; Literary Journalism; Literary; Lyric Essays; Memoir; Personal Essays; Travel

Poetry > *Any Poetic Form*

Send: Full text
How to send: Submittable
How not to send: Post; Email

Costs: A fee is charged upon submission. $3 submission fee.

Submissions for all fiction and nonfiction are open from August 15 until November 1 in the fall and from January 15 until March 14 in the spring. Poetry submissions are open from August 24 until September 7 in the fall and from January 15 until March 14 in the spring. Nonfiction submissions are open year-round.

M379 The Southern Review

Magazine
338 Johnston Hall, Louisiana State University, Baton Rouge, LA 70803
United States
Tel: +1 (225) 578-6467
Fax: +1 (225) 578-6461

southernreview@lsu.edu

https://thesouthernreview.org
https://www.facebook.com/lsusouthernreview
https://twitter.com/southern_review
https://soundcloud.com/lsupress_and_tsr

Fiction in Translation > *Short Fiction*

Fiction > *Short Fiction*

Nonfiction in Translation > *Essays*

Nonfiction > *Essays*

Poetry in Translation > *Any Poetic Form*

Poetry > *Any Poetic Form*

Closed to approaches.

Costs: A fee is charged upon submission. $3 per submission.

Strives to discover and promote a diverse array of engaging, relevant, and challenging literature—including fiction, nonfiction, poetry, and translation from literary luminaries as well as the best established and emerging writers.

M380 Southword Journal

Magazine
Frank O'Connor House, 84 Douglas Street, Cork
Ireland
Tel: +353 (0) 21 4322396

info@munsterlit.ie

http://www.munsterlit.ie/Southword%20Journal.html
https://www.facebook.com/Southword.Journal/
https://southword.submittable.com/submit/

Fiction > *Short Fiction*

Poetry > *Any Poetic Form*

Closed to approaches.

Accepts submissions during specific submission windows only. See website for details.

M381 Spelt Magazine

Magazine
United Kingdom

Speltmagazine@gmail.com

https://speltmagazine.com

Nonfiction > *Short Nonfiction*
Creative Nonfiction; Farming; Rural Living

Poetry > *Any Poetic Form*
Farming; Rural Living

Closed to approaches.

Publishes poetry and creative non-fiction that has something to say about the rural experience. Send up to six poems or up to two pieces of creative nonfiction (up to 1,500 words each) in the body of an email.

M382 Square Mile Magazine

Magazine
United Kingdom

https://squaremile.com
https://twitter.com/squaremile_com
https://www.facebook.com/squaremileuk/
https://instagram.com/squaremile_com

Magazine Publisher: Threadneedle Media

Nonfiction > *Articles*
Arts; Books; Boxing; Cars; Comedy / Humour; Culture; Films; Fitness; Food and Drink; Formula One; Golf; Investments; London; Motorbikes; Music; Property / Real Estate; Pubs; Sport; TV; Technology; Travel; Whisky; Wine; Yachts

Luxury lifestyle magazine targeting wealthy men working in London's financial districts.

Editor: Martin Deeson

M383 Stand Magazine

Magazine
School of English, Leeds University, Leeds, LS2 9JT
United Kingdom
Tel: +44 (0) 113 233 4794

engstand@leeds.ac.uk
enquiries@standmagazine.org

https://standmagazine.org
https://www.facebook.com/pages/Stand-Magazine/270598523017007
https://twitter.com/Stand_poetry

Fiction > *Short Fiction*: Literary

Poetry > *Any Poetic Form*

Send: Full text
How to send: Email

A well established magazine of poetry and literary fiction. Has previously published the work of, among others, Samuel Beckett, Angela Carter, Seamus Heaney, Geoffrey Hill, and Andrew Motion.

M384 Stickman Review

Online Magazine
United States

fiction@stickmanreview.com
nonfiction@stickmanreview.com
poetry@stickmanreview.com

http://www.stickmanreview.com

Fiction > *Short Fiction*: Literary

Nonfiction > *Essays*: Literary

Poetry > *Any Poetic Form*

Send: Full text
How to send: Email

Publishes literary fiction, poetry, and literary nonfiction. Accepts submissions February to April and August to October.

M385 The Stinging Fly

Magazine
PO Box 6016, Dublin 1
Ireland

stingingfly@gmail.com
submissions.stingingfly@gmail.com

https://stingingfly.org
https://www.facebook.com/StingingFly
http://twitter.com/stingingfly

Fiction in Translation > *Short Fiction*

Fiction
Graphic Short Fiction; *Novel Excerpts*; *Short Fiction*
Nonfiction
Essays: General
Interviews: Books; Creative Writing
Poetry in Translation > *Any Poetic Form*

Poetry > *Any Poetic Form*

Closed to approaches.

A literary magazine, a book publisher, an education provider, and an online platform. Independent and not for profit. Aims to seek out, nurture, publish and promote the very best new Irish and international writing.

Publisher: Declan Meade

M386 Story Unlikely

Magazine
United States

dan@storyunlikely.com

https://www.storyunlikely.com

Fiction > *Short Fiction*
General, and in particular: Adventure; Alternative History; Comedy / Humour; Crime; Cyberpunk; Fantasy; Horror; Literary; Magical Realism; Mystery; Romance; Satire; Science Fiction; Speculative; Suspense; Thrillers; Westerns

Nonfiction > *Short Nonfiction*
General, and in particular: Memoir; Narrative Nonfiction

How to send: Email

Seeks short stories of all genres and styles – as long as it's a story, we'll consider it. We prefer shorter fiction, but will accept up to 10,000 word pieces. We are concerned only with the quality of the story (both by the author's ability to write clean prose and their ability to in how to tell a story), and not by their pedigree (or lack there of).

M387 Strand Magazine

Magazine
33228 West 12 Mile Rd. #285, Farmington Hills, MI 48334
United States
Tel: +1 (800) 300-6652

strandmag@strandmag.com

https://strandmag.com
https://www.facebook.com/strandmagazine/
https://twitter.com/StrandMag
https://www.instagram.com/strandmag/?hl=en
https://www.pinterest.com/strandmag/

Fiction > *Short Fiction*: Mystery

Nonfiction
Articles: Creative Writing; Mystery
Interviews: Mystery
Reviews: Mystery; Thrillers

Originally founded in 1891 in England, but closed due to economic difficulties in the 1950s. Publishes mystery stories, and articles, interviews, and reviews related to the genre.

M388 Strange Horizons

Online Magazine
United States

management@strangehorizons.com

http://strangehorizons.com
https://strangehorizons.moksha.io/publication/strange-horizons/guidelines
https://www.facebook.com/groups/strangehorizons/
https://twitter.com/strangehorizons
https://www.patreon.com/strangehorizons

Fiction > *Short Fiction*
Fantasy; Science Fiction; Slipstream; Speculative

Nonfiction
Articles: Fantasy; Science Fiction; Slipstream; Speculative
Essays: Fantasy; Science Fiction; Slipstream; Speculative
Interviews: Fantasy; Science Fiction; Slipstream; Speculative
Reviews: Fantasy; Science Fiction; Slipstream; Speculative
Poetry > *Any Poetic Form*
Fantasy; Science Fiction; Slipstream; Speculative

Send: Full text
How to send: Moksha
How not to send: Email

Weekly online magazine of speculative fiction, poetry, and nonfiction on related topics. Submit via online submission system only.

M389 Strategic Finance
Magazine
United States

sfmag@imanet.org

https://sfmagazine.com

PROFESSIONAL > **Nonfiction** > *Articles*: Finance

Send: Query; Full text; Submission Form
How to send: Word file email attachment
How not to send: PDF file email attachment

Publishes articles that help financial professionals perform their jobs more effectively, advance their careers, grow personally and professionally, and make their organisations more profitable.

M390 Structo Magazine
Print Magazine; Online Magazine
United Kingdom

https://structomagazine.co.uk

Magazine Publisher: Structo Press

Fiction in Translation > *Short Fiction*

Fiction > *Short Fiction*

Poetry in Translation > *Any Poetic Form*

Poetry > *Any Poetic Form*

Closed to approaches.

Short stories of up to approximately 4,000 words will be considered, both original stories and new translations of non-English language texts; or up to three previously unpublished poems in English or new translations from other languages. Hybrid forms are welcome.

M391 Subtropics
Magazine
PO Box 112075, 4008 Turlington Hall, University of Florida, Gainesville, FL 32611-2075
United States

subtropics@english.ufl.edu

http://subtropics.english.ufl.edu
http://www.facebook.com/subtropicsmag/
https://twitter.com/subtropicsmag/

Fiction > *Short Fiction*: Literary

Nonfiction > *Essays*

Poetry > *Any Poetic Form*

Closed to approaches.

Costs: A fee is charged upon submission. $3.00 for each submission.

Publishes literary fiction, essays, and poetry, of any length. Submit via online submission

system during open windows. $3 charge per submission.

Editor: David Leavitt

Managing Editor: Mark Mitchell

Poetry Editor: Ange Mlinko

M392 Successful Meetings
Magazine
301 Route 17 N, Suite 1150, Rutherford, NJ 07070
United States
Tel: +1 (201) 902-1978

ledelstein@ntmllc.com

http://www.successfulmeetings.com

PROFESSIONAL > **Nonfiction** > *Articles*: Business

Magazine for multi-tasking meeting planners.

Editor: Loren Edelstein

M393 Suffolk Magazine
Magazine
United Kingdom

Magazine Publisher: Great British Life

M394 Sunshine Artist
Magazine
N7528 Aanstad Rd., Iola, WI 54945
United States
Tel: +1 (800) 597-2573

https://sunshineartist.com

Magazine Publisher: JP Media LLC

PROFESSIONAL > **Nonfiction** > *Reviews*
Arts; Crafts

Publishes reviews of fine art fairs, festivals, events, and small craft shows around the country, for professionals making a living through art shows.

Managing Editor: Melissa Jones

M395 Sunspot Literary Journal
Print Magazine; Online Magazine
Durham, NC
United States
Tel: +1 (919) 928-2245

Sunspotlit@gmail.com

https://sunspotlit.com
https://sunspotlit.submittable.com/submit

Fiction in Translation > *Short Fiction*

Fiction
  Graphic Short Fiction; *Short Fiction*
Nonfiction > *Essays*

Poetry in Translation > *Any Poetic Form*

Poetry > *Any Poetic Form*

Scripts
  Film Scripts; *Theatre Scripts*

How to send: Submittable

Costs: Offers services that writers have to pay for; A fee is charged upon submission in some cases. Offers a poetry feedback service and competitions for which there is an entry fee.

Since launching in January of 2019, this journal has amplified diverse multinational voices. New works have been published in their original language side-by-side with English translations. Boundaries that exclude meaningful and important works have been broken by accepting extremely long-form pieces, a rarity in publishing today.

M396 The Supplement
Magazine
Atlantean Publishing, 4 Pierrot Steps, 71 Kursaal Way, Southend-on-Sea, Essex, SS1 2UY
United Kingdom

atlanteanpublishing@hotmail.com

https://atlanteanpublishing.wordpress.com/
https://atlanteanpublishing.fandom.com/wiki/The_Supplement

Book Publisher / Magazine Publisher:
Atlantean Publishing (**P044**)

Fiction > *Short Fiction*

Nonfiction
  Articles: General
  News: Small Press
  Reviews: Books; Films
Poetry > *Any Poetic Form*

Closed to approaches.

Publishes small-press news and advertisements, reviews covering new publications from small presses, independent and mainstream books, films and much more beside, and various articles on an equally wide variety of topics — as well as the occasional poem or very short piece of fiction, often related to the non-fiction content.

Editor: David-John Tyrer

M397 Surface
Magazine
3921 Alton Road, Suite 413, Miami Beach, FL 33140
United States
Tel: +1 (212) 229-1500

editorial@surfacemag.com

https://www.surfacemag.com
https://twitter.com/SurfaceMag
https://www.instagram.com/surfacemag/
https://www.facebook.com/surfacemag
https://www.pinterest.com/surfacemag/
https://www.youtube.com/surfacemedia/videos

Magazine Publisher: Future Media Group

Nonfiction > *Articles*
  Architecture; Arts; Contemporary Culture; Design; Fashion; Travel

American magazine of global contemporary design. Covers architecture, art, design, fashion, and travel, with a focus on how these fields shape and are shaped by contemporary culture.

M398 Sussex Life

Magazine
United Kingdom

Magazine Publisher: Great British Life

M399 Sycamore Review

Print Magazine
Purdue University, Department of English, 500 Oval Drive, West Lafayette, IN 47907
United States

sycamore@purdue.edu

https://www.cla.purdue.edu/academic/english/publications/sycamore-review/index.html
https://sycamorereview.submittable.com/submit

Fiction in Translation > *Short Fiction*

Fiction > *Short Fiction*

Nonfiction in Translation > *Essays*

Nonfiction
  Essays: Personal Essays
  Interviews: General
  Reviews: Arts; Books
  Short Nonfiction: Literary Memoir

Poetry in Translation > *Any Poetic Form*

Poetry > *Any Poetic Form*

Closed to approaches.

Looking for original poetry, fiction, non-fiction and art. We accept unsolicited submissions of fiction, poetry, and non-fiction. Please query for art and book reviews. No outside interviews, previously published works, or genre pieces (conventional science fiction, romance, horror, etc.). Unless explicitly asked by an editor, submit no more than twice per year.

M400 Tahoma Literary Review

Magazine
United States

poetry@tahomaliteraryreview.com
fiction@tahomaliteraryreview.com
nonfiction@tahomaliteraryreview.com

https://tahomaliteraryreview.com

Fiction > *Short Fiction*
  Experimental; Literary

Nonfiction
  Essays: General, and in particular: Experimental; Lyric Essays
  Short Nonfiction: Narrative Nonfiction

Poetry
  Formal Poetry; *Free Verse*; *Long Form Poetry*

Closed to approaches.

Costs: A fee is charged upon submission; Offers services that writers have to pay for. $4 for poetry and flash prose; $5 for longer prose. Critiques available for an additional fee.

Publishes poetry, fiction, and nonfiction. Charges $4 submission fee for short works; $5 submission fee for long works. Submit online through online submission system.

M401 Takahe

Magazine
New Zealand

essays@takahe.org.nz
fiction@takahe.org.nz
poetry@takahe.org.nz
reviews@takahe.org.nz

https://www.takahe.org.nz
https://twitter.com/takahemagazine

Fiction > *Short Fiction*: Literary

Nonfiction
  Essays: Cultural Criticism; New Zealand; South Pacific
  Reviews: Books

Poetry > *Any Poetic Form*

Send: Full text; Author bio
How to send: Email attachment

Exists to foster and promote art and literature that represents the diverse voices of Aotearoa New Zealand within the global context. It does this by publishing innovative prose, poetry, art, and critique by emerging and established writers and artists.

Art Editor: Andrew Paul Wood

Essays Editor: Alie Benge

Fiction Editor: Zoë Meager

Poetry Editor: Erik Kennedy

Reviews Editor: Sile Mannion

M402 Take a Break's Take a Puzzle

Magazine
Media House, Peterborough Business Park, Lynch Wood, Peterborough, PE2 6EA
United Kingdom

https://www.puzzleshq.com/puzzles-magazines/mixed/take-a-puzzle/

Magazine: Take a Break
Magazine Publisher: Bauer Media Group

Nonfiction > *Puzzles*

Magazine of puzzles.

M403 Tammy Journal

Print Magazine
United States

thetjournal@gmail.com

https://www.tammyjournal.com

Book Publisher / Magazine Publisher: Tammy Chapbooks

Fiction > *Short Fiction*: Literary

Poetry > *Any Poetic Form*

Closed to approaches.

Costs: A fee is charged upon submission. $3 per submission. $15 to submit and receive a copy of the journal. $20 for expedited response.

Submit poetry up to to 10 pages, or fiction up to 20 pages.

M404 Tears in the Fence

Magazine
Flats, Durweston Mill, Mill Lane, Durweston, Blandford Forum, Dorset, DT11 0QD
United Kingdom
Tel: +44 (0) 7824 618708

tearsinthefence@gmail.com

https://tearsinthefence.com

Fiction > *Short Fiction*

Nonfiction
  Essays: General
  Interviews: General
  Reviews: General
  Short Nonfiction: Creative Nonfiction

Poetry
  Any Poetic Form; *Prose Poetry*

Send: Full text
How to send: Email attachment; In the body of an email

International literary magazine publishing poetry, fiction, prose poems, essays, translations, interviews and reviews. Publishes fiction as short as 100 words or as long as 3,500. Maximum 6 poems per poet per issue. No simultaneous submissions or previously published material. Send submissions by email as both an attachment and in the body of the email.

M405 Teen Breathe

Magazine
GMC Publications Ltd, 86 High Street, Lewes, BN7 1XU
United Kingdom
Tel: +44 (0) 1273 477374

hello@breathemagazine.com

https://www.teenbreathe.co.uk

YOUNG ADULT > **Nonfiction** > *Articles*
  Health; Lifestyle

Send: Full text

Magazine for young people who want to find time for themselves. Focuses on Wellbeing, Mindfulness, Creativity and Escaping. Experienced writers should send ideas with examples of previous work. New writers should submit complete articles. Submit using forms on website.

M406 The Temz Review
Online Magazine
London, ON
Canada

thetemzreview@gmail.com

https://www.thetemzreview.com

Fiction > *Short Fiction*: Literary

Nonfiction > *Reviews*: Literature

Poetry > *Any Poetic Form*

Send: Full text
How to send: Moksha

Quarterly online magazine. Submit one piece of fiction or creative nonfiction (or more than one if under 1,000 words) or 1-8 poems via online submission system. For reviews, send query by email.

M407 That's Life!
Magazine
The Lantern, 75 Hampstead Road, London, NW1 2PL
United Kingdom

stories@thatslife.co.uk

http://www.thatslife.co.uk

Types: Nonfiction
Formats: Articles; News
Subjects: Lifestyle
Markets: Adult

Publishes nonfiction true life stories. See website for details.

M408 the6ress
Print Magazine
United Kingdom

the6ress@gmail.com

https://the6ress.com
https://www.instagram.com/the6ress/
https://twitter.com/the6ress/

Poetry
  Any Poetic Form; Visual Poetry

Publishes poetry, art, and word art. See website for submission windows and issue themes.

M409 Thema
Magazine
Box 8747, Metairie, LA 70011-8747
United States

thema@cox.net

http://themaliterarysociety.com

Fiction > *Short Fiction*

Poetry > *Any Poetic Form*

How to send: Post; International Email
How not to send: Domestic Email

All issues are themed, so imperative to check website for upcoming themes before submitting. Material need not have specified theme as central to the plot, but must not be incidental.

See website for detailed submission guidelines.

Editor: Virginia Howard

Poetry Editor: Gail Howard

M410 Thin Air Magazine
Print Magazine
United States

https://thinairmagazine.org
https://www.instagram.com/thinairmagazine/
https://twitter.com/thinairmagazine
https://www.facebook.com/thinairmagazine/

Fiction > *Short Fiction*: Literary

Nonfiction > *Short Nonfiction*

Poetry > *Any Poetic Form*

Send: Full text
How to send: Submittable

Costs: A fee is charged upon submission. $3 per submission.

A non-profit, graduate-student-run, literary magazine. Submit up to three poems, or prose up to 3,000 words.

M411 Third Coast
Magazine
United States

editors@thirdcoastmagazine.com

http://thirdcoastmagazine.com
https://thirdcoastmagazine.submittable.com/submit
http://facebook.com/thirdcoastmagazine
http://twitter.com/thirdcoastmag
http://instagram.com/thirdcoastmag

Fiction > *Short Fiction*

Nonfiction > *Short Nonfiction*: Creative Nonfiction

Poetry > *Any Poetic Form*

Closed to approaches.

All submissions should be sent via Submittable, through the portals of their respective genres. All attachments sent by email will be deleted, and any submissions sent via postal mail or social media will not be read. Accepts simultaneous submissions, but not multiple submissions; please submit no more than one manuscript at a time. No previously published works.

Editor: Glenn Deutsch

M412 The Threepenny Review
Magazine
PO Box 9131, Berkeley, CA 94709
United States

wlesser@threepennyreview.com

http://www.threepennyreview.com

Fiction > *Short Fiction*: Literary

Nonfiction > *Articles*
  Arts; Culture; Literature

Poetry > *Any Poetic Form*

Closed to approaches.

National literary magazine with coverage of the visual and performing arts. Send complete MS by post with SASE or via online submission system. No previously published material, simultaneous submissions, or submissions from May to December. Prospective contributors are advised to read the magazine before submitting.

Editor: Wendy Lesser

M413 Tolka
Magazine
Ireland

https://www.tolkajournal.org
https://www.instagram.com/tolkajournal/
https://twitter.com/tolkajournal

Fiction > *Short Fiction*: Autofiction

Nonfiction
  Essays: Personal Essays
  Short Nonfiction: Memoir; Travel

Closed to approaches.

Biannual literary journal of non-fiction: publishing essays, reportage, travel writing, auto-fiction, individual stories and the writing that flows in between.

M414 Tor.com
Online Magazine
United States

blogsubmissions@tor.com

https://www.tor.com
https://www.tor.com/submissions-guidelines/

Nonfiction
  Articles: Fantasy; Science Fiction
  Essays: Fantasy; Science Fiction
  Reviews: Books; Fantasy; Science Fiction

Send: Pitch; Writing sample
How to send: Email

Most interested in pitches for essays, think pieces, list posts, reaction pieces, and reviews in the 1000-2500 word range (although also open to longer essays). If possible, please include 2-3 writing samples and/or links to your published work on other sites.

M415 Total Film
Magazine
11 West 42nd Street, 15th Floor, New York, NY 10036
United States

https://www.gamesradar.com/uk/totalfilm/

Magazine Publisher: Future US

Nonfiction
 Articles: Film Industry; Films
 News: Film Industry; Films

A cheeky, irreverent, but always passionate and authoritative look at every part of the film world. From all the latest blockbusters, comic-book tent poles and sci-fi extravaganzas to the very best Oscar-baiters, arthouse masterpieces, hidden gems and festival hits.

M416 Total Film (UK Edition)
Magazine
Quay House, The Ambury, Bath, BA1 1UA
United Kingdom

https://www.gamesradar.com/uk/totalfilm/

Magazine Publisher: Future

Nonfiction
 Articles: Film Industry; Films
 News: Film Industry; Films

"A cheeky, irreverent but always passionate and authoritative look at every part of the film world".

M417 Tributaries
Online Magazine
United States

https://www.thefourthriver.com
https://4thriver.submittable.com/submit

Magazine: The Fourth River (**M178**)

Fiction in Translation > *Short Fiction*

Fiction > *Short Fiction*

Nonfiction in Translation > *Short Nonfiction*

Nonfiction > *Short Nonfiction*

Poetry in Translation > *Any Poetic Form*

Poetry > *Any Poetic Form*

How to send: Submittable

Weekly online publication, showcasing the brief and the inspiring, that which sustains us and takes us through unexpected courses. Each week we will feature one short piece on our website. Submit one poem or up to 500 words of fiction or nonfiction prose, translations in any genre, and hybridity that addresses the mission. Multiple submissions are not accepted. Simultaneous submissions are fine as long as you notify us immediately. We do not accept previously published work.

M418 The Tusculum Review
Magazine
60 Shiloh Road, Greeneville, TN 37745
United States

review@tusculum.edu

https://ttr.tusculum.edu

Fiction > *Short Fiction*: Literary

Nonfiction > *Essays*

Poetry > *Any Poetic Form*

Scripts > *Theatre Scripts*: Drama

Send: Full text
How to send: Submittable

Costs: A fee is charged upon submission. $2.

We seek well-crafted writing that takes risks. We publish work in and between all genres: poetry, fiction, essays, and plays--we appreciate work in experimental and traditional modes. We accept prose submissions of less than 6,000 words (24 double-spaced pages) and poetry submissions under five pages. We publish scripts in the 10-minute format (10 pages).

M419 TV Times
Magazine
United Kingdom

https://www.futureplc.com/brand/tv-times/

Magazine Publisher: Future

Nonfiction > *Articles*
 Entertainment; TV

Magazine publishing television news, listings, and articles.

M420 UCity Review
Magazine
United States

editors@ucityreview.com

http://www.ucityreview.com

Types: Poetry
Subjects: Literary
Markets: Adult

Closed to approaches.

Online magazine accepting submissions of poetry year-round. Submit up to six poems in .doc or .docx format, by email.

M421 Ulster Business
Magazine
Belfast Telegraph House, 33 Clarendon Road, Clarendon Dock, Belfast, BT1 3BG
United Kingdom
Tel: +44 (0) 28 9026 4000

https://www.ulsterbusiness.com
https://www.belfasttelegraph.co.uk/business/ulsterbusiness/

Newspaper: Belfast Telegraph

PROFESSIONAL > **Nonfiction**
 Articles: Business
 Interviews: Business
 News: Business

Business magazine for Ulster, publishing news, articles, features, and interviews with local businessmen.

M422 Uncut
Magazine
United Kingdom

editors@www.uncut.co.uk

http://www.uncut.co.uk
https://www.facebook.com/UncutMagazine/
https://www.instagram.com/uncut_magazine/
https://twitter.com/uncutmagazine/

Nonfiction
 Articles: Films; Music
 Reviews: Films; Music

Magazine covering film and music.

M423 Under the Radar
Magazine
United Kingdom

mail@ninearchespress.com

https://ninearchespress.com/magazine
https://ninearchespress.submittable.com/submit

Book Publisher: Nine Arches Press (**P376**)

Fiction > *Short Fiction*

Poetry > *Any Poetic Form*

How to send: Submittable

A magazine of new contemporary poetry and fiction. Submit up to six poems, or short fiction up to 2,500 words. Submit only previously unpublished work.

M424 The Undercommons
Online Magazine
United States

https://www.commontonguezine.com

Fiction
 Novellas: Dark Fantasy
 Short Fiction: Dark Fantasy

Poetry > *Any Poetic Form*: Dark Fantasy

How to send: Online submission system

Dark fantasy magazine. Each issue includes one novella, one short story, and one poem.

M425 Understorey Magazine
Magazine
Alexa McDonough Institute for Women, Gender and Social Justice, Mount Saint Vincent University, 166 Bedford Highway, Halifax, NS, B3M 2J6
Canada

editor@understoreymagazine.ca

https://understoreymagazine.ca

Fiction > *Short Fiction*
 Feminism; Women's Issues; Women

Nonfiction > *Short Nonfiction*
 Creative Nonfiction; Feminism; Women's Issues; Women

Poetry > *Any Poetic Form*
 Feminism; Women's Issues; Women

Closed to approaches.

Publishes fiction, poetry, and creative nonfiction by Canadian women. Send prose up to 1,500 words or up to five poems by email. See website for full guidelines.

M426 Unthology

Magazine
Unthank Submissions (Unthology), PO Box 3506, Norwich, NR7 7QP
United Kingdom

unthology@unthankbooks.com

http://www.unthankbooks.com

Types: Fiction; Nonfiction
Formats: Essays; Short Fiction
Subjects: Experimental; Literary; Traditional
Markets: Adult

Closed to approaches.

Publishes the work of new or established writers and can include short stories of any length, reportage, essays or novel extracts from anywhere in the world. Allows space for stories of different styles and subjects to rub up against each other, featuring classic slice-of-life alongside the experimental, the shocking and strange. Submit by post with SAE and personal contact details, or by email.

M427 Urthona

Magazine
Old Abbey House, Abbey Road, Cambridge, CB5 8HQ
United Kingdom
Tel: +44 (0) 7443 499384

urthonamag@gmail.com

https://urthona.com

Nonfiction > *Essays*
Arts; Buddhism; Contemporary; Culture

Poetry > *Any Poetic Form*

How to send: Email

Magazine of Buddhism and the Arts, linking Buddhism and Western culture.

M428 Vagabond City

Online Magazine
United States

vagabondcitypoetry@gmail.com
vagabondcityfiction@gmail.com
vagabondcitynonfic@gmail.com
vagabondcityliterary@gmail.com
vagabondcityinterviews@gmail.com

https://vagabondcitylit.com

Fiction > *Short Fiction*

Nonfiction
Essays: Creative Nonfiction
Interviews: General
Reviews: Books

Poetry > *Any Poetic Form*

Send: Full text
How to send: Email

Electronic magazine featuring poetry, fiction, art, creative nonfiction and essays by marginalised creators. Also publishes book reviews and interviews. Submit up to five pieces at a time in the body of an email or as a Word file attachment. See website for full guidelines.

M429 Vallum

Magazine
5038 Sherbrooke West, P.O. Box 23077 CP Vendome Station, Montreal, Quebec, H4A 1T0
Canada
Tel: +1 (514) 937-8946
Fax: +1 (514) 937-8946

editors@vallummag.com

https://vallummag.com
https://www.facebook.com/VallumMagazine
https://twitter.com/vallummag
https://www.instagram.com/vallummag/
https://soundcloud.com/vallum-magazine
https://www.youtube.com/channel/
UCARH_nOH0vXwmpXSxzpgQZg

Nonfiction
Essays; *Interviews*; *Reviews*
Poetry > *Any Poetic Form*: Contemporary

Closed to approaches.

Send 4-7 poems, essays of 4-6 pages, interviews of 3-5 pages, reviews of 1-3 pages, through online submission system only. No fiction, plays, movie scripts, memoir, or creative nonfiction. Check website for submission windows and themes.

M430 Vestal Review

Online Magazine
United States

info@vestalreview.org

https://www.vestalreview.net
https://vestalreview.submittable.com/submit
https://www.facebook.com/VestalReview/
https://www.instagram.com/vestalreview/
https://twitter.com/VestalReview

Fiction > *Short Fiction*

Nonfiction
Interviews; *Reviews*

Closed to approaches.

Publishes flash fiction up to 500 words. Accepts submissions between February 1 and May 31, and between August 1 and November 30. Also accepts proposals for interviews and reviews.

M431 View From Atlantis

Online Magazine
United Kingdom

atlanteanpublishing@hotmail.com

https://viewfromatlantis.wordpress.com

Book Publisher / Magazine Publisher:
Atlantean Publishing (**P044**)

Fiction > *Short Fiction*
General, and in particular: Fantasy; Horror; Science Fiction; Speculative; Supernatural / Paranormal

Poetry
Any Poetic Form: General, and in particular: Fantasy; Horror; Science Fiction; Speculative; Supernatural / Paranormal
Prose Poetry: General, and in particular: Fantasy; Horror; Science Fiction; Speculative; Supernatural / Paranormal

How to send: In the body of an email

Primarily interested in speculative poetry (fantasy, science fiction, supernatural horror, etc), but literary poems and poetry from other genres will be considered as long as they fit the issue theme. Prose poems and flash fiction will also be considered. Please check the website for themes and submission periods. Submissions sent outside of submission periods will be deleted unread.

M432 The Virginia Quarterly Review

Magazine
5 Boar's Head Lane, PO Box 400223, Charlottesville, VA 22904
United States
Tel: +1 (434) 924-3675
Fax: +1 (434) 924-1397

editors@vqronline.org

https://www.vqronline.org
https://www.facebook.com/vqreview
https://twitter.com/vqr

Fiction > *Short Fiction*

Nonfiction > *Short Nonfiction*
Arts; Creative Nonfiction; Cultural Criticism; History; Literary Criticism; Politics

Poetry > *Any Poetic Form*

Does not want:

> **Fiction** > *Short Fiction*
> Fantasy; Romance; Science Fiction

Closed to approaches.

Strives to publish the best writing they can find. Has a long history of publishing accomplished and award-winning authors, but they also seek and support emerging writers.

M433 Virginia Wine & Country Life

Magazine
United States

Concierge@ivypublications.com
editor@ivylifeandstylemedia.com

https://wineandcountrylife.com
https://www.facebook.com/
WineAndCountryLife/
https://www.instagram.com/
wineandcountrylife/
https://www.pinterest.com/wclifeva/

Magazine Publisher: Ivy Life & Style Media

Nonfiction > *Articles*
Architecture; Arts; Beer Making; Country
Lifestyle; Entertainment; Farm Equipment;
Gardening; Interior Design; Literature;
Music; Virginia; Wine

Send: Query
How to send: Email

Celebrates elevated living in the heart of
Virginia wine country. Each issue highlights
architecture, interior design, music, literature,
gardening, entertaining, art, wine, equestrian
life in Hunt Country, beer making, and more.

M434 Virginia Wine & Country Weddings
Magazine
4282 Ivy Road, Charlottesville, VA 22903
United States
Tel: +1 (434) 984-4713

Concierge@ivypublications.com

https://wineandcountryweddings.com

Magazine Publisher: Ivy Life & Style Media

Nonfiction > *Articles*
Lifestyle; Virginia; Weddings

Send: Query
How not to send: Email

A uniquely curated magazine for creating the
elegant country wedding in Jefferson's
Virginia, one that will inspire couples as well
as top event planners across the nation from
New York City to Beverly Hills.

M435 Viz
Magazine
2nd Floor, Saunders House, 52-53 The Mall,
Ealing, W5 3TA
United Kingdom

hello@metropolis.co.uk

https://viz.co.uk
https://www.facebook.com/VizComic/
https://twitter.com/vizcomic

Magazine Publisher: Diamond Publishing

Fiction > *Cartoons*: Comedy / Humour

Nonfiction > *Articles*
Comedy / Humour; Satire

Magazine of adult humour, including cartoons,
spoof articles, etc.

M436 Waccamaw
Online Magazine
United States

http://waccamawjournal.com
https://www.facebook.com/Waccamaw-A-
Journal-of-Contemporary-Literature-
164290950299653/
https://twitter.com/waccamawjournal
https://www.instagram.com/waccamawjournal/

Book Publisher: Athenaeum Press (**P043**)

Fiction > *Short Fiction*: Literary

Nonfiction > *Essays*

Poetry > *Any Poetic Form*

Closed to approaches.

Online literary journal publishing poems,
stories, and essays. Submit prose up to 6,000
words or 3-5 poems between August 1 and
September 8 annually. Submit via online
submission system only.

M437 Walk Magazine
Magazine
United Kingdom

https://www.ramblers.org.uk/walkmag
https://twitter.com/walkmagazine

Nonfiction > *Articles*: Walking

Rambling magazine publishing features on any
aspect of walking in Britain. No general travel
articles.

M438 The Wallace Stevens Journal
Magazine
University of Antwerp, Prinsstraat 13, 2000
Antwerp
Belgium

https://www.press.jhu.edu/journals/wallace-
stevens-journal

ACADEMIC > **Nonfiction**
Articles: Biography; Literary Criticism;
Poetry as a Subject
Essays: Biography; Literary Criticism;
Poetry as a Subject
News: Literature
Reviews: Books

ADULT > **Poetry** > *Any Poetic Form*

Send: Full text
How to send: Email attachment

Publishes articles and essays on all aspects of
Wallace Stevens' poetry and life. Also accepts
poetry inspired by the poet. See website for full
submission guidelines.

Editor: Bart Eeckhout

M439 Wasafiri
Magazine
c/o School of English and Drama, Queen
Mary, University of London, Mile End Road,
London, E1 4NS
United Kingdom
Tel: +44 (0) 20 7882 2686

wasafiri@qmul.ac.uk

https://www.wasafiri.org
https://www.facebook.com/wasafiri.magazine
https://twitter.com/Wasafirimag
https://www.youtube.com/channel/UC4J-
lxAIL8iBiaRR2AOpGFg
https://www.linkedin.com/groups/8343914/
profile

Fiction > *Short Fiction*: Literary

Nonfiction
Articles: Culture; Literature
Essays: Culture; Literature
Poetry > *Any Poetic Form*

Send: Full text
How to send: Online submission system

The indispensable journal of contemporary
African, Asian Black British, Caribbean and
transnational literatures.

In over fifteen years of publishing, this
magazine has changed the face of
contemporary writing in Britain. As a literary
magazine primarily concerned with new and
postcolonial writers, it continues to stress the
diversity and range of black and diasporic
writers world-wide. It remains committed to its
original aims: to create a definitive forum for
the voices of new writers and to open up lively
spaces for serious critical discussion not
available elsewhere. It is Britain's only
international magazine for Black British,
African, Asian and Caribbean literatures. Get
the whole picture, get the magazine at the core
of contemporary international literature today.

Submit via online submissions portal only (see
website).

M440 Weber—The Contemporary West
Magazine
Weber State University, 1395 Edvalson Street,
Dept. 1405, Ogden, Utah 84408-1405
United States

weberjournal@weber.edu

https://www.weber.edu/weberjournal
https://www.facebook.com/weberjournal
https://twitter.com/WeberJournal

Fiction > *Short Fiction*
American West; Culture; Environment

Nonfiction
Essays: Personal Essays
Short Nonfiction: Commentary; Creative
Nonfiction
Poetry > *Any Poetic Form*
American West; Culture; Environment

Send: Full text
How to send: Email

Invites submissions in the genres of personal
narrative, critical commentary, fiction, creative
non-fiction, and poetry that offer insight into
the environment and culture (both broadly

defined) of the contemporary western United States.

M441 Welsh Country

Magazine
Aberbanc, Llandysul, Ceredigion, SA44 5NP
United Kingdom
Tel: +44 (0) 1559 372010

info@welshcountry.co.uk

https://www.welshcountry.co.uk

Nonfiction
  Articles: Arts; Crafts; Culture; Food and Drink; Gardening; History; Nature; Wales; Walking
  News: Wales

Magazine covering Welsh villages, history, wild life, walking and gardening. In addition we promote amazing local artisan Welsh food & drink producers, as well as a strong focus on the thriving Welsh arts & crafts scene.

M442 West Branch

Magazine
Stadler Center, Bucknell University, 1 Dent Drive, Lewisburg, PA 17837
United States

westbranch@bucknell.edu

https://westbranch.blogs.bucknell.edu

Fiction > *Short Fiction*

Nonfiction
  Essays; *Reviews*
Poetry > *Any Poetic Form*

Closed to approaches.

Send all submissions via online submission system, between August 1 and April 1 annually.

M443 West Essex Life

Magazine

Magazine Publisher: Archant

M444 Western Humanities Review

Magazine
Department of English, Languages & Communication BLDG, 255 S Central Campus Drive, Room 3500, SLC, UT 84112-0494
United States
Tel: +1 (801) 581-6168
Fax: +1 (801) 585-5167

managingeditor.whr@gmail.com

http://www.westernhumanitiesreview.com
https://www.facebook.com/WHReview/
https://whr.submittable.com/submit

Fiction > *Short Fiction*

Nonfiction
  Essays: General
  Reviews: Books

Poetry > *Any Poetic Form*

Send: Full text
How to send: Submittable

Costs: A fee is charged upon submission. $2 for poetry and prose submissions.

Send one story or essay, or up to five poems, via online submission system. Also accepts book reviews.

M445 The White Review

Magazine
A.103 Fuel Tank, 8-12 Creekside, London, SE8 3DX
United Kingdom

editors@thewhitereview.org

https://www.thewhitereview.org
http://www.facebook.com/thewhitereview
http://www.twitter.com/thewhitereview
http://www.instagram.com/thewhitereview

Fiction in Translation > *Short Fiction*: Literary

Fiction > *Short Fiction*: Literary

Nonfiction
  Essays: Arts; Literature
  Interviews: Arts; Literature
Poetry in Translation > *Any Poetic Form*

Poetry > *Any Poetic Form*

Closed to approaches.

Print and online arts and literature magazine. Publishes cultural analysis, reviews, and new fiction and poetry. Accepts submissions only in specific submission windows. Prose submissions should be a minimum of 1,500 words. See website for guidelines and submit by email.

M446 Willow Springs

Magazine
United States

willowspringsewu@gmail.com

http://willowspringsmagazine.org
https://willowsprings.submittable.com/submit

Fiction > *Short Fiction*

Nonfiction
  Essays; *Interviews*
Poetry > *Any Poetic Form*

How to send: Submittable

Costs: A fee is charged upon submission. $3 reading fee per submission. Writers who cannot afford the reading fee should contact by email to have the fee waived.

Publishes each spring and fall. Accepts fiction and poetry submissions between September 1 and May 31. Nonfiction is open year-round. Submit one packet of work at a time and wait to receive a response before submitting again.

M447 Woman & Home

Magazine
121-141 Westbourne Terrace, London, W2 6JR
United Kingdom
Tel: +44 (0) 20 3148 5000

https://www.womanandhome.com

Magazine Publisher: Future

Nonfiction > *Articles*
  Beauty; Fashion; Food; Health; Lifestyle; Travel; Wellbeing; Women's Interests

Our mission is to keep 40+ women informed on the subjects that matter to them, so they can live smarter, healthier and happier lives. We publish celebrity news for grown-ups, as well as informative, no-nonsense health and wellbeing features about subjects like the menopause. We speak to internationally renown experts to give up-to-date advice on dieting and weight-loss plans. We aim to delight you with delicious – and healthy – recipes. And to inspire your next holiday destinations with travel recommendations both near and far. We filter through the latest fashion and beauty noise to offer you advice on the trends you'll want to try, because they're flattering as well as stylish.

M448 Yachting Monthly

Magazine
United Kingdom

yachtingmonthly@futurenet.com

https://www.yachtingmonthly.com
http://www.youtube.com/user/YachtingMonthly
http://www.facebook.com/yachtingmonthlymag
http://twitter.com/yachtingmonthly

Magazine Publisher: Future

Nonfiction > *Articles*
  Sailing; Yachts

Magazine publishing articles and features on yachting and cruising.

M449 The Yale Review

Magazine
United States

theyalereview@yale.edu

https://yalereview.yale.edu
https://www.facebook.com/YaleReview/
https://www.instagram.com/yalereview/
https://twitter.com/YaleReview

Fiction > *Short Fiction*: Literary

Nonfiction > *Essays*
  Arts; Cultural Criticism; Films; History; Literary Criticism; Memoir; Music; Politics; TV

Poetry > *Any Poetic Form*

Send: Full text; Pitch
How to send: Submittable; Email

Opens for submissions of poetry, nonfiction, and fiction in September of each year, via online submission system. Accepts pitches for essays and criticism on a rolling basis by email.

Editor: Meghan O'Rourke

M450 Yellow Mama Webzine
Magazine
United States

crosmus@hotmail.com

http://blackpetalsks.tripod.com/yellowmama

Types: Fiction
Subjects: Horror; Literary
Markets: Adult

Send: Full text
How to send: Email

Webzine publishing fiction and poetry. Seeks cutting edge, hardboiled, horror, literary, noir, psychological / horror. No fanfiction, romance, swords & sorcery, fantasy, or erotica. Send submissions by email. See website for full guidelines.

M451 Yes Poetry Magazine
Online Magazine
United States

editor@yespoetry.com

https://www.yespoetry.com
https://twitter.com/yespoetry
https://yespoetry.tumblr.com/

Fiction > *Short Fiction*

Nonfiction
   Essays; Interviews; Reviews
Poetry > *Any Poetic Form*

Closed to approaches.

A lifestyle art publication that encourages deep analysis and thought, pushing for progressive change and identification.

Book Publisher: Yes Poetry Chapbooks (**P599**)

M452 Yorkshire Life
Magazine
United Kingdom

https://www.greatbritishlife.co.uk/magazines/yorkshire/

Magazine Publisher: Great British Life

Nonfiction

   Articles: Culture; Food and Drink; Houses; Lifestyle; Outdoor Activities; Travel; Walking; Yorkshire
   Interviews: Yorkshire

Magazine covering the people, places, history, arts, food and events of Yorkshire.

M453 Your Cat
Magazine
United Kingdom

https://www.yourcat.co.uk
https://www.facebook.com/yourcatmagazine
https://www.twitter.com/yourcatmagazine
https://www.instagram.com/yourcatmagazine
https://www.youtube.com/YourCatYourDog

Magazine Publisher: Warners Group Publications

Nonfiction > *Articles:* Cats

Practical magazine covering the care of cats and kittens.

Editor:

M454 Yours
Magazine
The Lantern, 75 Hampstead Road, London, NW1 2PL
United Kingdom

yours@bauermedia.co.uk

https://www.yours.co.uk
https://www.facebook.com/Yoursmagazine
https://twitter.com/yoursmagazine
https://www.pinterest.com/yoursmagazine/

Magazine Publisher: Bauer Media Group

Fiction > *Short Fiction*
   General, and in particular: Family; Nostalgia; Romance; Women's Fiction

Nonfiction
   Articles: Beauty; Fashion; Finance; Fitness; Food; Gardening; Health; Pets; Recipes; Relationships; Travel
   Interviews: Celebrity
   Short Nonfiction: Real Life Stories; Women

How to send: Email; Post

Magazine for women over 50. Publishes tips and expert advice on a range of topics from travel to financial guidance as well as discovering the latest fashion trends, beauty, and health tips. Also exclusive celebrity interviews and recipes for healthy meals or hearty treats. Publishes short stories of 950 words, or 3,000 words (serialised over three issues with cliff-hangers at the end of the first two parts).

Fiction Editor: Marion Clarke

M455 Yours Fiction – Women's Special Series
Print Magazine
The Lantern, 75 Hampstead Road, London, NW1 2PL
United Kingdom

yours@bauermedia.co.uk

https://www.yours.co.uk/yours-fiction/

Magazine Publisher: Bauer Media Group

Fiction > *Short Fiction*
   General, and in particular: Ghost Stories; Historical Fiction; Mystery; Romance; Saga

Closed to approaches.

Publishes 26 stories per issue. Stories can be of any genre, but we especially keen on romance, murder mystery, historical fiction, ghost stories, sagas and stories to make you smile. Any length between 450 and 2,700 words.

M456 Zoetrope: All-Story
Magazine
916 Kearny Street, San Francisco, CA 94133
United States

info@all-story.com

https://store.all-story.com

Fiction > *Short Fiction*

Closed to approaches.

Magazine of short fiction.

M457 Zone 3
Magazine
United States

https://www.zone3press.com

Book Publisher / Magazine Publisher: Zone 3 Press

Fiction > *Short Fiction*
   Contemporary; Literary

Nonfiction > *Short Nonfiction*
   Contemporary; Creative Nonfiction; Literary

Poetry > *Any Poetic Form*

Closed to approaches.

Costs: A fee is charged upon submission. $3.

Publishes fiction, poetry, and creative nonfiction. Accepts submissions through online submission system between August 1 and April 1 annually. $3 submission fee.

Book Publishers

For the most up-to-date listings of these and hundreds of other book publishers, visit https://www.firstwriter.com/publishers

To claim your free access to the site, please see the back of this book.

P001 Whitford Press
Publishing Imprint
United States

https://schifferbooks.com/pages/schiffer-imprints

Book Publisher: Schiffer Publishing (**P467**)

Nonfiction > *Nonfiction Books*
Mind, Body, Spirit; Supernatural / Paranormal

Publishes books on paranormal activities and mind and spirit lifestyles.

P002 1517 Media
Book Publisher
United States

https://1517.media

Publishing Imprint: Fortress Press (**P202**)

P003 23 House Publishing
Book Publisher
United States
Fax: +1 (214) 367-4343

editor@23house.com

http://www.23house.com

Nonfiction > *Nonfiction Books*
Ghosts; Regional

Currently looking for nonfiction, regional ghost story manuscripts. A prospective book should contain both the history and ghost stories of the specific region. The maximum word count is 65,000, and the minimum is 40,000 – photos, maps, and other visual aids are a major plus.

P004 4 Color Books
Publishing Imprint
United States

http://www.randomhousebooks.com/imprints/

Book Publishers: Random House; The Crown Publishing Group (**P148**)

Nonfiction > *Nonfiction Books*
Arts; Contemporary Politics; Cookery; Health; Sustainable Living

Collaborates with the most forward-thinking and groundbreaking BIPOC chefs, writers,

artists, activists, and innovators to craft visually stunning nonfiction books that inspire readers and give rise to a more healthy, just, and sustainable world for all.

P005 404 Ink
Book Publisher
United Kingdom

hello@404ink.com

https://www.404ink.com
https://www.facebook.com/404ink/
http://instagram.com/404ink
https://twitter.com/404Ink

Fiction
Novels; Short Fiction Collections
Nonfiction > *Nonfiction Books*
General, and in particular: Inspirational; Politics; Social Issues

Poetry > *Poetry Collections*

How to send: Through a literary agent

Publishes fiction, non-fiction, short stories and poetry. No children's books. Particularly likes humour, gritty women-led fiction, anti-heroes, parodies, the weird and wonderful, hard-hitting social issue non-fiction, inspirational stories and accessible political engagement. Would quite like to publish a crime book that's an unusual take on the genre.

P006 4RV Publishing
Book Publisher
249079 East 1000 Road, Hydro, OK 73048
United States
Tel: +1 (405) 820-9640

Administrator@4rvpublishingllc.com

https://www.4rvpublishing.com
https://www.facebook.com/4RV-Publishing-LLC-20479523692/
https://twitter.com/4RV
https://www.youtube.com/user/4RVPublishingLLC

ADULT
Fiction > *Novels*
General, and in particular: Christianity; Fantasy; Romance; Science Fiction

Nonfiction > *Nonfiction Books*

Poetry > *Poetry Collections*

CHILDREN'S > **Fiction**
Chapter Books; Early Readers; Middle Grade; Picture Books
TEEN > **Fiction** > *Novels*

YOUNG ADULT > **Fiction** > *Novels*

Does not want:

Fiction > *Novels*: Erotic

Send: Query; Synopsis; Writing sample
How to send: Email attachment

Accepts most genres of fiction and nonfiction books for all ages, including nonfiction, mystery, romance, mainstream, western, Christian, and science-fiction, as well as children's books, middle grade and young adult novels. No poetry or graphic sex or violence. Language should not be overly profane or vulgar. Accepts submissions by email from the US, UK, and Australia. Not accepting children's books as at May 2022. See website for current status and full guidelines.

Publishing Imprints: 4RV Biblical Based; 4RV Children's Corner; 4RV Fiction; 4RV Nonfiction; 4RV Tenacious (**P007**); 4RV Tweens & Teens; 4RV Young Adult

P007 4RV Tenacious
Publishing Imprint
United States

president@4rvpublishingllc.com
vp-o_ad@4rvpublishingllc.com

http://www.4rvpublishing.com/tenacious-submissions.html

Book Publisher: 4RV Publishing (**P006**)

Fiction > *Novels*
Adventure; Crime; Fantasy; Historical Fiction; Mystery; Romance; Science Fiction; Suspense; US Southern States; Women's Fiction

Nonfiction > *Nonfiction Books*

Send: Query; Synopsis; Writing sample
How to send: Email attachment

Genres wanted at this time include Action/Adventure, Science Fiction, Fantasy, Mystery/ Suspense/Crime, Romance (without graphic details), Nonfiction, Women's Lit, Southern-Lit, Historical Fiction.

P008 A-R Editions
Book Publisher
8401 Greenway Blvd, Suite 100, Middleton WI 53562
United States
Tel: +1 (608) 836-9000

info@areditions.com

https://www.areditions.com
https://www.facebook.com/areditions

Nonfiction > *Nonfiction Books*: Music

Send: Query; Proposal
How to send: Email; File sharing service

Publisher of modern critical editions of music based on current musicological research, aimed at scholars and performers. See website for submission guidelines.

Publishing Imprint: Greenway Music Press

P009 Aardwolf Press
Book Publisher
United States

aardwolfpress@aol.com

http://www.aardwolfpress.com

Fiction > *Novels*
Fantasy; Horror; Science Fiction; Speculative

Does not want:

> **Fiction** > *Novels*
> Hard Science Fiction; Space Opera

Send: Query; Outline; Writing sample
How to send: Email
How not to send: Email attachment

Small publisher of speculative fiction between 50,000 and 100,000 words. Send query by email with first five pages in the body of the text. No attachments, poetry, previously published books (including online in any form), children's, stories set mainly off the Earth or earlier than the 20th century, books about elves, dragons, wizards, quests for rings/jewels/swords etc. space opera or hard science fiction.

P010 ABC-CLIO
Book Publisher
147 Castilian Drive, Santa Barbara, CA 93117
United States
Tel: +1 (800) 368-6868
Fax: +1 (805) 968-1911

CustomerService@abc-clio.com

https://www.abc-clio.com/
https://www.facebook.com/ABCCLIO
https://twitter.com/ABC_CLIO
https://www.youtube.com/user/ABCCLIOLive
https://www.linkedin.com/company/abc-clio/

ACADEMIC > **Nonfiction** > *Reference*
General, and in particular: History; Sociology

Publishes academic reference works and periodicals primarily on topics such as history and social sciences for educational and public library settings.

Publishing Imprints: ABC-CLIO / Greenwood; Libraries Unlimited; Praeger

P011 Abdo Publishing Co
Book Publisher
1920 Lookout Drive, North Mankato MN 56003
United States
Tel: +1 (800) 800-1312
Fax: +1 (800) 862-3480

fiction@abdobooks.com

http://abdopublishing.com

Types: Fiction; Nonfiction
Subjects: Anthropology; Arts; Biography; Cookery; Crafts; Culture; Current Affairs; Design; Entertainment; History; Hobbies; Medicine; Politics; Religion; Science; Sociology; Sport; Technology; Travel; Warfare
Markets: Children's

Closed to approaches.

Publishes nonfiction, educational material for children up to the 12th grade, plus fiction series for children. Not accepting nonfiction submissions as at May 2017 (see website for current situation). Writers with a concept for a fiction series should send samples of manuscripts by email.

Editor: Paul Abdo

P012 ABI Professional Publications
Book Publisher
P.O. Box 149, St. Petersburg, FL 33731
United States
Tel: +1 (727) 556-0950
Fax: +1 (727) 556-2560

webmaster@vandamere.com

http://www.abipropub.com

PROFESSIONAL > **Nonfiction** > *Nonfiction Books*
Disabilities; Health; Medicine

Professional books and journals in the fields of Rehabilitation, Facial Prosthetics, Ophthalmic Prosthetics, Dentistry, Medical Research, and Healthcare Policy.

P013 Abson Books London
Book Publisher
5 Sidney Square, London, E1 2EY
United Kingdom
Tel: +44 (0) 20 7790 4737
Fax: +44 (0) 20 7790 7346

book.sales@absonbooks.co.uk

http://www.absonbooks.co.uk

Nonfiction > *Nonfiction Books*
Dialects; Slang

Publisher of pocket-size books on dialect and slang.

P014 Abuzz Press
Book Publisher
United States

https://www.abuzzpress.com

Fiction > *Novels*
General, and in particular: Adventure; Christianity

Nonfiction
Colouring Books: General
Nonfiction Books: Adventure; Christianity; How To

How to send: Online submission system

Publishes nonfiction, adult colouring books, how-to, new age, and exceptional fiction. No poetry, short story collections, books with colour interiors, or illegal material. Send submissions via form on website.

P015 Ad Hoc Fiction
Book Publisher
United Kingdom

helpdesk@adhocfiction.com

https://www.adhocfiction.com
https://twitter.com/AdHocFiction

Fiction > *Short Fiction Collections*

An award winning small independent publisher specialising in short-short fiction since 2015. Publishes anthologies of micro fiction, novellas-in-flash, and individual collections of flash fiction by local and international authors.

P016 Adlard Coles
Publishing Imprint
United Kingdom

adlardcoles@bloomsbury.com

https://www.bloomsbury.com/uk/connect/contact-us/writing-for-bloomsbury/

Book Publisher: Bloomsbury Publishing Plc (**P080**)

Nonfiction > *Nonfiction Books*: Nautical

Send: Query; Synopsis; Writing sample; Outline; Market info; Author bio
How to send: Email

Nautical imprint of large international publisher. Happy to accept unsolicited submissions, but response only if interested. Send all submissions by email with the word "submission" in the subject line.

P017 AdventureKEEN
Book Publisher
United States

Tel: +1 (800) 678-7006
Fax: +1 (877) 374-9016

info@adventurewithkeen.com

https://adventurewithkeen.com
https://www.instagram.com/
adventurewithkeen/
https://twitter.com/adventurekeen
https://www.facebook.com/adventurekeen/
https://www.pinterest.com/adventurekeen/
https://www.linkedin.com/company/
adventurekeen

Nonfiction > *Nonfiction Books*
   Adventure; Local History; Nature; Outdoor
   Activities; Sport; Travel

A nonfiction publisher of books on a wide
range of subjects, including adventure,
outdoors, travel, nature, local history, sports,
and more.

Publishing Imprint: Menasha Ridge Press
(P346)

P018 Algonquin Books
Publishing Imprint
PO Box 2225, Chapel Hill, NC 27515-2225
United States
Tel: +1 (919) 967-0108
Fax: +1 (919) 933-0272

inquiry@algonquin.com

https://www.hachettebookgroup.com/imprint/
workman-publishing-company/algonquin-
books/
http://twitter.com/algonquinbooks
http://facebook.com/AlgonquinBooks
http://instagram.com/algonquinbooks

Book Publisher: Workman Publishing
Company

Fiction > *Novels*

Nonfiction > *Nonfiction Books*

Closed to approaches.

Publishes both fiction and nonfiction. Does not
accept unsolicited submissions.

P019 Allen & Unwin
Book Publisher
SYDNEY:, 83 Alexander St, Crows Nest,
NSW 2065, MELBOURNE:, 406 Albert
Street, East Melbourne, Vic 3002
Australia
Tel: +61 (0) 2 8425 0100

fridaypitch@allenandunwin.com

https://www.allenandunwin.com
https://www.allenandunwin.com/about/
submission-guidelines/the-friday-pitch
https://www.facebook.com/
AllenandUnwinBooks
https://twitter.com/AllenAndUnwin
http://instagram.com/allenandunwin

ADULT
   Fiction > *Novels*

Nonfiction > *Nonfiction Books*

CHILDREN'S > **Fiction**
   *Board Books; Chapter Books; Early Readers;
   Middle Grade; Picture Books*
YOUNG ADULT > **Fiction** > *Novels*

Send: Query; Synopsis; Writing sample
How to send: Email

Publisher with offices in Australia, New
Zealand, and the UK. Accepts queries by
email. See website for detailed instructions.

P020 Allison & Busby Ltd
Book Publisher
11 Wardour Mews, London, W1F 8AN
United Kingdom
Tel: +44 (0) 20 3950 7834

susie@allisonandbusby.com

https://www.allisonandbusby.com
http://www.facebook.com/pages/Allison-
Busby-Books/51600359534
https://twitter.com/allisonandbusby
https://www.youtube.com/channel/
UCrYAc6ndJZWJWAONHCn8-Qw
https://www.tiktok.com/@allisonandbusby
https://www.instagram.com/allisonandbusby/

Fiction > *Novels*
   Contemporary; Crime; Fantasy; Historical
   Fiction; Mystery; Romance; Saga; Thrillers

Nonfiction
   Gift Books: General
   Nonfiction Books: Biography; Comedy /
   Humour; Crime; Memoir

How to send: Through a literary agent

Accepts approaches via a literary agent only.
No unsolicited MSS or queries from authors.

Publishing Director: Susie Dunlop

P021 Alternating Current Press
Book Publisher
PO Box 270921, Louisville, CO 80027
United States

alt.current@gmail.com

http://www.alternatingcurrentarts.com

ADULT
   Fiction > *Novels*
   Nonfiction > *Nonfiction Books*

CHILDREN'S > **Fiction** > *Chapter Books*

Indie press dedicated to publishing and
promoting incredible literature that challenges
readers and has an innate sense of self,
timelessness, and atmosphere:

Online Magazine: The Coil **(M103)**

P022 AMACOM Books
Book Publisher
United States
Tel: +1 (800) 250-5308

harpercollinsleadershipcc@harpercollins.com

https://www.harpercollinsleadership.com/
amacombooks/

Book Publisher: HarperCollins Leadership
(P247)

PROFESSIONAL > **Nonfiction** > *Nonfiction
Books*
   Business; Finance; Leadership; Management

Publishes business books only, covering such
topics as finance, management, sales,
marketing, human resources, customer
services, quality control, career growth, etc.

P023 Amato Books
Book Publisher; Magazine Publisher
United States
Tel: +1 (800) 541-9498

customerservice@amatobooks.com

https://amatobooks.com

Nonfiction > *Nonfiction Books*
   Alaska; Fishing; Fly Fishing; History; How
   To; Hunting; Offshore Gamefishing;
   Walking

Magazine: Flyfishing & Tying Journal **(M171)**

P024 Amber Books Ltd
Book Publisher
United House, North Road, London, N7 9DP
United Kingdom
Tel: +44 (0) 20 7520 7600

editorial@amberbooks.co.uk
enquiries@amberbooks.co.uk

https://www.amberbooks.co.uk
https://www.facebook.com/amberbooks
https://twitter.com/AmberBooks
https://www.pinterest.co.uk/amberbooksltd/
https://www.instagram.com/amberbooksltd/

Nonfiction > *Illustrated Books*
   General, and in particular: History; Military

Send: Synopsis; Table of Contents; Writing
sample; Author bio
Don't send: Full text
How to send: Post; Email

Publishes illustrated nonfiction books in a wide
range of formats and subject areas for an
international audience. Particularly interested
in submissions on military topics, but not
exclusively so, and welcomes good ideas on
any nonfiction subject suitable for treatment as
an illustrated book.

P025 Ammonite Press
Book Publisher
United Kingdom

https://www.ammonitepress.com
https://twitter.com/AmmonitePress
https://www.youtube.com/c/AmmonitePress
https://www.instagram.com/gmcpublications/

Nonfiction

Gift Books: General
Nonfiction Books: Biography; History; Personal Development; Photography; Popular Culture; Self Help; Wellbeing

Send: Synopsis; Writing sample

Publishes illustrated reference, guide and gift books that bring the worlds of photography and biography, pop culture and history, self-improvement and self-help into sharper focus.

Publisher: Jonathan Bailey

P026 And Other Stories
Book Publisher
Central Library, Surrey Street, Sheffield, S1 1XZ
United Kingdom

info@andotherstories.org

https://www.andotherstories.org
https://twitter.com/andothertweets
https://www.facebook.com/AndOtherStoriesBooks/
https://www.instagram.com/andotherpics/

Fiction in Translation > *Novels*: Literary

Fiction > *Novels*: Literary

Nonfiction in Translation > *Nonfiction Books*: Narrative Nonfiction

Nonfiction > *Nonfiction Books*: Narrative Nonfiction

Poetry > *Poetry Collections*

How to send: Through a literary agent

Our focus is on literary fiction and increasingly on non-fiction too, particularly narrative kinds of non-fiction. Also began publishing poetry collections in 2023.

P027 Angry Robot
Publishing Imprint
Unit 11, Shepperton House, 89 Shepperton Road, London, N1 3DF
United Kingdom
Tel: +44 (0) 20 3813 6940

incoming@angryrobotbooks.com

https://www.angryrobotbooks.com
https://twitter.com/#!/angryrobotbooks
https://www.instagram.com/angryrobotbooks
http://www.facebook.com/angryrobotbooks
https://www.youtube.com/channel/UC_2x8RXR5uL-_psvMmeBwNg
https://www.tiktok.com/@angryrobotbooks?lang=en

Book Publisher: Watkins Media

Fiction > *Novels*
 Cyberpunk; Fantasy; Hard Science Fiction; Horror; Science Fiction; Space Opera; Time Travel

How to send: Through a literary agent; Email

Publisher of science fiction and fantasy. Accepts submissions through literary agents

only, apart from a specific open door period held each year. See the company's social media for updates.

Black writers can submit directly. All other races must approach through a literary agent.

P028 Anhinga Press
Book Publisher
PO Box 3665, Tallahassee, FL 32315
United States

info@anhinga.org

http://www.anhinga.org
https://twitter.com/Anhinga_Press
https://www.facebook.com/anhingapress

Poetry
 Chapbooks; *Poetry Collections*

A non-profit, 501(c)3 operating in Tallahassee, Florida. Since 1974 our mission has been to bring quality poetry to a broad audience by publishing poetry, sponsoring poetry events and educational activities, participating in writers conferences, working with area colleges, making our books available as textbooks for students, and networking with other arts organizations as a good citizen of the arts community and the community at large.

P029 Anvil Press Publishers
Book Publisher
P.O. Box 3008, MPO, Vancouver, B.C., V6B 3X5
Canada
Tel: +1 (604) 876-8710

info@anvilpress.com

https://www.anvilpress.com
https://www.facebook.com/Anvil-Press-115437275199047/
https://www.twitter.com/anvilpress
https://www.instagram.com/anvilpress_publishers/

Fiction > *Novels*

Nonfiction > *Nonfiction Books*
 Arts; Photography

Poetry > *Poetry Collections*

Scripts > *Theatre Scripts*: Drama

Closed to approaches.

Publisher designed to discover and nurture Canadian literary talent. Considers work from Canadian authors only.

Editor: Brian Kaufman

P030 Apa Publications Group
Book Publisher
7 Bell Yard, London, WC2A 2JR
United Kingdom
Tel: +44 (0) 20 7403 0284

london@insightguides.com

https://www.insightguides.com
https://www.facebook.com/InsightGuides
https://twitter.com/insightguides
https://instagram.com/insightguides
https://www.pinterest.com/insightguides
https://www.linkedin.com/company/insight-guides

Nonfiction > *Nonfiction Books*: Travel

We've spent more than 45 years helping travellers to plan their next adventures. As well as our popular guidebooks, we now offer you the opportunity to book tailor-made private tours completely personalised to your interests and needs.

P031 Apex Publishing Ltd
Book Publisher
307 Holland Road, Holland on Sea, Essex, CO15 6PD
United Kingdom
Tel: +44 (0) 1255 812555

mail@apexpublishing.co.uk

http://www.apexpublishing.co.uk

Fiction > *Novels*: Contemporary

Nonfiction > *Nonfiction Books*
 Biography; Entertainment; Lifestyle; Memoir; Real Life Stories; Sport

Send: Submission Form
How to send: Post

Will consider publishing a wide range of high-quality non-fiction and also well-written works of contemporary fiction. Has a particular interest in real-life stories, biographies, memoirs, entertainment and lifestyle and sport.

P032 Arachne Press
Book Publisher
100 Grierson Road, London, SE23 1NX
United Kingdom
Tel: +44 (0) 20 8699 0206

https://arachnepress.com
https://arachnepress.submittable.com/submit
https://www.facebook.com/ArachnePress

Fiction > *Short Fiction Collections*

Poetry > *Poetry Collections*

How to send: Submittable

A small, independent publisher of award-winning short fiction, award winning poetry and (very) select non-fiction, for adults and children. Only accepts responses to call outs (mainly for inclusion in anthologies). See website for full details and current calls.

P033 Arcadia Books
Publishing Imprint
United Kingdom

https://www.quercusbooks.co.uk/landing-page/arcadia-books/

Publishing Imprint: MacLehose Press (**P331**)

Fiction in Translation > *Novels*

Fiction > *Novels*
Crime; Literary

Publisher of translated fiction, literary fiction and crime.

P034 Arcadia Publishing

Book Publisher
United States

https://www.arcadiapublishing.com
https://www.facebook.com/ArcadiaPublishing
https://twitter.com/arcadiapub
http://pinterest.com/imagesofamerica/
https://www.instagram.com/arcadia_publishing

Nonfiction
Nonfiction Books: African American; Agriculture; American Civil War; American History; Architecture; Asian American; Aviation; Baseball; Basketball; Boxing; Business; Catholicism; Crime; Education; Entertainment; Ethnic; Farming; Folklore, Myths, and Legends; Food and Drink; Football / Soccer; Ghosts; Golf; Horses; LGBTQIA; Maritime History; Music; NASCAR; Native Americans; Nature; Railways; Religion; School; Skiing; Sport; Supernatural / Paranormal; Surfing; Transport; Travel; Women; World War I; World War II
Reference: Birds

How to send: Online submission system

We bring together the best history books for a close-up look at American history, and our many series each provide a unique take on local history and culture.

Book Publisher: Pelican Publishing Company

P035 Arcturus Publishing Ltd

Book Publisher
26/27 Bickels Yard, 151-153 Bermondsey Street, London, SE1 3HA
United Kingdom
Tel: +44 (0) 20 7407 9400
Fax: +44 (0) 20 7407 9444

info@arcturuspublishing.com

https://arcturuspublishing.com
https://www.facebook.com/
ArcturusPublishing/
https://twitter.com/arcturusbooks
https://www.instagram.com/arcturusbooks/

ADULT > **Nonfiction**
Nonfiction Books: Classics / Ancient World; New Age; Practical Art
Puzzles: General
Reference: General

CHILDREN'S > **Nonfiction** > *Nonfiction Books*

Non-fiction ranges cover reference, practical art, new age, classics, puzzles and children's books.

P036 Arsenal Pulp Press

Book Publisher
202-211 East Georgia Street, Vancouver, BC, V6A 1Z6
Canada
Tel: +1 (604) 687-4233
Fax: +1 (604) 687-4283

submissions@arsenalpulp.com

https://arsenalpulp.com

ADULT
Fiction
Graphic Novels: General
Novels: LGBTQIA; Literary
Nonfiction
Graphic Nonfiction: General
Nonfiction Books: British Columbia; Crafts; Culture; LGBTQIA; Literary; Politics; Regional; Sociology; Youth Culture
CHILDREN'S
Fiction > *Novels*
Diversity; LGBTQIA

Nonfiction > *Nonfiction Books*
Diversity; LGBTQIA

YOUNG ADULT
Fiction > *Novels*
General, and in particular: LGBTQIA

Nonfiction > *Nonfiction Books*: LGBTQIA

How to send: Email; Post

Publishes Books by BIPOC and LGBTQ2S+ authors, including young adult and children's; Literary fiction and non-fiction (no genre fiction, such as mysteries, thrillers, or romance); Political/sociological studies; Cultural studies; Regional non-fiction, especially British Columbia; Graphic novels and graphic non-fiction; Youth culture and young adult literature; Books for children, especially those that emphasize diversity; Craft books. Prefers submissions by email, but will accept submissions by post.

P037 Arte Publico Press

Book Publisher
University of Houston, 4902 Gulf Fwy, Bldg. 19, Room 100, Houston, TX 77204-2004
United States

submapp@uh.edu

https://artepublicopress.com
https://www.facebook.com/artepublico/
https://twitter.com/artepublico
https://www.instagram.com/artepublico/
https://www.pinterest.com/artepublico/
http://artepublicopress.tumblr.com/

Fiction > *Novels*
Central America; Culture; History; Politics; South America

Nonfiction > *Nonfiction Books*
Central America; Culture; History; Politics; South America

Send: Writing sample
How to send: Online submission system
How not to send: Post

Publisher of contemporary and recovered literature by US Hispanic authors.

Publishing Imprint: Pinata Books (**P419**)

P038 Asabi Publishing

Book Publisher
United States

https://www.asabipublishing.com

ADULT
Fiction > *Novels*
Crime; Erotic; Historical Fiction; Horror; LGBTQIA; Mystery; Noir; Thrillers

Nonfiction > *Nonfiction Books*
Autobiography; Biography; Memoir; Narrative Nonfiction; Outdoor Survival Skills; Travel

CHILDREN'S
Fiction > *Novels*: Culture

Nonfiction > *Nonfiction Books*
Cultural History; Games

TEEN
Fiction > *Novels*: Culture

Nonfiction > *Nonfiction Books*
Cultural History; Games

YOUNG ADULT
Fiction > *Novels*: Culture

Nonfiction > *Nonfiction Books*
Cultural History; Games

Check website for submission windows. Submit query letter / proposal through form on website. No religious or spiritual books of any kind.

P039 Ascend Books, LLC

Book Publisher
11722 West 91st Street, Overland Park, Kansas 66214
United States
Tel: +1 (913) 948-5500

bsnodgrass@ascendbooks.com

http://ascendbooks.com
http://www.twitter.com/Ascend_Books

ADULT > **Nonfiction** > *Nonfiction Books*
Entertainment; Sport

CHILDREN'S > **Fiction**
Board Books; Picture Books

Send: Query; Self-Addressed Stamped Envelope (SASE)
How to send: Post
How not to send: Email

Highly specialised publishing company with a burgeoning presence in sports, entertainment and commemoration events. Send query by email.

Editor: Bob Snodgrass

P040 Astra House
Publishing Imprint
United States

Book Publisher: Astra Publishing House
(**P041**)

P041 Astra Publishing House
Book Publisher
United States

https://astrapublishinghouse.com/

Dedicated to publishing books for children and adults that celebrate excellent storytelling, have a strong point of view, and introduce readers to new perspectives about their everyday lives as well as the lives of others.

Publishing Imprints: Astra House (*P040*); Astra Young Readers (*P042*); Calkins Creek (*P101*); DAW Books (**P155**); Hippo Park (*P261*); Kane Press (**P300**); MineditionUS (*P355*); Toon Books (*P518*); WordSong (**P594**)

P042 Astra Young Readers
Publishing Imprint
United States

Book Publisher: Astra Publishing House
(**P041**)

P043 Athenaeum Press
Book Publisher
United States

https://theathenaeumpress.com
https://www.facebook.com/theathenaeumpress/
https://www.instagram.com/athenaeumpress/
https://twitter.com/athenaeum_press
http://www.amazon.com/shops/
athenaeumpress

Closed to approaches.

Online Magazine: Waccamaw (**M436**)

P044 Atlantean Publishing
Book Publisher; Magazine Publisher
4 Pierrot Steps, 71 Kursaal Way, Southend-on-Sea, Essex, SS1 2UY
United Kingdom

atlanteanpublishing@hotmail.com

https://atlanteanpublishing.fandom.com/wiki/
Atlantean_Publishing
https://atlanteanpublishing.wordpress.com/
https://www.facebook.com/Atlantean.
Publishing

Fiction > *Short Fiction*

Poetry > *Any Poetic Form*

Non-profit-making small press. Produces several serial publications and numerous one-off releases, specialising in poetry and short fiction, both 'general' and 'genre'.

Editor: David-John Tyrer

Magazines: Awen (**M046**); Bard (**M054**); Monomyth (**M280**); The Supplement (**M396**)

Online Magazines: 5-7-5 Haiku Journal (**M006**); View From Atlantis (**M431**)

P045 Atlantic Monthly Press
Publishing Imprint
United States

Book Publisher: Grove Atlantic Inc. (**P230**)

P046 Aurora Metro Press
Book Publisher
80 Hill Rise, Richmond, TW10 6UB
United Kingdom
Tel: +44 (0) 20 8948 1427

submissions@aurorametro.com
editor@aurorametro.com

https://aurorametro.com
https://www.facebook.com/
AuroraMetroBooks/
https://twitter.com/aurorametro

ADULT
  Fiction
    Novels; *Short Fiction*
  Nonfiction > *Nonfiction Books*
    Arts; Biography; History; Popular Culture; Travel; Wellbeing

  Scripts
    Film Scripts; *Theatre Scripts*
YOUNG ADULT > **Fiction** > *Novels*

Send: Query; Synopsis; Author bio; Writing sample

Publishes adult fiction, YA fiction, drama, and non-fiction biography and books about the arts and popular culture.

P047 Authentic Ideas
Publishing Imprint
85 Great Portland Street, First Floor, London, W1W 7LT
United Kingdom
Tel: +44 (0) 20 3745 0658

enquiries@integrity-media.co.uk

http://www.integrity-media.co.uk

Book Publisher: Integrity Media (**P287**)

Fiction > *Novels*
  Comedy / Humour; Crime; Drama; Fantasy; Horror; Literary; Mystery; Science Fiction; Thrillers

Send: Query; Synopsis; Writing sample
How to send: Email

Seeks to help up and coming authors to find their voice, display their creativity and deliver a novel of which they can be proud. It is our desire, that through this imprint our authors find their written voice and peace from their past. And through this imprint, a road for the future.

P048 Authentic Life
Publishing Imprint
85 Great Portland Street, First Floor, London, W1W 7LT
United Kingdom
Tel: +44 (0) 20 3745 0658

enquiries@integrity-media.co.uk

http://www.integrity-media.co.uk

Book Publisher: Integrity Media (**P287**)

Nonfiction > *Nonfiction Books*
  Autobiography; Biography; Health; Mental Health; Philosophy; Psychology; Self Help; Spirituality

Send: Query; Synopsis; Writing sample
How to send: Email

Focuses on relaying stories that cut to the heart of the society we all share. These are stories of normal individuals. Tales of hardship, suffering, injustice, endurance, strength, tenacity, resilience, faith and hope, that convey a picture of the world most of us witness and experience.

P049 Autumn Publishing Ltd
Publishing Imprint
Cottage Farm, Mears Ashby Road, Sywell, Northants, NN6 0BJ
United Kingdom
Tel: +44 (0) 1604 741116

customerservice@igloobooks.com

https://autumnpublishing.co.uk

Book Publisher: Igloo Books Limited (**P279**)

CHILDREN'S > **Nonfiction**
  Activity Books: General
  Nonfiction Books: English; Health; Mathematics; Nature; Science

Deals in books for babies and toddlers, activity books, early learning books, and sticker books. Publisher's philosophy is that children should enjoy learning with books, and to this end combines activity and learning by turning simple workbooks into activity books, allowing children to learn whilst they play.

Publishing Imprint: Byeway Books

P050 AUWA Books
Publishing Imprint
United States

https://auwabooks.com

Book Publisher: Macmillan Publishers (**P338**)

P051 Avalon Travel
Publishing Imprint
United States

https://www.avalontravelbooks.com

Book Publisher: Perseus Books

Nonfiction > *Nonfiction Books*: Travel

How to send: Through a literary agent

Publishes independent travel guides.

P052 Avon

Publishing Imprint
United Kingdom

https://corporate.harpercollins.co.uk/what-we-publish/avon/
https://www.facebook.com/AvonBooksUK/
https://twitter.com/AvonBooksUK

Book Publisher: HarperCollins UK

Fiction > *Novels*
  Commercial; Crime; Saga; Suspense; Thrillers

A commercial fiction division publishing predominantly crime, thrillers, suspense, feel-good general fiction, and saga.

P053 Avon Books

Publishing Imprint
United States

https://www.harpercollins.com
https://www.harpercollins.com/pages/avonromance
https://twitter.com/avonbooks
https://www.instagram.com/avonbooks/
https://www.facebook.com/avonromance

Book Publisher: HarperCollins

Fiction > *Novels*
  Contemporary Romance; Historical Romance; Romance; Romantic Comedy; Supernatural / Paranormal Romance

Publishing award-winning romance since 1941. Recognized for having pioneered the historical romance category and continues to publish in wide variety of other genres, including paranormal, urban fantasy, contemporary and regency.

P054 Bad Press Ink

Book Publisher
United Kingdom

enquiries@badpress.ink

https://badpress.ink
https://www.facebook.com/BADPRESS.iNKPublishing
https://twitter.com/badpressink
https://www.youtube.com/user/iainparkebadpress

Fiction > *Novels*

Publishes alternative books and niche lifestyle fiction. Complete online submission process on website.

Editors: Pat Blayney; Iain Parke

P055 Badger Learning

Book Publisher
Unit 55 Oldmedow Road, Hardwick Industrial Estate, King's Lynn, Norfolk, PE30 4JJ

United Kingdom
Tel: +44 (0) 1553 816082

info@badger-publishing.co.uk

https://www.badgerlearning.co.uk
https://twitter.com/@BadgerLearning
https://en-gb.facebook.com/badger.learning

ACADEMIC > **Nonfiction** > *Nonfiction Books*
  English; History; Mathematics; Science

CHILDREN'S
Fiction
  Chapter Books; *Early Readers*; *Middle Grade*
Nonfiction > *Nonfiction Books*

TEEN
Fiction > *Novels*
Nonfiction > *Nonfiction Books*

YOUNG ADULT
Fiction > *Novels*
Nonfiction > *Nonfiction Books*

Publishes books for UK schools, particularly books to engage reluctant and struggling readers.

P056 Baen Books

Book Publisher
PO Box 1188, Wake Forest, NC 27588
United States
Tel: +1 (919) 570-1640
Fax: +1 (919) 570-1644

https://www.baen.com
https://www.baen.com/slush/index/submit
https://twitter.com/BaenBooks

Fiction > *Novels*
  Fantasy; Science Fiction

Send: Full text
How to send: Online submission system
How not to send: Email

Publishes only science fiction and fantasy. Interested in science fiction with powerful plots and solid scientific and philosophical underpinnings. For fantasy, any magical system must be both rigorously coherent and integral to the plot. Work must at least strive for originality. Prefers manuscripts between 100,000 and 130,000 words. No submissions via email. Full manuscripts can be submitted online, in rtf format, via an electronic submission system. Postal submission accepted from those who are unable to submit electronically.

P057 Ballantine Books

Publishing Imprint

Book Publisher: Random House

P058 Baobab Press

Book Publisher
121 California Avenue, Reno, NV 89503

United States
Tel: +1 (775) 786-1188

info@baobabpress.com

https://baobabpress.com

ADULT
  Fiction
    Graphic Novels: General
    Novels: Contemporary; Literary
    Short Fiction: Contemporary; Literary
  Nonfiction
    Essays: General
    Short Nonfiction: Memoir

  Poetry > *Poetry Collections*

CHILDREN'S > **Fiction**
    Board Books; *Picture Books*

How to send: Submittable

Constantly strives to discover, cultivate, and nurture authors working in all genres. Publishes Creative Nonfiction, Short-Story, Novel, and Comic/Visual Narrative manuscripts (Comic/Visual Narrative manuscripts will not be considered without artwork). Also publishes children's picture and board books (send text with or without artwork). Submit via online submission system. Submit no more than one submission at a time.

P059 Barbican Press

Book Publisher
United Kingdom

martin@barbicanpress.com

https://barbicanpress.com
https://twitter.com/BarbicanPress1
https://www.instagram.com/barbicanpress/

ADULT
  Fiction > *Novels*
    General, and in particular: Historical Fiction; LGBTQIA; Science Fiction; Women's Fiction

  Poetry in Translation
    Nonfiction Books: General, and in particular: Sailing; Ships
    Poetry Collections: Classics / Ancient World

  Poetry > *Poetry Collections*

  Scripts > *Theatre Scripts*: Drama

CHILDREN'S
  Fiction
    Graphic Novels; *Short Fiction Collections*
  Scripts > *Theatre Scripts*: Drama

Closed to approaches.

Many of our titles were written as the creative elements of PhDs in Creative Writing. Universities can offer safe harbour for writers, challenging them with regular and expert feedback, giving them years in which their books achieve full voice without the necessity to compromise. Understandably, mainstream publishers tend to seek work that resembles other books that have made money. Breakout originality is harder to place. Those are the books we give a home to.

P060 Barbour Publishing
Book Publisher
United States
Tel: +1 (800) 852-8010

submissions@barbourbooks.com

https://www.barbourbooks.com
https://www.facebook.com/BarbourPublishing/
https://twitter.com/barbourbuzz
https://www.youtube.com/user/BarbourPublishing1
https://www.instagram.com/barbourbooks/

ADULT
Fiction > *Novels*
Amish; Contemporary; Historical Fiction; Romance; Suspense

Nonfiction
Nonfiction Books: Bible Studies; Bibles; Christian Living; Christianity; Evangelism; Inspirational
Puzzles: General

CHILDREN'S > **Nonfiction**
Activity Books: General
Nonfiction Books: Bible Stories; Bible Studies; Bibles
Puzzles: General

How to send: Through a literary agent

Publishes a range of fiction and nonfiction, but all must demonstrate a conservative, evangelical Christian world view, and speak to broad segments of the evangelical Christian market.

P061 Barefoot Books
Book Publisher
United States
Tel: +1 (866) 417-2369

help@barefootbooks.com
submission@barefootbooks.com

https://www.barefootbooks.com
https://www.facebook.com/barefootbooks
https://twitter.com/BarefootBooks
http://www.pinterest.com/BarefootBooks/
http://instagram.com/barefootbooks/
https://www.youtube.com/user/barefootbooks
https://www.tiktok.com/@barefootbooks

CHILDREN'S > **Fiction**
Board Books; *Picture Books*

How to send: Through a literary agent

An independent children's book publisher focusing on diverse, inclusive, beautifully illustrated board books and picture books for ages 0–12.

P062 Barricade Books
Book Publisher
2005 Palmer Ave, Ste 800, Larchmont, NY 10538
United States

Info@barricadebooks.com

http://www.barricadebooks.com

Nonfiction > *Nonfiction Books*

P063 Basalt Books
Publishing Imprint
WSU Press, Cooper Publications Building, PO Box 645910, Pullman, WA 99164-5910, 509-335-7630
United States

https://wsupress.wsu.edu/basalt-books-submission-guidelines/

Book Publisher: Washington State University Press (**P568**)

ADULT > **Nonfiction** > *Nonfiction Books*
Arts; Biography; Cookery; Culture; Environment; Food; History; Memoir; Nature; Pacific Northwest; Science

CHILDREN'S > **Nonfiction** > *Nonfiction Books*
Arts; Biography; Cookery; Culture; Environment; Food; History; Memoir; Nature; Pacific Northwest; Science

Send: Query; Market info; Table of Contents; Writing sample; Author bio
How to send: Email

Welcomes proposals for book projects anchored in the Pacific Northwest, particularly those focusing on the people, places, and cultures of the greater Northwest region. We encourage both established and first-time writers to contact us with your ideas. We are committed to publishing well-written and well-told stories.

P064 Basic Books
Publishing Imprint
United States

https://www.basicbooks.com
https://www.hachettebookgroup.com/imprint/basic-books/

Book Publisher: Perseus Books

Nonfiction > *Nonfiction Books*
Current Affairs; History; Politics; Psychology; Science; Sociology

Publishes award-winning books in history, science, sociology, psychology, politics, and current affairs.

P065 Basic Health Publications, Inc.
Publishing Imprint
United States

submissions@turnerpublishing.com

https://turnerbookstore.com/collections/basic-health

Book Publisher: Turner Publishing (**P528**)

Nonfiction > *Nonfiction Books*: Health

Send: Full text; Author bio; Market info
How to send: Word file email attachment; PDF file email attachment

Submit by email, including your manuscript as an attached Word Doc or PDF to your email (a completed manuscript is preferred, but partial manuscripts or detailed outlines/pitches are also accepted); author details including platform, following, qualifications, etc.; and pertinent marketing details, including intended audience and the sales angle of the book.

P066 BatCat Press
Book Publisher
c/o Lincoln Park Performing Arts Charter School, One Lincoln Park, Midland, PA 15059
United States

batcatpress@gmail.com

https://batcatpress.com

Fiction > *Short Fiction*

Nonfiction > *Nonfiction Books*: Creative Nonfiction

Poetry > *Any Poetic Form*

Closed to approaches.

Publishes literary fiction, poetry, and creative nonfiction. Submit via online submission system.

P067 Berghahn Books Ltd
Book Publisher
3 Newtec Place, Magdalen Rd, Oxford, OX4 1RE
United Kingdom
Tel: +44 (0) 1865 250011
Fax: +44 (0) 1865 250056

editorial@berghahnbooks.com

https://www.berghahnbooks.com
https://www.facebook.com/BerghahnBooks
https://twitter.com/berghahnbooks
https://www.youtube.com/channel/UCuh-JFDwm_HfzX1zJ92tzcw
https://www.instagram.com/berghahnbooks/

ACADEMIC > **Nonfiction** > *Nonfiction Books*
Anthropology; Archaeology; Culture; Education; Environment; Films; Gender; History; Politics; Sociology; TV; Warfare

Send: Query; Submission Form; Outline
How to send: Email attachment

Academic publisher of books and journals covering the social sciences. Download New Book Outline form from website, complete, and submit by email with an outline and/or chapter summary.

Editor: Marion Berghahn

P068 Berrett-Koehler Publishers
Book Publisher
1333 Broadway, Suite 1000, Oakland, CA 94612
United States
Tel: +1 (510) 817-2277
Fax: +1 (510) 817-2278

submissions@bkpub.com
bkpub@bkpub.com

https://www.bkconnection.com
https://www.facebook.com/BerrettKoehler
https://twitter.com/Bkpub
https://www.linkedin.com/company/berrett-koehler-publishers/
https://www.pinterest.com/berrettkoehler/
https://www.youtube.com/berrettkoehler

Nonfiction > *Nonfiction Books*
Business; Career Development; Communication; Creativity; Economics; Equality; Leadership; Management

Send: Proposal; Outline; Writing sample; Market info
How to send: PDF file email attachment; Word file email attachment

Connecting people and ideas to create a world that works for all. Publishes titles that promote positive change at personal, organizational, and societal levels.

P069 Bess Press
Book Publisher
3565 Harding Avenue, Honolulu, HI 96816
United States
Tel: +1 (808) 734-7159
Fax: +1 (808) 732-3627

submission@besspress.com

https://www.besspress.com

ACADEMIC > **Nonfiction** > *Nonfiction Books*
Hawai'i; Pacific

ADULT
Fiction > *Novels*
Hawai'i; Pacific

Nonfiction > *Nonfiction Books*
Biography; Hawai'i; Memoir; Pacific

CHILDREN'S > **Fiction**
Activity Books: Hawai'i; Pacific
Board Books: Hawai'i; Pacific
Picture Books: Hawai'i; Pacific

Send: Query
How to send: Email

Publishes books about Hawai'i and the Pacific. All submissions should be sent by email. See website for full guidelines.

P070 Between the Lines
Book Publisher
401 Richmond Street West, Studio 281,
Toronto, Ontario M5V 3A8
Canada
Tel: +1 (416) 535-9914

info@btlbooks.com
submissions@btlbooks.com

https://btlbooks.com
http://twitter.com/readBTLbooks
http://facebook.com/BTLbooks
https://www.instagram.com/btlbooks

Nonfiction > *Nonfiction Books*
Politics; Social Issues

How to send: Email

We publish nonfiction books that expose and challenge oppression in our society. We aim to amplify the struggles of Black, Indigenous, and racialized communities; migrants; women; queer folks; and working-class people. We are proudly left-wing and the books we publish reflect our activist roots and our commitment to social justice struggles. Our authors are academics, journalists, artists, and activists—all our authors hope their books will spark political and social change.

Acquisitions Editor: Paul Eprile

P071 BFI Publishing
Book Publisher
United Kingdom

https://www.bfi.org.uk
https://www.bfi.org.uk/bfi-book-releases-trade-sales
https://www.bloomsbury.com/uk/discover/bloomsbury-academic/authors/contacts-for-authors/

Book Publisher: Bloomsbury Academic **(P078)**

ACADEMIC > **Nonfiction** > *Nonfiction Books*
Film Industry; Films

Publishes film and television-related books and resources, both for schools and academic readerships, and more generally.

P072 Birlinn Ltd
Book Publisher
West Newington House, 10 Newington Road,
Edinburgh, EH9 1QS
United Kingdom
Tel: +44 (0) 1316 684371

info@birlinn.co.uk

http://birlinn.co.uk
https://www.facebook.com/birlinnbooks/
https://twitter.com/BirlinnBooks
https://www.youtube.com/channel/UChVAhFnMniUb_3XiVmXPT7Q
https://www.instagram.com/birlinnbooks/

Fiction

Novels: Comedy / Humour; Crime; Historical Fiction; Thrillers
Short Fiction Collections: General

Nonfiction > *Nonfiction Books*
Art History; Arts; Biography; Business; Comedy / Humour; Crime; Current Affairs; Folklore, Myths, and Legends; Food; Gaelic; Gardening; Geology; Local History; Memoir; Nature; Photography; Politics; Scotland; Sport; Traditional Music; Travel

Send: Query; Synopsis; Writing sample
How to send: Email
How not to send: Post

Focuses on Scottish material: local, military, and Highland history; humour, adventure; reference, guidebooks, and folklore. No longer accepting submissions for fiction, poetry, or children's books. Submissions for these areas must be made through a literary agent. Continues to accept direct submissions for nonfiction.

Publishing Imprint: Polygon **(P424)**

P073 Black Cat
Publishing Imprint
United States

Book Publisher: Grove Atlantic Inc. **(P230)**

P074 Black Velvet Seductions
Book Publisher
United States

https://blackvelvetseductions.com
https://www.facebook.com/blackvelvetseductions/
https://twitter.com/BVSBooks
https://www.instagram.com/bvsbooks/
https://www.pinterest.com/BVSPublishing/

Fiction > *Novels*
Adventure; Contemporary; Erotic; Fantasy; Historical Fiction; Supernatural / Paranormal; Thrillers; Westerns

Send: Full text; Synopsis
How to send: Online submission system

We are looking for a marriage of the romance genre (think Harlequin, Silhouette, MIRA) with a much higher degree of eroticism. We want all of the emotional impact, all the angst, all the character development, and all the conflict you would find in any traditional romance novel. But we want it to go several steps beyond the normal romance when it comes to sexual content and eroticism.

Stories may include any of the tried and true plot elements that have worked in romance novels for years. For example, authors can use secret baby, forced marriage, marriage of convenience, revenge, etc. as elements of their stories.

While we want a higher level of eroticism and a greater diversity of sexual activity in our books we do not want books that sacrifice the romance's story line in an effort to force a quick sexual pace. We believe the specific story and the make-up of the characters should decide the placement and frequency of sex scenes and we give authors wide latitude.

There are very few taboos in our line but the following are very firm. We do not want to see material containing bestiality, necrophilia or paedophilia.

P075 Blackstaff Press
Book Publisher
Jubilee Business Park, 21 Jubilee Road,
Newtownards, BT23 4YH
United Kingdom
Tel: +44 (0) 28 9182 0505

sales@colourpoint.co.uk

https://blackstaffpress.com
https://facebook.com/Blackstaffpressni
https://twitter.com/BlackstaffNI

Book Publisher: Colourpoint Educational
(**P136**)

Fiction > *Novels*

Nonfiction > *Nonfiction Books*
General, and in particular: Biography;
History; Ireland; Memoir; Northern Ireland;
Politics; Sport

Does not want:

> **Fiction** > *Novels*
> Erotic; Fantasy; Horror; Science
> Fiction

Closed to approaches.

Focuses on subjects of interest to the Irish market, both north and south. However, will consider other proposals if they are strong enough to generate interest from farther afield and specially if there is a connection to Ireland.

P076 Bloodaxe Books
Book Publisher
Eastburn, South Park, Hexham,
Northumberland, NE46 1BS
United Kingdom
Tel: +44 (0) 01434 611581

editor@bloodaxebooks.com
submissions@bloodaxebooks.com

https://www.bloodaxebooks.com

Poetry > *Poetry Collections*

Closed to approaches.

Submit poetry only if you have a track record of publication in magazines. If so, send sample of up to a dozen poems with SAE. No submissions by email or on disk. Poems from the UK sent without return postage will be recycled unread; submissions by email will be deleted unread. No longer accepting poets who have already published a full-length collection with another publisher. Considers poets from

beyond the UK and Ireland by invitation or recommendation only. See website for full details.

Editorial Director: Neil Astley

P077 Bloodhound Books
Book Publisher
Cambridge
United Kingdom

info@bloodhoundbooks.com
submissions@bloodhoundbooks.com

https://www.bloodhoundbooks.com
https://www.facebook.com/bloodhoundbooks/
https://twitter.com/Bloodhoundbook
https://www.instagram.com/bloodhound.books/

Fiction > *Novels*
Commercial; Crime; Historical Fiction;
Literary; Mystery; Psychology; Thrillers;
Women's Fiction

Send: Query; Synopsis; Full text
How to send: Email

Independent publishers of commercial fiction, focusing on crime, thriller, psychological, literary, historical, women's and mystery fiction.

P078 Bloomsbury Academic
Book Publisher
50 Bedford Square, London, WC1B 3DP
United Kingdom
Tel: +44 (0) 20 7631 5600

contact@bloomsbury.com

http://www.bloomsburyacademic.com

Book Publisher: Bloomsbury Publishing Plc
(**P080**)

ACADEMIC > **Nonfiction** > *Nonfiction Books*
Africa; Archaeology; Architecture; Arts;
Asia; Business; Classics / Ancient World;
Computer Science; Crime; Design; Drama;
Economics; Education; Engineering;
Environment; Ethnic Groups; Fashion;
Films; Food; Gender; Health; History;
Information Science; Interior Design;
Language; Legal; Literature; Management;
Mathematics; Media; Medicine; Middle East;
Music; Nursing; Philosophy; Politics;
Psychology; Psychotherapy; Religion;
Science; Sexuality; Society; Sociology;
Sport; Technology; Visual Culture;
Wellbeing

Publishes books for students, researchers, and independent thinkers.

Book Publisher: BFI Publishing (**P071**)

P079 Bloomsbury Professional
Book Publisher
50 Bedford Square, London, WC1B 3DP

United Kingdom
Tel: +44 (0) 20 7631 5600

contact@bloomsbury.com

https://www.bloomsburyprofessional.com
https://twitter.com/BloomsburyPro
https://www.linkedin.com/company/bloomsbury-professional

Book Publisher: Bloomsbury Publishing Plc
(**P080**)

PROFESSIONAL > **Nonfiction** > *Nonfiction Books*
Accounting; Legal; Taxation

Publishes high quality books and digital products for lawyers, tax practitioners, accountants and business professionals.

P080 Bloomsbury Publishing Plc
Book Publisher
50 Bedford Square, London, WC1B 3DP
United Kingdom

https://www.bloomsbury.com
https://www.facebook.com/BloomsburyPublishing/
https://www.instagram.com/bloomsburypublishing/
https://twitter.com/BloomsburyBooks
https://www.youtube.com/bloomsburypublishing

ACADEMIC > **Nonfiction** > *Nonfiction Books*

ADULT
  Fiction > *Novels*
  Nonfiction > *Nonfiction Books*

CHILDREN'S > **Fiction** > *Novels*

PROFESSIONAL > **Nonfiction** > *Nonfiction Books*

YOUNG ADULT > **Fiction** > *Novels*

Publishes books for the adult, academic, professional, children's, and young adult markets.

Book Publishers: Bloomsbury Academic
(**P078**); Bloomsbury Professional (**P079**)

Publishing Imprint: Adlard Coles (**P016**)

P081 Blue Guides
Publishing Imprint
Unit 2, Old Brewery Road, Wiveliscombe,
Somerset, TA4 2PW
United Kingdom

editorial@blueguides.com

https://www.blueguides.com

Book Publisher: Somerset Books (**P486**)

Nonfiction > *Nonfiction Books*: Travel

Send: Query
How to send: Email; Online contact form

Publishes travel guides. Always on the lookout for new authors. Contact by email in first instance, giving an indication of your areas of interest.

P082 Blue Jeans Books
Publishing Imprint
United Kingdom

submissions@sunpenny.com

https://www.sunpenny.com/imprints/

Book Publisher: Sunpenny Publishing (**P504**)

Fiction > *Novels*: Romance

Does not want:

> **Fiction** > *Novels*: Christian Romance

Romance genre imprint, non-Christian based.

P083 Blue Star Press
Book Publisher
Bend, OR
United States

brenna@bluestarpress.com
contact@bluestarpress.com

https://www.bluestarpress.com

Nonfiction > *Nonfiction Books*
Arts; Comedy / Humour; Creativity; Wellbeing

Send: Submission Form
How to send: Email

Focuses on the arts, creative processes, wellness, and witty non-fiction.

P084 BOA Editions, Ltd
Book Publisher
250 North Goodman Street, Suite 306, Rochester, NY 14607
United States
Tel: +1 (585) 546-3410

contact@boaeditions.org

https://www.boaeditions.org

Fiction > *Short Fiction Collections*: Literary

Nonfiction > *Nonfiction Books*
Literature; Poetry as a Subject

Poetry in Translation > *Poetry Collections*

Poetry > *Poetry Collections*

Send: Full text
How to send: Submittable

Publisher of literary fiction, poetry, and prose about poetry and poetics. Specific reading periods (see website). Also runs annual poetry and fiction competitions. See website for more details.

P085 Boathooks Books
Publishing Imprint
United Kingdom

submissions@sunpenny.com

https://www.sunpenny.com/imprints/

Book Publisher: Sunpenny Publishing (**P504**)

Nonfiction > *Nonfiction Books*
Boats; Sailing

Send: Query; Author bio; Marketing Plan; Synopsis; Full text
How to send: Email
How not to send: Post

Publishes books on boating of all kinds.

P086 Bonnier Books (UK)
Book Publisher
4th Floor, Victoria House, Bloomsbury Square, London, WC1B 4DA
United Kingdom
Tel: +44 (0) 20 3770 8888

hello@bonnierbooks.co.uk

https://www.bonnierbooks.co.uk

ADULT
Fiction > *Novels*
Nonfiction > *Nonfiction Books*

CHILDREN'S
Fiction
Chapter Books; *Early Readers*; *Picture Books*
Nonfiction > *Nonfiction Books*

How to send: Through a literary agent

Publishes adult fiction and nonfiction, and children's books. Accepts approaches through a literary agent only.

Publishing Imprints: Manilla Press (**P340**); Templar Books (**P510**)

P087 Bookouture
Book Publisher
United Kingdom

http://www.bookouture.com
https://twitter.com/bookouture

Book Publisher: Hachette UK (**P236**)

Fiction > *Novels*
General, and in particular: Book Club Fiction; Contemporary Romance; Cozy Mysteries; Crime; Domestic Suspense; Fantasy; Historical Fiction; Multicultural; Police Procedural; Psychological Thrillers; Romantic Comedy; Science Fiction; Thrillers; Women's Fiction

Send: Full text
How to send: Online submission system

Publishes commercial fiction.

For most authors outside the bestseller lists, traditional publishers simply aren't adding enough value to justify low royalty rates. And because authors aren't all experts in editing, design, or marketing, self-publishing doesn't get the most out of their books or time. Digital publishing offers incredible opportunities to connect with readers all over the world – but finding the help you need to make the most of them can be tricky.

That's why we bring both big publisher experience and small team creativity. We genuinely understand and invest in brands – developing long-term strategies, marketing plans and websites for each of our authors.

And we work with the most brilliant editorial, design and marketing professionals in the business to make sure that everything we do is perfectly tailored to you and ridiculously good.

Combine all of that with an incredible 45% royalty rate we think we're simply the perfect combination of high returns and inspirational publishing.

P088 Boxtree
Publishing Imprint
United Kingdom

Book Publisher: Pan Macmillan (**P398**)

P089 Brave Books
Book Publisher
United States

https://www.bravebooks.us
https://www.facebook.com/BraveBooksUS/
https://www.instagram.com/bravebooks.us/
https://twitter.com/bravebooksus

CHILDREN'S > **Fiction** > *Picture Books*: Conservative

Publishes conservative children's books set in a single world with its own map and set of characters. Partners with conservative figures to create stories that take place in this world, and teaches children either a topical or foundational conservative lesson.

P090 Breedon Books
Publishing Imprint
United Kingdom

Book Publisher: Brewin Books Ltd (**P091**)

P091 Brewin Books Ltd
Book Publisher
19 Enfield Ind. Estate, Redditch, Worcestershire, B97 6BY
United Kingdom
Tel: +44 (0) 1527 854228
Fax: +44 (0) 1527 60451

admin@brewinbooks.com

https://www.brewinbooks.com
http://www.facebook.com/brewinbooks
http://www.twitter.com/brewinbooks

ADULT
Fiction > *Novels*
Contemporary; Ghost Stories

Nonfiction > *Nonfiction Books*
Arts; Biography; Comedy / Humour; Creativity; Family; Health; History;

Memoir; Military History; Military; Music; Police; Social History; Sport; The Midlands; Transport; Wellbeing

CHILDREN'S
Fiction
Novels; *Picture Books*
Nonfiction > *Nonfiction Books*

Send: Query; Synopsis; Author bio
How to send: Email; Post

Publishes regional books on Midland history in the areas of the police, hospitals, the military, family, social and biographies. Also publishes contemporary fiction and books for children. Welcomes submissions from aspiring authors.

Authors: Rob Blakeman; Carl Chinn; Alton Douglas; Brian Drew; Audrey Duggan; Jean Field; Jill Fraser; Gwen Freeman; Patrick Hayes; Nick Owen; Shirley Thompson

Publishing Imprints: Breedon Books (*P090*); Brewin Books; History into Print; Hunt End Books (*P274*); Richards Publishing (*P444*)

P092 Bright Press
Publishing Imprint
18 Circus Street, Brighton, BN2 9QF
United Kingdom
Tel: +44 (0) 1273 727268

marketinguk@quarto.com

https://www.quartoknows.com/Bright-Press

Book Publisher: The Quarto Group, Inc.
(P430)

Nonfiction > *Illustrated Books*
Activities; Arts; Crafts; Culture; Food and Drink; Gardening; Lifestyle; Science

Dedicated to producing beautiful books that will inspire a wide range of enthusiasts, from beer lovers and science geeks to gardeners and artists.

P093 Bristol University Press
Book Publisher
1-9 Old Park Hill, Bristol, BS2 8BB
United Kingdom
Tel: +44 (0) 1173 746645

bup-info@bristol.ac.uk

http://bristoluniversitypress.co.uk
http://www.facebook.com/
BristolUniversityPress
http://twitter.com/BrisUniPress
https://www.youtube.com/ThePolicyPress
http://www.linkedin.com/company/bristol-university-press
http://www.instagram.com/
bristoluniversitypress

ACADEMIC > **Nonfiction** > *Nonfiction Books*
Business; Crime; Economics; Environment; Geography; International; Legal; Management; Politics; Science; Society; Sociology; Sustainable Living; Technology

Send: Query; Proposal; Outline; Author bio; Writing sample

Publishes scholarship in the social sciences and aligned disciplines.

Publishing Imprint: Policy Press

P094 British Library Publishing
Book Publisher
United Kingdom

publishing_editorial@bl.uk

https://www.bl.uk
https://www.bl.uk/publishing
https://twitter.com/BL_Publishing

Fiction > *Novels*
Crime; Science Fiction; Women's Fiction

Nonfiction > *Nonfiction Books*
Books; Food and Drink; History; Literature

Send: Query; Synopsis
How to send: Email

Alongside a range of award-winning exhibition catalogues, has also pioneered a market-leading list of classic crime fiction and is developing fast-growing strands of women's fiction, weird fiction and science fiction. Nonfiction encompasses history, literature, exploration, cartography, food and drink and books about books. Welcomes submissions from potential new authors for popular books relating to the Library's collections. No new fiction, drama, poetry, autobiographies or memoirs.

Editor: David Way

P095 The British Museum Press
Book Publisher
British Museum, Great Russell Street, London, WC1B 3DG
United Kingdom

publicity@britishmuseum.org

https://www.britishmuseum.org/commercial/british-museum-press

ACADEMIC > **Nonfiction** > *Nonfiction Books*
Archaeology; Arts; Culture; History

ADULT > **Nonfiction** > *Nonfiction Books*
Archaeology; Arts; Culture; History

Publishes books inspired by the collections of the British Museum, covering fine and decorative arts, history, archaeology and world cultures.

P096 Brown, Son & Ferguson, Ltd
Book Publisher
Unit 1A, 426 Drumoyne Road, Glasgow, G51 4DA
United Kingdom

Tel: +44 (0) 1418 830141
Fax: +44 (0) 1418 105931

info@skipper.co.uk

https://www.skipper.co.uk

ADULT > **Nonfiction** > *Nonfiction Books*
History; Model Ships and Boats; Sailing; Ships

PROFESSIONAL > **Nonfiction** > *Nonfiction Books*
Sailing; Shipping; Ships

Nautical publishers, printers and ships' stationers since 1832. Publishes technical and non-technical nautical textbooks, books about the sea, historical books, information on old sailing ships and how to build model ships.

P097 Burning Chair
Book Publisher
United Kingdom

info@burningchairpublishing.com

https://burningchairpublishing.com

Fiction > *Novels*
Adventure; Commercial; Crime; Historical Fiction; Horror; Mystery; Supernatural / Paranormal; Suspense; Thrillers

Closed to approaches.

We promise to always put our authors and their books first with: an open, supportive and collaborative approach; fair royalties; tailored, cutting edge production, marketing and promotion.

P098 Burning Eye Books
Book Publisher
United Kingdom

https://burningeyebooks.wordpress.com

Poetry > *Performance Poetry*

Closed to approaches.

Aims to create an inclusive representation of the best and most promising performance poets. Welcomes submissions from all human beings regardless of gender, race, religion, or any definition of origin or ethnicity. The only thing requirement is that you are active as a poet in the UK. No sexism / genderism, transphobia / homophobia, racism, ableism, or apologists for sexual assault and rape.

P099 C&T Publishing
Book Publisher
1651 Challenge Drive, Concord, CA 94520-5206
United States

ctinfo@ctpub.com

https://www.ctpub.com

Nonfiction > *Nonfiction Books*
Embroidery; Quilting; Sewing

Publishes books on sewing and related crafts.

Publishing Imprints: Crosley-Griffith; FunStitch Studio; Kansas City Star Quilts; Stash Books

P100 Caitlin Press Inc.

Book Publisher; Ebook Publisher
3375 Ponderosa Way, Qualicum Beach, BC, V9K 2J8
Canada
Tel: +1 (604) 741-4200

vici@caitlin-press.com

https://caitlin-press.com
http://facebook.com/caitlinbooks
http://twitter.com/caitlinpress
http://instagram.com/caitlinpress.
daggereditions

ADULT
Fiction
Novels; *Short Fiction Collections*
Nonfiction > *Nonfiction Books*
Arts; Biography; British Columbia; Environment; Feminism; History; LGBTQIA; Memoir; Outdoor Activities; Photography; Travel

Poetry > *Poetry Collections*

CHILDREN'S > **Fiction** > *Novels*

Send: Query; Outline; Author bio; Writing sample
Don't send: Full text
How to send: Post
How not to send: Email

Publishes books on topics concerning or by writers from the British Columbia Interior and stories about and by British Columbia women. No submissions by email. See website for full guidelines.

Editors: Sarah Corsie; Vici Johnstone

P101 Calkins Creek

Publishing Imprint
United States

Book Publisher: Astra Publishing House (**P041**)

P102 Cambridge University Press

Book Publisher
Shaftesbury Road, Cambridge, CB2 8EA
United Kingdom
Tel: +44 (0) 1223 553311

directcs@cambridge.org

https://www.cambridge.org
https://www.facebook.com/
CambridgeUniversityPress
https://twitter.com/CambridgeUP
https://www.youtube.com/CambridgeUP
https://www.linkedin.com/company/
cambridge-university-press
https://instagram.com/
cambridgeuniversitypress

ACADEMIC > **Nonfiction** > *Nonfiction Books*
Animals; Anthropology; Archaeology; Arts; Astronomy; Biology; Chemistry; Classics / Ancient World; Computer Science; Culture; Economics; Education; Engineering; Environment; Geography; History; Language; Legal; Literature; Management; Mathematics; Medicine; Music; Philosophy; Physics; Politics; Psychology; Religion; Science; Sociology; Statistics; Theatre

World's oldest publisher, with offices around the world. Publishes nonfiction, reference, academic textbooks, educational material, and academic journals. No fiction or poetry.

P103 Campbell Books

Publishing Imprint
United Kingdom

Book Publisher: Pan Macmillan (**P398**)

P104 Candlemark & Gleam

Book Publisher
United States

eloi@candlemarkandgleam.com
Morlocks@candlemarkandgleam.com

https://www.candlemarkandgleam.com

Fiction > *Novels*
Alternative History; Fantasy; Magical Realism; Science Fiction; Speculative

How to send: By referral

We specialize in speculative fiction—we're eager to explore infinite possibilities. We believe wholeheartedly in the power of the imagination, and we want to shape speculative fiction (science fiction, fantasy, magical realism, alternative history) as it deserves to develop: not a genre, but a way of looking at things with fresh eyes.

P105 Candy Jar Books

Book Publisher
Mackintosh House, 136 Newport Road, Cardiff, CF24 1DJ
United Kingdom
Tel: +44 (0) 2921 157202

hello@candyjarbooks.co.uk
submissions@candyjarbooks.co.uk

https://www.candy-jar.co.uk

ADULT
Fiction > *Novels*
Nonfiction > *Nonfiction Books*

CHILDREN'S > **Fiction** > *Middle Grade*

YOUNG ADULT > **Fiction** > *Novels*

Send: Query; Synopsis; Writing sample
How to send: Email; Post

Costs: Offers services that writers have to pay for. Also offers self publishing services through a sister imprint.

We are always on the lookout for new ideas and talent, for stories that are fresh and engaging. We'd love to read what you have been working on. If you have an agent, great, but don't worry if not; we welcome unsolicited manuscripts. We do not accept children's picture books.

Publishing Director: Shaun Russell

P106 Canterbury Press

Publishing Imprint
Hymns Ancient and Modern Ltd, 3rd Floor, Invicta House, 108-114 Golden Lane, London, EC1Y 0TG
United Kingdom
Tel: +44 (0) 20 7776 7540
Fax: +44 (0) 20 7776 7556

https://canterburypress.hymnsam.co.uk
https://twitter.com/canterburypress
https://www.facebook.com/Canterbury-Press-
176777199005586/

Book Publisher: Hymns Ancient & Modern Ltd

Nonfiction > *Nonfiction Books*
Biography; Christianity; Comedy / Humour; Spirituality; Travel

Supplier of popular religious books. Publishes a wide range of titles, covering liturgy, worship, mission, ministry, spirituality, biography, travel and even humour.

P107 Carina Press

Publishing Imprint
United States

submissions@carinapress.com
CustomerService@Harlequin.com

https://www.carinapress.com
https://www.writeforharlequin.com/carina-
press-submission-guidelines/
https://www.facebook.com/CarinaPress
https://carinapress.submittable.com/submit

Book Publisher: Harlequin Enterprises

Fiction > *Novels*
Contemporary Romance; Erotic Romance; Fantasy Romance; Historical Romance; Mystery; Romantic Suspense; Science Fiction; Supernatural / Paranormal Romance; Urban Fantasy

Send: Query; Full text; Synopsis
How to send: Submittable
How not to send: Email

Digital-first adult fiction imprint. See website for details submission guidelines and to submit via online submission system.

Editors: Kerri Buckley; Stephanie Doig

P108 Cassell

Publishing Imprint
United Kingdom

https://www.octopusbooks.co.uk/imprint/
octopus/cassell/page/cassell/

Book Publisher: Octopus Publishing Group
Limited

Nonfiction
Illustrated Books: Entertainment; Popular
Culture; Sport
Nonfiction Books: Business; Current Affairs;
Narrative Nonfiction; Popular Psychology;
Popular Science

Publishes illustrated non-fiction specialising in
popular culture, entertainment, sport and
reference titles, and non-illustrated narrative
non-fiction, including popular science,
business narrative, popular psychology and
current affairs.

P109 Caxton Press
Book Publisher
312 Main Street, Caldwell, Idaho 83605
United States
Tel: +1 (800) 657-6465

orders@caxtonpress.com

https://www.caxtonpress.com
https://www.facebook.com/pages/Caxton-
Press/201137615839
https://twitter.com/CaxtonPrint?lang=en

Fiction > *Novels*
Historical Fiction; Westerns

Nonfiction > *Nonfiction Books*
General, and in particular: American West;
Cookery; History; Travel

Send: Query; Proposal; Market info; Outline;
Table of Contents; Writing sample; Self-
Addressed Stamped Envelope (SASE)
How to send: Post

Publishes nonfiction trade books for general
audiences. May consider a manuscript on any
subject, but prefers nonfiction with a theme
such as western or frontier history, travel,
pictorials, narratives or western themed
cookbooks. Will consider historical fiction if it
deals with the West. No poetry.

P110 Celadon Books
Publishing Imprint
United States

Book Publisher: Macmillan Publishers (**P338**)

P111 CF4K
Publishing Imprint
United Kingdom

https://www.christianfocus.com

Book Publisher: Christian Focus Publications
(**P123**)

CHILDREN'S
Fiction
Board Books: Christianity; Evangelism
Chapter Books: Christianity; Evangelism
Early Readers: Christianity; Evangelism

Middle Grade: Christianity; Evangelism
Picture Books: Christianity; Evangelism
Nonfiction > *Nonfiction Books*
Christianity; Evangelism

Books for children, including Sunday school
and Home school titles.

P112 CGI (Chartered Governance Institute) Publishing
Book Publisher
Saffron House, 6–10 Kirby Street, London,
EC1N 8TS
United Kingdom
Tel: +44 (0) 20 7580 4741

https://www.cgi.org.uk
https://www.cgi.org.uk/shop
https://www.linkedin.com/school/cgiuki
https://www.facebook.com/CGIUKI
https://twitter.com/CGIUKI
https://www.flickr.com/photos/icsaglobal

PROFESSIONAL > **Nonfiction** > *Nonfiction Books*: Business

Practical governance books and media on
business skills; boards; risk and compliance;
company secretarial practice; governance; and
study texts.

P113 Chambers
Publishing Imprint
United Kingdom

enquiries@chambers.co.uk

https://chambers.co.uk
https://www.facebook.com/wordlovers/
https://twitter.com/chamberswords

Book Publisher: John Murray Press (**P296**)

Nonfiction
Puzzles: General
Reference: Language

Publishes dictionaries, thesauruses, and puzzle
books, including crosswords.

P114 Chapman Publishing
Book Publisher
4 Broughton Place, Edinburgh, EH1 3RX
United Kingdom
Tel: +44 (0) 131 557 2207

chapman-pub@blueyonder.co.uk

http://www.chapman-pub.co.uk

Fiction > *Short Fiction Collections*

Poetry > *Poetry Collections*

Scripts > *Theatre Scripts*

Closed to approaches.

**Note: No new books being undertaken as at
August 2022. Check website for current
status.**

Publishes one or two books of short stories,
drama, and (mainly) poetry by established and

rising Scottish writers per year. No novels.
Only considers writers who have previously
been published in the press's magazine. Only
publishes plays that have been previously
performed. No unsolicited MSS.

Magazine: Chapman (**M094**)

P115 Charisma House
Book Publisher
600 Rinehart Rd, Lake Mary, FL 32746
United States
Tel: +1 (407) 333-0600

info@charismamedia.com

https://charismahouse.com
https://www.facebook.com/CharismaHouse/
https://twitter.com/charismahouse
https://www.instagram.com/
charismahousebooks/

Media Company: Charisma Media

Fiction > *Novels*: Christianity

Nonfiction > *Nonfiction Books*
Christian Living; Christianity; Politics

Through the power of the Holy Spirit we
inspire people to radically change their world.
Providing Spirit-Filled Christians globally with
resources to empower them to change their
world through the power of the Holy Spirit.

P116 Charles River Press
Book Publisher
United States
Tel: +1 (508) 364-9851

info@charlesriverpress.com

http://www.charlesriverpress.com
https://www.facebook.com/charles.r.press/
https://twitter.com/CharlesRiverLLC
https://www.youtube.com/user/
CharlesRiverPress/

Fiction > *Novels*: Erotic

Nonfiction > *Nonfiction Books*: Sport

Send: Author bio; Market info; Synopsis; Full
text

Costs: Offers services that writers have to pay
for. Also offers editing and design services.

Currently accepting sports and erotica
manuscripts.

Authors: Richard Herrick; John McMullen;
Mike Ryan; Tony Schiavone; Jonathan
Womack; Rowena Womack

P117 Charlesbridge Publishing
Book Publisher
9 Galen Street, Watertown, MA 02472
United States
Tel: +1 (617) 926-0329

tradeeditorial@charlesbridge.com

https://www.charlesbridge.com
https://twitter.com/charlesbridge
https://www.facebook.com/
CharlesbridgePublishingInc
https://www.pinterest.com/charlesbridge/
https://www.instagram.com/
charlesbridgepublishing/
https://charlesbridgebooks.tumblr.com/
https://www.youtube.com/user/Charlesbridge1

CHILDREN'S
Fiction
Board Books; *Early Readers*; *Middle
Grade*; *Picture Books*
Nonfiction
Board Books: General
Early Readers: General
Middle Grade: Arts; Biography; History;
Mathematics; Nature; Science; Social
Issues
Picture Books: General

Send: Full text
How to send: Word file email attachment; PDF
file email attachment
How not to send: In the body of an email

Publishes books for children, with teen and
adult imprints.

Publishing Imprints: Charlesbridge Teen
(**P118**); Imagine Publishing (**P281**)

P118 Charlesbridge Teen
Publishing Imprint
9 Galen Street, Watertown, MA 02472
United States
Tel: +1 (800) 225-3214

ya.submissions@charlesbridge.com

https://charlesbridgeteen.com
https://twitter.com/CharlesbridgeYA
https://www.facebook.com/
CharlesbridgePublishingInc
https://www.pinterest.com/charlesbridge/
https://www.instagram.com/charlesbridgeteen/
http://charlesbridgebooks.tumblr.com/

Book Publisher: Charlesbridge Publishing
(**P117**)

YOUNG ADULT
Fiction > *Novels*
Nonfiction > *Nonfiction Books*

Send: Query; Synopsis; Writing sample;
Proposal; Outline
How to send: Email attachment

Features storytelling that presents new ideas
and an evolving world. Our carefully curated
stories give voice to unforgettable characters
with unique perspectives. We publish books
that inspire teens to cheer or sigh, laugh or
reflect, reread or share with a friend, and
ultimately, pick up another book. Our mission
– to make reading irresistible!

P119 Chartered Institute of Personnel and Development (CIPD) Publishing
Book Publisher
151 The Broadway, London, SW19 1JQ
United Kingdom
Tel: +44 (0) 20 8612 6202

https://www.cipd.co.uk
https://www.cipd.co.uk/learn/bookshop

ACADEMIC > **Nonfiction** > *Nonfiction
Books*
Business; Personal Development

PROFESSIONAL > **Nonfiction** > *Nonfiction
Books*
Business; Personal Development

Publishes professional and academic books,
looseleafs, and online subscription products,
covering topics relating to personnel, training,
and management.

Publishing Director: Stephen Dunn

P120 Child's Play (International) Ltd
Book Publisher
Ashworth Road, Bridgemead, Swindon,
Wiltshire, SN5 7YD
United Kingdom
Tel: +44 (0) 1793 616286

office@childs-play.com

http://www.childs-play.com
https://www.facebook.com/ChildsPlayBooks/
https://twitter.com/ChildsPlayBooks
http://pinterest.com/childsplaybooks/
http://www.instagram.com/childsplaybooks/
https://www.youtube.com/channel/
UCik8Eew5rGc2LfpggFgX4Qg

CHILDREN'S
Fiction
Activity Books; *Board Books*; *Picture
Books*
Poetry > *Picture Books*

Specialises in publishing books that allow
children to learn through play. No novels. No
AI-generated stories.

P121 Choc Lit
Book Publisher
Finsgate, 5 – 7 Cranwood Street, London,
EC1V 9EE
United Kingdom

info@choc-lit.com
submissions@choc-lit.com

https://www.choc-lit.com
https://twitter.com/choclituk
https://www.facebook.com/Choc-Lit-
30680012481/
https://www.instagram.com/choclituk/
https://www.youtube.com/channel/
UCLZBZ2qcR5gtOyDoqEjMbQw

Fiction > *Novels*

Contemporary Romance; Fantasy Romance;
Historical Romance; Romance; Romantic
Suspense; Timeslip Romance

Send: Query; Synopsis
How to send: Online submission system

Publishes romance suitable for an adult
audience, between 60,000 and 100,000 words
in length.

Author: Juliet Archer

Publishing Imprint: Ruby Fiction (**P451**)

P122 Chris Andrews Publications
Book Publisher
15 Curtis Yard, North Hinksey Lane, Oxford,
OX2 0LX
United Kingdom
Tel: +44 (0) 1865 723404
Fax: +44 (0) 1865 244243

enquiries@cap-ox.com

https://cap-ox.com
https://www.facebook.com/
ChrisAndrewsPublications/
https://twitter.com/capoxford
https://www.instagram.com/capoxford/

Nonfiction > *Coffee Table Books*
Photography; Travel

Publishes souvenir books with photography of
various locations.

Publisher: Chris Andrews

P123 Christian Focus Publications
Book Publisher
Geanies House, Fearn by Tain, Ross-shire,
IV20 1TW
United Kingdom
Tel: +44 (0) 1862 871011

info@christianfocus.com

https://www.christianfocus.com
https://twitter.com/christian_focus
https://www.facebook.com/christianfocus
https://www.linkedin.com/company/
christian%E2%80%93focus%E2%80%93publi
cations-limited

Nonfiction > *Nonfiction Books*: Evangelism

Send: Synopsis; Table of Contents; Writing
sample; Author bio; Submission Form
How to send: Email; Post

A conservative, evangelical publishing house.

Publishing Imprints: CF4K (**P111**); Christian
Focus; Christian Heritage; Mentor

P124 ChristLight Books
Publishing Imprint
United Kingdom

https://www.sunpenny.com/imprints/

Book Publisher: Sunpenny Publishing (**P504**)

Fiction > *Novels*: Christianity

Nonfiction > *Nonfiction Books*: Christianity

Send: Query; Author bio; Marketing Plan; Synopsis; Full text
How to send: Email

Publishes Christian fiction and nonfiction books.

P125 Chronicle Books LLC
Book Publisher
680 Second Street, San Francisco, California 94107
United States
Tel: +1 (415) 537 4200

submissions@chroniclebooks.com

https://www.chroniclebooks.com
https://facebook.com/ChronicleBooks
https://twitter.com/ChronicleBooks
https://pinterest.com/ChronicleBooks
https://instagram.com/ChronicleBooks

ADULT > **Nonfiction** > *Nonfiction Books*
Arts; Beauty; Cookery; Design; Fashion; Interior Design; Photography; Popular Culture; Relationships

CHILDREN'S
Fiction
Activity Books; *Board Books*; *Chapter Books*; *Early Readers*; *Middle Grade*; *Picture Books*
Nonfiction
Activity Books; *Board Books*; *Chapter Books*; *Early Readers*; *Middle Grade*; *Picture Books*

Send: Query; Outline; Writing sample; Market info; Author bio
How to send: Word file email attachment; PDF file email attachment

Publishes nonfiction for adults, and fiction and nonfiction for children. See website for full guidelines.

P126 Cinnamon Press
Book Publisher
Office 49019, PO Box 15113, Birmingham, B2 2NJ
United Kingdom

jan@cinnamonpress.com

https://www.cinnamonpress.com

Fiction > *Novels*

Nonfiction > *Nonfiction Books*

Poetry > *Poetry Collections*

Closed to approaches.

Small-press publisher of full length poetry collections, unique and imaginative novels, and practical and informative nonfiction with wide appeal. Willing to consider most genres as long as writing is thought-provoking, enjoyable, and accessible; but does not publish genre fiction (romantic, erotica, horror or crime), biography,

autobiography, academic, technical or how-to. No unsolicited MSS. See website for submission details.

Editor: Jan Fortune

P127 Clairview Books
Book Publisher
Russet, Sandy Lane, West Hoathly, West Sussex, RH19 4QQ
United Kingdom

office@clairviewbooks.com

https://www.clairviewbooks.com
https://www.facebook.com/Clairview-Books-190962737588974/

Nonfiction > *Nonfiction Books*
Arts; Current Affairs; History; Politics; Science; Spirituality

Send: Query; Proposal; Table of Contents; Writing sample
Don't send: Full text
How to send: Email; Post

Publishes nonfiction books which challenge conventional thinking. Send query by post or by email, with outline of around 200 words, list of chapters, and a sample chapter. No unsolicited MSS.

Authors: Wendy Cook; Howard Storm; Gore Vidal

Managing Director: Mr S. Gulbekian

P128 Claret Press
Book Publisher
51 Iveley Road, London, SW4 0EN
United Kingdom
Tel: +44 (0) 7736 716927

contact@claretpress.com

https://www.claretpress.com
https://www.facebook.com/ClaretPublisher
https://twitter.com/ClaretPress

Fiction > *Novels*
Mystery; Thrillers

Nonfiction > *Nonfiction Books*
Memoir; Politics; Travel

Closed to approaches.

A Micro Publisher specialising in narratives that encourage conversations about contemporary politics, issues and places. We love a great read about our shared world, about politics, people and places. Our page turners percolate with ideas, entertain and enlighten. We're London-based and the majority of our books are about Britain. But our travelogues take you around the world. So do many of our thrillers. Hearts and minds are opened by our memoirs and novels.

P129 Clarion Books
Publishing Imprint
United States

https://www.hmhbooks.com/imprints/clarion

Book Publisher: Houghton Mifflin Harcourt Books for Young Readers Division (**P272**)

CHILDREN'S
Fiction
Chapter Books; *Middle Grade*; *Picture Books*
Nonfiction > *Nonfiction Books*

Publishes fiction for children (including picture books) and nonfiction for all ages. Began publishing children's fiction and picture books in 1965 and has published many award-winning titles throughout the years. Its distinguished author list includes National Book Award winners, Caldecott, Newbery, Printz, and Sibert Medal and Honor recipients.

Authors: Eve Bunting; Eileen Christelow; Russell Freedman; Mary Downing Hahn; Kate Milford; Linda Sue Park; Catherine Reef; Marilyn Singer

P130 Classical Comics
Book Publisher
PO Box 177, Ludlow, SY8 9DL
United Kingdom
Tel: +44 (0) 845 812 3000
Fax: +44 (0) 845 812 3005

info@classicalcomics.com

http://www.classicalcomics.com
https://www.facebook.com/ClassicalComics/
https://www.instagram.com/classcomeducation

CHILDREN'S > **Fiction** > *Graphic Novels*: Literature

Publishes graphic novel adaptations of classical literature.

Creative Director: Jo Wheeler

Managing Director: Gary Bryant

P131 Cleis Press
Book Publisher
221 River St, 9th Fl, Hoboken, NJ 07030
United States
Tel: +1 (212) 431-5455

cleis@cleispress.com
acquisitions@cleispress.com

https://cleispress.com
https://instagram.com/cleis_press
https://twitter.com/cleispress
https://www.facebook.com/CleisPress.Page
https://www.pinterest.com/cleispress/
https://cleispress.tumblr.com/

Fiction > *Novels*
Erotic Romance; Erotic

Nonfiction > *Nonfiction Books*
Feminism; Health; LGBTQIA; Memoir; Relationships; Self Help; Sex; Sexuality; Women's Studies

Send: Query; Author bio; Writing sample
How to send: Email

The largest independent sexuality publishing company in the United States. With a focus on LGBTQ, BDSM, romance, and erotic writing for all sexual preferences.

P132 Coaches Choice
Book Publisher
311 – 21st Street, Camanche, IA 52730
United States
Tel: +1 (888) 229-5745

submissions@coacheschoice.com

https://coacheschoice.com

ADULT > **Nonfiction** > *Nonfiction Books*: Sports Coaching

PROFESSIONAL > **Nonfiction** > *Nonfiction Books*: Sports Coaching

Send: Query
How to send: Email

Always looking for people passionate about about sports instruction with the goal of improvement for coaches of all sports in all facets of their lives.

P133 Coal City Press
Book Publisher; Magazine Publisher
English Department, University of Kansas, Lawrence KS, 66045
United States

https://coalcity.org
http://www.facebook.com/CoalCityReviewAndPress/
http://twitter.com/CoalCityReview
http://instagram.com/coalcityreview

Poetry > *Poetry Collections*

Closed to approaches.

Submissions by invitation only.

Magazine: Coal City Review (**M101**)

P134 College Press Publishing
Book Publisher
1307 W 20th Street, Joplin, MO 64804
United States
Tel: +1 (417) 623-6280

collpressjoplin@gmail.com

https://collegepress.com
https://www.facebook.com/collpresspublishing/

Nonfiction > *Nonfiction Books*
   Bible Studies; Biography; Christianity; Evangelism; History

Send: Query; Proposal
How to send: Post; Email

Publishes Bible studies, topical studies (biblically based), apologetic studies, historical biographies of Christians, Sunday/Bible School curriculum (adult electives). No poetry, game or puzzle books, books on prophecy from a premillennial or dispensational viewpoint, or

any books that do not contain a Christian message.

Publishing Imprint: HeartSpring Publishing

P135 Collins
Book Publisher
Westerhill Road, Bishopbriggs, Glasgow, G64 2QT
United Kingdom

education@harpercollins.co.uk

https://collins.co.uk

Book Publisher: HarperCollins UK

ACADEMIC > **Nonfiction** > *Nonfiction Books*: Education

ADULT > **Nonfiction** > *Reference*
   Atlases; Dictionaries

Send: Author bio; Outline; Market info

Publishes reference books and educational resources.

P136 Colourpoint Educational
Book Publisher
Colourpoint House, Jubilee Business Park, 21 Jubilee Road, Newtownards, Northern Ireland, BT23 4YH
United Kingdom
Tel: +44 (0) 28 9182 0505

sales@colourpoint.co.uk

https://colourpointeducational.com
https://twitter.com/ColourpointEdu

ACADEMIC > **Nonfiction** > *Nonfiction Books*
   Biology; Chemistry; Design; Digital Technology; French; Gaelic; Geography; Health; History; Home Economics / Domestic Science; Legal; Lifestyle; Mathematics; Physical Education; Physics; Politics; Religion; Technology

Send: Query
How to send: Email

Provides textbooks, ebooks and digital resources for Northern Ireland students at Key Stage 3 level, and the CCEA revised specification at GCSE and AS/A2/A-level.

Book Publisher: Blackstaff Press (**P075**)

Editor: Wesley Johnston

P137 Columbia University Press
Book Publisher
61 West 62nd Street, New York, NY 10023
United States
Tel: +1 (212) 459 0600

https://cup.columbia.edu
https://www.facebook.com/ColumbiaUniversityPress
https://twitter.com/Columbiaup

http://www.pinterest.com/columbiaup
http://www.cupblog.org/

ACADEMIC > **Nonfiction** > *Nonfiction Books*
   African American; African Diaspora; Animals; Arts; Biography; Business; Climate Science; Economics; Films; Finance; Food; Gender; History; Journalism; Language; Literature; Media; Memoir; Middle East; New York City; Philosophy; Politics; Psychology; Religion; Science; Sexuality; Sociology

Send: Proposal; Table of Contents; Market info; Author bio
How to send: Email

American scholarly publisher based in New York.

Editorial Director: Jennifer Crewe

P138 Comma Press
Book Publisher
Studio 510a, 5th Floor, Hope Mill, 113 Pollard Street, Manchester, M4 7JA
United Kingdom

info@commapress.co.uk

http://commapress.co.uk
https://facebook.com/commapressmcr
https://twitter.com/commapress
https://instagram.com/commapress

Fiction > *Short Fiction*

A not-for-profit publisher and development agency specialising in short fiction from the UK and beyond.

P139 Concord Theatricals
Literary Agency; Book Publisher
250 W. 57th Street, 6th Floor, New York, NY 10107-0102
United States
Tel: +1 (866) 979-0447

info@concordtheatricals.com

https://www.concordtheatricals.com/

Scripts > *Theatre Scripts*

Closed to approaches.

Publishes plays and represents writers of plays. Deals in well-known plays from Broadway and London's West End.

P140 Concord Theatricals Ltd
Book Publisher
Aldwych House, 71 – 91 Aldwych, London, WC2B 4HN
United Kingdom
Tel: +44 (0) 20 7054 7298

acquisitions@concordtheatricals.co.uk

https://www.concordtheatricals.co.uk

Scripts > *Theatre Scripts*
   Drama; Musicals

Closed to approaches.

Publishes plays only. Send submissions by email only, following the guidelines on the website.

P141 Convergent
Publishing Imprint

Book Publisher: Random House

P142 Corazon Books
Book Publisher
Wyndham Media Ltd, 27 Old Gloucester Street, London, WC1N 3AX
United Kingdom

readers@greatstorieswithheart.com
b2b@greatstorieswithheart.com
pr@greatstorieswithheart.com

https://greatstorieswithheart.com

Fiction > *Novels*
  Crime; Family Saga; Historical Fiction; Medicine; Romance

Nonfiction > *Nonfiction Books*: Biography

Closed to approaches.

Publishes bestselling stories, specialising in romantic fiction, historical fiction, family sagas, medical fiction, biography and crime.

P143 Cornell Maritime Press
Publishing Imprint
United States

https://schifferbooks.com/pages/schiffer-imprints

Book Publisher: Schiffer Publishing (**P467**)

PROFESSIONAL > **Nonfiction** > *Nonfiction Books*
  Boats; Legal; Maritime History; Regional; Sailing

Titles for personnel in marine businesses, including texts for the Merchant Marine Academies, boating, water safety, maritime law, salvage, navigation, and regional maritime history.

P144 Coyote Arts
Book Publisher
PO Box 6690, Albuquerque, NM 87197-6690
United States

sales@coyote-arts.com

https://coyote-arts.com
https://www.facebook.com/coyoteartsllc/
https://twitter.com/coyoteartsllc
https://instagram.com/coyoteartsllc
https://www.pinterest.com/coyoteartsllc/

Fiction > *Novels*
  Arts; Literary

Nonfiction > *Nonfiction Books*: Arts

Poetry > *Any Poetic Form*

A literary arts publisher dedicated to the power of words and images to transform human lives and the environment we inhabit. Publishes works in the genres of poetry, fiction, non-fiction, and drama that engage the sense of wonder and possibility.

P145 Crabtree Publishing
Book Publisher
347 Fifth Ave, Suite 1402-145, New York, NY 10016
United States
Tel: +1 (800) 387-7650

https://crabtreebooks.com

ACADEMIC > **Nonfiction** > *Nonfiction Books*
  Arts; Biography; Earth Science; Economics; Finance; Geography; Health; History; Mathematics; Science; Sociology; Space; Technology; Visual Culture

CHILDREN'S
  Fiction
    Board Books: General
    Chapter Books: General
    Early Readers: Comedy / Humour; Fairy Tales; Fantasy; Horror; Magical Realism; Mystery
    Graphic Novels: General
    Picture Books: General

  Nonfiction > *Nonfiction Books*

Closed to approaches.

Publishes educational books for children. No unsolicited mss. All material is generated in-house.

P146 Croner-i Limited
Book Publisher
240 Blackfriars Road, London, SE1 8NW
United Kingdom
Tel: +44 (0) 800 231 5199

https://www.croneri.co.uk

PROFESSIONAL > **Nonfiction** > *Nonfiction Books*
  Accounting; Business; Taxation

Publishes books and resources for business professionals covering tax and accounting, human resources, health and safety, and compliance.

Online Magazine: Accountancy Daily (**M011**)

P147 Crown
Publishing Imprint
United States

https://crownpublishing.com/archives/imprint/crown-publishers
https://www.instagram.com/crownpublishing
https://twitter.com/CrownPublishing
https://www.facebook.com/CrownPublishing

Book Publisher: The Crown Publishing Group (**P148**)

Nonfiction > *Nonfiction Books*
  Biography; Business; Cultural Criticism; Current Affairs; Economics; History; Politics; Psychology; Science; Social Justice

Publishes across a wide range of nonfiction genres with an emphasis on politics, current affairs, social justice, personal narrative, biography, history, economics, business, cultural criticism, science, social science, and psychology. As a team, we are committed to publishing a diverse array of leading and emerging voices who enlarge our understanding of the world; help us navigate and succeed in a rapidly evolving climate; challenge legacy narratives; and harness the power of storytelling to illuminate, entertain, inspire, and connect readers everywhere.

P148 The Crown Publishing Group
Book Publisher
United States

https://crownpublishing.com
https://www.facebook.com/CrownPublishing
https://twitter.com/crownpublishing
http://instagram.com/crownpublishing
http://www.goodreads.com/user/show/2504245-crown-publishing-group
https://www.pinterest.com/crownpublishing/

Book Publisher: Penguin Random House

Nonfiction > *Nonfiction Books*
  Arts; Biography; Business; Comedy / Humour; Cookery; Crafts; Fitness; Gardening; Health; History; Hobbies; Memoir; Politics; Self Help

Division of large international publisher.

Publishing Imprints: 4 Color Books (**P004**); Clarkson Potter; Crown (**P147**); Currency; Ten Speed Press (**P511**); Watson-Guptill Publications

P149 The Crowood Press
Book Publisher
The Stable Block, Crowood Lane, Ramsbury, Marlborough, Wiltshire, SN8 2HR
United Kingdom
Tel: +44 (0) 1672 520320

enquiries@crowood.com
submissions@crowood.com

https://www.crowood.com
https://twitter.com/crowoodpress
http://www.facebook.com/TheCrowoodPress
https://www.instagram.com/thecrowoodpress/

Nonfiction > *Nonfiction Books*
  Architecture; Arts; Aviation; Cars; Crafts; Crocheting; Cycling; Dance; Dogs; Embroidery; Engineering; Equestrian; Films; Gardening; Home Improvement; Knitting; Lacemaking; Martial Arts; Military History; Model Making; Nature; Performing Arts; Photography; Railways; Sport; Theatre; Transport; Walking

Send: Query; Synopsis; Writing sample;
Author bio
Don't send: Full text
How to send: Email; Post

Publishes high-quality books packed with
detailed information on specialist interests.
Send proposals by post or by email.

Book Publisher: Robert Hale Publishers

Publishing Imprint: J.A. Allen

P150 Dahlia Books
Book Publisher
United Kingdom

submissions@dahliapublishing.co.uk

http://www.dahliapublishing.co.uk
https://twitter.com/dahliabooks

Fiction > *Short Fiction Collections*
  Contemporary; Diversity; Regional

Send: Query; Outline; Writing sample
How to send: Word file email attachment

We only accept proposals for short fiction and
short stories when presented as a collection
from UK based writers. Please do not send us
single short stories. We are particularly keen
on publishing diverse voices and actively
encourage submissions from first-time writers.

Print Magazine: Present Tense (**M331**)

P151 Dalkey Archive Press
Book Publisher
3000 Commerce Street, Dallas, Texas 75226
United States

toberead@deepvellum.org

https://www.dalkeyarchive.com
https://www.facebook.com/pages/Dalkey-
Archive-Press/128046170932
https://twitter.com/Dalkey_Archive

Fiction > *Novels*
  Avant-Garde; Experimental; Literary

Nonfiction > *Nonfiction Books*: Literary
Criticism

Poetry > *Any Poetic Form*

Send: Query
How to send: Email

Publishes primarily literary fiction, with an
emphasis on fiction that belongs to the
experimental tradition of Sterne, Joyce,
Rabelais, Flann O'Brien, Beckett, Gertrude
Stein, and Djuna Barnes. Occasionally
publishes poetry or nonfiction. Send
submissions by email. See website for full
guidelines.

P152 Dancing Girl Press
Book Publisher
United States

dancinggirlpress@yahoo.com

http://www.dancinggirlpress.com

Poetry > *Chapbooks*

Send: Full text

Publishes chapbooks by female poets between
12 and 32 pages. No payment, but free 10
copies and 40% discount on further copies.

P153 Darby Creek
Publishing Imprint
United States

https://lernerbooks.com/pages/our-imprints

Book Publisher: Lerner Publishing Group

CHILDREN'S > **Fiction**
  Chapter Books; *Middle Grade*
YOUNG ADULT > **Fiction** > *Novels*

How to send: Through a literary agent; By
referral

Publishes series fiction for emerging, striving,
and reluctant readers ages 8 to 18 (grades 4–
12). From chapter books to page-turning YA
novels, aims to engage readers with strong
characters, exciting premises, and accessible
formats. Makes reading an adventure instead of
a challenge or a chore.

P154 Daunt Books Publishing
Book Publisher
207-209 Kentish Town Rd, London, NW5 2JU
United Kingdom

publishing@dauntbooks.co.uk

https://dauntbookspublishing.co.uk
https://twitter.com/dauntbookspub

Fiction in Translation
  Novels: Literary
  Short Fiction Collections: Literary

Fiction
  Novels: Literary
  Short Fiction Collections: Literary

Nonfiction in Translation
  Essays: General
  Nonfiction Books: Memoir; Narrative
Nonfiction
Nonfiction
  Essays: General
  Nonfiction Books: Memoir; Narrative
Nonfiction

Closed to approaches.

We publish the finest and most exciting new
writing in English and in translation, whether
that's literary fiction – novels and short stories
– or narrative non-fiction including essays and
memoir. We also publish modern classics,
reviving authors who have been overlooked
and publishing them in bold editions with
introductions from the best contemporary
writers.

P155 DAW Books
Publishing Imprint
United States

https://astrapublishinghouse.com/imprints/
daw-books/

Book Publisher: Astra Publishing House
(**P041**)

Fiction > *Novels*
  Fantasy; Science Fiction

The first publishing company ever devoted
exclusively to science fiction and fantasy.
Seeks to publish a wide range of voices and
stories.

P156 Dead End Street
Book Publisher
320 North Carson Street, Carson City, Nevada
89701
United States

https://www.deadendstreet.com

Fiction > *Novels*

Nonfiction > *Nonfiction Books*

Formed in 1997 by three lifelong friends to
pioneer the still-nascent field of electronic
publishing. Through fits and starts and ups and
downs, the company continues to successfully
publish compelling reads long after its original
competitors folded.

Editor: John P. Rutledge

P157 Deep Overstock
Publishing
Book Publisher; Magazine Publisher
Portland, OR
United States

dop@deepoverstock.com
submissions@deepoverstock.com
editors@deepoverstock.com

https://deepoverstock.com
https://www.facebook.com/deepoverstock
https://www.instagram.com/deepoverstock
https://www.twitter.com/deepoverstock

Fiction > *Novels*

Nonfiction > *Nonfiction Books*

Poetry > *Poetry Collections*

Send: Pitch; Author bio
How to send: In the body of an email

Publishes full-length novels and longer works
by booksellers and book industry workers.

Magazine: Deep Overstock Magazine (**M136**)

P158 Del Rey
Publishing Imprint
United States

Book Publisher: Random House

P159 Denene Millner Books
Publishing Imprint

Book Publisher: Simon & Schuster Children's
Publishing (**P479**)

CHILDREN'S > Fiction > *Picture Books*

P160 Denis Kitchen Publishing Company Co., LLC

Book Publisher
P.O. Box 2250, Amherst, MA 01004
United States
Tel: +1 (413) 259-1627

help@deniskitchen.com

http://deniskitchenpublishing.com

Fiction
  Cartoons; *Comics*; *Graphic Novels*
Nonfiction > *Nonfiction Books*
  Arts; Comic Books

Publishes comics and graphic novels and books on the subject.

P161 DeVorss & Company

Book Publisher
PO Box 1389, Camarillo, CA 93011-1389
United States

editorial@devorss.com

https://www.devorss.com

ADULT > **Nonfiction** > *Nonfiction Books*
  Alternative Health; Inspirational; Lifestyle;
  Mind, Body, Spirit; Religion; Self Help;
  Spirituality

CHILDREN'S > **Nonfiction** > *Nonfiction Books*

Send: Query; Outline; Table of Contents;
Market info; Author bio
How to send: Email

Publishes New Thought, spirituality, self-improvement, alternative health and lifestyle, religion, children's books, and positive thinking. No poetry.

P162 Dewi Lewis Publishing

Book Publisher
8 Broomfield Road, Heaton Moor, Stockport,
SK4 4ND
United Kingdom
Tel: +44 (0) 1614 429450
Fax: +44 (0) 1614 429450

mail@dewilewispublishing.com
dewi.lewis@btconnect.com

https://www.dewilewis.com

Nonfiction > *Illustrated Books*: Photography

Closed to approaches.

Publishes books of photography.

Editors: Dewi Lewis; Caroline Warhurst

P163 The Dial Press

Publishing Imprint

Book Publisher: Random House

P164 Diversion Books

Book Publisher
United States
Tel: +1 (212) 961-6390

info@diversionbooks.com
submit@diversionbooks.com

http://www.diversionbooks.com

Nonfiction > *Nonfiction Books*
  Business; Crime; Current Affairs; History;
  Music; Sport

How to send: Through a literary agent

Currently accepting submissions through literary agents only.

Editors: Melanie Madden; Keith Wallman

P165 DK (Dorling Kindersley Ltd)

Book Publisher
One Embassy Gardens, 8 Viaduct Gardens,
London, SW11 7BW
United Kingdom
Tel: +44 (0) 1206 255678

adulteditorial@uk.dk.com
childreneditorial@uk.dk.com
travelguides@uk.dk.com

https://www.dk.com
https://www.facebook.com/dkbooks.uk
https://twitter.com/DKBooks
https://www.instagram.com/DKbooks/
https://www.youtube.com/user/DKinVideo
https://www.pinterest.co.uk/dkpublishing/

Book Publisher: Penguin Random House

ADULT > **Nonfiction**
  Nonfiction Books: Arts; Beauty; Business;
  Career Development; Comic Books; Crafts;
  Culture; Education; Films; Fitness; Food and
  Drink; Gardening; Health; History; Hobbies;
  Language; Medicine; Nature; Parenting;
  Photography; Pregnancy; Relationships;
  Religion; Science; Sport; TV; Transport;
  Travel
  Reference: General

CHILDREN'S > **Nonfiction** > *Nonfiction Books*

How to send: Through a literary agent

Publishes illustrated adult nonfiction and nonfiction for children. No unsolicited MSS. Approach via a literary agent only.

Book Publisher: DK Publishing (**P166**)

Publishing Imprints: Eyewitness Guides;
Eyewitness Travel Guides; Funfax

P166 DK Publishing

Book Publisher
1745 Broadway, 20th Floor, New York, NY
10019
United States

ecustomerservice@randomhouse.com

http://www.dk.com

Book Publisher: DK (Dorling Kindersley Ltd)
(**P165**)

ADULT > **Nonfiction**
  Nonfiction Books: Food; Gardening;
  Hobbies; Lifestyle; Travel; Wellbeing
  Reference: General

CHILDREN'S > **Nonfiction**
  Board Books; *Early Readers*; *Middle Grade*;
  Picture Books

How to send: Through a literary agent

Publishes highly visual nonfiction for children. Assumes no responsibility for unsolicited mss. Approach through an established literary agent.

P167 Dodo Ink

Book Publisher
United Kingdom

dodopublishingco@gmail.com

http://www.dodoink.com

Types: Fiction
Subjects: Literary
Markets: Adult

Closed to approaches.

Independent UK publisher aiming to publish three novels per year, in paperback and digital formats. Publishes risk-taking, imaginative novels, that don't fall into easy marketing categories. Closed to submissions as at June 2017.

Editor: Sam Mills

P168 Dogberry Books

Book Publisher
United Kingdom

https://www.dogberrybooks.com
https://twitter.com/DogberryLtd
https://www.facebook.com/literarymemoirs

Fiction > *Novels*
  Comedy / Humour; Literary

Nonfiction > *Nonfiction Books*
  Memoir; Narrative Nonfiction

Send: Query; Synopsis; Writing sample
How to send: Email; Online contact form

International publisher of memoir, other narrative non-fiction and literary fiction in English, particularly with an element of humour.

P169 Doubleday (UK)

Publishing Imprint
United Kingdom

https://www.penguin.co.uk/company/
publishers/transworld#Doubleday

Book Publisher: Transworld Publishers

Fiction > *Novels*

Nonfiction > *Nonfiction Books*: Narrative Nonfiction

A boutique literary imprint with a vibrant and dynamic list that publishes prize winners, international bestsellers and fresh new voices with passion and creative flair. We seek out ground-breaking books that engage the heart and mind; that speak to the zeitgeist but will also resonate for years to come.

Authors: Rosanna Amaka; Kate Atkinson; Sue Black; John Boyne; Bill Bryson; Tamsin Calidas; Nora Ephron; Alicia Garza; Rachel Joyce; John Lewis-Stempel; Hallie Rubenhold; Diane Setterfield; Curtis Sittenfeld; Clover Stroud; Francine Toon; Markus Zusak

P170 Dreamspinner Press
Book Publisher
5032 Capital Circle SW, Ste 2 PMB 279,
Tallahassee, FL 32305-7886
United States
Tel: +1 (800) 970-3759
Fax: +1 (888) 308-3739

contact@dreamspinnerpress.com
submissions@dreamspinnerpress.com

https://www.dreamspinnerpress.com
https://www.facebook.com/dreamspinnerpress/
https://twitter.com/dreamspinners
https://www.instagram.com/dreamspinner_press/

Fiction > *Novels*
Gay; Romance

Send: Synopsis; Full text
How to send: Email

Publishes gay male romance in all genres. While works do not need to be graphic, they must contain a primary or strong secondary romance plotline and focus on the interaction between two or more male characters. The main characters of the story must end in a gay or gay polyamorous relationship. Other relationships (heterosexual, lesbian, mixed gender polyamory) are acceptable in secondary pairings or as part of the development of a main character.

Authors: M. Jules Aedin; Rhianne Aile; Maria Albert; Eric Arvin; Mickie B. Ashling; Connie Bailey; Alix Bekins; Nicki Bennett; Sienna Bishop; Scarlett Blackwell; S. Blaise; Steven Blue-Williams; Anne Brooke; Bethany Brown; Janey Chapel; J. M. Colail; Jaymz Connelly; Lisa Marie Davis; Remmy Duchene; Giselle Ellis; Catt Ford; Lacey-Anne Frye; Reve Garrison; Andrew Grey; Felicitas Ivey; Ashlyn Kane; Sean Kennedy; V.B. Kildaire; Shay Kincaid; Marguerite Labbe; Clare London; Dar Mavison; Anais Morten; Chrissy Munder; Zahra Owens; D. G. Parker; Michael Powers; Angela Romano; Abigail Roux; Isabella Rowan; Steve Sampson; Ian Sentelik; Jane Seville; John Simpson; Jenna Hilary Sinclair; Dan Skinner; Sasha Skye; Sonja Spencer; Jaxx Steele; Jaelyn Storm; Rowena Sudbury; Fae

Sutherland; Ariel Tachna; Madeleine Urban; G.S. Wiley

Publishing Imprints: DSP Publications (**P171**); Harmony Ink Press (**P245**)

P171 DSP Publications
Publishing Imprint
5032 Capital Circle SW, Ste 2 PMB 279,
Tallahassee, FL 32305-7886
United States
Tel: +1 (800) 970-3759
Fax: +1 (888) 308-3739

contact@dsppublications.com

https://www.dsppublications.com
https://twitter.com/DSPPublications
https://www.facebook.com/dsppublications/

Book Publisher: Dreamspinner Press (**P170**)

Fiction > *Novels*
Fantasy; Historical Fiction; Horror; Mystery; Science Fiction; Spirituality; Supernatural / Paranormal

We are a boutique imprint producing quality fiction that pushes the envelope to present immersive, unique, and unforgettable reading experiences. We choose stories that beg to be told, tales that depart from mainstream concepts to create fantastic and compelling journeys of the mind.

P172 Duncan Petersen Publishing Limited
Book Publisher
80 Silverthorne Road, London, SW8 3HE
United Kingdom
Tel: +44 (0) 20 0147 8220

http://duncanpetersen.blogspot.com/

Nonfiction > *Nonfiction Books*
Cycling; Travel; Walking Guides

Travel publishing house based in London. Publishes Hotel Guides, along with a variety of walking and cycling guides for Britain.

P173 Dynasty Press
Book Publisher
19 New Road, Brighton, BN1 1UF
United Kingdom
Tel: +44 (0) 7970 066894

admin@dynastypress.co.uk

http://www.dynastypress.co.uk
https://www.facebook.com/dynastypress

Nonfiction > *Nonfiction Books*
Biography; History; Royalty

Publishes books connected to royalty, dynasties and people of influence.

P174 Eerdmans Books for Young Readers
Publishing Imprint
4035 Park East Court SE, Grand Rapids,

Michigan 49546
United States
Tel: +1 (616) 459-4591

info@eerdmans.com

https://www.eerdmans.com/youngreaders/

Book Publisher: William B. Eerdmans Publishing Co.

CHILDREN'S > *Fiction*
Middle Grade; *Picture Books*
YOUNG ADULT
Fiction > *Novels*
Nonfiction > *Nonfiction Books*

Send: Query; Synopsis; Writing sample; Full text
Don't send: Self-Addressed Stamped Envelope (SASE)
How to send: Post

Publishes picture books, middle reader and young adult fiction and nonfiction. Seeks manuscripts that are honest, wise, and hopeful; but also publishes stories that simply delight with their storyline, characters, or good humor. Stories that celebrate diversity, stories of historical significance, and stories that relate to contemporary social issues are of special interest at this time. Currently publishes 12 to 18 books a year. Submit by post only but do not include SASE. No return of materials or response unless interested.

P175 Eleusinian Press
Book Publisher
United Kingdom

shop@eleusinianpress.co.uk

http://www.eleusinianpress.co.uk
https://www.facebook.com/eleusinianpress

Nonfiction > *Nonfiction Books*
Music; Politics

A small publisher specialising in madness, music and radical politics.

Authors: Tristam Vivian Adams; Liz Albl; Graham Askey; Michael Burnett; Thomas D'Angelo; Zenon Gradkowski; Esther Leslie; Andrew Roberts; Richard Shrubb; Daniel Spicer; Jan Tchamani; Ben Watson; Kit Withnail; Dave Wood

P176 Elliott & Thompson
Book Publisher
2 John Street, London, WC1N 2ES
United Kingdom
Tel: +44 (0) 7973 956107

info@eandtbooks.com

http://www.eandtbooks.com
https://twitter.com/eandtbooks
https://www.instagram.com/elliottandthompson/

Fiction > *Novels*

Nonfiction

Gift Books: General
Nonfiction Books: Arts; Biography; Business; Comedy / Humour; Economics; History; Language; Music; Nature; Politics; Science; Sport

Publishes original and bestselling nonfiction and carefully selected fiction.

P177 Emperor's New Clothes Press

Book Publisher; Consultancy
United States

http://www.encpress.com
https://www.facebook.com/ENCPress/

Fiction > *Novels*

Closed to approaches.

Costs: Offers services that writers have to pay for.

Submissions on hold, but continue to act as consultants to those wishing to self-publish.

Editor: Olga Gardner Galvin

P178 ENC Press

Book Publisher
United States

sales@encpress.com

http://www.encpress.com
https://www.facebook.com/ENCPress/

Fiction > *Novels*: Comedy / Humour

Closed to approaches.

Publishes novels that blow up boundaries of genres and formulas and keep you guessing and turning pages until the end you didn't see coming. Funny novels. Sometimes bittersweet, but always with a chuckle.

Editor: Olga Gardner Galvin

P179 Encyclopedia Britannica (UK) Ltd

Book Publisher
2nd Floor, Unity Wharf, Mill Street, London, SE1 2BH
United Kingdom
Tel: +44 (0) 20 7500 7800
Fax: +44 (0) 20 7500 7878

enqbol@britannica.co.uk

https://britannica.co.uk

ACADEMIC > **Nonfiction** > *Reference*

ADULT > **Nonfiction** > *Reference*

Global digital educational publisher, publishing information and instructional products used in schools, universities, homes, libraries and workplaces throughout the world.

P180 Engram Books

Publishing Imprint
United Kingdom

submissions@sunpenny.com

https://www.sunpenny.com/imprints/

Book Publisher: Sunpenny Publishing (**P504**)

Nonfiction > *Nonfiction Books*
Autobiography; Biography; Disabilities; Memoir

Send: Author bio; Marketing Plan; Synopsis; Full text
How to send: Email
How not to send: Post

Imprint to focus on memoirs, auto-biographies, and biographies – including books about the challenges of disabilities. Especially interested in books that will be uplifting for the disabled community; that will reach out to others and let them know they are not alone, that others have gone through similar issues; how to deal with those issues; where to find help – and similar.

P181 EPTA Books

Publishing Imprint
United Kingdom

submissions@sunpenny.com

https://www.sunpenny.com/imprints/

Book Publisher: Sunpenny Publishing (**P504**)

Nonfiction > *Coffee Table Books*

Send: Query; Author bio; Marketing Plan; Synopsis; Full text
How to send: Email
How not to send: Post

Imprint for non-fiction books and coffee-table beauties.

P182 Ertel Publishing

Book Publisher
PO Box 838, Yellow Springs, OH 45387
United States
Tel: +1 (800) 767-5828

orders@ertelpublishing.com

https://ertelgiftshop.com

Nonfiction > *Nonfiction Books*
Cars; Farm Equipment; Military Vehicles; Railways; Recreational Vehicles

Publishes books for transportation enthusiasts.

P183 Essence Press

Book Publisher
United Kingdom

essencepress@btinternet.com

https://www.juliejohnstone.com/essence-press/

Poetry > *Poetry Collections*

Publishes the work of the editor, and occasionally the work of other poets and artists, usually working in collaboration to create handbound poem-objects or artists' books.

Editor: Julie Johnstone

P184 Evan-Moor Educational Publishers

Book Publisher
10 Harris Court, Ste C-3, Monterey, CA 93940
United States
Tel: +1 (800) 777-4362
Fax: +1 (800) 777-4332

customerservice@evan-moor.com

http://www.evan-moor.com
http://www.facebook.com/evanmoorcorp
https://twitter.com/evanmoor
https://www.youtube.com/channel/UCW1uyTjhrULw-vnU8PRwk0A
https://www.instagram.com/evanmoor_publisher/?hl=en

CHILDREN'S > **Nonfiction** > *Nonfiction Books*: Education

PROFESSIONAL > **Nonfiction** > *Nonfiction Books*: Education

Publishes practical, creative, and engaging PreK-8 educational materials.

P185 Everyman Chess

Publishing Imprint
United Kingdom

info@everymanchess.com

https://everymanchess.com
https://www.facebook.com/everymanchess
https://www.twitter.com/everymanchess
https://www.youtube.com/user/EverymanChessChannel
https://vimeo.com/everymanchess

Book Publisher: Gloucester Publishers (**P220**)

Nonfiction > *Nonfiction Books*: Chess

Describes itself as the world's preeminent chess book publisher.

P186 Everything With Words

Book Publisher
United Kingdom

info@everythingwithwords.com

http://www.everythingwithwords.com

ADULT > **Fiction** > *Novels*: Literary

CHILDREN'S > **Fiction** > *Novels*

Send: Query; Outline; Author bio; Writing sample
How to send: Email

We are open to submissions from both agents and authors.

At the moment, we don't publish picture books and we're not very interested in books with a strong moral or didactic aim — fine books do change people's view of the world but we find that books where the author's views are the main driving force tend to be heavy and predictable.

We don't publish adult horror fiction or crime.

Your book must be full length which means at least forty thousand words.

We try to respond to every query but we do receive a lot of submissions.

Please send a brief summary, something about yourself and three chapters or the first fifty pages.

P187 Facet Publishing
Book Publisher
7 Ridgmount Street, London, WC1E 7AE
United Kingdom
Tel: +44 (0) 20 4513 2831

info@facetpublishing.co.uk

https://www.facetpublishing.co.uk
https://www.facebook.com/facetpublishing
https://twitter.com/facetpublishing
https://www.youtube.com/user/facetpublishing
https://www.linkedin.com/company/facet-publishing

PROFESSIONAL > **Nonfiction** > *Nonfiction Books*
   Data and Information Systems; Information Science

Describes itself as the leading publisher of books for library, information and heritage professionals worldwide.

P188 Fairlight Books
Book Publisher; Online Publisher
Summertown Pavilion, 18-24 Middle Way, Oxford, OX2 7LG
United Kingdom
Tel: +44 (0) 1865 957790

contact@fairlightbooks.com
Submissions@FairlightBooks.com

https://www.fairlightbooks.co.uk
https://www.facebook.com/FairlightBooks/
https://twitter.com/FairlightBooks
https://www.instagram.com/fairlightbooks/

Fiction
   Novellas: Literary
   Novels: Literary
   Short Fiction: Literary

Send: Query; Synopsis; Writing sample; Full text

Publishes literary fiction. Accepts novels and novellas for print publication and short stories up to 10,000 words (including flash fiction) for online publication. Send query by email with synopsis and writing sample up to 10,000 words for long fiction, or full text for short stories.

P189 Familius
Book Publisher
United States

bookideas@familius.com

https://www.familius.com
https://www.facebook.com/familiustalk

https://www.instagram.com/familiustalk/?hl=en
https://twitter.com/familiustalk
https://www.pinterest.com/familius/
https://www.youtube.com/channel/UCe0DyumvESLsKkVQ86xQfAg?feature=emb_ch_name_ex

ADULT > **Nonfiction** > *Nonfiction Books*
   Cookery; Education; Family; Health; Parenting; Relationships; Self Help; Wellbeing

CHILDREN'S > **Fiction**
   Board Books: Family
   Picture Books: Family

YOUNG ADULT > **Nonfiction** > *Nonfiction Books*
   Health; Wellbeing

Send: Query; Outline; Writing sample; Market info; Author bio
Don't send: Full text
How to send: Email

Publishes nonfiction for adults, young adults, and children, focused on family as the fundamental unit of society. Submit by email or if necessary by post.

P190 Farrar, Straus & Giroux
Publishing Imprint
United States

Book Publisher: Macmillan Publishers (**P338**)

P191 Farshore Books
Publishing Imprint
United Kingdom

https://www.farshore.co.uk
https://www.facebook.com/FarshoreBooks
https://www.instagram.com/farshorebooks/
https://twitter.com/FarshoreBooks

Book Publisher: HarperCollins UK

CHILDREN'S > **Fiction**
   Chapter Books; *Early Readers*; *Middle Grade*; *Picture Books*

Aims to make every child a proud reader. This mission underpins every acquisition in their broad and inclusive portfolio of child-friendly picture books, fiction, non-fiction and brands, which offers children multiple ways into reading for pleasure.

P192 Fathom Books
Book Publisher
United States

editor@fathombooks.org

http://fathombooks.org
https://sharkpackpoetry.com/fathom-books/
https://spr.submittable.com/submit

Fiction > *Novels*
   Experimental; LGBTQIA; Literary; Philosophy; Women

Poetry > *Any Poetic Form*

Closed to approaches.

Costs: Offers services that writers have to pay for. Free to submit, but fee for expedited response.

Independent small press publishing volumes of poetry, very experimental fiction, hybrids, poetics, speculation, etc. Primary interest is text by women and queers. Accepts submissions via online submission system during specific windows only.

P193 The Feminist Press
Book Publisher
365 Fifth Avenue, Suite 5406, New York, NY 10016
United States

editor@feministpress.org

https://www.feministpress.org
https://www.facebook.com/FeministPress/
http://thefeministpress.tumblr.com/
https://www.youtube.com/channel/UCClCd_SsorK5JGKCE7rD7vw
https://twitter.com/FeministPress
https://www.instagram.com/feministpress/

ADULT
   Fiction
      Graphic Novels: Feminism
      Novels: Contemporary; Fantasy; Feminism; Mystery; Science Fiction
   Nonfiction > *Nonfiction Books*
      Activism; Africa; African American; Arts; Asia; Asian American; Biography; Education; Feminism; Films; Health; History; Italian American; Italy; Journalism; Judaism; LGBTQIA; Legal; Media; Medicine; Memoir; Middle East; Popular Culture; Postcolonialism; Science; Sexuality; South America

   Poetry > *Poetry Collections*: Feminism

CHILDREN'S > **Fiction** > *Novels*: Feminism

Closed to approaches.

Feminist publisher, publishing an array of genres including cutting-edge fiction, activist nonfiction, literature in translation, hybrid memoirs, children's books, and more.

P194 Fighting High
Book Publisher
23 Hitchin Road, Stotfold, Hitchin, Herts, SG5 4HP
United Kingdom
Tel: +44 (0) 7936 415843

fightinghigh@btinternet.com

https://fighting-high-books.myshopify.com
https://twitter.com/FightingHigh
https://www.facebook.com/groups/24337176057

Nonfiction > *Nonfiction Books*
   Adventure; Military History

Send: Query; Proposal; Synopsis; Writing sample
Don't send: Full text
How to send: Email

We specialise in non-fiction books that focus on human endeavour, particularly in a historical military setting. We also consider other stories of human enterprise and adventure.

P195 Filter Press
Book Publisher
400 Shy Circle, Westcliffe, CO 81252
United States
Tel: +1 (719) 481-2420

info@filterpressbooks.com
publisher@filterpressbooks.com

https://www.filterpressbooks.com
https://www.instagram.com/filterpressbooks/
https://twitter.com/filterpressllc

ADULT
  Fiction > *Novels*
    Colorado; Historical Fiction; Southwestern United States

  Nonfiction > *Nonfiction Books*
    Biography; Colorado; History; Travel

  Poetry > *Any Poetic Form*
    Colorado; Southwestern United States

CHILDREN'S > **Fiction**
  Chapter Books: Colorado; Historical Fiction; Southwestern United States
  Early Readers: Colorado; Historical Fiction; Southwestern United States
  Middle Grade: Colorado; Historical Fiction; Southwestern United States
  Picture Books: Colorado; Historical Fiction; Southwestern United States

Closed to approaches.

The publishing focus is on quality nonfiction and historical fiction with Southwest settings.

P196 Firefly
Book Publisher
Britannia House, Caerphilly Business Park, Van Road, Caerphilly, CF83 3GG
United Kingdom

submissions@fireflypress.co.uk
hello@fireflypress.co.uk

https://fireflypress.co.uk
https://www.facebook.com/FireflyPress/
https://twitter.com/FireflyPress
https://www.instagram.com/fireflypress/
https://www.youtube.com/channel/UCqzaLmXCoGJEQuaooZcnb4Q

CHILDREN'S > **Fiction**
  Early Readers; *Middle Grade*
TEEN > **Fiction** > *Novels*

YOUNG ADULT > **Fiction** > *Novels*

Closed to approaches.

Publishes fiction and nonfiction for children and young adults aged 5-19. Not currently accepting nonfiction submissions. Fiction submissions through agents only. Not currently publishing any picture books or colour illustrated book for any age group.

P197 Fiscal Publications
Book Publisher
United Kingdom
Tel: +44 (0) 800 678 5934

info@fiscalpublications.com

https://www.fiscalpublications.com

ACADEMIC > **Nonfiction** > *Nonfiction Books*
  Economics; Finance; Taxation

PROFESSIONAL > **Nonfiction** > *Nonfiction Books*
  Economics; Finance; Taxation

Send: Query
How to send: Email

Publishes academic and professional books specialising in taxation, public finance and public economics. Materials are relevant worldwide to policy-makers, administrators, lecturers and students of the economics, politics, law and practice of taxation.

P198 Flame Of The Forest Publishing Pte Ltd
Book Publisher
Blk 5 Ang Mo Kio Industrial Park 2A, #07-22/23, AMK Tech II, 567760
Singapore
Tel: (65) 6484 8887

editor@flameoftheforest.com

https://www.flameoftheforest.com

ADULT
  Fiction > *Novels*
  Nonfiction > *Nonfiction Books*

CHILDREN'S > **Fiction** > *Early Readers*

Send: Query; Synopsis; Writing sample
How to send: Email; Post

Submit a synopsis with a couple of sample chapters by email or by post. Submissions by post will not be returned.

Publishing Imprints: Angsana Books; Bamboo Books; Chiku Books

P199 Floris Books
Book Publisher
Canal Court, 40 Craiglockhart Avenue, Edinburgh, EH14 1LT
United Kingdom
Tel: +44 (0) 1313 372372

editorial@florisbooks.co.uk
floris@florisbooks.co.uk

https://www.florisbooks.co.uk
http://www.facebook.com/FlorisBooks

https://twitter.com/FlorisBooks
http://www.youtube.com/user/FlorisBooks
http://pinterest.com/florisbooks/

ADULT > **Nonfiction** > *Nonfiction Books*
  Arts; Astrology; Health; Holistic Health; Literature; Mind, Body, Spirit; Parenting; Philosophy; Religion; Space; Spirituality

CHILDREN'S
  Fiction
    Board Books; *Early Readers*; *Middle Grade*; *Novels*; *Picture Books*; *Short Fiction*
  Nonfiction > *Nonfiction Books*
    Activities; Crafts

Send: Synopsis; Writing sample; Table of Contents; Author bio
How to send: Online submission system
How not to send: Post

Publishes a wide range of books including adult nonfiction, picture books and children's novels. No poetry or verse, fiction for people over the age of 14, or autobiography, unless it specifically relates to a relevant nonfiction subject area. No submissions by email. Send via online form. See website for full details of areas covered and submission guidelines.

Publishing Imprint: Kelpies

P200 Forge
Publishing Imprint
United States

https://us.macmillan.com/tomdohertyassociates/
https://www.torforgeblog.com/
https://www.facebook.com/forgereads/

Publishing Imprint: Tor Publishing Group (**P520**)

Fiction > *Novels*
  Mystery; Thrillers; Westerns

Closed to approaches.

Publisher of Fiction, Thrillers, Mysteries, Westerns, and more. Open submission policy currently suspended due to COVID-19.

P201 Fort Publishing
Book Publisher
Old Belmont House, 12 Robsland Avenue, Ayr, KA7 2RW
United Kingdom
Tel: +44 (0) 1292 880693
Fax: +44 (0) 1292 270134

fortpublishing@aol.com

http://www.fortpublishing.co.uk

Nonfiction > *Nonfiction Books*
  History; Scotland; Sport

One of Scotland's leading independent publishers, specialising in sport, history and local interest.

Editor: James McCarroll

P202 Fortress Press

Publishing Imprint
411 Washington Ave N, 3rd Floor,
Minneapolis, MN 55401
United States
Tel: +1 (844) 993-3812
Fax: +1 (800) 722-7766

https://www.fortresspress.com
https://www.facebook.com/fortresspress/
https://twitter.com/fortresspress
https://www.youtube.com/user/FortressPress

Book Publisher: 1517 Media (**P002**)

ACADEMIC > **Nonfiction** > *Nonfiction Books*
   Bible Studies; Christianity; Culture; History;
   Literature; Philosophy; Social Justice

PROFESSIONAL > **Nonfiction** > *Nonfiction Books*: Christianity

Publisher of compelling theological, biblical,
and ethical engagements for the church and the
world in which it lives.

P203 Forum Books

Publishing Imprint

Book Publisher: Random House

P204 The Foundry Publishing Company

Book Publisher
PO Box 419527, Kansas City, MO 64141-6527
United States
Tel: +1 (816) 931-1900
Fax: +1 (816) 531-0923

rmcfarland@thefoundrypublishing.com

https://www.thefoundrypublishing.com
https://www.facebook.com/
TheFoundryPublishing/
https://twitter.com/WeAreTheFoundry
https://www.youtube.com/c/
TheFoundryPublishing
https://www.instagram.com/
thefoundrycommunity/

Nonfiction > *Nonfiction Books*
   Christianity; Evangelism

Poetry > *Any Poetic Form*: Christianity

Send: Table of Contents; Synopsis; Writing
sample
How to send: Word file email attachment

Publishes Christian books that reflect an
evangelical Wesleyan stance in accord with the
Church of the Nazarene. Also poems and
anecdotes. Send submissions by email.

P205 Franklin Watts

Publishing Imprint

Book Publisher: Hachette Children's Group
(**P235**)

P206 Free Spirit Publishing

Book Publisher
Attn: Acquisitions, 9850 51st Ave. N, Suite
100, Minneapolis, MN 55442
United States
Tel: +1 (714) 891-2273
Fax: +1 (888) 877-7606

acquisitions@freespirit.com

https://www.freespirit.com
https://freespiritpublishing.submittable.com/
submit
https://www.facebook.com/freespiritpublishing
https://twitter.com/FreeSpiritBooks
http://www.pinterest.com/freespiritbooks
https://www.instagram.com/
freespiritpublishing
http://www.youtube.com/user/
FreeSpiritPublishing

CHILDREN'S
   Fiction
      Board Books: Bullying; Disabilities;
      Personal Development; Wellbeing
      Novels: Bullying; Depression; Disabilities;
      Family; Health; Personal Development;
      Wellbeing
      Picture Books: Bullying; Disabilities;
      Personal Development; Wellbeing
   Nonfiction
      Board Books: Bullying; Disabilities;
      Education; Personal Development;
      Wellbeing
      Nonfiction Books: Bullying; Depression;
      Disabilities; Education; Family; Health;
      Personal Development; Social Justice;
      Wellbeing
      Picture Books: Biography; Bullying;
      Disabilities; Education; Personal
      Development; Wellbeing
TEEN
   Fiction > *Novels*
      Bullying; Depression; Disabilities; Family;
      Health; LGBTQIA; Personal Development;
      Wellbeing

   Nonfiction > *Nonfiction Books*
      Bullying; Depression; Disabilities;
      Education; Family; Health; LGBTQIA;
      Personal Development; Social Justice;
      Wellbeing

Send: Proposal
How to send: Post; Submittable

Publishes nonfiction books and learning
materials for children and teens, parents,
educators, counselors, and others who live and
work with young people. Also publishes fiction
relevant to the mission of providing children
and teens with the tools they need to succeed in
life, e.g.: self-esteem; conflict resolution, etc.
No general fiction or storybooks; books with
animal or mythical characters; books with
religious or New Age content; or single
biographies, autobiographies, or memoirs.
Submit by proposals by post or through online
submission system. See website for full
submission guidelines.

P207 Friends United Press

Book Publisher
101 Quaker Hill Drive, Richmond, IN 47374
United States
Tel: +1 (765) 962-7573

info@fum.org

https://bookstore.friendsunitedmeeting.org/
collections/friends-united-press
https://www.facebook.com/
friendsunitedmeeting/
https://www.instagram.com/
friendsunitedmeeting/

Nonfiction > *Nonfiction Books*: Quakerism

Publishes books by Quakers on Quaker history,
spirituality, and doctrine.

P208 Frontline Books

Publishing Imprint
47 Church Street, Barnsley, South Yorkshire,
S70 2AS
United Kingdom
Tel: +44 (0) 1226 734555
Fax: +44 (0) 1226 734438

info@frontline-books.com

https://www.frontline-books.com
https://twitter.com/frontline_books

Book Publisher: Pen & Sword Books Ltd
(**P407**)

Nonfiction > *Nonfiction Books*
   History; Warfare

Send: Query

Military history publisher. Publishes on a wide
range of military history topics and periods,
from Ancient Greece and Rome to the present
day. Welcomes submissions.

P209 Gale

Book Publisher
27555 Executive Dr. Ste 270, Farmington
Hills, MI 48331
United States
Tel: +1 (800) 877-4253
Fax: +1 (877) 363-4253

gale.customerexperience@cengage.com

https://www.gale.com
https://www.facebook.com/GaleCengage/
https://www.linkedin.com/company/gale
https://twitter.com/galecengage
https://www.youtube.com/user/GaleCengage

Book Publisher: Cengage

ACADEMIC > **Nonfiction**
   Nonfiction Books: Business; Chemistry;
   Computer Science; Earth Science;
   Economics; Education; Finance; Health;
   History; Legal; Literature; Mathematics;
   Medicine; Physics; Science; Sociology;
   Technology
   Reference: General

ADULT > **Nonfiction**

Nonfiction Books: Agriculture; Antiques; Arts; Astronomy; Business; Chemistry; Crafts; Earth Science; Economics; Education; Finance; Gardening; Health; History; Hobbies; Legal; Literature; Medicine; Science; Sport; Technology
Reference: General

PROFESSIONAL > Nonfiction
Nonfiction Books: Business; Economics; Education; Finance; Health; Legal; Medicine; Science; Sociology; Technology
Reference: General

Supplies businesses, schools, and libraries with books and electronic reference materials.

Book Publisher: KidHaven Press

Publishing Imprints: The Taft Group; Blackbird Press; Charles Scribner & Sons; Five Star; G.K. Hall & Co.; Graham & Whiteside Ltd; Greenhaven Publishing; KG Saur Verlag GmbH & Co. KG; Lucent Books; Macmillan Reference USA; Primary Source Media; Schirmer Reference; St James Press; Thorndike Press; Twayne Publishers; UXL; Wheeler Publishing

P210 Geared Up Publications
Publishing Imprint
United States

https://schifferbooks.com/pages/schiffer-imprints

Book Publisher: Schiffer Publishing (**P467**)

Nonfiction > *Nonfiction Books*: Deep Sea Fishing

Books on deep sea fishing and techniques for a robust catch.

P211 The Geological Society Publishing House
Book Publisher; Magazine Publisher
Unit 7, Brassmill Enterprise Centre, Brassmill Lane, Bath, BA1 3JN
United Kingdom

https://www.geolsoc.org.uk/publications

ACADEMIC > Nonfiction
Articles: Earth Science; Geology
Nonfiction Books: Earth Science; Geology; Memoir

Publishes postgraduate books and journals on the earth sciences.

Magazines: Geochemistry: Exploration, Environment, Analysis; Journal of the Geological Society; Petroleum Geoscience; Proceedings of the Yorkshire Geological Society; Quarterly Journal of Engineering Geology and Hydrogeology; Scottish Journal of Geology

P212 George Ronald Publisher
Book Publisher
United Kingdom

sales@grbooks.com

http://grbooks.com
http://www.facebook.com/pages/George-Ronald-Books/25850856123

Nonfiction > *Nonfiction Books*: Religion

Religious publisher, concentrating solely on books of interest to Baha'is.

P213 Gertrude Press
Book Publisher
United States

editor@gertrudepress.org

https://www.gertrudepress.org

Types: Fiction; Nonfiction; Poetry
Formats: Short Fiction
Subjects: Literary
Markets: Adult

Closed to approaches.

Publishes work by writers identifying as LGBTQ, both in online journal form and as chapbooks. Considers work for chapbook publication through its annual contests only. See website for details.

Online Magazine: Gertrude (**M189**)

P214 Ghostwoods Books
Book Publisher
United Kingdom

ghostwoodsbooks@gmail.com

http://gwdbooks.com
https://www.facebook.com/GhostwoodsBooks/

Fiction > *Short Fiction*

Closed to approaches.

A small, fair-trade publishing company. Publishes collections of short stories. Accepts submissions to specific calls only.

Editors: Tim Dedopulos; Salome Jones

P215 Gill
Book Publisher
Ireland

https://www.gill.ie

Publishing Imprints: Gill Books (**P216**); Gill Education (**P217**)

P216 Gill Books
Publishing Imprint
Hume Avenue, Park West, Dublin, D12 YV96
Ireland
Tel: +353 (01) 500 9500

https://www.gillbooks.ie
http://www.facebook.com/GillBooks
http://www.twitter.com/Gill_Books
http://www.instagram.com/GillBooks

Book Publisher: Gill (**P215**)

ADULT > Nonfiction

Gift Books: Ireland
Nonfiction Books: Biography; Comedy / Humour; Crafts; Crime; Current Affairs; Food and Drink; History; Hobbies; Ireland; Lifestyle; Mind, Body, Spirit; Nature; Parenting; Politics; Sport
Reference: General, and in particular: Ireland
CHILDREN'S
Fiction > *Novels*
Nonfiction > *Nonfiction Books*

Send: Query; Outline; Synopsis; Table of Contents; Writing sample; Author bio
How to send: Online submission system; Post

Publishes adult nonfiction and children's fiction and nonfiction. No adult fiction, poetry, short stories or plays. In general, focuses on books of Irish interest. Prefers proposals through online submission system, but will also accept proposals by post. See website for full submission guidelines.

P217 Gill Education
Publishing Imprint
Hume Avenue, Park West, D12 YV96
Ireland
Tel: +353 (1) 500 9500

secondarysubmissions@gill.ie

https://www.gilleducation.ie
https://www.facebook.com/GillEducation
https://twitter.com/GillEducation
https://www.instagram.com/GillEducation

Book Publisher: Gill (**P215**)

ACADEMIC > Nonfiction > *Nonfiction Books*
Accounting; Arts; Building / Construction; Business; Communication; Computer Programming; Design; Economics; Education; English; French; Geography; German; Graphic Design; Health; History; Home Economics / Domestic Science; Information Science; Irish (Gaeilge); Legal; Management; Marketing; Mathematics; Music; Nursing; Physical Education; Physics; Politics; Psychology; Religion; Science; Sociology

Send: Proposal
How to send: Email

Publishes books for the primary, secondary, and further education markets. Welcomes proposals from first time and experienced authors alike. All subject areas are of interest. See website for full guidelines.

P218 GL Assessment
Book Publisher
1st Floor Vantage London, Great West Road, Brentford, TW8 9AG
United Kingdom
Tel: +44 (0) 3301 235375

info@gl-assessment.co.uk

https://www.gl-assessment.co.uk

ACADEMIC > **Nonfiction** > *Nonfiction Books*

Publishes educational testing and assessment material.

P219 The Globe Pequot Press
Book Publisher
64 South Main Street, Essex, CT 06426
United States

GPSubmissions@rowman.com

http://www.globepequot.com
https://rowman.com/Page/GlobePequot
https://www.facebook.com/globepequot/
https://twitter.com/globepequot

Book Publisher: Rowman & Littlefield Publishing Group

Nonfiction > *Nonfiction Books*
Biography; Business; Cookery; Gardening; History; Mind, Body, Spirit; Nature; Travel

Send: Outline; Table of Contents; Writing sample; Author bio; Market info
How to send: Email; Post

Publishes books about iconic brands and people, regional interest, history, lifestyle, cooking and food culture, and folklore – books that hit the intersection of a reader's interest in a specific place and their passion for a specific topic.

Publishing Imprints: Applause; Astragal Press; Backbeat; Down East Books; FalconGuides; Lyons Press; Mcbooks Press; Muddy Boots; Pineapple Press (**P420**); Prometheus; Skip Jack Press; Stackpole Books; TwoDot; Union Park Press

P220 Gloucester Publishers
Book Publisher
36 Chapel Road, London, SE27 0TY
United Kingdom

https://find-and-update.company-information.service.gov.uk/company/04680814

Publishing Imprint: Everyman Chess (**P185**)

P221 GoldScriptCo
Book Publisher
United States

https://www.goldscriptco.com

Poetry > *Poetry Collections*

Co-founded by two writers as a means to share their own works as well as to support other writers and artists in their creative journeys.

P222 Goldsmiths Press
Book Publisher
Room 108, Deptford Town Hall, Lewisham Way, New Cross, London, SE14 6NW
United Kingdom

goldsmithspress@gold.ac.uk

https://www.gold.ac.uk/goldsmiths-press

ACADEMIC > **Nonfiction** > *Nonfiction Books*

Send: Query
Don't send: Full text

University press aiming to cut across disciplinary boundaries and blur the distinctions between theory, practice, fiction and non-fiction. See website for proposal forms and submit by email.

Editors: Adrian Driscoll; Sarah Kember; Ellen Parnavelas; Guy Sewell

P223 Goodman Beck Publishing
Book Publisher
United States

info@goodmanbeck.com

https://www.goodmanbeck.com
https://www.facebook.com/goodmanbeck
https://twitter.com/goodmanbeck

Fiction > *Novels*

Nonfiction > *Nonfiction Books*
Mental Health; Personal Development; Psychology; Self Help; Spirituality

Does not want:

> **Fiction** > *Novels*
> Fantasy; Romance; Science Fiction
>
> **Nonfiction** > *Nonfiction Books*
> How To; Politics; Religion

Send: Query
How to send: Email
How not to send: Post

Interested in helping people feel better about themselves and their lives. Focuses on mental health, personal growth, aging well, positive psychology, accessible spirituality, and overall self-help. Not interested in science fiction, fantasy, religious or political works, romance novels, textbooks, or how-to books.

Editor: Michael Pearson

P224 Goose Lane Editions
Book Publisher
Suite 330, 500 Beaverbrook Court, Fredericton, NB, E3B 5X4
Canada
Tel: +1 (506) 450-4251
Fax: +1 (888) 926-8377

info@gooselane.com

https://gooselane.com
https://www.twitter.com/goose_lane
https://www.facebook.com/GooseLaneEditions/
https://www.instagram.com/goose_lane

Fiction > *Novels*

Nonfiction > *Nonfiction Books*

Architecture; Arts; LGBTQIA; Military History; New Brunswick; Walking Guides

Send: Query; Author bio; Synopsis; Writing sample
How to send: Online submission system

Publishes literary fiction and nonfiction (and poetry through its poetry imprint) by established and up-and-coming Canadian authors. Submissions will only be considered from outside Canada if the author is Canadian and the book is of extraordinary interest to Canadian readers. No unsolicited MSS, children's, or young adult. See website for full submission details.

Editor: Angela Williams

Publishing Imprint: Icehouse (**P275**)

P225 Goss & Crested China Club
Book Publisher
Forestside House, Broadwalk, Forestside, Rowlands Castle, PO9 6EE
United Kingdom
Tel: +44 (0) 7738 842856

http://www.gosschinaclub.co.uk

ADULT > **Nonfiction** > *Reference*
Antiques; Collectibles

PROFESSIONAL > **Nonfiction** > *Reference*
Antiques; Collectibles

Publishes books on crested heraldic china and antique porcelain.

Managing Director: Andrew Pine

P226 Grant Books
Book Publisher
Pershore, Worcestershire
United Kingdom
Tel: +44 (0) 1386 803803

golf@grantbooks.co.uk

https://www.grantbooks.co.uk

Nonfiction > *Nonfiction Books*: Golf

Publishes golf-related books covering history, biography, course architecture, etc. No fiction, humour, or instructional.

Editor: H.R.J. Grant

P227 Granta Books
Book Publisher
12 Addison Avenue, London, W11 4QR
United Kingdom
Tel: +44 (0) 20 7605 1360

info@granta.com

https://granta.com/books/
https://www.facebook.com/grantamag/
https://twitter.com/GrantaMag/
https://www.instagram.com/granta_magazine/

Fiction > *Novels*: Literary

Nonfiction > *Nonfiction Books*
Autobiography; Culture; History; Literary
Criticism; Nature; Politics; Social Issues;
Travel

Closed to approaches.

Publishes around 70% nonfiction / 30% fiction.
In nonfiction publishes serious cultural,
political and social history, narrative history, or
memoir. Rarely publishes straightforward
biographies. No genre fiction. Not accepting
unsolicited submissions.

P228 **Graywolf Press**
Book Publisher
212 Third Avenue North, Suite 485,
Minneapolis, MN 55401
United States
Tel: +1 (651) 641-0077
Fax: +1 (651) 641-0036

wolves@graywolfpress.org

https://www.graywolfpress.org
https://graywolfpress.submittable.com/submit
https://www.facebook.com/GraywolfPress/
https://twitter.com/GraywolfPress
https://www.instagram.com/graywolfpress/

Fiction
Novels: Literary
Short Fiction Collections: Literary

Nonfiction
Essays: Creative Writing; Cultural Criticism;
Literary Criticism; Literary
Nonfiction Books: Creative Writing; Cultural
Criticism; Literary Criticism; Memoir
Poetry > *Poetry Collections*

Closed to approaches.

Publishes about 30 books annually, mostly
poetry, memoirs, essays, novels, and short
stories. Accepts submissions through literary
agents, or via competitions during specific
windows.

P229 **Green Books**
Book Publisher
UIT Cambridge Ltd, PO Box 145, Cambridge,
CB4 1GQ
United Kingdom

proposals@greenbooks.co.uk

https://www.greenbooks.co.uk
http://www.facebook.com/pages/Green-Books/
128608410501418
http://twitter.com/Green_Books
http://www.youtube.com/
greenbookspublishing

Nonfiction > *Nonfiction Books*
Agriculture; Arts; Business; Climate Science;
Culture; Economics; Environment; Food;
Gardening; Health; Literature; Nature;
Science; Sustainable Living; Transport; West
Country

Closed to approaches.

Set up in 1986 with the aim of spreading
awareness of ecological issues and providing
practical advice for those interested in living a
green lifestyle.

P230 **Grove Atlantic Inc.**
Book Publisher
154 West 14th Street, 12th Floor, New York,
NY 10011
United States
Tel: +1 (212) 614-7850
Fax: +1 (212) 614-7886

info@groveatlantic.com

https://groveatlantic.com

Fiction > *Novels*

Nonfiction > *Nonfiction Books*

How to send: Through a literary agent

Approach through an agent only. Publishes
general fiction and nonfiction.

Publishing Imprints: Atlantic Monthly Press
(*P045*); Black Cat (*P073*); Grove Press (*P231*);
The Mysterious Press (*P368*)

P231 **Grove Press**
Publishing Imprint
United States

Book Publisher: Grove Atlantic Inc. (**P230**)

P232 **Gryphon House, Inc.**
Book Publisher
PO Box 10, 6848 Leons Way, Lewisville, NC
27023
United States
Tel: +1 (336) 712-3490
Fax: +1 (877) 638-7576

info@ghbooks.com

https://www.gryphonhouse.com

ADULT > **Nonfiction** > *Nonfiction*
Books: Parenting

PROFESSIONAL > **Nonfiction** > *Nonfiction*
Books: Education

Send: Query; Market info; Table of Contents;
Writing sample; Author bio

Publishes books intended to help teachers and
parents enrich the lives of children from birth
to age eight. See website for proposal
submission guidelines.

P233 **Guppy Books**
Book Publisher
United Kingdom

https://guppybooks.co.uk
https://twitter.com/guppybooks
https://www.instagram.com/guppypublishin/

CHILDREN'S > **Fiction**
Chapter Books; *Early Readers*; *Middle*
Grade

How to send: Through a literary agent

A small and independent publisher of
children's fiction. No nonfiction or picture
books. No submissions from unagented or
unpublished authors.

P234 **Gwasg Carreg Gwalch**
Book Publisher
12 Iard yr Orsaf, Llanrwst, Conwy, LL26 0EH
United Kingdom
Tel: +44 (0) 1492 642031

llanrwst@carreg-gwalch.cymru

https://carreg-gwalch.cymru

ADULT > **Nonfiction** > *Nonfiction Books*
Folklore, Myths, and Legends; History;
Travel; Wales; Walking Guides

CHILDREN'S
Fiction
Novels: Wales
Picture Books: Wales

Nonfiction > *Nonfiction Books*
History; Wales

Publishes Welsh language books, and books in
English of Welsh interest, such as history and
folklore. Also publishes Welsh guides and
walks.

P235 **Hachette Children's**
Group
Book Publisher
3rd Floor, Carmelite House, 50 Victoria
Embankment, London, EC4Y 0DZ
United Kingdom

editorial@hachettechildrens.co.uk

https://www.hachettechildrens.co.uk
https://www.facebook.com/hachettekids/
https://twitter.com/hachettekids
https://www.instagram.com/hachettekids/

Book Publisher: Hachette UK (**P236**)

CHILDREN'S
Fiction
Board Books; *Chapter Books*; *Early*
Readers; *Gift Books*; *Middle Grade*;
Picture Books
Nonfiction
Board Books; *Gift Books*; *Nonfiction Books*

How to send: Through a literary agent

Aims to cater for every child, with baby and
pre-school books, picture books, gift, fiction,
non-fiction, series fiction, books for the school
and library market and licensed publishing.

Publishing Imprints: Franklin Watts (*P205*);
Hodder Children's Books (*P266*); Laurence
King Publishing (**P308**); Little, Brown Books
for Young Readers (*P316*); Orchard Books
(*P388*); Orion Children's Books (*P390*); Pat-a-
Cake (*P402*); Quercus Children's Books
(*P431*); Wayland Books (*P573*); Wren & Rook
(*P597*)

P236 **Hachette UK**
Book Publisher
Carmelite House, 50 Victoria Embankment,
London, EC4Y 0DZ
United Kingdom
Tel: +44 (0) 20 3122 6000

enquiries@hachette.co.uk

https://www.hachette.co.uk
https://www.facebook.com/HachetteBooksUK/
https://twitter.com/hachetteuk
https://www.instagram.com/hachetteuk/

Book Publisher: Hachette Livre

Fiction > *Novels*

Nonfiction > *Nonfiction Books*

How to send: Through a literary agent

Publishing group made up of ten autonomous publishing divisions and over fifty imprints with a rich and diverse history. Accepts submissions via literary agents only.

Book Publishers: Bookouture (**P087**); Hachette Children's Group (**P235**); John Murray Press (**P296**)

Publishing Imprints: Headline Publishing Group; Hodder & Stoughton; Hodder Education Group; John Murray; Laurence King Publishing (**P308**); Little, Brown Book Group; Octopus Publishing Group; Orion Publishing Group

P237 **Half Mystic Press**
Book Publisher
United States

hello@halfmystic.com

https://www.halfmystic.com
https://halfmystic.submittable.com/submit

Fiction
    Novellas; *Novels*; *Short Fiction Collections*
Nonfiction > *Nonfiction Books*
    Memoir; Music

Poetry > *Poetry Collections*

How to send: Submittable

Publishes poetry, essay, and short story collections; drama; memoirs; novellas; full-length novels; experimental work. See website for full submission guidelines.

Print Magazine: Half Mystic Journal (**M200**)

P238 **Halsgrove**
Book Publisher
Halsgrove House, Ryelands Business Park, Bagley Road, Wellington, Somerset, TA21 9PZ
United Kingdom
Tel: +44 (0) 1823 653777

sales@halsgrove.com

https://halsgrove.com
https://www.facebook.com/daa.halsgrove.1

https://www.instagram.com/halsgrove_publishing/

Nonfiction > *Nonfiction Books*
    Art History; Arts; Aviation; Leisure; Military; Nature; Political History; Politics; Regional; Transport

Send: Query; Synopsis
How to send: Email; Post

Publishes regional material covering various regions in the areas of contemporary art, art history, transport, aviation, politics, political history, natural history, exploration, military and leisure. Prefers approaches by email, but if contacting by post include email address for response.

P239 **Hammersmith Books**
Book Publisher
4/4A Bloomsbury Square, London, WC1A 2RP
United Kingdom

https://www.hammersmithbooks.co.uk
https://www.facebook.com/HammersmithHealthBooks
http://twitter.com/HHealthBooks
https://www.instagram.com/hhealthbooks/?hl=en
https://www.pinterest.com/hhealthbooks/

ACADEMIC > **Nonfiction** > *Nonfiction Books*
    Diet; Health; Medicine; Mental Health; Nutrition; Wellbeing

ADULT > **Nonfiction** > *Nonfiction Books*
    Diet; Health; Medicine; Mental Health; Nutrition; Wellbeing

PROFESSIONAL > **Nonfiction** > *Nonfiction Books*
    Diet; Health; Medicine; Mental Health; Nutrition; Wellbeing

Publisher of health, medicine, and nutrition books for the general public, health professionals, and academic markets.

Editor: Georgina Bentliff

P240 **Handspring Publishing**
Publishing Imprint
United Kingdom

Publishing Imprint: Jessica Kingsley Publishers (**P292**)

P241 **Happy Yak**
Publishing Imprint
1 Triptych Place, Second Floor, London, SE1 9SH
United Kingdom
Tel: +44 (0) 20 7700 9000

https://www.quartoknows.com/happy-yak

Book Publisher: The Quarto Group, Inc. (**P430**)

CHILDREN'S

Fiction
    Board Books; *Picture Books*
Nonfiction > *Nonfiction Books*

Send: Proposal
How to send: Email

A publisher of innovative preschool concepts, laugh-out-loud picture books, and illustrated nonfiction titles. If you have a book idea in one of our focus areas that you'd like to share with us, we'd love to hear it.

P242 **Harlequin Desire**
Book Publisher
195 Broadway, 24th floor, New York, NY 10007
United States
Tel: +1 (212) 207-7000

submissions@harlequin.com

https://www.harlequin.com

Types: Fiction
Subjects: Contemporary; Romance
Markets: Adult

Closed to approaches.

Publishes contemporary romances up to 50,000 words, featuring strong-but-vulnerable alpha heroes and dynamic, successful heroines, set in a world of wealth and glamour. See website for more details and to submit via online submission system.

Editor: Stacy Boyd

P243 **Harlequin Mills & Boon Ltd**
Book Publisher
Harlequin, 1 London Bridge Street, London, SE1 9GF
United Kingdom

info@millsandboon.co.uk

https://www.millsandboon.co.uk
https://www.instagram.com/millsandboonuk/
https://www.facebook.com/millsandboon/
https://twitter.com/MillsandBoon
https://harlequin.submittable.com/submit

Fiction > *Novels*: Romance

How to send: Submittable

Major publisher with extensive romance list and various romance imprints. Submit via online submission system.

Publishing Imprints: Harlequin MIRA; Mills & Boon Historical; Mills & Boon Medical; Mills & Boon Modern Romance; Mills & Boon Riva; Mills and Boon Cherish

P244 **Harmony**
Publishing Imprint

Book Publisher: Random House

P245 Harmony Ink Press
Publishing Imprint
United States

https://www.harmonyinkpress.com

Book Publisher: Dreamspinner Press (**P170**)

NEW ADULT > **Fiction** > *Novels*
Fantasy; LGBTQIA; Mystery; Romance;
Science Fiction; Supernatural / Paranormal

TEEN > **Fiction** > *Novels*
Fantasy; LGBTQIA; Mystery; Romance;
Science Fiction; Supernatural / Paranormal

Publishes Teen and New Adult fiction
featuring significant personal growth of
unforgettable characters across the LGBTQ+
spectrum.

P246 HarperCollins Focus
Book Publisher

focuscc@harpercollins.com

https://www.harpercollinsfocus.com

Book Publisher: HarperCollins

Book Publisher: HarperCollins Leadership
(**P247**)

P247 HarperCollins Leadership
Book Publisher

hcleadership@harpercollins.com

https://www.harpercollinsleadership.com
https://www.facebook.com/
harpercollinsleadership/
https://twitter.com/hcleadership
https://www.instagram.com/hcleadership/

Book Publisher: HarperCollins Focus (**P246**)

PROFESSIONAL > **Nonfiction** > *Nonfiction Books*: Leadership

Feeds your inner drive to grow as a leader with
integrated, values-based development
experiences that give you the inspiration and
insights you need to thrive in your current
role—and your next.

Book Publisher: AMACOM Books (**P022**)

P248 Harriman House Ltd
Book Publisher
3 Viceroy Court, Bedford Road, Petersfield,
Hampshire, GU32 3LJ
United Kingdom
Tel: +44 (0) 1730 233870

harriman@harriman-house.com

https://www.harriman-house.com

ADULT > **Nonfiction** > *Nonfiction Books*
Business; Economics; Finance; Lifestyle;
Personal Finance; Trade

PROFESSIONAL > **Nonfiction** > *Nonfiction Books*
Business; Finance

UK-based, but globally focussed independent
publisher operating in the business and finance
sector. Publishes books across a broad
spectrum of topics ranging from personal
finance and creative marketing titles through to
professional-level technical guides.

P249 Harvard Square Editions (HSE)
Book Publisher
2152 Beachwood Terrace, Hollywood, CA
90068
United States

submissions@harvardsquareeditions.org

https://harvardsquareeditions.org
http://www.youtube.com/watch?v=
EevUEEJH3GQ
https://twitter.com/harvardsquareed
https://www.facebook.com/
HarvardSquareEditions

Fiction > *Novels*
Dystopian Fiction; Environment; Fantasy;
International; Literary; Politics; Science
Fiction; Social Commentary; Spirituality;
Utopian Fiction

Send: Query; Synopsis; Writing sample
How to send: Online submission system

Looking for literary fiction of social, spiritual
and environmental value. Its mission is to
publish fiction that transcends national
boundaries, especially manuscripts that are
international, spiritual, political, literary, sci-fi,
fantasy, utopia and dystopia.

P250 Harvard University Press
Book Publisher
79 Garden Street, Cambridge, MA 02138
United States
Tel: +1 (617) 495-2600

contact_hup@harvard.edu

https://www.hup.harvard.edu
https://www.facebook.com/HarvardPress
https://twitter.com/Harvard_Press
https://www.instagram.com/harvardpress/
https://www.linkedin.com/company/harvard-
university-press-hup/
https://medium.com/@hup

ACADEMIC > **Nonfiction**
Nonfiction Books: Africa; American History;
Anthropology; Archaeology; Architecture;
Arts; Astronomy; Biography; Biology; Black
People; Business; Classics / Ancient World;
Earth Science; Economics; Engineering;
Environment; Ethnic Groups; Ethnic;
Evolution; Gender; Health; History;
Language; Legal; Literary Criticism;
Literature; Mathematics; Media; Medicine;
Music; Nature; Philosophy; Physics; Politics;
Popular Culture; Psychology; Religion;
Science; Social Issues; Sociology;
Technology; Travel
Reference: General

Publishes humanities, sciences, social sciences,
etc. Academic nonfiction only. See website for
manuscript guidelines and appropriate editorial
contacts.

Publishing Imprint: Belknap Press

P251 Haus Publishing
Book Publisher
4 Cinnamon Row, Plantation Wharf, London,
SW11 3TW
United Kingdom
Tel: +44 (0) 20 3637 9729

submissions@hauspublishing.com
haus@hauspublishing.com

https://www.hauspublishing.com
https://www.facebook.com/hauspublishing
https://www.twitter.com/hauspublishing
https://www.instagram.com/hauspublishing/
https://www.youtube.com/channel/
UCDSWSrh_wI5t_rflbyI3O7w

Fiction > *Novels*

Nonfiction > *Nonfiction Books*
Arts; Biography; Current Affairs; History;
Memoir; Politics; Travel

Send: Query; Proposal; Synopsis; Writing
sample; Author bio
How to send: Email; Through a literary agent

Accepts fiction submissions through literary
agents only. Nonfiction submissions may be
submitted direct by authors.

Book Publisher: The Armchair Traveller at the
bookHaus

Editor: Emma Henderson

Publishing Imprints: Armchair Traveller; Haus
Fiction; HausBooks; Life&Times

P252 Hawthorn Press
Book Publisher
1 Lansdown Lane, Stroud, Gloucestershire,
GL5 1BJ
United Kingdom
Tel: +44 (0) 1453 757040

info@hawthornpress.com

http://www.hawthornpress.com

Nonfiction > *Nonfiction Books*
Lifestyle; Self Help

Send: Query; Table of Contents; Author bio;
Self-Addressed Stamped Envelope (SASE);
Submission Form
How to send: Post

Publisher aiming to contribute to a more
creative, peaceful and sustainable world
through its publishing. Publishes mainly
commissioned work, but will consider
approaches. Send first two chapters with
introduction, full table of contents/book plan,
brief author biography and/or CV. Allow at
least 2-4 months for response.

P253 Hawthorne Books

Book Publisher
2201 NE 23rd Avenue Third Floor, Portland,
OR 97212
United States
Tel: +1 (503) 327-8849

rhughes@hawthornebooks.com

http://www.hawthornebooks.com
https://www.facebook.com/HawthorneBooks
http://twitter.com//hawthornebooks
http://pinterest.com/hawthornebooks/

Fiction > *Novels*: Literary

Nonfiction > *Nonfiction Books*
Memoir; Narrative Essays

How to send: Through a literary agent

An independent literary press based in
Portland, Oregon, with a national scope and
deep regional roots. Focuses on literary fiction
and nonfiction with innovative and varied
approaches to the relationships between essay,
memoir, and narrative.

Authors: Kassten Alonso; Poe Ballantine; Peter
Donahue; Monica Drake; D'Arcy Fallon; Peter
Fogtdal; Jeff Meyers; Mark Mordue; Scott
Nadelson; Toby Olson; Gin Phillips; Lynne
Sharon Schwartz; Tom Spanbauer; Michael
Strelow; Richard Wiley

P254 Hazel Press

Book Publisher
United Kingdom

https://hazelpress.co.uk
https://zirk.us/@hazelpress
https://twitter.com/hazel_press
https://www.instagram.com/
hazelpresspublisher/
https://www.youtube.com/channel/
UCOVRNv8pZw_l5DaoJ62IZug

Fiction > *Short Fiction*
Arts; Climate Science; Environment;
Feminism

Nonfiction > *Essays*
Arts; Climate Science; Environment;
Feminism

Poetry > *Poetry Collections*
Arts; Climate Science; Environment;
Feminism

Closed to approaches.

An independent publisher focusing on the
environment, the realities of the climate crisis,
feminism and the arts. Publishes short books of
poetry, essays and interdisciplinary work that
is intelligent, inspiring and has a strong sense
of place. Seeks to engage with ecological
issues in a collaborative and provocative way.

P255 Hearing Eye

Book Publisher
Box 1, 99 Torriano Avenue, London, NW5
2RX

United Kingdom
Tel: +44 (0) 20 7482 0044

https://hearingeye.org
https://www.facebook.com/hearingeyepoetry

Poetry > *Poetry Collections*

Small independent poetry publisher. Rarely
publishes unsolicited material.

P256 Helter Skelter Publishing

Book Publisher
United Kingdom

sales@helterskelterpublishing.com

http://www.helterskelterpublishing.com

Nonfiction > *Nonfiction Books*: Music

Publishes books on music.

P257 Henry Holt & Co.

Publishing Imprint
United States

Book Publisher: Macmillan Publishers (**P338**)

P258 Henry Holt Books for Young Readers

Publishing Imprint
United States

press.inquiries@macmillan.com

https://us.macmillan.com/mackids/

Book Publisher: Macmillan Children's
Publishing Group (**P334**)

CHILDREN'S > **Fiction**
Chapter Books; *Novels*; *Picture Books*

Publishes quality picture books, chapter books,
and novels for preschoolers through young
adults.

P259 High Stakes Publishing

Publishing Imprint
Harpenden, AL5 1EQ
United Kingdom
Tel: +44 (0) 1582 766348

https://highstakespublishing.co.uk

Book Publisher: Oldcastle Books Group

Nonfiction > *Nonfiction Books*: Gambling

Imprint publishing books on gambling.

P260 High Tide Press

Book Publisher
101 Hempstead Place Suite 1A, Joliet, Il 60433
United States
Tel: +1 (779) 702-5540

Submissions@HighTidePress.org
Greetings@HighTidePress.org

https://hightidepress.org
https://www.facebook.com/HighTidePress/
https://twitter.com/hightidepress

Nonfiction > *Nonfiction Books*

Leadership; Management; Mental Disorders;
Personal Development; Psychology;
Wellbeing

Send: Query; Outline; Market info; Author bio
Don't send: Full text
How to send: In the body of an email; Post
How not to send: Email attachment

Publishes titles on Person-Centered Planning;
Behavioral Health; Intellectual and
developmental disabilities; Positive
Psychology; Nonprofit management;
Leadership and management.

P261 Hippo Park

Publishing Imprint
United States

Book Publisher: Astra Publishing House
(**P041**)

P262 Hippocrene Books, Inc.

Book Publisher
171 Madison Avenue, Suite 1300, New York,
NY 10016
United States

editorial@hippocrenebooks.com
info@hippocrenebooks.com

https://www.hippocrenebooks.com
https://www.facebook.com/pages/Hippocrene-
Books-Inc/129993534671
https://twitter.com/hippocrenebooks
https://pinterest.com/hippocrenebooks

Nonfiction
Nonfiction Books: Cookery; Ethnic
Reference: Language

How to send: Email

Publishes general nonfiction, particularly
foreign language reference books and ethnic
cookbooks. No fiction. Send submissions by
email.

P263 Hiraeth Books

*Book Publisher; Ebook Publisher; Online
Publisher*
United States

hireath.sff@gmail.com
hiraethsubs@yahoo.com

https://www.hiraethsffh.com/
https://www.facebook.com/HiraethPublishing
https://twitter.com/HiraethSf

Fiction
Chapbooks: Fantasy; Horror; Science
Fiction; Speculative; Supernatural /
Paranormal
Colouring Books: Fantasy; Horror; Science
Fiction; Speculative; Supernatural /
Paranormal
Novellas: Fantasy; Horror; Science Fiction;
Speculative; Supernatural / Paranormal
Novels: Fantasy; Horror; Science Fiction;
Speculative; Supernatural / Paranormal

Short Fiction Collections: Fantasy; Horror; Science Fiction; Speculative; Supernatural / Paranormal
Short Fiction: Fantasy; Horror; Science Fiction; Speculative; Supernatural / Paranormal
Poetry > *Poetry Collections*
Fantasy; Horror; Science Fiction; Speculative; Supernatural / Paranormal

Send: Synopsis; Writing sample
How to send: Email attachment

We publish what we consider the very best in speculative fiction: science fiction, fantasy, horror, paranormal, anything out of the ordinary. We welcome new and established authors and artists equally, as talent is often found in out-of-the-way places. We are a family friendly company, but we don't shy away from strong language or tough situations if the story or artwork calls for it.

We publish novels, novellas, chapbooks, coloring books, anthologies, collections, even short stories online in the effort to showcase the many talented writers and artists how have entrusted us with their creations. We do our best to present their work in an attractive package that will gain the most attention and entertain the most readers.

Online Magazine / Print Magazine: Scifaikuest **(M361)**

P264 The History Press
Book Publisher
97 St George's Place, Cheltenham, Gloucestershire, GL50 3QB
United Kingdom
Tel: +44 (0) 1242 895310

web@thehistorypress.co.uk

https://www.thehistorypress.co.uk
https://www.facebook.com/thehistorypressuk/
https://twitter.com/TheHistoryPress/
https://www.pinterest.com/thehistorypress/

Nonfiction > *Nonfiction Books*: History

Send: Query; Synopsis; Author bio; Market info; Proposal
Don't send: Full text
How to send: Email

Publishes books on history, from local to international. Welcomes submissions from both new and established authors. Send query by email. No unsolicited mss. See website for full guidelines.

Publishing Imprint: Phillimore

P265 Hodder & Stoughton Ltd
Book Publisher
Carmelite House, 50 Victoria Embankment, London, EC4Y 0DZ
United Kingdom
Tel: +44 (0) 20 3122 6777

enquiries@hachette.co.uk

https://www.hodder.co.uk
https://www.facebook.com/hodderbooks/
https://twitter.com/HodderBooks
https://www.instagram.com/hodderbooks/

Fiction > *Novels*

Nonfiction > *Nonfiction Books*

How to send: Through a literary agent

Large London-based publisher of nonfiction and fiction.

Book Publisher: Hodder Faith

Publishing Imprint: Nicholas Brealey Publishing

P266 Hodder Children's Books
Publishing Imprint

Book Publisher: Hachette Children's Group **(P235)**

P267 Hogs Back Books
Book Publisher
34 Long Street, Devizes, Wiltshire, SN10 1NT
United Kingdom

enquiries@hogsbackbooks.com
submissions@hogsbackbooks.com

http://www.hogsbackbooks.com

CHILDREN'S
 Fiction
  Early Readers; *Picture Books*
 Nonfiction > *Nonfiction Books*

TEEN > **Fiction** > *Novels*

YOUNG ADULT
 Fiction > *Novels*
 Nonfiction > *Nonfiction Books*

Send: Full text; Synopsis; Writing sample
How to send: Email; Post

Publishes picture books and nonfiction for children up to 10, early readers for children up to 14, teenage fiction and young adult fiction and nonfiction. Send submissions by email or by post to an address in France (see website for details). All responses are by email.

P268 Holtzbrinck Publishing Group
Book Publisher
Germany

Book Publisher: The Macmillan Group **(P336)**

P269 Honest Publishing
Book Publisher
United Kingdom

info@honestpublishing.com

https://www.honestpublishing.com
https://www.facebook.com/HonestPublishing
https://twitter.com/HonestPublisher

Fiction
 Novels; *Short Fiction*

Poetry > *Poetry Collections*

Closed to approaches.

A British independent book publisher of both fiction and nonfiction. Founded by three friends in 2010, the company strives to publish alternative, original voices, and to provide an audience for unique writers neglected by the mainstream.

P270 HopeRoad
Book Publisher
PO Box 55544, Exhibition Road, London, SW7 2DB
United Kingdom

info@hoperoadpublishing.com

https://www.hoperoadpublishing.com
https://www.facebook.com/
HopeRoadPublishing
https://twitter.com/hoperoadpublish
https://www.instagram.com/
hoperoadpublishing/
https://www.youtube.com/channel/
UCd3aU4rc8zWAnB3dgnV-xhw?view_as=
subscriber

ADULT > **Fiction** > *Novels*
 Africa; Asia; Caribbean; Culture; Disabilities; Social Justice

YOUNG ADULT > **Fiction** > *Novels*
 Africa; Asia; Caribbean; Culture; Disabilities; Social Justice

How to send: Through a literary agent

Promotes the best writing from and about Africa, Asia and the Caribbean, with themes of identity, cultural stereotyping, disability and injustices of particular interest.

P271 Host Publications
Book Publisher
PO BOX 302920, Austin, TX 78703
United States

annar@hostpublications.com

https://hostpublications.com
https://hostpublications.submittable.com/
submit
https://www.facebook.com/HostPublications
https://twitter.com/Hostpublication

Fiction in Translation > *Short Fiction Collections*

Fiction > *Short Fiction Collections*

Poetry in Translation > *Poetry Collections*

Poetry > *Poetry Collections*

Closed to approaches.

Publishes literature from across the United States and around the world, including Nobel Prize winners. In 2018, shifted its focus from international authors to authors based in the United States, and committed to creating a seat at the table for marginalized groups: primarily women, people of color, immigrants, and LGBTQ+ writers.

P272 Houghton Mifflin Harcourt Books for Young Readers Division
Book Publisher

Book Publisher: Houghton Mifflin Harcourt

Publishing Imprint: Clarion Books (**P129**)

P273 How to Books Ltd
Publishing Imprint
Carmelite House, 50 Victoria Embankment, London, EC4Y 0DZ
United Kingdom
Tel: +44 (0) 20 3122 7000

howtobooks@littlebrown.co.uk

https://www.howto.co.uk
https://www.facebook.com/lbhowtouk/
http://www.twitter.com/LittleBrownUK/
https://www.instagram.com/howto.uk/

Publishing Imprint: Little, Brown Book Group

Nonfiction > *Nonfiction Books*
Business; Food; How To; Lifestyle; Parenting; Personal Finance; Relationships; Wellbeing

How to send: Through a literary agent

Publishes books that inspire you to make positive changes in your life, whether you're looking to advance your career, improve your relationships, boost your business, revitalise your health or develop your mind.

P274 Hunt End Books
Publishing Imprint
United Kingdom

Book Publisher: Brewin Books Ltd (**P091**)

P275 Icehouse
Publishing Imprint
Canada

https://gooselane.com/pages/poetry-submission

Book Publisher: Goose Lane Editions (**P224**)

Poetry > *Poetry Collections*

How to send: Online submission system

Publishes full-length poetry collections of roughly 48-100 pages, by new and established writers. Consider submissions by Canadian citizens or permanent residents only. Accepts submissions annually between April 1 and June 30.

P276 IDW Publishing
Book Publisher
2355 Northside Drive, Suite 140, San Diego, CA 92108
United States

info@idwpublishing.com

https://www.idwpublishing.com

ADULT > Fiction
Comics; *Graphic Novels*; *Novels*
CHILDREN'S > Fiction
Comics; *Graphic Novels*; *Novels*
YOUNG ADULT > Fiction
Comics; *Graphic Novels*; *Novels*

Publisher of comic books and graphic novels based on well known intellectual properties, for both children and adults.

P277 Idyll Arbor
Book Publisher
2432 39th Street, Bedford, IN 47421
United States
Tel: +1 (812) 675-6623

sales@idyllarbor.com

https://www.idyllarbor.com

ADULT > Nonfiction > *Nonfiction Books*: Health

PROFESSIONAL > Nonfiction > *Nonfiction Books*
Health; Medicine

Send: Query; Author bio; Outline; Writing sample

Publishes books that provide practical information on the current state and art of health care practice. Currently emphasizes books for recreational therapists, for activity directors working with the elderly, and for social services professionals. The books must be useful for the health practitioner who meets face to face with patients or for instructors of undergraduate and graduate level classes.

Another line of books is aimed at health care consumers. These books are intended to provide information about a single health topic (e.g., sickle cell anemia). The level of information should include enough information for a patient to be on an equal footing with a primary care physician.

P278 Ig Publishing
Book Publisher
PO Box 2547, New York, NY 10163
United States
Tel: +1 (718) 797-0676

robert@igpub.com

http://igpub.com
https://twitter.com/Igpublishing
https://www.facebook.com/pages/Ig-Publishing/176428769078839
https://www.pinterest.com/igpublishing/
https://www.instagram.com/igpublishing/

Fiction > *Novels*: Literary

Nonfiction > *Nonfiction Books*
Culture; Politics

Send: Query
How to send: Email

A New York-based award-winning independent press dedicated to publishing original literary fiction and political and cultural nonfiction. Send query by email only.

Editor-in-Chief: Robert Lasner

P279 Igloo Books Limited
Book Publisher
Cottage Farm, Mears Ashby Road, Sywell, Northants, NN6 0BJ
United Kingdom
Tel: +44 (0) 1604 741116

customerservice@igloobooks.com

https://igloobooks.com
https://www.facebook.com/igloobooks/
https://instagram.com/igloobooks/
https://www.tiktok.com/@igloobooks

ADULT > Nonfiction
Activity Books; *Colouring Books*; *Gift Books*; *Puzzles*
CHILDREN'S
Fiction
Board Books; *Picture Books*
Nonfiction
Activity Books; *Board Books*; *Reference*

Publishes nonfiction and gift and puzzle books for adults, and fiction, nonfiction, and novelty books for children.

Publishing Imprint: Autumn Publishing Ltd (**P049**)

P280 Image
Publishing Imprint

Book Publisher: Random House

P281 Imagine Publishing
Publishing Imprint
United States

https://www.imaginebooks.net
https://twitter.com/Imagine_CB
https://www.facebook.com/ImaginePress/
https://www.pinterest.com/charlesbridge/adult-books-from-imagine-publishing/
https://www.instagram.com/imagine_cb/

Book Publisher: Charlesbridge Publishing (**P117**)

Nonfiction
Coffee Table Books: General
Nonfiction Books: Arts; Comedy / Humour; Cookery; History; Nature; Politics; Women's Studies
Puzzles: General

Closed to approaches.

Publishes 8-10 titles a year, primarily focused on history, politics, women's studies, and nature.

P282 Indiana University Press
Book Publisher
IU Office of Scholarly Publishing, Herman B

Wells Library E350, 1320 E 10th Street E4,
Bloomington, IN 47405-3907
United States
Tel: +1 (812) 855-8817

iuorder@indiana.edu

https://iupress.org
https://www.facebook.com/iupress
https://twitter.com/iupress
https://www.instagram.com/iu.press/
https://www.youtube.com/c/
IndianaUniversityPress/videos

ACADEMIC > **Nonfiction** > *Nonfiction
Books*
Africa; American Civil War; American
Midwest; Eastern Europe; Films; Folklore,
Myths, and Legends; Gender; International;
Ireland; Jewish Holocaust; Judaism; Media;
Middle East; Military History; Music;
Paleontology; Performing Arts; Philosophy;
Railways; Refugees; Regional; Religion;
Russia; Sexuality; Transport

Send: Proposal; Outline; Table of Contents;
Writing sample; Author bio
How to send: Online submission system

Submit proposals via online proposal
submission form.

P283 Indigo Dreams Publishing
Book Publisher
24 Forest Houses, Halwill, Beaworthy, Devon,
EX21 5UU
United Kingdom

publishing@indigodreams.co.uk

https://www.indigodreams.co.uk
https://twitter.com/IndigoDreamsPub

Poetry > *Poetry Collections*

Closed to approaches.

Publishes poetry collections up to 60/70 pages
and poetry pamphlets up to 36 pages. See
website for submission guidelines.

Authors: Roselle Angwin; Frances
Galleymore; Paula Rae Gibson; Seema Gill;
Charlie Hill; James Lawless; Robert Leach;
Dennis Loccoriere; Angela Locke; Char
March; Ann Pilling; Cyril Tawney

Editor: Ronnie Goodyer

Magazines: The Dawntreader (**M135**); Reach
(**M344**); Sarasvati (**M359**)

P284 Influx Press
Book Publisher
United Kingdom

https://www.influxpress.com
http://instagram.com/influxpress
http://twitter.com/influxpress

Fiction > *Novels:* Gender

Nonfiction > *Nonfiction Books:* Creative
Nonfiction

Closed to approaches.

Publishes innovative and challenging fiction,
poetry and creative non-fiction from across the
UK and beyond.

P285 Ink & Willow
Publishing Imprint

Book Publisher: Random House

P286 The Innovation Press
Book Publisher
United States

submissions@theinnovationpress.com
info@theinnovationpress.com

https://www.theinnovationpress.com
http://www.facebook.com/theinnovationpress
https://twitter.com/InnovationPress
http://instagram.com/theinnovationpress

CHILDREN'S
Fiction
*Chapter Books; Graphic Novels; Middle
Grade; Picture Books*
Nonfiction
*Activity Books; Chapter Books; Middle
Grade; Picture Books*

Send: Synopsis; Writing sample; Author bio
How to send: Email

Publishes memorable children's books that
inspire learning, enliven creative thinking, and
spark imaginations. From innovative activity
books to clever fiction.

P287 Integrity Media
Book Publisher
85 Great Portland Street, First Floor, London,
W1W 7LT
United Kingdom
Tel: +44 (0) 20 3745 0658

enquiries@integrity-media.co.uk

http://www.integrity-media.co.uk

A publishing company with a unique objective.
We aim to provide a platform and portal for
those suffering poor mental health, to find
release, acceptance and growth through
literature. Whether they wish to write an
autobiographical work or simple write
creatively.

While the above is our primary motivation, we
accept submissions from all authors who fit
within our areas of interest.

Online Magazine: Authentic Shorts (**M044**)

Publishing Imprints: Authentic Ideas (**P047**);
Authentic Life (**P048**)

P288 International Society for Technology in Education (ISTE)
Book Publisher
2111 Wilson Boulevard, Suite 300, Arlington,
VA 22201, 621 SW Morrison Street, Suite

800, Portland, OR 97205
United States
Tel: +1 (503) 342-2848
Fax: +1 (541) 302-3778

iste@iste.org

https://www.iste.org
https://www.iste.org/professional-
development/books
https://twitter.com/iste
https://www.instagram.com/isteconnects/
https://www.facebook.com/ISTEconnects
https://www.iste.org/youtube

ACADEMIC > **Nonfiction** > *Nonfiction
Books*
Computer Programming; Digital Technology

PROFESSIONAL > **Nonfiction** > *Nonfiction
Books*
Computer Programming; Digital
Technology; Education

Publishes books and resources focused on
technology in education.

P289 InterVarsity Press (IVP)
Book Publisher
Studio 101, The Record Hall, 16-16A
Baldwins Gardens, London, EC1N 7RJ
United Kingdom
Tel: +44 (0) 20 7592 3900

submissions@ivpbooks.com

https://ivpbooks.com
https://www.facebook.com/ivpbooks
https://www.instagram.com/ivpbooks/
https://twitter.com/IVPbookcentre

ACADEMIC > **Nonfiction** > *Nonfiction
Books:* Religion

ADULT > **Nonfiction** > *Nonfiction Books*
Biography; Christian Living; Church
History; Contemporary Culture; Religion

Closed to approaches.

Aims to produce quality, Evangelical books for
the digital age. Send query through form on
website.

P290 Iron Press
Book Publisher
5 Marden Terrace, Cullercoats, North Shields,
Northumberland, NE30 4PD
United Kingdom
Tel: +44 (0) 191 253 1901

peter@ironpress.co.uk

https://www.ironpress.co.uk

Fiction
Short Fiction Collections; Short Fiction
Poetry
Any Poetic Form; Poetry Collections

Closed to approaches.

Poetry and fiction publisher championing
quality new writing since 1973. Publishes
poetry, (including haiku), collections of short

stories, and anthologies of verse and prose. No novels or unsolicited mss. Send query by email in first instance.

Editor: Peter Mortimer

P291 Jacaranda Books Art Music Ltd
Book Publisher
27 Old Gloucester Street, London, WC1N 3AX
United Kingdom

office@jacarandabooksartmusic.co.uk

https://www.jacarandabooksartmusic.co.uk

Types: Fiction
Subjects: Arts; Autobiography; Beauty; Commercial; Crime; Fashion; History; Literary; Music; Photography; Science Fiction; Women's Interests
Markets: Adult

Closed to approaches.

Publishes adult fiction and nonfiction, including crime, romance, illustrated books, biography, memoir, and autobiography. Particularly interested in books where the central character or theme relates to minority groups and/or has strong female protagonists. Also interested in original works from or about African, African-American, Caribbean and black British artists working in the fields of photography, fine art, fashion, and contemporary and modern art, and artists of calibre from the soul, blues, R&B and reggae traditions. Send query with writer CV, detailed synopsis, and 20-30 pages of consecutive text. See website for full submission guidelines.

Publisher: Valerie Brandes

P292 Jessica Kingsley Publishers
Publishing Imprint
Carmelite House, 50 Victoria Embankment, London, EC4Y 0DZ
United Kingdom
Tel: +44 (0) 20 3122 6000

hello@jkp.com

https://www.jkp.com
https://jkp.submittable.com/submit
https://www.facebook.com/jessicakingsleypublishers
https://twitter.com/JKPBooks
http://www.pinterest.com/jkpbooks
http://instagram.com/JKPbooks

Book Publisher: John Murray Press (**P296**)

ACADEMIC > **Nonfiction** > *Nonfiction Books*
Autism; Culture; Gender Issues; Health; Mental Health; Parenting; Religion; Social Issues

PROFESSIONAL > **Nonfiction** > *Nonfiction Books*
Autism; Culture; Gender Issues; Health; Mental Health; Parenting; Religion; Social Issues

Send: Proposal
How to send: Submittable

Publishes books on autism, social work and arts therapies.

Publishing Imprints: Handspring Publishing (*P240*); Singing Dragon (**P481**)

P293 JMD Media / DB Publishing
Book Publisher
United Kingdom
Tel: +44 (0) 7914 647382

https://www.jmdmedia.co.uk

Fiction > *Novels*

Nonfiction > *Nonfiction Books*
Autobiography; Biography; Comedy / Humour; Crime; Football / Soccer; Ghosts; Local History; Local; Magic; Motorsports; Social History; Sport; Supernatural / Paranormal; Travel; Walking

Send: Query; Outline; Author bio
How to send: Email
How not to send: Post

Considers all types of books, but focuses on local interest, sport, biography, autobiography and social history. Approach by email or phone – no submissions by post. See website for full guidelines.

Editor: Steve Caron

P294 Jo Fletcher Books
Publishing Imprint
United Kingdom

info@jofletcherbooks.co.uk
submissions@jofletcherbooks.co.uk

https://www.jofletcherbooks.com
https://www.facebook.com/jofletcherbooks
https://twitter.com/JoFletcherBooks
https://www.youtube.com/channel/UCU2vJMMmmWwI-B5cHwKKSFQ

Book Publisher: Quercus Books

Fiction > *Novels*
Fantasy; Horror; Science Fiction

Send: Query; Synopsis; Writing sample
How to send: Word file email attachment

Specialist science fiction, fantasy and horror imprint. Send query by email with synopsis and first three chapters or first 10,000 words.

P295 Joffe Books
Book Publisher
United Kingdom

submissions@joffebooks.com

https://www.joffebooks.com
https://www.facebook.com/joffebooks

https://twitter.com/joffebooks
https://www.instagram.com/joffebooks

Fiction > *Novels*
Cozy Mysteries; Crime; Domestic Noir; Historical Fiction; Mystery; Police Procedural; Psychological Thrillers; Romance; Saga; Suspense; Women's Fiction; World War II

Send: Full text; Synopsis; Author bio
How to send: Email

Publishes crime fiction, mysteries, psychological thrillers, cosy crime, police procedurals, chillers, suspense and domestic noir. Will also consider women's fiction, historical fiction and romance novels, including WWII romances and sagas. Manuscripts must be at least 60,000 words. Send query by email with complete manuscript as an attachment, a synopsis in the body of the email, and 100 words about yourself. Include "submission" in the subject line. Reply not guaranteed unless interested. See website for full guidelines.

Editor: Jasper Joffe

P296 John Murray Press
Book Publisher
Carmelite House, 50 Victoria Embankment, London, EC4Y 0DZ
United Kingdom
Tel: +44 (0) 20 3122 7222

enquiries@hachette.co.uk

https://www.johnmurraypress.co.uk

Book Publisher: Hachette UK (**P236**)

Fiction > *Novels*

Nonfiction > *Nonfiction Books*

Publisher of fiction and nonfiction, founded in the eighteenth century.

Publishing Imprints: Chambers (**P113**); Jessica Kingsley Publishers (**P292**)

P297 The Johns Hopkins University Press
Book Publisher
2715 North Charles Street, Baltimore, Maryland 21218-4363
United States
Tel: +1 (410) 516-6900

https://www.press.jhu.edu
https://twitter.com/JHUPress
https://www.facebook.com/JohnsHopkinsUniversityPress
https://www.youtube.com/user/JHUPJournals
https://www.pinterest.com/jhupress/

ACADEMIC > **Nonfiction** > *Nonfiction Books*
Architecture; Arts; Business; Classics / Ancient World; Economics; Education; Health; History; Language; Legal; Literature; Mathematics; Medicine; Music; Politics;

Recreation; Religion; Science; Sociology; Sport

Publishes titles in history, science, higher education, health and wellness, humanities, classics, and public health. Provides authors with a reputable forum for evidence-based discourse and exposure to a worldwide audience.

Editor-in-Chief: Trevor Lipscombe

Magazine: African American Review (**M014**)

P298 Jolly Learning
Book Publisher
Tailours House, High Road, Chigwell, Essex, IG7 6DL
United Kingdom
Tel: +44 (0) 20 8501 0405
Fax: +44 (0) 20 8500 1696

info@jollylearning.co.uk

https://www.jollylearning.co.uk
https://www.facebook.com/Jolly-Learning-195770143786043/
http://www.twitter.com/jollylearning
https://www.youtube.com/user/jollylearning/videos

CHILDREN'S
  Fiction > *Early Readers*
  Nonfiction > *Early Readers*

PROFESSIONAL > **Nonfiction** > *Nonfiction Books*: Education

Publishes books for children to help with reading, using the synthetic phonics method of teaching the letter sounds in a way that aims to be fun and multi-sensory.

P299 JournalStone Publishing
Book Publisher
United States

journalstone.submissions@gmail.com

https://journalstone.com

Fiction > *Novels*
  Gothic; Horror; Psychological Horror

Publishes horror in all its forms – from literary to weird, Gothic to psychological, and (almost) everything in between.

P300 Kane Press
Publishing Imprint
United States

kpsubmissions@astrapublishinghouse.com

https://astrapublishinghouse.com/imprints/kane-press/

Book Publisher: Astra Publishing House (**P041**)

CHILDREN'S
  Fiction
    Chapter Books; *Early Readers*; *Middle Grade*; *Picture Books*

Nonfiction > *Nonfiction Books*
  Arts; Engineering; Mathematics; Science; Technology

Send: Proposal
How to send: Email; Through a literary agent

An award-winning publisher of illustrated STEAM and literacy titles. Fiction and nonfiction books for ages 3–11 feature fun stories with curriculum connections and are the perfect springboard for learning in classrooms, libraries, and homes. Currently accepting proposals for series only, from published authors and literary agents.

P301 Kensington Publishing Corp.
Book Publisher
119 West 40th Street, New York, NY 10018
United States
Tel: +1 (800) 221-2647

https://www.kensingtonbooks.com
https://www.facebook.com/kensingtonpublishing
https://twitter.com/KensingtonBooks
https://www.instagram.com/kensingtonbooks/
https://www.youtube.com/user/KensingtonPublishing
https://www.pinterest.co.uk/kensingtonbooks/
https://www.tiktok.com/@kensingtonbooks

ADULT
  Fiction
    Comics: General
    Graphic Novels: General
    Novels: Cozy Mysteries; Fantasy; Literary; Mystery; Romance; Thrillers; Westerns
  Nonfiction
    Nonfiction Books: Activities; Autobiography; Biography; Business; Comedy / Humour; Computers; Cookery; Crafts; Crime; Economics; Education; Engineering; Family; Fitness; Games; Gardening; Health; History; Hobbies; Houses; Language; Legal; Medicine; Mind, Body, Spirit; Music; Nature; Performing Arts; Pets; Philosophy; Photography; Politics; Psychology; Recreation; Relationships; Religion; Science; Self Help; Sociology; Sport; Technology; Transport; Travel
    Reference: General

CHILDREN'S > **Fiction** > *Novels*

YOUNG ADULT
  Fiction > *Novels*
  Nonfiction > *Nonfiction Books*

Send: Query
Don't send: Full text
How to send: In the body of an email

Send query only, in the body of the email. Submit to one editor only. See website for full guidelines and individual editor contact details.

Editor: John Scognamiglio

Publishing Imprints: Aphrodisia; Brava; Citadel Press; Dafina; Holloway House; John Scognamiglio Books; KTeen; KTeen Dafina; Kensington Hardcover; Kensington Mass-Market; Kensington Trade Paperback; Lyle Stuart Books; Lyrical Caress; Lyrical Liaison; Lyrical Press; Lyrical Shine; Lyrical Underground; Pinnacle; Rebel Base Books; Zebra; Zebra Shout

P302 Kluwer Law International
Book Publisher
25 Canada Square, Canary Wharf, London, E14 5LQ
United Kingdom

https://kluwerlawonline.com

Book Publisher: Wolters Kluwer (**P590**)

PROFESSIONAL > **Nonfiction** > *Nonfiction Books*: Legal

Send: Query
Don't send: Full text

Publisher of international law titles, including looseleafs and journals. Welcomes unsolicited synopses and ideas on relevant topics.

P303 Kore Press
Book Publisher
PO Box 42315, Tucson, AZ 85733
United States

https://korepress.org

Types: Fiction; Nonfiction; Poetry
Subjects: Autobiography; Culture; Literary; Literary Criticism
Markets: Adult

Closed to approaches.

Publishes fiction, poetry, nonfiction, hybrid, and cultural criticism. Accepts submissions both through open submission windows and competitions.

Managing Editor: Ann Dernier

P304 Korero Press
Book Publisher
London
United Kingdom
Fax: +44 (0) 7906 314098

info@koreropress.com
contact@koreropress.com

https://www.koreropress.com
https://www.facebook.com/koreropress
https://twitter.com/KoreroPress
http://www.pinterest.com/koreropress
https://instagram.com/koreropress/

Nonfiction > *Illustrated Books*
  Arts; Drawing; Erotic; Fantasy; Horror; How To; Painting; Popular Culture; Science Fiction

Send: Query; Outline; Author bio; Market info
How to send: Email

A London-based publisher with a love of lowbrow and kustom kulture. List is mainly made up of pop culture, street art, erotica and horror titles. Publishes illustrated books only. No novels.

P305 Kube Publishing
Book Publisher
MCC, Ratby Lane, Markfield, Leicestershire, LE67 9SY
United Kingdom
Tel: +44 (0) 1530 249230

info@kubepublishing.com

https://www.kubepublishing.com
https://kubepublishing.submittable.com/submit
https://www.facebook.com/kubepublishing
https://twitter.com/Kube_Publishing
http://pinterest.com/kubepub/
https://www.instagram.com/kubepublishing/
http://www.youtube.com/user/KubeVideos/feed
https://www.tiktok.com/@kubepublishing?lang=en

ACADEMIC > **Nonfiction** > *Nonfiction Books*: Islam

ADULT > **Nonfiction** > *Nonfiction Books*
Biography; Creativity; Culture; Current Affairs; History; Islam; Memoir; Politics; Spirituality

CHILDREN'S
  Fiction
    Board Books: Islam
    Chapter Books: Islam
    Early Readers: Islam
    Middle Grade: Islam
    Picture Books: Islam

  Nonfiction
    Activity Books: Islam
    Nonfiction Books: Islam
    Picture Books: Islam

  Poetry > *Any Poetic Form*: Islam

Send: Query
How to send: Submittable

Independent publisher of general interest, academic, and children's books on Islam and the Muslim experience. Publishes nonfiction for children, young people, and adults, but fiction and poetry for children. See website for full guidelines.

P306 Langmarc Publishing
Book Publisher
PO Box 90488, Austin, Texas 78709-0488
United States
Tel: +1 (512) 394-0989

langmarc@booksails.com

https://www.langmarc.com

Fiction > *Novels*

Nonfiction > *Nonfiction Books*

Closed to approaches.

Started primarily as a publishing house for church resources and inspirational/motivational books. Now publishes novels and nonfiction.

Publishing Imprints: Harbor Lights Series; North Sea Press

P307 Lantana Publishing
Book Publisher
Clavier House, 21 Fifth Road, Newbury, RG14 6DN
United Kingdom

submissions@lantanapublishing.com

https://www.lantanapublishing.com
https://www.instagram.com/lantana_publishing/
https://www.facebook.com/lantanapublishing
https://twitter.com/lantanapub
https://www.youtube.com/channel/UC_edBCMh3Y2wDID2X9qMSkA

CHILDREN'S
  Fiction
    Chapter Books; *Early Readers*; *Graphic Novels*; *Middle Grade*; *Picture Books*
  Poetry > *Any Poetic Form*

Send: Full text
How to send: Email

We are looking for manuscripts and book dummies by authors and illustrators from under-represented groups. We particularly love stories that make us laugh, cry or move us in some way.

P308 Laurence King Publishing
Publishing Imprint
Carmelite House, 50 Victoria Embankment, London, EC4Y 0DZ
United Kingdom
Tel: +44 (0)20 3122 6444

commissioning@laurenceking.com

https://www.laurenceking.com
https://twitter.com/LaurenceKingPub
https://www.instagram.com/LaurenceKingPub/
https://www.facebook.com/LaurenceKingPublishing
https://www.pinterest.co.uk/LaurenceKingPub/
https://vimeo.com/laurencekingpublishing
https://www.youtube.com/user/laurencekingpub

Book Publishers: Hachette UK (**P236**); Hachette Children's Group (**P235**)

ACADEMIC > **Nonfiction** > *Nonfiction Books*
Architecture; Arts; Beauty; Design; Fashion; Films; Music; Nature; Photography; Popular Culture; Popular Science

ADULT > **Nonfiction** > *Nonfiction Books*
Architecture; Arts; Beauty; Design; Fashion; Films; Music; Nature; Photography; Popular Culture; Popular Science

CHILDREN'S > **Nonfiction** > *Illustrated Books*

Send: Query; Synopsis; Market info; Author bio
How to send: Email

Publisher of books on the creative arts. Send proposal by email.

P309 Leapfrog Press
Book Publisher
PO Box 1293, Dunkirk, NY 14048
United States

leapfrog@leapfrogpress.com

https://leapfrogpress.com
https://www.facebook.com/Leapfrogpress
https://twitter.com/leapfrogpress1
https://instagram.com/leapfrogpress

ADULT
  Fiction > *Novels*
  Nonfiction > *Nonfiction Books*
  Poetry > *Poetry Collections*

CHILDREN'S > **Fiction** > *Middle Grade*

YOUNG ADULT > **Fiction** > *Novels*

Publisher with an eclectic list of fiction, poetry, and nonfiction, including paperback originals of adult, young adult and middle-grade fiction, and nonfiction.

P310 LexisNexis
Book Publisher
Lexis House, 30 Farringdon Street, EC4A 4HH
United Kingdom
Tel: +44 (0) 330 161 1234

BIS@lexisnexis.co.uk

https://www.lexisnexis.com/en-gb

PROFESSIONAL > **Nonfiction** > *Reference*: Legal

Publishes books, looseleafs, journals etc. for legal professionals.

Book Publisher: Jordan Publishing

P311 Lighthouse Trails Publishing
Book Publisher
PO Box 307, Roseburg, OR 97470
United States
Tel: +1 (541) 391-7699

editors@lighthousetrails.com
david@lighthousetrails.com

https://www.lighthousetrails.com
https://www.facebook.com/LighthouseTrailsResearch
http://www.twitter.com/LTrails
http://www.youtube.com/joiful77

ADULT
  Fiction > *Novels*: Christianity
  Nonfiction > *Nonfiction Books*: Christianity

CHILDREN'S > Nonfiction
 Activity Books: Christianity
 Nonfiction Books: Christianity
 Picture Books: Christianity
 Puzzles: Christianity

Publishes Christian books that promote Jesus Christ.

P312 Lightning Books
Publishing Imprint
United Kingdom

dan@eye-books.com

https://www.eye-books.com

Book Publisher: Eye Books

Fiction > *Novels*

Send: Query; Pitch; Synopsis; Writing sample
How to send: Word file email attachment

Query by email with the word SUBMISSION in capitals at the beginning of the subject field, followed by your name and book title. Attach a single Word file containing a pitch of up to 250 words, a synopsis of up to 500 words, and the first three chapters, up to 10,000 words.

P313 Lillenas Music
Book Publisher
PO Box 419527, Kansas City, MO 64141-6527
United States
Tel: +1 (800) 363-2122
Fax: +1 (800) 849-9827

customercare@lillenas.com

https://lillenas.com

ADULT > **Nonfiction** > *Nonfiction Books*
 Choral Music; Church Music; Hymnals

CHILDREN'S > **Nonfiction** > *Nonfiction Books*
 Choral Music; Church Music; Hymnals

YOUNG ADULT > **Nonfiction** > *Nonfiction Books*
 Choral Music; Church Music; Hymnals

Closed to approaches.

Publishes religious music books.

P314 The Lilliput Press
Book Publisher
62-63 Sitric Road, Arbour Hill, Dublin 7
Ireland

editorial@lilliputpress.ie
contact@lilliputpress.ie

https://www.lilliputpress.ie

Fiction > *Novels*: Ireland

Nonfiction
 Nonfiction Books: Architecture; Arts; Biography; Cultural Criticism; Environment; Food; Genealogy; History; Ireland; Literary Criticism; Literature; Local History; Memoir; Mind, Body, Spirit; Music; Nature; Philosophy; Photography; Travel

 Reference: Ireland

Poetry > *Any Poetic Form*: Ireland

Closed to approaches.

Publishes books broadly focused on Irish themes. Send query by email with one-page synopsis and three sample chapters. See website for full guidelines.

P315 Little Bigfoot
Publishing Imprint
United States

Book Publisher: Sasquatch Books (**P462**)

CHILDREN'S
 Fiction > *Picture Books*
 General, and in particular: American West; Nature; Pacific Northwest

 Nonfiction > *Nonfiction Books*
 General, and in particular: American West; Nature; Pacific Northwest

P316 Little, Brown Books for Young Readers
Publishing Imprint

Book Publisher: Hachette Children's Group (**P235**)

P317 Llewellyn Worldwide Ltd
Book Publisher
Acquisitions Department, 2143 Wooddale Drive, Woodbury, MN 55125
United States
Tel: +1 (612) 291-1970
Fax: +1 (612) 291-1908

submissions@llewellyn.com

http://www.llewellyn.com

Nonfiction > *Nonfiction Books*
 Alternative Health; Angels; Astral Projection; Astrology; Chakras; Cryptozoology; Ghost Hunting; Kabbalah; Meditation; Mind, Body, Spirit; Paganism; Psychic Abilities; Reiki; Reincarnation; Shamanism; Spirit Guides; Spirituality; Tarot; UFOs; Wicca; Witchcraft; Yoga

Send: Query; Proposal; Full text; Outline; Table of Contents; Market info; Author bio
How to send: Word file email attachment; Post

As the world's oldest and largest independent publisher of books for body, mind, and spirit, we are dedicated to bringing our readers the very best in metaphysical books and resources. Since 1901, we've been at the forefront of holistic and metaphysical publishing and thought. We've been a source of illumination, instruction, and new perspectives on a wealth of topics, including astrology, tarot, wellness, earth-based spirituality, magic, and the paranormal.

P318 LMBPN Publishing
Book Publisher
United States

https://lmbpn.com
https://www.facebook.com/
LMBPNPublishing/
https://twitter.com/lmbpn
https://www.instagram.com/lmbpn_publishing

Fiction > *Novels*
 Fantasy; Mystery; Science Fiction; Thrillers; Urban Fantasy

P319 Loft Press, Inc.
Book Publisher
9293 Fort Valley Road, Fort Valley, VA 22652
United States
Tel: +1 (540) 933-6210
Fax: +1 (540) 933-6523

books@loftpress.com

http://www.loftpress.com

ADULT
 Fiction > *Novels*

 Nonfiction > *Nonfiction Books*
 History; Memoir; Philosophy

 Poetry > *Poetry Collections*

PROFESSIONAL > **Nonfiction** > *Nonfiction Books*
 Business; Logistics; Supply Chain Management; Transport; Warehousing

Does not want:

> **Fiction** > *Novels*
> Coming of Age; Fantasy; Feminism; Gender; Science Fiction; Women's Fiction

Send: Query; Writing sample; Outline; Market info; Self-Addressed Stamped Envelope (SASE)
How to send: Post
How not to send: Email

Publishes books for both the business community and the general reading public. Business books specialize in transportation loss and damage, logistics, warehousing, and supply chain management. For the general reading public, publishes Poetry, history, philosophy, and memoirs. Publishes very little fiction. No "coming of age" works, science fiction, fantasy, feminist-, gender-, or women-oriented works, or any manuscript with inappropriate coarse language.

P320 Logaston Press
Book Publisher
The Holme, Church Road, Eardisley, Herefordshire, HR3 6NJ
United Kingdom
Tel: +44 (0) 1544 327182

info@logastonpress.co.uk

https://logastonpress.co.uk
https://twitter.com/LogastonPress

Nonfiction > *Nonfiction Books*
Archaeology; Architecture; Biography;
Breconshire; Gloucestershire; Herefordshire;
Local History; Montgomeryshire;
Radnorshire; Shropshire; Walking Guides;
Worcestershire

Send: Query; Submission Form; Table of
Contents; Writing sample; Author bio
How to send: Email

Publishes local history, biography,
archaeology, architecture, landscape and
topography, and walk guides; and also books
about the Southern Marches region: the
English counties of Herefordshire, Shropshire,
Worcestershire and Gloucestershire, and the
Welsh counties of Radnorshire, Breconshire
and Montgomeryshire.

Publishing Imprint: Fircone Books Ltd

P321 Lonely Planet
Book Publisher
Australia

https://www.lonelyplanet.com
https://www.facebook.com/lonelyplanet
https://twitter.com/lonelyplanet
https://www.pinterest.com.au/lonelyplanet/

Nonfiction > *Nonfiction Books*: Travel

Book Publishers: Lonely Planet China (**P322**);
Lonely Planet India (**P323**); Lonely Planet UK
(**P324**); Lonely Planet USA (**P325**)

P322 Lonely Planet China
Book Publisher
OB5A, Office Tower B, East Gate Plaza, No.
29 Dongzhong Street, Dongcheng District,
Beijing 100027
China

https://www.lonelyplanet.com

Book Publisher: Lonely Planet (**P321**)

Nonfiction > *Nonfiction Books*: Travel

P323 Lonely Planet India
Book Publisher
302 DLF City Court, Sikanderpur|Gurgaon
122002
India

https://www.lonelyplanet.com

Book Publisher: Lonely Planet (**P321**)

Nonfiction > *Nonfiction Books*: Travel

Publishes travel guides.

P324 Lonely Planet UK
Book Publisher
United Kingdom

Book Publisher: Lonely Planet (**P321**)

Nonfiction > *Nonfiction Books*: Travel

P325 Lonely Planet USA
Book Publisher
1101 Red Ventures Drive, Fort Mill, SC 29707
United States

https://www.lonelyplanet.com

Book Publisher: Lonely Planet (**P321**)

Nonfiction > *Nonfiction Books*: Travel

P326 Loyola Press
Book Publisher
8770 W Bryn Mawr Ave, Suite 1125, Chicago,
IL 60631
United States
Tel: +1 (773) 281-1818
Fax: +1 (773) 281-0152

submissions@loyolapress.com

https://www.loyolapress.com
https://www.facebook.com/LoyolaPress
https://twitter.com/loyolapress
https://instagram.com/loyolapress/
https://www.youtube.com/user/LoyolaPress

Nonfiction > *Nonfiction Books*
Catholicism; Ignation Spirituality

Send: Query
How to send: Email; Post

Provides resources for readers of all ages
interested in Ignatian spirituality and prayer,
and supports parish ministry leaders and
catechists especially in their roles of fostering
and passing on a living faith.

Publishing Imprint: Loyola Classics

P327 Lund Humphries Limited
Publishing Imprint
The Alphabeta Building, 18 Finsbury Square,
London, EC2A 1AH
United Kingdom
Tel: +44 (0) 20 7440 7530

info@lundhumphries.com

https://www.lundhumphries.com
http://facebook.com/LHArtBooks
https://www.twitter.com/LHArtBooks
https://instagram.com/lhartbooks
https://www.youtube.com/channel/UCt-
2V5NDuUGTzJOxNGSqR7w

Book Publisher: Ashgate Publishing Ltd

ACADEMIC > **Nonfiction** > *Nonfiction
Books*
Architecture; Arts; Design

ADULT > **Nonfiction** > *Nonfiction Books*
Architecture; Arts; Design

PROFESSIONAL > **Nonfiction** > *Nonfiction
Books*
Architecture; Arts; Design

Send: Query; Proposal
How to send: Email

Publishes books on art, art history, and design.
See website for guidelines on submitting a
proposal.

Editor: Lucy Clark

P328 The Lutterworth Press
Publishing Imprint
PO Box 60, Cambridge, CB1 2NT
United Kingdom
Tel: +44 (0) 1223 350865
Fax: +44 (0) 1223 366951

publishing@lutterworth.com

https://www.lutterworth.com
https://lutterworthpress.wordpress.com
https://twitter.com/LuttPress
https://www.facebook.com/JamesClarkeandCo
https://www.instagram.com/lutterworthpress

Book Publisher: James Clarke & Co.

ADULT > **Nonfiction** > *Nonfiction Books*
Anthropology; Antiques; Archaeology;
Architecture; Arts; Biography; British
History; Church Architecture; Church Art;
Church History; Classics / Ancient World;
Crafts; Education; Environment; European
History; Games; History; Leisure; Literary
Criticism; Literature; Nature; New Age;
Philosophy; Poetry as a Subject; Politics;
Psychology; Religion; Science; Sociology;
Sport; Technology

CHILDREN'S
Fiction > *Novels*

Nonfiction > *Nonfiction Books*: Religion

Send: Submission Form
How to send: Post; Fax; Email

Publisher of religious books. Handles
nonfiction for adults, and fiction and nonfiction
for children. No adult fiction, cookery books,
or drama or poetry.

Not currently accepting children's books.

P329 LW Books
Publishing Imprint
United States

https://schifferbooks.com/pages/schiffer-
imprints

Book Publisher: Schiffer Publishing (**P467**)

Nonfiction > *Nonfiction Books*
Ceramics; Collectibles

Specialized books with price guides for
collectibles, especially ceramics.

P330 M. Evans & Company
Publishing Imprint
United States

https://rowman.com/action/search/cop/m.
%20evans%20&%20company

Book Publisher: Rowman & Littlefield
Publishing Group

Nonfiction > *Nonfiction Books*
General, and in particular: Health;
Psychology

Publishes general nonfiction, but best known
for popular psychology and health books.

P331 MacLehose Press
Publishing Imprint
United Kingdom

Book Publisher: Quercus Books

Publishing Imprint: Arcadia Books (**P033**)

P332 Macmillan
Publishing Imprint
United Kingdom

Book Publisher: Pan Macmillan (**P398**)

P333 Macmillan Children's Books
Publishing Imprint
United Kingdom

https://www.panmacmillan.com/mcb
https://twitter.com/MacmillanKidsUK
https://www.facebook.com/
panmacmillanbooks/
https://www.instagram.com/panmacmillan
https://www.tiktok.com/@panmacmillan

Book Publisher: Pan Macmillan (**P398**)

CHILDREN'S > **Fiction**
Board Books; Chapter Books; Middle Grade;
Picture Books
YOUNG ADULT > **Fiction** > *Novels*

How to send: Through a literary agent

One of the UK's leading children's publishers,
creating and publishing absorbing and exciting
stories for children of all ages for over 150
years.

P334 Macmillan Children's Publishing Group
Book Publisher

Publishing Imprint: Henry Holt Books for
Young Readers (**P258**)

P335 Macmillan Digital Audio
Publishing Imprint
United Kingdom

Book Publisher: Pan Macmillan (**P398**)

P336 The Macmillan Group
Book Publisher
United States

https://macmillan.com

Book Publisher: Holtzbrinck Publishing Group
(**P268**)

Book Publisher: Macmillan Publishers (**P338**)

P337 Macmillan New Writing
Publishing Imprint
United Kingdom

Book Publisher: Pan Macmillan (**P398**)

P338 Macmillan Publishers
Book Publisher
175 Fifth Avenue, New York, NY 10010
United States

press.inquiries@macmillan.com

https://us.macmillan.com

Book Publisher: The Macmillan Group (**P336**)

Types: Fiction; Nonfiction
Markets: Adult; Children's; Young Adult

How to send: Through a literary agent

US office of international publisher of
hardcover, trade paperback, and paperback
books for adults, children, and teens.

Publishing Imprints: AUWA Books (**P050**);
Castle Point Books; Celadon Books (*P110*);
Farrar, Straus & Giroux (*P190*); Flatiron
Books; Henry Holt & Co. (**P257**); MCD Books
(**P343**); Macmillan Audio; Metropolitan
Books; Minotaur Books (*P357*); Picador
(*P417*); Quick and Dirty Tips; St Martin's
Press; St Martin's Press (*P490*); St. Martin's
Essentials (*P491*); St. Martin's Griffin (*P492*);
St. Martin's Publishing Group (*P493*); Tor
Publishing Group (**P520**); Wednesday Books

P339 Mango Publishing Group
Book Publisher
2850 Douglas Road, 2nd Floor, Coral Gables,
FL 33134
United States
Tel: +1 (305) 428-2299

support@mangopublishinggroup.com

https://mangopublishinggroup.com
https://www.facebook.com/mangopublishing
https://twitter.com/MangoPublishing
https://www.instagram.com/mangopublishing/
https://www.pinterest.com/mangomediainc/
https://www.linkedin.com/company/
mangopublishing/

ADULT
Fiction > *Novels*

Nonfiction
Nonfiction Books: Adventure; Business;
Cookery; Crafts; Entertainment;
Environment; Feminism; Films; Finance;
Health; Hobbies; LGBTQIA; Science; Self
Help; Spirituality; Technology; Veganism
Reference: General

Poetry > *Poetry Collections*

CHILDREN'S > **Nonfiction** > *Nonfiction
Books*

YOUNG ADULT > **Nonfiction** > *Nonfiction
Books*

An innovative independent publisher based in
Miami. Publishes books from the freshest,
most distinctive voices of our time, and seeks
to stretch the boundaries of our online culture,
social media and ideas.

P340 Manilla Press
Publishing Imprint
United Kingdom

https://www.bonnierbooks.co.uk/imprints/
manilla-press/

Book Publisher: Bonnier Books (UK) (**P086**)

Fiction > *Novels*

Nonfiction > *Nonfiction Books*

How to send: Through a literary agent

A boutique literary imprint dedicated to
publishing unique author-led fiction and nonfiction. Boasting a carefully curated list and
international reach, our books aspire to capture
the mood of the times and the hearts and minds
of our readers.

A home for novelists, journalists, memoirists,
thinkers, dreamers, influencers, and experts.
We are driven by our passion for bold and
distinctive storytelling – seeking out a broad
range of voices and underrepresented talents as
we publish for readers from all walks of life.

P341 Margaret K. McElderry Books
Publishing Imprint
United States

http://simonandschusterpublishing.com/
margaret-k-mcelderry-books/

Book Publisher: Simon & Schuster Children's
Publishing (**P479**)

CHILDREN'S
Fiction
Middle Grade: Contemporary; Historical
Fiction; Literary Fantasy
Picture Books: General

Poetry > *Any Poetic Form*

TEEN
Fiction > *Novels*
Contemporary; Historical Fiction; Literary
Fantasy

Poetry > *Any Poetic Form*

Publisher of literary author-driven fiction and
nonfiction for the teen, middle grade, picture
book, and poetry markets. Specializes in high
quality literary fantasy, contemporary, and
historical fiction, as well as character-driven
picture books and poetry for all ages.

P342 Maryland Historical Society Press
Book Publisher
Maryland Center for History and Culture, 610

Park Ave., Baltimore, MD 21201
United States

mkado@mdhistory.org

https://www.mdhistory.org/publications/book-publishing/

Nonfiction > *Nonfiction Books*
    History; Maryland

Send: Query
How to send: Post; Email

Publishes books on the history and people of Maryland. Send query by post or by email. See website for full guidelines.

Editors: Patricia Dockman Anderson; Robert Cottom

P343 MCD Books
Publishing Imprint
United States

https://www.mcdbooks.com
https://twitter.com/mcdbooks
https://www.instagram.com/mcdbooks/
https://www.facebook.com/MCDBooks/

Book Publisher: Macmillan Publishers (**P338**)

P344 McGraw Hill EMEA
Book Publisher
Unit 4, Foundation Park, Roxborough Way, Maidenhead, SL6 3UD
United Kingdom
Tel: +44 (0) 1628 502500

emea_uk_ireland@mheducation.com
emea_me@mheducation.com
emea_europe@mheducation.com

https://www.mheducation.co.uk
https://www.facebook.com/mheducationemea
https://twitter.com/mhe_emea
https://www.linkedin.com/showcase/27094331/admin/
https://www.youtube.com/channel/UCmbIrRJdSlo0J99kFa5uYfA

Book Publisher: McGraw-Hill Education

ACADEMIC > **Nonfiction** > *Nonfiction Books*: Education

PROFESSIONAL > **Nonfiction** > *Nonfiction Books*
    Engineering; Health; Medicine; Science

Publisher of books for the professional and academic markets, particularly healthcare, medical, engineering, and science.

P345 Media Lab Books
Publishing Imprint

https://us.macmillan.com/publishers/media-lab-books

P346 Menasha Ridge Press
Publishing Imprint
United States

https://adventurewithkeen.com/menasha-ridge-press-submissions-form/

Book Publisher: AdventureKEEN (**P017**)

Nonfiction > *Nonfiction Books*
    Cookery; Food; History; Outdoor Activities; Travel; Wilderness Sports; Wildlife

Send: Query; Pitch; Outline
How to send: Online submission system

Independent publisher covering the outdoors, wilderness sports, wildlife, cooking, history, dining, and travel worldwide.

P347 Mensch Publishing
Book Publisher
United Kingdom

enquiries@menschpublishing.com

https://menschpublishing.com

Nonfiction > *Nonfiction Books*

No mission statement nor other worthy but meaningless platitudes. Its aim is simply to help authors reach readers with minimal intervention and maximum impact and to reward them proportionately.

P348 Mentor Books
Book Publisher
43 Furze Road, Sandyford Industrial Estate, Dublin 18
Ireland
Tel: 01 2952112

admin@mentorbooks.ie

https://www.mentorbooks.ie

ACADEMIC > **Nonfiction** > *Nonfiction Books*
    Biology; Business; Economics; English; French; Geography; German; History; Irish (Gaeilge); Religion; Science; Spanish

PROFESSIONAL > **Nonfiction** > *Nonfiction Books*: Education

Publishes educational books.

P349 Menus and Music
Book Publisher
1462 66th Street, Emeryville, CA 94608
United States
Tel: +1 (510) 658-9100

info@menusandmusic.com

https://www.menusandmusic.com
https://www.facebook.com/menusandmusic
https://twitter.com/menusandmusic
https://www.pinterest.com/menusandmusic/
https://www.instagram.com/menusandmusic/

Nonfiction > *Nonfiction Books*
    Arts; Food; Music; Travel

Publishes books combining inspiring food, music, art and travel.

Editor: Sharon O'Connor

P350 Merriam Press
Book Publisher; Ebook Publisher
489 South Street, Hoosick Falls NY 12090
United States
Tel: +1 (866) 357-7377

merriampress@gmail.com

https://www.merriam-press.com
https://www.facebook.com/MerriamPress

Nonfiction > *Nonfiction Books*
    Military History; World War II

Closed to approaches.

Military history publisher, focusing on World War II.

P351 Methuen Publishing Ltd
Book Publisher
Orchard House, Railway Street, Slingsby, York, YO62 4AN
United Kingdom
Tel: +44 (0) 1653 628152
Fax: +44 (0) 1653 628195

editorial@methuen.co.uk

http://www.methuen.co.uk
https://twitter.com/MethuenandCo

Fiction > *Novels*

Nonfiction
    Essays: General
    Nonfiction Books: Autobiography; Biography; Classics / Ancient World; Literature; Politics; Sport; Theatre; Travel; World War II

Send: Query
How to send: Email
How not to send: Phone

No unsolicited submissions. Send query by email only, stating the subject area of your manuscript. No phone calls regarding submissions.

P352 Metro Publications Ltd
Book Publisher
United Kingdom
Tel: +44 (0) 20 8533 7777

info@metropublications.com

https://metropublications.com
https://twitter.com/metrolondon
https://www.instagram.com/metropublications/
https://www.linkedin.com/company/metro-publications-limited

Nonfiction > *Nonfiction Books*
    Arts; Culture; Food; London; Walking Guides

Publisher of guide books on many aspects of London life.

P353 Milkweed Editions
Book Publisher
1011 Washington Avenue South, Open Book,

Suite 300, Minneapolis, MN 55415
United States

orders@milkweed.org

https://milkweed.org
http://www.facebook.com/milkweed.books
http://twitter.com/#!/Milkweed_Books
https://www.instagram.com/milkweed_books/
http://www.youtube.com/MilkweedEditions
https://www.pinterest.com/Milkfolk/

Fiction > *Novels*

Nonfiction > *Nonfiction Books*

Poetry > *Poetry Collections*

Closed to approaches.

An independent publisher of fiction, nonfiction, and poetry.

P354 Mills & Boon
Publishing Imprint
1 London Bridge Street, London, SE1 9GF
United Kingdom

info@millsandboon.co.uk
submissions@harlequin.com

https://www.millsandboon.co.uk
https://harlequin.submittable.com/submit
https://www.facebook.com/millsandboon/
https://twitter.com/MillsandBoon
https://www.instagram.com/millsandboonuk/
https://www.tiktok.com/@millsandboonuk

Book Publishers: Harlequin Enterprises; HarperCollins UK

Fiction > *Novels*
   Adventure; Crime; Historical Romance; Medicine; Romance; Romantic Suspense; Romantic Thrillers

How to send: Submittable

Across every romance genre, from historical to contemporary, rom-com to erotica, our compelling, uplifting romances guarantee an instant escape to fantasy worlds, and the heart-warming reassurance of 'happily ever after'. We are proud to publish over 1,300 authors, 700 new titles a year, with manuscripts from 200 authors living in the UK and a further 1,300 worldwide.

P355 MineditionUS
Publishing Imprint
United States

Book Publisher: Astra Publishing House (**P041**)

P356 Minnesota Historical Society Press
Book Publisher
345 Kellogg Blvd. West, Saint Paul, MN 55102-1906
United States
Tel: +1 (651) 259-3205
Fax: +1 (651) 297-1345

https://www.mnhs.org/mnhspress
https://www.facebook.com/Mnhspress
https://twitter.com/MNHSPress
https://www.youtube.com/playlist?list=
PLRrmlN6cO7LvpRkbuLYO6paOGLjrKCoX
P

Nonfiction > *Nonfiction Books*
   American Midwest; Culture; History; Minnesota

Send: Query; Market info; Author bio; Table of Contents; Outline; Writing sample
How to send: Email; Post

Publishes books on the history and culture of America's Upper Midwest. Submit proposal by post including author info, working title, description of the book, table of contents/outline, intended readership, outline of the market and potential competition, the book's length, your schedule for completing it, and 15-25 sample pages. See website for detailed guidelines.

Publishing Imprint: Borealis Books

P357 Minotaur Books
Publishing Imprint
United States

Book Publisher: Macmillan Publishers (**P338**)

P358 Mirror Books
Book Publisher
One Canada Square, Canary Wharf, London, E14 5AP
United Kingdom

submissions@mirrorbooks.co.uk

https://mirrorbooks.co.uk

Nonfiction > *Nonfiction Books*
   Celebrity; Crime; Memoir; Nostalgia

Send: Query; Outline; Synopsis; Table of Contents; Writing sample; Author bio; Marketing Plan
How to send: Email

Currently accepting submissions with a focus on nonfiction real-life (memoir, crime, nostalgia, personalities and celebrities). Send submissions by email.

P359 The MIT Press
Book Publisher
One Broadway, 12th Floor, Cambridge, MA 02142
United States
Tel: +1 (617) 253-5646

https://mitpress.mit.edu
https://www.facebook.com/mitpress
https://twitter.com/mitpress
https://www.linkedin.com/company/11587565/
https://www.pinterest.com/mitpress/
https://www.instagram.com/mitpress/
https://www.youtube.com/c/TheMITPress

ACADEMIC > **Nonfiction** > *Nonfiction Books*
   Arts; Design; Science; Sociology; Technology

University press publishing books and journals at the intersection of science, technology, art, social science, and design.

Acquisitions Editors: Matthew Browne; Susan Buckley; Beth Clevenger; Katie Helke; Victoria Hindley; Justin Kehoe; Philip Laughlin; Marc Lowenthal; Gita Manaktala; Jermey Matthews; Robert Prior; Elizabeth Swayze; Emily Taber; Thomas Weaver

P360 The Monacelli Press
Publishing Imprint
Attn: Acquisitions, 65 Bleecker Street, 8th Floor, New York, New York 10012
United States

submissions@themonacellipress.com

https://www.phaidon.com/store/the-monacelli-press/

Book Publisher: Phaidon Press (**P415**)

Nonfiction > *Nonfiction Books*
   Architecture; Arts; Gardening; Interior Design; Photography

How to send: Post; Email

Will review book proposals in the fields of architecture and landscape architecture, fine and decorative arts, design, and photography.

P361 Monday Books
Book Publisher
Festival House, Jessop Avenue, Cheltenham, GL50 3SH
United Kingdom
Tel: +44 (0) 1242 633717

info@mondaybooks.com

http://www.mondaybooks.com

Nonfiction > *Nonfiction Books*

Closed to approaches.

Independent publisher of strongly written nonfiction covering a range of subjects.

P362 Mortimer Books
Publishing Imprint
United Kingdom

Book Publisher: Welbeck Publishing Group (**P580**)

P363 Mud Pie Books
Book Publisher
Oxford, OX2 6HY
United Kingdom
Tel: +44 (0) 7985 935320

info@mudpiebooks.com

https://mudpiebooks.com

Fiction > *Novels*: Buddhism

Nonfiction > *Nonfiction Books*: Buddhism

Poetry > *Poetry Collections*: Buddhism

Publishes books about Buddhism, and books for Buddhists.

P364 Mudfog Press
Book Publisher
C/o Arts and Events, Culture and Tourism, P.O Box 99A, Civic Centre, Middlesbrough, TS1 2QQ
United Kingdom

paulinepoethughes@gmail.com

https://www.mudfog.co.uk

Fiction > *Short Fiction Collections*

Poetry > *Poetry Collections*

Send: Writing sample; Synopsis
How to send: Post; Email

Publishes poetry and short fiction by writers in the Tees Valley area. Send query with 15-20 poems or 2-3 stories, or a sample of 10-15 pages for other genres, with synopsis.

P365 Multnomah
Publishing Imprint

Book Publisher: Random House

P366 Myriad Editions
Book Publisher
United Kingdom

submissions@myriadeditions.com

https://myriadeditions.com

Types: Fiction; Nonfiction
Subjects: Autobiography; Contemporary; Crime; History; Literary; Medicine; Politics; Thrillers
Markets: Adult

Closed to approaches.

Publishes literary fiction: contemporary and historical; crime fiction: psychological and political thrillers with strong female characters; graphic novels: documentary comics, graphic reportage, fiction, memoir and life writing, graphic medicine; and literary or political nonfiction: feminist, literary nonfiction, memoir. No young adult fiction, children's books, horror, science fiction, fantasy, plays or poetry, or books that have been previously published or self-published (in print or as ebooks) unless you are a graphic novelist. Do not send proposals – send complete manuscript by email. See website for full guidelines.

P367 Myrmidon Books Ltd
Book Publisher
Rotterdam House, 116 Quayside, Newcastle upon Tyne, NE1 3DY
United Kingdom
Tel: +44 (0) 1912 064005
Fax: +44 (0) 1912 064001

ed@myrmidonbooks.com

http://www.myrmidonbooks.com

Fiction > *Novels*
Commercial; Literary

Send: Query; Writing sample; Author bio
How to send: Post
How not to send: Email; Fax

Submit your initial three chapters and a one-page covering letter providing information about yourself and your work. A synopsis or structure plan may be useful for a non-fiction proposal, but a synopsis is not required for fiction submissions and will not be read.

P368 The Mysterious Press
Publishing Imprint
United States

Book Publisher: Grove Atlantic Inc. (**P230**)

P369 Naturegraph & Keven Brown Publications
Book Publisher
United States

naturegraph@gmail.com

http://www.naturegraph.com

Nonfiction in Translation > *Nonfiction Books*: Islamic Philosophy

Nonfiction > *Nonfiction Books*
California; Native Americans; Nature

Publishes mainly books on nature, Native American subjects, and translations of Islamic philosophy.

Editors: Barbara Brown; Keven Brown

P370 NBM Publishing
Book Publisher
160 Broadway, Suite 700 East Wing, New York, NY 10038
United States

tnantier@nbmpub.com

https://nbmpub.com
https://twitter.com/NBMPUB
https://www.facebook.com/NBMGraphicNovels
https://www.instagram.com/nbmgraphicnovels/
https://www.tiktok.com/@nbmgraphicnovels
https://www.youtube.com/@NBMGraphicNovels

Fiction > *Graphic Novels*
General, and in particular: Comedy / Humour; Erotic; Fantasy; Literary; Mystery; Science Fiction

Nonfiction > *Graphic Nonfiction*
General, and in particular: Autobiography; Biography; Crime; How To; Journalism

Send: Query; Synopsis; Self-Addressed Stamped Envelope (SASE)
How to send: Email; Post

We are interested in literary fiction, non-fiction and biographies. We are not interested in superheroes or any genre. We have no need for illustrations alone including covers. To submit please send a one-page synopsis of your story which will include any pertinent background and some character development. For the art, please send copies of a few finished pages or pencils for the project or at least of previous work in the same style you plan on using. Please do not at first send a complete finished story as that will only delay an answer greatly. To submit electronically: Send a low-resolution pdf of no more than 10 megs as attachment. You may submit a link to a website as an extra source but not by itself. If sending by mail and you want anything back, including an answer, please include a SASE.

Editor: Terry Nantier

P371 Nell James Publishers
Book Publisher
United Kingdom

info@nelljames.co.uk

https://nelljames.co.uk
https://twitter.com/NJamesPublisher

Nonfiction > *Nonfiction Books*
Contemporary; Social Issues

Send: Outline; Synopsis; Pitch; Market info; Author bio; Submission Form
How to send: Email

An independent publisher of nonfiction books, bringing awareness to issues in modern society. Download submission form from website and return by email.

Currently closed to fiction and poetry submissions.

P372 New American Press
Book Publisher
PO Box 1094, Grafton, WI 53024
United States

https://newamericanpress.com
https://www.facebook.com/New-American-Press-110522495698111/
https://www.instagram.com/newamericanpress/
https://twitter.com/newamerpress

Fiction in Translation > *Novels*: Literary

Fiction > *Novels*: Literary

Nonfiction in Translation > *Nonfiction Books*

Nonfiction > *Nonfiction Books*

Poetry in Translation > *Any Poetic Form*

Poetry > *Any Poetic Form*

Send: Query
Don't send: Full text
How to send: Online contact form

An independent nonprofit literary press that publishes fiction, poetry, nonfiction, and works in translation. Does not regularly accept unsolicited manuscripts, but queries are welcome.

P373 New Harbinger Publications

Book Publisher
5674 Shattuck Avenue, Oakland, CA 94609
United States

proposals@newharbinger.com

https://www.newharbinger.com
https://www.facebook.com/NewHarbinger
https://www.instagram.com/newharbinger/
https://twitter.com/NewHarbinger
https://www.linkedin.com/company/new-harbinger-publications/
https://www.youtube.com/newharbinger

ADULT > **Nonfiction** > *Nonfiction Books*
Health; Mental Health; Psychology; Self Help

PROFESSIONAL > **Nonfiction** > *Nonfiction Books*
Health; Mental Health; Psychology

Send: Query; Proposal; Market info; Author bio; Writing sample
How to send: Email

Publishes psychology and health self-help books that must be simple and easy to understand, but also complete and authoritative. Most authors for this publisher are therapists or other helping professionals. See website for extensive author guidelines.

P374 New Walk Editions

Book Publisher
c/o Nick Everett, School of English, Leicester University, University Road, Leicester, LE1 7RH
United Kingdom

newwalkmagazine@gmail.com

https://newwalkmagazine.com

Poetry > *Poetry Collections*

Send: Full text; Author bio
How to send: Word file email attachment; Post

A small press specialising in extremely high quality poetry pamphlets. Interested in poetic plurality: equally interested in established and new poets, and a broad church stylistically and thematically. Send 12-24 pages of poems by email or by post.

Editor: Nick Everett

P375 Nightfire

Publishing Imprint
United States

nightfiresubmissions@tor.com

https://us.macmillan.com/tomdohertyassociates/
https://nightfire.moksha.io/publication/nightfire/guidelines

Publishing Imprint: Tor Publishing Group **(P520)**

Fiction > *Novels*
Dark Fantasy; Horror; Supernatural / Paranormal

Closed to approaches.

Publishes fiction that unsettles and delights, exploring the full range of horror, dark fantasy, and the supernatural.

P376 Nine Arches Press

Book Publisher
Unit 14, Frank Whittle Business Centre, Great Central Way, Rugby, Warwickshire, CV21 3XH
United Kingdom
Tel: +44 (0) 1788 226005

mail@ninearchespress.com

https://ninearchespress.com
https://ninearchespress.submittable.com/submit
https://twitter.com/NineArchesPress

Poetry > *Poetry Collections*

Closed to approaches.

Publishes poetry collections. Accepts submissions during specific submission windows. See website for details.

Magazine: Under the Radar **(M423)**

P377 No Starch Press, Inc.

Book Publisher
245 8th Street, San Francisco, CA 94103, MAILING ADDRESS:, 329 Primrose Road, #42, Burlingame, CA 94010-4093
United States
Tel: +1 (415) 863-9900
Fax: +1 (415) 863-9950

editors@nostarch.com
support@nostarch.com

https://nostarch.com

ADULT > **Nonfiction** > *Nonfiction Books*
Arts; Computer Programming; Computer Science; Computers; Design

CHILDREN'S > **Nonfiction** > *Nonfiction Books*
Arts; Computer Programming; Computer Science; Computers; Design

Send: Query; Outline; Synopsis; Market info; Author bio
How to send: Email

Publishes unique books on computer programming, security, hacking, alternative operating systems, STEM, and LEGO.

P378 Northern Eye Books

Book Publisher
22 Crosland Terrace, Helsby, Frodsham, Cheshire, WA6 9LY
United Kingdom
Tel: +44 (0) 1829 770309

tony@northerneyebooks.com

https://www.northerneyebooks.co.uk
https://www.facebook.com/NorthernEyeBooks/
https://twitter.com/northerneyeboo
https://www.pinterest.co.uk/tony9709/

Nonfiction > *Nonfiction Books*: Walking Guides

Send: Query

Publishes walking books for the Lake District, Peak District, Yorkshire Dales, other UK National Parks, the Wales Coast Path, South West Coast Path, Wales and Cheshire. Most books are commissioned, but willing to consider ideas or a sample chapter.

Editor: Tony Bowerman

P379 Northern Illinois University Press

Publishing Imprint
Sage House, 512 East State Street, Ithaca, NY 14850
United States
Tel: +1 (607)253-2338

cupressinfo@cornell.edu

https://www.cornellpress.cornell.edu/imprints/northern-illinois-university-press/

Book Publisher: Cornell University Press

ACADEMIC > **Nonfiction** > *Nonfiction Books*
American Midwest; Christianity; Culture; European History; History; Philosophy; Politics; Religion; Russia; South-East Asia

ADULT > **Nonfiction** > *Nonfiction Books*
American Midwest; Christianity; Culture; European History; History; Philosophy; Politics; Religion; Russia; South-East Asia

Publishes scholarly and trade books in the humanities and social sciences for both specialists and general readers. The Press has long published major works in Russian and Eurasian studies and has additional series in Orthodox Christianity and Southeast Asian studies. Also publishes books on politics, philosophy, religion, European history, and American Midwest history and culture.

P380 NorthSouth Books

Book Publisher
600 Third Avenue, 2nd Floor, NY, NY 10016
United States
Tel: +1 (917) 699-2079

info@northsouth.com
submissionsnsb@gmail.com

https://northsouth.com

CHILDREN'S > Fiction
Board Books; Picture Books

Closed to approaches.

Publishes picture books for children up to 1,000 words. Seeks fresh, original fiction on universal themes that would appeal to children aged 3-8. Generally does not acquire rhyming texts, as must also be translated into German. Send submissions by email as Word document or pasted directly into the body of the email. Authors do not need to include illustrations, but if the author is also an illustrator sample sketches can be included in PDF or JPEG form.

P381 Nosy Crow
Book Publisher
The Crow's Nest, 14 Baden Place, Crosby Row, London, SE1 1YW
United Kingdom
Tel: +44 (0) 20 7089 7575

hello@nosycrow.com

https://nosycrow.com
https://www.facebook.com/NosyCrow
https://www.instagram.com/nosycrow/
https://twitter.com/nosycrow
https://www.youtube.com/user/NosyCrow

CHILDREN'S
   Fiction
      Board Books; Chapter Books; Middle Grade; Picture Books
   Nonfiction > *Nonfiction Books*

Closed to approaches.

Publishes child-focused, parent-friendly children's books for ages 0-12. No submissions from white people.

P382 Oghma Creative Media
Book Publisher
United States

submissions@oghmacreative.net

https://oghmacreative.com

ADULT
   Fiction > *Novels*
      Contemporary Romance; Contemporary; Crime; Diversity; Environment; Fantasy; High / Epic Fantasy; Historical Fiction; Historical Romance; Horror; LGBTQIA; Mainstream; Military; Mystery; Nautical; Police Procedural; Romance; Romantic Comedy; Romantic Thrillers; Science Fiction; Secret Intelligence; Space Opera; Supernatural / Paranormal; Thrillers; Traditional; Westerns

   Nonfiction > *Nonfiction Books*
      Biography; Entertainment; History; Military; Mind, Body, Spirit; Music; TV

CHILDREN'S > Fiction

Chapter Books; Middle Grade; Picture Books
NEW
ADULT > **Fiction** > *Novels*: Contemporary Romance

YOUNG ADULT > **Fiction** > *Novels*

Send: Query; Synopsis; Full text
How to send: Email; Through a literary agent

A traditional publisher reaching out to authors who don't want to take the self-publishing route. Provides a team of editors, designers, and marketers to help bring your work to its finished form. Aims to develop long-term relationships with authors and artists. Closed to submissions between November 1 and April 1.

Currently only accepting submissions from agents and authors who have already published with them.

P383 The Ohio State University Press
Book Publisher
United States
Tel: +1 (773) 702-7000

OSUPInfo@osu.edu

https://ohiostatepress.org

ACADEMIC > **Nonfiction** > *Nonfiction Books*
      19th Century; Central America; Classics / Ancient World; Comic Books; Communication; Creative Nonfiction; Culture; Disabilities; Ethnic Groups; Films; Gender; History; Language; Literature; Media; Medieval; Ohio; Politics; Sexuality; South America; United States

ADULT
   Fiction > *Novels*
   Poetry > *Poetry Collections*

Send: Query; Outline; Table of Contents; Writing sample; Market info; Author bio
How to send: Email attachment

Publishes mainly academic nonfiction, but also has imprints for regional books that are of interest to the citizens of the state of Ohio, primarily about their history, environment, and culture; and creative works, including the winners of the poetry and prose prizes.

Acquisitions Editor: Ana Maria Jimenez-Moreno

Acquisitions Editor / Managing Editor: Tara Cyphers

Associate Editor: Becca Bostock

Editorial Director: Kristen Elias Rowley

Publishing Director: Tony Sanfilippo

P384 Old Street Publishing Ltd
Book Publisher
Notaries House, Exeter, EX1 1AJ

United Kingdom
Tel: +44 (0) 20 8787 5812

info@oldstreetpublishing.co.uk

http://www.oldstreetpublishing.co.uk
https://twitter.com/oldstpublishing

Fiction > *Novels*

Nonfiction > *Nonfiction Books*

Send: Query; Outline
Don't send: Full text
How to send: Email

Independent British publisher of fiction and nonfiction.

P385 Oneworld Publications
Book Publisher
10 Bloomsbury Street, London, WC1B 3SR
United Kingdom
Tel: +44 (0) 20 7307 8900

submissions@oneworld-publications.com

https://oneworld-publications.com
https://www.facebook.com/oneworldpublications
https://twitter.com/OneworldNews
https://www.instagram.com/oneworldpublications/
https://www.youtube.com/user/oneworldpublications

ADULT
   Fiction in Translation > *Novels*

   Fiction > *Novels*
      General, and in particular: Crime; Thrillers

   Nonfiction
      Gift Books: General
      Nonfiction Books: Anthropology; Arts; Baha'i; Biography; Buddhism; Business; Christianity; Comedy / Humour; Current Affairs; Economics; Feminism; Gender; Health; Hinduism; History; Islam; Judaism; Literature; Memoir; Middle East; Nature; Philosophy; Politics; Popular Psychology; Popular Science; Psychology; Religion; Science; Self Help; Spirituality
CHILDREN'S > **Fiction** > *Novels*

Send: Query; Submission Form
How to send: Email

Not accepting fiction submissions as at May 2022. Hopes this will change in the near future, but has been hoping this since at least 2018. Check website for current status.

Nonfiction authors must be academics and/or experts in their field. Approaches for fiction must provide a clear and concise synopsis, outlining the novel's main themes. See website for full submission guidelines, and forms for fiction and nonfiction, which should be submitted by email.

P386 Ooligan Press
Book Publisher
PO Box 751, Portland, OR 97207

United States
Tel: +1 (503) 725 9748
Fax: +1 (503) 725-3561

https://www.ooliganpress.com
https://ooliganpress.submittable.com/submit
https://www.facebook.com/ooliganpress/
https://twitter.com/ooliganpress
https://www.instagram.com/ooliganpress
https://www.youtube.com/user/OoliganPress
https://sk.pinterest.com/ooliganpress/_saved/

ADULT
Fiction > *Novels*: Literary

Nonfiction > *Nonfiction Books*
General, and in particular: Memoir;
Publishing; Sustainable Living; Writing

YOUNG ADULT > **Fiction** > *Novels*

Does not want:

Nonfiction > *Nonfiction Books*
Religion; Self Help

Send: Query; Proposal
How to send: Submittable

A student-run trade press rooted in the Pacific
Northwest dedicated to cultivating the next
generation of publishing professionals.
Prioritizes literary equity and inclusion. Strives
to publish culturally relevant titles from local,
marginalized voices in order to make literature
accessible and redefine who has a place within
its pages.

P387 Orange Mosquito
Publishing Imprint
United Kingdom

Book Publisher: Welbeck Publishing Group
(P580)

P388 Orchard Books
Publishing Imprint
United Kingdom

Book Publisher: Hachette Children's Group
(P235)

P389 Orenda Books
Book Publisher
16 Carson Road, West Dulwich, London, SE21
8HU
United Kingdom

info@orendabooks.co.uk
submissions@orendabooks.co.uk

https://orendabooks.co.uk
https://twitter.com/orendabooks
https://www.facebook.com/orendabooks
https://www.instagram.com/orendabooks

Fiction in Translation > *Novels*

Fiction
Novels: Adventure; Comedy / Humour;
Crime; Ghost Stories; Historical Fiction;
Horror; Legal Thrillers; Literary; Mystery;

Political Thrillers; Psychological Thrillers;
Romance; Suspense; Thrillers
Short Fiction Collections: General

Closed to approaches.

Publishes literary fiction and upmarket genre
fiction (in particular, crime fiction) only. No
nonfiction, screenplays, children's books, or
young adult. Send one-page synopsis and full
ms (or three-chapter sample) by email.

P390 Orion Children's Books
Publishing Imprint

Book Publisher: Hachette Children's Group
(P235)

P391 Ouen Press
Book Publisher
United Kingdom

submissions@ouenpress.com

http://www.ouenpress.com
https://www.facebook.com/ouenpress
https://twitter.com/ouenp

Fiction > *Novels*: Contemporary

Nonfiction > *Nonfiction Books*
Biography; Travel

Send: Query; Outline; Author bio; Writing
sample
How to send: Email
How not to send: Post; Email attachment

Seeking to publish well written Contemporary
Fiction, Travel Literature, and Biography if
edgy! No genre, no children's books, no
poetry, no single short stories, no guide books,
no recipe books. Response only if interested. If
no response after 60 days, assume rejection.

P392 Our Sunday Visitor
Book Publisher
200 Noll Plaza, Huntington, IN 46750
United States
Tel: +1 (260) 356-8400

https://www.osv.com

Nonfiction > *Nonfiction Books*: Catholicism

Non-profit Catholic publisher particularly
interested in Apologetics and Catechetics,
reference and prayer, heritage and saints, the
family, and the parish.

P393 Out-Spoken Press
Book Publisher
United Kingdom

press@outspokenldn.com

https://www.outspokenldn.com
https://out-spoken.submittable.com/submit
https://www.facebook.com/outspokenldn
https://twitter.com/OutSpokenLDN
https://instagram.com/outspokenldn

Poetry > *Poetry Collections*

Send: Query; Author bio; Writing sample
How to send: Submittable

A London-based independent publisher of
poetry and critical writing with the aim of
providing a platform for compelling writing
from voices that were (and remain) underrepresented in mainstream publishing.
Publishes full-length poetry collections and
pamphlets.

P394 Pacific Press Publishing Association
Book Publisher
1350 North Kings Road, Nampa, ID 83687
United States
Tel: +1 (208) 465-2500
Fax: +1 (208) 465-2531

booksubmissions@pacificpress.com

https://www.pacificpress.com

ADULT > **Nonfiction** > *Nonfiction Books*
Bible Studies; Biography; Christian Living;
Christianity; Church History; Cookery;
Health; Parenting; Relationships

CHILDREN'S
Fiction
Chapter Books: Christianity
Middle Grade: Christianity
Picture Books: Christianity

Nonfiction
Chapter Books: Christianity
Middle Grade: Christianity
Picture Books: Christianity

Send: Query
How to send: Email
How not to send: Post

Seventh-day Adventist publisher publishing
mainly nonfiction, but some fiction especially
children's fiction. All titles are religious and
Christian and confirm to Seventh-day
Adventist beliefs. Send query by email only.

P395 Pale Fire Press
Book Publisher
United States
Tel: +1 (520) 282-1442

http://palefirepress.com

Fiction > *Novels*: Literary

Closed to approaches.

Closed to submissions as at January 2020.
Check website for current status.

P396 Palgrave Macmillan
Book Publisher
United Kingdom

https://www.palgrave.com

Book Publisher: Springer Nature

ACADEMIC > **Nonfiction**
Nonfiction Books: Business; Culture;
Economics; Environment; Films; Geography;

Health; History; International; Journalism; Language; Literature; Media; Neuroscience; Philosophy; Politics; Psychology; Sociology; TV; Theatre
Reference: Business; Philosophy
PROFESSIONAL > **Nonfiction** > *Nonfiction Books*
  Business; Management

Send: Query; Submission Form; Author bio; Writing sample
How to send: Online submission system

Submit via online submission system.

P397 Pan
Publishing Imprint
United Kingdom

Book Publisher: Pan Macmillan (**P398**)

P398 Pan Macmillan
Book Publisher
Cromwell Place, Hampshire International Business Park, Lime Tree Way, Basingstoke, Hampshire, RG24 8YJ
United Kingdom

webqueries@macmillan.co.uk
TorUKSubmissions@macmillan.com

https://www.panmacmillan.com
https://www.facebook.com/pages/Pan-Macmillan/246973468695197
https://twitter.com/panmacmillan
https://www.instagram.com/panmacmillan

ADULT
  Fiction > *Novels*
    Crime; Fantasy; Historical Fiction; Literary; Romance; Science Fiction; Thrillers

  Nonfiction > *Nonfiction Books*
    Biography; Crime; History; Nature; Politics; Science; Self Help; Wellbeing

  Poetry > *Any Poetic Form*

CHILDREN'S
  Fiction
    Board Books; Chapter Books; Middle Grade; Picture Books
  Poetry > *Any Poetic Form*

YOUNG ADULT > **Fiction** > *Novels*
  Dystopian Fiction; Fantasy; Friends; Romance; Science Fiction

How to send: Through a literary agent; Email

Accepts submissions for science fiction and fantasy direct from authors. Submissions in all other areas must come via a literary agent.

Book Publisher: Pan Macmillan Australia (**P399**)

Publishing Imprints: Bello; Bluebird; Boxtree (*P088*); Campbell; Campbell Books (*P103*); Kingfisher; Macmillan (*P332*); Macmillan Children's Books (**P333**); Macmillan Digital Audio (*P335*); Macmillan New Writing

(*P337*); Mantle; Pan (*P397*); Picador; Sidgwick & Jackson (*P478*); Tor; Two Hoots

P399 Pan Macmillan Australia
Book Publisher
Australia

pan.reception@macmillan.com.au

https://www.panmacmillan.com.au

Book Publisher: Pan Macmillan (**P398**)

ADULT
  Fiction > *Novels*
    Contemporary; Crime; Drama; Historical Fiction; Literary; Psychological Suspense; Saga; Thrillers

  Nonfiction > *Nonfiction Books*
    Contemporary; Crime; Health; History; Lifestyle; Memoir; Mind, Body, Spirit; Narrative Nonfiction

CHILDREN'S > **Fiction** > *Middle Grade*

YOUNG ADULT > **Fiction** > *Novels*

Send: Query; Author bio; Market info; Synopsis; Proposal; Writing sample
How to send: Online submission system

Accepts submissions via online submission system.

P400 Parthian Books
Book Publisher
The Old Surgery, Napier Street, Cardigan, SA43 1ED
United Kingdom
Tel: +44 (0) 7890 968246

info@parthianbooks.com

https://www.parthianbooks.com

Fiction
  Novels: Literary
  Short Fiction: Literary

Nonfiction > *Nonfiction Books*

Poetry > *Poetry Collections*

Closed to approaches.

Publisher of poetry, fiction, and creative nonfiction, of Welsh origin, in the English language. Also publishes English language translations of Welsh language work. Send query with SAE, and (for fiction) a one-page synopsis and first 30 pages, or (for poetry) a sample of 15-20 poems. No email submissions, genre fiction of any kind, or children's / teenage fiction. See website for full submission guidelines.

Author: Richard Owain Roberts

P401 Partisan Press
Book Publisher
PO 11417, Norfolk, VA 23517
United States

red-ink@earthlink.net

https://www.partisanpress.org
https://www.angelfire.com/va/bcr/ptsn.html

Poetry > *Poetry Collections*: Working Class

Not for profit publisher of working class poetry. Aims to create an awareness of and involvement in working class culture as well as to promote a progressive vision that will move our class and our society forward toward a more just and peaceful future.

Magazine: Blue Collar Review (**M075**)

P402 Pat-a-Cake
Publishing Imprint

Book Publisher: Hachette Children's Group (**P235**)

P403 Patrician Press
Book Publisher
Manningtree, Essex
United Kingdom

patricia@patricianpress.com

https://patricianpress.com
https://www.facebook.com/PatricianPress

Fiction
  Novels: General, and in particular: Italy
  Short Fiction Collections: General, and in particular: Italy; Politics
Nonfiction > *Essays*
  General, and in particular: Italy; Politics

Poetry > *Poetry Collections*
  General, and in particular: Italy; Politics

Closed to approaches.

Small and independent non-profit press, with the aim of encouraging and promoting writers of high quality fiction and poetry. Imprint publishes books for children. Contact by email only.

Publishing Imprint: Pudding Press

P404 Pavilion Books
Book Publisher
The News Building, 1 London Bridge St, London, SE1 9GF
United Kingdom
Tel: +44 (0) 20 8741 7070

https://www.pavilionbooks.com
https://www.instagram.com/pavilionbooks/
https://twitter.com/PavilionBooks
https://uk.pinterest.com/pavilionbook

Book Publisher: HarperCollins UK

ADULT > **Nonfiction** > *Illustrated Books*
  Arts; Comedy / Humour; Crafts; Design; Fashion; Food and Drink; Games; Gardening; History; Lifestyle; Popular Culture

CHILDREN'S
  Fiction
    Board Books; Early Readers; Picture Books

Nonfiction
Activity Books; *Colouring Books*

Closed to approaches.

A London-based publisher specialising in illustrated books for the UK and international markets. At the core of the business are specialist lists such as craft, cookery and children's.

Publishing Imprints: Batsford; Collins & Brown; National Trust; Pavilion; Pavilion Children's; Portico

P405 Peepal Tree Press
Book Publisher
17 King's Avenue, Leeds, LS6 1QS
United Kingdom
Tel: +44 (0) 113 245 1703

contact@peepaltreepress.com

https://www.peepaltreepress.com

Fiction > *Short Fiction Collections*
Black People; Caribbean Diaspora; Caribbean

Nonfiction > *Nonfiction Books*
Arts; Black People; Caribbean Diaspora; Caribbean; Cultural Criticism; Literary Criticism; Memoir

Poetry > *Poetry Collections*
Black People; Caribbean Diaspora; Caribbean

Publishes international Caribbean, Black British, and south Asian writing. Submit through online submission system.

P406 Pen & Ink Designs Publishing
Book Publisher; Self Publishing Service; Editorial Service
United Kingdom

https://www.penandinkdesigns.co.uk

ADULT
Fiction
Novels: Crime; Historical Fiction; Mystery
Short Fiction Collections: General

Nonfiction > *Nonfiction Books*: Self Help

Poetry > *Poetry Collections*

CHILDREN'S > **Fiction**
Chapter Books; *Colouring Books*; *Novels*; *Picture Books*; *Short Fiction Collections*
YOUNG ADULT > **Nonfiction** > *Nonfiction Books*: Self Help

Send: Query
How to send: Online contact form

Costs: Offers services that writers have to pay for.

The publisher has been operating since 2012 on a small basis originally by publishing a selection of children's picture books and other short story books. This was followed by the publication of an award winning historical novel and due to a physical move of the business to Wales the company began working with another small independent publisher. Due to the pandemic this publisher had to retire from the business leaving the business to continue under the ownership of the original proprietor. Since then the publisher has become a member of and been accepted as a small independent Welsh Publisher by the CCPW Group (backed by Literature Wales). They have published a small quantity of manuscripts both fiction and non-fiction and offer a variety of services aimed at assisting new and developing writers.

P407 Pen & Sword Books Ltd
Book Publisher
George House, Units 12 & 13, Beevor Street, Off Pontefract Road, Barnsley, South Yorkshire, S71 1HN
United Kingdom
Tel: +44 (0) 1226 734222
Fax: +44 (0) 1226 734438

editorialoffice@pen-and-sword.co.uk

https://www.pen-and-sword.co.uk

Nonfiction > *Nonfiction Books*
Local History; Maritime History; Military Aviation; Military History

Send: Query
Don't send: Full text

Publishes across a number of areas including military history, naval and maritime history, aviation, local history, family history, transport, discovery and exploration, collectables and antiques, nostalgia and true crime. In 2017, launched a new lifestyle imprint which publishes books on areas such as health and diet, hobbies and sport, gardening and wildlife and space. Submit proposal using form on website.

Editor: Lisa Hooson

Publishing Imprints: Frontline Books (**P208**); Leo Cooper; Pen & Sword Aviation; Pen & Sword Maritime; Remember When (**P442**); Wharncliffe Books (**P582**); White Owl

P408 Penguin Random House Verlagsgruppe
Book Publisher
Germany

https://www.penguinrandomhouse.de

Book Publisher: Penguin Random House

Book Publisher: Prestel Publishing Ltd (**P426**)

P409 Persephone Books
Book Publisher
8 Edgar Buildings, Bath, BA1 2EE
United Kingdom
Tel: +44 (0) 1225 425050

info@persephonebooks.co.uk

https://persephonebooks.co.uk
http://instagram.com/persephonebooks
https://twitter.com/PersephoneBooks

Fiction > *Novels*

Nonfiction > *Nonfiction Books*

Closed to approaches.

Publisher of neglected fiction and nonfiction by mid-twentieth century (mostly) women writers, all in elegant matching grey editions.

P410 Peter Lang
Book Publisher
John Eccles House, Science Park, Robert Robinson Avenue, Littlemore, OX4 4GP
United Kingdom

Publishing@peterlang.com
info@peterlang.com

https://www.peterlang.com
https://www.facebook.com/pages/Peter-Lang-Oxford/260315267419469
https://twitter.com/peterlangoxford
http://peterlangoxford.wordpress.com/

Book Publisher: Peter Lang Group (**P411**)

ACADEMIC > **Nonfiction** > *Nonfiction Books*
Arts; Communication; Culture; Economics; Education; English; France; Germany; History; Italy; Language; Legal; Management; Media; Philosophy; Politics; Religion; Romania; Science; Slavs; Society; Spain

Send: Query
How to send: Email

Select appropriate editor from website and query by email.

Editor: Na Li

Publishing Director: Lucy Melville

Senior Editors: Tony Mason; Dr Laurel Plapp

P411 Peter Lang Group
Book Publisher
Place de la Gare 12, 1003 Lausanne
Switzerland

https://www.peterlang.com

Book Publisher: Peter Lang (**P410**)

P412 Peter Lang Publishing
Book Publisher
80 Broad St, Fl 5, New York, NY 10004-4145
United States
Tel: +1 (844) 882-0928

editorial@peterlang.com

https://www.peterlang.com
https://www.facebook.com/PeterLangPublishingUSA
https://twitter.com/PeterLangUSA

https://www.instagram.com/
peterlangpublishing

ACADEMIC > **Nonfiction** > *Nonfiction Books*
Arts; Communication; Culture; Economics; Education; English; France; Germany; History; Italy; Language; Legal; Management; Media; Philosophy; Politics; Religion; Romania; Science; Slavs; Society; Spain

Send: Query
How to send: Online submission system

International academic publisher. Submit query via web form.

P413 **Peter Owen Publishers**
Book Publisher
Somerset House, Strand, London, WC2R 1LA
United Kingdom

books@pushkinpress.com

https://www.peterowen.com
https://twitter.com/PeterOwenPubs
https://www.facebook.com/peter.owen.publishers
https://www.instagram.com/peterowenpublishing

Book Publisher: Pushkin Press

Fiction > *Novels*
International; Literary

Nonfiction > *Nonfiction Books*

Does not want:

> **Nonfiction** > *Nonfiction Books*
> Memoir; Self Help; Spirituality; Sport

Closed to approaches.

Publishes general nonfiction and international literary fiction. No first novels, short stories, poetry, plays, sport, spirituality, self-help, or children's or genre fiction. Accepts query by email only, including cover letter, synopsis, and one or two sample chapters. No submissions by post. Prefers fiction to come from an agent or translator as appropriate.

Editorial Director: Antonia Owen

P414 **Peter Pauper Press**
Book Publisher
3 International Drive, Suite 310, Rye Brook, NY 10573-7501
United States
Tel: +1 (914) 681-0144
Fax: +1 (914) 681-0389

customerservice@peterpauper.com
orders@peterpauper.com

https://www.peterpauper.com
https://www.facebook.com/pages/Peter-Pauper-Press-Inc/137389080124
https://twitter.com/PeterPauperPres
https://pinterest.com/peterpauperpres/

ADULT > **Nonfiction** > *Gift Books*
CHILDREN'S > **Nonfiction** > *Activity Books*
Closed to approaches.

Described as a preeminent gift and stationery publisher.

P415 **Phaidon Press**
Book Publisher
United Kingdom

submissions@phaidon.com

https://www.phaidon.com
https://www.instagram.com/phaidonsnaps/
https://twitter.com/Phaidon
https://www.facebook.com/phaidoncom/
https://youtube.com/phaidonpress
https://linkedin.com/company/phaidon-press

ADULT > **Nonfiction** > *Nonfiction Books*
Architecture; Arts; Contemporary; Cookery; Cultural History; Culture; Design; Fashion; Films; Food; Interior Design; Music; Performing Arts; Photography; Travel
CHILDREN'S > **Nonfiction** > *Nonfiction Books*

Send: Outline; Author bio
How to send: Email

Publishes books in the areas of art, architecture, design, photography, film, fashion, contemporary culture, decorative arts, interior design, music, performing arts, cultural history, food, and cookery, travel, and books for children. No fiction or approaches by post. Send query by email only, with CV and short description of the project. Response only if interested.

Publishing Imprint: The Monacelli Press (**P360**)

P416 **Piatkus Books**
Publishing Imprint
50 Victoria Embankment, London, EC4Y 0DZ
United Kingdom
Tel: +44 (0) 20 3122 7000

info@littlebrown.co.uk

https://www.littlebrown.co.uk/imprint/piatkus/page/lbbg-imprint-piatkus/
https://business.facebook.com/piatkusfiction/?business_id=873802706096561
https://twitter.com/PiatkusBooks

Publishing Imprint: Little, Brown Book Group

Fiction > *Novels*
Fantasy; Historical Fiction; Popular; Romance; Supernatural / Paranormal; Suspense

Nonfiction > *Nonfiction Books*
Business; Health; Mind, Body, Spirit; Parenting; Personal Development; Popular Psychology; Self Help

How to send: Through a literary agent

No longer accepts unsolicited submissions. Accepts material through a literary agent only.

P417 **Picador**
Publishing Imprint
United States

Book Publisher: Macmillan Publishers (**P338**)

P418 **Piccadilly Press**
Publishing Imprint
United Kingdom
Tel: +44 (0) 20 3770 8888

hello@bonnierbooks.co.uk

https://www.bonnierbooks.co.uk/imprints/piccadilly-press/
https://www.instagram.com/piccadilly.press/
https://twitter.com/piccadillypress
https://www.facebook.com/piccadillypressbooks/

CHILDREN'S > **Fiction**
Chapter Books; *Early Readers*; *Middle Grade*

Publishes books primarily for readers aged 5 to 12 years old. Publishes fun, engaging, family-orientated stories in any genre that will capture the imagination of readers and listeners.

P419 **Pinata Books**
Publishing Imprint
Arte Publico Press, University of Houston, 4902 Gulf Fwy, Bldg 19, Rm100, Houston, TX 77204-2004
United States
Fax: +1 (713) 743-2847

submapp@uh.edu

https://artepublicopress.com/pinata-books/

Book Publisher: Arte Publico Press (**P037**)

CHILDREN'S > **Fiction** > *Novels*
Central America; Culture; South America
YOUNG ADULT > **Fiction** > *Novels*
Central America; Culture; South America

Send: Query; Synopsis; Writing sample
How to send: Online submission system

Publishes children's and young adult literature that authentically and realistically portrays themes, characters, and customs unique to US Hispanic culture. Submit via form on website.

P420 **Pineapple Press**
Publishing Imprint
64 South Main Street, Essex, CT 06426
United States

http://pineapplepress.com
https://www.facebook.com/PineapplePress/

Book Publisher: The Globe Pequot Press (**P219**)

ADULT
Fiction > *Novels*
Florida; Folklore, Myths, and Legends

Nonfiction
   Nonfiction Books: Animals; Arts; Florida;
   Gardening; History; Nature; Travel
   Reference: Florida
CHILDREN'S
   Fiction > *Novels*: Florida

   Nonfiction > *Nonfiction Books*: Florida

Send: Query; Outline; Table of Contents;
Writing sample; Author bio; Market info
How to send: Email; Post

Publishes quality books that educate and
entertain while making the real Florida
accessible to readers nationwide. Topics
include gardening, nature, art, folklore, history,
travel, and children's books and fiction that
feature the sunshine state.

P421 Platypus Media
Book Publisher
725 8th Street, SE, Washington DC 20003
United States
Tel: +1 (202) 546-1674

info@platypusmedia.com
submissions@platypusmedia.com

https://www.platypusmedia.com
https://www.facebook.com/PlatypusMedia/
https://twitter.com/PlatypusMedia

ADULT > **Nonfiction** > *Nonfiction Books*
   Family; Parenting

CHILDREN'S > **Nonfiction** > *Nonfiction
Books*
   Animals; Family

PROFESSIONAL > **Nonfiction** > *Nonfiction
Books*
   Education; Family

Send: Query; Author bio; Writing sample; Full
text; Market info; Self-Addressed Stamped
Envelope (SASE)
How to send: Post
How not to send: Email

Publishes books focusing on the family and
child development, including fiction and
nonfiction for children, and parenting guides
for adults. Send material with SASE for
response.

P422 Plexus Publishing, Inc.
Book Publisher
143 Old Marlton Pike, Medford, NJ 08055
United States
Tel: +1 (609) 654-6500, ext. 330
Fax: +1 (609) 654-6760

info@plexuspublishing.com
rcolding@plexuspublishing.com

https://www.plexuspublishing.com

ACADEMIC > **Nonfiction** > *Nonfiction
Books*
   Biology; Environment; Medicine

ADULT

Fiction > *Novels*: New Jersey

Nonfiction > *Nonfiction Books*
   Biology; Environment; History; Medicine;
   Nature; New Jersey; Travel

Send: Query; Synopsis; Table of Contents;
Market info; Marketing Plan; Author bio;
Writing sample; Proposal
How to send: Post

In addition to being a regional book publisher,
publishes practical, popular, and scholarly
titles in the fields of biology, ecology, and
clinical research. New Jersey regional book
program encompasses numerous topics and
genres including history, nature and the
environment, and travel/tourism. Publishes a
limited amount of fiction, including original
novels and new editions of worthy out-of-print
works with regional appeal.

P423 Pocket Mountains
Book Publisher
The Old Church, Annanside, Moffat, DG10
9HB
United Kingdom
Tel: +44 (0) 1683 221641

robbie@pocketmountains.com

https://pocketmountains.com
https://www.facebook.com/Pocket-Mountains-
Ltd-107054847745288/
https://twitter.com/pocketmountains
https://www.instagram.com/
pocketmountainsltd/

Nonfiction > *Nonfiction Books*
   Adventure; Cycling; Nature; Running;
   Walking Guides

Publishes accessible and inspiring pocket-sized
guidebooks for anyone who likes a bit of an
adventure, including cycling, easy walking,
wildlife and running guides to various parts of
Scotland, England and Wales.

Editors: Robbie Porteous; April Simmons

P424 Polygon
Publishing Imprint
West Newington House, 10 Newington Road,
Edinburgh, EH9 1QS
United Kingdom
Tel: +44 (0) 1316 684371

info@birlinn.co.uk

https://birlinn.co.uk/polygon/

Book Publisher: Birlinn Ltd (**P072**)

Fiction > *Novels*: Literary

Poetry > *Poetry Collections*

Send: Query; Synopsis; Writing sample
How to send: Email

Publishes literary fiction and poetry, both
classic and modern. Send query by email with
synopsis and sample material.

P425 Press 53
Book Publisher
560 N. Trade Street, Suite 103, Winston-
Salem, NC 27101
United States
Tel: +1 (336) 770-5353

editor@press53.com

https://www.press53.com

Fiction > *Short Fiction Collections*

Poetry > *Poetry Collections*

Publishes collections of poetry and short
stories by US-based authors. No novels or
book length fiction. Finds authors through its
competitions, and through writers being active
in the literary community and literary
magazines.

Editor: Kevin Morgan Watson

P426 Prestel Publishing Ltd
Book Publisher
16-18 Berners Street, London, W1T 3LN
United Kingdom
Tel: +44 (0) 20 7323 5004

sales@prestel-uk.co.uk

https://prestelpublishing.penguinrandomhouse.
de

Book Publisher: Penguin Random House
Verlagsgruppe (**P408**)

Nonfiction > *Nonfiction Books*
   Architecture; Arts; Design; Photography

Send: Proposal
How to send: Email

One of the world's leading publishers in the
fields of art, architecture, photography and
design. The company has its headquarters in
Munich, offices in New York and London, and
an international sales network.

P427 Prufrock Press
Publishing Imprint
United States

https://www.routledge.com/go/prufrock-press

Book Publisher: Routledge

ACADEMIC > **Nonfiction** > *Nonfiction
Books*
   Arts; Language; Mathematics; Science;
   Society

CHILDREN'S > **Nonfiction** > *Nonfiction
Books*

PROFESSIONAL > **Nonfiction** > *Nonfiction
Books*
   Arts; Education; Language; Mathematics;
   Science; Society

Publisher of professional learning resources,
gifted child identification instruments, and
curricula designed for gifted students,
advanced learners, and twice-exceptional
children. Comprehensive line of more than 500

titles across the areas of Language Arts, Math, Science, Social Studies, Children's Nonfiction, and more, Offers teachers and parents exciting, research-based resources for helping gifted, advanced, and special needs learners succeed.

Editor: Misha Kydd

P428 Puffin (UK)
Book Publisher
United Kingdom

https://www.penguin.co.uk/brands/puffin.html

Book Publisher: Penguin Random House Children's

CHILDREN'S
  Fiction
    Chapter Books; *Middle Grade*; *Novels*; *Picture Books*
  Nonfiction > *Nonfiction Books*

Publishing Imprint: Tamarind Books (**P507**)

P429 Purdue University Press
Book Publisher
504 Mitch Daniels Blvd., West Lafayette, IN 47907-2058
United States
Tel: +1 (765) 494-2038

pupress@purdue.edu

https://thepress.purdue.edu
https://www.facebook.com/purduepress
https://twitter.com/purduepress

ACADEMIC > **Nonfiction** > *Nonfiction Books*
  Agriculture; Animals; Central Europe; Culture; Dementia; Engineering; Environment; Genocide; History; Indiana; Jewish Holocaust; Literature; Politics; Public Health; Science; Technology

ADULT > **Nonfiction** > *Nonfiction Books*
  Agriculture; Animals; Central Europe; Culture; Dementia; Engineering; Environment; Genocide; History; Indiana; Jewish Holocaust; Literature; Politics; Public Health; Science; Technology

Send: Query; Author bio; Table of Contents; Proposal; Writing sample
How to send: Email

Dedicated to publishing works for academic and general readers. Welcomes proposals in its core subjects, which should be emailed to the Director.

Editorial Directors: Andrea Gapsch; Justin Race

Publishing Imprint: PuP

P430 The Quarto Group, Inc.
Book Publisher
1 Triptych Place 2nd Floor, 185 Park Street, London, SE1 9SH
United Kingdom
Tel: +44 (0) 20 7700 9000

https://www.quarto.com
https://www.instagram.com/quartobooksus
https://www.youtube.com/channel/UCg6_9Q3TbEXRPspas_bqPHw
https://www.pinterest.com/quartoknows
https://www.tiktok.com/@quartobooks

ADULT > **Nonfiction** > *Nonfiction Books*

CHILDREN'S > **Nonfiction** > *Nonfiction Books*

Publisher of illustrated nonfiction books for adults and children.

Publishing Imprints: Book Sales; Bright Press (**P092**); Burgess Lea Press; Cool Springs Press; Epic Ink; Fair Winds Press; Frances Lincoln Children's Books; Happy Yak (**P241**); Harvard Common Press; Iqon Editions; Ivy Kids; Ivy Press; Leaping Hare Press; Lincoln First Editions; Motorbooks; Quarry; Quarto Children's Books; Quarto Publishing; Race Point Publishing; Rock Point Gift & Stationery; Rockport Publishing; SmartLab Toys; Union Books; Voyageur Press; Walter Foster Jr.; Walter Foster Publishing; Wellfleet Press; White Lion Publishing; Wide-Eyed Editions (**P584**); Words & Pictures (**P593**); becker&mayer! books; becker&mayer! kids; small world creations

P431 Quercus Children's Books
Publishing Imprint

Book Publisher: Hachette Children's Group (**P235**)

P432 Quill Driver Books
Publishing Imprint
2006 South Mary Street, Fresno, CA 93721
United States
Tel: +1 (800) 345-4447
Fax: +1 (559) 233-6933

kent@lindenpub.com

https://quilldriverbooks.com

Book Publisher: Linden Publishing

Types: Nonfiction
Subjects: Architecture; Arts; Biography; Business; Comedy / Humour; Crime; Health; Hobbies; Lifestyle; Self Help; Spirituality; Technology; Travel
Markets: Adult

Closed to approaches.

Publishes nonfiction only. Send a book proposal including synopsis; commercial info; author platform; and sample chapters or supporting materials. See website for full guidelines.

Editor: Kent Sorsky

P433 Quiller Publishing Ltd
Book Publisher
The Hill, Merrywalks, Stroud, GL5 4EP

United Kingdom
Tel: +44 (0) 1939 261616

info@quillerbooks.com

https://www.quillerpublishing.com
https://www.facebook.com/QuillerPublishing
https://twitter.com/QuillerBooks
https://www.pinterest.co.uk/QuillerPublishing/
https://instagram.com/quillerpublishing/

Nonfiction > *Nonfiction Books*
  Archery; Arts; Biography; Canoeing; Climbing; Country Lifestyle; Crafts; Deer; Dogs; Environment; Equestrian; Falconry; Farming; Fishing; Food and Drink; History; Shooting

Send: Proposal; Synopsis; Writing sample; Table of Contents; Market info; Author bio; Self-Addressed Stamped Envelope (SASE)
How to send: Email; Post

Publishes books for all lovers of fishing, shooting, equestrian and country pursuits. Accepts unsolicited MSS from authors. Send submissions as hard copy only, with email address for reply or SAE if return of ms is required. Proposals may be sent by email.

Editor: Andrew Johnston

Publishing Imprints: The Sportsman's Press; Kenilworth Press; Quiller Press

P434 R D Publishers
Book Publisher
Robert D. Reed Publishers, POB 1992, Bandon, OR 97411,
United States
Tel: +1 (541) 347-9882
Fax: +1 (531) 347-9883

4bobreed@msn.com

https://rdrpublishers.com

Types: Fiction; Nonfiction; Scripts
Formats: Film Scripts; TV Scripts
Subjects: Arts; Comedy / Humour; Commercial; Drama; Entertainment; Fantasy; Lifestyle; Media; Psychology; Romance; Science; Science Fiction
Markets: Adult; Children's; Young Adult

Closed to approaches.

This company is looking for developing authors with a drive and the talent to submit ready manuscripts in for film, television, and print publication. They have a proven track record of success and are willing to work with the right author who has the right ideas for a saleable market.

Authors: Arun Gandhi; Daniel Quinn; Bernie Siegel

P435 Rand McNally
Book Publisher
United States
Tel: +1 (877) 446-4863

tndsupport@randmcnally.com

https://www.randmcnally.com
https://www.randmcnally.com/publishing

ADULT > Nonfiction
Activity Books: Travel
Reference: Road Atlases; Travel
CHILDREN'S > Nonfiction > *Activity*
Books: Travel

Publishes road atlases and activity books for adults and children, focusing on travel.

P436 **Random House Worlds**
Publishing Imprint

Book Publisher: Random House

P437 **Ransom Note Press**
Book Publisher
United States

editorial@ransomnotepress.com

http://www.ransomnotepress.com

Fiction > *Novels*
Mystery; Suspense

Send: Query; Synopsis; Author bio; Writing sample
Don't send: Full text
How to send: In the body of an email
How not to send: Email attachment; Post

Publishes mystery and suspense novels only. Accepts approaches via email only. See website for full submission guidelines.

P438 **Ravenstone**
Publishing Imprint
Canada

info@turnstonepress.com

https://www.turnstonepress.com/books/ravenstone.html
https://www.facebook.com/turnstone.press.3
https://twitter.com/turnstonepress
http://www.pinterest.com/turnstonepress/
https://www.instagram.com/turnstone_press/
https://www.youtube.com/user/TurnstonePress
http://www.goodreads.com/user/show/16275125-turnstone-press

Book Publisher: Turnstone Press

Fiction > *Novels*
Mystery; Noir; Thrillers

Send: Full text
How to send: Online submission system

Publishes literary mysteries, thrillers, noir, speculative fiction, and urban fantasy.

P439 **Red Feather**
Publishing Imprint
United States

proposals@schifferbooks.com

https://redfeathermbs.com
https://www.facebook.com/REDFeatherMindBodySpirit/

https://www.instagram.com/redfeather.mbs/
https://www.youtube.com/channel/UCbx_ahvb0yoOUgUKhYV5vng
https://twitter.com/RedFeatherMBS

Book Publisher: Schiffer Publishing (**P467**)

Nonfiction > *Nonfiction Books*
Astrology; Fortune Telling and Divination; Health; Lifestyle; Meditation; Mind, Body, Spirit; Numerology; Palmistry; Psychic Abilities; Spirituality

Send: Pitch; Author bio; Table of Contents; Writing sample
How to send: Email

Seeks to create groundbreaking sacred tools with a purpose that are made with pride, giving honor to the subject matter of each and every project.

P440 **Red Ferret Press**
Publishing Imprint
United States

thedude@weaselpress.com

https://www.weaselpress.com/red-ferret-press
https://www.facebook.com/redferretpress
https://twitter.com/redferretpress
http://www.instagram.com/systmaticwzl

Book Publisher: Weasel Press (**P575**)

Fiction
Chapbooks: Erotic
Novelette: Erotic
Novellas: Erotic
Novels: Erotic

Closed to approaches.

A publisher of erotic/adult fiction. Publishes sex and sex related topics: queer works, works from furries, pet players, kinksters, Hookup Stories. No Christian or religious erotica.

P441 **Red Squirrel Publishing**
Book Publisher
Suite 235, 15 Ingestre Place, London, W1F 0DU
United Kingdom

https://www.redsquirrelbooks.com

Nonfiction > *Nonfiction Books*
Culture; Society; United Kingdom

Publishes books aimed at helping people pass the British Citizenship test. No fiction, poetry, or children's.

Managing Director: Henry Dillon

P442 **Remember When**
Publishing Imprint
47 Church Street, Barnsley, South Yorkshire, S70 2AS
United Kingdom
Tel: +44 (0) 1226 734222
Fax: +44 (0) 1226 734438

editorialoffice@pen-and-sword.co.uk
enquiries@pen-and-sword.co.uk

https://www.pen-and-sword.co.uk
https://www.pen-and-sword.co.uk/Remember-When/i/6

Book Publisher: Pen & Sword Books Ltd (**P407**)

Nonfiction > *Nonfiction Books*
Antiques; History; Nostalgia

Send: Synopsis; Market info; Author bio
How to send: Online submission system

Publishes books on nostalgia and antique collecting. Submit proposals via online submission system. See website.

P443 **RFF Press**
Book Publisher
1616 P St. NW, Suite 600, Washington, DC 20036
United States
Tel: +1 (202) 328-5000
Fax: +1 (202) 939-3460

info@rff.org

https://www.rff.org

ACADEMIC > Nonfiction > *Nonfiction*
Books: Environment

ADULT > Nonfiction > *Nonfiction*
Books: Environment

PROFESSIONAL > Nonfiction > *Nonfiction*
Books: Environment

Publishes books about important issues in environmental and natural resource policy.

P444 **Richards Publishing**
Publishing Imprint
United Kingdom

Book Publisher: Brewin Books Ltd (**P091**)

P445 **Rising Stars**
Book Publisher
Carmelite House, 50 Victoria Embankment, London, EC4Y 0DZ
United Kingdom
Tel: +44 (0) 20 3122 6000

primary@hachette.co.uk

https://www.risingstars-uk.com
https://www.youtube.com/channel/UCTO7hZc1TrfzBKFEo4i8qkQ
https://twitter.com/risingstarsedu
https://www.facebook.com/Rising-Stars-547479242046479/timeline/
https://www.instagram.com/risingstarsedu

Book Publisher: Hodder Education

ACADEMIC > Nonfiction > *Nonfiction*
Books: Education

Send: Query
How to send: Online submission system

Publisher of educational books and software for children aged 3-18. Always looking for people bursting with ideas and imagination and a view of primary education. Complete survey online in first instance.

Publishing Director: Ben Barton

P446 Roc Lit 101
Publishing Imprint

Book Publisher: Random House

P447 Rocky Nook
Book Publisher
1010 B Street, Ste 350, San Rafael, CA 94901
United States

editorial@rockynook.com
info@rockynook.com

https://rockynook.com
https://www.facebook.com/rockynookinc/
https://rockynook.com/wp-content/uploads/2017/05/tw-rn.png
https://www.instagram.com/rocky_nook/

Nonfiction > *Nonfiction Books*
   Crafts; Drawing; Graphic Design; Painting; Photography

Send: Author bio; Query; Outline; Writing sample; Market info
How to send: Email

A small, independent publishing company with the goal of helping photographers of all levels improve their skills in capturing those moments that matter. Creates books that help you master the technology, find inspiration, and hone your craft in order to create better pictures. Also now publishing books on drawing, painting, graphic design, crafts, and much more.

P448 Rodale
Publishing Imprint

Book Publisher: Random House

P449 Rose and Crown Books
Publishing Imprint
United Kingdom

submissions@sunpenny.com

https://www.sunpenny.com/imprints

Book Publisher: Sunpenny Publishing (**P504**)

Fiction > *Novels*
   Christian Romance; Inspirational

Send: Author bio; Marketing Plan; Synopsis; Full text
How to send: Email
How not to send: Post

We were the first publishers in the UK to start publishing Christian / Inspirational Romance as a genre. Later, others followed, but we were proud to be the first.

P450 Round Hall
Publishing Imprint; Magazine Publisher
Spaces, Office 313, 77 Sir John Rogerson's Quay, Block C, Dublin 2, D02YK60
Ireland

https://www.sweetandmaxwell.co.uk/roundhall/

Book Publisher: Thomson Reuters

PROFESSIONAL > **Nonfiction**
   Articles: Legal
   Nonfiction Books: Legal

Send: Query
How to send: Email

Publishes information on Irish law in the form of books, journals, periodicals, looseleaf services, CD-ROMs and online services. Contact by email.

Company Director: Martin McCann

Editor: Pamela Moran

P451 Ruby Fiction
Publishing Imprint
Finsgate, 5-7 Cranwood Street, London, EC1 V 9EE
United Kingdom

info@rubyfiction.com
submissions@rubyfiction.com

https://www.rubyfiction.com
https://twitter.com/rubyfiction
https://www.facebook.com/pages/RubyFiction

Book Publisher: Choc Lit (**P121**)

Fiction > *Novels*
   Romance; Thrillers; Women's Fiction

Send: Author bio; Synopsis
How to send: Online submission system

Publishes thrillers, women's fiction and romances without the hero's point of view, between 60,000 and 100,000 words, suitable for a female adult audience.

P452 Rutgers University Press
Book Publisher
106 Somerset St., 3rd Floor, New Brunswick, NJ 08901
United States

https://www.rutgersuniversitypress.org
https://www.pinterest.com/rutgersuniv0180/
http://www.facebook.com/pages/Rutgers-University-Press/212072346925
https://www.instagram.com/RutgersUPress/
https://twitter.com/RutgersUPress
https://www.youtube.com/user/RutgersUPress

ACADEMIC > **Nonfiction**
   Nonfiction Books: General, and in particular: 18th Century; African American; Anthropology; Architecture; Arts; Asia; Asian American; Biography; Business; Caribbean; Comic Books; Crime; Culture; Environment; Ethnic Groups; Films; Food;

Gardening; Gender; Health; History; Judaism; LGBTQIA; Leadership; Legal; Leisure; Literature; Management; Media; Medicine; Memoir; Middle East; Military History; Music; Nature; New Jersey; New York City; New York State; Philosophy; Politics; Regional; Religion; Science; Social Issues; Sociology; South America; Sport; Travel; United States; Urban; Women's Studies
   Reference: General

Send: Outline; Table of Contents; Writing sample; Market info; Author bio
How to send: Post; Email

Publishes scholarly books, regional, social sciences and humanities. No original fiction or poetry. See website for full submission guidelines and individual editor contacts.

P453 RYA (Royal Yachting Association)
Book Publisher
RYA House, Ensign Way, Hamble, Southampton, Hampshire, SO31 4YA
United Kingdom
Tel: +44 (0) 23 8060 4100

https://www.rya.org.uk/
https://www.facebook.com/RoyalYachtingAssociation
https://twitter.com/rya
https://www.youtube.com/user/RYA1875
https://www.instagram.com/royalyachtingassociation/
https://www.linkedin.com/company/royal-yachting-association

Nonfiction > *Nonfiction Books*
   Boats; Sailing; Yachts

Publisher of books on boating and sailing.

Editor: Phil Williams-Ellis

P454 Ryland Peters & Small and CICO Books
Book Publisher
United Kingdom

enquiries@rps.co.uk

https://rylandpeters.com
https://www.facebook.com/RylandPetersandSmall
https://twitter.com/rylandpeters
https://www.pinterest.co.uk/rpscicobooks/
https://www.instagram.com/rylandpetersandsmall/
https://www.youtube.com/channel/UC-zcYDB1m8QxPJhWhRmytjA

ADULT > **Nonfiction** > *Illustrated Books*
   Comedy / Humour; Crafts; Food and Drink; Health; Interior Design; Mind, Body, Spirit; Popular Culture

CHILDREN'S > **Nonfiction** > *Illustrated Books*
   Crafts; Gardening; Science

Send: Query; Synopsis; Table of Contents; Author bio; Writing sample
How to send: Email

Independent, illustrated publisher creating books in the areas of interior design, food and drink, craft, mindfulness and spirituality, health, humour and pop culture. Also produces gifts and stationery, as well as books for kids.

P455 Safari Press
Book Publisher
15621 Chemical Lane, Huntington Beach, CA 92649
United States

info@safaripress.com

https://www.safaripress.com
https://www.facebook.com/SafariPress

Nonfiction > *Nonfiction Books*
   Firearms; Hunting

Publisher of big-game hunting, wingshooting, and sporting-firearms books.

P456 Safer Society Press
Book Publisher
PO Box 340, Brandon, VT 05733-0340
United States
Tel: +1 (802) 247-3132
Fax: +1 (802) 247-4233

davidprescott@safersociety.org

https://safersocietypress.org
http://twitter.com/@SaferSocietyFI
https://www.facebook.com/
safersocietyfoundation/timeline
https://www.pinterest.com/safersociety/

PROFESSIONAL > **Nonfiction** > *Nonfiction Books*
   Health; Mental Health; Psychiatry

Send: Query; Outline; Author bio; Market info
Don't send: Full text
How to send: Email

Publishes books and other resources for professionals who treat, educate, supervise, and provide social services to children and adolescents whose life circumstances place them at risk of poor social, emotional, and physical health, cognitive difficulties, and problematic behaviors throughout their lives.

P457 Sage Publications
Book Publisher; Magazine Publisher
1 Oliver's Yard, 55 City Road, London, EC1Y 1SP
United Kingdom
Tel: +44 (0) 20 7324 8500
Fax: +44 (0) 20 7324 8600

info@sagepub.co.uk

https://uk.sagepub.com

Types: Nonfiction
Subjects: Anthropology; Archaeology; Arts; Business; Crime; Finance; Health; History;

Media; Medicine; Politics; Psychology; Religion; Science; Sociology; Technology
Markets: Academic; Professional

Publishes academic books and journals. See website for guides for authors and making submissions, etc.

Book Publisher: CQ Press

Magazine: Feminist Review (**M160**)

P458 Saguaro Books, LLC
Book Publisher
16201 E. Keymar Drive, Fountain Hills, AZ 85268
United States
Tel: +1 (480) 372-1362
Fax: +1 (480) 284-4855

mjnickum@saguarobooks.com

https://www.saguarobooks.com

CHILDREN'S > **Fiction** > *Middle Grade*

YOUNG ADULT > **Fiction** > *Novels*

Send: Query
How to send: Email

Publishes books for children and young adults aged 10-18, by first-time authors over the age of 18. Send query by email describing your submission in first instance. Exclusive submissions only. No fan fiction or submissions from literary agents.

Editor: Mary Nickum

P459 Salt Publishing
Book Publisher
12 Norwich Road, CROMER, Norfolk, NR27 0AX
United Kingdom

submissions@saltpublishing.com

https://www.saltpublishing.com
https://twitter.com/saltpublishing
https://www.facebook.com/SaltPublishing
https://instagram.com/saltpublishing/

Fiction
   Novels: Contemporary
   Short Fiction Collections: General

Poetry > *Poetry Collections*

Closed to approaches.

Publishes contemporary novels and collections of poetry and short stories, by British and Irish authors. Prefers to work with writers living in the British Isles. See website for full guidelines.

P460 Saqi Books
Book Publisher
Gable House, 18-24 Turnham Green Terrace, London, W4 1QP
United Kingdom
Tel: +44 (0) 20 7221 9347

submissions@saqibooks.com

https://saqibooks.com
http://www.twitter.com/SaqiBooks
https://www.facebook.com/SaqiBooks/
https://www.youtube.com/channel/
UCqvwvEp1N5rHauJEmmXq16g
http://instagram.com/saqibooks

ACADEMIC > **Nonfiction** > *Nonfiction Books*
   Middle East; North Africa

ADULT > **Nonfiction** > *Nonfiction Books*
   Middle East; North Africa

Send: Query; Synopsis; Table of Contents; Writing sample; Author bio; Market info
How to send: Email

Publisher of books related to the Arab world and the Middle East. See website for full submission guidelines.

Publishing Imprint: Telegram Books

P461 SAS Press
Book Publisher
SAS Campus Drive, Cary, NC 27513-2414
United States
Tel: +1 (919) 677-8000
Fax: +1 (919) 677-4444

https://support.sas.com/en/books/publish.html

ACADEMIC > **Nonfiction** > *Nonfiction Books*
   Data and Information Systems; Leadership; Software

ADULT > **Nonfiction** > *Nonfiction Books*
   Data and Information Systems; Leadership; Software

PROFESSIONAL > **Nonfiction** > *Nonfiction Books*
   Data and Information Systems; Leadership; Software

How to send: Online submission system

Publishes books on the use of and programming for the software of the parent company only, and its application in solving real-world, business, and academic challenges.

Editor-in-Chief: Julie M. Platt

P462 Sasquatch Books
Book Publisher
1904 Third Avenue, Suite 710, Seattle, Washington 98101
United States

editorialdepartment@sasquatchbooks.com

https://sasquatchbooks.com
https://www.facebook.com/
SasquatchBooksSeattle/
https://twitter.com/sasquatchbooks
https://www.instagram.com/sasquatchbooks/

Nonfiction > *Nonfiction Books*
   Arts; Business; Family; Food; Gardening; Literature; Nature; Politics; Wine

Send: Query; Proposal; Full text
How to send: Email

Publishes books by the most gifted writers, artists, chefs, naturalists, and thought leaders in the Pacific Northwest and on the West Coast, and brings their talents to a national audience. Welcomes agented and unagented submissions from both debut and experienced writers.

Publishing Imprints: Little Bigfoot (**P315**); Spruce Books (*P489*)

P463 Schiffer Craft
Publishing Imprint
4880 Lower Valley Road, Atglen, PA 19310
United States
Tel: +1 (610) 593-1777
Fax: +1 (610) 593-2002

proposals@schifferbooks.com

https://www.schiffercraft.com
https://www.facebook.com/schiffercraft/
https://www.instagram.com/schiffercraft/

Book Publisher: Schiffer Publishing (**P467**)

Nonfiction > *Nonfiction Books:* Crafts

Send: Outline; Pitch; Author bio; Table of Contents; Writing sample; Market info
How to send: Email

Publishes to help energize maker and craft communities worldwide. Dedicated to publishing high quality books and kits that inspire, instruct, and educate. Aims to enrich lives through craft.

P464 Schiffer Fashion Press
Publishing Imprint
United States

https://schifferbooks.com/pages/schiffer-imprints

Book Publisher: Schiffer Publishing (**P467**)

Nonfiction > *Nonfiction Books:* Fashion

An imprint of fashion-related books that provides inspiration, historical reference, and instruction to all areas of the fashion community.

P465 Schiffer Kids
Publishing Imprint
4880 Lower Valley Road, Atglen, PA 19310
United States
Tel: +1 (610) 593-1777
Fax: +1 (610) 593-2002

proposals@schifferbooks.com

https://www.schiffer-kids.com
https://www.facebook.com/schifferkids/
https://twitter.com/schifferkids
https://www.instagram.com/schifferkids/

Book Publisher: Schiffer Publishing (**P467**)

CHILDREN'S

Fiction
Activity Books; Board Books; Early Readers; Graphic Novels; Middle Grade; Picture Books
Nonfiction
Activity Books; Board Books; Early Readers; Middle Grade; Picture Books

Send: Query; Outline; Pitch; Author bio; Table of Contents; Writing sample; Market info
How to send: Email

Our mission is to build the knowledge base for SEED and STEAM learning through content that promotes critical thinking, opens up conversations, and ultimately inspires young minds. Our award-winning titles explore concepts such as managing emotions, forming positive relationships, and making informed behavioral decisions. As a platform for the leading voices in social and emotional education, we support the SEED learning process by elevating their voices.

P466 Schiffer Military
Publishing Imprint
United States

proposals@schifferbooks.com

https://www.schiffermilitary.com
https://schifferbooks.com/pages/schiffer-imprints

Book Publisher: Schiffer Publishing (**P467**)

Nonfiction > *Nonfiction Books*
Aviation; History; Military

Send: Query; Outline; Pitch; Author bio; Table of Contents; Writing sample; Market info
How to send: Email

Dedicated to publishing definitive books on military and aviation history by the world's leading historians.

P467 Schiffer Publishing
Book Publisher
4880 Lower Valley Road, Atglen, PA 19310
United States
Tel: +1 (610) 593-1777
Fax: +1 (610) 593-2002

proposals@schifferbooks.com

https://schifferbooks.com
https://www.facebook.com/schifferpublishing
https://twitter.com/Schifferbooks
https://www.instagram.com/SchifferPublishing/
https://www.youtube.com/user/SchifferPublishing1
https://schifferpublishing.tumblr.com/
https://pinterest.com/schifferbooks/

Nonfiction > *Nonfiction Books*
Antiques; Architecture; Arts; Fashion; Health; Lifestyle; Popular Culture; Regional; Transport

Send: Query; Outline; Pitch; Author bio; Table of Contents; Writing sample; Market info
How to send: Email

Focused on creating publications that inspire, educate, and inform inquisitive readers seeking trusted content to enrich their lives and passions.

Publishing Imprints: Whitford Press (**P001**); Cornell Maritime Press (**P143**); Geared Up Publications (**P210**); LW Books (**P329**); Red Feather (**P439**); Schiffer Craft (**P463**); Schiffer Fashion Press (**P464**); Schiffer Kids (**P465**); Schiffer Military (**P466**); Tidewater Publishers (**P514**)

P468 Scholastic UK
Book Publisher
Euston House, 1 London Bridge, London, SE1 9BG, WITNEY:, Unit 18F, Thorney Leys Park, Witney, OXON, OX28 4GE, SOUTHAM:, Westfield Road, Southam, Warwickshire, CV47 0RA
United Kingdom
Tel: +44 (0) 1993 893453

enquiries@scholastic.co.uk

https://www.scholastic.co.uk
https://www.facebook.com/ScholasticUK
https://twitter.com/scholasticuk
https://instagram.com/scholastic_uk
https://www.pinterest.co.uk/scholasticuk
https://www.youtube.com/user/scholasticfilmsuk

Book Publisher: Scholastic

CHILDREN'S
Fiction
Board Books; Chapter Books; Early Readers; Middle Grade; Novels; Picture Books
Nonfiction
Board Books; Chapter Books; Early Readers; Middle Grade; Nonfiction Books; Picture Books

Publisher of fiction and nonfiction for children, as well as educational material for primary schools.

Book Publisher: Scholastic Children's Books

P469 SCM Press
Publishing Imprint
United Kingdom

https://scmpress.hymnsam.co.uk

Book Publisher: Hymns Ancient & Modern Ltd

Nonfiction > *Nonfiction Books:* Christianity

Publishes books which engage academic theology with the wider church and with society. We release around 40 new books a year across biblical studies, practical theology, ecclesiology and ethics.

P470 Seal Press

Publishing Imprint
1290 Avenue of the Americas, New York, NY
10104
United States

Seal.Press@hbgusa.com

https://www.sealpress.com
https://www.facebook.com/sealpress
https://twitter.com/sealpress
https://www.instagram.com/sealpress/

Publishing Imprint: Da Capo Press

Nonfiction > *Nonfiction Books*: Feminism

Founded in 1976 and stands as one of the most
enduring feminist publishing houses to emerge
from the women's press movement of the
1970s. Publishes radical and groundbreaking
books that inspire and challenge readers, that
humanize urgent issues, that build much-
needed bridges in divisive times, and help us
see the world in a new light.

P471 Seaworthy Publications

Book Publisher
6300 N Wickham Road, Unit #130-416,
Melbourne, FL 32940
United States
Tel: +1 (321) 610-3634

queries@seaworthy.com

http://www.seaworthy.com

Nonfiction > *Articles*
   Boats; Sailing

Send: Full text

Nautical book publisher specialising in
recreational boating. Send query by email
outlining your work and attaching sample table
of contents and two or three sample chapters.
See website for full submission guidelines.

P472 Sentient Publications

Book Publisher
PO Box 1851, Boulder, CO 80306
United States
Tel: +1 (303) 443-2188

submissions@sentientpublications.com

https://www.sentientpublications.com

Fiction > *Novels*: Literary

Nonfiction > *Nonfiction Books*
   Education; Holistic Health; Spirituality

Send: Query; Author bio; Synopsis; Full text;
Writing sample
How to send: Email

We have typically published titles with content
related to the areas of holistic health,
alternative education, and spirituality. While
our primary focus is non-fiction in those
genres, we're open to evaluating very well-
written literary fiction and other work which
may cross over into new territory for us.

P473 September Publishing

Book Publisher
United Kingdom
Tel: +44 (0) 20 3637 0116

info@septemberpublishing.org
submissions@septemberpublishing.org

https://www.septemberpublishing.org

Nonfiction > *Nonfiction Books*
   Adventure; Arts; Creativity; Current Affairs;
   Folklore, Myths, and Legends; Memoir;
   Nature; Personal Development; Photography;
   Politics; Trains; Travel

Send: Synopsis; Writing sample
How to send: Email

Currently accepting nonfiction submissions for
a general, adult readership. Send a synopsis
and three sample chapters by email.

P474 Seren Books

Book Publisher
Suite 6, 4 Derwen Road, Bridgend, CF31 1LH
United Kingdom
Tel: +44 (0) 1656 663018

seren@serenbooks.com
poetrysubmissions@serenbooks.com
mickfelton@serenbooks.com

https://www.serenbooks.com
https://www.facebook.com/SerenBooks
http://www.twitter.com/SerenBooks
http://www.pinterest.com/SerenBooks

Fiction
   Novels: Literary
   Short Fiction: Literary

Nonfiction > *Nonfiction Books*
   Arts; Biography; Current Affairs; Drama;
   History; Literary Criticism; Memoir; Music;
   Photography; Sport; Travel

Poetry > *Poetry Collections*

Send: Query; Full text; Proposal; Author bio;
Synopsis; Outline; Market info
How to send: Email; Post

Publishes fiction, nonfiction, and poetry.
Specialises in English-language writing from
Wales and aims to bring Welsh culture, art,
literature, and politics to a wider audience.
Accepts nonfiction submissions by post or by
email. Prefers poetry submissions by email, but
will accept hard copies. Accepts fiction only
from authors with whom there is an existing
publishing relationship.

Poetry Editor: Amy Wack

Publisher: Mick Felton

P475 Severn House Publishers

Book Publisher
Eardley House, 4 Uxbridge Street, London,
W8 7SY
United Kingdom
Tel: +44 (0) 20 7467 0840

info@severnhouse.com

https://severnhouse.com
https://www.facebook.com/severnhouse/
https://twitter.com/severnhouse
https://www.instagram.com/
severnhouseimprint/

Fiction > *Novels*
   Cozy Mysteries; Historical Fiction; Horror;
   Police Procedural; Romance; Science
   Fiction; Thrillers

Dedicated to publishing unputdownable genre
fiction: from gritty procedurals to cosy
mysteries and tense thrillers, as well as sci-fi,
horror, romance, historical fiction, and more.

P476 Shambhala Publications

Book Publisher
2129 13th Street, Boulder, CO 80302
United States

submissions@shambhala.com
editors@shambhala.com

https://www.shambhala.com
http://www.facebook.com/
ShambhalaPublications
http://www.instagram.com/
shambhala_publications/

Fiction > *Novels*: Adventure

Nonfiction > *Nonfiction Books*
   Activities; Arts; Buddhism; Christianity;
   Crafts; Creativity; Hinduism; Judaism;
   Martial Arts; Meditation; Memoir; Parenting;
   Philosophy; Psychology; Religion; Sufism;
   Taoism; Theravada Buddhism; Yoga; Zen

Poetry > *Poetry Collections*
   Classics / Ancient World; Contemporary;
   Inspirational; Spirituality

Send: Proposal
How to send: Email
How not to send: Post

Specialises in books that present creative and
conscious ways of transforming individuals,
society, and the planet. Focuses mainly on
religion and philosophy, but covers a wide
range of subjects including sciences, arts,
Buddhism, Christianity, literature, poetry,
psychology, etc. See website for full range of
books published.

P477 Shipwreckt Books Publishing Company

Book Publisher
153 Franklin Street, Winona, MN 55987
United States

contact@shipwrecktbooks.com

https://shipwrecktbooks.press
https://shipwrecktbooks.submittable.com/
submit
https://www.facebook.com/SWBPC/
https://twitter.com/shipwrecktbook/

Fiction

Novels; *Short Fiction Collections*
Nonfiction
Essays: General
Nonfiction Books: General, and in
particular: Biography; Family; Memoir
Poetry > *Poetry Collections*

Closed to approaches.

Publishes books and literary magazine. Submit
query letter, brief bio, synopsis, and/or writing
sample via online submission system.

Print Magazine: Lost Lake Folk Opera
Magazine (**M260**)

Publishing Imprints: Lost Lake Folk Art;
Rocket Science Press; Up On Big Rock Poetry

P478 Sidgwick & Jackson
Publishing Imprint
United Kingdom

Book Publisher: Pan Macmillan (**P398**)

P479 Simon & Schuster Children's Publishing
Book Publisher
United States

https://www.simonandschuster.com/kids
https://www.facebook.com/simonandschuster
https://twitter.com/SimonSchuster
https://www.youtube.com/user/
SimonSchusterVideos
https://instagram.com/simonandschuster

Book Publisher: Simon & Schuster

CHILDREN'S
Fiction
Board Books; *Chapter Books*; *Early
Readers*; *Middle Grade*; *Picture Books*
Nonfiction
Board Books; *Middle Grade*; *Picture Books*
YOUNG ADULT > **Fiction** > *Novels*

Closed to approaches.

Does not review, retain or return unsolicited
materials or artwork.

Publishing Imprints: Aladdin; Atheneum;
Beach Lane Books; Denene Millner Books
(**P159**); Little Simon; Margaret K. McElderry
Books (**P341**); Paula Wiseman Books; Saga
Press; Salaam Reads; Simon & Schuster Books
for Young Readers; Simon Spotlight

P480 Simon Element
Publishing Imprint
United States

https://www.simonelement.com

Book Publisher: Simon & Schuster Adult
Publishing

Nonfiction > *Nonfiction Books*
Business; Cookery; Design; Diet; Domestic;
Drinks; Fitness; Food; Health; How To;
Inspirational; Lifestyle; Memoir; Narrative
Nonfiction; Parenting; Personal

Development; Popular Culture;
Relationships; Science; Self Help;
Spirituality; Wellbeing; Wine

Publishes books addressing topics that are
foundational to how we live—from the meals
we eat to the relationships we nurture, the
households we manage, and the personal and
professional goals we set and strive to achieve.

P481 Singing Dragon
Publishing Imprint
Carmelite House, 50 Victoria Embankment,
London, EC4Y 0DZ
United Kingdom
Tel: +44 (0) 20 3122 6000

hello@singingdragon.com
proposals@singingdragon.com

https://uk.singingdragon.com
https://jkp.submittable.com/submit
https://twitter.com/Singing_Dragon_
https://www.facebook.com/SingingDragon
http://instagram.com/singingdragonbooks

Publishing Imprint: Jessica Kingsley
Publishers (**P292**)

ADULT > **Nonfiction**
Graphic Nonfiction: Alternative Health;
Health; Wellbeing
Nonfiction Books: Alternative Health;
Aromatherapy; Ayurveda; Childbirth;
Chinese Medicine; Fertility; Health; Herbal
Remedies; Lifestyle; Martial Arts; Nutrition;
Pregnancy; Qigong; Tai Chi; Taoism;
Wellbeing; Yoga
CHILDREN'S > **Nonfiction** > *Nonfiction
Books*
Depression; Mental Health; Wellbeing

PROFESSIONAL > **Nonfiction** > *Nonfiction
Books*
Career Development; Health; Medicine

Send: Proposal
How to send: Submittable

Publishes authoritative books on
complementary and alternative health, Tai Chi,
Qigong and ancient wisdom traditions for
health, wellbeing, and professional and
personal development. Our books are for
professionals and general readers. We also
publish graphic novels across our subject areas,
and books for children on issues such as
bereavement, depression and anger.

P482 Sinister Stoat Press
Publishing Imprint
United States

https://www.weaselpress.com/
sinisterstoatpress
https://www.facebook.com/sinisterstoat
https://twitter.com/sinisterstoat

Book Publisher: Weasel Press (**P575**)

Fiction

Chapbooks: Dark Fantasy; Furries; Ghost
Stories; Horror; LGBTQIA; Psychological
Horror; Science Fiction; Sex; Supernatural /
Paranormal Horror; Vampires; Werewolves
Novellas: Dark Fantasy; Furries; Ghost
Stories; Horror; LGBTQIA; Psychological
Horror; Science Fiction; Sex; Supernatural /
Paranormal Horror; Vampires; Werewolves
Novels: Dark Fantasy; Furries; Ghost Stories;
Horror; LGBTQIA; Psychological Horror;
Science Fiction; Sex; Supernatural /
Paranormal Horror; Vampires; Werewolves
Short Fiction Collections: Dark Fantasy;
Furries; Ghost Stories; Horror; LGBTQIA;
Psychological Horror; Science Fiction; Sex;
Supernatural / Paranormal Horror; Vampires;
Werewolves

Closed to approaches.

Horror publisher publishing Furry works,
Queer Horror, Extreme Horror, Splatter Punk,
Slashers, Paranormal Horror, Weird Horror,
Vampires, Werewolves, Monsters, Cryptids
(within reason), Sci-Fi horror, and Dark
Fantasy. Only accepting work from Authors of
Color, Authors who Identify as LGBTQ+,
Authors with Disabilities, and Current and
Former Sex Workers.

P483 Slope Editions
Book Publisher
United States

https://www.slopeeditions.org
https://twitter.com/SlopeEditions
http://slopeeditions.tumblr.com/
http://instagram.com/slopeeditions
https://www.facebook.com/slopeeditions

Poetry
Chapbooks; *Poetry Collections*

Aims to present readers with a fine and eclectic
array of poetry being written in English today.
Releases each year one to two well-chosen and
stylistically diverse softcover, perfect-bound
books and chapbooks that defy convention and
categorization.

Editor-in-Chief: Ethan Paquin

P484 Society for Promoting Christian Knowledge (SPCK)
Book Publisher
The Record Hall, 16-16A Baldwins Gardens,
London
United Kingdom

contact@spck.org.uk

https://spckpublishing.co.uk
https://www.facebook.com/pages/SPCK-
Publishing/205059496214486
https://www.instagram.com/spck_publishing/
https://twitter.com/SPCKPublishing

ADULT
Fiction > *Novels*: Christianity

Nonfiction > *Nonfiction Books*

Arts; Bible Studies; Biography; Christian Living; Christianity; Culture; Family; Health; History; Meditation; Personal Development; Relationships; Society; Spirituality

CHILDREN'S > Fiction > *Picture Books*: Christianity

Send: Query; Table of Contents; Outline; Market info
How to send: Online submission system

A recognised market-leader in the areas of Theology and Christian Spirituality. Nearly all books are commissioned so rarely accepts unsolicited projects for publication.

P485 Society of Genealogists
Book Publisher
Unit 2, 40 Wharf Road, London, N1 7GS
United Kingdom
Tel: +44 (0) 20 7251 8799

membership@sog.org.uk

https://www.sog.org.uk
https://facebook.com/societyofgenealogists
https://twitter.com/soggenealogist
https://www.pinterest.co.uk/societyofgeneal/

Nonfiction > *Nonfiction Books*
Genealogy; History

Publishes a wide variety of family history and genealogy publications.

P486 Somerset Books
Book Publisher
United Kingdom

https://www.somersetbooks.com

Nonfiction > *Nonfiction Books*: Travel

Publishing Imprint: Blue Guides (**P081**)

P487 Somerville Press
Book Publisher
Dromore, Bantry, Co. Cork
Ireland
Tel: 353 (0) 28 32873

somervillepress@gmail.com

http://www.somervillepress.com
https://somervillepress.company.site

Fiction > *Novels*

Nonfiction > *Nonfiction Books*

Publishes fiction and nonfiction, mainly of Irish interest.

P488 Sourcebooks
Book Publisher
1935 Brookdale Rd, Suite 139, Naperville, IL 60563
United States
Tel: +1 (800) 432-7444
Fax: +1 (630) 961-2168

info@sourcebooks.com
editorialsubmissions@sourcebooks.com

https://www.sourcebooks.com
https://linkedin.com/company/50434/
https://twitter.com/sourcebooks
https://facebook.com/sourcebooks
https://www.pinterest.com/sbjabberwockykids/
https://www.instagram.com/sourcebooks/
https://www.sourcebooks.com/contact-us.html

ADULT
Fiction > *Novels*
General, and in particular: Mystery; Romance

Nonfiction
Gift Books: General
Nonfiction Books: General, and in particular: Beauty; Biography; Business; Education; Entertainment; Health; History; Memoir; Parenting; Psychology; Relationships; Self Help; Women's Issues
Reference: General, and in particular: Education

CHILDREN'S > Nonfiction > *Nonfiction Books*

YOUNG ADULT > Fiction > *Novels*

Send: Query; Synopsis; Author bio; Table of Contents; Writing sample; Market info
Don't send: Full text
How to send: Email
How not to send: Post

We are interested in books that will establish a unique standard in their subject area. We look for books with a well-defined, strong target market. Our list includes most nonfiction categories, including memoir, history, college reference and study aids, entertainment, general self-help/psychology, business, parenting and special needs parenting, health and beauty, reference, education, biography, love and relationships, gift books and women's issues.

Publishing Imprints: Sourcebooks Casablanca; Sourcebooks Hysteria; Sourcebooks Landmark; Sourcebooks MediaFusion; Sphinx Publishing

P489 Spruce Books
Publishing Imprint
United States

Book Publisher: Sasquatch Books (**P462**)

P490 St Martin's Press
Publishing Imprint
United States

Book Publisher: Macmillan Publishers (**P338**)

P491 St. Martin's Essentials
Publishing Imprint
United States

Book Publisher: Macmillan Publishers (**P338**)

P492 St. Martin's Griffin
Publishing Imprint
United States

Book Publisher: Macmillan Publishers (**P338**)

P493 St. Martin's Publishing Group
Publishing Imprint
United States

Book Publisher: Macmillan Publishers (**P338**)

P494 Stairwell Books
Book Publisher
161 Lowther Street, York, YO31 7LZ
United Kingdom

rose@stairwellbooks.com

https://www.stairwellbooks.co.uk
https://twitter.com/StairwellBooks

ADULT
Fiction
Novels: Crime; Environment; Fantasy; Historical Fiction; Science Fiction
Short Fiction: General

Nonfiction > *Nonfiction Books*
Climate Science; Memoir

Poetry > *Any Poetic Form*

Scripts > *Theatre Scripts*

CHILDREN'S > Fiction > *Novels*

YOUNG ADULT > Fiction > *Novels*

Send: Query
How to send: Email

Small press publisher specialising in poetry anthologies, short stories, and novels from new writers. Send query by email. See website for full details.

Editor: Rose Drew

P495 Stanford University Press
Book Publisher
485 Broadway, First Floor, Redwood City CA 94063-8460
United States
Tel: +1 (650) 723-9434

https://www.sup.org
http://www.facebook.com/stanforduniversitypress
http://www.twitter.com/stanfordpress
https://www.youtube.com/channel/UCmd8xj7yu0WGcLRqL39UjLA
http://instagram.com/stanfordupress

ACADEMIC > Nonfiction > *Nonfiction Books*
Anthropology; Asia; Business; Economics; Finance; History; Judaism; Legal; Literature; Middle East; Philosophy; Politics; Religion; Sociology; South America

Send: Query; Proposal; Author bio; Table of Contents
How to send: Email; Post

Submit proposals by post, or see website for list of editors and submit proposal to the appropriate editor by email.

P496 Stanley Gibbons
Book Publisher; Magazine Publisher
United Kingdom

support@stanleygibbons.com

https://www.stanleygibbons.com
https://www.stanleygibbons.com/publishing/publishing-house
https://www.facebook.com/stanleygibbonsgroup
https://twitter.com/StanleyGibbons
https://www.instagram.com/stanleygibbons/

Nonfiction > *Reference*: Stamp Collecting

Publishes handbooks and reference guides on stamps and stamp collecting.

P497 Starscape
Publishing Imprint
United States

https://us.macmillan.com/torpublishinggroup/

Publishing Imprint: Tor Publishing Group (**P520**)

CHILDREN'S > **Fiction** > *Middle Grade*
General, and in particular: Fantasy; Science Fiction

Publishes books for young readers aged 10 and up.

P498 Steerforth Press
Book Publisher
31 Hanover Street, Suite 1, Lebanon, NH 03766
United States
Tel: +1 (603) 643-4787

submissions@steerforth.com
info@steerforth.com

https://steerforth.com
https://twitter.com/SteerforthPress
https://www.instagram.com/steerforthpress/
https://www.facebook.com/steerforthpress

Nonfiction > *Nonfiction Books*
Crime; History; Investigative Journalism; Literary Journalism; Narrative Nonfiction

Send: Query; Proposal
Don't send: Full text
How to send: Email

Exclusively considering works of narrative nonfiction, such as investigative or literary journalism, true crime and history for a general audience.

Fiction Editor / Poetry Editor: Roland Pease

Publishing Imprints: For Beginners; Playboy Press; Zoland Books; Zoland Poetry

P499 Steward House Publishers
Book Publisher
2307 Steamboat Lp E #202, Port Orchard, WA 98366
United States

query@stewardhouse.com
submissions@stewardhouse.com

https://www.stewardhouse.com

Fiction > *Novels*

Nonfiction > *Nonfiction Books*

Send: Full text; Query; Synopsis; Writing sample
How to send: Email attachment

Generally publishes works between 15,000 and 150,000 words in length, and is open to a variety of genres, both fiction and non-fiction, if the writing shows skill and care with words. Not accepting book proposals: only finished manuscripts will be considered for publication. All submissions must contain either a full manuscript (preferred) or a partial manuscript that includes at least three sample chapters, a cover letter, and a synopsis of the whole manuscript.

P500 The Stinging Fly Press
Book Publisher; Magazine Publisher
Ireland

submissions.stingingfly@gmail.com
editor@stingingfly.org
info@stingingfly.org

https://stingingfly.org
https://www.facebook.com/StingingFly
http://twitter.com/stingingfly

Fiction > *Short Fiction Collections*

Closed to approaches.

Publishes single-author short-story collections and multiple-author anthologies.

Publisher: Declan Meade

P501 Strata Publishing, Inc.
Book Publisher
PO 1303, State College, PA 16804-1303
United States
Tel: +1 (814) 234-8545

stratapub@stratapub.com

http://www.stratapub.com

ACADEMIC > **Nonfiction** > *Nonfiction Books*
Communication; Journalism

PROFESSIONAL > **Nonfiction** > *Nonfiction Books*
Communication; Journalism

Send: Query; Outline; Market info; Table of Contents; Author bio
How to send: Post
How not to send: Email attachment

An independent publishing house producing books for college students, scholars, and professionals in communication and journalism. Send query letter giving the working title, the course(s) for which the book is intended, brief description of your general approach, major competitors, and how your book is different from them.

Editor: Kathleen Domenig

P502 Sublunary Editions
Book Publisher; Magazine Publisher
Seattle
United States

support@sublunaryeditions.com

https://sublunaryeditions.com
https://oleada.io/publication/sublunary-editions
https://twitter.com/sublunaryeds
https://instagram.com/sublunaryeditions

Fiction
Novellas: Experimental; Literary
Short Fiction: Experimental; Literary
Nonfiction > *Essays*
Experimental; Literary
Poetry
Any Poetic Form; *Experimental Poetry*

Started as a small-scale, DIY project in early 2019. For the first several months, the press's sole output as a regular envelope of new writing mailed (the old fashioned way) to subscribers. Since then, the press has expanded to publish 8-10 brief books every year, and, as of early 2021, a quarterly magazine

Magazine: Firmament (**M165**)

P503 Sunberry Books
Publishing Imprint
United Kingdom

submissions@sunpenny.com

https://www.sunpenny.com/imprints/

Book Publisher: Sunpenny Publishing (**P504**)

CHILDREN'S > **Fiction** > *Novels*

YOUNG ADULT > **Fiction** > *Novels*

Send: Author bio; Marketing Plan; Synopsis; Full text
How to send: Email
How not to send: Post

Imprint set up for children's books and YA (Young Adults).

P504 Sunpenny Publishing
Book Publisher
United Kingdom

submissions@sunpenny.com

https://www.sunpenny.com

ADULT
  Fiction > *Novels*
    General, and in particular: Christian
    Romance; Christianity; Inspirational;
    Romance

  Nonfiction > *Nonfiction Books*
    General, and in particular: Boats;
    Christianity

CHILDREN'S > **Fiction** > *Novels*

TEEN > **Fiction** > *Novels*

Send: Author bio; Marketing Plan; Synopsis;
Full text
How to send: Email
How not to send: Post

An independent small publishing house
focusing particularly on encouraging and
developing new talent in writing – in fiction
and non-fiction, and in Christian and romantic
works.

We have a soft spot for travel, sailing,
adventure, crime/detective, courage and
overcoming, self-help, gift books and coffee-
table books. We enjoy wit and humour,
entertainment, upliftment. Sunpenny promotes
beauty and excellence in publishing. Books do
not have to be Christian in either topic or
nature, but they do have to keep to acceptable
value standards.

What we won't even consider: Unless it is
suitably within an overall context of
"overcoming", we do not accept depressive or
self-contemplative styles, 'black comedy',
racism, gratuitous sex or violence or foul
language, or anything else that does not
conform to good mainstream family values
(and we get to be the judge!) ... our taste also
does not run to the gothic – vampires,
werewolves, and the like, or horror generally;
nor do we enjoy the crass and the crude, no
matter how witty. If it's seedy or seamy, please
don't even try. And let's not even go into the
futuristic games-type wild fantasy adventure "I
have the power!" stuff. Intelligent sci-fi, yes.
Silliness, no. Aliens, probably not. And if you
have a book that expounds theories/religions
such as The Big Bang, Evolution and suchlike
– why even waste your time sending it to a
Christian publisher? Save yourself the money.
:-)

Please visit our web site and read ALL our
guidelines carefully before querying.

Authors: Cheryl Cain; Rowland Evans; JS
Holloway; Lucy McCarraher; Julie McGowan;
Terri Tiffany

Editor: Jo Holloway

Publishing Imprints: Blue Jeans Books (**P082**);
Boathooks Books (**P085**); ChristLight Books
(**P124**); EPTA Books (**P181**); Engram Books
(**P180**); Rose and Crown Books (**P449**);
Sunberry Books (**P503**)

P505 Sweet Cherry Publishing
Book Publisher
Unit 4U18, The Book Brothers Business Park,
Tolwell Road, Leicester, LE4 1BR
United Kingdom
Tel: +44 (0) 1162 536796

submissions@sweetcherrypublishing.com

https://www.sweetcherrypublishing.com
http://www.facebook.com/
sweetcherrypublishing
https://twitter.com/sweetcherrypub
https://www.instagram.com/
sweetcherrypublishing/

CHILDREN'S > **Fiction**
    Board Books; *Chapter Books*; *Middle Grade*;
    Picture Books
YOUNG ADULT > **Fiction** > *Novels*

Send: Query; Writing sample; Synopsis;
Author bio
How to send: Email

Publishes picture and board books, chapter
books, middle-grade fiction, and young adult
fiction. Specialises in sets and series, so
unlikely to take on a stand-alone title. Send
submissions by email. See website for full
submission guidelines.

Editor: Abdul Thadha

P506 Sweetgum Press
Book Publisher
United States

https://sweetgumpress.com

Fiction > *Short Fiction Collections*
    American Midwest; Historical Fiction;
    Missouri

Poetry > *Poetry Collections*
    American Midwest; History; Missouri

Closed to approaches.

Publishes book-length works (70-250 pages)
by writers from the Midwest, particularly
Missouri. The editors look for manuscripts that
are unlikely to attract mainstream publishers
but are worthy of publication because of one or
more qualities, among them originality,
authenticity, beauty, regional or historical
appeal.

P507 Tamarind Books
Publishing Imprint
United Kingdom

puffin@penguinrandomhouse.co.uk

https://www.penguin.co.uk/puffin/tamarind.
html

Book Publisher: Puffin (UK) (**P428**)

CHILDREN'S
  Fiction
    Chapter Books: Diversity
    Middle Grade: Diversity
    Novels: Diversity

Nonfiction > *Nonfiction Books*: Diversity

Publishes children's books and picture books
with black, Asian, or mixed race children as
the main protagonists.

P508 Taylor & Francis Group
Book Publisher
4 Park Square, Milton Park, Abingdon, OX14
4RN
United Kingdom
Tel: +44 (0) 20 8052 0500

enquiries@taylorandfrancis.com

https://taylorandfrancis.com
https://www.facebook.com/
TaylorandFrancisGroup
https://twitter.com/tandfonline
https://www.linkedin.com/company/taylor-&-
francis-group/
https://www.instagram.com/tandfscience/

Book Publisher: Informa PLC

ACADEMIC > **Nonfiction** > *Nonfiction Books*
    Agriculture; Arts; Biomedical Science;
    Business; Chemistry; Computer Science;
    Earth Science; Economics; Education;
    Engineering; Environment; Finance;
    Geography; Health; History; Information
    Science; Language; Legal; Literature;
    Management; Mathematics; Medicine;
    Nursing; Philosophy; Physics; Politics;
    Psychiatry; Psychology; Religion; Science;
    Sociology; Statistics; Sustainable Living;
    Technology

PROFESSIONAL > **Nonfiction** > *Nonfiction Books*
    Agriculture; Biomedical Science; Business;
    Chemistry; Computer Science; Earth
    Science; Economics; Education;
    Engineering; Environment; Finance;
    Geography; Health; History; Information
    Science; Language; Legal; Literature;
    Management; Mathematics; Medicine;
    Nursing; Philosophy; Physics; Politics;
    Psychiatry; Psychology; Religion; Science;
    Sociology; Statistics; Sustainable Living;
    Technology

One of the leading research publishers in the
world, serving academia and professionals in
industry and government.

Book Publishers: Ashgate Publishing Limited;
Focal Press; Routledge

Publishing Imprint: Psychology Press

P509 TCK Publishing
*Book Publisher; Ebook Publisher; Audio Book
Publisher*
16641 Brick Road, Granger, IN 46530
United States

info@tckpublishing.com
submissions@tckpublishing.com

https://www.tckpublishing.com

ADULT
Fiction > *Novels*
General, and in particular: Adventure;
Fantasy; Historical Fiction; Horror;
Mystery; Romance; Science Fiction;
Suspense; Thrillers

Nonfiction > *Nonfiction Books*
General, and in particular: Business;
Finance; Gardening; Health; How To;
Nature; Personal Development;
Relationships; Self Help; Spirituality;
Wellbeing

CHILDREN'S > **Fiction** > *Middle Grade*

NEW ADULT > **Fiction** > *Novels*

YOUNG ADULT > **Fiction** > *Novels*

Send: Full text
How to send: Online submission system

A traditional book publisher that pays 50%
gross royalties. We love to publish meaningful
and inspirational fiction and nonfiction books
that inspire and educate readers.

P510 Templar Books
Publishing Imprint
United Kingdom
Tel: +44 (0) 20 3770 8888

hello@bonnierbooks.co.uk

https://www.bonnierbooks.co.uk/childrens-
imprints/templar-books/
https://www.instagram.com/templarbooks/
https://twitter.com/templarbooks
https://www.facebook.com/templarbooks/
https://www.tiktok.com/@booksforkidsuk

Book Publisher: Bonnier Books (UK) (**P086**)

CHILDREN'S
Fiction > *Picture Books*

Nonfiction
Board Books; Gift Books; Illustrated Books

From vibrant board and picture books for early
readers to beautiful gift and novelty books that
capture the imagination of the whole family,
has become one of the world's most respected
children's imprints, building a reputation for
innovation and creativity over nearly forty-five
years.

Renowned for its cleverly-conceived concept
publishing with an emphasis on paper
innovation, stylish design, and contemporary
illustration for an international audience, its
stories are truly immersive, playful reading
experiences that get inside the world of a child.

P511 Ten Speed Press
Publishing Imprint
United States

https://crownpublishing.com/archives/imprint/
ten-speed-press

Book Publisher: The Crown Publishing Group
(**P148**)

Nonfiction > *Illustrated Books*
Design; Food and Drink; Gardening; Health;
Popular Culture

Known for creating beautiful illustrated books
with innovative design and award-winning
content. Actively seeks out new and
established authors who are authorities and
tastemakers in the world of food, drink, pop
culture, graphic novels, illustration, design,
reference, gardening, and health.

Publishing Imprint: Crossing Press

P512 Thames & Hudson Inc.
Book Publisher
500 Fifth Avenue, New York, NY 10110
United States
Tel: +1 (212) 354-3763
Fax: +1 (212) 398-1252

bookinfo@thames.wwnorton.com

https://www.thamesandhudsonusa.com
https://www.instagram.com/
thamesandhudsonusa
https://twitter.com/ThamesHudsonUSA
https://www.facebook.com/
ThamesandHudsonUSA

Book Publisher: Thames and Hudson Ltd

ADULT
Fiction > *Novels*

Nonfiction
Nonfiction Books: Animals; Anthropology;
Antiques; Archaeology; Architecture; Arts;
Biography; Business; Classics / Ancient
World; Comedy / Humour; Comic Books;
Crafts; Design; Evolution; Fashion; Films;
Fitness; Folklore, Myths, and Legends;
Food; Games; Gardening; Health; History;
Houses; Interior Design; Literary
Criticism; Medicine; Military History;
Music; Nature; Philosophy; Photography;
Religion; Science; Spirituality; Sport; TV;
Theatre; Travel
Reference: General

Poetry > *Poetry Collections*

CHILDREN'S
Fiction
*Chapter Books; Early Readers; Picture
Books*
Nonfiction
*Activity Books; Nonfiction Books; Picture
Books*

Send: Query
Don't send: Full text
How to send: In the body of an email
How not to send: Email attachment

Send proposals up to six pages by email. No
attachments or unsolicited mss.

P513 Thistle Publishing
Book Publisher
London
United Kingdom

info@thistlepublishing.co.uk

http://www.thistlepublishing.co.uk
http://twitter.com/ThistleBooks
https://www.facebook.com/ThistlePublishing/

Fiction > *Novels*

Nonfiction > *Nonfiction Books*

Send: Query; Synopsis; Author bio; Writing
sample; Outline
How to send: Email

London-based publisher of quality fiction and
nonfiction. Welcomes submissions. For
nonfiction, send synopsis, author profile,
sample chapter, and brief chapter summaries;
for fiction, send synopsis and three sample
chapters.

P514 Tidewater Publishers
Publishing Imprint
United States

https://schifferbooks.com/pages/schiffer-
imprints

Book Publisher: Schiffer Publishing (**P467**)

ADULT > **Nonfiction** > *Nonfiction Books*
Chesapeake Bay; History; Lifestyle

CHILDREN'S > **Nonfiction** > *Nonfiction
Books*
Chesapeake Bay; History; Lifestyle

Life and history in the Chesapeake Bay region
for children and adults.

P515 Tiger of the Stripe
Book Publisher
50 Albert Road, Richmond, Surrey, TW10
6DP
United Kingdom
Tel: +44 (0) 20 8940 8087

https://tigerofthestripe.co.uk

Fiction > *Novels*

Nonfiction > *Nonfiction Books*
Architecture; Books; Food; History;
Language; Medieval; Music

Eclectic but with an emphasis on well-
researched academic or semi-academic works.
Also interested in biographies, history,
language textbooks, cookbooks, typography.
Not currently accepting new fiction.

Authors: Gerrish Gray; Jay Landesman; Julia
Scott

Editor: Peter Danckwerts

P516 Tiny Owl
Book Publisher
366 Woodstock Road, Oxford, OX2 8AE
United Kingdom

info@tinyowl.co.uk

https://tinyowl.co.uk
https://www.facebook.com/tinyowlpublishing/
https://twitter.com/tinyowl_books

https://www.youtube.com/channel/
UCJkMec_cxEVzTf2iUGvk2Pg
https://www.instagram.com/
tiny_owl_publishing/

CHILDREN'S > **Fiction** > *Picture Books*

Closed to approaches.

Publisher of picture books for children.

P517 Toad Hall Editions
Book Publisher; Self Publishing Service;
Magazine Publisher
United States

hello@toadhalleditions.ink

https://www.toadhalleditions.ink
https://www.instagram.com/toadhalleditions/

Fiction
Novels; *Short Fiction Collections*
Nonfiction > *Nonfiction Books*
Creative Nonfiction; Memoir; Personal
Essays

Poetry > *Poetry Collections*

Does not want:

> **Fiction** > *Novels*
> Fantasy; Historical Fiction; Horror;
> Mystery; Romance; Science Fiction;
> Thrillers
>
> **Nonfiction** > *Nonfiction Books*
> Finance; Motivational Self-Help

Costs: Offers services that writers have to pay
for.

Small press publisher that also provides self-
publishing services. Publishes 1-3 per year,
written by women or gender-diverse people.

Magazines: Buttered Toast (**M086**); Kerning
(**M244**)

P518 Toon Books
Publishing Imprint
United States

Book Publisher: Astra Publishing House
(**P041**)

P519 Tor
Publishing Imprint
United States

https://us.macmillan.com/
tomdohertyassociates/
https://www.torforgeblog.com/

Publishing Imprint: Tor Publishing Group
(**P520**)

Fiction > *Novels*
Fantasy; Science Fiction

Closed to approaches.

Particular emphasis on science fiction and
fantasy. Open submission policy currently
suspended due to COVID-19.

Publishing Imprints: Orb; Tor; Tor/Seven Seas

P520 Tor Publishing Group
Publishing Imprint
120 Broadway, New York, NY 10271
United States

https://us.macmillan.com/torpublishinggroup/
https://www.facebook.com/torbooks
https://twitter.com/torbooks
https://www.youtube.com/user/torforge

Book Publisher: Macmillan Publishers (**P338**)

ADULT > **Fiction** > *Novels*
Fantasy; Horror; Mystery; Science Fiction;
Thrillers

TEEN > **Fiction** > *Novels*
Fantasy; Science Fiction; Speculative

Publisher of Science Fiction, Fantasy, Horror,
Mystery, Thriller and Suspense, and Other
Speculative Fiction.

Publishing Imprints: Forge (**P200**); Nightfire
(**P375**); Starscape (**P497**); Tor (**P519**); Tor
Teen (**P521**); Tor.com Publishing (**P522**)

P521 Tor Teen
Publishing Imprint
United States

torteenpublicity@torteenbooks.com

https://torteen.com
https://www.instagram.com/torteen/
https://twitter.com/torteen
https://www.facebook.com/torteen
http://torteen.tumblr.com/

Publishing Imprint: Tor Publishing Group
(**P520**)

TEEN > **Fiction** > *Novels*
General, and in particular: Fantasy; Science
Fiction

YOUNG ADULT > **Fiction** > *Novels*
General, and in particular: Fantasy; Science
Fiction

Launched as an imprint dedicated to publishing
quality science fiction, fantasy, and general
fiction for young adults.

P522 Tor.com Publishing
Publishing Imprint
United States

https://publishing.tor.com

Publishing Imprint: Tor Publishing Group
(**P520**)

Fiction
Novellas: Fantasy; Science Fiction
Novels: Fantasy; Science Fiction

An imprint for science fiction and fantasy
novellas and novels, a line that provides a
home for emerging and established writers to
tell focused, engaging stories in exactly the
number of words they choose. Most titles are

available globally in print and DRM-free
ebook format.

P523 Torrey House Press, LLC
Book Publisher
370 S 300 E, Suite 103, Salt Lake City, UT
84111
United States

Gray@TorreyHouse.org

https://www.torreyhouse.org
https://torreyhousepress.submittable.com/
submit/
https://www.facebook.com/TorreyHousePress/
https://twitter.com/torreyhouse
https://www.instagram.com/torreyhousepress

ADULT
Fiction
Graphic Novels: General
Novels: Contemporary; Fantasy; Futurism;
Historical Fiction; Horror; LGBTQIA;
Literary; Magical Realism; Mystery;
Romance; Science Fiction; Thrillers; Urban
Short Fiction Collections: General

Nonfiction
Essays: General
Nonfiction Books: Creative Nonfiction;
Investigative Journalism; Literary
Journalism; Memoir
Poetry > *Poetry Collections*

YOUNG ADULT > **Fiction** > *Novels*

How to send: Submittable

Interested in great writing that engages, in a
wide variety of ways, with place, the natural
world, and/or issues that link the Western
United States to the past, present, and future of
the ever-changing Earth. Originally founded
with a specific focus on the Intermountain
West but, over the past thirteen years, has
expanded its scope to include literature from
the plains to the Pacific. (And yes, that
includes Alaska and Hawaii!)

Editors: Kirsten Johanna Allen; Mark Bailey

P524 TouchWood Editions
Book Publisher
Canada

submissions@touchwoodeditions.com

https://www.touchwoodeditions.com

Fiction
Novels: Contemporary; Historical Fiction;
Mystery; Supernatural / Paranormal
Short Fiction Collections: General

Nonfiction
Essays: General
Nonfiction Books: Alberta; Arctic; Arts;
Beer; Biography; British Columbia;
Contemporary; Cookery; Food; Gardening;
History; Memoir; Nature; Painting; Pets;
Photography; Travel; Vancouver Island;
Wine; Women

Send: Query; Outline; Proposal; Synopsis; Marketing Plan; Author bio; Writing sample
How to send: PDF file email attachment

Accepts submissions by email only. Response only if interested. Publishes Canadian authors only. See website for full guidelines.

P525 Travelers' Tales / Solas House

Book Publisher
2320 Bowdoin Street, Palo Alto CA 94306
United States
Tel: +1 (650) 462-2110
Fax: +1 (650) 462-6305

ttales@travelerstales.com

https://travelerstales.com
https://www.facebook.com/Travelers-Tales-197098590465058/
https://twitter.com/travelerstales

Nonfiction
Nonfiction Books: Travel
Short Nonfiction: Travel

How to send: Online submission system
How not to send: Post; Email

Publishes books and anthologies of true travel tales, whether funny, adventurous, frightening, or grim. No fiction. Submit through online submission system only. No submissions by post or email. Response only if interested.

P526 Troika Books

Book Publisher
United Kingdom
Tel: +44 (0) 7710 412830

kidglovesbooks@gmail.com

https://www.troikabooks.com
https://twitter.com/TroikaBooks
https://youtube.com/channel/UCmc3CUxge0slDJwLs57WLJw

CHILDREN'S
Fiction
Novels; Picture Books
Poetry > *Any Poetic Form*

Closed to approaches.

Publishes picture books, fiction, and poetry for children.

Editor: Martin West

P527 TTA Press

Magazine Publisher; Book Publisher
United Kingdom

http://www.ttapress.com

Magazines: Black Static (**M073**); Crimewave (**M126**)

P528 Turner Publishing

Book Publisher
Nashville, TN
United States

submissions@turnerpublishing.com

https://turnerbookstore.com
https://www.facebook.com/turner.publishing/
https://twitter.com/TurnerPub
https://www.pinterest.com/turnerpub
https://www.instagram.com/turnerpub/

ADULT
Fiction > *Novels*
Fantasy; Historical Fiction; Horror; Literary; Mystery; Romance; Science Fiction; Suspense; Thrillers

Nonfiction > *Nonfiction Books*
Animals; Autobiography; Biography; Business; Cookery; Crafts; Crime; Drinks; Entertainment; Family; Genealogy; Health; History; Hobbies; Medicine; Mind, Body, Spirit; Nature; Pets; Politics; Relationships; Religion; Science; Travel; Wellbeing

CHILDREN'S
Fiction
Chapter Books; Comics; Graphic Novels; Middle Grade; Novels; Picture Books
Nonfiction > *Nonfiction Books*

TEEN > **Fiction** > *Novels*

YOUNG ADULT > **Fiction** > *Novels*

Send: Proposal; Full text
How to send: Email

An award-winning, independent publisher of books. The company is in the top 101 independent publishing companies in the U.S. as compiled by Bookmarket.com and has been named five times to Publishers Weekly's Fastest Growing Publishers List. Accepts submissions of manuscripts and/or proposals. Submissions can be made by agents or authors directly.

Publishing Imprints: Basic Health Publications, Inc. (**P065**); Jewish Lights Publishing

P529 Two Fine Crows Books

Publishing Imprint
United States

https://twofinecrowsbooks.com
https://saddleroadpress.submittable.com/submit

Book Publisher / Ebook Publisher: Saddle Road Press

Nonfiction > *Nonfiction Books*
Nature; Spirituality

Publishes books of nature and spirit.

P530 Tyndale House Publishers, Inc.

Book Publisher
351 Executive Drive, Carol Stream, IL 60188
United States
Tel: +1 (855) 277-9400
Fax: +1 (866) 622-9474

https://www.tyndale.com
https://facebook.com/TyndaleHouse
https://twitter.com/TyndaleHouse
https://pinterest.com/TyndaleHouse/
https://instagram.com/tyndalehouse/
https://youtube.com/user/TyndaleHP/

ADULT
Fiction > *Novels*
Allegory; Christianity; Contemporary Romance; Contemporary; Historical Fiction; Mystery; Romantic Suspense; Suspense; Thrillers; Westerns

Nonfiction
Nonfiction Books: Archaeology; Arts; Autobiography; Biography; Business; Christian Living; Christianity; Comedy / Humour; Culture; Current Affairs; Education; Finance; Health; History; Judaism; Leadership; Leisure; Memoir; Mental Health; Personal Development; Politics; Sport; Travel
Reference: Christianity

CHILDREN'S
Fiction
Chapbooks: Christianity
Picture Books: Christianity

Nonfiction > *Nonfiction Books*
Christian Living; Christianity

TEEN
Fiction > *Novels:* Christianity

Nonfiction > *Nonfiction Books*
Christian Living; Christianity; Relationships; Sex

How to send: Through a literary agent

Christian publisher, publishing bibles, nonfiction, fiction, and books for kids and teens.

P531 Ugly Duckling Presse

Book Publisher
The Old American Can Factory, 232 Third Street, #E303 (corner Third Avenue), Brooklyn, NY 11215
United States
Tel: +1 (347) 948-5170

office@uglyducklingpresse.org

https://uglyducklingpresse.org

Nonfiction > *Nonfiction Books:* Experimental

Poetry in Translation > *Poetry Collections*

Poetry > *Poetry Collections*

Closed to approaches.

Nonprofit publisher of poetry, translation, experimental nonfiction, performance texts, and books by artists. Check website for specific calls for submissions.

Print Magazine: Second Factory (**M366**)

P532 Ulverscroft Ltd
Book Publisher
The Green, Bradgate Road, Anstey, Leicester,
LE7 7FU
United Kingdom
Tel: +44 (0) 116 236 4325

customersupport@ulverscroft.co.uk

https://www.ulverscroft.com
https://www.facebook.com/Ulverscroft
https://www.instagram.com/ulverscroftltd

Fiction > *Novels*

Nonfiction > *Nonfiction Books*

Publishes a wide variety of large print titles in
hard and soft cover formats, as well as
abridged and unabridged audio books. Many
titles are written by the world's favourite
authors.

Editor: Mark Merrill

P533 Ulysses Press
Book Publisher
32 Court Street, Suite #2109, Brooklyn, New
York 11201
United States

acquisitions@ulyssespress.com
ulysses@ulyssespress.com

https://ulyssespress.com
https://www.instagram.com/ulyssespress/
https://www.facebook.com/ulyssespress
https://twitter.com/UlyssesPress

ADULT
  Fiction > *Novels*

  Nonfiction > *Nonfiction Books*
  Comedy / Humour; Cookery; Crime;
  Education; Fitness; Health; Home
  Improvement; Popular Culture; Self Help

CHILDREN'S
  Fiction > *Picture Books*
  Nonfiction > *Nonfiction Books*

YOUNG ADULT
  Fiction > *Novels*
  Nonfiction > *Nonfiction Books*

Send: Query; Synopsis; Table of Contents;
Author bio; Market info; Writing sample
How to send: Email

Our publishing program seeks to move along
the cultural cutting edge. We stay ahead of the
competition by publishing books at the
forefront of emerging trends and by finding
unique angles on established topics unexplored
by other publishers.

When it comes to finding new books, we are
especially interested in titles that fill
demonstrated niches in the trade book market.
We seek books that take a specific and unique
focus, a focus that can differentiate a book and
make it stand out in a crowd.

P534 Unbound Press
Book Publisher
20 St Thomas Street, London, SE1 9RS
United Kingdom
Tel: +44 (0) 20 3997 6790

support@unbound.com

https://unbound.com
https://facebook.com/unbound
https://twitter.com/unbounders
https://instagram.com/unbounders

Fiction > *Novels*

Nonfiction > *Nonfiction Books*

Send: Full text

Crowdfunding publisher. Submit manuscripts
via form on website.

P535 Unicorn
Publishing Imprint
United Kingdom

https://www.unicornpublishing.org/page/about/

Book Publisher: Unicorn Publishing Group
(**P536**)

Nonfiction > *Nonfiction Books*
  Cultural History; Visual Arts

Send: Query
How to send: Email

We are always looking for new and exciting
projects relating to the visual arts and cultural
history. Email the chairman in the first
instance.

Chair: Ian Macpherson

P536 Unicorn Publishing Group
Book Publisher
Charleston Studio, Meadow Business Centre,
Ringmer, Lewes, East Sussex, BN8 5RW
United Kingdom
Tel: +44 (0) 1273 812066

ian@unicornpublishing.org

https://www.unicornpublishing.org
https://www.facebook.com/UnicornPressLtd/
https://www.linkedin.com/company/unicorn-
publishing-group/
https://twitter.com/UnicornPubGroup/
https://www.instagram.com/
UnicornPubGroup/

Fiction > *Novels*: Historical Fiction

Nonfiction > *Nonfiction Books*
  Cultural History; Health; Military History;
  Philosophy; Visual Arts

How to send: Email; Post

Publishes books on the visual arts and cultural
history, military history, and historical fiction,
through four separate imprints. Approach by
email or by post.

Chair: Ian Macpherson

Publishing Director: Lucy Duckworth

Publishing Imprints: Unicorn (**P535**); Uniform
(**P537**); Unify (**P538**); Universe (**P540**)

P537 Uniform
Publishing Imprint
United Kingdom

https://www.unicornpublishing.org/page/about/

Book Publisher: Unicorn Publishing Group
(**P536**)

Nonfiction > *Nonfiction Books*: Military
History

P538 Unify
Publishing Imprint
United Kingdom

https://www.unicornpublishing.org/page/about/

Book Publisher: Unicorn Publishing Group
(**P536**)

Nonfiction > *Nonfiction Books*
  Health; Philosophy

Imprint publishing health and philosophy titles.

P539 Unity
Book Publisher
1901 NW Blue Parkway, Unity Village, MO
64065--0001
United States
Tel: +1 (816) 524-3550

unitycustomerservice@unityonline.org

https://www.unity.org

Nonfiction > *Nonfiction Books*
  Health; Lifestyle; Philosophy; Relationships;
  Self Help; Spirituality

Publisher of books on Spirituality, New
Thought, personal growth, spiritual leadership,
mind-body-spirit, and spiritual self-help.

P540 Universe
Publishing Imprint
United Kingdom

https://www.unicornpublishing.org/page/about/

Book Publisher: Unicorn Publishing Group
(**P536**)

Fiction > *Novels*: Historical Fiction

P541 The University of Akron Press
Book Publisher
185 E. Mill St., University of Akron, Akron,
OH 44325-1703
United States

uapress@uakron.edu

https://www.uakron.edu/uapress/
https://theuniversityofakronpress.
submittable.com/submit

ACADEMIC > **Nonfiction** > *Nonfiction Books*
  Culture; History; Ohio; Poetry as a Subject; Politics; Psychology

ADULT
  Nonfiction > *Nonfiction Books*
  Cookery; Culture; Food; History; Ohio; Sport

  Poetry > *Poetry Collections*

Closed to approaches.

For nonfiction, download and complete form on website, or submit through online submission system. Also publishes books of poetry, mainly through its annual competition.

P542 University of Alaska Press
Book Publisher
Editorial Department, University of Alaska Press, PO Box 756240, 104 Eielson Building, Fairbanks, AK 99775-6240
United States
Tel: +1 (720) 406-8849
Fax: +1 (720) 406-3443

https://upcolorado.com/university-of-alaska-press

ACADEMIC > **Nonfiction** > *Nonfiction Books*
  Alaska; Biography; Culture; History; Language; Memoir; Nature; Politics; Science

ADULT
  Fiction > *Short Fiction Collections*: Alaska

  Poetry > *Poetry Collections*: Alaska

Send: Query; Proposal
How to send: Online submission system

Publishing books on politics and history, Native languages and cultures, science and natural history, biography and memoir, poetry, fiction and anthologies, and original translations, all with an emphasis on the state of Alaska.

P543 University of Arizona Press
Book Publisher
1510 E. University Blvd., P.O. Box 210055, Tucson, AZ 85721-0055
United States

https://uapress.arizona.edu
http://www.facebook.com/AZPress
http://www.twitter.com/AZPress

ACADEMIC > **Nonfiction** > *Nonfiction Books*
  Anthropology; Archaeology; Arizona; Environment; Ethnic Groups; Gender; History; Native Americans; South America; Southwestern United States; Space

ADULT > **Poetry** > *Any Poetic Form*

Publishes the work of leading scholars from around the globe. Invites proposals from authors of appropriate works.

Acquisitions Editor: Allyson Carter

P544 University of Georgia Press
Book Publisher
Main Library, Third Floor, 320 South Jackson Street, Athens, GA 30602
United States

books@uga.edu

https://ugapress.org
https://www.facebook.com/UGAPress
https://twitter.com/UGAPress
https://www.instagram.com/ugapress/
https://www.goodreads.com/user/show/23695305-university-of-georgia-press
https://ugapress.wordpress.com/

ACADEMIC > **Nonfiction** > *Nonfiction Books*
  African American; American History; American Literature; Current Affairs; Environment; Food; Geography; Georgia (US State); National Security; Nature; US Southern States; United States; Urban

ADULT > **Nonfiction** > *Nonfiction Books*
  African American; American History; American Literature; Current Affairs; Environment; Food; Geography; Georgia (US State); National Security; Nature; US Southern States; United States; Urban

Send: Query; Proposal; Author bio; Market info
How to send: Email

Publishes scholarly and general-interest books in the areas indicated. See website for full submission guidelines.

P545 University of Hawai'i Press
Book Publisher
2840 Kolowalu Street, Honolulu, HI 96822
United States
Tel: +1 (808) 956-8255
Fax: +1 (800) 650-7811

uhpbooks@hawaii.edu

https://uhpress.hawaii.edu
https://www.facebook.com/UniversityofHawaiiPress/
https://www.instagram.com/uhpress/
https://twitter.com/uhpressnews?lang=en

ACADEMIC > **Nonfiction** > *Nonfiction Books*
  Anthropology; Architecture; Arts; Asia; Buddhism; Environment; Hawai'i; History; Language; Literature; Pacific; Popular Culture; Religion; South-East Asia

Send: Query; Outline; Market info; Author bio; Table of Contents; Writing sample
How to send: Email; Post

Focuses on books in the humanities, social sciences, and natural sciences in areas that include history, religion, anthropology, literature, art and architecture, the environment, and languages. Also publishes or distributes more than 25 scholarly journals that reflect the university's regional and international focus in the aforementioned subjects.

Publishing Imprints: Kolowalu Books; Latitude 20

P546 University of Illinois Press
Book Publisher; Magazine Publisher
1325 South Oak Street, Champaign, IL 61820-6903
United States
Tel: +1 (217) 333-0950

uipress@uillinois.edu

https://www.press.uillinois.edu
https://www.facebook.com/UniversityofIllinoisPress/
https://www.youtube.com/user/univofillinoispress
https://www.instagram.com/illinoispress/
https://open.spotify.com/user/462orqowlbwnk44jrfkk16tcb
https://twitter.com/illinoispress
https://soundcloud.com/user-511256562

ACADEMIC > **Nonfiction** > *Nonfiction Books*
  18th Century; Africa; African American; Agriculture; American History; American Midwest; Animal Rights; Animals; Anthropology; Appalachia; Archaeology; Architecture; Asia; Asian American; Biography; Biology; Business; Caribbean; Chicago; Children; Classics / Ancient World; Comedy / Humour; Communication; Computers; Crime; Culture; Dance; Economics; Education; Engineering; Environment; European History; Films; Folklore, Myths, and Legends; Food; France; Geography; Germany; Illinois; Information Science; International; Ireland; Italy; Jewish Holocaust; Judaism; Language; Legal; Literature; Marxism; Mathematics; Media; Medicine; Medieval; Middle East; Military History; Mormonism; Music; Native Americans; Nature; Philosophy; Photography; Poetry as a Subject; Politics; Popular Culture; Psychology; Renaissance; Science Fiction; Science; Sexuality; Sociology; South America; Sport; Travel; Urban

ADULT > **Fiction** > *Novels*

Supports the mission of the university through the worldwide dissemination of significant scholarship, striving to enhance and extend the reputation of the university.

P547 University of Iowa Press
Book Publisher
119 West Park Road, 100 Kuhl House, Iowa City IA 52242-1000
United States
Tel: +1 (319) 335-2000
Fax: +1 (319) 335-2055

uipress@uiowa.edu

https://www.uipress.uiowa.edu

ACADEMIC > **Nonfiction** > *Nonfiction Books*
American Midwest; Archaeology; Books; Culture; Food; History; Literature; Military; Nature; Poetry as a Subject; Theatre; Writing

ADULT
Fiction
Novels; Short Fiction
Poetry > *Any Poetic Form*

Send: Outline; Market info; Table of Contents; Writing sample; Author bio
How to send: Email; Through a contest

Send proposals for nonfiction by email. Accepts short fiction and poetry through annual competitions only. Also publishes novels.

P548 University of Massachusetts Press
Book Publisher
East Experiment Station, 671 N. Pleasant St, Amherst, MA 01003
United States
Fax: +1 (413) 545-1226

admin@umpress.umass.edu

https://www.umasspress.com
https://www.facebook.com/umasspress/
https://twitter.com/umasspress

ACADEMIC > **Nonfiction** > *Nonfiction Books*
19th Century; 20th Century; African American; American Civil War; Anthropology; Architecture; Arts; Autobiography; Biography; Children; Cultural History; Culture; Disabilities; Drama; Education; Environment; Films; Food; Health; History; Journalism; Judaism; LGBTQIA; Legal; Literature; Media; Medicine; Military History; Music; Native Americans; New England; Political History; Popular Culture; Recreation; Religion; Renaissance; Science; Social Class; Sociology; Sport; Technology; United States; Urban

ADULT
Fiction > *Novels*

Nonfiction > *Nonfiction Books*
General, and in particular: Creative Nonfiction

Poetry > *Poetry Collections*

Focuses primarily on books in the field of American studies, including books that explore the history, politics, literature, culture, and environment of the United States – as well as works with a transnational perspective. In addition to publishing works of scholarship, the Press produces books of more general interest for a wider readership. Also publishes poetry and fiction via its annual competitions only.

Editor-in-Chief: Matt Becker

P549 University of Nevada Press
Book Publisher
Mail Stop 0166, Reno, NV 89557-0166
United States

cvickers@unpress.nevada.edu

https://www.unpress.nevada.edu
https://twitter.com/UNVPress
https://www.facebook.com/universityofnevadapress
https://www.instagram.com/universitynevadapress
https://www.linkedin.com/company/74920592/admin/

ACADEMIC > **Nonfiction** > *Nonfiction Books*
American West; Architecture; Arts; Autobiography; Biography; Business; Drama; Economics; Education; Engineering; Family; Gambling; Games; History; Language; Legal; Literary Criticism; Medicine; Nature; Nevada; Performing Arts; Philosophy; Politics; Psychology; Relationships; Technology; Transport

ADULT
Fiction
Novels: American West; Nevada
Short Fiction Collections: American West; Nevada
Nonfiction > *Nonfiction Books*
American West; Cookery; Fitness; Health; Mind, Body, Spirit; Nevada; Recreation; Sport; Travel

Poetry > *Any Poetic Form*
American West; Nevada

Send: Outline; Market info; Proposal; Author bio; Table of Contents; Writing sample
How to send: Online submission system

Publishes regionally focused works that contribute to our understanding of Nevada, the Great Basin, and American West. Also publishes scholarly books in the humanities and social sciences in the fields of environmental studies, public health, mining studies, Native American studies, urban studies, Basque studies, and gambling and commercial gaming. The Press publishes select fiction as well. Submit a book proposal, which

includes a CV, detailed table of contents, and sample chapter.

Editor: JoAnne Banducci

P550 University of North Texas Press
Book Publisher
1155 Union Circle #311336, Denton, TX 76203-5017
United States
Tel: +1 (940) 565-2142

https://untpress.unt.edu
https://www.facebook.com/UniversityOfNorthTexasPress/
https://twitter.com/untpress/
https://www.pinterest.com/untpress0263/

ACADEMIC > **Nonfiction** > *Nonfiction Books*
Crime; Culture; Environment; Folklore, Myths, and Legends; Food History; History; Legal; Military History; Multicultural; Music; Nature; Texas; Women's Studies

ADULT
Fiction > *Short Fiction*
Poetry > *Any Poetic Form*

Send: Query
How to send: Post; Email
How not to send: Phone

Publishes in the humanities and social sciences, with an emphasis on Texas. Also publishes fiction and poetry through its annual competitions. See website for more details.

P551 University of Oklahoma Press
Book Publisher
2800 Venture Drive, Norman, OK 73069-8216
United States

https://www.oupress.com

ACADEMIC > **Nonfiction** > *Nonfiction Books*
Arts; Autobiography; Biography; Business; Comedy / Humour; Cookery; Crafts; Drama; Economics; Education; Engineering; Family; Fitness; Health; History; Hobbies; Language; Legal; Literature; Music; Nature; Performing Arts; Pets; Philosophy; Photography; Politics; Psychology; Relationships; Religion; Science; Self Help; Sociology; Sport; Technology; Transport; Travel

How to send: Online submission system

Publishes scholarly books of significance to the state, region, nation, and world, both to convey the results of current research to other scholars and to offer broader presentations for the general public.

P552 University of Pennsylvania Press
Book Publisher
3905 Spruce Street, Philadelphia, PA 19104-4112
United States

custserv@pobox.upenn.edu

https://www.upenn.edu/pennpress

ACADEMIC > **Nonfiction** > *Nonfiction Books*
African Diaspora; Atlantic; Culture; History; Intellectual History; Judaism; Literary Criticism; Medieval; North America; Political History; Renaissance; South America

Send: Query
How to send: Email

Send query by email to appropriate editor.

Associate Editor: Jenny Tan

Editor-in-Chief: Walter Biggins

Senior Editor: Robert Lockhart

P553 University of Pittsburgh Press
Book Publisher
7500 Thomas Boulevard, Pittsburgh, PA 15260
United States

https://upittpress.org

ACADEMIC > **Nonfiction** > *Nonfiction Books*
Architecture; Arts; Asia; Biography; Eastern Europe; Environment; History; Literature; Medicine; Pennsylvania; Photography; Pittsburgh; Russia; Science; South America; Technology; Travel; Urban

ADULT > **Poetry** > *Any Poetic Form*

Send: Query
Don't send: Full text

Publishes books on Latin American studies, Russian and East European studies, Central Asian studies, composition and literacy studies, environmental studies, urban studies, the history of architecture and the built environment, and the history and philosophy of science, technology, and medicine. Describes its poetry series as representing many of the finest poets active today.

Acquisitions Editor: Joshua Shanholtzer

Editorial Director: Abby Collier

P554 University of Tennessee Press
Book Publisher
110 Conference Center, Knoxville, TN 37996-4108
United States
Tel: +1 (865) 974-3321
Fax: +1 (865) 974-3724

utpress@utk.edu

https://utpress.org
https://www.facebook.com/utennpress/
https://twitter.com/utennpress

ACADEMIC > **Nonfiction** > *Nonfiction Books*
American Civil War; American History; Anthropology; Folklore, Myths, and Legends; Literature; Music; Popular Culture; Religion; Sport

Send: Query; Table of Contents; Writing sample; Author bio

The press is committed to preserving knowledge about Tennessee and the region and, by expanding its unique publishing program, it promotes a broad base of cultural understanding and, ultimately, improves life in the state.

Acquisitions Editor: Scot Danforth

P555 University of Texas Press
Book Publisher
3001 Lake Austin Blvd, 2.200, Stop E4800, Austin, TX 78703-4206
United States

https://utpress.utexas.edu

ACADEMIC > **Nonfiction** > *Nonfiction Books*
Anthropology; Archaeology; Architecture; Arts; Biography; Caribbean; Classics / Ancient World; Comic Books; Cookery; Environment; Films; Food; Gender; History; Judaism; Literary Criticism; Literature; Media; Middle East; Music; Nature; Photography; Sexuality; South America; Southwestern United States; Texas; United States

ADULT > **Nonfiction** > *Nonfiction Books*
Art History; Arts; Culture; Current Affairs; Food; History; Music; Nature; Texas

Send: Query; Proposal; Table of Contents; Writing sample; Author bio; Submission Form
How to send: Email

Send query with proposal, table of contents, sample chapter, and CV. Publishes scholarly books and some general readership nonfiction. See website for full details.

P556 University of Virginia Press
Book Publisher
P.O. Box 400318, Charlottesville, VA 22904-4318
United States
Tel: +1 (434) 924-3468
Fax: +1 (434) 982-2655

vapress@virginia.edu

https://www.upress.virginia.edu/

ACADEMIC > **Nonfiction** > *Nonfiction Books*
18th Century; Africa; African American; American Civil War; American History; Anthropology; Archaeology; Architecture; Arts; Autobiography; Biography; Business; Caribbean; Cookery; Culture; Current Affairs; Education; Environment; European History; Food; Geography; History; Legal; Literary Criticism; Literature; Memoir; Nature; Philosophy; Photography; Politics; Publishing; Religion; Science; Sociology; Technology; Virginia; Women's Studies

ADULT
Nonfiction > *Nonfiction Books*: Virginia

Poetry > *Any Poetic Form*

Send: Submission Form

Has a reputation for publishing quality scholarship in American history and government, eighteenth-century and Victorian literature, Afro-Caribbean studies, cultural religion, architectural and environmental history, and trade books of regional interest.

P557 The University of Wisconsin Press
Book Publisher
728 State Street, Suite 443, Madison, WI 53706
United States
Tel: +1 (608) 263-1110
Fax: +1 (608) 263-1173

uwiscpress@uwpress.wisc.edu

https://uwpress.wisc.edu
https://www.facebook.com/universityofwisconsinpress
https://twitter.com/UWiscPress
https://www.instagram.com/uwiscpress
https://www.goodreads.com/user/show/24113667-university-of-wisconsin-press
https://uwpress.wisc.edu/blog.html

ACADEMIC > **Nonfiction** > *Nonfiction Books*
Africa; African American; American Civil War; American Midwest; Anthropology; Asia; Autobiography; Brazil; Caribbean; Cinemas / Movie Theaters; Classics / Ancient World; Dance; Earth Science; Eastern Europe; Environment; Ethnography; Folklore, Myths, and Legends; Germany; History; Ireland; Judaism; LGBTQIA; Media; Native Americans; Outdoor Activities; Politics; Popular Culture; Russia; Scandinavia; South America; Travel; Wisconsin

ADULT
Fiction > *Novels*
General, and in particular: Mystery

Poetry > *Any Poetic Form*

Publishes scholarly, general interest nonfiction books and books featuring the American midwest, along with a limited number of novels and short story and poetry collections.

P558 University Press of Colorado
Book Publisher
1624 Market St., Ste 226, PMB 39883, Denver, CO 80202-1559
United States
Tel: +1 (720) 406-8849

https://upcolorado.com
https://twitter.com/UPColorado
https://www.facebook.com/profile.php?id=100069378078836

ACADEMIC > **Nonfiction** > *Nonfiction Books*
American West; Anthropology; Archaeology; Colorado; Environment; Ethnic; History; Native Americans; Science

Send: Proposal; Table of Contents; Market info; Author bio
How to send: Online submission system

Currently accepting manuscript proposals in anthropology, archaeology, ethnohistory, environmental justice, history of the American West, indigenous studies, and the natural sciences as well as projects about the state of Colorado and the Rocky Mountain region.

Publishing Imprint: Utah State University Press

P559 University Press of Mississippi
Book Publisher
United States

https://www.upress.state.ms.us

ACADEMIC > **Nonfiction** > *Nonfiction Books*
African American; Caribbean; Comic Books; Culture; Films; Folklore, Myths, and Legends; History; Literature; Media; Music; Popular Culture; US Southern States

How to send: Email

Publishes books that interpret the South and its culture to the nation and the world, scholarly books of the highest distinction, and books vital to readers in African American studies, Caribbean studies, comics studies, film and media studies, folklore, history, literary studies, music, and popular culture.

P560 Unseen Press
Book Publisher
United States

https://www.unseenpress.com
https://www.facebook.com/ghosttoursIN/
https://twitter.com/ghosts_IN
https://www.youtube.com/channel/UCinXzwCZ2_qj-xRO62SULaw
https://instagram.com/ghosts_in/

Nonfiction
Colouring Books: Crime; Folklore, Myths, and Legends; Ghosts; History; Indiana; Supernatural / Paranormal
Nonfiction Books: Crime; Folklore, Myths, and Legends; Ghosts; History; Indiana; Supernatural / Paranormal

Dedicated to bringing the information about ghosts to the public. Promotes ghost research as a source of folklore and also as viable scientific area of study.

P561 Unthank Books
Book Publisher
United Kingdom

information@unthankbooks.com

https://www.unthankbooks.com
https://www.facebook.com/UnthankBooks/
https://twitter.com/@unthankbooks

Fiction
Novels: Literary
Short Fiction Collections: Literary

An independent publisher nurturing distinct and vibrant literature, both in the novel and short form.

P562 Valley Press
Book Publisher; Publishing Service
Woodend, The Crescent, Scarborough, YO11 2PW
United Kingdom

hello@valleypressuk.com

https://www.valleypressuk.com
https://www.facebook.com/valleypress
https://twitter.com/valleypress
https://www.pinterest.com/valleypress

Fiction
Novels; Short Fiction Collections
Nonfiction > *Nonfiction Books*
Memoir; Travel

Poetry > *Poetry Collections*

Closed to approaches.

Costs: Offers services that writers have to pay for.

Publishes poetry, fiction, and nonfiction.

P563 VanderWyk & Burnham
Book Publisher
1610 Long Leaf Circle, St. Louis, MO 63146
United States
Tel: +1 (314) 432-3435
Fax: +1 (314) 993-4485

quickpublishing@sbcglobal.net

http://www.vandb.com

Nonfiction > *Nonfiction Books*
Alzheimer's; Animals; Cookery; Disabilities; Education; Family; Memoir; Nature; Nursing; Personal Development; Pets;

Society; Spirituality; Stress Management; Travel

Closed to approaches.

Not accepting unsolicited proposals or submissions as at May 2023.

P564 Vinspire Publishing
Book Publisher
107 Clearview Circle, Goose Creek, SC 29445
United States
Tel: +1 (843) 695-7530

vinspirepublishingeic@gmail.com

https://www.vinspirepublishing.com

ADULT
Fiction > *Novels*
African American; Contemporary Romance; Historical Fiction; Historical Romance; Inspirational; Literary; Mystery; Romance; Supernatural / Paranormal Romance

Nonfiction > *Nonfiction Books*

CHILDREN'S > **Fiction**
Middle Grade; Picture Books
YOUNG ADULT > **Fiction** > *Novels*

Send: Query; Author bio; Outline; Synopsis
How to send: In the body of an email

Now open to the following limited submissions that do not require an agent: Young Adult; Historical Romance; and African-American Contemporary Romance.

P565 Virago Books
Publishing Imprint
50 Victoria Embankment, London, EC4Y 0DZ
United Kingdom
Tel: +44 (0) 20 3122 7000

https://www.virago.co.uk
https://www.facebook.com/ViragoPress
https://twitter.com/viragobooks
https://www.instagram.com/viragopress/

Publishing Imprint: Little, Brown Book Group

Fiction
Graphic Novels: Women
Novels: Women's Fiction; Women's Issues; Women
Nonfiction > *Nonfiction Books*
Feminism; Women's Issues; Women's Studies; Women

How to send: Through a literary agent

Publishes books by women. Founded in 1973 to put women centre stage; to explore the untold stories of their lives; above all to champion women's talent. Publishes award-winning fiction, agenda-setting non-fiction, a rich list of rediscovered classics – and most recently a boutique list of graphic novels.

Authors: Maya Angelou; Margaret Atwood; Jennifer Belle; Waris Dirie; Sarah Dunant; Germaine Greer; Daphne du Maurier; Michele

Roberts; Gillian Slovo; Talitha Stevenson; Natasha Walter; Sarah Waters; Edith Wharton

Publishing Imprints: Virago Modern Classics; Virago.

P566 W.W. Norton & Company Ltd
Book Publisher
15 Carlisle Street, London, W1D 3BS
United Kingdom
Tel: +44 (0) 20 7323 1579

crussell1@wwnorton.com

https://wwnorton.co.uk
https://twitter.com/wwnortonUK
https://www.instagram.com/wwnortonuk/
https://medium.com/@W.W.NortonUK
https://www.pinterest.com/wwnortonuk/

ACADEMIC > **Nonfiction** > *Nonfiction Books*
African American; Anthropology; Astronomy; Biology; Chemistry; Classics / Ancient World; Computer Science; Films; Geology; History; Literature; Music; Philosophy; Physics; Politics; Psychology; Religion; Sociology; Statistics

ADULT
Fiction
Graphic Novels; *Novels*
Nonfiction
Essays: General
Nonfiction Books: Adventure; African American; Archaeology; Architecture; Arts; Astronomy; Biography; Business; Classics / Ancient World; Comedy / Humour; Crafts; Crime; Culture; Current Affairs; Design; Drama; Economics; Education; Environment; Films; Folklore, Myths, and Legends; Food and Drink; Games; Gardening; Health; History; Hobbies; Houses; LGBTQIA; Legal; Literature; Medicine; Memoir; Music; Nature; Neuropsychology; Neuroscience; Oceanography; Parenting; Pets; Philosophy; Photography; Politics; Psychology; Psychotherapy; Religion; Self Help; Sociology; Sport; Statistics; Technology; Transport; Travel; Women's Studies; Writing
Poetry > *Poetry Collections*

CHILDREN'S
Fiction
Chapter Books; *Early Readers*; *Picture Books*
Nonfiction > *Nonfiction Books*

PROFESSIONAL > **Nonfiction** > *Nonfiction Books*
Addiction; Anxiety Disorders; Architecture; Autism; Child Psychotherapy; Couple Therapy; Depression; Design; Eating Disorders; Education; Family Therapy; Genetics; Geriatrics; Health; Hypnosis; Juvenile Psychotherapy; Medicine; Neurobiology; Neuropsychology;

Neuroscience; Personal Coaching; Post Traumatic Stress Disorder; Psychiatry; Psychoanalysis; Psychological Trauma; Psychotherapy; Self Help; Sexuality; Writing

UK branch of a US publisher. No editorial office in the UK – contact the main office in New York (see separate listing).

P567 W.W. Norton & Company, Inc.
Book Publisher
500 Fifth Avenue, New York, NY 10110
United States
Tel: +1 (212) 354-5500
Fax: +1 (212) 869-0856

https://wwnorton.com
https://www.facebook.com/wwnorton/
https://twitter.com/wwnorton
https://www.instagram.com/w.w.norton/

ACADEMIC > **Nonfiction** > *Nonfiction Books*
Anthropology; Architecture; Arts; Astronomy; Biology; Chemistry; Communication; Computer Science; Design; Economics; Education; English; Films; Geology; History; Literature; Mathematics; Music; Science; Sociology

ADULT
Fiction
Graphic Novels: General
Novels: Adventure; African American; Alternative History; Animals; Asian American; Coming of Age; Crime; Culture; Disabilities; Dystopian Fiction; Epistolary; Erotic; Family; Fantasy; Folklore, Myths, and Legends; Mystery; Thrillers
Short Fiction Collections: General

Nonfiction
Nonfiction Books: Architecture; Biography; Business; Comedy / Humour; Cookery; Design; Economics; Education; History; Hobbies; Houses; Legal; Literary Criticism; Mathematics; Memoir; Mental Health; Mind, Body, Spirit; Performing Arts; Philosophy; Politics; Psychology; Religion; Visual Arts
Reference: General

Poetry > *Poetry Collections*

PROFESSIONAL > **Nonfiction** > *Nonfiction Books*: Education

How to send: Through a literary agent

No longer accepts submissions directly – submissions through a literary agent only.

P568 Washington State University Press
Book Publisher
Cooper Publications Building, PO Box 645910, Pullman, WA 99164-5910
United States

Tel: +1 (509) 335-7630
Fax: +1 (509) 335-8568

wsupress@wsu.edu

https://wsupress.wsu.edu

Types: Nonfiction
Subjects: Biography; Cookery; Culture; History; Nature; Politics; Westerns
Markets: Academic; Adult

Send: Query
Don't send: Full text

Send query by post or by email (preferred) with author CV, summary of proposed work, sample bio, and one or two sample chapters. Specialises in the American West, particularly the prehistory, history, environment, politics, and culture of the greater Northwest region. No fiction, poetry, or literary criticism. See website for full guidelines.

Editor-in-Chief: Linda Bathgate

Publishing Imprint: Basalt Books (**P063**)

P569 Waterbrook
Publishing Imprint

Book Publisher: Random House

P570 Watkins Publishing
Book Publisher
Unit 11, Shepperton House, 89 Shepperton Road, London, N1 3DF
United Kingdom
Tel: +44 (0) 20 3813 6940

enquiries@watkinspublishing.com

https://www.watkinspublishing.com

Book Publisher: Watkins Media

Types: Nonfiction
Subjects: History; Lifestyle; Religion; Self Help
Markets: Adult

Closed to approaches.

Publishes books in the field of Mind, Body and Spirit. Not accepting submissions as at April 2019. Check website for current status.

P571 Wave Books
Book Publisher
1938 Fairview Avenue East, Suite 201, Seattle, WA 98102
United States
Tel: +1 (206) 676-5337

info@wavepoetry.com

https://www.wavepoetry.com
http://twitter.com/WavePoetry
http://www.facebook.com/pages/Wave-Books/325354873993
http://wavepoetry.tumblr.com/

Poetry > *Poetry Collections*: Contemporary

Closed to approaches.

Independent poetry press based in Seattle. Accepts submissions only in response to specific calls for submissions posted on the website (see the submissions page).

Publisher: Charlie Wright

P572 Waverley Books
Publishing Imprint
Unit 31, Six Harmony Row, Glasgow, G51 3BA
United Kingdom
Tel: +44 (0) 1413 751996

https://www.waverley-books.co.uk
https://www.facebook.com/pages/
WAVERLEY-BOOKS/110565462291036
https://twitter.com/WaverleyBooks

Book Publisher: Gresham Books Ltd

ADULT
 Fiction
  Graphic Novels: Scotland
  Novels: General, and in
  particular: Romantic Comedy; Scotland
  Nonfiction > *Nonfiction Books*
  Comedy / Humour; Food and Drink;
  History; Scotland; Travel

CHILDREN'S
 Fiction
  Novels: General, and in particular: Scotland
  Picture Books: General, and in
  particular: Scotland
  Nonfiction > *Nonfiction Books*
  History; Scotland

Publishes history, fiction, nostalgia, food and drink, humour, children's, graphic novels, and Scottish interest.

P573 Wayland Books
Publishing Imprint

Book Publisher: Hachette Children's Group **(P235)**

P574 Wayne State University Press
Book Publisher
4809 Woodward Avenue, Detroit, Michigan 48201-1309
United States

https://www.wsupress.wayne.edu

ACADEMIC > **Nonfiction** > *Nonfiction Books*
  African American; Detroit; Fairy Tales;
  Films; Health; Judaism; Media; Michigan;
  Regional; TV

ADULT
 Fiction > *Short Fiction Collections*

 Nonfiction > *Nonfiction Books*: Creative Nonfiction

 Poetry > *Poetry Collections*

Send: Query; Proposal; Author bio; Writing sample

Don't send: Full text
How to send: Email

Actively acquiring books in African American studies, media studies, fairy-tale studies, Jewish studies, citizenship studies, and regional studies: books about the state of Michigan, the city of Detroit, and the Great Lakes region. Send query to appropriate acquisitions editor (see website for details and individual contact details).

P575 Weasel Press
Book Publisher
United States

thedude@weaselpress.com

https://www.weaselpress.com
https://weaselpress.submittable.com/submit
https://www.facebook.com/weaselpress
https://twitter.com/weaselpress
http://www.instagram.com/weaselpress

Poetry > *Poetry Collections*
  Dark; Erotic; Furries; Horror; LGBTQIA;
  Personal Experiences; Prostitution; Punk;
  Realistic; Science Fiction; Speculative

Scripts > *Theatre Scripts*
  Dark; Disabilities; Ethnic Groups; Furries;
  LGBTQIA; Personal Experiences;
  Prostitution; Speculative

How to send: Submittable

Only accepts submissions from authors of color; queer and trans authors; authors with disabilities; and current or former sex workers.

Publishing Imprints: Red Ferret Press **(P440)**; Sinister Stoat Press **(P482)**

P576 Weidenfeld & Nicolson
Book Publisher
United Kingdom

https://www.weidenfeldandnicolson.co.uk
https://twitter.com/wnbooks/
https://www.facebook.com/
WeidenfeldandNicolson/
https://www.instagram.com/orionbooks/?hl=en

Book Publisher: The Orion Publishing Group Limited

Fiction > *Novels*: Literary

Nonfiction > *Nonfiction Books*

Describes itself as one of the most prestigious and dynamic literary imprints in British and international publishing, home to a wide range of literary fiction and non-fiction, modern classics, prizewinning debuts and worldwide bestsellers.

P577 Welbeck Children's
Publishing Imprint
United Kingdom

Book Publisher: Welbeck Publishing Group **(P580)**

P578 Welbeck Editions
Publishing Imprint
United Kingdom

Book Publisher: Welbeck Publishing Group **(P580)**

P579 Welbeck Flame
Publishing Imprint
United Kingdom

Book Publisher: Welbeck Publishing Group **(P580)**

P580 Welbeck Publishing Group
Book Publisher
20 Mortimer Street, London, W1T 3JW
United Kingdom
Tel: +44 (0) 20 7612 0400
Fax: +44 (0) 20 7612 0401

submissions@welbeckpublishing.com

https://www.welbeckpublishing.com
https://www.facebook.com/welbeckpublish/
https://www.instagram.com/welbeckpublish/
https://twitter.com/welbeckpublish
https://www.youtube.com/
welbeckpublishinggroup
https://www.linkedin.com/company/
welbeckpublishinggroup/

ADULT
 Fiction > *Novels*
  Commercial; Popular

 Nonfiction
  Illustrated Books: Comedy / Humour;
  Entertainment; Fashion; History; Lifestyle;
  Sport
  Nonfiction Books: Biography; Business;
  Crime; History; Memoir; Military;
  Narrative Nonfiction; Popular Culture;
  Popular Science; Psychology; Self Help;
  Sport
  Puzzles: General

CHILDREN'S
 Fiction > *Middle Grade*

 Nonfiction
  Illustrated Books: Environment; History;
  Hobbies; Mental Health; Nature
  Nonfiction Books: General
  Picture Books: General

Send: Query
Don't send: Full text

Publishes illustrated reference, sport, entertainment, commercial fiction and children's nonfiction. Synopses and ideas for suitable books are welcomed, but no unsolicited MSS, academic, or poetry. Send query by email only with short synopsis, author bio, market info, and up to two chapters up to a maximum of 20 pages. See website for full guidelines.

Publishing Imprints: Mortimer Books (*P362*); Orange Mosquito (*P387*); Welbeck Children's (*P577*); Welbeck Editions (*P578*); Welbeck Flame (*P579*)

P581 Wesleyan University Press
Book Publisher
215 Long Lane, Middletown, CT 06459
United States
Tel: +1 (860) 685-7727
Fax: +1 (860) 685-7712

stamminen@wesleyan.edu

https://www.weslpress.org

ACADEMIC > **Nonfiction** > *Nonfiction Books*
  Dance; Music

ADULT > **Poetry** > *Poetry Collections*

Send: Query; Proposal
Don't send: Full text
How to send: Email; Submittable

Accepting proposals in the areas of poetry, dance and music. See website for submission guidelines.

P582 Wharncliffe Books
Publishing Imprint
United Kingdom

https://www.pen-and-sword.co.uk/Wharncliffe-Books/i/8

Book Publisher: Pen & Sword Books Ltd (**P407**)

Nonfiction > *Nonfiction Books*
  History; Regional

Send: Query; Synopsis
How to send: Online submission system

Publishes local history books covering areas across the UK.

Editor: Rupert Harding

P583 Whitecap Books Ltd
Book Publisher
Suite 209, 314 West Cordova Street, Vancouver, BC, V6B 1E8
Canada

hdoll@fitzhenry.ca

https://www.whitecap.ca
http://www.pinterest.com/whitecapbooks/
https://twitter.com/whitecapbooks
https://www.facebook.com/whitecapbooks

Nonfiction > *Nonfiction Books*
  Food; Health; Regional History; Wellbeing; Wine

Closed to approaches.

Publishes visually appealing books on food, wine, health and well-being, regional history, and regional guidebooks.

P584 Wide-Eyed Editions
Publishing Imprint
1 Triptych Place, Second Floor, London, SE1 9SH
United Kingdom
Tel: +44 (0) 20 7700 9000

QuartoExploresSubmissions@Quartous.com

https://www.quartoknows.com/Wide-Eyed-Editions

Book Publisher: The Quarto Group, Inc. (**P430**)

CHILDREN'S > **Nonfiction** > *Nonfiction Books*
  Arts; Nature; Travel

Send: Query
Don't send: Full text

Publishes books on the arts, natural history and armchair travel. Send query with proposal by email. See website for full guidelines.

P585 Wild Goose Publications
Book Publisher
The Iona Community, Suite 9, Fairfield, 1048 Govan Road, Glasgow, G51 4XS
United Kingdom
Tel: +44 (0) 1414 297281

admin@ionabooks.com

https://www.ionabooks.com

Nonfiction > *Nonfiction Books*: Christianity

Publisher of an ecumenical community of people from different walks of life and different traditions in the Christian church.

P586 Wild Places Publishing
Book Publisher
PO Box 100, Abergavenny, NP7 9WY
United Kingdom
Tel: +44 (0) 1873 737707

books@wildplaces.co.uk

https://wildplaces.co.uk

Nonfiction > *Nonfiction Books*: Caving and Potholing

Publisher specialising in caving-related publications.

P587 Wilderness Press
Book Publisher
c/o Keen Communications, 2204 First Avenue South, Suite 102, Birmingham, AL 35233
United States
Tel: +1 (800) 678-7006

info@adventurewithkeen.com

https://shop.adventurewithkeen.com

Nonfiction > *Nonfiction Books*
  Nature; Outdoor Activities; Travel; Walking Guides

Publisher of books on the outdoors, travel, and outdoor activities.

P588 Wisdom Publications
Book Publisher
199 Elm Street, Somerville, MA 02144
United States

submissions@wisdompubs.org

https://wisdomexperience.org
https://twitter.com/wisdompubs
https://www.facebook.com/wisdompubs
https://instagram.com/wisdompubs
https://www.youtube.com/channel/UCKrdx4usaugOhLzjvYmzpIg

Nonfiction > *Nonfiction Books*: Buddhism

Send: Submission Form
How to send: Email

Will only consider books directly related to Buddhism, written by people with relevant credentials. Download submission questionnaire from website, then complete and return by email.

P589 Wolfpack Publishing
Book Publisher
9850 S. Maryland Parkway, STE. A-5 #323, Las Vegas, NV, 89183
United States

submissions@wolfpackpublishing.com

https://wolfpackpublishing.com
https://www.goodreads.com/group/show/138635-wolfpack-publishing
https://www.facebook.com/WolfpackPub/
https://twitter.com/wolfpackpub

Fiction > *Novels*
  Adventure; Crime; Historical Fiction; Thrillers; Westerns

How to send: Through a literary agent

An award winning indie publisher that began life as a small Western Fiction publishing company, but which now publishes across a variety of genres.

P590 Wolters Kluwer
Book Publisher
PO Box 1030, 2400 BA, Alphen aan den Rijn
Netherlands

Book Publishers: Kluwer Law International (**P302**); Wolters Kluwer (UK) Ltd

P591 WordCrafts Press
Book Publisher
912 E. Lincoln St, Tullahoma, TN 37388
United States
Tel: +1 (615) 397-8376

wordcrafts@wordcrafts.net

https://www.wordcrafts.net

ADULT
  Fiction > *Novels*

Christianity; Contemporary; Dystopian Fiction; Fantasy; Historical Fiction; Horror; Literary; Mystery; Romance; Suspense; Women's Fiction

Nonfiction > *Nonfiction Books*
Animals; Bible Studies; Biography; Business; Cars; Christian Living; Comedy / Humour; Education; History; Memoir; Philosophy; Self Help; Sport; Travel

Poetry > *Poetry Collections*
General, and in particular: Christianity

Scripts > *Theatre Scripts*

CHILDREN'S > **Fiction**
Middle Grade; Picture Books
YOUNG ADULT > *Fiction* > *Novels*
General, and in particular: Fantasy

Send: Proposal
How to send: Query Manager

We publish fiction, nonfiction, and stage plays for both the Christian market and the general market. We do not publish erotica.

Acquisitions Editors: Kristen Ownby; Mike Parker

Authors: Gail Kittleson; Dan Kulp; Robert G. Lee; Jason Lee McKinney; Joey Monteleone; Carrie Anne Noble; Darden North; Paula K. Parker

P592 WordFarm
Book Publisher
140 Lakeside Ave, Suite A-303, Seattle, WA 98122-6538
United States
Tel: +1 (312) 281-8806

info@wordfarm.net

http://www.wordfarm.net

Fiction > *Novels:* Literary

Nonfiction > *Nonfiction Books:* Literary

Poetry > *Any Poetic Form*

Closed to approaches.

Publishes collections of poetry, short fiction, essays, and single works of fiction or literary nonfiction.

Authors: Stacy Barton; Ruth Goring; Erin Keane; Jack Leax; Lynda Rutledge; Luci Shaw; Paul Willis

Editor: Andrew Craft

P593 Words & Pictures
Publishing Imprint
1 Triptych Place, Second Floor, London, SE1 9SH
United Kingdom
Tel: +44 (0) 20 770 9000

QuartoHomesSubmissions@Quarto.com

https://www.quartoknows.com/words-pictures

Book Publisher: The Quarto Group, Inc. (**P430**)

CHILDREN'S > **Fiction** > *Picture Books*

How to send: Email

Always on the lookout for authors and artists with creative ideas to enhance and broaden their list of children's books. See website for submission guidelines.

Publisher: Holly Willsher

P594 WordSong
Publishing Imprint
815 Church Street, Honesdale, PA 18431
United States
Tel: +1 (570) 253-1164

submissions@boydsmillspress.com

https://www.boydsmillspress.com

Book Publisher: Astra Publishing House (**P041**)

Types: Poetry
Markets: Children's

Send: Full text

Describes itself as "the only children's imprint in the United States specifically dedicated to poetry". Send book-length collection of poetry by post with SASE. Do not make initial query prior to submission.

P595 Wordsonthestreet
Book Publisher; Magazine Publisher
Six San Antonio Park, Salthill, Galway
Ireland

publisher@wordsonthestreet.com

http://www.wordsonthestreet.com

Fiction
Novellas; Novels; Short Fiction Collections
Poetry > *Poetry Collections*

Closed to approaches.

Independent publisher based in Galway, Ireland, publishing novels, novellas, short story and poetry collections, and Ireland's premier fiction and poetry magazine.

Editor: Tony O'Dwyer

Magazine: Crannog Magazine (**M121**)

Publishing Imprint: 6th House

P596 Wordsworth Editions
Book Publisher
PO Box 13147, Stansted, CM21 1BT
United Kingdom
Tel: +44 (0) 1920 465167

enquiries@wordsworth-editions.com

http://www.wordsworth-editions.com
https://twitter.com/WordsworthEd
https://en-gb.facebook.com/wordsworth.editions/

ADULT
Fiction > *Novels*
Poetry > *Poetry Collections*

CHILDREN'S > **Fiction** > *Novels*

Publishes out-of-copyright titles.

Managing Director: Helen Trayler

P597 Wren & Rook
Publishing Imprint

Book Publisher: Hachette Children's Group (**P235**)

P598 Yale University Press (London)
Book Publisher
47 Bedford Square, London, WC1B 3DP
United Kingdom
Tel: +44 (0) 20 7079 4900

trade@yaleup.co.uk

https://www.yalebooks.co.uk

ADULT > **Nonfiction**
Nonfiction Books: Architecture; Arts; Biography; Business; Computers; Current Affairs; Economics; Fashion; Health; History; Language; Legal; Literature; Mathematics; Medicine; Memoir; Music; Philosophy; Politics; Religion; Science; Society; Sociology; Technology; Wellbeing
Reference: General

CHILDREN'S > **Nonfiction** > *Nonfiction Books:* Education

Send: Query; Author bio; Market info; Table of Contents; Writing sample
How to send: Post; Email

Publishes world class scholarship for a broad readership.

Editors: Mark Eastment; Joanna Godfrey; Julian Loose; Heather McCallum; Sophie Neve

P599 Yes Poetry Chapbooks
Book Publisher
United States

editor@yespoetry.com

https://www.yespoetry.com

Online Magazine: Yes Poetry Magazine (**M451**)

Poetry > *Chapbooks*

Closed to approaches.

Has published a poetry magazine since 2010, and since 2016 has also published poetry chapbooks. Closed to chapbook submissions as at October 2019. Check website for current status.

P600 YesYes Books
Book Publisher
1631 Broadway St #121, Portland, OR 97232-

1425
United States
Tel: +1 (503) 446-3851

info@yesyesbooks.com

https://www.yesyesbooks.com
https://www.facebook.com/yesyesbooks/
https://twitter.com/YesYesBooks
https://www.instagram.com/yesyesbooks

Fiction
   Novellas; Novels; Short Fiction Collections
Poetry > *Poetry Collections*

A dynamic independent press that publishes poetry and prose collections from bold fresh voices.

P601 ZED Press
Book Publisher
Canada

zedpresschapbook@gmail.com

https://zedpresswindsor.wordpress.com

Types: Poetry
Subjects: Experimental; Literary
Markets: Adult

Closed to approaches.

Publishes poetry chapbooks. Looks for experimental work and seeks to highlight voices that are underrepresented in literature. Accepts manuscripts up to 32 pages in length, by email. See website for full guidelines.

P602 Zibby Books
Book Publisher
United States

info@zibbybooks.com
kathleen.harris@zibbybooks.com

https://www.zibbybooks.com
https://www.instagram.com/zibbybooks
https://www.facebook.com/zibbybooks
https://twitter.com/zibbybooks

Fiction > *Novels*

Nonfiction > *Nonfiction Books*: Memoir

How to send: Through a literary agent

A publishing home for fiction and memoir.

P603 ZigZag Education
Book Publisher
Unit 3, Greenway Business Centre, Doncaster Road, Bristol, BS10 5PY
United Kingdom
Tel: +44 (0) 1179 503199

support@ZigZagEducation.co.uk

https://zigzageducation.co.uk

ACADEMIC > **Nonfiction** > *Nonfiction Books*
   Arts; Business; Classics / Ancient World; Computer Science; Crime; Design; Drama; Economics; English; Films; Food; Geography; Health; History; Language; Legal; Mathematics; Media; Music; Nutrition; Philosophy; Physical Education; Politics; Psychology; Religion; Science; Sociology; Technology; Travel

Educational publisher publishing photocopiable and digital teaching resources for schools and colleges. Register on publisher's author support website if interested in writing or contributing to resources.

P604 Zondervan
Book Publisher
United States

submissions@zondervan.com

https://www.zondervan.com

Book Publisher: HarperCollins

Nonfiction > *Nonfiction Books*: Christianity

Send: Proposal; Table of Contents; Market info; Author bio
How to send: Email

A world leading Bible publisher and provider of Christian communications.

Publishing Imprints: Zonderkidz; Zondervan Academic; Zondervan Books (*P605*); Zondervan Fiction (*P606*); Zondervan Gift (*P607*); Zondervan Reflective (*P608*)

P605 Zondervan Books
Publishing Imprint
United States

Book Publisher: Zondervan (**P604**)

P606 Zondervan Fiction
Publishing Imprint
United States

Book Publisher: Zondervan (**P604**)

P607 Zondervan Gift
Publishing Imprint
United States

Book Publisher: Zondervan (**P604**)

P608 Zondervan Reflective
Publishing Imprint
United States

Book Publisher: Zondervan (**P604**)

Index

Arts

See more specifically: Art Criticism; Art History; Church Art; Drawing; Painting; Performing Arts; Photography; Practical Art; Visual Arts

China

See more broadly: South-East Asia

Chinese Medicine

See more broadly: Alternative Health

Choral Music

See more broadly: Music

Christian Living

See more broadly: Christianity

Christian Romance

See more broadly: Romance
See more specifically: Amish Romance

Christianity

See more broadly: Religion
*See more specifically: Amish; Bible Stories; Bible
    Studies; Bibles; Catholicism; Christian
    Living; Evangelism; Methodism;
    Mormonism; Quakerism*

Crime Thrillers
See more broadly: Crime; Thrillers
Hannah Sheppard Literary Agency L283
Crocheting
See more broadly: Crafts
Crowood Press, The P149
Cryptozoology
See more broadly: Supernatural / Paranormal
Llewellyn Worldwide Ltd P317
Cuba
See more broadly: Caribbean
Cultural Commentary
See more broadly: Commentary; Culture
Carter, Rebecca L103
Pande, Ayesha L487
Whelan, Maria L645
Cultural Criticism
See more broadly: Culture
American Book Review M023
Chang, Nicola L110
Crown P147
Eisenmann, Caroline L193
Feminist Studies M161
Fuentes, Sarah L236
Gillespie, Claire L248
Graywolf Press P228
Lewis, Alison L388
Lilliput Press, The P314
McQuilkin, Rob L435
Mendia, Isabel L438
New England Review M291
Peepal Tree Press P405
Power, Anna L511
Rabble Review M338
Takahe M401
Virginia Quarterly Review, The M432
Wong-Baxter, Jade L659
Yale Review, The M449
Cultural History
See more broadly: Culture; History
Asabi Publishing P038
Derviskadic, Dado L165
Keren, Eli L352
Kirby, Robert L358
McCormick Literary L432
Perez Literary & Entertainment L495
Perez, Kristina L496
Phaidon Press P415
Ramer, Susan L518
Seymour, Charlotte L564
Unicorn P535
Unicorn Publishing Group P536
University of Massachusetts Press P548
Culture
*See more specifically: Contemporary Culture;
   Cultural Commentary; Cultural Criticism;
   Cultural History; Ethnic; Folklore, Myths,
   and Legends; Jewish Culture; Multicultural;
   Popular Culture; Postcolonialism; Sub-
   Culture; Visual Culture; Youth Culture*
Abdo Publishing Co P011
African American Review M014
American Heritage M024
Antigonish Review, The M028
Arsenal Pulp Press P036
Art Papers M032
Art Times Journal M034
Arte Publico Press P037
Asabi Publishing P038
Atlanta Magazine M039
Atlantic Northeast M041
Baffler, The M050
Bal, Emma L042
Barr, Anjanette L046
Basalt Books P063
Bear Deluxe Magazine, The M060

Hobbies

See more specifically: Embroidery; Gardening;
    Knitting; Motorcycling; Numismatics (Coin /
    Currency Collecting); Quilting; Rock
    Collecting / Rockhounding; Sewing; Stamp
    Collecting

Hockey

See more broadly: Sport

Holiday Homes

See more broadly: Holidays

Holidays

See more specifically: Holiday Homes

Holistic Health

See more broadly: Health

Home Economics / Domestic Science

Home Improvement

See more broadly: Houses

Midwifery
See more broadly: Nursing

Military
See more broadly: Warfare
*See more specifically: Military Aviation; Military
    Vehicles; Special Forces*

Military Aviation
See more broadly: Aviation; Military

Military History
See more broadly: History; Warfare

Military Vehicles
See more broadly: Military; Vehicles

Mind, Body, Spirit
See more broadly: Health
See more specifically: Meditation; Yoga

Minerals
See more broadly: Geology

Mini Cars
See more broadly: Cars

Minnesota
See more broadly: United States

Missouri
See more broadly: United States

Model Aircraft
See more broadly: Model Making

Model Making
See more broadly: Crafts
*See more specifically: Model Aircraft; Model
    Ships and Boats*

Model Ships and Boats
See more broadly: Model Making

Modern History
See more broadly: History

Montgomeryshire
See more broadly: Wales

Mormonism
See more broadly: Christianity

Motherhood
See more broadly: Parenting

Motivational Self-Help
See more broadly: Self Help

*Claim your free access to **www.firstwriter.com**: See p.391*

Science Journalism
   See more broadly: Journalism; Science

Scotland
   See more broadly: United Kingdom
   See more specifically: Shetland

Scripts

Scuba Diving
   See more broadly: Diving

Search and Rescue
   See more broadly: Emergency Services

Secret Intelligence
   See more broadly: Warfare
   See more specifically: CIA

Self Help
   See more broadly: Personal Development
   See more specifically: Motivational Self-Help

Shropshire
See more broadly: England
Skiing
See more broadly: Leisure; Sport

UFOs
See more broadly: Supernatural / Paranormal

US Southern States
See more broadly: United States

United Kingdom
See more broadly: Europe
See more specifically: England; Northern Ireland;
   Scotland; Wales

United States
See more broadly: North America
See more specifically: Alaska; American Midwest;
   American West; Americana; Appalachia;
   Arizona; California; Chesapeake Bay;
   Colorado; Florida; Georgia (US State);
   Hawai'i; Illinois; Indiana; Louisiana;
   Maine; Maryland; Michigan; Minnesota;
   Missouri; Nevada; New England; New
   Jersey; New York State; Ohio; Ozarks;
   Pacific Northwest; Pennsylvania;
   Southwestern United States; Tennessee;
   Texas; US Southern States; Utah; Virginia;
   Wisconsin

Upmarket
See more specifically: Upmarket Commercial
   Fiction; Upmarket Contemporary Fiction;
   Upmarket Crime; Upmarket Romance;
   Upmarket Thrillers; Upmarket Women's
   Fiction

Upmarket Commercial Fiction
See more broadly: Commercial; Upmarket

Upmarket Contemporary Fiction
See more broadly: Contemporary; Upmarket

Upmarket Crime
See more broadly: Crime; Upmarket

Upmarket Romance
See more broadly: Romance; Upmarket

Upmarket Thrillers
See more broadly: Thrillers; Upmarket

Upmarket Women's Fiction
See more broadly: Upmarket; Women's Fiction

Youth Culture
  See more broadly: Culture
Yukon
  See more broadly: Canada
Zen
  See more broadly: Mahayana Buddhism
Zombies
  See more broadly: Horror

Get Free Access to the firstwriter.com Website

To claim your free access to the firstwriter.com website simply go to the website at https://www.firstwriter.com/subscribe and begin the subscription process as normal. On the second page, enter the required details (such as your name and address, etc.) then for "Voucher / coupon number" enter the following promotional code:

- **1XPT-49GB**

This will reduce the cost of creating a subscription by up to $18 / £15 / €18, making it free to create a monthly, quarterly, or combination subscription. Alternatively, you can use the discount to take out an annual or life subscription at a reduced rate.

Continue the process until your account is created. Please note that you will need to provide your payment details, even if there is no up-front payment. This is in case you choose to leave your subscription running after the free initial period, but there is no obligation for you to do so.

When you use this code to take out a free subscription you are under no obligation to make any payments whatsoever and you are free to cancel your account before you make any payments if you wish.

If you need any assistance, please email support@firstwriter.com.

If you have found this book useful, please consider leaving a review on the website where you bought it.

What you get

Once you have set up access to the site you will be able to benefit from all the following features:

Databases

All our databases are updated almost every day, and include powerful search facilities to help you find exactly what you need. Searches that used to take you hours or even days in print books or on search engines can now be done in seconds, and produce more accurate and up-to-date information. Our agents database also includes independent reports from at least three separate sources, showing you which are the top agencies and helping you avoid the scams that are all over the internet. You can try out any of our databases before you subscribe:

- Search dozens of **current competitions**.
- Search **over 2,400 literary agents and agencies.**
- Search **over 2,200 magazines**.
- Search **over 2,700 book publishers** that **don't** charge fees.

Plus advanced features to help you with your search:

- Save searches and save time – set multiple search parameters specific to your work, save them, and then access the search results with a single click whenever you log in. You can even save multiple different searches if you have different types of work you are looking to place.
- Add personal notes to listings, visible only to you and fully searchable – helping you to organise your actions.
- Set reminders on listings to notify you when to submit your work, when to follow up, when to expect a reply, or any other custom action.
- Track which listings you've viewed and when, to help you organise your search – any listings which have changed since you last viewed them will be highlighted for your attention!

Daily email updates

As a subscriber you will be able to take advantage of our email alert service, meaning you can specify your particular interests and we'll send you automatic email updates when we change or add a listing that matches them. So if you're interested in agents dealing in romantic fiction in the United States you can have us send you emails with the latest updates about them – keeping you up to date without even having to log in.

User feedback

Our agent, publisher, and magazine databases all include a user feedback feature that allows our subscribers to leave feedback on each listing – giving you not only the chance to have your say about the markets you contact, but giving a unique authors' perspective on the listings.

Save on copyright protection fees

If you're sending your work away to publishers, competitions, or literary agents, it's vital that you first protect your copyright. As a subscriber to firstwriter.com you can do this through our site and save 10% on the copyright registration fees normally payable for protecting your work internationally through the Intellectual Property Rights Office.

Monthly newsletter

When you subscribe to firstwriter.com you also receive our monthly email newsletter – described by one publishing company as "the best in the business" – including articles, news, and interviews for writers. And the best part is that you can continue to receive the newsletter even after you stop your paid subscription – at no cost!

Terms and conditions

The promotional code contained in this publication may be used by the owner of the book only to create one subscription to firstwriter.com at a reduced cost, or for free. It may not be used by or disseminated to third parties. Should the code be misused then the owner of the book will be liable for any costs incurred, including but not limited to payment in full at the standard rate for the subscription in question. The code may be used at any time until the end of the calendar year named in the title of the publication, after which time it will become invalid. The code may be redeemed against the creation of a new account only – it cannot be redeemed against the ongoing costs of keeping a subscription open. In order to create a subscription a method of payment must be provided, but there is no obligation to make any payment. Subscriptions may be cancelled at any time, and if an account is cancelled before any payment becomes due then no payment will be made. Once a subscription has been created, the normal schedule of payments will begin on a monthly, quarterly, or annual basis, unless a life Subscription is selected, or the subscription is cancelled prior to the first payment becoming due. Subscriptions may be cancelled at any time, but if they are left open beyond the date at which the first payment becomes due and is processed then payments will not be refundable.

Made in the USA
Middletown, DE
13 December 2023

45451688R00223